Good Reasoning Matters!

Good Reasoning Matters!

A Constructive Approach to Critical Thinking

Third Edition

Leo A. Groarke & Christopher W. Tindale

OXFORD

UNIVERSITY PRESS

1904 ❧ 2004

100 YEARS OF
CANADIAN PUBLISHING

OXFORD
UNIVERSITY PRESS

70 Wynford Drive, Don Mills, Ontario M3C 1J9
www.oup.com/ca

Oxford University Press is a department of the University of Oxford.
It furthers the University's objective of excellence in research, scholarship,
and education by publishing worldwide in

Oxford New York

Auckland Bangkok Buenos Aires Cape Town Chennai
Dar es Salaam Delhi Hong Kong Istanbul Karachi Kolkata
Kuala Lumpur Madrid Melbourne Mexico City Mumbai Nairobi
São Paulo Shanghai Taipei Tokyo Toronto

Oxford is a trade mark of Oxford University Press
in the UK and in certain other countries

Published in Canada
by Oxford University Press

National Library of Canada Cataloguing in Publication

Groarke, Leo
Good reasoning matters! : a constructive approach to critical
thinking / Leo A. Groarke, Christopher W. Tindale. — 3rd ed.

Includes index.
First ed. by J. Frederick Little, Leo Groarke and Christopher Tindale.
ISBN 0-19-541904-9

1. Reasoning. I. Tindale, Christopher W. (Christopher William)
II. Little, J. Frederick. Good reasoning matters. III. Title.

BC177.G76 2004   168   C2003-906416-6

2 3 4 - 07 06 05 04

Cover Design: Joan Dempsey
Cover Images: Digital Vision

This book is printed on permanent (acid-free) paper ∞.
Printed in Canada

CONTENTS

Introduction   xi
Acknowledgements   xvii

1   **GETTING STARTED: Looking for an Argument**   1
    1.   Arguments   2
    2.   An Example   3
         Exercise 1A   4
    3.   Arguers, Audiences, and Opponents   5
    4.   Simple and Extended Arguments   9
         Exercise 1B   11
    5.   Distinguishing Arguments from Non-arguments   13
         Exercise 1C   18
    6.   Arguments and Explanations   20
    7.   Argument Narratives   24
         Exercise 1D   25
         Major Exercise 1M   27

2   **ARGUMENT DIAGRAMS: Pointing the Way**   33
    1.   Argument Diagrams   33
    2.   Linked and Convergent Premises   38
    3.   Supplemented Diagrams   42
         Exercise 2A   44
    4.   Diagramming Your Own Arguments   46
         Exercise 2B   47
         Major Exercise 2M   48

3   IMPLICIT ARGUMENT COMPONENTS: Filling in the Blanks   51
    1. Speech Acts and the Principles of Communication   52
        Exercise 3A   56
    2. Abbreviated Arguments   56
        Exercise 3B   64
    3. Non-verbal Elements in Argument   65
        Exercise 3C   77
    4. A Note on Argument Construction   77
        Exercise 3D   78
        Major Exercise 3M   78

4   DEFINITIONS: Saying What You Mean   83
    1. Using Words Precisely   84
        Exercise 4A   86
    2. Vagueness and Ambiguity   87
        Exercise 4B   91
    3. Formulating Definitions   93
    4. Rules for Good Definitions   97
        Exercise 4C   100
    5. Expressing Your Intended Meaning   103
        Major Exercise 4M   104

5   BIAS: Reading Between the Lines   109
    1. Bias and Perspective   109
        Exercise 5A   116
    2. Detecting Illegitimate Biases   116
        Exercise 5B   126
        Major Exercise 5M   127

6   STRONG AND WEAK ARGUMENTS: Preparing for Evaluations   133
    1. Strong Arguments   134
    2. Argument Criticism   137
    3. Acceptability   138
    4. Valid and Invalid Arguments   139
        Exercise 6A   142
    5. Argument Schemes   144
    6. Invalid Arguments   147
        Major Exercise 6M   150

7   SYLLOGISMS I: Classifying Arguments   156
    1. Categorical Statements   157
        Exercise 7A   161
    2. Immediate Inferences   162
        Exercise 7B   166

3. Categorical Syllogisms   166
    Exercise 7C   169
4. Venn Diagrams   170
    Major Exercise 7M   180

8   **SYLLOGISMS II: Testing Classes**   185
    1. Full Schematization   185
    2. Rules of Validity   187
    3. Applying the Rules   188
    4. Procedural Points   190
        Major Exercise 8M   192

9   **PROPOSITIONAL LOGIC I: Some Ifs, Ands, and Buts**   195
    1. Simple and Complex Propositions   196
        Exercise 9A   203
    2. Translation   204
        Exercise 9B   208
    3. Propositional Schemes and Proofs   210
        Exercise 9C   219
        Major Exercise 9M   222

10 **PROPOSITIONAL LOGIC II: Conditionals, Dilemmas,**
    and Reductios   226
    1. Conditional Proofs   226
        Exercise 10A   229
    2. Reductio ad Absurdum   229
        Exercise 10B   232
    3. Dilemmas   232
        Exercise 10C   236
    4. De Morgan's Laws   237
        Exercise 10D   238
    5. Summary: Rules of Inference   238
        Major Exercise 10M   239

11 **ORDINARY REASONING: Assessing the Basics**   247
    1. Ordinary Reasoning   248
    2. Acceptability   250
        Exercise 11A   263
    3. Relevance   265
        Exercise 11B   272
    4. Sufficiency   274
        Exercise 11C   277
    5. Applying the Criteria   278
        Major Exercise 11M   281

12 EMPIRICAL SCHEMES OF ARGUMENT: Nothing but the Facts   286
   1. Generalizations   287
      Exercise 12A   293
   2. Polling   294
      Exercise 12B   300
   3. Causal Reasoning   302
      Exercise 12C   311
   4. Appeals to Ignorance   313
      Exercise 12D   315
   5. The Methods of Science   315
      Exercise 12E   321
      Major Exercise 12M   322

13 MORAL AND POLITICAL REASONING: Schemes of Value   329
   1. Slippery-Slope Arguments   330
      Exercise 13A   334
   2. Arguments from Analogy   335
      Exercise 13B   340
   3. Appeals to Precedent   342
      Exercise 13C   344
   4. Two-Wrongs Reasoning   345
      Exercise 13D   353
      Major Exercise 13M   354

14 ETHOTIC SCHEMES: Judging Character   359
   1. *Pro Homine*   360
      Exercise 14A   362
   2. *Ad Populum* Arguments   362
      Exercise 14B   363
   3. Arguments from Authority   364
      Exercise 14C   369
   4. *Ad Hominem*   369
      Exercise 14D   372
   5. Arguments against Authority   372
      Exercise 14E   374
   6. Guilt (and Honour) by Association   374
      Exercise 14F   377
   7. Other Cases   378
      Exercise 14G   380
      Major Exercise 14M   380

15 **ARGUMENTATIVE WRITING: Essaying an Argument**   387
    1. The Good Evaluative Critique   388
        Exercise 15A   391
    2. The Good Argumentative Essay   395
        Exercise 15B   399
    3. A Student's Paper   400
    4. Conclusion   409
        Major Exercise 15M   410

Selected Answers   411

Index   467

For
Jazz, Katie & Scott
Caitlyn & Jonathan

INTRODUCTION

A Note to the Student

> *What is right or wrong*
> *I don't know who to believe in*
> *My soul sings a different song*
>
> *I am right and you are wrong*
> *I am right and you are wrong*
> *I am right and you are wrong*
> *No one's right and no one's wrong*
>
> —Creed, 'In America'

It is often said that we live in an 'information age'. During the last few decades, rapid technological changes have revolutionized the way we receive and process information. Unless we divorce ourselves from ordinary life, we are inundated by the messages we see, hear, and read on the Internet, television, and radio, in magazines and books, on bumper stickers and billboards. Any space, public or private, can now accommodate a message. In part because of this, the world is now a 'global village'. Events happening a hundred, a thousand, or ten thousand miles away can be conveyed to us immediately.

Our sources of information and the myriad of messages they convey all vie for our attention, soliciting our support. Debates rage, arguments and counter-arguments are offered, and advertisements tell us we should buy this and do that. Those involved in these exchanges push us to take a stand, but the influx of contradictory messages is confusing. How are we to decide who is right, what is acceptable, and even what ideas or points of view we should spend our time, energy, and money exploring? If we care about the world or the people and things around us, we must find a way to respond reasonably to a wide range of personal and public issues. Most of us are poorly equipped to do so—not because we lack the thinking skills this requires, but because these skills are not sufficiently developed.

This book is designed to help you improve your reasoning, so that you can reach your own conclusions about whatever topics you address. We hope that you will emerge a reasoner who is proficient at assessing the arguments you encounter, and who is able to construct convincing arguments of your own. The thinking skills you will develop can be applied to all aspects of your life, and are particularly important in a democracy, for its success depends on the ability of citizens to make significant political decisions about complex social and economic issues. It is at least arguable that the focus on personality that characterizes many of our election campaigns and coverage reflects a widespread inability to assess the logic of the arguments propounded by competing candidates.

In the process of developing your reasoning skills you should expect to work. Practice makes perfect, and this is especially true in honing your reasoning skills. Many people think they are good at reasoning because they like to argue and are willing to defend a position 'to the bitter end'. But there is much more to reasoning. Among other things, a good arguer must be able to recognize and judge

- what counts as a good reason for a claim;
- when claims are relevant to an argument, and when they are not;
- what conclusions reasonably follow from different kinds of evidence;
- the difference between sufficient and insufficient evidence; and
- the expectations that attend different contexts and different audiences.

The key to success is not memorizing the principles of good reasoning but attempting, repeatedly, to apply them in practice. We encourage you to apply the critical skills you will be developing by doing the exercises in this book, and by making a concerted effort to employ a critical attitude in other contexts (in talking with friends, in reading the newspaper, in writing essays for your other courses, and so on). On the website associated with this text (<www.oup.com/ca/he/companion/groarketindale>) you will find some links and a glossary that are meant to help you in this endeavour.

The study of good reasoning may also prompt you to ask why we reason the way we do. How did we come to hold the set of beliefs we take for granted? What do we learn about ourselves, and about knowledge, when we pay attention to aspects of reasoning? How can we choose reasonably between the different perspectives that characterize different audiences? What should convince us to hold a position quite different from the one to which we do not ascribe? A willingness to think about these questions can help you better understand objectivity and fairness—notions that must play a central role in reasonable decisions.

In working through the exercises in this book, and when you apply your reasoning skills elsewhere, keep in mind that reasoning is rarely final and definitive. As you develop your ability to think critically, you will find that many claims, issues, views, and arguments are open to differing interpretations. In preparing and analyzing the examples in this book, we, the authors, have made an effort to be fair and to consider all reasonable points of view. We have done the same in providing answers to selected (starred) exercises at the back of the book. But it is always possible that you will disagree with our analysis of a particular example. When this happens, make sure you discuss your point of view with your instructor or another student. Because consultation of this sort is essential to good reasoning, and good reasoning matters, your willingness to discuss your point of view with others will help you put into practice the principles we champion in this text.

A NOTE TO THE INSTRUCTOR

Continued innovations in informal logic, critical thinking, the study of rhetoric, and communication studies have reinforced our belief that a range of texts is vital to the development of argumentation theory, which has become one of the most significant areas of pedagogy and inquiry to emerge in the last two decades. Our approach is one among many of value, but we believe that it continues to provide an introduction to argument that features aspects of argument that are missing from many other texts. Having engaged all the major contemporary perspectives on argument in our research and our teaching, we think that this book is distinctive in four ways that are worth noting.

First—and we regard this as foremost—this is a text that pays a great deal of attention to the construction (and not just the analysis) of arguments. Everyone agrees that the attempt to teach argumentation/critical thinking must include teaching the skills for evaluating arguments. We would add that the ability to *construct* good arguments is as important a skill (or set of skills), and we have designed our text with this in mind. In our experience, the expectation that people will argue well because they can analyze other people's arguments (often by applying fallacy labels) is a hit-and-miss affair. We have tried to explain more consciously to students how they can present their own arguments clearly, how they can avoid problems with issues of language and inference, and how they can construct good arguments in a manner that is in keeping with a variety of argumentation schemes. We have included many exercises that ask students to construct their own arguments, along with exercises that ask them to analyze the arguments of others. The account of argumentative essay writing in the final chapter is an attempt to pull together the different issues that arise in the construction of good arguments in a way that will be relevant to virtually every college and university student, regardless of their discipline.

The second distinctive feature of our text, which follows from the first, is our discussion of a variety of argument schemes. One might contrast this aspect of our approach with another popular approach to the teaching of critical thinking and informal logic: the identification and assessment of fallacies. We believe that something can be learned from the latter approach, and we continue to benefit from the insights it makes possible, but we find that it is an unduly negative way to teach students how to reason. In our own experience, it fosters a negative attitude in students, who come to believe that logic is a tool for finding fault with almost every argument and arguer.

Our doubts about the fallacy approach have been fuelled by the conclusion that many types of argument that have been treated as fallacies constitute good argument schemes if they are used properly (a conclusion that is also evident in the work of commentators like Govier, Walton, and Wreen). *Ad hominem* arguments are a good example. According to the account still found in many logic texts, this is a term synonymous with a particular kind of faulty reasoning. This view persists even though a number of argumentation theorists have demonstrated that it is erroneous, and that instances of *ad hominem* can be reasonable arguments if they are properly constructed. It is possible to develop the fallacy approach in a way that makes room for this (by saying that there are exceptional cases where *ad hominem* arguments are not to be deemed fallacious), but we believe this is confusing. A poorly constructed inductive generalization or *reductio ad absurdum* can properly be called a bad argument, but we would not on these grounds classify inductive generalization or *reductio ad absurdum* as a fallacy. Pedagogically, we think there are other problems with the fallacy approach, for the overriding emphasis it places on poor instances of *ad hominem* encourages the dismissal of an *ad hominem* as soon as it is identified rather than the careful analysis of the reasoning in each case.

In most cases, the counter-side of a traditional fallacy is a legitimate argument scheme, i.e. an identifiable set of conditions and structure that define some proper form of argument. In helping to expand and deepen students' ability to construct good arguments, this text emphasizes these schemes. An argument scheme like 'appeal to authority' is, therefore, presented in a manner designed to show students how to compose good arguments by authority. Our emphasis on argument schemes of this sort gives our text a constructive, positive tone. Even when students are required to assess other people's arguments, we think that our approach encourages a thorough analysis and avoids the hasty application of a fallacy label.

A third feature that sets our book apart is its discussion of the rhetorical features of argument, something that has characterized earlier editions of this text. Though audiences have traditionally been ignored in logic books, contemporary research increasingly recognizes that a failure to consider audiences is difficult to reconcile with the reality of ordinary arguments, which do not arise in a vacuum. Everyday arguments are directed at audiences and constructed with them in mind. All of us (even logicians) continually pick and choose arguments that suit the particular audience we are addressing, whether it be a spouse, a colleague, the public, a boss, or a particular group or organization. We therefore stress both the specific and the 'universal' audience for arguments—that is, the specific audience to which an argument is directed, and the 'universal audience' that can help us establish standards of good reasoning by which the ultimate strength of an argument must be judged.

A fourth distinctive feature of this text is our attempt to recognize and include insights on aspects of argument that have come to light in the field of argumentation theory, a field of study that has grown dramatically in way that has engaged philosophers, logicians, communication theorists, rhetoricians, linguists, computer scientists, and others. The aspects of this text that reflect developments in the field are its account of argumentative communication, its discussion of visual (and other non-verbal) forms of argument, and its attempt to recognize the dialectical aspects of argument (what Johnson calls the 'dialectical tier' of an argument) and the role that dialectics must play in argument assessment.

Though we are familiar with the controversy surrounding the use of formal logic to teach ordinary reasoning, we wanted to create a text that would allow instructors to decide for themselves whether they wished to include a discussion of some (very limited) aspects of formal logic in a course on argument. The book has been written in a way that will allow instructors who do not wish to use the chapters on formal logic to use the other chapters of the text as the basis of a complete and uninterrupted course. Though there are some aspects of formal logic (truth tables, truth trees, the predicate calculus, etc.) which are, we think, of minimal use in the attempt to teach most students natural-language reasoning, we continue to believe that some formal rules of inference can help introduce students to rigorous reasoning and to some simple principles that are applicable to good everyday reasoning. The emphasis we place on argument schemes rather than fallacies in our later chapters can be seen as a natural evolution beyond the deductive schemes of arguments introduced in the chapters on formal logic. In this manner, our approach to argument can be seen as an approach that blends formal and informal reasoning.

In organizing the text, we have tried to write it in a way that makes it cumulative. Skills taught in earlier chapters are required in later chapters, and the problems in the exercises are arranged in order of increasing complexity. The exercises grouped at the end of a major section of a chapter cultivate the skills discussed in that section. The exercises at the end of the chapter include a 'major' exercise that usually requires the application of all the ideas that have been introduced in that chapter and, where relevant, in preceding chapters.

Like our earlier editions, this edition of *Good Reasoning Matters!* has benefited from contemporary research on the theory of argument. In some cases, chapters have been rewritten to keep them current with the terminology in the field. (We have, for example, replaced our previous talk of argument 'forms' with a discussion of argument 'schemes'.) In the course of our revisions we have also tried to benefit from our own and others' pedagogical experiences. Among other things, we have reorganized some chapters to emphasize more clearly the focus on arguments and good arguments, and have reordered some of the material within chapters, moving subsections to places that may make for a better pedagogical fit.

In response to comments from instructors who have used our text, we have made many minor changes and rearranged the material in the early chapters to improve their pedagogical development. This has resulted in an additional chapter of this introductory material. We have also added a new chapter devoted to an account of factual (causal) arguments and some of the principles of scientific reasoning. While these modifications have involved considerable rewriting and reorganization, users of earlier editions will have no difficulty recognizing the same basic approach to argument, with the same focus on good reasoning, audience, and argument schemes. Most of the earlier topics and types of reasoning are still discussed, though there are some cases where these discussions have been altered in some way or occur in different places in the text.

Finally, we have revised the text by adding many new examples of actual argument. These examples have been inserted both in the body of the text and in the exercises. In many cases, we have tried to update the issues we use to introduce critical thinking skills, as in the final chapter, where we have focused on the question of human cloning. Despite the introduction of many new contemporary examples, we have not hesitated to use historical examples when we think they can make a valuable contribution to the discussion in the book. As a general rule, we believe it is important to introduce students to a wide range of arguments that will encourage them to consider views and perspectives they might not be otherwise exposed to.

As we have added new examples to our exercises, we have enlarged the section on 'Answers to Selected Exercises' that is included at the back of the book (answers are provided for all starred questions in the exercises). In most cases, the nature of the material inevitably means that our answers are not definitive; they might be better described as 'reasonable possibilities'. We encourage instructors (and students) to challenge and suggest alternatives to our analyses. In the process of rewriting the text we have also constructed a website for instructors. It includes a full glossary of important terms, many more examples of argument, an explanation of our approach to the different topics we discuss, teaching hints and suggestions, a number of fully analyzed examples, and suggestions for further reading that correspond to each chapter of the book. The website is located at <www.oup.com/ca/he/companion/groarketindale>. The material for instructors is password-protected and not available to students. We have tried to construct the website in a way that will make it a convenient teaching tool that will be especially helpful to new instructors.

Instructors who would like to comment on the text or the website should feel free to contact either author.

Leo A. Groarke (lgroarke@wlu.ca)

Christopher W. Tindale (ctindale@trentu.ca)

ACKNOWLEDGEMENTS

The authors would like to thank everyone who contributed to the completion of this edition. This includes instructors who have used previous versions of the book and passed along suggestions for improvement as well as the anonymous reviewers, whose comments have helped strengthen some aspects of the text. We are particularly grateful to Dana Snow for preparing the illustrations, and to Daniel Farr for collecting examples and generally assisting with the preparation of the manuscript.

We would like to thank our editors at Oxford, Laura Macleod and Mark Piel, for their enthusiasm at every stage of the project, and our copy editor, Eric Sinkins, for his perceptive editing of the manuscript.

Like the previous editions of *Good Reasoning Matters!*, this one has benefited from the wealth of scholarship and literature produced by current research in the burgeoning fields of informal logic, rhetoric, and argumentation studies. While no uniform approach to argument and reasoning has resulted, or seems likely to result in the near future, we have striven to take account of the state of art in the field as it has developed since our last edition appeared. We owe a word of thanks to the many colleagues whose research informs good pedagogy. We could not name them all here without risking serious omissions.

C.D.B. Bryan. Excerpt from *Close Encounters of the Fourth Kind: Alien Abduction, UFOs, and the Conference at M.I.T.* (New York: Alfred A. Knopf, 1995).

Patrick Clawson. Excerpts from 'Sanctions as Punishment, Enforcement, and Prelude to Further Action' originally appeared in *Ethics and International Affairs* 7 (1993), © 1993 by Carnegie Council on Ethics and International Affairs, reprinted by permission.

Kate Cox. Excerpts from '$40,000-plus for eggs of clever, pretty women', *The Sydney Morning Herald* (15 Dec. 2002), <http://www.smh.com.au/articles/2002/12/14/1039656259779.html>.

Robert Fisk. Excerpts from 'When journalists forget that murder is murder', Z *Magazine* (18 Aug. 2001), <http://www.zmag.org/meastwatch/fiskmurd.htm>.

Augie Fleras. Excerpts from '"Crude" Form of Protest a Maori Tradition', *Kitchener-Waterloo Record* (1 Apr. 1986), reprinted by permission of the author.

Maggie Fox. 'Inquest says mad cow disease killed Briton' (19 Aug. 1996), © Reuters Limited, reprinted by permission of Reuters Limited.

Janet George. Excerpts from 'Saboteurs—the Real Animals', *The Guardian* (28 Feb. 1993), © The Guardian, reprinted by permission of The Guardian.

Mary Gordon. Excerpt from *Joan of Arc* (New York: Lipper/Viking, 2000).

Ronald M. Green. Excerpt '…unlike an embryo…lives of children and adults' from the sidebar 'The Ethical Considerations', appearing with the article 'The First Human Cloned Human Embryo' by Jose B. Cibelli et al (Jan. 2002), copyright © 2002 by Scientific American, Inc. All rights reserved.

Greg Gutfeld. Excerpts from 'Be a Jerk', copyright 1995 by Rodale, Inc., reprinted by permission of *Men's Health* Magazine. All rights reserved.

Norman Kretzmann. Excerpt from the introduction to *William Sherwood's Introduction to Logic*, translated by Norman Kretzmann (Minneapolis, MN: University of Minnesota Press, 1968), reprinted by permission of University of Minnesota Press.

Ralph H. Johnson and J. Anthony Blair. Excerpts from *Logical Self-Defense* (New York: McGraw-Hill, 1994), copyright © The McGraw-Hill Companies, Inc., reprinted by permission of The McGraw-Hill Companies, Inc.

Paul Koring. Excerpt from 'Pressure rises for Bush to slow down on Iraq war', *The Globe and Mail* (23 Jan. 2003), reprinted with permission from The Globe and Mail.

Samuel V. LaSelva. Excerpt from 'Pluralism and Hate: Freedom, Censorship, and the Canadian Identity', in *Interpreting Censorship in Canada*, ed. K. Petersen and A.C. Hutchinson (Toronto: University of Toronto Press, 1999).

Anne McIlroy. Excerpts from 'Most smokers so addicted they need fast hit', *The Globe and Mail* (21 Jan. 1999), reprinted with permission from The Globe and Mail.

Paul Martin. Excerpts from 'Cult Proofing Your Kids', *AFF News*, vol. 2, no. 1 (1997).

Rex Murphy. Excerpts from 'Selling Something, Dr Suzuki?', *The Globe and Mail* (28 Sept. 2003), reprinted by permission of the author.

'Poll: Majority of Muslims view U.S. unfavorably', adapted from <http://www.cnn.com/2002/US/02/26/gallup.moslems/index.html>.

Daniel D. Polsby. Excerpt from 'The False Promise of Gun Control', *The Atlantic Monthly* (Mar. 1994), reprinted by permission of The Atlantic Monthly.

'Poultry in Motion'. Excerpts are reprinted from *Wall Street Journal* (4 June 2003).

Tim Radford. 'Genes say boys will be boys and girls will be sensitive', *The Guardian* (22 June 1997), © The Guardian, reprinted by permission of The Guardian.

Hugh Rawson. Excerpts from *Devious Derivations*, copyright © 1994 by Hugh Rawson, reprinted with permission of the author.

Tom Rockmore. Excerpts from 'On Heidegger's Nazism and Philosophy', <http://www.friesian.com/rockmore.htm> (accessed 4 Feb. 2003), copyright © 2000 by Kelley L. Ross, reprinted by permission.

Carl Sagan. Excerpt from *The Dragons of Eden: Speculations on the Evolution of Human Intelligence* (New York: Random House, 1977).

Edward Said. Excerpts from 'Palestinian Elections Now', *Al-Ahram Weekly Online*, no. 590 (13–19 June 2002).

Margaret Somerville. Excerpt from *The Ethical Canary*, © 2000 Margaret A. Somerville, reprinted by permission of Penguin Group (Canada), a Division of Pearson Penguin Canada Inc.

Robert Sullivan. Excerpt from 'Adventure: An Attempt at a Definition', in *Life: The Greatest Adventures of All Time*, by the Editors of *Life* Magazine (New York: Life Books, Time Inc, 2000).

'The corrosion of the death penalty', editorial, *The Globe and Mail* (21 May 2002), reprinted with permission from The Globe and Mail.

'Toxic Teeth'. Excerpts reprinted from a report of an Oakland, California, press conference of Consumers for Dental Choice, <http://toxicteeth.net/8-3-01.html>, by permission of Consumers for Dental Choice.

'...while US students own up to cheating'. Excerpt reprinted from *Nature*, vol. 390, no. 6659 (4 Dec. 1997) by permission of Nature.

Ian Wilmut, Keith Campbell, and Colin Tudge. Excerpts from *The Second Creation*, copyright © 2000 by Ian Wilmut, Keith Campbell, and Colin Tudge, reprinted by permission of Farrar, Straus and Giroux, LLC.

1

GETTING

STARTED:

LOOKING FOR AN ARGUMENT

Our basic unit of reasoning is the 'argument'. In introducing arguments, the present chapter discusses

- the nature of arguments and their components;
- the contexts, audiences, and opponents that arguments address;
- logical indicators that are signs of argument;
- the difference between arguments and explanations; and
- argument narratives.

In a famous skit in *Monty Python's Flying Circus*, a man enters a room and asks: 'Is this the right room for an argument?'

Almost everyone has heard the expression 'room for argument'. 'There's room for argument' means that some claim is open to debate. But not at Monty Python's 'argument clinic', where the expression 'room for argument' denotes a room where arguments take place.

In real life, there are no 'argument rooms' designed as places to sell an argument. But there are many rooms in which arguments take place. They include all the rooms in which we carry on our professional and personal lives. In view of this, the ability to argue is a skill that every one of us employs. The present text attempts to teach you how to improve this skill. It contains chapters that explain the difference between strong and weak arguments, and the ways you can assess the reasoning that arguments contain. We begin with an account of arguments, and the differences that distinguish arguments and non-arguments.

1. ARGUMENTS

The Monty Python skit continues. In answer to the question 'Is this the right room for an argument?' the man sitting at the desk responds:

'I've told you *once*.'

[man looking for an argument:] 'No you haven't.'

. . . 'Yes I did!'

'Didn't.'

'Did.'

'Didn't.'

'I'm telling you I did!'

'You did not!'

Exasperated, the man looking for an argument finally exclaims: 'Look, this isn't an argument, it's just a contradiction'.

Sometimes we use the word 'argument' to mean 'disagreement', and especially a vehement disagreement: a harangue, a quarrel, a yelling match characterized by impassioned contradictions. In this sense, the two men in Monty Python's argument clinic *are* arguing. Arguments of this sort are a significant and sometimes painful reality we must contend with. But this is not the kind of argument that this book discusses. For philosophers, logicians, and those who study argumentation, an argument is an attempt to go beyond a simple contradiction and provide evidence for some point of view.

Consider the kind of argument attributed to the mythical detective Sherlock Holmes. It begins with a claim, which is usually unexpected and usually amazes his companion Watson. Let's say the claim is

The crime was committed by someone in the house.

When Watson protests, Holmes does not stop there. He does not raise his voice and simply disagree with Watson. Instead, he backs his claim with reasons that support it. Suppose he provides the following reasons:

(1) Although the living room window is open, there are no footprints outside, despite the softness of the ground after yesterday's rain.

(2) The clasp on the box was not broken but opened with a key that had been hidden behind the clock.

(3) The dog did not bark.

Holmes has now given us three reasons that support his claim. He has provided us with an argument, based on three observations, that supports the claim that the crime was an 'inside job'.

Unlike the men in the Monty Python skit, Holmes has given an 'argument' in the sense in which the term is used in logic. For this is a context in which an *argument* is *a set of reasons offered in support of a claim*. Arguments of this sort are the essence of reasoning, which is a rational attempt to decide what should be believed. Arguments may be presented orally, in a written text, or by means of photographs, pictures, symbols, and other visual images (visual arguments are discussed in detail in Chapter 3). The claim an argument supports is called its *conclusion*. The reasons offered in support of a conclusion are called its *premises*.

The simplest arguments have one premise. In the Monty Python skit that we began with, an argument in our sense emerges when the man looking for an argument, exasperated, denies that an argument can be the same as a contradiction, retorting, 'No it can't. An argument is a connected series of statements intended to establish a definite proposition.'

This is a one-premise argument that can be summarized as follows:

> PREMISE: An argument is a connected series of statements intended to establish a definite proposition.
> CONCLUSION: It can't be the same as a contradiction.

In the Holmes example, the conclusion is supported by three premises. In other arguments, conclusions may be supported by more or fewer premises. Most of the arguments that we use in our day-to-day lives are complex combinations of premises and conclusions that contain a main argument and a number of sub-arguments that support the premises the main argument depends on.

Arguments are motivated by the intentions of arguers. First and foremost, an arguer's intention is to convince an audience—someone or some group of people—that a given claim is acceptable, or that a proposed course of action is or is not justified. A strong argument convinces an audience because its premises are acceptable rather than unacceptable, and because they justify the conclusion. We shall have much to say about the difference between strong and weak (and good and bad) arguments in later chapters of this book. In the present chapter, we focus on the nature of arguments and their components, as this is the best way to prepare for that discussion.

2. AN EXAMPLE

We will take our first example of real argument from the lead article in the Plaistow, New Hampshire, *Rockingham News* on 30 August 2002. Entitled 'Dog-fight leader gets prison', it recounts the case of a man who was tried for cruelty to animals after he trained 43 pit bull terriers to fight in matches he staged. Like other cases tried before the courts, this is a paradigm example of a context in which arguments occur.

In the case in question, Judge Gillian Abrahamson presented an argument when she said that the actions of the man who trained the dogs and staged the fights, Christopher DeVito, were disturbing because he had 'inflicted such pain and torture on helpless animals for fun and profit.' She presented another argument when she remarked that the severity of the 37 counts of 'Exhibition of Fighting Animals' justified a sentence in a state prison rather than a county jail.

The attorney for the defendant, Michael Natola, argued when he asserted that the sentence handed down by Judge Abrahamson did not fit the crime because it was 'unprecedented in its length'. A coordinator for the Humane Society of the United States New England Regional Office, Hillary Twining, argued for a contrary conclusion when she supported the prison sentence, claiming that 'the minor penalties associated with misdemeanour convictions are not a sufficient deterrent.' They were not sufficient, she claimed, because 'dog fighting yields such large profits for participants [that dog fighters] merely absorb these fines as part of the cost of doing business.'

Like other legal and social issues, this is one that is characterized by many conflicting arguments. Both the prosecuting attorney and the lawyer defending Mr DeVito presented arguments to the court. The judge responded with a decision backed by argument. The lawyers and the judge argued in a broader context that included arguments that were presented in newspapers, in letters to the editor, in public meetings, and in many public and private conversations. All of these arguments took place in an even broader context characterized by debate about the rights of animals and cruelty to animals.

Arguments in real life usually occur in complex contexts of this sort. In most cases, contrary arguments are possible, and a variety of issues may be discussed and debated. In part because of this, argumentation is a complex, open-ended process that may develop and evolve in a variety of ways.

Exercise 1A*

1. The discussion of the report in the *Rockingham News* notes a number of arguments that emerged in the trial of Christopher DeVito. Identify three of these arguments by specifying the premise(s) and conclusion of each.

2.*The discussion of the dog-trainer's case might easily evolve in a way that considers many related issues. Given that it is wrong to be cruel to animals, one might ask, why is it permissible to kill them and eat them, for isn't killing animals a form of cruelty? Identify the premise and conclusion in this argument and construct your own argument for the conclusion that it is (or is not) wrong to kill animals to eat them (use no more than three premises in your argument). Identify the premises and the conclusion of your argument.

3. Someone defending those who stage dog fights might argue that we permit boxing, so we should permit dog fighting. Should these two sports be treated similarly? Why or why not? Construct an argument (with no more than three premises) for a conclusion one way or the other.

4. Do you think that animals should be used in scientific experiments? Write a short argument (one paragraph) that supports your view.

5. Explain how someone with an opposing point of view might argue against the argument you prepared in answer to question 4.

*In this and other exercise sets, answers to starred questions are provided in the 'Selected Answers' section at the back of this book.

3. ARGUERS, AUDIENCES, AND OPPONENTS

Traditional logic analyzes arguments in terms of premises and conclusions. This is an important perspective, but there are other ways to look at arguments. Because argumentation is a communicative act, what is sometimes called a 'speech act', arguments should also be analyzed in terms of three parties who play a central role in argument.

The first party to an argument is the arguer—the party who forwards the argument. Usually this party is an individual, but it may also be a group of people or a corporate body of some sort—a company, a branch of government, or some other organization. When we ourselves construct arguments we are, of course, arguers. Arguers construct arguments in contexts that are characterized by disagreement and debate or in which these have the potential to arise. It is in such contexts that an arguer may want to reinforce a point of view with reasons that support it. In judging arguments, we often judge the arguer as well as the argument they provide, because their credibility is essential to their trustworthiness (an indication of their character, or what argumentation theorists call their *ethos*). An arguer's credibility will probably determine our willingness to accept many aspects of the claims they make. The importance of an arguer's character in the assessment of argument gives rise to a whole family of arguments—called *ethotic* arguments—which we discuss in Chapter 14.

A second party to an argument is the *audience* to whom the argument is addressed. We use arguments when we want to convince an audience—someone or some group of people—that a given claim is true or false or acceptable, or that some course of action is or is not justified. In some circumstances we act as our own audience. Sherlock Holmes probably reasons through to his conclusion privately before he presents an argument to Watson. He may begin with a hypothesis, then look to see if there is evidence to support it. On another occasion, he may be struck by one or more pieces of evidence, and reason from these to his conclusion, reinforcing his argument with other premises that present additional evidence. Holmes acts as his own audience as he develops the argument in his mind.

After Holmes is satisfied with his conclusion, he sets about convincing another audience that it is correct—in this case, Watson. Poor reasoners often fail to distinguish between audiences, assuming that whatever convinces them of some conclusion will and should convince other audiences. In cases where two people (say, Holmes and Watson) share very similar points of view, this is a reasonable assumption. But it is an erroneous assumption in broader contexts, and especially in contexts in which we must interact and argue with audiences who do not share our point of view. In such contexts, it is egocentric to believe that the things that we care about are characteristic of our audience, which may have a very different set of beliefs and values. This is often the case given that arguments are the principal means we use to try to convince those who have different points of view that they should accept our own conclusions.

The role that audiences play in arguments is often evident in historical examples. These examples can be instructive because they were designed to appeal to audiences who had different attitudes, beliefs, and concerns than we do. When we read these arguments, such differences may jump out at us, making the arguments seem peculiar. Consider the following 1940s advertisement for Philip Morris cigarettes:

Medical authorities know <u>this</u> <u>one</u> is superior—
  Philip Morris
Scientifically proved less irritating to the nose and throat.
When smokers changed to Philip Morris, <u>substantially</u> <u>every</u> <u>case</u> <u>of</u> <u>irritation</u> of nose and throat—due to smoking—cleared up completely, or definitely improved!
That is the <u>findings</u> of <u>distinguished</u> <u>doctors</u>, in clinical tests of men and women smokers—reported in an authoritative medical journal.
Solid *proof* that this finer-tasting cigarette is *less irritating* to the nose and throat!
Call for Philip Morris
  America's <u>finest</u> cigarette

Today, it seems peculiar to cite 'distinguished doctors' and 'medical authorities' in an advertisement for cigarettes, for we live at a time when it has been clearly demonstrated that smoking is injurious to one's health. We all know that medical authorities would recommend not that one smoke a particular brand of cigarette, but that one *should not smoke*. The only medical studies likely to be cited in such a context are studies that demonstrate that smoking contributes to particular kinds of ailment. Because of this, the Philip Morris argument has little impact on contemporary audiences.

Another feature of the Philip Morris advertisement that is worth noting in this context is a slogan—'Buy more war bonds'—that appears with it. This tag is characteristic of North American advertisements during the Second World War, when advertisers felt a pressing need to assert their patriotism, something that was necessary if their advertisements were to appeal to a population that was wholly preoccupied with the war effort. It is for this reason that a full-page advertisement for Camel cigarettes on the back of *Life* (27 July 1942) features photos of a woman labourer working in a cockpit and a pilot flying a B-24 Bomber, with the caption:

When Bombers are your Business
  — ON THE ASSEMBLY LINE — ON THE FRONT LINE
  YOU WANT STEADY NERVES
  IMPORTANT TO STEADY SMOKERS:
    The <u>smoke</u> of
      slow-burning
      CAMELS
      contains
      LESS NICOTINE

Like the Philip Morris ad, this Camel advertisement tries to strike a responsive chord in the audience of the day—in this case, by producing an ad that associates the alleged mildness of Camel cigarettes with the ongoing war effort. This is an association that is underscored by other aspects of the ad, which features quotes from women who are working on the manufacture of the B-24 and a note that, 'With men in the Army, Navy, Marines, Coast Guard, the favourite cigarette is Camel. (Based on actual sales records in Post Exchanges and Canteens.)'

Similar attempts to engage an audience preoccupied with war characterize other advertisements of the same era. In an advertisement in *Life* (11 October 1943) Nestle's chocolate bars are advertised under the title of a column written by the famous war correspondent Ernie Pyle. Underneath the title ('U.S. Troops Fight On Chocolate Diet') one reads that:

> This is the way famed war correspondent Ernie Pyle started one of his columns that are appearing daily in the Scripps-Howard newspapers . . . Yes, chocolate is a fighting food, it supplies the greatest amount of nourishment in the smallest possible bulk. So wherever America fights, the Army uses chocolate in the form of emergency rations, selected because it contains so much quick energy . . .

The preoccupation with World War II that is reflected in arguments and advertisements of this period is accompanied by other assumptions and values that characterize the audience of the day. The Campbell Soup advertisement we have adapted below (p. 8)—'Put A Feather in Mrs. Canada's Cap'—is addressed to women readers of the Canadian magazine *Star Weekly*. It suggests that they should buy Campbell's cream of mushroom soup because it is 'unusual and especially good' and, much more importantly, because it will make a good impression on their families, an achievement for these women to take pride in—a 'feather in their cap'. Underlying the advertisement is the assumption that women are homemakers and that they should aspire to perform their housework in ways that will earn them the approval of their families.

These advertisements—and other arguments of the past—strike us as odd because we are not the audience they address. The audience of the past had a different set of attitudes, beliefs, and concerns that made these arguments seem natural and appropriate. Some would argue that the appeal to a war effort against fascism has now been replaced by an appeal to comfort, sex, and an ever higher standard of living. Whether this is so or not, it is likely that future audiences who look at our advertisements and arguments will find many of them peculiar, for they will assume a different point of reference that is characterized by a different set of beliefs and values. With hindsight, it is often easy to point to naive or misguided beliefs and convictions in the arguments of the past. Though other naive and misguided beliefs and convictions probably characterize our own arguments, it is much more difficult to identify them because we take them for granted. Logic can help us develop a critical attitude to arguments that will enable us to identify questionable assumptions more easily.

Sophisticated arguers recognize that arguments need to be attuned to audiences and respond to the views and the perspective of whatever audience they address. If we want to convince you that you should vote for a particular politician, and we know that you are concerned about budget overspending, we may appeal to her record of fiscal responsibility. If we are arguing with someone who thinks that poverty is the most

important social issue, we may argue on the basis of her record of commitment to the poor. It would be dishonest to say in the first case that she will decrease social spending and in the second that she will increase it. But it would be equally wrongheaded to assume that the same argument is appropriate for different audiences whose views differ radically. Each audience has its own issues, values, and concerns, and a good reasoner is obligated to recognize and respond to these.

Sometimes arguers take advantage of audiences, playing on their biases and taking advantage of their lack of knowledge. In part, this is possible because many audiences are made up of people who do not reason well, and who can be persuaded by arguments that do not satisfy the criteria for good reasoning. This is especially true in the case of audiences that have not developed a good sense of reasonableness. By promoting the study of reasoning, we aim to neutralize the power of bad arguments both by developing the logical acumen of audiences (for we are all audiences) and by teaching the ability to persuade with good reasoning. Our goal is 'reasonable persuasion' rather than mere 'persuasion'.

One way to ensure that we argue in a reasonable way that does not take advantage of an audience is by respecting obligations that we have to a third party to an argument. This party is made up of those who oppose our conclusion and our point of view—individuals we might loosely call the argument's *opponents*. Even when they are not included in our immediate audience, these opponents are important, for arguments develop in controversial contexts that are characterized by a process of argument and counter-argument (what argumentation theorists call 'dialectical' contexts). If we are arguing for a public medicare system, this means that we should take seriously (and, ideally, anticipate) the objections to our arguments that are likely to be forwarded by those who are opposed to publicly supported healthcare. If we are arguing against the use of animals in medical experiments, we will need to respond to the views of those who think that such use is justified because it is necessary for the development of medicine.

A commitment to pay attention to the arguments of opponents forces us to take objections to our views seriously. In Judaism, a Rabbi who meets with someone who wishes to convert is obligated to make three genuine attempts to convince them that this is *not* a good idea. This is a version of the principle that one should take objections to one's conclusions seriously. In this case, the idea is that one is not ready for such a momentous decision unless one is certain enough not to be persuaded by objections to it. More generally, a commitment to reason well requires that we take objections to our views seriously whenever we make important decisions or argue for particular points of view.

4. SIMPLE AND EXTENDED ARGUMENTS

A *simple argument* is an argument that has one conclusion that is supported by one or more premises. Simple arguments represent the basic unit of reasoning. An *extended argument* is an argument that has a main conclusion supported by premises, and some premises that are supported by other arguments. The following example illustrates how simple arguments can evolve into extended arguments.

In a book expounding the Christian notion of grace, *What's So Amazing About Grace?* (Zondervan/Harper Collins, 1997, p. 247), Philip Yancey writes that, 'For all its flaws the church at times has, fitfully and imperfectly to be sure, dispensed Jesus' message of grace to the world. It was Christianity, and only Christianity, that brought an end to slavery, and Christianity that inspired the first hospitals and hospices to treat the sick. The same energy drove the early labour movement, women's suffrage, prohibition, human rights campaigns, and civil rights.' This passage is naturally interpreted as a simple argument, for it presents a claim (that the Christian church has, despite its flaws, made Jesus' message of grace manifest in the world) and backs it with reasons for thinking that this is so (it was only Christianity that brought an end to slavery; it was Christianity that inspired the first hospitals and hospices; and so on and so forth).

Yancey's argument appears in a book that is written for Christian readers. His argument may, when it is taken in conjunction with his other claims and arguments, convince this audience that there is something valuable and worthwhile in the Christian church. But it is easy to see how his simple argument may quickly evolve into an extended argument. For one's willingness to accept the argument will depend on one's willingness to accept the premises, and those skeptical of his Christian point of view are not likely to accept them without debate. Skeptics are, for example, likely to reject the claim that it was only Christianity that brought an end to slavery, or that Christianity made women's suffrage possible.

Defending Yancey's argument to a broader audience that includes those skeptical of religion requires that one build arguments for his premises. In the process, one turns his initial argument into an extended argument. In the course of real debate about the Christian church, it is likely that all of Yancey's premises will have to be defended. Some of the premises used to support his premises may have to be backed by further argument. It is in this way that a simple argument naturally evolves into a complex extended argument made up of a principal argument and sub-arguments that back its premises.

DEFINITIONS

➤ An *argument* is a set of reasons designed to support a claim. The reasons are called *premises*. The claim they support is called the *conclusion*. The sentence, 'She's a better chess player than he is, so he'll never date her,' expresses an argument. Its conclusion is the claim that he'll never date her. It has one premise, which is the statement that she's a better chess player than he is.

➤ An *audience* is an individual or group to whom an argument is directed. Arguments are a way to convince particular audiences of some point of view. The audience for any arguments we make in this text is you, the reader.

> ➤ The **opponents** are those individuals who hold an opposing point of view. In preparing arguments, we are obligated to try to answer the objections that the opponents might propose.
> ➤ A **simple argument** is an argument that has one conclusion supported by one or more premises. An **extended argument** is an argument that has a main conclusion supported by premises, some of which are conclusions of subsidiary arguments.

Exercise 1B

1. Describe two different audiences to whom you might present an argument for or against the use of animals in scientific experiments (each audience may be an individual or a collective). What are the issues that are likely to matter to each audience?

2. *What is the argument in the following ad from *Family* (May/June 1996), which features a large photo of a baby, accompanied by text? Who is the intended audience? How can you tell?

   > YOU'RE THE ONE WHO HAS PROMISED TO PROTECT HER. PROTECT HER SCALP FROM IRRITATION WITH NEW IMPROVED JOHNSON'S BABY SHAMPOO, THE <u>ONLY</u> <u>ONE</u> <u>CLINICALLY</u> <u>PROVEN</u> <u>HYPOALLERGENIC</u>.

3. You are in the process of buying a new house. You must decide between three different options: (A) You buy a deluxe condominium on Lakeshore Boulevard; (B) You buy a modest bungalow on Northfield Road; (C) You decide to give up on the house and move into a downtown apartment. Option A will let you live the lifestyle you will most enjoy; option B will save you a significant amount of money; option C will place you within walking distance of a good grade school for your children. Pick an option and write an argument for it that is addressed to (a) your spouse, (b) your children, (c) your parents.

4. In recent years, dentists, medical researchers, and health activists have debated the risks of 'silver' amalgam fillings. The principal ingredient in these fillings is mercury, which is toxic to human beings. Those opposed to amalgam fillings argue that the mercury in the fillings does not remain inert and enters the body, where it can cause serious illness and multiple side effects. Those committed to amalgam fillings (including professional dentistry associations) have argued that there is no convincing evidence to back these claims. In order to explore the argumentation in this debate,

   a) go to the World Wide Web, find a site that discusses amalgam fillings, and identity the premises and conclusion in one argument it contains;

b) identify and analyze the argument forwarded in the following excerpt from the website of the American Dental Association <http://www.ada.org/public/faq/fillings.html#safe> (18 Dec. 2002), explaining how one would turn it into an extended argument.

Are dental amalgams safe?

Yes. Dental amalgam has been used in tooth restorations worldwide for more than 100 years. Studies have failed to find any link between amalgam restorations and any medical disorder. Amalgam continues to be a safe restorative material for dental patients.

5. The following illustration is a copy of a 1997 recruitment poster used by the British Army (see *The Guardian Weekly*, 19 Oct. 1997, p. 9). It is a revised version of a famous World War I recruitment poster that depicted Lord Kitchener in the same pose, his gloved hand pointing at the viewer while he declares 'Your country needs YOU'. During the war and afterwards, the poster was widely recognized as a patriotic symbol. In the 1997 version, the face of a black officer is superimposed over the face of Lord Kitchener. There is an argument being conveyed in the poster. What is it? Identify the premises and conclusion and discuss it from the point of view of audience.

5. Distinguishing Arguments from Non-arguments

We have defined an argument as a conclusion and a set of supporting statements ('premises'). The first step in argument analysis is recognizing arguments and their components. It is important to distinguish the identification of an argument from an assessment of it. When we say here that something is an argument, we are not saying that it is a good argument. It may be strong or weak, plausible or implausible, convincing or unconvincing, but we leave the determination of this for later chapters. As part of your approach to good reasoning, you should separate the attempt to identify and summarize an argument from the attempt to decide whether it is a good one. In the early chapters of this book, our concern is the former rather than the latter.

Sometimes enthusiastic students (or pugnacious individuals) are inclined to interpret almost anything as an argument. This is a mistake, for many claims and remarks are not properly developed as attempts to provide evidence for some conclusion. We use language for many purposes other than arguing—to report facts, to convey our feelings, to ask questions, to propose hypotheses, to express our opinions, etc. The first step in learning how to analyze arguments is, therefore, learning how to distinguish between arguments and non-arguments.

Logical Indicators

In deciding whether or not a set of sentences is an argument, it is important to remember that verbal arguments are expressed in a variety of ways. Sometimes the conclusion comes first and is followed by premises. Sometimes the premises come first and are followed by the conclusion. At other times, some of the evidence is given first, followed by the conclusion, followed by further evidence.

'Logical indicators' are signposts that tell us that particular statements are premises or conclusions. The expressions 'consequently', 'thus', 'so', 'hence', 'it follows that', 'therefore', and 'we conclude that' are *conclusion indicators*. When you come across these and other words and phrases that function in a similar way, it usually means that the statement that follows them is the conclusion of an argument. Consider the following examples:

> All the senior managers here are members of the owner's family. *So* I'll have to move if I want to get promoted.

> A human being is constituted of both a mind and a body, and the body does not survive death; *therefore* we cannot properly talk about personal immortality.

In cases as simple as these, we can easily identify the premises, for they are the statements that remain after we identify the argument's conclusion. Remember, here we are simply identifying arguments without making any judgment about the quality of the reasoning.

In other cases arguments are designated by *premise indicators*. Common premise indicators include the expressions 'since', 'because', 'for', and 'the reason is'. The argument in our last example can be expressed with a premise rather than a conclusion indicator by wording it as follows:

> *Since* a human being is constituted of both a mind and a body, and the body does not survive death, we cannot properly talk about personal immortality.

Here are two more arguments that use premise indicators:

> Nothing can be the cause of itself; *for* in that case it would have to exist prior to itself, which is impossible.

> Sheila must be a member of the cycling club, *because* she was at last week's meeting and only members were admitted.

In these and cases like them, premise indicators clearly identify the reasons offered for some conclusion. The conclusion of the argument is the statement they support. In the last case, the conclusion is the claim, 'Sheila must be a member of the cycling club.'

Arguments may contain both premise and conclusion indicators, but this is unusual, for once we know the premises or conclusion of an argument, its other components are usually obvious. An argument with a premise *or* a conclusion is usually a clear argument. In constructing your own arguments, the important point is that you should use logical indicators so that other people can clearly recognize that they are arguments and note what evidence you are offering for what conclusion.

COMMON LOGICAL INDICATORS

PREMISE INDICATORS

since	because
for	given that
as	the reasons are
can be deduced from	

CONCLUSION INDICATORS

consequently	thus
so	hence
therefore	we conclude that
it follows that	

Arguments without Indicator Words

Logical indicators are signposts that help us identify arguments and differentiate their premises and conclusions. But arguers often do not use logical indicators in their arguments. Very few advertisements contain logical indicators, for example, but most of them invite us to reason to the conclusion that we should buy this or that. To deal with cases such as these, we need to be able to determine when arguments occur without premise or conclusion indicators.

In trying to decide whether a group of sentences without a logical indicator is an argument, we need to consider whether the context in which the sentence group appears is a context in which something is in dispute or controversial: is the situation one in which someone should justify some claim by offering reasons in support of it? Argumentative contexts can be illustrated with Stephen Brunt's book *Facing Ali: The Opposition Weighs In* (Alfred Knopf, 2002), which is made up of interviews with the opponents who boxed against Muhammed Ali. On the back of the jacket cover, there are three quotes under the heading *Praise for* FACING ALI. The following quote is assigned to Bert Sugar, who is identified as the 'co-author of *Sting Like a Bee* and former editor and publisher of *Ring Magazine*':

> Just when you think that everything about Muhammad Ali and his career has been written, re-written and over written, along comes Stephen Brunt to give us a valuable new perspective to the Ali story in this extraordinary look at the parties of the second part: his opponents. *Facing Ali* has 'winner' written all over it. And through it.

This passage contains no premise or conclusion indicators—no 'therefore', 'since', or 'because'. But it is plausibly taken as an argument. For the quotes on the back of the book jacket are not there simply to inform us; they are there to convince prospective readers that Stephen Brunt's book is a book worth reading and, more fundamentally, that it is a book that they should buy. This is the function of the information that is typically included on the cover of a book. In the case of Brunt's book, the quote from Bert Sugar is plausibly interpreted as the argument that the book is worth reading—that it 'has "winner" written all over it'—because it unexpectedly provides a 'valuable new perspective to the Ali story' and 'an extraordinary look' at his opponents. This simple argument can in turn be plausibly construed as an argument for a further conclusion that is unstated, i.e. that one should buy this book.

It is important to recognize contexts that are argumentative contexts, for they are contexts in which we need to adopt a critical attitude that asks whether the reasons given for some claim are convincing. We need to recognize that we are dealing with an attempt to convince us to purchase Mary Gordon's *Joan of Arc* (Weidenfeld & Nicholson/Penguin, 2000) when, on the inside cover of the book, we read, 'In this book Mary Gordon, with the passion and grace that mark her bestselling novels about women and faith, penetrates this cultural icon . . .' along with quotes of praise for her other books. In this context, we need to ask how strongly quotes from two newspaper reviews (two reviews out of possibly thousands, in a context where reviewers may disagree radically) support the conclusion that we should buy the book.

When arguments are presented without premise or conclusion indicators—as though they were simple statements of fact—it is easy to forget that they need to be queried and evaluated. In many cases, it is possible that indicators are not used precisely because the author of an argument wants to present it as a matter of fact that is not open to dispute. If we fail to raise questions in such cases, we fail to adopt the critical stance that a healthy attitude to argument requires.

Context is one important factor that can help us decide whether a set of sentences with no logical indicators should be classified as an argument. In making this decision, we should also pay attention to other clues that may be found in the wording of the sentences themselves. Suppose, for example, we find the following paragraph in a letter on the history of South America:

> The artistic motifs that characterize the ruins of ancient Aztec pyramids are very similar to those found in Egypt. And the animals and vegetation found on the eastern coasts of South America bear a striking resemblance to those of West Africa. From all appearances, there was once a large land mass connecting these continents.

This passage does not contain standard indicator words. Yet its first two sentences report observational data that appear to justify a speculative third statement—a statement that is the kind of statement that needs to be supported. This appears to be confirmed by the expression 'from all appearances', which acts as a bridge between the first two sentences and the third. In this way, the internal clues in the passage convince us that this is a case in which the author offers his first two statements as premises for his last.

Borderline Cases

The ability to detect arguments on the basis of context and internal clues is a skill that everyone has to some degree, but it is a skill that improves with practice. The more time you spend looking for, detecting, and analyzing arguments, the better you will be at distinguishing arguments from non-arguments, though no amount of skill will resolve all of the issues raised by difficult cases. The kinds of questions that arise in the latter situations are illustrated in the following example, adapted from a letter to the *Hamilton Spectator*, written on the occasion of a strike by steel workers in the city:

> Haven't we had enough letters to the editorial page of the *Spectator* every day and from cry-baby steel workers talking about how the Stelco strike is killing them? I am sure there are hundreds of pro-union letters going into the *Spectator* office, but only the anti-union ones are printed. I would not be a bit surprised if Stelco and the *Spectator* were working together to lower the morale of the steel workers who chose to strike for higher wages.

It is difficult to say whether or not this passage contains an argument. Certainly an opinion is expressed. But does the author offer reasons to support it?

If we want to distill an argument from the letter, it might look something like this:

PREMISE: We have had enough letters to the editorial page from cry-baby steel workers talking about how the Stelco strike is killing them.

PREMISE: I am sure there are hundreds of pro-union letters going into the *Spectator* office, but only the anti-union ones are printed.

CONCLUSION: There is reason to believe that Stelco and the *Spectator* are working together to lower the morale of steel workers.

This interpretation of the letter contains some linguistic adjustments. The final sentence in the published letter reads like a privately held suspicion. We have reworded it so that it carries the impact of a conclusion (but in a way that is in keeping with the tentative tone of the author's comments). Given that the writer has decided to express such a controversial claim publicly, it is plausible to suppose that she wants to convince readers that it is true, on the basis of the considerations she has raised in the earlier sentences of her letter. For this reason we have interpreted 'I would not be a bit surprised if . . .' as the claim, 'There is reason to believe that . . .'

In creating our first premise we have put into statement form what appeared in the letter as a question, changing 'Haven't we had enough letters . . .?' to 'We have had enough letters . . .' This is not an arbitrary change, for it highlights a common stylistic feature shared by many ordinary-language arguments. Genuine questions are not statements but requests for information, so they cannot function as a premise or conclusion in an argument. But not all questions are requests. Some are implicit statements or assertions that are expressed as questions for 'rhetorical' effect. They are used because they involve the person who hears or reads the argument in the argument, forcing them to answer the question in the way intended. We call such questions *rhetorical questions*. In the case at hand, the writer is not genuinely asking whether there have or have not been enough letters to the editorial page. Rather, her question is a way of asserting that there *have* been enough letters. Our revised wording clarifies this meaning.

We could have constructed a more complex representation of the chain of reasoning that seems to be contained in this letter about steel workers. We could have identified as an intermediary conclusion, or 'sub-conclusion', the statement, 'the *Spectator* presents a biased view of the Stelco strike,' which is implied in the second premise. This sub-conclusion could itself be construed as a premise for the main conclusion, that Stelco and the *Spectator* are working together to lower the morale of the steel workers. In this and many other cases, alternative interpretations and representations of the same argument are possible. In the present case, the proposed premises and conclusion are sufficient for our purposes.

The question remains: does the writer argue? Does she assert a claim and provide evidence for it? Do our proposed premises and conclusion capture reasoning in the letter? Is this a context in which reasons have been given for some conclusion? Perhaps so, perhaps not. It is always difficult to discern someone else's intentions if they do not use explicit or even oblique indicator words. While this is a context in which an argument would be appropriate—the letter is, after all, published in the context of a debate about the steel workers' strike—you may think that there is not enough internal evidence to show that the author of the letter should be attributed the argument we have suggested.

We have chosen this example precisely because it is difficult to say whether the letter in question should be treated as an argument. In dealing with borderline cases of this sort, you will do well to recognize that there is no certain way to establish whether the author of the letter intended it as an argument. The only evidence we have is the letter itself, and it might be interpreted as an argument or not. Rather than attempt to do the impossible and decide between these two alternatives, you will do better to acknowledge this uncertainty and then deal with the issues that it raises. This can be done in a way that recognizes that the intentions of the author are somewhat unclear. We can, for example, respond to the *Spectator* letter by remarking that

> The author of this letter suggests that the *Spectator* is acting in collusion with Stelco. She appears to believe that this is so on the grounds that . . . If this is her reasoning, then she has failed to adequately back her claims. . . .

Here the expressions 'She appears to believe' and 'If this is her reasoning' clearly recognize that it is possible that the author of the letter intends it in a different way. But our remarks also allow us to deal with the argumentative issues that are raised by her letter in view of the argument it *may* contain. And dealing with these issues in this way is the proper way to further the discussion and debate.

In cases where we wish to analyze a possible argument, we can recognize the ambiguity of the arguer's intention by introducing our discussion with a statement like the following:

> It is not clear whether the author intends to argue for the claim that . . . He appears to think that this claim can be justified on the grounds that . . . If this is what he intends, then it must be said that . . .

We can then go on to outline the tentative argument we wish to discuss, and to analyze it as we would analyze other arguments. The caveat that we add to such analyses allows us to deal with possible arguments that are worth discussing even if their author intended them in another way. The simple fact that someone might interpret their claims in this way warrants this discussion.

When we do attempt to identify and assess arguments it is important to remember the risk that we may misinterpret someone's claims. When we construct our own arguments we want to construct them in a way that prevents misinterpretation. In dealing with other people's claims, we must be particularly careful not to interpret their claims as bad arguments they may not have intended (the principle that we should adopt a charitable interpretation is called the 'Principle of Charity'). As someone involved in argumentative discussion, which is characterized by controversy and debate, you need to remember that the attempt to avoid misinterpretation does not mean that you should avoid issues that are raised by someone's remarks. If it is unclear what they intend, you should say so, but this should not stop you from discussing whatever issues are raised by their remarks (intentionally or unintentionally). It is by pursuing such discussion that you will best contribute to the clearer understanding that is the ultimate goal of argument.

EXERCISE 1C

1. The following passage is a variant of the second proof of God's existence found in St Thomas Aquinas's *Summa Theologica* (the argument is sometimes called the 'argu-

ment from first cause'). Identify all the premise and conclusion indicators used in the passage, and identify the structure of the argument, i.e. what premises lead to what conclusions.

> The second proof of God's existence is from the nature of cause and effect. In the world we find that there is an order of causes and effects. There is nothing which is the cause of itself; for then it would have to be prior to itself, which is impossible. Therefore things must be caused by prior causes. So there must be a first cause, for if there be no first cause among the prior causes, there will be no ultimate, nor any intermediate cause, for to take away the cause is to take away the effect. If there were an infinite series of causes, there would be no first cause, and neither would there be an ultimate effect, nor any intermediate causes; all of which is plainly false. Therefore it is necessary to admit a first cause, to which everyone gives the name of God.

2. Insert premise or conclusion indicators, and/or revise the following sentences, in a way that clarifies the argument.
   a)* [from a travel brochure] You'll like the sun. You'll like the beach. You'll like the people. You'll like Jamaica.
   b) [from a letter to *New Woman* (July 1995)] I am disgusted that *New Woman* printed the letter from B.A. Showalter . . . Showalter said, 'You don't see straight people pushing their lifestyle on everyone else.' But straight people and straight society do just that. From day one, children are assumed to be heterosexual. They are exposed to tales of heterosexual romance, pushed to enjoy the company of the opposite sex, and given little opportunity to explore the alternative.
   c)* [adapted from a letter in defence of the decision by the Serbian military to take UN peacekeepers hostage, in *Time* (3 July 1995)] The Serbs have responded in accordance with appropriate military procedure. Proper military procedure makes soldiers Prisoners of War, not hostages. Those individuals taken are soldiers in combat. They have the right to fire and bomb.
   d) [adapted from Aristotle, in *Metaphysics*, 1084a, pp. 1–4] Number must be either infinite or finite. But it cannot be infinite. An infinite number is neither odd nor even, but numbers are always odd or even.

3. Are the following passages arguments? Borderline cases? What would you say about the passage if you were responding to it?
   a) [Martha Beck, in 'Looking for Dr Listen-Good', *The Oprah Magazine* (Jan. 2003), p. 42] You can steer clear of all these nightmare councillors by remembering Goethe's phrase 'Just trust yourself, then you will know how to live.' Rely on this truth at every stage of the therapeutic process. Trust yourself when your aching heart tells you it needs a compassionate witness. Trust yourself when your instincts warn you that the therapist your mother or a minister recommended isn't giving you the right advice. Trust yourself when, sitting in a relative stranger's office, you suddenly feel a frightening, exhilarating urge to tell truths you've never known until that very moment.

b)   She's the best boss I've ever had. She buys everyone a present on their birthday.

c)*   [from a letter to *National Geographic* (Nov. 1998)] The laboratory where I am a consultant obtained a hair sample of an alleged 1,200-year-old Peruvian mummy. Our analysis revealed levels of lead, cadmium, and aluminum 5 to 13 times higher than would be acceptable in the typical patient of today . . . consensus was that he received the contaminants from improperly glazed clay pottery.

d)   [from *Life Extension* (Dec. 2002), p. 32] . . . the fact is that millions of women all over the world don't need Premarin because they don't get the [menopause] symptoms Western women get. By now most people have heard that the Japanese have no word for 'hot flash'. But did you know that the Mayan and Navajo indigenous peoples don't either? The women in these cultures don't get 'hot flashes'. In fact, they get virtually no menopausal symptoms at all. And it's not because they have strange rituals or odd lifestyles. They simply eat differently. Sounds boring, but these women incorporate things in their diet that keep menopausal symptoms away.

e)*   [from *PC Gamer* (Dec. 2002)] **No other action game** has so brilliantly mixed ground combat with aerial support in a multiplayer setting. In Battlefield 1942, airpower is a strong weapon, . . . but it comes with high dangers. Ground-based anti-aircraft guns can chop you to pieces with flak, and enemy fighters are a constant dogfighting threat. But when you land your payloads, it's a devastating blow to the enemy.

f)   [from the same article] American, British, Russian, German, and Japanese forces are all modelled. Each map pits two forces against one another in a re-creation of a historic battle.

6. ARGUMENTS AND EXPLANATIONS

Attempting to distinguish arguments from non-arguments can sometimes be confusing because the indicator words used to indicate premises and a conclusion are sometimes used in other ways. In the sentence 'Since you arrived on the scene my life has been nothing but trouble,' the word 'since' does not act as a premise indicator but signals the passage of time. In the sentence 'I work for IBM,' the word 'for' is not a premise indicator, and 'thus' does not indicate a conclusion in 'You insert the CD in the CD-ROM drive thus.'

In cases like the ones just noted, it is obvious that indicator words do not function as a way to signal premises and conclusions. In other cases, this may not be obvious, especially in cases where indicators like 'so', 'since', 'therefore', and 'because' are used in giving explanations. To understand why these words are used in explanations—and to appreciate the difference between arguments and explanations—you need to understand two different meanings that characterize our ordinary talk of 'reasons'.

When we talk of 'reasons' in logic we mean 'reasons for believing something'. It is in this sense that premises are reasons for believing some conclusion. In other circumstances, the word 'reasons' means 'causes' rather than 'premises'. In this kind of context, the *reason* something happened is the *cause* that brought it about. Consider Hugh Rawson's opening remarks in a book on folk etymology (*Devious Derivations*, Castle Books, 2002, p. 1): 'One of the most basic of all human traits is the urge to find reasons for why things are as they are. Ancient peoples heard thunder and created gods of thunder. They witnessed the change of seasons, and devised stories to explain the coming of winter and the miraculous rebirth of spring. The tendency is universal, appearing in every aspect of human thought and endeavor.'

In this context, the reasons alluded to are those things that bring about—i.e. cause—thunder, the seasons, and everything else that humans aspire to explain. Among the contemporary issues we want to explain are global warming, why some people manage to live so long, and why Mad Cow disease became a human problem. In explaining such phenomena we often use indicator words. We say that global warming has intensified *since* we burn too much fossil fuel; that Aunt Sally lived so long *because* she didn't drink or smoke and avoided arguments; or that the protein molecules that cause Mad Cow disease are not contained in milk, *so* one cannot contract the disease by drinking milk.

In deciding whether indicator words are being used to indicate an argument or an explanation, you need to consider the status of the claim that is backed by reasons. Consider the claim 'X, therefore Y'. If this is an argument, it is Y (the conclusion) that is in dispute. If it is an explanation, it is X (the reasons given for Y) that is in dispute. In an explanation, we know what happened and are trying to determine the reasons for it. In an argument (at least if it is a good argument), we know the reasons we cite and are using them to establish some further conclusion that is in doubt.

The claim 'The house burnt down because they were smoking in bed' is an explanation. If we put it into the form 'X, therefore Y', then X would be equivalent to 'They were smoking in bed', and Y would equal 'The house burnt down'. In such a case, Y is not in doubt. The issue is what reasons explain why Y occurred. It would, therefore, be a mistake to interpret the claim as the following argument:

> PREMISE: They were smoking in bed.
> CONCLUSION: Their house burnt down.

In dealing with such cases, you should ask yourself whether the 'concluding' statement or state of affairs that is indicated by an indicator word is an issue of disagreement or debate. If the controversy surrounds the reasons (the 'premise' material) provided to account for the event, you are dealing with an explanation. If, on the other hand, the conclusion is controversial, and the reasons are assumed to be acceptable, then we have an argument.

Consider another example. Imagine a courtroom in which an expert witness makes the following remarks in explaining what happened in an accident:

> The minivan was carrying a load in excess of the maximum recommended and was hauling a trailer that had been improperly attached to the vehicle. Consequently, when the driver veered suddenly to the left—trying to avoid a stalled truck—he lost control of the vehicle and crashed into the oncoming vehicle.

These remarks give the reasons why (according to the expert) the accident occurred. The remarks make it clear that no one doubts that the crash occurred. What is in question is the cause of the crash, and it is this that the expert explains. Of course, the explanation offered for the crash might be debated. It probably will be debated if it is expert testimony in a trial that accuses the driver of breaking the law. In such a context, an explanation may *generate* an argument. But it is not itself an argument, and it would be a mistake to interpret it as one because it uses a word ('consequently') that is often used as a conclusion indicator.

You can usually distinguish arguments and explanations by putting them into the general scheme 'X, therefore Y' (or 'Y because X') and asking whether they are an attempt to explain the cause of Y or an attempt to argue the claim that Y is true. Alternatively, you can ask whether X or Y is in dispute. If Y (the conclusion) is in dispute, the sentences are an argument. If X (the set of reasons) is in dispute, they form an explanation.

Arguments within Explanations

Complex cases arise in situations in which explanations contain arguments. These situations occur because arguments can also be causes. We have already said that good reasoners are convinced by good arguments. In this way, good arguments cause them to hold certain beliefs. To explain the beliefs that people hold, and the behaviours that follow from them, we often need to explain the arguments that led people to such beliefs. In such cases, an explanation will contain an argument (the one ascribed to the person or persons whose belief is in question), and we will, in the process of identifying and assessing arguments, want to recognize and analyze it.

Consider an example. Imagine that it is January. You live in Detroit. Your daughter, Clara, gets up in the morning, looks out the window, and sees a blizzard raging. Instead of getting dressed and setting off to school she smiles and goes back to bed. Let's suppose she reasoned as follows: 'The schools close down whenever there is a blizzard, so there will be no school today.' It is clear that this is an argument. It is an argument that convinces Clara that she does not need to go to school.

When you bang on Clara's bedroom door and ask her why she isn't ready for school, she explains: 'Because there's a blizzard outside and they close the schools whenever there's a blizzard.' Clara is now offering an explanation. She is explaining why she isn't ready for school. If we put her explanation into the standard 'X, therefore Y' format, then X = There's a blizzard outside and they close the schools whenever there's a blizzard, and Y = I'm still not ready for school. This is clearly an explanation—it explains a cause, and it is the reasons (X) that led to it that are in question (Clara is not disputing that she is still in bed). But this is an explanation with a difference, for it is an explanation that explains the reasoning behind Clara's decision to stay in bed. In this way, her explanation outlines an argument, which might be summarized as follows:

> PREMISE 1: There's a blizzard outside.
> PREMISE 2: They close the schools whenever there's a blizzard.
> CONCLUSION: There's no need to get ready for school.

In the process of recognizing this argument, we recognize that this is a case in which an explanation contains an argument, and a case in which the word 'because' indicates both a causal explanation *and*, less directly, a set of premises in an argument.

Once we recognize Clara's argument, it can be assessed and analyzed in the ways that we analyze other arguments. Given that her explanation is, in part, an attempt to convince you that she does not need to get ready for school, you are likely to respond by evaluating her inference. You might look out the window and accept her premise, and accept the conclusion she has inferred. But you might disagree. You might challenge the suggestion that the snowfall outside qualifies as a 'blizzard', or you might remind Clara of times when Detroit schools (or her school) remained open, even in the middle of a blizzard. In all these situations, you intuitively recognize that her explanation contains an argument.

Another example can illustrate the difference between explanations that do and do not contain an argument. Suppose someone tells you that 'Germany lost the war because Hitler turned his attention to Russia when he had England at his mercy.' This is the kind of statement that is likely to elicit discussion in a conversation about World War II. Many would say it is a simplistic explanation of Germany's fall from strength. But it is not an argument. This is a case where 'because' indicates an explanation rather than an argument. For the statement that Germany lost the war is not a matter of dispute. In attempting to provide a causal explanation for why this happened, the speaker offers a controversial opinion, but they have not as yet attempted to provide evidence to support it.

Imagine that someone challenges the proposed explanation of Hitler's defeat. Suppose the speaker answers the challenge as follows:

> Sun Tzu's famous book *The Art of War* says that a successful military campaign must move swiftly. No army can sustain a war for a protracted period of time. Hitler ignored this wisdom. His decision to attack Russia committed him to a long and protracted war. Therefore, he failed.

In this remark our imaginary interlocutor *explains* the reasons that led to Hitler's fall. In view of this, the word 'therefore' functions as an explanation indicator. But this is a case in which the explanation contains an argument. For it indicates a chain of reasoning that might cause one to believe that Hitler was bound to lose the war when he decided to turn his attention to Russia instead of finishing the war against England. This chain of reasoning can be summarized as follows:

> PREMISE 1: Sun Tzu's famous book *The Art of War* tells us that a successful military campaign must move swiftly—no army can sustain a military operation for a protracted period of time.
> PREMISE 2: Hitler's decision to attack Russia ignored this wisdom, committing him to a protracted war.
> CONCLUSION: Once Hitler decided to attack Russia, he was bound to fail.

Once we recognize that the explanation contains this argument, we may ask a variety of questions that pertain to it. Does Sun Tzu say what our interlocutor claims? Is the proposed principle of military success debatable? Are there counter-examples that cast doubt upon it? Did the decision to attack Russia inevitably mean a long war? Were there other factors that extended it? Putting aside the answers to these questions, the important point is that this is another case where an explanation contains an argument that may be assessed.

These examples show that arguments and explanations are not in every case distinct. In logic, we have an argument whenever we have reasons forwarded as premises for a conclusion. Some explanations contain reasoning and can be said to contain an argument. In classifying sets of sentences as arguments and non-arguments we need, therefore, to distinguish between explanations that do and do not contain arguments.

7. ARGUMENT NARRATIVES

The most obvious examples of arguments are 'first-hand' arguments. They are arguments that are conveyed to us by the words of the arguer. Most of the examples in this book are first-hand arguments. In the cases that are unclear, the lack of clarity is inherent in the words of the author of the argument in question.

We have already seen that the situation is more complex when one deals with arguments that are contained in explanations. In such cases, the argument leads to the conclusion that one should accept the belief or behaviour that is explained. On other occasions, both in this book and in day-to-day reasoning, we will want to analyze second- (or third-) hand arguments that are similar in the sense that they are not expressed in the words of the actual arguer.

Consider an example from a novel. In the novel *Redwork*, Michael Bedard describes a liaison between one of his main characters, Alison, and a philosophy Ph.D. student she nicknames 'Hegel'. When her liaison with Hegel leads to pregnancy, 'His solution to the problem was as clear, clean and clinical as a logical equation—get rid of it. Instead, she had got rid of him. She hadn't had much use for philosophy since' (p. 24). In this passage, the narrator provides a second-hand account of reasoning, or 'argument narrative', which he attributes to Alison. We do not have the reasoning expressed in her own words, but it is clear that it was Alison's negative experience with her boyfriend that convinced her that she had no use for philosophy. We might summarize her argument as 'Hegel is a philosopher who deals with human situations in ways typical of a philosopher (in ways as clean and clinical as a logical equation), so philosophy is of no use to me.'

Like borderline cases, such argument narratives have to be treated with care, for it is always possible that the person who narrates the argument is not presenting it accurately. The kinds of problems this poses are highlighted in historical discussions of ancient thinkers whose written works have not survived. An extreme example is the ancient philosopher Pyrrho, who is famous for a radical skepticism that has exerted a great deal of influence on the history of philosophy. The closest we come to his views is an account of them provided by Eusebius, the fourth-century bishop of Caesarea, who quotes a passage in Aristocles' *On Philosophy*, which is an account of Pyrrho's philosophy given by his follower, Timon of Phlius. This long chain of reporting makes Eusebius's account a fourth-hand account of Pyrrho's views, written more than 500 years after Pyrrho died. In as extreme a case as this, the issues of accuracy that arise in the analysis of narrated arguments make it very difficult to establish, with any certainty, the argument the original arguer espoused.

The limited access we have to an arguer's own words when we deal with second-hand arguments calls for caution in such contexts, but we can still usefully analyze argument narratives in the way in which we analyze other arguments. In doing so we must be sure to recognize that we are, in such a case, analyzing the argument *someone else* has attributed to the arguer. Provided we have reasonable faith in the person who is attributing the argument, it may be worth analyzing for the same reason that other arguments are worth analyzing—because it can shed light on significant issues we want to explore and understand.

EXERCISE 1D

1. For each of the following passages, discuss whether it contains an explanation and/or argument. Identify any argument (or explanation) indicators in the text and discuss what needs to be said in responding to each passage. In the case of arguments, identify their premises and conclusion.

    a) The company lost a lot of money last year, so we are not getting a wage increase this year.

    b)* I believe that drugs should be legal because the attempt to ban them creates more problems than it solves.

    c) [adapted from a letter to the *TLS* (17 Jan. 2003)] Galileo was faced with the choice of whether to recant the Copernican theory or face almost certain death by torture at the hands of the Inquisition. He chose the disgrace of recanting, rather than an honourable death as a martyr to science, because his work was not complete. He was subsequently able to develop, among other things, a physics involving concepts of constant velocity and acceleration that were crucial to Newton's development of the laws of motion.

    d) [Emily Carr, in 'Klee Wyck', *The Emily Carr Collection* (2002), p. 23] Everything looked safe, but Jimmie knew how treacherous the bottom of Skedans Bay was; that's why he lay across the bow of his boat, anxiously peering into the water and motioning to Louisa his wife, who was at the wheel.

    e) [from an ad in *Oprah's Magazine* (Jan. 2003)] Over 34 million people are affected by nail fungus, a recurring infection that can spread and lead to serious consequences. So it's important to begin treatment at the first sign of symptoms.

    f)   [David Lodge, in *Small World* (1984), p. 231] Half the passengers on transatlantic flights these days are university teachers. Their luggage is heavier than average, . . . and bulkier, because their wardrobes must embrace both formal wear and leisure wear, clothes for attending lectures in, and clothes for going to the beach in, or the Museum, or the Schloss, or the Duomo, or the Folk Village. For that's the attraction of the conference circuit: it's a way of converting work into play . . .

    g)* [from Peter King's website <http://users.ox.ac.uk/~worc0337/note.html> (accessed 19 Dec. 2002)] The smug and offensive (and ignorant) tone of this [comment from another website] gets up my nose, and is a sure-fire way of ensuring that I don't include a link to the site in question.

2.   Provide two examples of each of the following:
    a)* argument
    b)   logical indicator
    c)   premise indicator
    d)* rhetorical question
    e)   audience
    f)   conclusion
    g)   conclusion indicator
    h)* opponent
    i)   second-hand argument

3.   Each of the following passages is taken from the discussion in this chapter, though the wording has sometimes been adapted for the purposes of this exercise. Each contains a simple argument. In each case, identify any logical indicators as well as the premises and conclusion.
    a)* We have defined an argument as a unit of discourse that contains a conclusion and supporting statements or premises. Since many groups of sentences do not satisfy this definition, and cannot be classified as arguments, we must begin learning about arguments in this sense by learning to differentiate between arguments and non-arguments.
    b)   In other cases, indicator words are used, but not to indicate premises and a conclusion. When you come across indicator words that have more than one use, you must therefore be sure that the word or phrase is functioning as a logical indicator.
    c)* In logic, we have an argument whenever we have reasons suggested as premises for a conclusion. Explanations can contain reasoning in this sense and can, therefore, be classified as arguments.
    d)   [Clara explaining why she isn't ready to go to school] 'Because there's a blizzard outside and they close Detroit schools whenever there's a blizzard.'
    e)   Sun Tzu's famous book *The Art of War* tells us that a successful military force must act swiftly and cannot sustain a military operation for a protracted period of time. But Hitler's decision to attack Russia inevitably committed him to a

long war. Because of this, he was bound to fail once he decided to attack Russia.

f)   It is important that you be alert to variations from the usual indicator words, for the richness of our language makes many variations possible.

g)   We have already seen that an argument is a unit of discourse consisting of a group of statements. But genuine questions are not statements, but requests for information. As such, a genuine question cannot serve as a premise or conclusion.

h)   Misinterpreting someone else's thinking is a serious mistake and we should therefore proceed with caution when we are trying to decide whether a particular discourse is or is not an argument.

4.   Explain why you are reading this book. As this explanation will have to explain your reasoning, it will contain an implicit argument. Identify the premises and conclusion in this argument.

Major Exercise 1M

For each of the following, decide whether an argument and/or explanation is present and explain the reasons for your decision. Be sure to qualify your remarks appropriately when dealing with borderline cases. In the case of arguments, provide the premises and conclusion.

a)*   Religion is nothing but superstition. Historians of religion agree that it had its beginnings in magic and witchcraft. Today's religious belief is just an extension of this.

b)*   [a comment by an observer who visited the seal hunt on the east coast of Newfoundland] The first time I went out onto the ice and saw the seal hunt it sickened me. I could not believe that a Canadian industry could involve such cruelty to animals and callous brutalization of men for profit.

c)*   The island of Antigua, located in the Caribbean, boasts secluded caves and dazzling beaches. The harbour at St John's is filled with the memories of the great British navy that once called there.

d)   [from an ad for Ceasefire, the Children's Defense Fund and Friends (1995)] Each year, hundreds of children accidentally shoot themselves or someone else. So if you get a gun to protect your child, what's going to protect your child from the gun?

e)   [from a passage in John Grisham's *The Chamber* (1994), where his protagonist, Adam, and the Governor discuss whether his client will name an accomplice and be granted clemency] It won't happen, Governor. I've tried. I've asked so often, and he's denied so much, that it's not even discussed any more.

f)*   [Donald Wildmon, quoted in *Time* (2 June 2003)] Could somebody have a husband and a woman partner at the same time and be a Christian? . . . I doubt that seriously.

g) [Richard Stengel, in *(You're Too Kind) A Brief History of Flattery* (Simon & Schuster, 2000), p. 11c] People who do not suffer fools gladly, gladly suffer flatterers. (Ergo, flatterers are no fools.)

h)* [Stengel, p. 14] In many ways, flattery works like a heat seeking missile, only what the missile homes in on is our vanity. And vanity, as the sages tell us, is the most universal human trait. . . . Flattery almost always hits its target because the target—you, me, everybody—rises up to meet it. We have no natural defense system against it.

i)* [from *Time* (2 June 2003), p. 4] As a single father who, when married, held down a demanding job and fully participated in child rearing and household chores, I was offended by Pearson's fatuous attempt to mine the worn-out vein of humour about useless males. She defines a husband as 'a well-meaning individual often found reading a newspaper'. None of the fathers and husbands I know come anywhere close to this stereotype. I was dismayed that *Time* would publish such tired pap and think it's funny or relevant.

j) [overheard at a train station] These trains are *never* on time. The last time I took one it was two hours late.

k) [from an ad in *University Affairs* (Mar. 2003), p. 51] UBC hires on the basis of merit and is committed to employment equity. We encourage all qualified people to apply. There is no restriction with regard to nationality or residence, and the position is open to all candidates. Offers will be made in keeping with immigration requirements associated with the Canada Research Chairs program.

l) [Orlo Miller, in *The Donnellys Must Die* (Macmillan, 1962), p. 231] The body of criminal law is more designed for the punishment of the individual offence than for the execution of judgment against a corporate criminal conspiracy. In witness of this we need only consider the American experience in dealing with organized crime. Even in international law a charge of genocide is difficult to sustain against an individual member of a state conspiracy.

m) [Hugh Rawson, in *Devious Derivations* (Castle Books, 2002), p. 2] False conclusions about the origins of words also arise . . . as a result of the conversion of Anglo-Saxon and other older English terms into modern parlance. Thus a *crayfish* is not a fish but a crustacean (from the Middle English *crevis*, crab). A *helpmate* may be both a help and a mate, but the word is a corruption of *help meet*, meaning suitable helper . . . *Hopscotch* has nothing to do intrinsically with kids in kilts; *scotch* here is a moderately antique word for a cut, incision, or scratch, perhaps deriving from the Anglo-French *escocher*, to notch or nick.

By the same token, people who eat *humble pie* may have been humbled, but only figuratively. The name of the dish comes from *umbles*, meaning the liver, heart, and other edible animal innards.

n) [from a local church pamphlet] None of us on the Leadership Team, here at Brant Community Church, would claim to have received an infallible picture of the future, but we do believe that forecasting and planning is part of the job that God has called us to do.

o) [a quote from 'Midwifery on Trial', *Quarterly Journal of Speech* (Feb. 2003),
    p. 70] The difficulty I find with the judge's decision [to dismiss a charge against
    a midwife] . . . is that these people are completely unlicensed. They are just a
    group of people, some with no qualifications, whose only experience in some
    cases is having watched five or six people give birth. They have no comprehen-
    sion of the complications that can arise in childbirth . . . we are about to
    embrace totally unqualified people . . . I think the judge is out of his mind.

p) [from the *Disability Discrimination Act* of the United Kingdom, available online
    at <http://www.parliament.the-stationery-office.co.uk/pa/ld200102/ldbills/040/
    2002040.htm> (accessed 8 Jan. 2003)] Where (a) any arrangements made by or
    on behalf of an employer, or (b) any physical feature of premises occupied by the
    employer, place the disabled person concerned at a substantial disadvantage in
    comparison with persons who are not disabled, it is the duty of the employer to
    take such steps as it is reasonable, in all the circumstances of the case, for him to
    have to take in order to prevent the arrangements or feature having that effect.

q) [from a letter to *Sport's Illustrated* (14 Feb. 1984)] True. Wayne Gretzky's scor-
    ing streak is amazing. But to compare Gretzky's streak with Joe DiMaggio's 56-
    game gem is ludicrous—it's no contest. Gretzky kept his streak alive by scoring
    into an empty net in the closing seconds of a game against Chicago. Tell me,
    how many times did Joe D. come to bat in the bottom of the ninth with no one
    playing in the outfield? Case closed!

r)* [from a letter in *National Geographic* (May 1998), which is a comment on an
    article on the aviator Amelia Earhart, who disappeared on a flight over the
    Pacific in July 1937] I was sorry to see Elinor Smith quoted, impugning
    Amelia's flying skills, in the otherwise excellent piece by Virginia Morell.
    Smith has been slinging mud at Earhart and her husband, George Putnam, for
    years, and I lay it down to jealousy. Amelia got her pilot's license in 1923 (not
    1929 as Smith once wrote) and in 1929 was the third American woman to win
    a commercial license.

s) [John Beifuss, in 'Timing's right for Kissinger portrait', a review of the film
    Trials, at gomemphisgo.com *Movie Reviews*, <http://www.gomemphis.com/mca/
    movie_reviews/ article/0,1426,MCA_569_1592636,00.html> (accessed 24 Dec.
    2002)] At the very least, *Trials* serves as an overdue corrective to the still active
    cult of Kissinger. Even viewers who aren't convinced that the former national
    security adviser, Secretary of State and Nobel Peace Prize winner fits the defini-
    tion of 'war criminal' likely will emerge shocked that presidents still call for
    advice from the man who may have been responsible for such clandestine and
    illegal foreign policy initiatives as the 1969 US carpet bombing of Cambodia,
    the 1970 overthrow and murder of democratically elected Chilean president
    Salvador Allende and the 1972 'Christmas Bombing' of North Vietnam, which
    Hitchens, in an onscreen interview, describes as 'a public relations mass murder
    from the sky'. As journalist Seymour Hersh comments: 'The dark side of Henry
    Kissinger is very, very dark.'

t)   [an exchange attributed to a reporter interviewing a former Miss Alabama:] *Question*: If you could live forever, would you and why? *Answer*: I would not live forever because we should not live forever because if we were supposed to live forever then we would live forever but we cannot live forever which is why I would not live forever.

u)   [Nicholas Lezard, in *Guardian Weekly* (12 Oct. 1997), commenting on Edward de Bono's *Textbook of Wisdom*] This book contains some of the most mindless rubbish I've ever been privileged to hear from an adult. . . . I won't quote any because cleaning vomit from computer keyboards is nasty, time-consuming work. Just trust me when I say that you will become wiser if you gently smear your nose against any section of this newspaper—adverts included. No correspondence, please.

v)*   [from a letter to *New Woman* (July 1995) in support of a commitment to cover New Age issues] When I was going through a recent bout with depression, I discovered the 'goddess spirituality' movement. I chose Artemis as the goddess I would seek comfort in. . . . I built an altar to her in my room, burned incense, and meditated, and I found comfort in these ritualistic practices. I think this type of paganism can be an important tool for women to discover their inner strengths.

w)   [Jonelle P. Weaver, in 'Salad Days', *New Woman* (July 1996)] Today, there is a tendency to reduce oil [in vinaigrette salad dressing] and make up the volume in acidic liquid. That is a gross error, because the tongue-puckering results annihilate the gentle flavors of other ingredients.

x)   [from a letter to the *Kitchener-Waterloo Record*, entitled 'We're Different' (28 Sept. 1993)] The Sept. 20 article, Waterloo Restaurant Charged, outlined the various charges laid against the Golden Griddle Restaurant on Weber Street, Waterloo. This restaurant was charged by the Waterloo Region health unit for various violations under the Provincial Offences Act, including unsanitary conditions and mishandling of food.

    As an employee of a neighbouring Golden Griddle in Kitchener, I feel that it is important to point out that the practices of one restaurant are not indicative of the quality of food, service or cleanliness of other Golden Griddle Restaurants, especially the Kitchener location.

    The Kitchener Golden Griddle on Highland Road is the highest-ranked restaurant in the chain having been awarded the number one position among the 64 Golden Griddle restaurants across Canada. Each month a 'mystery guest' hired by the head office rates each chain restaurant on 57 dimensions that fall under three categories: service, quality of food and cleanliness.

    The owners/managers and staff have worked hard over the last nine months to achieve and to maintain this number one standing. It would be unfortunate and unfair for the Kitchener Golden Griddle's reputation to be tarnished by another restaurant's transgressions.

    The quality, service and cleanliness in any restaurant is a direct reflection of the staff and the management who dedicate their time and effort to their jobs.

y) [The following is adapted from a Wilson Sports advertisement from 1943. Identify two arguments it contains. How do they compare to arguments in advertisements today?]

SPORTS EQUIPMENT IS FIGHTING EQUIPMENT
take care of what you have

Every piece of sports equipment you own has a part to play in our total war effort. America's sports must be *kept up* to *keep* America *strong*.

The Player's Pledge

Whereas - American sports play a vital part in the physical fitness and morale of civilian America, and,

Whereas - There is just so much of various types of sports equipment available for the duration,

Therefore - I pledge myself to follow the Wilson "Share the Game" Plan - to help preserve sports for the good of all - to make my present equipment last by using it carefully, and - if I buy NEW equipment, to see that my old equipment is made available to some other American who needs exercise, too.

BUY "WILSON" QUALITY

If you need new equipment, specify *Wilson* quality. It not only insures *better* play but *longer* play. Once you get new equipment, take good care of it. Never has sports equipment been as precious as now. See your Professional or dealer.

z)   [What is the argument propounded in the following advertisement?]

ARGUMENT

DIAGRAMS:

POINTING THE WAY

Having identified arguments, we need to set them out in diagrams that show the relations between the components. The present chapter discusses

- ♦ argument diagrams;
- ♦ linked and convergent premises within arguments;
- ♦ supplemented diagrams; and
- ♦ diagramming your own arguments.

1. ARGUMENT DIAGRAMS

Once we recognize an argument, we need to delineate its structure as a first step in deciding how we should assess it. This is not always easy, for arguments in their natural state are frequently confusing. A conclusion may be stated first or last, or may be sandwiched by the premises. Premise and conclusion indicators may or may not be used, and the same ideas may be repeated in a number of different ways. Extraneous comments, digressions, and diversions (insinuations, jokes, insults, complements, etc.) may be interspersed with that content that really matters to the argument.

We call remarks and comments that accompany but are not integral to an argument 'noise'. In analyzing arguments, you will need to begin by eliminating noise. Sometimes it exists in the form of introductory information that sets the stage or background for an argument that follows. Sometimes it consists of statements that are intended only as asides—statements that have no direct bearing on the argument but may add a flourish or a dash of humour. In discarding noise, you must be careful to ensure that you do not, at the same time, discard something that is integral to the argument.

We can discard the noise that accompanies an argument by drawing an argument 'diagram' that maps and clarifies its structure. Diagramming is an especially important tool when you are first learning how to understand an argument (your own or someone else's), for it teaches you how to isolate an argument's essential components and plot their relationship to each other. Even when you have developed your logic skills, diagramming will be an invaluable aid when you must deal with complex arguments, or with arguments that are presented in confusing ways, something that is common in ordinary discourse.

We begin to diagram an argument by extracting its components. It is easiest to begin with the conclusion, because it is the point of the whole argument. After we determine the conclusion, we can identify the premises by asking what evidence is given to support the conclusion. When we are creating a diagram, we create a 'legend' that designates the argument's premises as P1, P2, etc, and the conclusion as C. In an extended argument, we list the intermediary secondary conclusions as C1, C2, etc., and designate the main conclusion as MC. Once we have constructed a legend for a diagram, we use the legend symbols (P1, P2, MC, C1, etc.) to represent the argument's premises and conclusion, and connect them with arrows that indicate what follows from what.

When we wish to diagram the argument 'Thinking clearly and logically is an important skill, so all students should study the rudiments of logic,' we create a legend as follows:

P1 = Thinking clearly and logically is an important skill.
C = All students should study the rudiments of logic.

Once we have this legend, we can diagram the argument as:

This diagram portrays the essential structure of our argument. It shows that our argument consists of one premise that leads to one conclusion. Together with our legend, the diagram shows the argument's components and their relationship. The only thing that might seem missing is the conclusion indicator 'so', but this is represented by the arrow in the argument, which tells us the direction of the inference.

In our first example, our diagram is so simple it may seem redundant. But we have purposely begun with a simple argument that requires no interpretation. Should someone using this argument draw a further conclusion from C, such as 'Courses on critical thinking should be mandatory' then the corresponding diagram would be a 'serial' diagram:

When diagramming most arguments, especially extended ones, we must make many linguistic adjustments. We have already seen that we delete indicator words, since the arrows and symbols in our diagram will perform the task of indicating premises and conclusions and the ways in which they are connected. A more difficult task is eliminating sentences that repeat ideas, as well as remarks, words, and phrases that are, for some other reason, properly classified as noise. In many cases, changes in the wording (but not the meaning) of an argument's premises and conclusion will make the diagram read more smoothly. We may also need to change verb tenses and reformulate exclamations, rhetorical questions, and sentence fragments so that they will be recognized as implicit statements that function as a premise or conclusion.

The following excerpt will help to illustrate the kinds of linguistic changes that may be necessary in order to diagram an argument. It is taken from an article entitled '$40,000-plus for eggs of clever, pretty women', by Kate Cox, posted on the *Sydney Morning Herald* website <http://www.smh.com.au/articles/2002/12/14/1039656259779.html> (15 Dec. 2002):

> Karen Synesiou, a director of Egg Donation, Inc., said women [in Australia who are willing to donate their eggs to American couples] could earn up to $US25,000 ($44,000), although the average payment was between $US5,000 and $US10,000. . . . American fertility specialist and former model Shelley Smith, who runs the Egg Donor Program in the US, said it was unethical for US agents to tout for business overseas. 'I vehemently oppose what they do,' she said.
>
> 'We work frequently with Australian couples, more and more over the years because they just can't find donors there. But we don't import Australian donors.
>
> 'It's just terrible that they purposely take a woman from there and bring them here when there are dozens of couples desperately needing donors in their own country. It's a roundabout way . . . and it really exploits everybody, the girls and the couples. Everybody gets hurt.'
>
> Ms Smith said recipient couples would most likely receive less information about their donor and Australian egg donors would be offered less than US citizens get paid for their eggs, not have adequate access to counselling services, and possibly regret it later.

Once we recognize that this passage contains an argument, we can proceed to diagram it. It should immediately be clear that the first sentence in the excerpt is noise that provides background information rather than the content of an argument: it explains the context of Smith's argument, but it is not a part of it. Hence, while the first sentence is important, it contains nothing that needs to be included in our diagram.

In this and other cases, you should always begin your analysis of an argument by trying to identify the principal point the arguer is trying to establish. In the process, you will cut through the noise the argument contains. In this case, this way of proceeding means that we should begin to diagram Smith's argument by trying to determine her main conclusion. We find this early in the excerpt, when she is attributed the claim that it is unethical for US agents to tout for business overseas. This claim is emphatically reinforced in her statements: 'I vehemently oppose what they do,' and 'it really exploits everybody, the girls and the couples. Everybody gets hurt.' As the discussion is clearly a discussion of the use of Australian women donors, we will identify the main conclusion as:

> MC = It is unethical for American companies to solicit human egg donations from Australia.

Having established the main conclusion in the argument, we need to ask what evidence Smith gives in support of it. We detect a number of premises. The first piece of evidence that demands some comment is included in Smith's suggestion that 'Australian egg donors would not have adequate access to counselling services and possibly regret it later.' This is plausibly interpreted as a sub-argument, for it suggests that Australian women may possibly regret their decision later *because* they will not have adequate access to counselling services. In order to capture this aspect of the reasoning we need to include the following premise and conclusion in our legend:

> P1 = Australian egg donors will not have adequate access to counselling services.
> C1 = Australian egg donors who donate to American couples may regret their decision later.

We detect three other premises in the argument, which we identify as follows:

> P2 = It's just terrible that they purposely take a woman from Australia and bring them here when there are dozens of Australian couples desperately needing donors.
> P3 = American couples involved in such transactions will most likely receive less information about their donor.
> P4 = Australian egg donors will likely be offered less money than US citizens get paid for their eggs.

This completes our legend, allowing us to diagram the argument attributed to Smith:

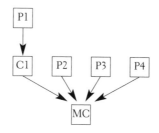

This example is more complex than our first and better illustrates the process by which we 'translate' ordinary-language arguments into diagrams. It is especially important to observe the way we created a clear diagram by eliminating the background information, digressions, and significant repetition of the original. The diagram gives us important information that will be invaluable in an evaluation of the reasoning: it shows us how many lines of support there are for the main conclusion, and how many of those lines are also supported. As diagramming is a skill that improves with practice, it is by repeating exercises such as this that you will learn how to recognize language that needs to be adjusted to suit a diagram, and how to make the linguistic adjustments that are appropriate in different cases.

DIAGRAMMING: A SHORTCUT METHOD

In most cases in this book we will present a diagram by defining our legend in the way we have already outlined. But in dealing with arguments on a more casual basis, we often use a quicker method. Instead of writing out each premise and conclusion, we circle the relevant statements in a passage and number them consecutively. We can then sketch a diagram that shows the relationships between the numbered statements. Those sentences or words that can be considered 'noise' can be crossed out or left unnumbered.

1 (Thinking clearly and logically is an important skill), so

2 (all students should study the rudiments of logic)

In diagramming with this shortcut method, our first example might be diagrammed as follows:

This shortcut method of diagramming can help you complete practice exercises much more quickly than the long method, which requires you to write out an argument's premises and conclusion in full. Use the shortcut when it is convenient, as

we will on occasion, but be aware that there are cases in which this method is unsuitable. In these cases, the premises and/or conclusion of the argument need to be identified by making revisions to the actual statements that the arguer uses (in order to eliminate 'noise', to clarify the arguer's meaning, to recognize the argument's implicit components, or for some other reason).

2. LINKED AND CONVERGENT PREMISES

In order to make diagrams a more effective way to represent the structure of an argument, we draw them in a way that distinguishes between premises that are 'linked' and those that are 'convergent'. *Linked premises* work as a unit—they support a conclusion only when they are conjoined. *Convergent premises* are separate and distinct, and offer independent evidence for a conclusion.

Some simple examples can illustrate the difference between linked and convergent premises, and the ways in which they can be represented in a diagram. Consider, as a first example, the Sherlock Holmes argument we discussed in Chapter 1 (see p. 2). It can be diagrammed as follows:

P1 = Although the living room window is open, there are no footprints outside despite the softness of the ground after yesterday's rain.
P2 = The clasp on the box was not broken but opened with a key that had been hidden behind the clock.
P3 = The dog did not bark.
 C = The crime was committed by someone in the house.

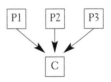

The premises in this argument are convergent: each premise has a separate arrow leading to the conclusion indicating that it provides an independent reason for that conclusion. You can see this by imagining that the only premise in the argument is either P1 or P2 or P3. In each case, our reasoning would be weaker, but the single premise would still provide some evidence for C. The premises do not require each other to provide support for the conclusion.

The situation would be very different if Sherlock Holmes used the following reasoning to conclude that the crime could not have been committed by the butler, George:

It is clear that the crime was committed by someone who is very strong. But George is singularly weak. So he cannot be the culprit.

In this new argument, the premises are linked: they provide support for the conclusion *only* if they are considered as a unit. The first premise—the claim that the crime was committed by someone very strong—provides *no* support for the conclusion that George 'cannot be the culprit' unless we combine it with the second premise—that George is singularly weak. Similarly, the second premise provides no support for the conclusion unless it is combined with the first.

In an argument diagram, we will recognize the linked nature of these two premises by placing a plus sign (+) between them, drawing an underline beneath them, and using a single arrow to join the two of them to the conclusion. Our finished diagram looks like this:

    P1 = The crime was committed by someone very strong.
    P2 = George is singularly weak.
    C = George cannot be the culprit.

We can easily imagine Sherlock Holmes combining this argument with further reasoning. If he has already decided that 'Either George or Janice is guilty of the crime,' he may now conclude that Janice is the culprit, for the argument above has eliminated the only other possibility. In this case, Holmes' entire chain of reasoning may be diagrammed by extending our initial diagram:

    P1 = The crime was committed by someone very strong.
    P2 = George is singularly weak.
    C1 = George cannot be the culprit.
    P3 = Either George or Janice is guilty of the crime
    MC = Janice is guilty of the crime.

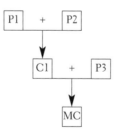

In this new diagram, C1 and P3 are linked premises for the main conclusion, for they support it only when they are combined.

In drawing diagrams, it is important to make sure that you distinguish between linked and convergent premises, for this distinction will determine how you assess particular premises. If you have difficulty deciding whether some premise P is linked to other premises, ask yourself whether P provides any support for the conclusion when it is considered independently of the other premise(s). If the answer is yes, then draw an arrow from P to the conclusion. If the answer is no, then ask yourself which of the other premises must be combined with P to make it support the conclusion. After you have answered this question, join P to these other premises with a + sign, underline them, and draw one arrow from this set of premises to the conclusion.

Some Examples

To better acquaint you with argument diagrams we have designed the following three diagrams to illustrate the application of our diagramming method to particular arguments.

EXAMPLE 1

Argument

The ruins of ancient Aztec pyramids are very similar to those found in Egypt. Also, animals and vegetation found on the eastern coasts of South America bear a striking resemblance to those of West Africa. From all appearances, there was once a large land mass connecting these continents. Which implies that the true ancestors of the indigenous peoples of South America are African.

Diagram

P1 = The ruins of ancient Aztec pyramids are very similar to those found in Egypt.

P2 = Animals and vegetation found on the eastern coasts of South America bear a striking resemblance to those of West Africa.

C1 = There was once a large land mass connecting these continents.

MC = The true ancestors of the indigenous peoples of South America are African.

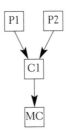

EXAMPLE 2

Argument

[In a famous incident in Homer's *Odyssey*, Odysseus and his men land on an island inhabited by one-eyed giants called 'Cyclopes'. When Odysseus speaks to a Cyclops inside a cave he reminds him that Zeus requires the Cyclopes to treat guests well. The Cyclops responds with the following argument.] 'Stranger, you must be a fool, or must have come from very far afield. For you warn me to take care of my responsibilities to Zeus and we Cyclopes care nothing about Zeus and the rest of the gods . . .'

Diagram

P1 = You warn me to take care of my responsibilities to Zeus.
P2 = We Cyclopes care nothing about Zeus and the rest of the gods.
C = You must be a fool or have come from very far afield.

EXAMPLE 3

Argument

[adapted from a letter to the *Globe and Mail* (9 Oct. 1998)] Re. Lord Elgin's Greek Marbles: Robert Fulford advocates that the sculptures should be kept at the British museum. He's wrong. I can think of three reasons why the marbles should be returned to Greece. They are part of the cultural heritage of Greece, not Britain. They were taken from Greece with the consent of the Ottoman empire, which had no cultural claim on the antiquities. And there is no evidence that the marbles were in danger of 'destruction or dispersal', as he puts it, when Lord Elgin shipped them off to Britain.

Mr Fulford should think again.

Diagram

P1 = The Elgin Marbles are part of the cultural heritage of Greece, not Britain.
P2 = The Elgin Marbles were taken from Greece with the consent of the Ottoman empire, which had no cultural claim on the antiquities.
P3 = There is no evidence that the marbles were in danger of 'destruction or dispersal' (as Fulford puts it) when Lord Elgin shipped them off to Britain.
C1 = The Marbles should be returned to Greece.
MC = Robert Fulford is wrong when he advocates that Lord Elgin's Greek Marbles should be kept at the British Museum.

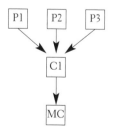

> ## DIAGRAMMING AN ARGUMENT
>
> 1. Determine the main conclusion of the argument: the major point the arguer is trying to establish.
> 2. Mark the text into blocks that have a unified logical purpose, such as stating a premise or drawing a conclusion.
> 3. Cross out digressions and noise.
> 4. Express the content of each block in statement form. In doing so, try to capture the author's intended meaning.
> 5. Create a legend listing the premises as P1, P2, etc., the subsidiary conclusions as C1, C2, C3, etc. and the main conclusion as MC.
> 6. Join each independent premise to the conclusion it supports with an arrow.
> 7. Conjoin linked premises with a plus sign (+) and an underline, and connect them to the appropriate conclusion with an arrow.

3. Supplemented Diagrams

A diagram is an efficient way to summarize the content of an argument. Its legend presents the premises and conclusion(s). The diagram itself provides a visual representation of the relationships that exist between them. When we want to assess an argument, constructing a diagram is a good way to begin our assessment of the reasoning it contains.

It is important to remember that, as useful as they may be, diagrams do not, in themselves, provide all the information we need to assess any argument. We have already noted that there is more to an argument than premises and conclusions. Arguments are situated in a context of communication that includes arguers, audiences, and opponents. A careful analysis of an argument must frequently discuss these parties. In order to prepare the way for this discussion, we may, in drawing the diagram for an argument, decide to identify one or more of them. In discussing the strength of the argument, this information may provide the basis for a discussion of the arguer (which may address their credibility or our past experience in dealing with their arguments, etc.), the audience for whom the argument is constructed (which may explain aspects of the argument that might otherwise make little sense), or the opponents (for we may need to assess the extent to which the arguer has adequately dealt with objections to their view).

A *supplemented* diagram is a diagram of an argument to which has been added information about the arguer, the audience to which the argument is directed, or those who oppose this point of view. A *fully supplemented* argument contains information on all three. An example that can be used to illustrate the construction of a fully supplemented diagram is the following advertisement for Scotiabank, which appeared in a variety of university newspapers in an effort to promote the bank among students:

**Being a student
has its advantages.**

Being a student can be tough, but it does have its advantages, like the no-fee Scotia Banking Advantage Plan.

It gives you a daily interest chequing account, a ScotiaCard banking card and a Classic VISA card.

We also offer low-interest Scotia Student Loans.

Sign up for the Scotia Banking Advantage Plan before November 10th, you'll automatically get a chance to win an IBM ThinkPad PS/Note 425 notebook computer.

Just drop into any Scotia branch for full details or call 1-800-9-SCOTIA.

Scotiabank

To construct a fully supplemented diagram for this argument, we proceed by preparing a standard diagram, combining it with an account of the arguer, the audience, and the opponents. When we do so, the resulting account of the argument might look like this:

The *arguer* is Scotiabank

The *audience* is students, for this particular advertisement speaks only to students, not to other potential customers.

The *opponents* include competing banks, who are likely to argue that their banks are as student-friendly as Scotiabank, as well as those who might oppose banking in a more fundamental way. The latter may believe that there are moral reasons that show that we should not use banks and should support credit unions in their place.

P1 = The no-fee Scotia Banking Advantage Plan gives you a daily interest chequing account, a ScotiaCard banking card, and a Classic VISA card.

P2 = We also offer low-interest Scotia Student Loans.

P3 = If you sign up for the Scotia Banking Advantage Plan before November 10th, you'll automatically get a chance to win an IBM ThinkPad PS/Note 425 notebook computer.

C = You should drop into a Scotiabank branch or call 1-800-9-SCOTIA for details.

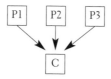

This fully supplemented diagram provides a very complete background for argument analysis. On the one hand, it clearly delineates the premises and conclusion of the argument, and the pattern of support within the reasoning. At the same time, it provides us with the information on the arguer, the audience, and the opponents that may play an important role in our attempt to determine whether this is a good argument. For example, the recognition that the arguer is Scotiabank is not inconsequential, for this is a case where the arguer has an obvious vested interest, where there are financial benefits that accrue to Scotiabank if the intended audience accepts its conclusion. This is something we may need to consider in deciding whether the argument is biased in a way that reflects this vested interest.

In dealing with most arguments we will not provide fully supplemented diagrams. Why? Because this is a time-consuming task, especially if we are analyzing a whole series of arguments. Instead of providing fully supplemented diagrams, we will normally provide diagrams that are supplemented only with whatever information about the arguer, the audience, or the opponents we believe is relevant to a critical assessment of the argument. We suggest you do the same, while keeping in mind that someone who fully understands an argument should be able to provide a fully supplemented diagram that discusses the features of argument we have outlined in this and the previous chapter. Even when you don't provide a fully supplemented argument, you should, in principle, be able to do so.

EXERCISE 2A

1. Illustrate each of the following concepts with two examples of your own.
    a)* diagram legend
    b) linked premises
    c) convergent premises
    d) supplemented diagrams

2. Say whether each of the following passages is an argument. If it is an argument, provide a supplemented diagram that illustrates its structure.
    a) [Richard Stengel, in (You're Too Kind) A Brief History of Flattery (Simon & Schuster, 2000), p. 234] Compliments, favours, and self-enhancement aren't good bets when ingratiating upward because they seem manipulative and even impertinent.
    b) [from a letter to the Globe and Mail (4 June 2003), p. A16] If the committee that ranked Brian Mulroney second among recent Canadian prime ministers applied the same criteria to prime ministers of the United Kingdom, they would place Neville Chamberlain above Winston Churchill. . . . Something is wrong here.
    c) [from a university debate over the proposed North American 'missile shield', which would protect North America from incoming missiles] The proposed missile defence system would be the first step toward weapons in space. So far, space has been preserved as a military free zone. It is important—for the safety of us all—that we keep it that way. So we should reject the proposed missile shield.
    d)* [Hilary Clinton, quoted by David Heinzmann in the Chicago Tribune (28 Oct. 1999)] '[I]n many ways, the story of Chicago blues is the story of the African-

American experience,' she said. 'The blues found its beat with the polyrhythms of Africa; gained words and form and pain and emotion on the plantations of the South; travelled up the Mississippi; collaborated with white musicians and discovered electricity, volume and fame right here in the Windy City.'

e)* [adapted from <http://www.openair.org/maxwell/hillary1.html> (accessed 4 June 2003)]

Urge Hillary Clinton to Save Maxwell Street, An American Treasure

Hilary Clinton has an appreciation for and understanding of the blues and played an instrumental role in ensuring that the Chess Studios have been saved and rehabbed. If preserving the Chess Studios is essential to the legacy of the Blues, certainly Maxwell Street must be preserved also. Blues is, at root, a folk idiom. Its creation comes from the folk at the grassroots street level. The music got recorded at Chess, VJ, and other labels but it got created on Maxwell Street.

f) [adapted from an advertisement in *University Affairs* (May 2003)]

UNIVERSITY COLLEGE BAHRAIN

University College Bahrain is a new private university in the Kingdom of Bahrain. The college seeks qualified candidates in a range of disciplines. It's an opportunity you should explore. We provide competitive salaries and a renewable 3-year contract, although visiting positions for one year are also available. The benefits package includes (1) Suitable furnished housing, (2) Medical Insurance, (3) Annual round-trip excursion air tickets from Bahrain to place of residence for the employee, spouse, and up to 2 dependent children under the age of 18, (4) Educational allowance for the teaching of children up to BD4,000 for both children from KG2 through Grade 12 level, (5) Annual paid leave of 60 days, (6) Moving allowance and (7) One month's salary as gratuity for each year of service completed at the University paid annually.

g) [Robert Sullivan, in 'Adventure: An Attempt at a Definition', *Life: The Greatest Adventures of All Time* (Life Books, Time Inc., 2000), pp. 8–9] We will not deny that when the Norwegian Viking Leif Eriksson sailed to Vinland in the year 1000, . . . he had quite an adventure. We will not deny that when Marco Polo traveled the Silk Road at the end of the 13th century, he had many adventures. We will not deny the adventurousness of Christopher Columbus . . . But adventurers first? We would argue not. Most were explorers, principally, while others were variously conquistadors, missionaries and mercenaries. Among their reasons for venturing, adventure was low on the list. . . . Yes, on paper an explorer may look quite the same as an adventurer. They share several traits—boldness, stoicism, strength. But the reason for the enterprise is fundamentally different, and an adventurer is, therefore, a very different beast.

h)* [from *Time* (2 June 2003), p. 23] Swing voters have always been elusive creatures, changing shape from election to election. . . . This axiom is proving true again with that most-talked-about slice of American political demography: the Soccer Mom. Since 9/11, polls suggest she has morphed into Security Mom . . . The sea change in these women has already reshaped voting patterns. Their new attitude helps explain why the gender gap that had worked to the Democrats' advantage since Ronald Reagan was in office narrowed sharply in last year's congressional elections.

i)   [Hugh Rawson, in *Devious Derivations* (Castle Books, 2002), pp. 131–2] **loo**. The standard British euphemism for the toilet . . . is of comparatively recent vintage but of unknown provenance. This has not prevented—on the contrary, it has encouraged—a wealth of speculation about its origin. Among the more frequently encountered theories . . .

1. *Loo* is a mangled translation of the French *lieu*, place, as in *lieux d'aisance*, places of comfort, i.e. comfort stations. This theory accords with the tendency of English speakers to lapse into French when touching on delicate topics. . . . On the other hand, the evidence for *lieux* as the source of loo is only circumstantial, and it is odd that the conversion into English was not made much earlier than seems to have been the case.

2. *Loo* is a clipping of Waterloo, a word that is never far removed from the patriotic Briton's consciousness, possibly with an allusion to yet another euphemism—W.C. or *water closet*. The association was in the mind of James Joyce . . . But Joyce was always making connections of this sort, and the fact he made this one is not a proof of the *Waterloo* origin. . . .

The various 'explanations' for *loo* are passed along with confident but sadly misplaced assurance.

j)   [Hugh Rawson, from the same book, p. 123] **kick the bucket**. The 'obvious' explanation—that the reference is to standing on a pail and kicking it away in order to hang oneself from a rafter may not be correct. *Bucket* also is an antique word, perhaps from the Old French *buquet*, balance, for a beam or yoke from which anything may be carried or hung. Thus, the reference might also be to the beam from which slaughtered pigs are suspended by their heels . . .

The earliest known example of kick the bucket in print is from Captain Francis Grose's *A Classical Dictionary of the Vulgar Tongue* (1785), where the phrase is defined simply as 'to die'. The use of the expression at this date to refer to death in general rather than suicide in particular argues in favor of the bucket-as-beam theory, as does the existence of such similar phrases as *kick up [one's] heels* and *kick [one's] clogs*, also meaning simply 'to die'.

4. DIAGRAMMING YOUR OWN ARGUMENTS

Our examples have already demonstrated that diagramming is a useful tool when we need to plot the structure of someone else's argument. We will end our discussion by noting that diagramming can also be used to analyze and construct arguments of our own. How extensively you use diagrams will depend on your own inclinations. Some people find a diagrammatic representation of an argument an invaluable tool in argument construction. Others who are not inclined to visual representations may not make extensive use of them. Though you will need to decide what works for you, there are two ways in which a supplemented diagram can help you construct an argument, especially if you feel some trepidation as you approach the task before you.

First, a diagram will provide you with a precisely defined set of premises and conclusions, and illustrate the way in which the premises support particular conclusions. Because the structure in a diagram is clear, using a diagram will encourage you to plot straightforward patterns of argument with clear lines of reasoning. Second, diagramming will help you see for yourself whether the premises you provide work independently to support a conclusion or rely upon each other to provide support.

Once you sketch a diagram, turning it into a written or a spoken argument is a simple task. It requires only that you substitute premise or conclusion indicators for the arrows in the argument, and make any minor adjustments the sense of the argument requires. If there are sub-arguments, you will want to include them as separate paragraphs (or separate sections) in a written argument. The argument that results will have a clear structure because it has been built upon a structure that was clearly delineated in your diagram.

A supplemented diagram is an especially useful tool when preparing an argument, because it will force you to think about the audience and opponents of your argument and their own beliefs and attitudes. This can help you develop an argument that takes them into account. A long extended argument should appeal to the beliefs, convictions, and concerns of the audience, and should address counter-arguments that opponents to your position are likely to raise. The ability to prepare supplemented diagrams will be important to your development as a reasoner.

The arguments you present should be arguments that can easily be diagrammed. Because your argument should be expressed precisely, it should not be difficult for someone who wishes to diagram it to specify your premises and conclusions in a legend. Premise and conclusion indicators should make clear which premises are tied to which conclusions, allowing an observer to easily determine how arrows should connect the different components of the argument, and whether premises should be linked in the diagram or left to converge on the conclusion.

EXERCISE 2B

1. Go back to Exercise 1M (see p. 27). Pick four arguments in the exercise. In each case, dispute the argument's conclusion by providing a supplemented diagram (specifying an audience and an opponent) for a simple argument for the opposite conclusion. Present the argument in a paragraph.

2. Construct and diagram simple arguments supporting or disputing five of the following ten claims. In each case, let the audience be the general public, and define some group of likely opponents. Present the argument you have diagrammed in a paragraph.
   a)* A college education is a privilege rather than a right.
   b)* Genetic experiments should be banned.

c)* Capital punishment is wrong.

d) The threat of terrorism justifies greater security measures in airports.

e) History has vindicated capitalism.

f) The drinking age should be a uniform 21 across the nation.

g) Newspapers should not exploit their position by supporting causes.

h) Violent pornography should be censored.

i) The right to bear arms does not extend to assault weapons designed for killing humans.

j) University education should be free for all who qualify.

A Cautionary Note

Having extolled the virtues of diagramming, we offer you a few words of caution and some practical suggestions. In diagramming—and in constructing arguments—aim for simplicity. Plot the structure of your argument so that it is relatively simple and stands out as clearly as possible. Do not defeat your purpose by creating a small-scale version of a Greek labyrinth. Do not push the possibilities for diagramming to extremes. All you need is a diagram that shows clearly the role that each premise plays in the total scheme of your argumentation. Too much elaboration tends to be confusing.

PREPARING ARGUMENTS

1. Diagram an argument for your conclusion.
2. Diagram an argument against likely objections.
3. Keep your diagrams as simple as possible.
4. Base your finished argument on your diagrams.

MAJOR EXERCISE 2M

Decide whether each of the following contains an argument, and explain the reasons for your decision. Diagram any arguments you find. In at least four cases, provide a fully supplemented diagram of the argument.

a)* The room was sealed from the inside. Hence, no one could have left it. Therefore, the murderer was never in the room.

b) Few monographs are successful in introducing readers to the manifold benefits of a new theory or idea while at the same time making clear its weaknesses and limitations. The author is to be commended for what she has accomplished here.

c)* Literacy skills are essential for the development of productive citizens. This program has been teaching people basic literacy skills for over two decades. Providing continued funding for the program is clearly justified.

d) Active euthanasia, or assisting someone to die, is a practice that will come to be accepted in the future. For when people become old or debilitated by illness, they may lack the strength to end their own lives. Such individuals may try many times, unsuccessfully, to end their own lives, causing themselves and others great suffering. Therefore, the need to have assistance in ending terminal pain is becoming more evident.

e) [Josef Joffe, discussing America's role in the world, in *Time* (7 Mar. 1995)] Why not be a 'cheap hawk', letting the others take care of the world's business? The answer is easy. The Japanese won't take care of free trade . . . The Russians, if left alone, will happily sell nuclear-weapons technology to Iran, and the French would be similarly obliging about lifting the embargo on Iraq. And who will contain China, the next superpower?

f) [from one of the first printed reviews of the Rolling Stones, included in Tony Sanchez, *Up and Down with the Rolling Stones* (Blake, 1991)] The Stones are destined to be the biggest group in the R & B scene—if that scene continues to flourish. Three months ago only fifty people turned up to see the group. Now Gomelski has to close the doors at an early hour—with over 400 fans crowding the hall. . . . Fact is that, unlike all other R & B groups worthy of the name, the Rolling Stones have a definite visual appeal. . . . They are genuine R & B fanatics themselves . . . They can also get the sound that Bo Diddley gets—no mean achievement. . . . They know their R & B numbers inside out and have a repertoire of about 80 songs, most of them ones that the real R & B fans know and love.

g)* [from the website of the US Food and Drug Administration Center for Devices and Radiological Health, <http://www.fda.gov/cdrh/consumer/amalgams.html> (accessed 5 Jan. 2003)] FDA and other organizations of the US Public Health Service (USPHS) continue to investigate the safety of amalgams used in dental restorations (fillings). However, no valid scientific evidence has ever shown that amalgams cause harm to patients with dental restorations, except in the rare case of allergy.

The safety of dental amalgams has been reviewed extensively over the past ten years, both nationally and internationally. In 1994, an international conference of health officials concluded there is no scientific evidence that dental amalgam presents a significant health hazard to the general population, although a small number of patients had mild, temporary allergic reactions. The World Health Organization (WHO), in March 1997, reached a similar conclusion. They wrote: 'Dental amalgam restorations are considered safe, but components of amalgam and other dental restorative materials may, in rare instances, cause local side effects or allergic reactions. The small amount of mercury released from amalgam restorations, especially during placement and removal, has not been shown to cause any other adverse health effects.' Similar conclusions were reached by the USPHS, the European Commission, the National Board of Health and Welfare in Sweden, the New Zealand Ministry of Health, Health Canada and the province of Quebec.

h) [from 'Toxic Teeth', a report of an Oakland, California, press conference, <http://www.toxicteeth.net/8-3-01.html> (accessed 5 Jan. 2003)] 'The State of California Dental Board, acting as an arm of the American Dental Association, continues to cover up the dangers of Mercury in dental fillings, in defiance of the law and the increasing scientific evidence,' said Charles G. Brown, the lead attorney in the national legal battle against Mercury in dentistry and a former West Virginia state Attorney General. 'It is long past time for the Dental Board to "open wide" and start using the "M" word. By refusing to adopt an accurate, full disclosure Fact Sheet, they continue to deceive consumers into thinking amalgam fillings are made of silver, when in fact the major component—about 50 per cent—is Mercury and only about 25 per cent of a Mercury amalgam filling is composed of silver.

'Mercury is universally recognized as an extremely dangerous toxin,' Brown continued. 'One filling contains 750 milligrams of Mercury, enough to contaminate a small lake. The Dental Board and the ADA [American Dental Association] are out of the medical mainstream in claiming that Mercury is safe for use in human beings. . . .'

'The Dental Board, like the ADA and the CDA, is out of step not only with the rest of the medical community, but with California law,' said attorney Shawn Khorrami, who has sued the Dental Board, the ADA and CDA in California Superior Court. 'The State of California identifies Mercury as a toxic substance, and under Prop. 65, therefore, dentists are required to warn their patients about it. Our complaint is not with individual dentists, many of whom share our concern about the use of Mercury, but with the Dental Board, too many of whose members seem to have a vested interest in the continued use of Mercury.'

'We believe that the dental industry has not taken responsibility for the toxic Mercury that they release into our waters every day,' said Lena Brook of Clean Water Action, speaking for her organization as well as Health Care Without Harm and the California Public Interest Research Group. 'Waste from dental offices and from people with Mercury fillings gets into our sewer systems and eventually into the waters that we fish. Eating fish contaminated with Mercury, a potent neurotoxin, has been proven to affect brain development in children. In fact, according to recent estimates by the Centers for Disease Control, one in ten women of childbearing age are now at risk of having children with neurological defects due to Mercury exposure.'

IMPLICIT

ARGUMENT

COMPONENTS:

FILLING IN THE BLANKS

> Communication is a complex process. It frequently depends on an ability to understand what isn't said, or what is said obliquely. To help understand and diagram arguments of this sort, this chapter presents
>
> - three basic principles of communication;
> - abbreviated arguments;
> - hidden premises and hidden conclusions; and
> - verbal, non-verbal, and visual arguments.

The examples of argument we have examined so far are relatively straightforward. They were chosen because they are, in most cases, explicit combinations of premises and conclusions that are easily interpreted. Arguments can be more difficult to diagram and assess in cases that require more interpretation. This is especially true of arguments that depend on claims or assumptions that are not explicit but are left unstated or are said obliquely. The problems of interpretation that arise in such cases might be compared to the problems we have already noted in our discussion of arguments that lack explicit premise or conclusion indicators.

When diagramming and assessing arguments that depend on components that are not explicit, you must 'fill in the blanks' by identifying what an argument assumes or implicitly asserts. To help you deal with the issues this raises, this chapter presents principles of communication that can be applied to cases of this sort. By developing your ability to apply and abide by these principles, you will hone the skills you need to interpret and diagram other people's arguments, and to create clear and meaningful arguments of your own.

1. SPEECH ACTS AND THE PRINCIPLES OF COMMUNICATION

Because speech is the paradigm way in which we communicate, attempts to communicate are commonly called 'speech acts'. As their name suggests, speech acts are actions commonly performed by uttering certain kinds of statements. We will follow this convention, noting that we engage in speech acts whenever we communicate, even when we do so without using spoken words. A comment made to a friend is a speech act, but so is a paragraph in a term paper, a wave to a friend, a 'thumbs up' gesture, or a map that someone draws to show you where they live.

The three basic principles of communication we will emphasize can be expressed in terms of speech acts. They are broad principles that inform all kinds of communication. We will emphasize their application to argumentative exchange, but will state them in a general way, as directions you should follow whenever you attempt to interpret a speech act, and especially a speech act that has a meaning that is not fully explicit:

Principle 1. Assume that a speech act is intelligible.
Principle 2. Interpret a speech act in a way that fits the context in which it occurs.
Principle 3. Interpret a speech act in a way that is in keeping with the meaning of its explicit elements (the words, gestures, music, etc., it explicitly contains).

The first of these three principles tells us that we should assume that a speech act is meaningful and strive to understand it. The second and third principles tell us how to understand a speech act, i.e. by considering its immediate and broader context (the other speech acts it is connected to, but also the broader social context in which it occurs), and by interpreting it in a way that is in keeping with the meaning of its explicit elements.

We all use these three principles when we interpret many non-argumentative remarks and gestures. We also use them when we interpret instances of poetry and art, which count as speech acts because they are attempts to engage in communication. We invite you to think about the application of the principles of communication in the latter contexts. In this book we will, however, restrict our attention to their use in the attempt to interpret, diagram, and assess argumentative exchange. Our aim is a discussion that will teach you how to use these principles to unearth and identify implicit components that need to be recognized and identified in such contexts.

It may be helpful to begin by saying that we have implicitly appealed to our three principles of communication in the earlier chapters of this book. The role our principles play in ordinary diagramming and analysis can be illustrated with an example. The following excerpt is taken from a letter to *Atlantic Monthly* (December 2002). It is a response to an article in which Philip Jenkins predicted the rise of 'The Next Christianity', first in the southern hemisphere and then globally.

> Philip Jenkins accurately points out the profound demographic shift of Christianity toward the Third World, particularly in Africa. However, the competition between Christianity and Islam, particularly in Africa, may be the real story. . . .
>
> AIDS could have profound consequences for the relative performances of Christianity and Islam, particularly in the sub-Saharan Africa. Muslim North and West Africa has been largely spared the devastation that has torn through Christian East and South Africa. Not only are Muslims less likely to engage in social practices that lead to viral transmission (an imperfect defense at best), but circumcised males in Africa become infected and pass on infection at substantially lower rates with a similar level of viral exposure. Unless Christian Africa can find a way to halt the HIV epidemic, the demographic ascent of Christianity may be significantly blunted.

This letter is plausibly read as an extended argument that supports a conclusion expressed in its last sentence. The argument can be diagrammed as follows:

P1 = Muslim North and West Africa have been largely spared the devastation that has torn through Christian East and South Africa.

P2 = Not only are Muslims less likely to engage in social practices that lead to viral transmission (an imperfect defense at best), but circumcised males in Africa become infected and pass on infection at substantially lower rates with a similar level of viral exposure.

C1 = The spread of AIDS may have a more negative impact on Christianity than on Islam, especially in Africa.

MC = Unless Christian Africa can find a way to halt the HIV epidemic, the demographic ascent of Christianity may be significantly blunted.

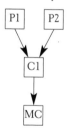

This is a relatively straightforward diagram. You should have no difficulty recognizing that this diagram represents the author's reasoning, even though some features of the argument are not explicit in the letter, which contains no premise and conclusion indicators, and does not explicitly assert C1.

The author comes closest to C1 when he says that 'AIDS could have profound consequences for the relative performances of Christianity and Islam, particularly in the sub-Saharan Africa.' Taken in isolation, this is a weaker claim than C1, for it does not explicitly state that the effects of AIDS are likely to affect Christianity *more* than Islam. It is nonetheless clear that C1 is the claim intended by the author of the letter, for this is the only interpretation that fits with his other claims (claims that do not leave open the possibility that Islam will be more seriously affected). In recognizing C1 in our diagram, we are implicitly invoking our second principle of communication, which tells us to understand claims and other speech acts in a way that is in keeping with their context. We made another appeal to this principle when we interpreted the letter as an argument on the grounds that this is the best way to make sense of the arguer's attempt to engage in argumentative exchange.

In reading the various sentences in the *Atlantic* letter, we rely upon our third principle of communication, which tells us to interpret a speech act by considering the words it explicitly employs. In this case, the meaning of the arguer's sentences is clear and obvious, for it is determined by the conventions we associate with the words they contain. In this and cases like it, it may seem that the application of the third principle of communication is straightforward (for it is as easy as understanding language), but argumentative exchanges often contain violations of the principle. They occur because we often read and listen carelessly, especially when we are dealing with speech acts that present views that we do not agree with.

An exchange from the *Windsor Star*, reported by Ralph H. Johnson and J. Anthony Blair (in their book *Logical Self-Defense*; McGraw Hill, 1994, pp. 94–6) provides a good example of the ways in which the third principle of communication is often violated. It begins with the following letter, which a Dr LaFave wrote in response to the *Star*'s coverage of police attitudes toward capital punishment:

> The vast majority of . . . police appear to favour capital punishment, especially when one of their colleagues is murdered in the line of duty. These policemen are entitled to their opinion. However, the public should not take their views on this subject seriously and the mass communications media . . . should not continue to give so much space to their views.

In answer to this criticism, the *Star* responded to LaFave's letter with the following:

> Wrong, Dr LaFave. The police are entitled to their opinion, as your letter says. But police—and any other group—are also entitled to express their opinions and have them reported. . . . And on the subject of capital punishment, a good case can be made for greater attention to the view of police groups . . .
>
> The *Star* agrees with Dr LaFave in his opposition to capital punishment, and disagrees with the anti-abolition stand that he feels is the majority view of Canadian police officers. But the *Star* does not agree that the views should be suppressed, censored, or ignored.

If you read Dr LaFave's original letter carefully, you should see that the *Star* has misinterpreted his remarks. He claims that the mass communications media 'should not continue to give so much space to' the views of the police on capital punishment, which implies that they should not get as much attention as they do, but he does not claim that their views should be 'suppressed, censored, or ignored'. In interpreting LaFave in this way, the *Star* fails to respect our third principle of communication, for there is no way to interpret LaFave's explicit words as conveying the strong claim the *Star* attributes to him.

Arguments of this sort are called 'straw-man' arguments because they attack a fake opponent rather than a real one. They do so by attributing to a real opponent a position they do not really hold. We shall have more to say about straw-man arguments in later chapters of this book. For the moment, we need to continue with our discussion of the principles of communication and their application in contexts in which arguments depend on implicit components.

ARGUMENT DIALOGUES

The principles of communication require that we engage in acts of communication that make sense in the contexts in which they occur. In many cases, this means that different contexts—often referred to as 'argument dialogues'—call for different kinds of argument. In collective bargaining, for example, both sides are involved in a complex argumentative process governed by labour law, by commonly accepted standards and expectations, and by complex relations that tie a bargainer to a union and its membership, or to management. In such a context, it is considered 'bargaining in bad faith' if the company's chief bargainer argues directly with the members of the union, for this circumvents the bargaining table, where the real bargaining is supposed to take place.

A courtroom is another context in which a very specific kind of argumentative dialogue is called for. If one is the defence lawyer, then one acts improperly if one argues in a wholly impartial manner. As a defence lawyer, one is not there to be impartial, but to put together the best possible arguments that can convince a judge or a jury that one's client is innocent. (This does not mean that the ultimate aim is not impartiality, but only that courts try to achieve impartiality in a different way.) In presenting their arguments, lawyers are bound by laws and practices that dictate that they must argue in very specific ways.

It would be possible to write a book on the complexities of argumentative dialogue in law, in collective bargaining, and in other unique contexts, but these are topics that lie beyond the scope of this book. In the present context, it is enough to say that we should be aware of specialized contexts of this sort and try to recognize the different argumentative ideals they incorporate.

THE PRINCIPLES OF COMMUNICATION

Principle 1. Assume that a speech act is intelligible.
Principle 2. Interpret a speech act in a way that fits the context in which it occurs.
Principle 3. Interpret a speech act in a way that is in keeping with the meaning of its explicit components.

EXERCISE 3A

1. Take four of the arguments you analyzed in completing Exercise 2M. Explain how the principles of communication were implicitly applied in your analysis of the argument.

2. Suppose you are writing a term paper on the ancient sophist Protagoras and on his claim that 'Humans are the measure of all things.' According to the principles of communication, how should you go about trying to understand this claim?

2. ABBREVIATED ARGUMENTS

We have already seen that a rhetorical question can function as a premise or a conclusion in an argument. A rhetorical question can function in this way because it is not a real question. Rather, it is used as an oblique way to make a statement of the answer to the question. In diagramming an argument with a rhetorical question, we recognize the question as a statement in our legend. In a similar way, when diagramming 'abbreviated' arguments, we must recognize premises and/or conclusions that are unstated or stated obliquely. We call these components 'hidden' premises and conclusions. In analyzing arguments and constructing diagrams, we need to identify these hidden components so that their role in the argument can be recognized and assessed.

In keeping with the principles of communication, you can identify an argument's hidden premises and conclusions by looking for clues in its explicit components, and by considering the context in which the argument occurs. In the process of doing so, you will need to be mindful of two competing concerns. You will, on the one hand, want to identify all the hidden components that are relevant to the argument: you want to recognize the *whole* argument. You will, on the other hand, want to make sure that you do not add components that are not a part of the original argument: you want to avoid the possibility that you are misrepresenting the intentions of the arguer. In identifying hidden components, you need to work like an archaeologist rather than an architect: instead of adding to the argument, you want to discover what is already there, though it is there implicitly.

Hidden Conclusions

An argument has a hidden conclusion when its premises invite a conclusion that is left unstated. Often the argument will contain some indication that the arguer is offering reasons for accepting the conclusion. Consider the following comment on seatbelts:

> I think there is enough evidence to justify a reasonable conclusion. In the vast majority of cases that have been examined, wearing seatbelts has prevented injuries that would have resulted from automobile accidents. And these cases appear to vastly outnumber the relatively few cases in which people have avoided injury because they were not wearing seatbelts and were thrown clear of a vehicle.

The first sentence in these remarks suggests that a conclusion follows from the evidence that is given. No conclusion is explicitly stated, but the rest of the passage makes it clear that the hidden conclusion is the claim that wearing seatbelts is a good way to avoid injuries in automobile accidents. In order to recognize the hidden conclusion in this abbreviated argument, we diagram it as follows:

P1 = In the vast majority of cases that have been examined, wearing seatbelts has prevented injuries that would have resulted from automobile accidents.

P2 = These cases appear to vastly outnumber the relatively few cases in which people have avoided injury because they have been thrown clear of a vehicle.

HC = It is reasonable to believe that wearing a seatbelt is a good way to avoid injuries in automobile accidents.

Within legends and diagrams, we indicate hidden components by prefixing 'H' to the symbols that we use to represent them. In this case, that means that our conclusion is represented as 'HC'. In this way, a diagram clearly indicates when we are dealing with a hidden, rather than an explicit, component.

In supplying the hidden conclusion in this example we have tried to do so in a way that captures the tone and content of the author's explicit statements. It is significant that she emphasizes that some of the accidents investigated do not confirm her point, that she qualifies one of her statements with the word 'appear', and that she says her conclusion is 'reasonable to believe' rather than certain. In the midst of such qualifications, we would overstate her intentions if we expressed the conclusion as 'Wearing seat belts always prevents injury.' A conclusion of the form 'The wearing of seat belts should be required by law' would be also out of place, for it introduces a new issue the writer has not touched upon, namely that of legislation. For all we know, the author may not believe in legislation (perhaps because she is a libertarian opposed to government regulation) and only advocates the voluntary use of seat belts.

Here are two further examples of abbreviated arguments with hidden conclusions, in this case taken from a set of advertisements for 'PSYCHICS' in a magazine:

Voted #1 Psychic Michelle Palmer will bring lover back to stay forever. Removes evil influences. **817-772-3345**

ESP Psychic/Harvard PhD Melinda Meyers
God-gifted spiritualist, 20 yrs. Discovers problems, solutions in 1st minutes of conversation. **817-776-0039** Returns lovers within hours. Successful!

These are cases where context tells us that we are dealing with arguments, for it is obvious that these are advertisements that are trying to present reasons why we should call these psychics for advice. The evidence they forward is presented succinctly (for one pays for such ads by the word), but it is unlikely to be misunderstood.

In diagramming the arguments, we express each piece of information provided as a premise. The argument of the first advertisement can be diagrammed as follows:

P1 = Michelle Palmer was voted the number-1 psychic.
P2 = Michelle Palmer will bring lovers back to stay forever.
P3 = Michelle Palmer removes evil influences.
HC = You should call Michelle Palmer for advice.

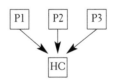

Although this will likely strike you as a poor argument in several ways (premise P1 is vague—we are not told who voted Palmer the number-1 psychic—and there is no solid evidence to back the claims about her abilities), it must still be classified as an argument, for it is a clear attempt to give us reasons for believing a hidden conclusion.

Leaving the second advertisement for you to diagram, we'll consider a different kind of example. The following is a paragraph from a commentary in the naturalist magazine *Seasons* (Winter 2002, p. 42). The commentary, by Jason Thorne, is a criticism of the Ontario government's plan to create a 'superhighway' through the

Niagara Peninsula, where it would 'cut a massive gash into the Niagara Escarpment, a World Biosphere Reserve.' The following is a paragraph from the commentary:

> Its proponents claim that the new highway is needed to handle the expected . . . growth in commercial vehicle traffic crossing the two Niagara bridges to the United States. On an average day, 7,100 trucks cross these bridges carrying a combined $280 million worth of goods. But just how many of these trucks would take the new road? Anyone who has examined the proposal carefully would conclude that the mid-peninsula highway clearly is intended as a toll highway. Anyone who has driven the 407 [a new toll highway] knows that transport trucks do not take toll roads. Also, the new highway's path to the Greater Toronto Area will be several kilometres longer than the current route along the QEW, making it much more costly for truckers to use.

In this example, the author makes a clear attempt to identify the views of his opponents, providing reasons why he thinks their views are mistaken. Though he never explicitly states his conclusion, the logic of the passage makes it plain. Certainly it makes no sense to suppose he is supporting the views of those who favour the construction of the superhighway. The principles of communication, which require that we look for an intelligible meaning in all speech acts, do not allow this interpretation. We will, therefore, diagram the implicit argument as follows:

P1 = Anyone who takes the 407 knows that trucks do not take toll roads.

P2 = The new highway's path to the Greater Toronto Area will be several kilometres longer than the current route along the QEW, making it much more costly for truckers to use.

C1 = Few trucks will take the new road.

HMC = Proponents of the new highway are mistaken when they claim that it is justified because it will alleviate the growing traffic problem on the bridges to the United States.

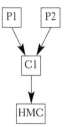

There is much that might be said about the reasoning in this example. While the argument is not definitive, it is notable that the author has made a conscious effort to understand and address the views of his opponents. This is an important part of good argument that we will be discussing later. But in the present context it is more important to put aside such issues and complete our account of hidden argument components by turning to hidden premises.

> ## FINDING HIDDEN CONCLUSIONS
>
> Ask yourself whether the remarks in question defend or invite some unstated conclusion. If the answer is 'yes', represent this claim as a hidden conclusion, 'HC'.

Hidden Premises

Hidden premises are unstated claims an argument depends on. Without assuming them, there is no way to logically move from the argument's explicit premises to the conclusion. We include a hidden premise in a diagram when we think that premises do not support the conclusion unless some bridge between them is supplied. When arguments contain hidden premises, you will often feel a gap in the reasoning from premises to conclusion. As in the case of hidden conclusions, we can identify hidden premises by applying our three principles of communication, which tell us to interpret an argument as an intelligible speech act that has a meaning that matches its context and the explicit components it contains.

Consider the following example we have adapted from a letter to *Time*, which was a response to an article on reproductive technologies (surrogate motherhood, *in vitro* fertilization, cloning, etc.) used to help infertile couples have children of their own. In response to the article, the author writes:

> We should stop aborting innocents, as that would eliminate the need for bizarre and unnatural methods of making babies.

This is an intriguing example because the argument is so condensed. Looking at the explicit claims the arguer makes, we can see that she is opposed to abortion, which she describes as 'aborting innocents', and to technological methods of dealing with infertility, which she describes as 'bizarre and unnatural'. Once we recognize her attitude to these issues, we can identify her argument, which maintains that abortion is objectionable because it creates a shortage of babies that must be remedied by making babies in 'bizarre and unnatural' ways.

We will diagram the argument as follows:

P1 = By stopping the abortion of innocent fetuses we could eliminate the need for bizarre and unnatural methods of making babies.

C = We should stop aborting fetuses.

You may sense that there is something right and something wrong with this diagram. This is the general structure of the reasoning, but there is something missing. There is a gap in the reasoning that must be bridged. Someone could accept P1 and not draw the proposed conclusion, so the author must be committed to some other premise that establishes C. If you think about it, you will see that this extra premise is the claim that unnatural methods of making babies are wrong and should, if possible, be avoided. It is this claim *together with* P1 that takes us to the conclusion.

When we recognize the hidden premise in the argument, our diagram becomes the following:

P1 = By stopping the abortion of innocent fetuses we could eliminate the
      need for bizarre and unnatural methods of making babies.
HP2 = Unnatural methods of making babies are wrong.
  C = We should stop aborting fetuses.

It is important to recognize hidden premises when they are controversial claims. In the present case, many people would take issue with HP2, for they would argue that unnatural methods of making babies are not wrong. They might back this claim by arguing that we all depend on unnatural methods of doing things (driving, flying, e-mailing, etc.) that are based on technological innovation. The point here is not to debate such questions but to recognize the hidden premise in the person's argument.

In diagramming, we supply the hidden components of an argument so they can be scrutinized. Our aim is a diagram that makes explicit all aspects of the argument we may want to discuss when we are ready to assess it. This sometimes means that we will identify hidden premises that are assumptions that the arguer has taken for granted. In doing so we distinguish between assumptions that are debatable and assumptions that are not, and identify the former but not the latter as hidden premises. We cannot treat every assumption as a hidden premise, for every argument presupposes an endless number of assumptions that are too numerous to be catalogued. For instance, in the above argument we have not treated as hidden premises the obvious assumptions that 'Abortion is a way of killing a fetus,' that 'Science has made unnatural ways of making babies possible,' that 'Making babies naturally is not wrong,' and that 'The words used in this argument are meaningful English words.' Every argument makes many assumptions of this sort. There is no reason to enumerate them when they are not controversial assumptions, for they do not need to be discussed. They can be taken for granted because they are assumptions that reflect widespread agreement about the world, about language, and about what is right and wrong. In contrast, those assumptions that are speculative or debatable are represented as hidden premises in the diagramming of an argument. Failure to include them results in an incomplete diagram.

Identifying hidden premises may sometimes require you to choose between different possibilities. In such cases, we encourage you to be cautious. Be charitable when you identify the hidden premises in an argument. Make sure any unstated claim you attribute the arguer is both necessary to the argument and something the arguer would accept.

Consider the following example that comes from a response to a Canadian Senate Committee's recommendation in the Fall of 2002 that marijuana use be decriminalized. One supporter of the report wrote the following to the *Globe and Mail* (6 September 2002):

> Adults should have the right to decide whether or not to use it because no scientific study has ever shown marijuana to be even as harmful as alcohol.

The premise indicator 'because' shows us that the second statement is intended as support for the first, and hence we have an argument. Initially, we might diagram it as:

P1 = No scientific study has ever shown marijuana to be even as harmful as alcohol.

C = Adults should have the right to decide whether or not to use marijuana.

It should be clear that there is something missing from this diagram. Indeed, the reasoning is somewhat peculiar, for why should the absence of a scientific study showing marijuana to be as harmful as alcohol count as a reason for adults having the right to use it? One possibility, which focuses on the references to a scientific study and harm, is that the arguer believes that adults have a right to decide for themselves in cases where a significant harm has not been scientifically proven. Adopting this interpretation, the hidden premise in the argument is:

HP2 = Adults have a right to decide for themselves in cases where a significant harm has not been scientifically proven.

The diagram becomes

The difficulty with this interpretation, even though it is plausible, is that it commits the arguer to a very general claim that may have applications beyond her or his intention. Because we are committed to as charitable an interpretation of the argument as possible, we prefer a different diagram that uncovers an assumption that commits the author to no more than we can be fairly sure he or she believes. Thus, we identify the hidden premise in the argument as:

HP2 = Adults have the right to decide whether or not to use alcohol.

This is a weaker claim than our first HP2. While that claim was controversial, the new HP2 reports a state of affairs known to exist and hence a belief we can expect the arguer to hold. With this HP, we are able to see the connection between the expressed components of the argument; without it, we could not.

In choosing this as our hidden premise, we are not saying that the argument is a good one. Only that this hidden premise is sufficient to explain the inference it incorporates. A decision about the strength of the argument would require an investigation of P1 and HP2, which we will not embark on here.

Our next example of a hidden premise comes from the same dispute over the Canadian Senate report on the decriminalization of marijuana:

> The criminalization of marijuana use cannot be justified. In spite of the eagerness of the police to devote many hours to the enforcement of pot legalization, the logical course of action would leave the police free to investigate crimes that actually hurt people.

We can diagram the expressed reasoning by establishing the following legend:

P1 = In spite of the eagerness of the police to devote many hours to the enforcement of pot legalization, the logical course of action would leave the police free to investigate crimes that actually hurt people.

C = The criminalization of marijuana use cannot be justified.

In this case, the move from P1 to C depends on at least two assumptions that may be identified as hidden premises. The first is the assumption that the enforcement of pot legislation requiring many hours of police work is not logical. The second is the assumption that marijuana use does not hurt people. It is only by accepting these two assumptions that one can move from P1 to the conclusion, yet both need to be supported. Thus we need to include them as two hidden premises on which the reasoning depends.

Our final example of a hidden premise is taken from an article on Chinese–American relations published in *Time* (July 1995). It describes poor relations with China that began with 'the bloody suppression of the Tiananmen Square democracy movement'. According to the article, relations worsened in the wake of a series of subsequent disputes. '[T]he only logical conclusion' the Chinese have been able to draw 'is that Washington is making a concerted and coordinated attack' on the Chinese government. In making this claim, the article functions as an argument narrative that attributes the following reasoning to the Chinese:

P1 = A series of disputes has arisen with the United States.
C = Washington is making a concerted and coordinated attack on us.

Again, we can see that something is missing from this diagram, for the stated conclusion follows only if one accepts another premise, i.e. that America has a coordinated policy on China. We can express this hidden premise as:

HP2 = The US must be acting according to a coordinated plan.

The amended diagram becomes

In the *Time* article, there is support for this interpretation in a remark by Charles Freeman, an assistant secretary of Defense, who is quoted saying that 'The Chinese are congenitally incapable of believing that a great country can conduct foreign policy by spastic twitching.'

FINDING HIDDEN PREMISES

Ask yourself whether the stated premises lead directly to the conclusion or depend on some unstated assumption. If the latter, and if this assumption needs to be assessed, present the unstated assumption as a hidden premise.

EXERCISE 3B

1. You are shopping for a used car and go to a car lot with four friends (Sam, Jari, Francesca, and Darryl). Each offers you an opinion. Each opinion can be understood as an argument with hidden components. Diagram the arguments contained in their remarks.
    a) Sam: Buy this Suzuki Swift. It's cheap and gets 60 miles to the gallon.
    b)* Jari: Buy this Volvo. They are built to German standards. It will last forever.
    c) Francesca: Buy this sports car. We can fly down the highway with the top down. It'll be so cool.

d) Darryl: Buy this old Cadillac. You'll look like a VIP.

2. Suppose you decide to accept the salesman's argument that 'You should buy this used Ford Escort. It is 10 years old but has only 40,000 miles on the odometer. It was owned by an old lady who only drove it to church. It is the best deal on the lot.' Provide a fully supplemented diagram representing your own reasoning to the conclusion that you should buy the Ford Escort.

3. Each of the following passages can be read as a simple argument but with hidden components that should be made explicit. Diagram each argument. (A number of these examples are taken or adapted from examples on Mark B. Mayer's website <http://faculty-staff.ou.edu/M/Mark.B.Mayer-1/T4.htm>, accessed 29 December 2002).

a)* God is all good. So God is benevolent.

b) You can't rely on what that witness said. He has perjured himself in the past.

c) Politicians of today are no longer leaders. They do whatever will get them elected.

d) Let's go see the *Lord of the Rings*. The first two episodes were great.

e) We shouldn't elect Charmaine president. She's too pushy.

f) Drugs should not be legalized because legalization would increase the number of drug addicts.

g)* Sports are good for kids because they teach discipline.

h) Father-only families are single-parent families. So we should make special efforts to help them.

i) We should strengthen the Endangered Species Act because doing so will preserve genetic diversity on the planet.

j) The Endangered Species Act is too stringent. It severely damages the economy.

k) Cheerleading should be considered a sport because cheerleaders belong to squads (or teams), try out, train, compete, and hone specialized skills.

l)* It's morally wrong to treat human beings as mere objects. So it is wrong to genetically engineer human beings.

m) It is morally acceptable for humans to eat animal flesh. Humans have teeth designed for eating animal flesh.

n) We have a duty to provide food for future generations. So we have a duty to develop genetically engineered crops.

3. Non-verbal Elements in Argument

In interpersonal argument, we frequently use gestures, facial expressions, and other non-verbal means of communication. Especially as information technology has made it easier to convey images and sounds, public arguments may also be conveyed in ways that extend beyond mere words. The arguments you encounter frequently exploit images, music, and other non-verbal carriers of meaning. In trying to understand and diagram these arguments you must be able to identify and interpret their non-verbal aspects. This is less difficult than it might at first appear, for these non-verbal speech acts can, like the verbal aspects of argument, be understood by applying the principles of communication we outlined at the beginning of this chapter. Principle 1 suggests that there is a 'logic' to non-verbal attempts to communicate argumentative ideas, i.e. that these speech acts are in principle intelligible. Principles 2 and 3 suggest that we must try to make sense of them by considering the contexts in which they occur and the explicit components (visual, musical, etc.) they employ.

In analyzing the non-verbal parts of argument, it is useful to distinguish four different kinds of non-verbal speech acts that frequently occur in argumentative exchange. An argument that incorporates non-verbal elements may use any or all of them. For reasons that will become clear as we proceed, we will call these different speech acts 'argument flags', 'demonstrations', 'symbolic references', and 'metaphors'.

Argument Flags

Sometimes non-verbal acts of communication accompany an argument without playing a significant role in it. A visual backdrop to an argument often has no argumentative significance. When an arguer presents a case in a room or a location that has no special relationship to the argument, it need not be considered in argument analysis. In other cases, the background to an argument is significant and needs to be discussed, for it has been chosen specifically to facilitate the argument in one way or another.

In the simplest cases, an image or some other non-verbal speech act functions as an *argument flag* that draws attention to an argument. In such cases, the non-verbal elements are used to attract us to an argument and make us pay attention to it. An arguer may, for example, arrange to have his or her argument announced by a drum roll or piece of music; present it before a stunning natural landscape or while sitting in the high-backed chair of a judge; or have it presented by an announcer with eye-catching good looks. Insofar as these non-verbal means are intended as attempts to attract our attention (and not as content in the actual argument) they are all examples of argument flags. A historical example of a visual flag is the illustration below of a cricket, featured in an early ad campaign for home insurance (see p. 67). This image is properly classified as a visual argument flag because it was used to attract the reader's attention to the argument that accompanied it. In doing so, it exploited the way a picture on a page may 'jump out' at you. In this case, the image's ability to catch the viewer's eye was enhanced by the quality of the artwork, and by the vivid colour in the original, which was published at a time when colour printing was rare and remarkable.

In cases like this, the non-verbal cue that catches our eye is only a flag and not itself an argument or part of an argument. For the flag is not used to convey the message of the argument, and only functions as a means of directing us to the text that conveys the actual argument. Within that text, we are told that the painting is of a field cricket building a home, a theme that introduces the argument that we should purchase life insurance, for we, too, care about our homes.

Visual and musical flags are often used in contemporary argument. Arguers exploit them as a means of attracting our attention, especially in contexts in which there are many other arguments that vie for our attention. Argument flags can be an effective way to attract our attention, for we are naturally drawn to a stunning photograph or piece of music. But argument flags are (insofar as they function as argument flags and not in other ways) not themselves arguments or argument components. In interpreting arguments with non-verbal elements that function only as argument flags we will, therefore, treat them as noise rather than a component of the argument. They can be compared with many headlines and verbal claims that introduce an argument but are not themselves a part of its premises and conclusion.

Non-verbal Demonstrations

The most basic way in which non-verbal elements function as arguments occurs when music, sounds, images, or even aromas are used in non-verbal demonstrations. Demonstrations of this sort appeal directly to some kind of evidence in favour of a conclusion. Before-and-after photographs that vividly present the weight loss that can be achieved through a particular weight loss program, video evidence in a court case, a clip of a recording used to advertise a CD, and the scent sprayed from a sample bottle of perfume are all instances of non-verbal demonstration. In each case, they are a means of supporting some conclusion the arguer hopes to convey to you—that you can lose *this* kind of weight, that *this* person robbed the jewellery store, that this CD sounds *this* good, or that this perfume smells *this* good.

A famous example of non-verbal demonstration is described in the traditional biography of Aesop, the ancient fabulist credited with fables like 'The Tortoise and the Hare' and 'The Boy Who Cried Wolf'. According to the *Life of Aesop*, Aesop was born an ugly slave who could not speak, with few prospects for the future. Despite his initial handicap, he proved his ingenuity when two other slaves ate his master's finest figs and blamed it on Aesop, thinking that his inability to speak would undermine his ability to defend himself. Aesop managed to outwit them and avoid his master's wrath by motioning for warm water, swallowing it, and forcing himself to regurgitate. The results show that he has nothing in his stomach. One might summarize this as the simple argument:

P1 = If I was the one who ate the figs, I would have regurgitated them.
P2 = I did not regurgitate them.
C = I was not the one who ate the figs.

When Aesop motions to the other slaves, the master forces them to do the same and the evidence against them falls from their own mouths.

Traditionally, non-verbal demonstrations have been highly regarded forms of argument, for they more directly present evidence than an argument expressed in mere words. A witness who tells us she saw a person wearing a ring that was stolen from us may be lying: all we have for evidence is her words. If she, in contrast, presents the person with the ring on his right hand, the claim that this person is wearing our ring cannot be dismissed as a lie. A photograph or video is one step removed from this kind of presentation, but it, too, attempts to capture evidence in a relatively direct way. Non-verbal demonstrations are attempts to directly engage the world. Verbal claims are, at best, attempts to present a view of reality that we ourselves construct.

Especially in an age where technology has made it relatively easy to reproduce sounds and visual images, non-verbal demonstrations are a common form of argument. This is a problem as well as a blessing, for the technological advances that have made it easier to present non-verbal evidence have also made it easier to manipulate this evidence. Given that images and recordings and videos can be edited and 'doctored', it would be naive to assume that they necessarily convey 'things as they are'. Particularly where professional photography is involved, you must remember that any image or recording is the result of a conscious decision to approach a particular subject in a particular way—to emphasize a particular camera angle, background, time of day, theme, and so on and so forth.

These caveats being noted, non-verbal demonstrations are a reasonable form of argument in some circumstances. The image in the advertisement for Newfoundland and Labrador that we have reproduced below (p. 69) is a case in point. Especially if it

Here, the history of the earth's creation is told in stone. A land carved by time and glaciers. Still fjords held close by ancient rock walls.

This is the place where sky, land & water embrace like old friends.

Gros Morne National Park. A UNESCO World Heritage Site.

NEWFOUNDLAND & LABRADOR
CANADA
www.gov.nf.ca/tourism/

For more information or to order your free travel guide, call Eileen at 1-800-563-NFLD

'The glacier-carved freshwater fjord at Western Brooke Pond', provided by the Government of Newfoundland and Labrador.

is considered together with the many other photographs posted on the website of their provincial tourism office (<http://www.gov.nf.ca/tourism/welcome/default.htm>), it is a reasonable way to demonstrate some of the sights that one can expect to see on a trip to Newfoundland and Labrador. We might diagram the intended argument as:

> P1 = If you visit Newfoundland and Labrador, you will be able to see sights like these.
> HP2 = Seeing sights like these is an experience worth pursuing.
> C = You should visit Newfoundland and Labrador.

We have included HP2 as a premise in this diagram because the principal premise — that you will see sights like these in Newfoundland and Labrador — warrants the conclusion if one assumes that this is an experience worth pursuing. It is a hidden premise because it is assumed rather than stated in the argument. In contrast, P1 is an explicit premise. It is not expressed verbally, but it is expressed non-verbally, through the images in question.

It is difficult to assess this example in a general way, for its force will vary greatly, depending on the audience that considers it. Given this, our own critical assessment of the conclusion that we should visit Newfoundland and Labrador must take account of our concerns and attitudes—on the extent to which we value scenic beauty (rather than, say, an urban night life), on our ability to pay for such a trip, on what we can discover about accommodations in Newfoundland, etc. That said, the images in question provide reasonable (and if we value scenic beauty, powerful) evidence in favour of such a trip.

Symbolic References

Non-verbal demonstrations are the most direct form of non-verbal argument. But a non-verbal argument may not be a demonstration. A political cartoon that depicts a politician caught embezzling as a devil with horns employs non-verbal elements, but it is not a demonstration. In this and similar cases, the non-verbal elements of arguments function as symbols that can replace words, represent some idea, or refer to someone or something. You use and interpret non-verbal symbols every day. You know that a crucifix represents Christ, that a skull represents death, that the 'Star Spangled Banner' symbolizes the United States of America, that a peace sign stands for peace, that a thumbs-up means 'Okay!', and that a 'swoosh' represents Nike sports equipment. If you follow the NHL, you know that a blue maple leaf stands for the Toronto Maple Leafs.

In contexts of argument, non-verbal symbols are often used either to state a position or to make a case for one. An example is the message we have reproduced below (p. 71), which was widely circulated (often by e-mail) as a response to US president George W. Bush's comments on Iraq. It reproduces photos of George Bush and his father, and quotes President Bush's claim that 'We shall not exonerate Saddam Hussein for his actions. We will mobilize to meet this threat to vital interests in the Persian Gulf until an amicable solution is reached. Our best strategy is to be prepared. Failing that, we are coming.' The intended message is conveyed visually, by inserting the logos of international corporations within the quote, replacing particular words with certain corresponding logos. For instance, the phrase 'shall not' becomes 'Shell not', 'exonerate' becomes 'EXXONerate', 'be prepared' becomes 'BP repared', etc.

As in other cases, we can understand this speech act by applying our principles of communication. They tell us that some intelligible message is being conveyed by the author, and that this message needs to be distilled by considering the context of the message and the elements it contains. In this case, the broader context is the debate over President Bush's remarks on Iraq, which have been quoted in the message. Its elements are both the words and sentences in the quote, and the images they have been combined with. The photo of Bush functions as a way to ascribe the quote to him. The photo of his father suggests that he and his father share the same perspective. The logos of the international corporations are a way of suggesting that President Bush's real agenda in Iraq is not his claimed concerns but the protection of the interests of corporations like Shell, Exxon, Mobil, Gulf, Amoco, BP, and Arco. Visually, the message presents itself as an exposé of the president's remarks, one that reveals the true message behind his remarks (much as a visual demonstration tries to reveal the true nature of reality).

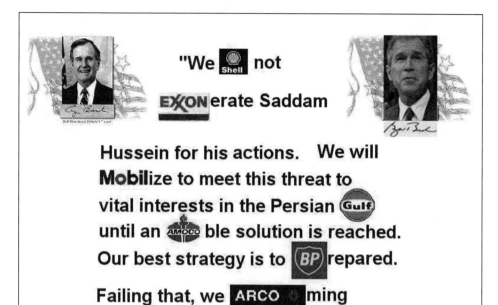

It is significant that this message can only be classified as a statement or an explanation of Bush's attitude to Iraq and not as an argument. The statement it forwards may contribute to an argument or precipitate debate, but it does not itself qualify as an argument, for it does not provide reasons to support the proposed interpretation of President Bush's remarks. In a different speech act, someone might assemble evidence — verbally, visually, and otherwise — that would support the claim the message makes, but it is not provided in this instance. Though its analysis of Bush may have merit, and though its cleverness is worth noting (and is likely to be enjoyed by those who oppose Bush's stance), the absence of reasons gives it little argumentative force. A persuasive conclusion about Bush and his agenda would need evidence in its support.

Metaphors

A fourth kind of non-verbal meaning is conveyed when arguments use non-verbal metaphors. A metaphor describes one thing as though it were another. 'Jill is a block of ice' and 'The world's a stage' are verbal metaphors. They make no sense if we try to understand them literally, for people are not made of ice and the world is not a theatre. We therefore understand them, in a figurative way, as the claims that Jill is unfriendly, and that our lives are like roles in a stage play.

Non-verbal metaphors operate in a similar way. They use non-verbal elements metaphorically to ascribe some characteristic to a person or a thing (because these elements may be non-verbal symbols, many non-verbal metaphors employ symbolic references). Political cartoons are a visual genre that uses visual metaphors to make a

How Jean Chretien Makes the Decisions
that Matter to Canadians

point. An example is the cartoon we have reproduced above. It depicts former Canadian prime minister Jean Chrétien on a weather vane, making 'the decisions that matter to Canadians'. The implicit claim might be described as the view that Chrétien made such decisions not by following the dictates of strongly held convictions but by doing whatever the winds of public opinion dictated. Published in the context of an election, this cartoon functions as an argument against Chrétien, for it provides an (alleged) reason why he should not be voted for.

It is worth noting here that this criticism of Chrétien is one that has often been directed at democratically elected politicians, who are said to be more interested in maintaining the support of the electorate than in voting as their conscience dictates. In view of this, the visual metaphor exploited in this cartoon could easily be amended so that it functions as a remark on some other politician, simply by substituting a different figure for the drawing of Chrétien atop the wind vane. Indeed, a similar image displaying an American senator rather than Jean Chretein (drawn by Mischa Richter) is found in Charles Press's *The Political Cartoon* (Farleigh Dickinson University Press, 1981). Visual (and verbal) metaphors are frequently used this way, one metaphor inspiring another that makes a similar comment on another person or thing.

Other good examples of non-verbal metaphors are found in a series of radio advertisements that have helped Durex Condoms become the largest condom manufacturer in the world (available on the Durex website <http://www.durex.com/

index.html>). One of the ads (which the company calls 'Guitar') can be summarized as follows:

1. [an enticing female voice:] 'This is what sex is like with an ordinary condom.'
2. [One hears the sound of:] A pedestrian, slow march.
3. [The female voice returns:] 'This is what sex is like with a Durex Sheik condom.'
4. [One hears the sound of:] A rock and roll tune with a driving beat.
5. [The female voice returns:] 'Feel what you've been missing. Set yourself free with the condom designed for excitement. Durex Sheik condoms. For super sensitivity. So you can enjoy all of love's pleasures. Now safer sex doesn't have to feel like safe sex. Set yourself free with Durex Sheik condoms.'

The crux of this advertisement is the difference between the two pieces of music it contains, the first representing ordinary condoms, the second representing Durex. In a context in which Durex is obviously promoting its condoms, we have no problem recognizing that the energy and the driving beat in the second clip, when contrasted with the boredom and lack of vigour conveyed in the first piece of music, suggests that sex with an ordinary condom is ho-hum in comparison to sex with a Durex condom, and that Durex condoms can 'set you free' so that you can 'enjoy all of love's pleasures'.

If we eliminate the repetition in the argument and isolate the reasons it provides for its conclusion, we can diagram it as follows:

P1 = Durex Sheik condoms will provide a more exciting sex life than ordinary condoms (one that includes all of love's pleasures; one that doesn't feel like safe sex).

P2 = Durex Sheik condoms are designed for super sensitivity.

C = Your should use Durex Sheik condoms.

When you recognize and diagram this argument, it may occur to you that it is very weak. Durex is attempting to convince us that we should buy Durex Sheik condoms on the grounds that they will make our sex life more exciting. But there is no proof that they will do so. Indeed, this claim is inherently peculiar. For why should we think that a particular condom can turn a pedestrian sex life into one that we would associate with rock and roll? There are ways in which one might plausibly argue for Durex Sheik condoms (by comparing their properties to those of competing brands, by appealing to testimony, etc.), but the radio ad for Durex is a clear instance of a company deciding to try to sell their product by charming us with music and humour, not by engaging in a reasonable attempt at argument.

A Complex Example

Non-verbal means of communication have a strong emotional appeal. Images and music captivate us. They make us laugh and smile, and can play upon our fears and frustrations, our likes and dislikes. At times, the emotional pull of non-verbal messages can be used legitimately in argument. For instance, in an attempt to convince you that you should help the homeless, photographs (or an actual tour of a shelter) may be the best way to convey to you the needs of homeless people.

But there are many circumstances in which arguments are couched in non-verbal terms because this encourages us to be emotional *rather* than critical when we relate to them. It is important to recognize the communicative role that non-verbal elements play in many arguments, because this will encourage us to properly recognize them as something that needs to be subjected to criticism and inquiry. The Durex radio advertisements are clever and witty, but we need to see them as something more than this, especially if we are considering buying condoms, i.e. if we are part of the audience to which the advertisements are directed. In that case, we should be concerned that this attempt to persuade us to buy Durex condoms rather than some other brand has little argumentative force because it fails to provide reasons.

Of course, many of the arguments we encounter are complex combinations of verbal and non-verbal elements. In cases such as this, we need to interpret the argument as a whole. Consider Mazda's popular 'zoom, zoom' advertisements for the Mazda Tribute, its new sport-utility vehicle. These advertisements have been carefully crafted to include stirring music with an African beat, stunning visuals, and a verbal commentary that all lead to the inevitable conclusion that one should drive a Tribute. In diagramming and analyzing the argument, we need to recognize that these are all parts of a package and need to be interpreted together. We might begin by summarizing the advertisement for the Tribute, which unfolds as follows:

1. Music
2. [male voice:] 'What would happen if an SUV was raised by a family of sports cars?'
3. pause with visuals (wheat blowing in the wind)
4. [A boy in a suit whispers:] 'Zoom, zoom.'
5. [male voice:] 'Introducing the 200 horsepower Mazda Tribute, the SUV with the soul of a sports car.'
6. [One hears a driving African beat, scat singing with the sounds:] 'zoom, zoom, zoom . . . heh, . . . zoom, zoom, zoom . . . yah . . . zoom, zoom, zoom . . .'
7. The music is accompanied by scenes on the open road, where a Mazda Tribute weaves its way through a pack of sports cars racing along a highway.
8. After the Tribute emerges at the front of the pack it refuses to take a turn in the highway, and races off the road into open country.

What is the message conveyed in this advertisement? Clearly, it is an attempt to sell the Mazda Tribute. But what are the reasons it offers for the conclusion that this is a car one would want to own? To understand these reasons, we need to understand both the verbal and the non-verbal elements of the ad. The non-verbal elements include instances of all the forms of non-verbal communication we have already noted. They might be summarized as follows:

- **Argument flags**. The vivid music and the visuals function as argument flags that capture our attention.
- **Non-verbal demonstrations**. The visuals demonstrate the principal message of the ad—that the Mazda Tribute combines the qualities of a sports car (the speed, the handling, etc.) with the SUV's ability to drive off road. The qualities of the sports car are demonstrated as the Tribute weaves its way through a pack of sports cars. The off-road capability is demonstrated when it refuses to take a turn and drives off the highway into the outback.
- **Metaphor**. The 'zoom, zoom' theme is Mazda's (highly successful) attempt to adopt a slogan that captures what it has called 'the joy of motion'. This is a theme enunciated in the words that accompany the ad, and in the music, which is strong, fun, lively, energizing. The Tribute itself is alleged to embody all these traits.
- **Symbolic references**. The boy in the suit may initially seem perplexing. Why a boy? Boys don't drive automobiles. And why a boy in a suit? Boys don't wear suits. To understand this aspect of the advertisement we need to consider the implicit symbolism. Men are the traditional market for automobile advertisements. And the professional men who can afford a Mazda Tribute wear suits. The boy in the ad is the boy who still exists inside the businessman—the boy who still enjoys the simple thrill of motion. It is this 'inner child' who whispers the crucial 'zoom, zoom' in the advertisement. He whispers because his comment is a thought inside the head of the man that he is speaking to—the man thinking about the Mazda Tribute.

When we combine these non-verbal elements with the statements made in the advertisement, we can see an argument that we can begin to diagram as follows:

P1 = The Mazda Tribute combines the driving qualities of a sports car (the speed, the handling, etc.) with the SUV's ability to handle off-road driving.
C1 = The 200 horsepower Mazda Tribute is an SUV with the soul of a sports car.
P2 = Driving the Mazda Tribute (like driving other Mazdas) is boyishly fun, thrilling, and energizing.
MC = You should purchase a Mazda Tribute.

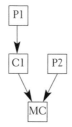

We can develop this further by recognizing that the sub-argument from P2 to MC depends on two unstated premises that can be expressed as follows:

HP3 = One should purchase an automobile that is fun, thrilling, and energizing.
HP4 = The tribute is *more* fun, thrilling, and energizing than the competition.

HP3 is needed because the fun of driving a Tribute provides significant support for the conclusion that one should purchase the Tribute only if this is what really matters in an automobile (and not safety, economy, etc.). We can see why we must add HP4 to our diagram if we imagine that the Tribute is *not* more fun than its competitors. For in these circumstances, the assumption that one should buy a car that is fun and appeals to one's youthful sense of play (HP3) may lead to the conclusion not that one should purchase a Tribute, but that one should purchase a competing vehicle. Our full diagram is:

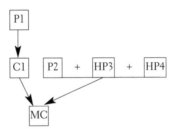

Once we have this diagram, a number of debatable aspects become apparent. Despite its emotional appeal (especially to the 'boy inside the man' that Mazda is targeting), HP3 could easily be debated. HP4 is also open to debate, as is the staged visual presentation that is supposed to demonstrate the qualities claimed in P1.

But these and other concerns lie beyond the scope of our present discussion, where we want only to demonstrate that complex arguments employing non-verbal elements can be identified and diagrammed by recognizing the different forms of non-verbal meaning we have noted. Once we have identified and diagrammed the elements of such arguments, we can assess them in the same ways we will assess other arguments, by asking whether their premises are plausible and their conclusions follow.

FOUR KINDS OF NON-VERBAL MEANING

There are four kinds of non-verbal elements that may function in an argument:

➤ **Argument flags** are used to draw our attention to an argument.
➤ **Non-verbal demonstrations** are used to provide some direct evidence for a conclusion.
➤ **Symbolic references** are used to make a non-verbal reference to some idea, person, or thing.

> ➤ **Metaphors** are used to figuratively ascribe some characteristic to the subject of the metaphor.
>
> In some complex arguments, all four kinds of non-verbal meaning may be used. Sometimes the same non-verbal elements (e.g. a particular piece of music) may convey more than one kind of non-verbal meaning.

EXERCISE 3C

1. Take one of the visual arguments in Exercise 1M (p. 27) and explain how the principles of communication were applied in your treatment of the argument. What kinds of non-verbal meaning are evident in these cases?

2. Go to your university or college website. Go to the section entitled 'Prospective Students'. Analyze the images and statements (and sounds, if there are some). What messages do they communicate? Find an argument and diagram it.

3. The Gap, Calvin Klein, and United Colors of Benetton are all famous for their advertisements, which are almost wholly visual. Find one of their advertisements and analyze it according to the discussion of non-verbal meaning included in this chapter.

4. A NOTE ON ARGUMENT CONSTRUCTION

In many circumstances, we communicate in ways that are not entirely explicit. This is not a bad thing. If we could communicate only in ways that were fully explicit, and used only words, communication would be cumbersome, difficult, and mundane. But there are circumstances in which explicitness is a goal that we should aim for. The attempt to identify and diagram an argument is one such case, for it is an attempt to reveal *all* the important parts of the argument. Identifying these parts prepares us for the inspection of them that will allow us to decide whether the argument is strong or weak.

In the process of identifying and diagramming arguments, we can 'fill in the blanks' and recognize their implicit aspects by applying the three basic principles of communication outlined at the beginning of this chapter. They suggest that the interpretation of any speech act should aim for a coherent meaning that is in keeping with its context and its explicit elements. In earlier chapters, we implicitly relied on the process of interpretation this suggests in deciding what is and is not an argument, and in deciding how the components of ordinary arguments should be identified and diagrammed. In this chapter we have explained how this process can be used in identifying hidden premises and conclusions, and in understanding the non-verbal elements of many arguments.

In constructing arguments of your own, your goal should be arguments that do not depend on implicit elements in a way that makes them difficult to interpret or easy to misconstrue. The first step towards this goal is a commitment to use premise and conclusion indicators whenever you construct an argument. This is the only way to ensure that your arguments will be recognized as arguments.

In the body of your arguments you can avoid confusion by using words and, if you decide to use them, non-verbal elements that clearly and precisely express what you want to say. Though no one can expect to avoid hidden premises in every circumstance (because our audiences will, in some cases, want to take issue with assumptions that seem to us obvious and unproblematic), you should try to explicitly express any important premise your argument depends on. In Chapter 1 we introduced the device of imagining an opponent for your argument to help you see what objections might be raised. You can use the same device to anticipate what statements will be controversial. If you can reasonably expect a premise to be controversial to such an opponent, then you should not hide it. Instead, you should create an extended argument that includes a sub-argument to support the premise in question.

In constructing arguments, especially in public contexts that are conducive to images, music, and other elements, do not hesitate to use non-verbal elements that may be appropriate, but be sure not to abuse them. In many cases, they are attempts to substitute purely emotional appeals for combinations of premises and conclusions that will stand up to scrutiny. We encourage you to be clever, witty, and creative, but not in a way that undermines the force of the arguments you construct.

EXERCISE 3D

Construct an extended argument for or against the death penalty (no more than three paragraphs long). Use non-verbal elements if you choose. After you have constructed the argument, discuss it from the point of view of clarity: How have you presented your argument and structured it so that it is clear what you are saying? What potential confusions did you need to avoid? How have you avoided them? What mistakes might occur in a poorly constructed version of your argument?

MAJOR EXERCISE 3M

1.   For each of the following passages, say whether it contains an argument. If it contains an argument, diagram it, adding hidden premises and conclusions as necessary. (Don't assume that all passages are arguments, or that all contain hidden components. Qualify your discussion of borderline cases.)

   a)   Section 598b of the California Penal Code makes it illegal to eat domesticated animals like cats and dogs. But the only community in California that eats such animals is the Vietnamese community. So section 598b of the California Penal Code discriminates against the Vietnamese community.

b)* [adapted from a column in the *Detroit Free Press*] Airlines are funny. They make sure you aren't carrying a weapon of destruction and then sell you all the booze you can drink.

c) [patterned after an old-fashioned advertisement] ARE YOU GULLIBLE? Then our product is for you. For years people believed there was no simple cure for this ailment. People who succumbed to its ravages were considered beyond help. They studied critical thinking, they worked hard to develop a critical attitude. All with little chance of success. Why work so hard? Now there's TINDALE'S CREDULITY FORMULA. $25 for the completely gullible. Smaller bottles, priced at only $10, are available for the slightly gullible.

d) [Nancy Clarke, in 'Why do we hate big, black birds?' *Seasons* (winter 2002)] Surely our attitudes toward animals are culturally based. The animals we choose as companions, sacred objects, villains, and food vary depending on where we come from. Thus, North Americans eat cows and worship domestic cats and dogs, while people in some parts of Asia do the reverse.

e)* [from a discussion of Bill Moyers' PBS television series on poetry in *Time* (7 Mar. 1995)] Moyers makes virtually no attempt to place the poet in a larger social context—to view poetry as a profession (or, perhaps more to the point, to analyze what it means that ours is a culture where it's all but impossible to be a professional poet). Ezra Pound once pointed out that history without economics is bunk. To which one might add that poetry without economics—without some sense of the ebb and flow of the megamercantile society surrounding the poet—is bunk too.

f)* [from a philosophy class discussion] Abortion is not murder. The soul does not enter the body until the first breath is taken. Up to this point, the fetus is a biological entity only.

g) [from a comment on an article that appeared in *National Geographic* (Nov. 1999), which declared the Archaeraptor Fossil to be 'a true missing link in the complex chain that connects dinosaurs to birds'] How did *National Geographic* come to publish the fraud with such fanfare? This was due to the fossil's origins being cloaked in mystery since it was discovered in China, and to there being insufficient time to have the article peer-reviewed [reviewed by experts in the field].

h)* [Odysseus in the *Odyssey*, 7.215] For nothing in the world is so shamelessly demanding as a man's confounded stomach. However afflicted he may be and sick at heart, it calls for attention so loudly that he is bound to obey it.

i) [Pierre Théberge, the organizer of an exhibit of automobiles at the Montreal Museum of Fine Arts (1995)] In design circles the automobile is still something of an 'orphan', because it has been looked upon as essentially an outgrowth of technological development.

j) [Gene Laczniak and Patrick Murphy, in *Ethical Marketing Decisions* (Pearson, 1993), p. 263] A final argument that can be made for televised political advertising is that it motivates voters. TV advertising is thought to reach and vitalize individuals who otherwise might not participate in the election.

k) [Robert Bly, in *The Key and the Pillow*] Since the Wild Man cannot stay in civilization, the boy has no choice at last but to go off with the Wild Man and overcome . . . his fear of irrationality, intuition, emotion, the bodily and primitive life.

l) Cigarettes are the greatest public health problem we have, and the most flagrant example of drug pushing, since most tobacco is pushed on teenagers, who are led by advertising into thinking it's cool to smoke.

m)* [a sign on a public bench] You just proved Bench Advertising Works.

n) [from a radio advertisement for a Subaru four-wheel drive] Have you ever seen an agile dog on two legs? For better agility and handling, see your Subaru dealer today.

o) [from *The Economist* (21 Dec. 2002), p. 38] The pithiest explanation of why Cameroonians have to put up with all this came from the gendarme at road-block 31. He had invented a new law about carrying passengers in trucks . . . When it was put to him that the law he was citing did not, in fact, exist, he patted his holster and replied: 'Do you have a gun? No. I have a gun, so I know the rules.'

2. Construct fully supplemented diagrams for the arguments in the following advertisements. Discuss the non-verbal aspects of the arguments, and any other aspects of the arguments that are worthy of note.

a) a World War II advertisement for American Motor Lines

TO KEEP THE FLAMES OF FREEDOM BURNING
. . . Intercity Buses Bring Up the Manpower

MOTOR BUS LINES OF AMERICA
NATIONAL ASSOCIATION OF MOTOR BUS OPERATORS, WASHINGTON, D. C.

b) an ad for the National Center for Tobacco-Free kids (reprinted by permission of the National Center for Tobacco-Free kids, www.tobaccofreekids.org)

Does RJR Nabisco Lie About Marketing To Kids?

In public they say:

"I do not want to sell tobacco to children. I'd fire anyone on the spot if I found they were doing it." (Steven Goldstone, CEO, RJR Nabisco Holdings Corp., 12/6/96).

But a 1976 RJR internal memo stated:

"Evidence is now available to indicate that the 14-to-18-year-old group is an increasing segment of the smoking population. RJR-T must soon establish a successful new brand in this market if our position in the industry is to be maintained over the long term."

You Decide.

In 1988, RJR introduced Joe Camel. Subsequently, Camel's share of the kids' market quadrupled. Camel is now the second most popular cigarette among children, and kids were found to be as familiar with Joe Camel as Mickey Mouse.

Tell your elected officials to support restrictions on tobacco marketing to children, including the Food and Drug Administration rule.

Tobacco vs. Kids.
Where America draws the line.

CAMPAIGN for TOBACCO-FREE Kids

To learn more, call 1-800-284-KIDS.

This ad supported by: American Cancer Society; American Lung Association; American Heart Association; Center for Women Policy Studies; National Federation of State High School Associations; Committee for Children; Intercultural Cancer Council; Interreligious Coalition on Smoking OR Health; Youth Service America; American College of Preventive Medicine; Girl Scouts USA; Child Welfare League of America; National Association of Secondary School Principals; National Association of Elementary School Principals; American Federation of Teachers; Women's Legal Defense Fund; Association of State and Territorial Health Officials.

The National Center for Tobacco-Free Kids, 1707 L Street NW, Suite 800, Washington, DC 20036

3. The following images are public-domain images from the American Fish and Wildlife Service. Use them to construct a poster promoting the 'St George Environmental Fund'. Or find an image of your own and create a poster on another topic. After you have created the poster, analyze it in terms of the account of non-verbal communication provided in this chapter.

4

DEFINITIONS:

SAYING

WHAT YOU MEAN

In Chapter 3 we discussed the principles of communication that arguments depend on. In this chapter we continue our study of language, discussing it in the context of the issues that arise when we construct or analyze an argument. To this end, we look at

- vagueness and ambiguity;
- equivocation and verbal disputes;
- extensional, intensional, and stipulative definitions; and
- ways to ensure you express what you mean.

We have all been interrupted in the course of an argument by someone who asks us to clarify something we have said. The point or term that is unclear may have seemed perfectly clear to us. In such circumstances, we may be surprised to find that our meaning has not been communicated in the way that we expected.

When this occurs in conversation we can usually explain ourselves. The problem is more difficult if a similar confusion arises in an argument we are trying to communicate in writing. In an ongoing exchange we may have the opportunity to clarify our meaning, but there will be many circumstances in which we have only one opportunity to convey what we mean. In such cases, our ability to argue convincingly may depend upon our ability to convey our meaning well. This chapter is designed to teach you how to communicate clearly and precisely in argumentative contexts. It explains some of the common ways in which meanings are lost or misconstrued, and how you can avoid such problems. You will need to keep these concerns in mind when you are constructing arguments (especially written arguments) and be able to discuss them when you analyze and critique other people's reasoning.

One of the principal ways in which we can make our meanings clearer is by using definitions to explain important terms we use. The ability to evaluate definitions and construct them is, therefore, a crucial skill in the good reasoner's repertoire. This is especially important because many disputes are founded on arguments about the meaning of some term or concept, or the way it should be defined. We have recognized the significance of definitions in good reasoning by making definitions and the arguments that hinge on them a central topic in this chapter.

1. Using Words Precisely

Human cloning is an important contemporary issue. Suppose you are involved in a discussion of the rights and wrongs of cloning. Imagine that someone sitting across the table from you declares that 'human cloning contravenes the most fundamental requirements of reverence in dealing with human life.' You want to evaluate this statement. As you will see when we introduce the principles of argument evaluation, your evaluation will turn on the question of whether this premise—that 'human cloning contravenes the most fundamental requirements of reverence dealing with human life'—is a good reason for the conclusion that 'human cloning is wrong.'

But we cannot decide whether a claim is a good reason for a conclusion unless we are clear about what it means. To this end, we must isolate the different terms and phrases used and be sure we understand them. In the case in question, we need to ask what is meant by 'the fundamental requirements of reverence', and more fundamentally, what is meant by 'reverence'. The answers to these questions may lie elsewhere in an arguer's discussion, so we must pay careful attention to all that has been said. We cannot evaluate whether a particular statement is a reasonable premise—or conclusion—in an argument if we cannot establish what that statement or one of its component terms means.

In approaching the words used in arguments, and in using them ourselves, we need to remember that languages change over time. Dictionaries are constantly updated because language is fluid and the meanings of words shift. New words are coined, and old words acquire additional meanings or different meanings. Consider, to take one example, how the evolution of computer technology has affected our language, introducing terms like 'software' and 'Internet' as well as new meanings for old terms like 'crash' or 'mouse' or 'web' or 'ring'. It is important to remember the fluid nature of language when you are reviewing the arguments of arguers from previous generations: it would be wrong to artificially impose on their arguments the meanings that words have for us today.

In contexts in which our own use of language may be misunderstood, we need to take steps to avoid this possibility. If we are using a term in an idiosyncratic way that does not correspond to the standard meaning of the term, we need to say so. If there are different uses of a term that need to be distinguished, we need to make clear which use we are employing. If our use differs from that of an author we are quoting, we must note the distinction. What we require of ourselves and other arguers is precision in the use of terms.

Euphemisms and Emotional Language

Euphemisms substitute mild and indirect ways of speaking for words that might seem blunt and harsh. They may neutralize remarks that would otherwise be filled with emotion. Many euphemistic words and phrases play an integral role in our ordinary vocabulary. In the interests of social grace or politeness they function as inoffensive substitutes for coarse, harsh, or inelegant expressions. We say that someone 'passed away' instead of saying that they 'died'. We do not say that a veterinarian 'kills' a family pet, but that she 'puts it to sleep'. Euphemisms of this sort are in many circumstances acceptable. Insofar as they soften a harsh reality, they may be advantageous, as long as they do not muddle someone's intended meaning.

In contrast, there are times when meanings and claims are distorted by the use of euphemisms. Political activists often accuse politicians and the military of using intentionally misleading euphemisms to soften the images of weapons and their effects. The term 'smart bomb' may, for example, promote a positive attitude to this kind of device (for we admire things that are smart) and suggest that it is much less likely to cause unwarranted destruction than other explosives. The American philosopher and peace activist John Somerville argued that the term 'nuclear war' is fundamentally misleading, and proposed that we replace it with the term 'omnicide', formed by analogy with terms like 'infanticide', 'fratricide', and 'genocide', to capture nuclear war's capacity to kill all things. According to Somerville, nuclear war is as different from other kinds of war as murder and suicide are from disease, and we invite confusing conclusions if we treat it as something that is comparable (John Somerville, 'Human Rights and Nuclear War', *The Churchman* 196, January 1982).

Other euphemisms that may be disturbing include terms that are used to refer to business notions like 'restructuring' and 'downsizing' (sometimes called 'rightsizing'). Such terms are, critics argue, specifically designed to allow us to talk about important moral and social issues without properly addressing the dire consequences they can have. George Orwell famously expressed these sentiments in 'Politics and English Language', where he wrote that 'political language has to consist largely of euphemisms, question-begging and sheer cloudy vagueness. . . . Such phraseology is needed if one wants to name things without calling up [disquieting] mental pictures of them.'

In contrast to euphemism, which softens or neutralizes emotional content, *emotional language* consists of words or phrases infused with an emotional charge. This kind of language is often used by arguers who are strongly attached to the issues they address. In many cases a hasty emotional response to an issue is unintentionally substituted for a careful argument. When the Supreme Court of Canada ruled that homosexuals must be included under Alberta's human-rights legislation, a group calling itself Canada's Civilized Majority attacked the court's decision in a full-page advertisement in a national newspaper. The ad railed against 'the barbaric agenda of militant homosexuals' and accused the Supreme Court of imposing a 'bathhouse morality'.

Many readers who thought the advertisement crossed the line of tolerance and good taste wrote letters to the editor attacking the newspaper for agreeing to run it. But many of these letters used language that was just as incendiary as the original ad, saying that the ad was guilty of a 'horrifying viciousness and bigotry'; a 'hysterical and sensationalistic tone' that indicated 'outright fear-mongering and exploitation'; and a 'misinformed and hateful rhetoric'. In each of these instances, emotionally charged phrases were used instead of reasoned argument.

Perhaps the authors of these letters believed, as writers overcome with rage or dismay often do, that the viciousness, hysteria, or exploitation was obvious. You will see that this sort of appeal to obviousness cannot resolve the issue if you consider the fact that the sentiments of outrage expressed by those who placed the original advertisement were equally strong. In the present context, the important point is that emotional language is no substitute for argument. Indeed, it invites problems and confusion, for it tends to violate the principle that we should use language with precision. For instance, in the example we have just noted, there is no precise meaning to such expressions as 'a barbaric agenda', 'bathhouse morality', 'horrifying viciousness and bigotry', 'outright fearmongering and exploitation', and so on. It might be possible to explain some of these terms, but no serious effort was made to do so and they are, therefore, a weakness rather than a strength of the remarks expressed.

We will have much more to say about emotional language when we look at illegitimate biases and slanting in the next chapter. For the moment, it suffices to note that emotion-laden language is, like the use of unacceptable euphemisms, another obstacle to the clear communication of arguments.

EXERCISE 4A

The following is from an advertisement in *Mother Jones* magazine (June/July 1987). Provide a fully supplemented diagram of the argument it contains. Circle all the terms within it that might need to be discussed or defined. How might someone argue that this is a case of overly emotional language? How might someone argue that it is, in fact, exposing an illegitimate use of language?

In America Violence Starts Young!

Of all western countries only in the United States are helpless infant boys routinely strapped to a board, spread-eagled and without anesthesia their foreskins are clamped, slit, torn, crushed and sliced off while they scream and struggle from the diabolical torture, usually vomiting and excreting before losing consciousness. The bloody stumps that result from this mutilation are open to constant irritation from hot, urine-soaked diapers and faeces. Infection is an obvious problem in addition to the needless accidents where too much foreskin is removed or a tiny penis is totally destroyed. For lists of medical pamphlets and groups working to stop this savage custom, send a stamped, self-addressed envelope to CIRCUMCISION IS CHILD ABUSE.

2. VAGUENESS AND AMBIGUITY

The use of words or phrases that are vague or ambiguous is one common way in which arguers fail to be clear and precise. In assessing other arguers' arguments we need to be able to recognize vagueness and ambiguity. In creating our own arguments, we need to make sure that we construct arguments that are not undermined by either.

A word or phrase is *vague* if it has no clearly specifiable meaning. Words like 'the American dream', 'existential situation', 'conservative' and 'liberal', when used without qualification, are vague terms. When we use such terms, we allow our audience to read into them whatever meanings they prefer, and we run the risk of miscommunication.

Vagueness can affect whole sentences as well as single words and phrases. A professor who was asked to provide support for a student requesting more funding for research that had been prematurely terminated explained that 'the student had legitimate problems related to the maintenance and survival of his experimental organisms.' What this meant would not have been clear to the review committee if the student had not provided his own straightforward explanation: 'My fish died.' Similarly, advertisers may purposely use vagueness in their copy. A claim that a laundry detergent 'gets clothes up to 50 per cent cleaner' appears to promise a great deal until we realize how difficult it is to understand precisely what the company has promised: for what does '50 per cent cleaner' mean? Cleaner than what? And how is the 50 per cent to be measured?

It is important to try to resolve instances of vagueness when preparing an argument diagram, which should present premises and conclusions in clear language that remains true to the intended meaning of the arguer. Sometimes an 'initial vagueness' can be resolved by reading the context in which the argument arises, including any previous argumentation on the issue. If so, the argument has been expressed in a weak way, but our analysis of it will not be seriously hindered. In contrast, cases in which the claims of an arguer and the context cannot help us determine a clear meaning of a term or phrase involve serious weaknesses in the argument. In the most difficult cases, we will not be able to evaluate the argument. The problem is less serious when the vagueness is restricted to a sub-argument in the reasoning. Then we may be able to proceed with our evaluation.

Like vagueness, ambiguity may undermine our ability to fully evaluate an argument. Words or phrases are *ambiguous* when they can have more than one specifiable meaning in the context in which they arise. An 'amphibole' (also called a 'syntactic ambiguity') is an ambiguity that results from a confusing grammatical construction. A person who says, 'Last night I shot a burglar in my pyjamas,' has said something ambiguous because the structure of the sentence makes it unclear whether the man or the burglar was wearing the pyjamas. Other cases of ambiguity (called 'semantic ambiguity') result when words with multiple meanings are not used carefully. In puns, such ambiguity is intentional. The joke 'The trouble with being a writer in a dictatorship is that the government keeps revoking your poetic licence' elicits a smile because 'poetic licence' in this context can be interpreted to mean an official permit, or a writer's freedom to violate rules of syntax, rhyme, and the like.

Equivocation and Verbal Disputes

Although ambiguity is indispensable in entertainment and creative writing, it is usually a problem in argumentative discourse. When an arguer conflates two or more meanings of a term or phrase we charge them with the fallacy *equivocation* (a 'fallacy' is a common mistake in reasoning). Consider the following argument:

> If, as scientists tell us, energy neither comes into being nor goes out of being, I can't understand why there should be an energy crisis.

The problem with the reasoning in this comment is rooted in the meaning of the term 'energy'. In its first occurrence it refers to the total amount of energy in the universe. In its second, it refers to our diminishing supplies of gas and oil and electricity. The premise, that scientists tell us that energy neither comes into being nor goes out of being, does not really support the conclusion that there shouldn't be an energy crisis, because the two statements refer to different things. The ambiguity of the word 'energy' makes the confusion possible.

Consider a second example:

> Science has discovered many laws of nature. This surely constitutes proof that there is a God, for wherever there are laws, there must be a lawgiver. Consequently, God must exist as the Great Lawgiver of the universe.

We can diagram this argument as follows.

> P1 = Science has discovered many laws of nature.
> P2 = Wherever there are laws there must be a lawgiver.
> C = [Science shows us that] God, the Great Lawgiver of the universe, must exist.

Initially, this argument might seem convincing. But not if you think carefully about the meaning of the word 'laws', which is used in two different senses. The laws laid down by a legislative body or lawgiver are 'prescriptive' laws. In contrast, 'descriptive'

laws identify regularities or patterns in the world. Once we make this distinction, we can see that premise P1 holds only if the word 'laws' is interpreted to mean 'descriptive laws'. But P2 holds only if 'laws' is interpreted to mean 'prescriptive laws'. The conclusion seems to follow only because the argument equivocates on these two different meanings of the word 'law'.

When a group of arguers is involved in discussion or debate, an equivocation may take the form of a *verbal dispute*, which can be contrasted with a *real dispute*. In a real dispute, the parties to the dispute must utter opposing statements. In a verbal dispute, the disputants appear to disagree, but this is an illusion that reflects different meanings they assign to some key term or phrase. What appears to be a real difference is only verbal.

We have already noted an instance of a verbal dispute at the beginning of this book. You will remember that we began with an account of Monty Python's 'argument room' skit. At one point in the exchange, the paying client and the professional arguer enter into a long debate about whether they have had an argument. The professional arguer maintains they have; the client maintains they have not. It is unclear from the discussion that they really disagree because they are, as we have already noted, using the word 'argument' in two different ways. According to one meaning (used by the professional arguer) an argument is any disagreement. According to the other (used by the client) an argument is a connected series of propositions, which approximates the notion of argument we have developed in this book. In such a context, there is, despite the emotion that often accompanies verbal disputes, no genuine dispute. The arguers agree about what is going on in the argument room—it appears otherwise only because they have decided to use the word 'argument' in two contrasting ways.

Of course, verbal disputes often take place in more serious contexts. Imagine two people arguing about the morality of euthanasia (popularly known as 'mercy-killing'). Suppose they are debating the question of whether it should be legalized. One maintains that euthanasia is morally justifiable because it allows terminally ill patients the opportunity to die with dignity rather than prolonging their lives with life-support machines. The other argues that you cannot disguise the reality with euphemisms, and that euthanasia is morally wrong because it is, in the final analysis, nothing less than murder. In this context, the opposing conclusions—'Euthanasia is morally justifiable' and 'Euthanasia is not morally justifiable'—appear to signify a real dispute. This is possible, but not necessarily so. The first person may be talking about 'passive' euthanasia, which occurs when one withholds extraordinary systems of life-support (thereby allowing the individual to die), while the second may be talking about 'active' euthanasia, which occurs through interference in the process by means of, for example, the injection of a lethal drug. In such a context, there is no real dispute. Not because it is impossible to debate the morality of either type of euthanasia, but because these two disputants are focusing on different aspects of the issue.

Like disputes, agreements may be merely verbal. A real agreement must be built upon a mutual understanding of crucial terms and phrases. Two individuals who think they share a belief in 'capitalism' may in fact disagree because one of them believes in a completely unrestrained capitalism that leaves no room for government intervention in the economy, while the other believes in a capitalism that allows government regulation in order to establish minimum wages and protect the environment.

Even in a debate, disputants may mistakenly think that they agree upon the meaning of key terms that they use. Creationists and evolutionists seem to be speaking the same language when they debate whether there is any 'proof' of the theory of evolution. An evolutionist who puts forward proofs may be perplexed by a creationist who denies that what has been put forward constitutes a proof. In such a case, the assumption that the two disputants use the term 'proof' in the same way may be mistaken. Some Christian groups will use the word 'proof' to mean a 'proof with holy text'. According to this notion, any scientific notion, if it is to be considered credible, must be backed by Scripture. When a creationist of this ilk says that there is 'no proof' of evolution, they may mean that there are no Scriptures that support it. The evolutionist who claims that there is proof may, on the other hand, mean that evolution has been tested and is supported by the biological and geological evidence available. The point here is not to comment on the merits of the positions in the dispute, but to recognize how confusion over a central term like 'proof', which seems to have a common meaning but does not, can impede understanding in the debate itself.

Avoiding vagueness and ambiguity in our own disputes is not easily accomplished. Like other aspects of good reasoning, it demands an ability to view one's own work from a different perspective. Often, we are so close to our own arguments that we are unable to appreciate the confusions they may foster. We do not see the vagueness and the ambiguity in what we have said or written.

You can combat such problems by preparing drafts of arguments, setting them aside, and coming back to them. A few days later, you may have achieved a little distance and can probably read your work with a more critical eye. In doing so, ask yourself whether your intended meaning is clear and unambiguous. Clarify your meaning where necessary. Do not worry about implausible meanings that might be artificially attached to your remarks. Good reasoners will be judicious and charitable, and will not assign outlandish interpretations to what you say.

For your own part, you should not waste your time worrying about implausible meanings that might be attributed to someone else's arguments. In those cases where more than one plausible meaning might be applied, try to resolve the ambiguity by looking at the context and considering your knowledge of the author and the background. In cases in which you cannot resolve the ambiguity, you will want to charge the arguer with a problematic argument or claim, depending on the impact the ambiguity has on their argument and your ability to evaluate it. In some cases, it may be possible to continue by offering alternative evaluations of an argument that depend on the different ways existing ambiguities might be resolved. In such cases, you will still want to say that there is a major problem with the argument.

EXERCISE 4B

1. Are the following claims vague or ambiguous or both? If vague, explain why. If ambiguous, state whether it is a case of amphibole (syntactic ambiguity) or semantic ambiguity, and provide at least two alternative interpretations.
    a) [first sentence in a report in the *Toronto Star* (20 Aug. 1998), p. A2] Bank tellers are harder on low-income Canadians than bank presidents.
    b)* Jennifer is a wealthy woman.
    c) [professor to a student submitting an overdue essay] 'I'll lose no time reading your essay.'
    d) 'The best investigator is one who will stop at nothing,' Holmes asserted confidently.
    e)* Vitamin E is good for aging people.
    f) [from Cleveland Amory, *The Cat Who Came for Christmas*] I, for example, am a terrible dream-rememberer.
    g) Democracy is government by the people.
    h) You say nothing eloquently.
    i) [sign in a shop window] Watch repairs here.
    j) [a title from an advertisement in *University Affairs*]

    University of Victoria
    Assistant or Associate Professor
    Centre on Aging Faculty Position

    k)* [from Shakespeare's *Henry VI*] The duke yet lives that Henry shall depose.
    l) [A politician responds to the demand that he apologize for calling a colleague a liar.] I called him a liar. It is true, and I am sorry for it.
    m) A recent survey shows that teenagers are smoking and drinking less than they were four years ago.

2. The following are 'medical bloopers' that were circulated on a list that claimed that 'this varicose vein of anguished English has in no way been doctored.' In each case, diagnose the problem (vagueness, ambiguity, or something else) and, if possible, rewrite the medical comment to make it clear and precise.
    a)* The patient has been depressed ever since she began seeing me in 1983.
    b) Patient has chest pain if she lies on her left side for over a year.
    c) Discharge status: Alive but without permission.
    d) By the time he was admitted, his rapid heart had stopped, and he was feeling better.
    e)* The patient refused an autopsy.
    f) The patient's past medical history has been remarkably insignificant with only a 40-pound weight gain in the past three days.
    g) The patient left the hospital feeling much better except for her original complaints.

i)   The bugs that grew out of her urine were cultured in the ER and are not available.

3. Each of the following claims has two plausible senses that might easily give rise to equivocation or a verbal dispute. To practise avoiding such problems, distinguish the senses and express each interpretation in a way that makes it clearer than the original.
    a)* Convicted criminals must be made to pay for their crimes.
    b) The good life is a life of pleasure.
    c)* Life continues after death.
    d) The universe is a giant thought.
    e)* Enabling legislation should be introduced to make euthanasia possible.
    f) Genetic experimentation must be restricted.
    g) Rape trials are unfair to victims.
    h) When I made that decision, I could have decided differently.
    i) Machines can think.
    j) God is omnipotent.

4. The following arguments involve instances of ambiguity, vagueness, or equivocation. Diagram the arguments and discuss the seriousness of the problem with language. Are we able to use context to resolve the vagueness or ambiguity?
    a)* Every society is, of course, repressive to some extent. As Sigmund Freud pointed out, repression is the price we pay for civilization.
    b) [This argument refers to the debate over the use of human embryos in research to find cures for serious illnesses that affect many people. Concerns are raised when embryos used in this kind of research are destroyed.] As a moral being, I cannot understand the debate. We all agree that it is the potential of the embryo that is important. It should have the potential to help other people through its role in research. It can liberate millions of lives that might be helped by the results of the research.
    c)* [Rt Hon. David Blunkett, home secretary of Great Britain, in 'Integration with Diversity: Globalisation and the Renewal of Democracy and Civil Society', *Rethinking Britishness* (The Foreign Policy Centre, 16 Sept. 2002)] The military engagement in Afghanistan illustrates not a war of competing civilisations, but a defence of democratic states from terrorist attacks sponsored by deep oppression and brutalisation. But democracy is not only defended in military terms—it is defended in depth through the commitment of its citizens to its basic values. When the people of New York pulled together after 11 September, they were displaying not just mutual sympathy, support, and solidarity, but a patriotic commitment to their democracy. By that I mean patriotism in its most decent, and deeply expressed sense, of civil virtue—a commitment to one's community, its values and institutions.

    It follows that the strongest defence of democracy resides in the engagement of every citizen with the community, from activity in the neighbourhood, through to participation in formal politics.

d) [from an advertisement for Flair pens, *Reader's Digest* (May 1982), p. 51]

> OUR POINT . . . CAN MAKE YOUR POINT . . . PRECISELY
>   Want to be precise and to the point?
>   Try an Ultra Fine Flair pen.
>   You see, Ultra Fine has a precision point that delivers
>   an incredibly smooth line of vivid Flair ink. So everything
>   you write will be precise and to the point.
> Look for Ultra Fine and refillable Ultra Fine where Flair pens are
> sold.

e) [Rex Murphy, in 'Selling Something, Dr Suzuki?', *Globe and Mail* (28 Sept. 2002). Mr Murphy is responding to remarks made by David Suzuki at a press conference hosted by Canadian doctors advocating the ratification of the Kyoto Accord. Among the claims advanced was that 16,000 Canadian deaths are caused each year by global warming.] That 16,000 Canadians die every year is a very particular claim. It must be scientific. And if it is a piece of proven science that 16,000 of us die every year because of global warming, then only those people who don't care about the deaths of a horrifying number of fellow citizens would oppose ratifying Kyoto.

I don't buy the 'science' of the press conference for a minute. These are 'advocacy' numbers. They have as much science, in the strict sense, as that phrase 'more dentists recommend . . .' that used to pop up so unpersuasively in toothpaste commercials. The point of advocacy numbers is to pump a cause, not make a finding. Advocacy numbers are the rhetoric of an age that can't write perorations; they are argumentative quickies, meant to sidestep the preliminaries, finesse the intermediate niceties, and get the meeting over with.

3. FORMULATING DEFINITIONS

In an interview about his book *Animal Rights and Wrongs* (*Philosophy Now*, June/July 2000), the British philosopher Roger Scruton criticized people who use the term 'animal rights' in what he considers 'a very loose way':

> . . . when people refer to animal rights, either they are making a mistake about the nature of animals, or they are using the word 'rights' in a very loose way to refer to our duties towards animals. If animals really have rights in the way we do, then they have to be fully part of the moral realm, the realm of negotiation. Therefore, they must be accorded not only the benefits of morality, but also the burdens, which are huge. Cats would have to be treated as serial killers, for a start. And we don't want to inflict the penalties on them that that would imply.

Scruton's remarks can be interpreted as an instance of the argument scheme called an 'Appeal to Precedent', which we discuss in Chapter 13. In the present context, we are interested in the way that his argument depends upon a particular understanding of the key term 'rights'. He assumes a traditional account that ties rights to responsibilities. On the basis of this account, he argues that the notion of animal rights entails certain consequences, and those who use the term must be committed to those consequences.

Consider another example. In their groundbreaking report 'The First Cloned Human Embryo' (*Scientific American*, 24 Nov. 2001), scientists from Advanced Cell Technology described the processes they used to clone early-stage human embryos—processes that put therapeutic cloning (cloning to further medical treatments) within reach. The authors of the report were acutely aware of ethical concerns that their work could provoke. They countered these concerns in part in a sidebar to the report ('The Ethical Considerations') prepared by their ethics advisory board. They argued that the organisms produced in the process of human therapeutic cloning are not like ordinary human embryos and don't merit the moral respect and protection afforded to human embryos:

> . . . unlike an embryo, a cloned organism is not the result of fertilization of an egg by a sperm. It is a new type of biological entity never before seen in nature. Although it possesses some potential for developing into a full human being, this capacity is very limited. At the blastocyst stage, when the organism is typically disaggregated to create an embryonic stem cell line, it is a ball of cells no bigger than the period at the end of this sentence. . . . It has no organs, it cannot possibly think or feel, and it has none of the attributes thought of as human. Although board members understood that some people would liken this organism to an embryo, we preferred the term 'activated egg', and we concluded that its characteristics did not preclude its use in work that might save the lives of children and adults.

This passage uses the argument scheme 'disanalogy' in order to distinguish embryos and an entity the authors of the report call an 'activated egg'. This is another scheme that we will discuss later. In this chapter, the important point is that this is an argument about a definition. The authors are proposing a new term and arguing for the legitimacy of doing so.

These two examples illustrate the central role that definitions play in many arguments. This is one reason why a good reasoner must understand the different kinds of definition and the ways in which they can be used. Another reason is the need to use definitions to resolve problems of vagueness and ambiguity that make the meaning of a remark or argument unclear.

The purpose of a definition is to enable your reader or audience to understand quickly and precisely how you are using a particular term. When you are writing and when you are attempting to make explicit the meaning of a term used by another author, you should recognize that there are several kinds of definition. We will look at three kinds and then discuss how these can be drawn for our own purposes in constructing arguments.

Three Different Kinds of Definition

In the examples presented above, both Roger Scruton and the scientists from Advanced Cell Technology make implicit reference to the way in which we naturally classify things. By this we mean that one of the principal ways in which we use language is to create or refer to categories and assign things to them. Scruton understands that we all use the category 'rights', but he is insisting that the subcategories of 'animal rights' and 'human rights' do not necessarily coincide, so that we cannot transfer the meaning of one to the other. In a similar way, the scientists of Advanced Cell Technology are creating a new category, 'activated egg', that they define to distinguish it from the category 'embryo'.

Quite often when we use definitions, we are either attempting to identify the classes or categories to which things belong or to draw attention to some distinguishing features that differentiate things within the same category.

Extensional definitions clarify a term by identifying members of the class of things it names. The following are examples of extensional definitions:

'That', as one points to people engaged in a particular activity, 'is a game.'

'Humanistic studies' means 'studies in language, literature, philosophy, fine arts, religion, and music'.

Extensional definitions may be constructed by pointing to or naming instances of the things to which the term applies, as in our first example; or, as in the second case, by noting how the larger class of things comprises a series of representative subclasses.

Intensional definitions clarify the meaning of a term by identifying the essential qualities that make something a member of the class of things it names, that is, by reference to its meaning, or 'intension'. The following are examples of intensional definitions:

'Rubella' means 'measles'.

'Scapula' means 'shoulder blade'.

'Nom de plume' means 'pseudonym'.

These are all instances of the simplest form of intensional definition, which substitutes a familiar term for an unfamiliar one. By invoking the familiar term, the definition explains to an audience the essential characteristics of the thing in question.

In formal situations, where we take pains to ensure that something is defined as precisely as possible, we may employ an intensional definition by *genus and differentia*. It designates the class to which a thing belongs (its *genus*) and the characteristics that distinguish it from other members of the class (its *differentia*). The following are definitions by genus and differentia.

A 'chair' is 'a piece of furniture (genus) designed for the purpose of seating one person and providing a support for the back (differentia).'

Happiness is a state of mind (genus) characterized by the satisfaction that one has achieved what one deems to be worthwhile, and by the absence of mental anguish (differentia).'

In each of these examples, the definition identifies the larger class to which something belongs, and then specifies the way in which it is distinguished from other members of this class. Though they can be difficult to construct, the details that definitions by genus and differentia require can make them the best way to clarify a contentious term or phrase.

A third important class of definition is the *stipulative definition*. With the exception of the term 'activated egg', the terms in our examples above have been associated with a conventional definition. A conventional definition reports how a term is customarily used within the community of people who share a language. In most circumstances, conventional understandings suffice. But there will be times when conventional meanings do not fit your precise purpose, and you will need to indicate that you are using a term or phrase in a very specific way. In a sociology paper, you may want to restrict the meaning of 'the unemployed' to 'those people who are actively seeking employment' and define 'actively seeking employment' as 'making at least two inquiries a week'. In such circumstances, we stipulate the meaning of a term or phrase.

Stipulative definitions can help you avoid vagueness, ambiguity, and verbal disputes. Even if your audience—an instructor, perhaps—does not agree with your definition, he or she will be able to better understand what you mean because you have used it to explicitly say how you intend a key term or phrase to be understood. 'Democracy' normally means 'government by the people either directly or through elected representatives'. But you may want to use the term in a more restricted sense. You may use an extensional definition: 'By the term "democracy" I mean the kind of rule by the people found in Canada and the US, not in Korea and Singapore.' Or you could use an intensional definition: 'By the term "democracy" I mean rule by the people through the representatives chosen by popular votes in free multi-party elections.' The most important thing is that you inform your audience that the definition you are providing is a stipulative one, so that they understand how you are using it.

Many arguments and remarks are difficult to understand because authors use familiar words as key terms in specific ways without stipulating their meaning—often because they take their meaning to be self-evident. Consider the claim 'The law of the church forbids the marriage of priests.' Suppose that the context does not make it clear whether the marriage of priests is forbidden by the church's understanding of the will of God or by the church's administration for strictly practical purposes. The former circumstance would make the non-marriage of priests a 'divine law', the latter an 'ecclesiastical law'. The claim, then, is subject to two interpretations: (1) divine law forbids the marriage of priests, and (2) ecclesiastical law forbids the marriage of priests. Because the alternative meanings pivot on the single term 'law', this is the kind of situation that could easily give rise to an equivocation or a verbal dispute.

In using definitions, you need to remember that the different kinds of definition have different strengths that make them appropriate in different kinds of contexts. Extensional definitions link our words and our arguments to the world of experience. If terms did not have extensions, the definitions in our dictionaries would be circular, for they would, in every case, define terms by means of other terms that had no foothold in reality. In view of such considerations, we can use an extensional definition to anchor the meaning of an important word in the world beyond our language. On the other hand, an extensional definition is rarely able to indicate every application of the term defined. For practical reasons, it can, in most cases, do no more than indicate a sample of the things included in a term's extension. A large and representative list would be unwieldy. And even if we provided such a list, this definition would not identify the common features that establish that the items it lists are included in the extension.

Because it focuses on the essential features shared by those things in a term's extension, an intensional definition that defines a term in a single, relatively simple, well-constructed sentence is, in many cases, the clearest and most convenient way to proceed. Even when you are using a stipulative definition, it will help to try and emulate the merits of good intensional definitions. If you are unsure how you should construct such a definition, you might try a definition by genus and differentia. Begin by specifying the kind of thing you are defining and proceed to an account of the differences between it and other things of the same sort.

In constructing your own arguments, be prepared to define key terms, especially unfamiliar and technical terms as well as terms that are vague or ambiguous, or ones that are used in a way that deviates from conventional usage. This task may sound more formidable than it is. Normally the number of terms that require definition is not large. The vast majority of the words you use will be common ones that have a meaning that your audience will appreciate. Even in cases where you use words with several meanings, the context will usually make the intended meaning clear.

DEFINITIONS

➤ *Extensional definitions* define a term by referring to its *extension*, the group of things to which it refers.
➤ *Intensional definitions* define a term by referring to its *intension*, the set of characteristics that determines what it refers to.
➤ *Stipulative definitions* define how a term or phrase is to be understood in a specific context.

4. Rules for Good Definitions

To help you construct definitions, we will provide you with four rules that good definitions must follow.

Rule 1: The Rule of Equivalence

➡ *The defining phrase should include neither more nor less than the term being defined.*

If 'A' stands for the term defined and 'B' for the defining phrase, then A and B must be equivalent. Those things designated by A must be the same as those things designated by B. The definition of 'violin' as 'a stringed musical instrument' is too broad because there are many stringed musical instruments that are not violins. The definition of 'portrait' as 'a large oil painting of a person's head and shoulders' is too narrow because portraits are not necessarily large and are not always done in oils. The rule of equivalence is respected in the extensional definition *'That* [pointing to a cow] is a cow' because it is understood that the extension includes all animals of this sort.

Rule 2: The Rule of Essential Characteristics

➡ *In an intensional definition, the defining phrase must specify the essential features of the thing defined, i.e. the traits that are indispensable to its being what it is, rather than accidental features.*

The definition of 'the moon' as 'the large object in the sky that is sometimes said to be made of green cheese' satisfies the rule of equivalence (for there is only one astronomical object with this reputation), but it does not pick out the moon in a useful way because it has fastened on an aspect of it that is not particularly informative. In most contexts, we will do better to define the moon as 'the earth's natural satellite, which shines at night by the sun's reflected light'.

In specifying essential characteristics, keep in mind that different characteristics may be counted as essential in different contexts. In introducing a book on the history of comic strips, one might begin by defining human beings as 'the only animals that read comic strips'. In such a context, this may be what matters, though a similar definition of human beings would probably be unhelpful in a lecture on moral responsibility.

Rule 3: The Rule of Clarity

➡ *The defining phrase must clarify the meaning of the term defined by using words that make it readily understood by the intended audience.*

Since we use definitions precisely when we want to clarify meaning, we undermine our definitions when they do not successfully explain our meaning to our intended audience. Plato's definition of 'time' as 'the moving image of eternity' presupposes familiarity with his theory of reality. In another context and, some would argue, even against the background of his theory, this definition of 'time' violates the principle of clarity. An attempt to define 'architecture' in terms of 'frozen music' might suit an informal talk on the aesthetics of architecture, but only if it is backed by an explanation that makes it clear how this comparison is to be understood.

The rule of clarity is often violated by arguments that make use of *circular definitions*. A circular definition defines a word in terms of the word itself or, in some cases, by using terms or phrases so similar that the meaning of the original term is not made any clearer. If someone says, 'By "human rights" I mean the rights of human beings,' they can be charged with a circular definition. We need, instead, a definition like 'Human rights are rights (such as freedom from unlawful imprisonment, torture, and execution) that are believed to belong to all human beings.' In cases like this, the repetition of some part of the term defined is permissible, provided it will not confuse the audience. When we define a term like 'isosceles triangle' or 'watchdog', we will probably want to repeat the modified term ('triangle', 'dog') within our definition. If the use of the term 'rights' in our definition of human rights is likely to confuse our audience, then it must itself be defined, perhaps, as 'something to which one has a just claim'.

In subtle cases, circular definitions use defining phrases that include obvious synonyms and correlative phrases without properly explaining the idea that the term or its synonyms refer to. The definition 'a homosexual is a gay person' uses a synonym and does not explain what a homosexual, or a gay person, is. The definition 'a cause is something that produces an effect' illustrates the use of correlative terms. There may be rare contexts in which these definitions are useful (as when someone who does not speak English well understands the synonym or the correlative term, but not the term defined). However, in most circumstances, these definitions will count as circular definitions.

Like synonyms, antonyms may also violate the rule of clarity. An 'evil person' can be defined as 'a person who is not good', and 'night' as 'not day', but such definitions rarely explain these notions to an unsure audience.

Rule 4: The Rule of Neutrality

➥ *The defining phrase must avoid terms heavily charged with emotion.*

Earlier in this chapter we noted the problems that arise when arguers use euphemisms and emotional language. These problems are compounded when arguers offer or assume persuasive definitions that betray ulterior motives. One violates the rule of neutrality if one defines 'socialism' as 'that form of government that steals wealth from energetic people and divides it among the lazy poor', or 'capitalism' as 'a system built on greed that ensures that the poor suffer and the rich get richer'. In the next chapter, we discuss the problems of 'slanting' that can be caused by definitions of this sort.

Constructing Good Definitions

The rules for good definition are easier to understand than to apply. In dealing with real definitions, you will find that many of them violate more than one of the rules, or that the same problem might be described in terms of different rules. You will also find it can be difficult to identify the unique, essential, and defining differentia that distinguish one group of things from the other members of a larger class.

In some cases, defining properties are not at all obvious. What are the unique defining characteristics of a 'human being'? Rationality? A capacity to create symbols and communicate by means of them? A sense of moral responsibility? The ability to create and use sophisticated tools? If you see the last three of these characteristics as expressions of human rationality, where do you propose to draw the line between 'higher animals', such as chimpanzees, and human beings with a very low IQ?

Especially in moral contexts, where our judgments of individuals may depend on a definition, controversies surrounding the meaning of a term are common. When President Clinton claimed he did not have sex with Monica Lewinsky and later claimed that he did not think that the word 'sex' included oral sex, *Time* magazine ran a poll to see how the public defined sex. While 87 per cent of those answering the questions agreed that oral sex was included under the term 'sex', there were significant differences of opinion in other regards. While 53 per cent of those in the survey thought that romantic kissing counted as sexual relations, 40 per cent did not. And though 59 per cent believed that the touching of breasts or buttocks (but not the genital area) through clothing counted as sex, 35 per cent did not.

The problems that arise when one tries to define a word like 'human being' or 'sex' can be seen as expressions of the difficulties that arise when we try to decide the extension of important terms. Does the human embryo (or 'activated egg') belong within or outside the class of 'human beings'? If outside, then at what point does it become a human being? If within, is it entitled to 'rights and freedoms', including the right to life, liberty, and security of the person? The bearing of these considerations on the debate surrounding human cloning is apparent.

In constructing your own definitions, and in judging those of others, remember that good definitions must recognize the audiences to which they are directed and be suitable to their intended purpose. The definition of 'water' as 'a liquid compound of 11.188 per cent hydrogen and 88.812 per cent oxygen by weight, which freezes at 0 and boils at 100 degrees Celsius' may be useful in an introductory science lecture, but it would be quite unserviceable in a talk or magazine article about sailing or about what measures to take when our bodies retain too much water.

A good arguer constructs an argument in a way that makes it clear and convincing to the intended audience. In formulating definitions, a good arguer constructs them with the same concerns in mind.

EXERCISE 4C

1. What kind of definition is each of the following?
   a) By 'western Canadian provinces' I mean Saskatchewan, Alberta, and British Columbia.
   b)* A kitten is an immature cat.
   c) A textbook is the sort of thing you are now reading.
   d) A human being is a featherless biped who uses language and is capable of higher emotions such as indignation and resentment.

e) 'Macabre' means 'gruesome'.

f) 'Terrorism' is a form of violence to achieve political goals.

g)* By 'social sciences' is meant economics, history, anthropology, sociology, and psychology.

h) By 'primary caregiver' I mean that parent who bears greater responsibility for the raising of a child.

i) An argument consists of at least two statements, one of which is a conclusion and the other a premise.

j) An 'activated egg' is a biological entity that is not the result of fertilization of an egg by a sperm.

2. What rule(s) of definition, if any, does each of the following definitions violate? In each case explain your answer in one sentence.

a)* Child abuse is the physical and/or psychological violence inflicted on a child as an expression of parental anger and frustration.

b) [the definition of 'obscenity' in the *Canadian Criminal Code*] For the purposes of this Act, any publication a dominant characteristic of which is the undue exploitation of sex. . . .

c) Noon means 12 o'clock.

d) Nonsense is what one is speaking or writing when what one speaks or writes is devoid of all sense.

e)* Prayer is a form of religious mumbo-jumbo.

f) Sonar is a system using transmitted and reflected acoustic waves.

g) 'Terrorism' is the tactic or policy of engaging in terrorist acts.

h)* Canada is a country that lies north of the 49th parallel.

i) Taxation is a form of theft in which the government acts as a criminal victimizing citizens by taking a big bite of their income without their willing co-operation.

j) A circle is a geometric plane figure.

k) A laser printer is the pen of the contemporary scribe.

l)* Distance is the space between two points measured by the yard.

m)*'Terrorism' is a method of war that consists in intentionally attacking those who ought not to be attacked.

3. The following passages involve terms or phrases that have controversial meanings. Identify the terms or phrases in question and their importance to the arguments concerned. What kinds of definitions are given? Are the definitions given adequate? Do they respect the rules of good definitions?

a) [Michael Ignatieff, in 'The Value of Toleration', *The Rushdie File*, ed. L. Appignanesi & S. Maitland (Fourth Estate, 1989), p. 251] In the heated competition to appear full of conviction, some liberals have taken to saying that they hold freedom sacred. This, I think, is a misuse of 'sacred'. If the word means anything it means something that is inviolate to criticism or rational scrutiny. Freedom is not a holy belief, nor even a supreme value. It is a contestable concept.

b) [from a Wilfrid Laurier University pamphlet on harassment] Harrassment: One of a series of vexatious comments or conduct related to one or more of the prohibited grounds (Human Rights Code Sections 5.1, 5.2, 7.2, 7.3.a and 7.3b) that is known or might reasonably be known to be unwelcome/unwanted, offensive, intimidating, hostile or inappropriate. Examples include but are not limited to gestures, remarks, jokes, taunting, innuendo, display of offensive materials, offensive graffiti, threats, verbal or physical assault, imposition of academic penalties, hazing, stalking, shunning or exclusion related to the prohibited grounds.

c)* The distinguishing characteristic of a 'person' is rationality: being able to reflect on one's own existence, remember one's past, and project oneself into the future. It follows from this that a person is a creature of culture, capable of sophisticated, higher-order brain activity. A person is able to enjoy art, literature, and culture. No matter what respectful status we accord to non-human primates, they will never be persons.

d) [from the law of blasphemy in England, as formulated in article 214 of *Stephen's Digest of the Criminal Law* 9th edn (1950)] Every publication is said to be blasphemous that contains any contemptuous, reviling, scurrilous or ludicrous matter relating to God, Jesus Christ or the Bible, or the formularies of the Church of England as by law established. It is not blasphemous to speak or publish opinions hostile to the Christian religion, or to deny the existence of God, if the publication in couched in decent and temperate language. The test to be applied is as to the manner in which the doctrines are advocated and not to the substance of the doctrines themselves.

e)* [from a statement by Andrea Dworkin and Catharine McKinnon] Pornography does not include erotica (defined as sexually explicit materials premised on equality) and it does not include *bona fide* sex education materials, or medical or forensic literature. In short, we define pornography as depicting a combination of the sexual objectification and subordination of women, often including violation and violence.

f) [Barbara Dority, in 'Feminist Moralism, "Pornography", and Censorship', *The Humanist* (Nov./Dec. 1989)] 'Pornography' is the depiction of erotic behavior (as in pictures or writing) intended to cause sexual excitement.

g) [from the Vegetarian Society UK Information sheet <http://www.vegsoc.org/info/definitions.html>] A vegetarian is someone living on a diet of grains, pulses, nuts, seeds, vegetables and fruits with or without the use of dairy products and eggs (preferably free-range). A vegetarian does not eat any meat, poultry, game, fish, shellfish or crustacea, or slaughter by-products such as gelatine or animal fats.

4. You must define a key term for the audience you are addressing. Formulate a definition that would be appropriate for each of the following circumstances.

a) You are telling your grandparents what is meant by computer 'spam'.
b) You are explaining to your parents, who are not college or university graduates, the nature of the discipline (anthropology, sociology, etc.) in which you are majoring.
c)* You are a candidate in a forthcoming election addressing a public meeting on the merits of 'liberalism'.
d) You are a financial adviser speaking to a group of middle- and upper-class homemakers about 'preferred shares'.
e) You are explaining AIDS to a high school class.
f)* You are the keynote speaker at a convention of newspaper journalists talking about 'objectivity' in reporting.
g) You are a participant at a political rally speaking to whoever will listen about 'peace activism'.
h) You are writing a letter to the editor of your local newspaper arguing for more 'international aid'.
i) You are addressing an assembly of college and university students on sexual 'ethics'.
j) You are urging the local Board of Education to adopt a sabbatical policy as a measure to prevent teachers' 'burnout'.

5. Expressing Your Intended Meaning

For a variety of reasons you will often find yourself at a loss to grasp clearly the claim an arguer is making. The problem may be psycho-social. As individuals, we have different backgrounds, environmental influences, peer groups, political commitments, problems, loves, and loyalties, all of which contribute to a network of beliefs that we bring to bear on arguments we encounter. This network colours our interpretation of all arguments. (We discuss arguments and belief systems in Chapter 11.)

Alternatively, the problem may arise in the context of the issues discussed in this chapter. A claim will be unclear whenever the person to whom it is directed does not understand a term or phrase. Often this is because the term is vague or ambiguous. It is the author's responsibility to ensure that any key terms he or she uses are used consistently throughout the text. An author who shifts between two different meanings of a term is guilty of equivocation. If an author uses a crucial but familiar term without stipulating the specialized sense in which it is being used, you must identify alternative senses that are possible within that context. If an arguer uses an unfamiliar term without providing a definition, you will have to identify the meaning or meanings justified by the arguer's use of it, perhaps with the help of a dictionary. In your own arguments, you will want to spare your audience such frustrations by carefully considering your choice of words, by using the different kinds of definitions as appropriate, and by employing your terms consistently.

Even after you have addressed the problems of meaning that stem from an author's use of specific words and phrases, you may find that a claim is open to alternative senses or interpretations. Once you have established plausible meanings of an author's claims, you will need to determine which interpretation the author intended. This is something you can do by a process of elimination that is guided by a sense of fidelity to the text, common sense, and the principle of charity. Use whatever hints you can locate in the rest of the author's writing. If one of the plausible senses stands in blatant contradiction to what is clearly the main claim of the text, then common sense (and the principles of communication we introduced in the previous chapter) dictates that you reject it. If other interpretations appear irrelevant or trivial or uninteresting or obviously false, you should eliminate them unless you have good reason for not doing so. Eventually you should be left with a plausible interpretation of the author's intended meaning or, perhaps, two different interpretations that could each qualify as the intended meaning.

This entire procedure should not be necessary, and would not be necessary if the author had communicated clearly and precisely. The lesson for you, as you go about constructing extended units of informative and argumentative discourse, should be clear. Be willing to endure some labour pains in the process of giving birth to your claims and arguments. After you formulate a claim, think about it; ask yourself whether it says precisely what you mean or if it can be interpreted in different ways. Be prepared to amend it—several times, if necessary. Don't be satisfied until you have a way of expressing your views that communicates exactly what you mean.

MAJOR EXERCISE 4M

1. Diagram the reasoning in each of the following arguments and then, in a few paragraphs, assess the strengths and weaknesses of the language employed. Look in particular for problematic instances of vagueness, ambiguity, and emotional language. Determine also whether any key terms are left undefined, and in the case of definitions provided and argued for, assess them according to the ideas of this chapter.

    a)* You can consult all the experts you like, write reports, make studies, etc., but the fact that pornography corrupts lies within the common sense of everybody. If people are affected by their environments, by the circumstances of their lives, then they certainly are affected by pornography. The mere nature of pornography makes it impossible that it should ever effect good. Therefore, it must necessarily effect evil. Even a fool has the sense to see that someone who wallows in filth is going to get dirty. This is intuitive knowledge. People who spend millions of dollars to try and prove otherwise are malicious or misguided, or both.

    b)* [Victor P. Maiorana, in *Critical Thinking Across the Curriculum: Building the Analytical Classroom* (1992)] The purpose of critical thinking is, therefore, to achieve understanding, evaluate view points, and solve problems. Since all three areas involve the asking of questions, we can say that critical thinking is the questioning or inquiry we engage in when we seek to understand, evaluate, or resolve.

c)   [Daniel J. Kurland, in *I Know What It Says . . . What does it Mean?* (1995)] Broadly speaking, critical thinking is concerned with reason, intellectual honesty, and open-mindedness, as opposed to emotionalism, intellectual laziness, and closed-mindedness. Thus, critical thinking involves: following evidence where it leads; considering all possibilities; relying on reason rather than emotion; being precise; considering a variety of possible viewpoints and explanations; weighing the effects of motives and biases; being concerned more with finding the truth than with being right; not rejecting unpopular views out of hand; being aware of one's own prejudices and biases, and not allowing them to sway one's judgment.

d)   [John Ralston Saul, in *The Devil's Dictionary*, p. 41] In his *Philosophical Dictionary* Voltaire points out that bees seem superior to humans because one of their secretions is useful. Nothing a human secretes is of use; quite the contrary. Whatever we produce makes us disagreeable to be around.

e)   [from *Consumers Reports* (July 1980)] Langendorf Natural Lemon Flavored Creme Pie contains no cream. It does contain sodium propionate, certified food colors, sodium benzoate, and vegetable gum.

That's natural? Yes indeed, says L.A. Cushman, Jr, chairman of American Bakeries Co., the Chicago firm that owns Langendorf. The 'natural', he explains, modifies 'lemon flavored', and the pie contains oil from lemon rinds. 'The lemon flavour', Cushman states, 'comes from natural lemon flavor as opposed to artificial lemon flavor,' assuming there is such a thing as artificial lemon flavor.

f)   [Mark Elliott, in 'It Ain't a Sport', in a university student newspaper, *The Cord* (22 Sept. 1994)] Last week it became official—the World Series has been cancelled for the first time in 90 years. I, for one, will not be shedding any tears for the loss of this game. I say game, not sport, for a reason. A sport is a structured activity that involves some perspiration, a game involves some skill that does not necessarily have to be physical. The only time you see a baseball player sweat is on a hot day. There is very little physical activity required. . . .

Don't get me wrong. Baseball is not an easy game, it is just bereft of anything physical. Baseball is similar to pool and golf as incredible skill is needed but without any exertion. Although, golfers do walk around for 18 holes.

The terminology in the game helps my argument. The pitcher misses 4 times and you get a walk to first. . . . There are 'pinch runners' so that the team can substitute a couple of real athletes in the game every now and then. . . .

g)* [from Stuart Umpleby, <http:www.asc-cyberneticcs.org/foundations/defs.htm> (1982; rev. 2000)] Cybernetics takes as its domain the design or discovery and application of principles of regulation and communication. Cybernetics treats not things but ways of behaving. It does not ask 'what is this thing?' but 'what does it do?' and 'what can it do?' Because numerous systems in the living, social and technological world may be understood in this way, cybernetics cuts across many traditional disciplinary boundaries. The concepts that cyberneticians develop thus form a metadisciplinary language through which we may better understand and modify our world.

h) [adapted from a letter to the *New York Times* (Mar. 1982)] As a true American, I wish to speak for what is near and dear to the hearts of Americans. I wish to speak against what is as foreign to these shores as communism, socialism, totalitarianism, and other foreign 'isms', except of course Americanism. I speak of the administration's Medicare bill, better known as 'socialized medicine'.

If Medicare is sound, then a government-sponsored, -financed, and -controlled program is sound for every aspect of our life. But this principle must be rejected. As Americans, freedom must be our watchword. And since freedom means no control, no regulation, no restraint, government programs like Medicare are quite contrary to the American concept of freedom.

Unlike pseudo-Americans who want to socialize this country, I believe that socialized medicine would be an insult to true Americans. For true Americans don't want handouts. They want to stand on their own feet. They're willing to meet their obligations. They're willing to work and pay for their medical bills. As convincing proof of this, the AMA has advertised that it will give free medical care to anyone who wants it, and practically no one responds to these ads.

i) [from a letter to the *Globe and Mail* (25 Mar. 1996)] The analysis of many of those who oppose the principle of prohibiting discrimination on the basis of sexual orientation is fundamentally flawed . . . They say that because sexual orientation is 'a personal choice' (which of course is highly debatable, given recent studies indicating that sexual orientation is likely genetically determined), it does not deserve human-rights protection. Well, religion is also 'a personal choice', but we rightly prohibit discrimination on the basis of a person's creed.

The principle is this: If there is evidence that people are being discriminated against because they possess a particular personal characteristic, that characteristic is a suitable candidate for human-rights protection. 'Sexual orientation' clearly meets the test. Put simply: There is no evidence that being gay (or being Protestant) affects job performance. Is it fair then to allow employers to deny someone a job because that person is gay (or Protestant)? Unless we put sexual orientation in the federal Human Rights Code (as we have done with religious creed), we are in effect saying 'yes'.

j)   The central question is whether the state has a right to prevent an adult citizen from consuming materials that, though not dangerous, are considered by other citizens to be disgusting. Is it proper to make criminals out of people who wish to produce, show, or transmit these socially benign materials? Does the state have the right to impose the values of moralistic meddlers upon the rest of us? The state has no such right in a free and democratic society.

k)   [Ian Wilmut, Keith Campbell, and Colin Tudge, in *The Second Creation: Dolly and the Age of Biological Control* (Farrarr, Straus and Giroux, 2000), p. 9] Beyond technology, and in harness with it, is science. People conflate the two: Most of what is reported on television by 'science' correspondents is in fact technology. Technology is about changing things, providing machines and medicine, altering our surroundings to make our lives more comfortable and to create wealth. Science is about understanding, how the universe works and all the creatures in it. The two pursuits are different, and not necessarily linked. Technology is as old as human kind: Stone tools are technology. People may produce fine instruments and weapons, cathedrals, windmills, and aqueducts, without having any formal knowledge of the underlying science — metallurgy, mechanics, aerodynamics, and hydrodynamics. In contrast, science at its purest is nothing more nor less than 'natural philosophy', as it was originally known, and needs produce no technologies at all.

l)* [from an example discussed by George Orwell in his essay 'Politics and the English Language' (1946)] If a new spirit is to be infused into this old country, there is one thorny and contentious reform that must be tackled, and that is the humanization and galvanization of the B.B.C. Timidity here will bespeak canker and atrophy of the soul. The heart of Britain may be sound and of strong beat, for instance, but the British lion's roar at present is like that of Bottom in Shakespeare's *A Midsummer Night's Dream* — as gentle as any sucking dove. A virile new Britain cannot continue indefinitely to be traduced in the eyes, or rather ears, of the world by the effete languors of Langham Place, brazenly masquerading as 'standard English'. When the Voice of Britain is heard at nine o'clock, better far and infinitely less ludicrous to hear aitches honestly dropped than the present priggish, inflated, inhibited, school-ma'amish arch braying of blameless bashful mewing maidens!

m)   [Patrick Ryan, in *AFF [American Family Foundation] News*, vol. 2, no. 1 (1997)] When an ex-cultist returns to the 'high' after leaving a cult, it is called 'floating'. It is also called 'floating' when one snaps back into the shame-based motivations experienced while in the cult and believes anew that the cult was right. Floating is handled by discovering what triggers the episodes and then dealing with the triggers . . . The first step in recovery from floating is to identify these triggers and the loaded language that gives meaning to the visual trigger. For example, the visual trigger may be a book that has been forbidden by the cult. Seeing the book causes thoughts like, 'This is the work of the devil.' Loaded language is any thought-stopping cliché that is used in manipulative groups to prevent critical thinking. For example, simple tiredness is reinterpreted as 'running in the flesh', and is used to discourage people from claiming fatigue or stress. Not wanting to go to every scheduled meeting is labelled 'rebellion' and as possessing a[n] . . . 'independent spirit'. . . . Such loaded language is not easily forgotten even after exiting a cult. It sidetracks critical analysis, disrupts communication, and may produce confusion, anxiety, terror, and guilt.

BIAS:

READING

BETWEEN THE LINES

Chapters 1–4 introduced arguments. They explained how one identifies arguments, premises, and conclusions. In this chapter we begin our discussion of strong and weak reasoning by considering the contexts in which good, and especially bad, reasoning is likely to occur. We highlight

- bias and perspective;
- vested interest;
- conflict of interest; and
- slanting by omission and distortion.

In our previous chapters, we discussed arguments and their components. In this chapter, we begin our discussion of good and bad reasoning by examining the kinds of contexts in which good, and especially bad, reasoning is likely to occur. We continue our discussion of the implicit aspects of argument in our account of the implicit judgments that often characterize argument contexts. In dealing with arguments that reflect illegitimate biases, we will show you how you can 'read between the lines' to detect and expose implicit judgments that undermine the balance that must accompany good reasoning.

1. BIAS AND PERSPECTIVE

The *Oxford English Dictionary* defines 'bias' as an 'inclination or prejudice for or against'. When we say that an arguer or argument is biased, we usually mean that they unfairly favour a particular point of view. But all arguers favour the positions they believe in and argue for. Everyone has a perspective. It is a mistake to think that there is something wrong with this.

All of us rely on our commitments and beliefs when we formulate our opinions. Problems arise only when our inclinations illegitimately influence the way we argue in support of the claims we defend or interfere with our ability to listen to the reasons that others advance for their own points of view. In such cases, we may be said to have *illegitimate biases*. Good reasoners work hard to maintain a perspective that is not characterized by biases of this sort.

We need to be wary of illegitimate biases, especially our own, for all of us have a natural tendency to favour some positions over others. Many studies conducted by social psychologists have demonstrated the extent to which reasoning is influenced by our beliefs and by those things we would *like* to believe. In a classic study, Hastorf and Cantril showed that the supporters of competing football teams who viewed the same footage of a game reached opposite conclusions about the conduct of the players ('They Saw A Game: A Case Study', in Young, Becker, Pike, eds, *Rhetoric: Discovery & Change*, 1970). In a broad review of the psychological literature on 'motivated reasoning', Ziva Kunda cites many studies that provide 'considerable evidence' that people try to arrive at those conclusions 'they want to arrive at' (*Psychological Bulletin*, vol. 108, no. 3, 1990).

One of the studies Kunda mentions concludes that smokers are less likely than non-smokers to be persuaded by the scientific evidence against smoking. In another study, a group of women were asked to read an article that argued that caffeine was bad for women. Those women from the group who normally drank caffeinated beverages were much more skeptical of the article than those women who did not. In a third study, subjects who were given negative results after an intelligence test showed a marked tendency to agree with arguments that maintained that such tests were not reliable. In these and many other studies, a person's judgment of an issue seems to be determined not by a careful look at the quality of the arguments they encounter but by their desire to preserve their beliefs or to believe a particular conclusion that attracts them.

Though such forces make illegitimate biases a common feature of everyday argument, we must be careful when we charge someone with biases of this sort, for such charges are often made unfairly. Consider the following letter to the *National Post* (31 Oct. 1998), written in response to an editorial cartoon that suggested that a doctor who performed abortions was murdered by a pro-life advocate:

> As a long-time pro-lifer, I was saddened by your cartoon. I have no idea about the identity of the cruel person who killed Dr Slepian, but I do know that he or she is not pro-life. For pro-lifers, there is no difference between an unborn child and a baby, child, teen, adult or older person.

This arguer probably overstates her conclusion when she says that she 'knows' that the murderer was not pro-life, but her argument is still clear. It can be diagrammed as follows:

P1 = For pro-lifers, there is no difference between an unborn child and a baby, child, teen, adult, or older person.

HC1 = For pro-lifers, it is wrong to kill not only unborn children but also children, teens, adults, and older people.

MC = The cruel person who killed Dr Slepian is not pro-life.

This is an argument by a pro-life advocate who is defending pro-life advocates against the suggestion that one of them was responsible for the murder of Dr Slepian. Given that the arguer is so clearly committed to the pro-life perspective she defends, you might wonder whether we should dismiss the argument as biased.

We think the question may be clearer if we rephrase it to ask whether this is a case in which an arguer's strong commitment to the position they defend creates an illegitimate bias that interferes with their judgment or their reasoning. We can find no reason to think so. The arguer is open about her commitments, and there is no obvious way in which they distort her views, her arguments, or her depiction of opposing points of view. She presents her argument in a way that leaves us free to evaluate her argument in an open-minded way.

Illegitimate biases arise when arguers present arguments that do not accurately represent their own views or the views of their opponents. In such cases, arguers present issues in a way that favours a particular perspective. Usually this perspective is rooted in their own convictions, but there are cases in which arguments are biased because they reflect perspectives that originate not in the arguer but in arguments, articles, reports, and other material they rely on. Whatever their origin, and whether or not the arguer is aware of them, illegitimate biases lead to arguments that minimize, ignore, or dismiss evidence that invites a conclusion other than the one proposed.

In the final analysis, the question of whether a particular argument reflects illegitimate biases must be answered by carefully assessing the extent to which the arguer has fairly and accurately presented their own and their opponents' points of view. In diagramming arguments where there is some risk of illicit bias, it is particularly useful to supplement the diagram with information on the arguer's opponents. Because someone with an illegitimate bias will usually misrepresent the views of their opponents, the attempt to identify these views can help us determine whether we are dealing with a case of problematic bias.

As we write this chapter, one of the most successful business people in the world, Martha Stewart, has been implicated in an insider trading scandal in which she is alleged to have improperly traded shares in the stock market. Following a criminal probe of her actions, Stewart was indicted by federal prosecutors. She currently faces criminal charges that include securities fraud, obstruction of justice, making false statements, and perjury. In spite of this, her supporters have been vocal. The SAVE MARTHA website (at <http://www.savemartha.com/>) is complete with the latest news, SAVE MARTHA T-shirts, form letters designed to be sent to the media, and extensive commentary that contains many arguments for the conclusion that she has been unfairly accused and unfairly treated by the media.

This is the kind of case in which we might reasonably wonder if arguments are biased. This is not because we presuppose any conclusion about what Stewart did or didn't do. Rather, our concern is that those who are proud to call themselves 'fans' of Martha Stewart are obviously predisposed to defend her and reject evidence against her. While this does not mean that you should jump to the conclusion that the arguments on the SAVE MARTHA website are illegitimately biased, you should be aware of the possibility that this is so and treat arguments coming from such a source with care. To establish any illegitimate bias in this case, you must carefully examine the arguments against a broad background that includes objective reports of the Martha Stewart situation, as well as arguments of those who are critical of Stewart.

Vested Interests

The danger of illegitimate bias is particularly strong in any situation in which an arguer has a *vested interest*. This occurs when an arguer will benefit in some significant way if they and other arguers see issues in a particular way. In such circumstances, an arguer may be attracted to a conclusion for the wrong reason—because it benefits them—and not because there are convincing premises that show that it is true.

In the most obvious cases, an arguer's vested interest is financial. Patricia Bickers discusses a good example in an essay on the relationship between art and fashion that she has published in *Art Monthly* ('Marriage à la Mode', Nov. 2002). For artists, the underlying issue is whether fashion design is an art form, and whether art galleries and the art establishment should treat it as such. Bicker discusses specific cases that have been the cause of controversy, in particular, a show of Armani designs sponsored by the Guggenheim Museum in New York. In debates about this show, the central issue was whether the Guggenheim genuinely judged Armani designs to be worthy of the label 'art', or reached this conclusion because Armani offered a gift of $15 million dollars to the Guggenheim Museum. From the point of view of argumentation, the issue is whether those deciding on the Armani show (who were deciding whether they would show Armani or some other artist or designer) were influenced by an illegitimate bias founded on a vested interest. The vested interest was the $15 million dollars they were able to procure for their museum.

According to Bickers,

> . . . Armani was perceived by many commentators at the time not only to have bought himself a show at the Guggenheim but to have taken over from the

curators . . . none of the famous suits were included, for instance, instead the emphasis was on the designer's more recent, more glamorous—and still available—designs. It is no secret that in most art retrospectives many of the works discreetly labeled . . . are in fact for sale . . . The Armani show, however, seemed to suggest that the museum itself was for sale—or at least for hire.

The arguments that Bickers here reports suggest not only that the Guggenheim decision was a case of illegitimate bias, but that Armani himself was illegitimately biased when he decided which of his designs he would show. This, Bickers explains, was said to be reflected in his decision to pick designs that emphasized not his classic creations but recent works that were still for sale. According to the reasoning proposed, he did so because the latter allowed him to benefit financially, and in this way served his vested interests rather than the interests of design, history, or art.

Another good example of vested interest is portrayed in the famous 1913 cartoon we have reproduced below. Drawn by Art Young, it is a biting satire on 'The Freedom of the Press' that (metaphorically) compares newspaper owners and journalists to women working in a brothel. The owner and editor is pictured as a madam who courts a hefty client with a large wallet. In case we fail to understand the symbolism, Young has explicitly labelled the client 'Railroad – Mining – Dept. Stores, etc.' We can summarize his argument with the following supplemented diagram:

THE FREEDOM OF THE PRESS

AUDIENCE = the public
OPPONENTS = newspapers and large advertisers
P1 = The Press is willing to prostitute themselves and do whatever they need to do to please large advertisers who will pay them.
C = 'The Freedom of the Press' is a sham.

In making the case that newspapers are illegitimately biased (because they are willing to say whatever large advertisers want), Young emphasizes two different sets of vested interests—those of the newspapers, who benefit financially when they please their advertisers, and those of the advertisers, who don't wish to be criticized in a way that interferes with their business operations.

In cases that involve advantages other than financial benefits, vested interests may be less obvious. In dealing with such contexts, it is helpful to remember that an arguer may benefit from a particular perspective in all kinds of ways that are not directly tied to monetary gains. For instance, the acceptance of particular conclusions may serve one's pride or one's view of right and wrong rather than one's wallet. An arguer may, for example, be attracted to a particular conclusion because it increases the prestige of the institution from which they graduated, because it vindicates a stand they have publicly defended, because it fosters a particular image of their congregation, ethnic group, or political party, or because it promotes policies or beliefs that are in some ways in keeping with their loyalties and commitments.

In detecting vested interests, always remember that the existence of a vested interest does not in itself show that an argument is mistaken. When an arguer has a vested interest, you should treat their arguments with caution. You should be more circumspect, and more likely to ask whether they are characterized by illegitimate biases and have fairly presented the issues that are to be discussed. But an arguer may have a vested interest in an issue and still offer strong premises for a conclusion. Anyone defending themselves against a charge that they have done wrong has a considerable vested interest in the discussion of their case. It would be a mistake to think their arguments can be dismissed offhandedly on this account. It is important to detect an arguer's vested interests, and to be aware of their biases. But the question of whether an argument is to be accepted or rejected should lie with the quality of the premises and their relationship to the conclusion.

Conflict of Interest
In some cases, vested interests are so significant that they give rise to a *conflict of interest*. It occurs when someone, usually in a professional situation, is in a position to make a decision that might unfairly provide them with important benefits. Though the legal and ethical issues that arise in such contexts are too complex to be discussed in detail here, it can generally be said that someone who has a conflict of interest has a duty to declare it, and to refrain from the decision it might interfere with.

The following are three examples of conflict of interest:

EXAMPLE 1

The Case
You are a shareholder in a corporation that has been accused of polluting the river that runs through the city in which you live. The government has decided to investigate. They appoint you to the expert panel that has been established to investigate the matter.

The Conflict of Interest
You have something to lose from a decision that the corporation acted wrongly. It could affect share prices and decrease the value of the shares you hold.

EXAMPLE 2

The Case
You are a judge in criminal court. Your sister, Bridget, has been charged with theft and break and enter. You are assigned the case.

The Conflict of Interest
You have something to gain by deciding that she is innocent, both because it will save someone you love from unpleasant consequences and because it will save you the embarrassment that you might feel if you had a sister who was a convicted thief.

EXAMPLE 3

The Case
You are a member of the hiring committee of the Archaeology department at your university or college. Your committee plays a major role in deciding who is hired for new appointments that are open. The department has advertised an opening for an expert in Near Eastern archaeology. Your partner, who is qualified, has decided to apply.

The Conflict of Interest
You have a great deal to gain by favouring your partner in the selection process, because hiring that person will substantially increase your combined revenue and award a very significant benefit to someone you are very close to. It may provide you with other advantages as well, by increasing your power and influence in the department.

In cases of conflict of interest, the issue is someone's ability to act as an impartial decision-maker in some circumstance in which they have a vested interest in the outcome of the decision. In such contexts, the very possibility that one might be swayed by personal interest is enough to undermine one's role as a decision-maker, for this is a possibility that could cast doubt on the validity of the process by which the decision is made.

EXERCISE 5A

1. Suppose the federal government has established an initiative program that provides grants to businesses in order to stimulate the economy in depressed areas of the country. It is discovered that a good friend of the president or prime minister has received a large grant to support the building of a golf and country club. Is this a case of conflict of interest? Why or why not? What would you need to know to be certain?

2. Go to the SAVE MARTHA website mentioned above. Do you think it is characterized by vested interest or illegitimate bias? Why or why not? What would you have to find out to be sure?

3. Many of those who have argued that global warming is not the result of human activity have been closely associated with the oil industry, an industry that would be seriously affected by any significant attempt to reduce emissions of greenhouse gases. Is this a case of vested interest that produces an illegitimate bias? Why or why not? Find arguments against (or for) the claim that global warming is the result of human activity and discuss whether they are illegitimately biased.

2. DETECTING ILLEGITIMATE BIASES

In some cases, illegitimate biases are obvious. Consider the following letter, which we have adapted from an actual letter written to a university student newspaper after an incident in a student pub ('Fed Hall'). According to the author, her boyfriend had been 'set up' by a 'punk-rocker'. The letter appeared under the headline, 'My Larry was obviously set up':

> To the editor:
> After a recent incident at Fed Hall, I feel that it is necessary to bar punk-rockers from the premises. They have no class and should be kept from entering a class establishment. During Friday night my boyfriend, Larry, and his friends were in the washroom talking when they noticed a punker come in. He had a blond mohican-style haircut, army boots, and a leather jacket with inch high spikes on the shoulders. It was obvious he was only there to cause trouble. Larry asked him what his problem was and who he was trying to impress, but the punker wouldn't answer and gave my boyfriend a dirty look. Then after several attempts at finding out whether he was there to fight, the punker became violently deranged and they had to hold him from attacking them. When Larry tried to grab hold of him, the punk punched him several times in the face and kicked his friend in the kidney area. Larry was obviously set up.
>
> Larry ended up in the hospital that night with a badly broken nose and several stitches under his lip. We went to the police and they said nothing could be done because the punker was outnumbered and that it sounded like Larry had been at fault for harassing the punker into fighting.

I know that Larry and his friends would not start a fight.

If someone is reading this to you, punker, it is only fair to warn you that if my boyfriend ever sees you again at Fed Hall or the Turret, he and his friends will make you pay dearly for this. I can only hope, for your sake, that you have the temporary intelligence to stay away from there for good.

The most notable feature of this letter is the author's inability to appreciate how illegitimately biased her conclusions are. Even if we restrict our attention to her account of the evening, the evidence suggests that Larry was *not* set up, and that he and his friends harassed the punk-rocker into fighting (as the police had in fact suggested). The author's inability to see the situation for what it is is striking, especially when she claims that Larry and his friends would not start a fight, but then goes on to warn the punk rocker that they will make him 'pay dearly' for this, suggesting that they will assault him.

Though this is an extreme example, it usefully displays some of the common features that characterize illegitimate biases. They include an inability to see that one is biased, as well as strong opinions that leave no room for the possibility that one might look at a situation in a different way. As in the letter about Larry, problems with illegitimate bias are particularly common in circumstances in which arguers are dealing with matters that are of great importance to them—matters that pertain directly to themselves, their loved ones, their livelihood, or their cherished beliefs and convictions. Illegitimate biases are common in these contexts because they are contexts in which it is difficult to dispassionately weigh the evidence.

Slanting by Omission and Distortion

Even in cases that are not as obvious as our first example there are ways to detect illegitimate biases, for they tend to manifest themselves in techniques that are used to distort reports and arguments. Learning these techniques of 'slanting' can help you detect arguments that have been distorted by biases of one sort or another. Even more importantly, it can help you avoid such techniques in the construction of your own arguments.

The first technique of slanting is called *slanting by omission*. Anyone who describes a situation must select particular facts and issues to emphasize. Given that time and space are limited, it is unavoidable that other facts or issues must be summarized or ignored entirely. In the process of deciding what will and will not be reported and emphasized, it is relatively easy for an arguer to report those facts and details that favour the impression they wish to create. In the process, the arguer can downplay or leave out altogether those facts that suggest an alternative conclusion. The arguer does present 'nothing but the truth' but fails to give 'the whole truth', by avoiding aspects of the situation that may raise doubts about their perspective.

The following is the opening of a newspaper article that appeared in the *Halifax Chronicle-Herald*:

NO VIABLE ENERGY ALTERNATIVE TO NUCLEAR POWER, CHURCHMEN TOLD

Sackville (Special)—Two professors from the University of New Brunswick in Saint John told United Churchmen here Saturday that there is no viable alternative to nuclear energy if Canadians wish to maintain their present lifestyle.

The rest of this article expands on this opening remark, outlining the views of the two professors. The article was accurate in this regard, but it neglected to point out that there were *three* professors who spoke to United Churchmen. The third offered a critique of nuclear energy and the positions of the other two professors. By omitting this central fact, the article slanted its story in favour of the arguments that were offered for the pro-nuclear position. The conclusion that there is no viable alternative to nuclear power may be the correct one, but one is guilty of an illegitimate bias if one establishes it in this way. Proper reasoning on a controversial issue of this sort must demonstrate such conclusions by recognizing opposing arguments, especially when they have been an explicit part of the discussion.

We take our next example from a news feature on the website of the University of Waterloo, one of Canada's major universities (<http://www.uwaterloo.ca/>). Every year, Canadian universities are ranked in a national survey that is popular among prospective students, who use it to help them decide where they will go to university. On 1 January 2003, the University of Waterloo website had this to say about the university's place in the national rankings:

> The annual *Maclean's* magazine survey gives UW the highest ranking for reputation in its category of universities, including 'most innovative', 'highest quality', and top source of 'leaders of tomorrow'. The icing on the cake: opinion leaders across the country ranked Waterloo 'best overall' among all universities for the 11th year in a row.

Reading this message, one might easily conclude that 'the icing on the cake' is the University of Waterloo's standing as 'best overall'—i.e. number 1 in Canada—for 11 years in a row. This is at best misleading, for it fails to provide the context that is necessary if one is to understand the university's performance. We can provide the necessary background in a more balanced version of the university's press release, which might read as follows:

> In the annual Maclean's magazine survey, <u>UW was ranked second to the University of Guelph in the 'comprehensive' category</u>, <u>where it is ranked with ten other universities</u>. The university continues to perform strongly in the reputational ranking <u>that accounts for 20 per cent of every institution's score in the national rankings</u>. There, UW achieved the highest ranking for reputation in the category of <u>comprehensive</u> universities, including 'most innovative', highest quality', and top source of 'leaders of tomorrow'. Opinion leaders across the country ranked Waterloo 'best overall' among all universities for the 11th year in a row.

In our version of the press release we have underscored relevant information that was omitted from the notice on the university website. While the university can still claim to have performed well in the national rankings, this information may significantly change one's view of the result. Especially if one is at an institution that is competing with the University of Waterloo, one is likely to feel that the news item has not presented the university's results in the national rankings—and the results of competing institutions—fairly. We charge the university with slanting by omission.

As in the University of Waterloo case, slanting by omission is common in circumstances characterized by pronounced vested interest. It is also common in news reporting that promotes short accounts of a news story rather than in-depth analysis. Most notably, slanting by omission is a problem in television news, which relies on short, memorable copy with accompanying visuals. Two minutes is a long television news report, and it is difficult to fit all the relevant aspects of a complex issue into such a short span of time. Some critics conclude that TV news is inevitably misleading, for it always omits crucial aspects of the issues and events that it reports on. In place of the important—albeit boring—details that an informed report requires, it frequently substitutes sensational pieces of information and captivating visuals that grab our attention. An understanding of slanting by omission can help you combat these tendencies, not only when you watch television, but in any context in which you are gathering the kind of information that may play a role in argumentative discussion.

A second slanting technique is called *slanting by distortion*. It occurs when one describes or exaggerates or colours the facts that one is reporting in a manner that enhances an impression one wishes to create. A newspaper reporter or editor can, for example, twist the facts that they report by using terms with suggestive overtones in place of words that are neutral and descriptive; by inserting insinuating phrases; or by using headlines, the position on a page, or accompanying illustrations to foster the perspective that they favour.

Slanting by distortion can be very subtle, because it can be hard to find words that are entirely neutral and easy to use descriptions that lean one way or another. The adage that 'a half empty glass is half full' well captures the point that the same fact can be cast in a positive or negative light. A good historical example of slanting by distortion is provided in the following Paris newspaper headlines, which announced the journey of Napoleon across France on his return from Elba (9–22 March 1815; this example is given by Eleanor MacLean in *Between the Lines: Detecting Bias and Propaganda*). Each headline reports that Napoleon is in such-and-such a place but colours this report in a way that sends more extreme messages that change according to the bias of the newspaper in which the headline is reported. In this case, the slanted messages are not themselves arguments, but it is easy to imagine how they might provide the background for argumentative debate.

9 March

THE ANTHROPOPHAGUS [the monster who eats people] HAS QUITTED HIS DEN

10 March

THE CORSICAN OGRE HAS LANDED AT CAPE JUAN

11 March

THE TIGER HAS ARRIVED AT CAP

12 March

THE MONSTER SLEPT AT GRENOBLE

13 March

THE TYRANT HAS PASSED THROUGH LYONS

14 March

THE USURPER IS DIRECTING HIS STEPS TOWARDS DIJON

18 March

BONAPARTE IS ONLY SIXTY LEAGUES FROM THE CAPITAL

He has been fortunate to escape his pursuers

19 March

BONAPARTE IS ADVANCING WITH RAPID STEPS, BUT HE WILL NEVER ENTER PARIS

20 March

NAPOLEON WILL, TOMORROW, BE UNDER OUR RAMPARTS

21 march

THE EMPEROR IS AT FONTAINBLEAU

22 March

HIS IMPERIAL AND ROYAL MAJESTY

arrived yesterday evening at the Tuileries amid the joyful acclamations of his devoted and faithful subjects

None of these headlines explicitly says that Napoleon is good, bad, loved, feared, hated, admired, or despised, but the choice of words very clearly implies a variety of claims in this regard. The slanting by distortion that results reflects the vested interests of the newspapers that carried these headlines, for they are, of course, more likely to be furthered by positive headlines as Napolean comes closer and closer to Paris.

A second example of slanting by distortion that can illustrate the power of very slight changes in the wording of a sentence is found in Cassandra Pybus's book *The Woman Who Walked to Russia* (Thomas Allen Publishers, 2002). It is the story of a New York immigrant (Lillian Ailling) who reportedly 'walked to Russia' during the days of the Klondike. According to the accounts of her journey, she did so by walking a remarkable path through the wilds of British Columbia to the Yukon, to Nome, Alaska, and across the Bering Strait. Pybus retraces much of Ailling's alleged journey, looking for clues as to what really happened, coming to the conclusion that Ailling could not have been trying to walk to Russia.

Pybus's thesis seems at odds with an article in the *Dawson News* that is one of the few extant articles based on an actual interview with Ailling. In response to this apparent counterevidence, Pybus defends her theory by remarking that 'The *Dawson News* reported that she "gave it out" that she was going to Nome and then to Siberia, although the paper is careful not to quote her' (p. 196). This one sentence contains a pithy argument that might be diagrammed as follows.

AUDIENCE = The readers of Pybus's book.

OPPONENTS = Those who believe that Ailling was trying to walk to Russia.

P1 = Though the *Dawson News* reported that she 'gave it out' that she was going to Nome and then to Siberia, the paper is careful not to quote her.

HC1 = The *Dawson News* was presenting its *own* view of Ailling's destination rather than views that were actually expressed by Ailling.

MC = It is quite possible that the *News* got it wrong, and was mistaken when it reported that Ailling was trying to walk to Russia.

But Pybus's account is a slanted reading of the evidence. Her slanting by distortion is evident in a single word in her account—the word 'careful'. The problems with this word may be evident if we consider her argument from the point of view of her opponents. They will rightly say that Pybus has presented the evidence in the *Dawson News* as though it is very much in keeping with her account. For her description of the situation makes it sound as though they were careful to not quote Ailling, in order to make it clear that they were offering an opinion she did not corroborate. But how can she know that the *News* was 'careful' not to quote Ailling? All we know is that the *News* did not quote her. There is, in contrast, no way of knowing that they were *careful* not to quote her. Perhaps they did not quote her because they were *careless* rather than careful. Perhaps the *Dawson News* didn't think a quote important. Perhaps the reporter wanted to keep his piece brief and decided not to use a quote he had. All of these possibilities are as compatible with the evidence in the *Dawson News* as the possibility that Pybus has fastened upon. She is guilty of slanting by distortion because she arbitrarily describes the situation in a way that reads into it evidence that favours her conclusions rather than opposing points of view.

Slanting by distortion or omission is a likely possibility whenever an individual or group has a perspective, a product, or a cause they are dedicated to promote. Slanting is found not only in newspaper and television news but in strategic analyses, feasibility studies, union and management reports, political platforms, scholarly defences of particular points of view, and attempts to promote 'special interests' of one sort or another (milk producers, the dot-com industries, a particular religious perspective, a sports franchise, etc.). The crux of slanting is the use of omission and distortion to create an illegitimate bias that insinuates a particular interpretation of the facts or issues that are reported and debated. A good reasoner recognizes when someone arguing has imposed a particular 'slant' on the issues.

Slanting is particularly evident in propaganda, which the *Oxford English Dictionary* defines as 'information, especially of a biased or misleading nature, used to promote a political cause or point of view'. Propagandists are willing to exaggerate in extreme ways that employ self-serving analogies, shifts of meaning in the use of key terms in the course of an argument, controversial hidden premises, and an aura of certainty that is often promoted by name-dropping and pseudo-technical jargon. Ironically, the extreme slanting that characterizes propaganda often makes their lack of objectivity transparent, making their arguments unconvincing rather than convincing. Films like *Reefer Madness*, which shows high-school kids smoking pot and quickly doing insane things, and *The Atomic Café*, which parodies the extreme propaganda that promoted things like the atomic bomb, have become popular comedies because we can, in hindsight, see how crude and heavy-handed earlier attempts at propaganda were.

Looking for Balance

Slanting is an indication of illegitimate biases that can help us determine how we should respond to arguers and arguments. But an argument may be influenced by such bias even if it is not obvious that it is slanted. Someone reading the article from the *Halifax Chronicle Herald*, noted earlier, will not know that it has left out important details unless they were at the colloquium on nuclear power it discusses, or have learned, in some other way, about the events of the evening. In many circumstances, an article or argument may not appear slanted to someone who does not have a comprehensive understanding of the issues or the circumstances it discusses.

This underscores the point that a decision on the question whether an argument is illegitimately biased may in some cases depend on an examination of arguments forwarded by those who have opposing points of view. Especially when assessing an arguer's attempt to provide a comprehensive overview of some issue or concern, it is important to see what those with opposing views maintain, for this is the only way we can be sure that the comprehensive overview is fair to them and their arguments. In order to judge whether the arguments on the SAVE MARTHA website are illegitimately biased, we may have to spend time looking at the arguments of those who are critical of Martha Stewart. In this way, an attempt to consider bias and perspective must often evolve into an attempt to understand the broader context in which debates, arguments, and controversies occur.

In trying to determine whether arguments are affected by illegitimate biases, you may follow a three-step method, outlined as follows:

(1) Note vested interests.
(2) Look for slanting.
(3) Survey opposing views.

In dealing with many arguments, there is no need to survey opposing views, which can be a long and labourious task. If an arguer has no vested interests, if their claims are relatively straightforward, or if there is little reason to believe that they are misrepresenting their or their opponents' points of view, then the argument they present can be considered on its own terms, without a survey of the broader argumentative context in which it occurs. However, if there is good reason to think that bias may be a problem, you should remember that surveying opposing views is the best way to determine whether, and to what extent, an argument is illegitimately biased.

Difficult Cases

In some circumstances, issues of bias will make it very difficult for you to know how you should regard particular arguments or issues. In difficult cases of this sort, don't be shy about identifying the problems and recognizing the limits of your analysis.

Consider a sensational case of alleged child abuse that surfaced in 1992, when a Manitoba woman robbed a bank at gun point and took the money to the Manitoba minister of Justice, declaring 'Here's some money to help my abusive husband get into a treatment program.' In the hearings that followed, one of the central issues that arose was whether or not the woman's husband, Ambrose, was guilty of child abuse. We include below a list of some of the charges and countercharges that were made during the course of the case:

Charge: Ambrose, in his affidavit, stated that Mary Ann admitted to his lawyer that she fabricated the abuse charge. Mary Ann admitted this in her second affidavit.

Countercharge: Mary Ann claimed she was under a great deal of pressure to say whatever Ambrose wanted.

Charge: An independent witness swore in an affidavit that Mary Ann told him the accusation was false.

Countercharge: Mary Ann accused the witness of lying.

Charge: Mary Ann and her supporters made much of the point that Ambrose pleaded guilty to a charge of abuse.

Countercharge: Ambrose said that Mary Ann promised to reconcile with him if he pleaded guilty, and Mary Ann admitted in court that she had threatened to keep the child away if he didn't plead guilty.

This is only a small segment of the charges and countercharges that characterized this case. Even if we ignore the others, they usefully demonstrate how clashes of vested interest and the possibility of illegitimate bias may make it almost impossible to decide what should be believed.

If two individuals are implicated in a murder and the only account of the situation we have is their two reports, how can we reconcile their accounts if each points a finger at the other? Each has a substantial vested interest (to be free from blame and punishment), and there are good reasons to suspect that each one of them may be providing an account of the situation that is illegitimately biased in their favour. In some circumstances (in which one of them has divulged 'what really happened', to a friend, perhaps) there may be a way to get to the bottom of the situation, but there are cases in which we have no way to choose between them.

A case that illustrates these issues in a visual context is provided by archaeological research, which has often debated the extent to which our distant ancestors are similar to contemporary humans. In books on archaeology, this debate is reflected in illustrations of early humans that must be reconstructed from the limited evidence that archaeological discoveries make available. Because this evidence is compatible with different interpretations of what early humans 'looked like', different illustrators produce illustrations of early humans that suggest very different views of their relationship to us. The examples below illustrate two contrasting perspectives in this regard. It does not take a detailed analysis to show that one promotes the view that early humans were much more primitive than contemporary humans, the other the view that they were similar.

Illustration from *Prehistoric Man*, by Josef Augusta and Zdenek Burian (London: Paul Hamlyn, 1960).

Illustration by Angel Martin from *Grain Collection: Humans' Natural Ecological Niche* by Sergio Treviño (New York: Vantage Press, 1991).

Both of these illustrations might be criticized for the way in which they embellish what is known about early humans. The second illustration might, in particular, be criticized, for the picture it presents is absurdly contemporary (one viewer has described it as 'flower children after Woodstock'). In the final analysis there is, however, no way to be sure what early humans looked like, hence no way to be sure how significant the problem of illegitimate bias is. In a case like this, and in other cases where we have a limited ability to judge problems of bias, we will do best to recognize the potential biases and say that we have no definitive way to establish how serious these problems are.

Balancing Your Arguments

In the course of constructing your own arguments, be mindful of the dangers of illegitimate biases and do your best to avoid them. If your perspective is informed by vested interests and previous commitments that are pertinent to the case at hand, be open about them. Be explicit about your views, and do your best to ensure that any opinions or feeling you express are justified by an unbiased understanding of opposing views of the issue or situation you discuss.

In the process of putting your arguments together, be cautious about emotionally charged modes of expression. It is appropriate to feel strongly about some things, but strong claims need to be backed by convincing arguments, and you must be cautious of overstatement and terms that colour your claims in a way that is slanted in favour of your own view. In the end, the strength of your own perspective will depend on your willingness to be fair to the views of your opponents. The most convincing argument is one that recognizes and fairly states opposing points of view, and then deals adequately with the issues that they raise.

In constructing your own arguments, you will need to judge those of other people. In many cases, the manoeuvres used in slanting can alert you to the possibility of its presence. Obvious symptoms of slanting—and possible symptoms of propaganda—include the use of inflammatory terms where neutral ones suffice, sensational words that promote moralistic judgments, unnecessary phrases filled with innuendo, and suggestions that are implied but never explicitly stated. As you read an argument, you should be able to identify some of the facts an argument depends on. Once you do, you can ask if the account proposed is slanted. As you read or watch or listen, ask yourself: Does this commentary push its audience unreasonably toward a particular perspective? By assessing the facts and issues in a loaded way, or by letting the facts 'speak for themselves'? Has the arguer made appropriate judgments in deciding which details should be emphasized and which should be treated as inconsequential or as secondary matters? Could one 'juggle the facts' in a way that creates a very different impression?

In many cases, you will be aware of slanting only when someone who has been offended raises their voice to correct some omission or some distorted commentary. But there are ways to take a more active role in diagnosing and exposing illegitimate biases. If you detect significant vested interests (and especially vested interests that have not been declared), or if the terms used in an argument jump out at you, try to compare the argument before you with a report or argument written by someone with a competing point of view. Studying two reports of the same event—especially reports from sources with opposing commitments and loyalties—is one of the best ways to establish a more accurate understanding of the issues you discuss.

DETECTING BIAS

> ➤ Note vested interests.
> ➤ Look for slanting.
> ➤ Survey opposing views.
> ➤ Admit the problems with difficult cases.

EXERCISE 5B

Read the lead article from your daily newspaper (in print or on the web).
a)   Is the article illegitimately biased? Slanted? Why or why not?
b)   Rewrite the article in a slanted way that unfairly promotes a different view of the situation than that suggested in the article.

c) Write a mock letter to the editor criticizing your own article on the grounds that it is illegitimately biased.

d) Rewrite the original article in another way that reflects a different set of illegitimate biases (your first rewrite might be from a liberal point of view, the second from a conservative point of view, etc.).

Major Exercise 5M

1. Consider the following arguments or reports and identify any concerns about vested interest and possible bias (provide supplemented diagrams for any arguments you find):

a)* [Ms Pat Curran, Canadian Automobile Association, quoted in *TransMission* (1995)] We at the CAA believe that reducing the speed to 30 kilometers per hour on city streets would be unreasonable and unenforceable. Motorists will only obey the speed limits that they perceive as reasonable. Further, we feel that such a low speed limit . . . could have the detrimental effect of increasing fuel consumption and exhaust pollution.

b) [from an advertisement in *Wired* (Jan. 2003)]

WE COULD TELL YOU HOW WE GOT THESE NUMBERS BUT THEN WE'D HAVE TO KILL YOU.

OUR MISSION: BECOME THE LEADER IN MANAGED HOSTING

MISSION STATISTICS:

0
Seconds to talk to a real person

97%
Of our customers would recommend us

100%
Network uptime for the last 18 months

6,000+
Servers managed at Rackspace

550,000+
Domains hosted

rackspace MANAGED HOSTING

c)* [adapted from a public advertisement from the Post Office in favour of 'Advertising Mail', which is popularly referred to as 'junk mail'] The people who send you ads-in-the-mail do a lot of nice things for you, and for us. Advertising Mail allows you to shop from the comfort of your home. Advertising Mail adds $50,000,000 revenue to the Post Office and that keeps postal rates down. Advertising Mail creates employment for tens of thousands of men and women . . . Probably someone you know.

d)   [from a news report at <http://www.newsmax.com/showinside.shtml?a=2002/12/30/104929> (accessed 2 Jan. 2003)]

Clonaid Founder: I'd Clone Hitler

. . .

RAEL: I know some people tell me, 'One day, what if we can find Adolf Hitler and clone Adolf Hitler?' And let's imagine we can bring back his memory and personality. I think that's beautiful and the Jews—the Jewish people will be happy to judge him.
HOPKINS: To judge the clone of Adolf Hitler?
RAEL: Absolutely. If it's the same person and he has the same personality and memory—yes.

. . .

Before he announced that he thought cloning Hitler would be beautiful, Rael said that he had turned over total control of Clonaid to Dr Boisselier four years ago, explaining, 'I gave her the company and she's taking care of it and I have no interest in it.'

e)   [from the introduction to an article in O: *The Oprah Magazine* (Jan. 2003)]

IS SHE THE MOST
SHOCKING
WOMAN
ON TELEVISION?

She looks like a plainspoken, modest, homey grandmother. In fact, cable TV sex therapist Sue Johanson is an authority on (among other things) vibrators, clitoral sensitivity, and how to get semen out of silk. Lise Funderburg sits down with Canada's favorite lay person.

f)   [from an article in *Wired* (Jan. 2003)]

Google Sells Its Soul
. . . It's inevitable that a company of Google's size and influence will have to compromise on purity. There's a chance that, in five years, Google will end up looking like a slightly cleaner version of what Yahoo! has become. There's also a chance that the site will be able to make a convincing case to investors that long-term user satisfaction trumps short-term profit. The leadership of the Internet is . . . [Google's] to lose. For now, at least, in Google we trust.

g)   [from 'Marx after communism', in *The Economist* (21 Dec. 2002)] When Soviet communism fell apart towards the end of the 20th century, nobody could say that it failed on a technicality. A more comprehensive or ignominious collapse—moral, material, and intellectual—would be difficult to imagine. Communism had tyrannized and impoverished its subjects, and slaughtered them in the tens of millions. For decades past, in the Soviet Union and its satellite countries, any allusion to the avowed aims of communist doctrine—equality, freedom from exploitation, true justice—had provoked only bitter laughter.

2. Each of the following passages is a comment on the kinds of issues discussed in this chapter. Explain what the author is saying in terms of vested interest, illegitimate bias, conflict of interest, slanting, and any other concepts introduced in this chapter. If the passage contains an argument, diagram it. Do you think this is a case of illegitimate bias? Why or why not? If you would need more evidence to decide the issue, where would you go to get it? Make sure you explain what the author is saying *before* you judge their claims.

a)* [a letter to *The Economist* (May 1997)] Sir: Your assertion that public smoking should not be banned, on the grounds that 'other people's freedoms . . . sometimes get in your eyes,' is biased. Our societies ban or restrict any number of activities that are minor irritants: begging, loud music, nudity, skateboarding. Although each of these restrictions on individual liberty is the result of intolerance, *The Economist* seldom champions their causes; yet your newspaper seems unable to mention tobacco without commenting on dangers to the rights of smokers.

b) In an article on Google in *Wired* (Jan. 2003), one of the search provider's founders suggests that there is nothing wrong with their decision to sell advertising space to companies interested in promoting their sites and products on the Google website. According to Google, we need to distinguish between the way that Google does this and the way it is done by search engines like Overture, for sites like the latter don't clearly indicate what listings are and are not paid for. In contrast, Google clearly indicates its paid listings to ensure that there is no chance that a Google user could, say, be directed to breast cancer information paid for by a drug company without knowing that its listing has been paid for.

c) Some have suggested that we make Pulp Press Publishers a publicly owned company. We could make a great deal of money by doing so. But we think we would pay in a different way. As a private company, Pulp Press Publishers answers to one master: the readers it has cultivated for a unique brand of pulp fiction. As a public company, Pulp Press would have shareholders to worry about. And shareholders are primarily concerned with profits.

   Pulp Press has demonstrated its loyalty to its readers by continuing to publish unique titles with a small but devoted readership. If Pulp Press goes public, will it cave to pressure from its shareholders and streamline its publishing list if stock prices begin to cave?

d) [from a letter to the *Toronto Sun* (1 Apr. 1996) concerning police violence in a controversial strike] It was okay for the union goons to harass citizens crossing the picket lines to the point of tears or even scuffle or skirmish, but as soon as the shoe was on the other foot they wimped out and cried police brutality.

e)* [a 'disclaimer' pasted into high school biology textbooks in Clayton County, Georgia:] This textbook may discuss evolution, a controversial theory some scientists present as a scientific explanation for the origin of living things, such as plants, animals and humans. . . . No human was present when life first appeared on earth. Therefore, any statement about life's origins should be considered a theory, not fact.

f) [from an advertisement for a vitamin pill called 'Within', in *Ms.* (Aug. 1987)]

> *Most multivitamins don't know you from Adam.*
> *WITHIN*
> *With the extra calcium and extra iron women need*
> *. . . The most complete multivitamin created for women.*

g) [from a letter to the *Toronto Sun* (9 Mar. 1987)] I think it is sad that some members of our society still enjoy watching a spectacle like the Media Pig Race (page 2, Aug. 27 *Sun*). Those pigs were not racing. They were terrified animals running in a panic from the noise of the crowd. It is a display of cruelty that the *Sun* should not condone by endorsing one of the unfortunate participants. We kill pigs for food. We do not need to torment them first.

h) [from <http://www.vix.com/men/media/manucon.html> (accessed 2 Jan. 2003)] Statistics show that men and women suffer roughly equal rates of violence. Media coverage of male victimization, however, is virtually non-existent. . . . [In a study I did on newspaper headlines,] I found that the few headlines on men were quantitative, providing data on the amount of violence they experienced without placing it in any societal context. Headlines on women were rarely quantitative: those that were used words like 'epidemic' or provided statistics only on women . . . In the end, I argued that while the media appeared willing to address violence against women, and rightly so, the media did not appear willing to address a second type of violence, that against men, although statistics show that rates of violence against men are at least as high as those for women.

i) [David L. Katz, in 'How to Spot a Diet Scam', *O: The Oprah Magazine* (Jan. 2003)] Ads for fad diets generally offer convincing quotes from highly satisfied customers. These are as easy to obtain as they are meaningless. The quotes may come from the brief period of peak satisfaction. How do these folks feel six months later, when the weight is likely to have come back? The ads don't say.

j) [under the headline 'The Times's Slip is Showing', in 'The Goldberg File', from *The National Review* <http://www.nationalreview.com/goldberg/goldberg052499.html> (3 Jan. 2003)] Speaking of hegemonic liberal orthodoxy (was that what I was speaking about? I can't remember), today's *New York Times* is a great example. The *Times* has a huge article on the US Court of Appeals for the Fourth Circuit. It wrings its hands about the fact that this cell of conservatives is trying to do conservative things and it's succeeding. Is it possible to think that the *Times* would ever run a hand-wringing piece about a liberal circuit succeeding at doing liberal things?

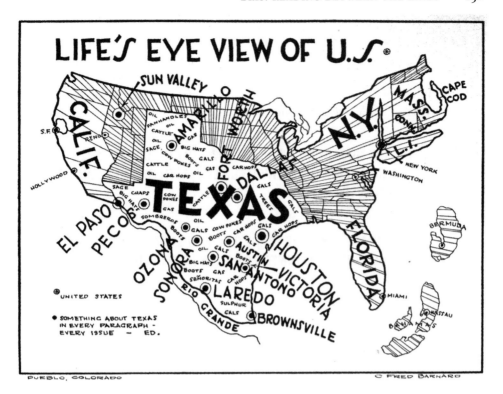

LIFE'S EYE VIEW OF U.S.

PUEBLO, COLORADO   © FRED BARNARD

k) [The map above is one of the United States 'according to *Life*', drawn by a dis-
    gruntled reader in 1943]

l) [from Robert Fisk, in 'When journalists forget that murder is murder', *Z-magazine*
    <http://www.zmag.org/meastwatch/fiskmurd.htm> (18 Aug. 2001)] What on
    earth has happened to our reporting of the Middle East? George Orwell would
    have loved a Reuter's dispatch from the West Bank city of Hebron last Wednes-
    day. 'Undercover Israeli soldiers', the world's most famous news agency reported,
    'shot dead a member of Yasser Arafat's Fatah faction yesterday in what Palestini-
    ans called an assassination.' The key phrase, of course, was 'what Palestinians
    called an assassination'. Any sane reader would conclude immediately that
    Imad Abu Sneiheh, who was shot in the head, chest, stomach and legs by 10
    bullets fired by Israeli 'agents' had been murdered, let alone assassinated. But
    no. Reuters, like all the big agencies and television companies reporting the
    tragedy of the Palestinian–Israeli conflict, no longer calls murder by its real
    name.

m) [from <http://www.newsmax.com/showinside.shtml?a=2002/12/30/104929> (3
    Jan. 2003)] Clonaid founder 'Rael', whose disciple Dr Brigitte Boisselier conned
    almost the entire media over the weekend into covering her claim that Clonaid
    scientists had successfully cloned a human being, announced Saturday that he
    would clone Nazi Fuhrer Adolf Hitler if he had the chance.

While the press has taken note of Mr Rael . . . reporters were apparently too embarrassed over their own gullibility to cover the Clonaid founder's comments to Fox News Channel's Page Hopkins on Saturday. But we think Hopkins and Fox performed a genuine public service by exposing the media's ill-considered rush to report Clonaid's claims, with her probing questions of the group's white-suited, shoulder-padded, ponytailed cult leader.

n) [from the cover of a 'prize envelope']

YOU ARE NOW IN POSSESSION OF A COLOUR-CODED PRIZE SEAL THAT COULD MAKE YOU RICH FOR LIFE WITH OUR BIGGEST CASH AWARD EVER.

If you reply in time and win, we'll say . . .

LEO GROARKE, YOU'VE MADE THE FINAL CUT—YOU'RE ONE OF TEN LUCKY PRIZE WINNERS GUARANTEED UP TO $11,000,000!

STRONG

AND WEAK

ARGUMENTS:

PREPARING FOR EVALUATIONS

In chapters 4 and 5 we discussed issues of meaning that may affect the quality of an argument. In this chapter we introduce principles of argument evaluation that determine whether an argument that is understandable is strong or weak. In doing this, we discuss

- ♦ strong and weak arguments;
- ♦ acceptability and burden of proof;
- ♦ valid and invalid arguments; and
- ♦ schemes of argument.

In evaluating arguments, we can usefully distinguish between those that are strong and those that are weak. We shall provide a definition of a strong argument later in this chapter. For the moment, we can say that a 'strong' argument provides evidence that should convince a reasonable audience that its conclusion should be accepted; a 'weak' argument does not. The goal of good reasoning is the production of strong arguments.

We describe good and bad reasoning in terms of 'strong' and 'weak' arguments because these two terms indicate that the strength of an argument is not a black-and-white affair. A strong argument should convince a reasonable audience, but it will rarely be so strong that it cannot be strengthened. A weak argument may be so weak that it cannot be rehabilitated or else weak but capable of strengthening (by adding more premises, for example). Argument evaluation encompasses a continuum from very weak to very strong that contains abundant, perhaps infinite, shades of grey.

We have already seen that the first prerequisite of good reasoning is clarity. An arguer's audience should have no trouble recognizing that the argument has specific premises that lead to a clear conclusion. But strong arguments require more than clarity. In this chapter, we begin to elaborate the features of strong arguments, features that make them instances of good rather than bad or questionable reasoning. After a general overview of the requirements for strong arguments, we focus on one type of reasoning that encompasses the kinds of arguments we will discuss in chapters 7, 8, 9, and 10.

1. STRONG ARGUMENTS

An argument can be compared to a trip from one place to another. The premises are the vehicle that takes an audience to the conclusion. In order to accomplish this, a strong argument must do two things.

First, a strong argument must provide *acceptable premises*, i.e. evidence its intended audience should accept. If an audience does not accept the premises of an argument, it will be difficult for these premises to take the audience to the conclusion. The audience are like passengers who refuse to get on a bus that cannot, in view of this, take them to its destination. Ideally, all the premises of a strong argument are acceptable, but there may be times when an argument is convincing even though there is a problem with one or more of its premises.

Having provided acceptable premises, a strong argument must provide *a conclusion that follows from these premises*. The conclusion is the destination the arguer is aiming for. The argument cannot serve its intended purpose if its premises do not take the audience in the right direction. Even if it has acceptable premises, an argument with a conclusion that does not follow from them is like a bus that fails to arrive at its intended destination.

We will recognize these aspects of strong arguments in the following definition:

> A strong *argument is an argument with* (1) *acceptable premises and* (2) *a conclusion that follows from them.*

A *weak* argument is, as this implies, an argument without acceptable premises or with a conclusion that does not follow from them, and possibly both.

Our definition of a strong argument explains in more detail what was implied in our earlier suggestion that a strong argument provides evidence that will convince a reasonable audience that its conclusion should be accepted. The qualities of strong arguments can be illustrated with an argument that Arthur Conan Doyle attributes to Sherlock Holmes, his fictional detective. It occurs in A *Scandal In Bohemia*, a story in which the King of Bohemia hires Holmes to find out who is blackmailing him and threatening to undermine his upcoming marriage. At the end of the story, Holmes explains to the King why it would be best if the woman who is blackmailing him loves her husband:

Because it would spare your majesty all fear of future annoyance. If the lady loves her husband, she does not love your majesty. If she does not love your majesty, there is no reason why she should interfere with your majesty's plan.

This explanation gives reasons for believing that it would be best if the woman who is blackmailing the king loves her husband; therefore, we can treat it as an argument. In doing so, we need to recognize that the word 'would' in Holmes' first sentence tells us that it is a statement about what would be the case if the woman loves her husband. In view of this, we can express the premises and conclusion in Holmes' reasoning as follows:

> P1 = If she loves her husband, she does not love your majesty.
> P2 = If she does not love your majesty, there is no reason why she should interfere with your majesty's plan.
> C1 = If the lady loves her husband, it would spare your majesty all fear of future annoyance.
> HMC = It would be best if the lady blackmailing the king loves her husband.

To be sure that we have fully captured Holmes' reasoning to C1, we can make the connection between P2 and C1 clear by adopting as HP3 the implicit claim that 'If there is no reason why she should interfere with your majesty's plan, then this should spare your majesty all fear of future annoyance.' Once this is done, we can construct a supplemented diagram for the argument as follows:

AUDIENCE = King and Watson

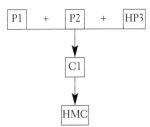

As the King himself admits, this is a strong argument that is difficult to criticize. It is worth noting that this means that it is a strong argument for the intended audience. Another audience—one that includes the woman who is blackmailing the king, for example—might not accept the conclusion, because it does not accept the assumption that it would be best if the King's plans were not interfered with. But such an audience does not matter in this context. For the audience that matters, the argument is strong because it has the properties shared by all strong arguments. In this case, this means that P1, P2, and HP3 are acceptable premises; that C1 follows from them; that C1 is (in consequence) acceptable; and that HMC follows from C1. Like many (but not all) of the examples that make Holmes a famous detective, this argument is characterized by the two essential ingredients of strong arguments.

Our second example comes from an article entitled 'The Trouble With Dams', which appeared in *Atlantic Monthly* (Aug. 1995). According to the author, American water policy should be changed to enforce conservation measures, because 'we squander so much [water] that following through on just the easiest conservation measures would save vast amounts of water.' We can diagram the intended argument as follows:

P1 = Following through on just the easiest water conservation measures
    would save vast amounts of water.
 C = We should follow through on conservation measures.

If we want to be sure that the diagram captures all of the author's reasoning, we may include, as a hidden premise, HP2, the implied assumption that it is wrong to waste water that could easily be saved. The diagram then appears as follows:

A detailed analysis of P1 and HP2 is beyond the scope of our present discussion, so we will simply say that we find both of them acceptable. (In support of P1, for example, we could cite studies of conservation measures.) Because the premises are acceptable, and the conclusion follows from them, this is another example of a strong argument.

While we have judged this argument a strong one, we recognize that someone might wish to debate P1. In the article from which we have excerpted our example, this possibility is addressed with arguments that support P1 (making the author's argument an extended argument). In arguing about controversial issues, it is difficult to treat them in a definitive way without entering into a long and protracted argument. This is especially the case with moral and political debates, which typically involve a variety of issues that can be discussed from different points of view. When practical circumstances make a protracted argument impossible, our attempts at argument evaluation may have to end with provisional judgments that we may revise after further scrutiny. We all operate in this manner in our daily lives, for we all accept conclusions we later reject when further evidence comes to light. In both our provisional and our final (or merely less provisional) judgments, we must judge arguments in terms of the criteria for strong argument.

2. ARGUMENT CRITICISM

In keeping with our definition of strong arguments, a weak argument is an argument that fails to satisfy one or both of the criteria for strong arguments. Our definition of a weak argument thus explains the essentials of good argument criticism, which is criticism that exposes one or both of these flaws.

We will take an example of good argument criticism from an essay on baseball that Steve Marantz published in *The Sporting News* (24 July 1995). Within the essay, Marantz takes issue with the common claim that major-league pitching has declined. In the course of his discussion, he criticizes a comment by the general manager of the New York Mets, who backs the claim that pitching has declined with the remark, 'Go watch a high-school pitcher. Nine of ten have major mechanical flaws.'

We can represent the general manager's argument as follows:

P1 = Nine of ten high-school pitchers have major mechanical flaws.
HP2 = Such flaws were not so prevalent in earlier years.
C = Pitching in the majors is declining.

We include the hidden premise HP2 in the diagram because the issue that the general manager is addressing is whether pitching is poorer now than in the past. Without HP2, it would make no sense to conclude that the general quality of pitching has declined.

Having diagrammed the general manager's argument, let's turn to Marantz's criticism of it. He argues that the GM's conclusion makes two unfounded assumptions:

> One . . . is that those flaws carry into the major leagues. Another is that in a long-ago golden age of sandlot baseball, mechanical flaws were nonexistent.

Consider the second criticism first. Its talk of a 'golden age' is overstated, but it raises a good question about the GM's argument. It is, as Marantz suggests, a weak argument because it assumes, without evidence, that mechanical flaws in high-school pitchers were not *as* prevalent in a previous era. Put in the terms we would use, the problem is that the argument is founded on a questionable premise that needs support before it could become acceptable, HP2.

Marantz's other criticism raises doubts that are associated with the second criterion of strong arguments, which requires that the conclusion of an argument follow from its premises. For suppose that we ignore the problems with HP2 and assume that P1 and HP2 are true. Even in that case, C does not clearly follow. For though P1 and HP2 lead to the conclusion that pitching has declined in *high school*, it does not follow that it has declined in the *majors*, for we do not know that the mechanical flaws in high-school pitching carry over to the big leagues. If they are routinely corrected—say, in the minor leagues—then their existence does not lead to the conclusion that pitching has declined in the major leagues.

Though his comments are somewhat overstated, Marantz's criticism of the argument he ascribes to the general manager of the New York Mets follows the general pattern one looks for in good argument criticism. In the process of raising his two criticisms, Marantz adopts the stance of a good arguer, showing that an argument is weak because it fails to satisfy the two criteria for strong arguments.

STRONG AND WEAK ARGUMENTS

➤ A *strong* argument is an argument with (1) acceptable premises and (2) a conclusion that follows from them.
➤ A *weak* argument is, as this implies, an argument that has unacceptable premises, or a conclusion that does not follow from them, or both.

---

3. ACCEPTABILITY

Taking our account of strong arguments one step further requires that we introduce several aspects of good reasoning. These will be developed in more detail in later chapters, but you should understand that they can receive only a limited discussion in an introductory text.

Truth and Acceptability

In discussing the criteria for good reasoning, some would say that the premises of an argument must be 'true' rather than 'acceptable'. Because acceptable premises are premises that should be accepted as true by an audience (even if only provisionally), truth still plays an implicit role in our account of arguments and argument evaluation. We will, however, judge premises by asking whether they are acceptable rather than true, both because 'true' seems too rigorous a requirement and because we cannot discuss the complex questions that the notion of truth raises (questions addressed by philosophical theories of truth). Suffice it to say, the premises of a strong argument may be acceptable even though a reasonable audience might hesitate to go so far as to call them 'true'.

Burden of Proof

Another complex issue that arises in theoretical discussions of argument is called 'burden of proof'. The mention of 'proof' might confuse you here. As we suggested with regard to 'truth', we would rarely expect someone to *prove* a claim in the sense in which we might use that term in mathematics (a context in which proofs are often thought to establish certainty). In the phrase 'burden of poof' the emphasis is not on the word 'proof' but the word 'burden'. A burden is something that is carried. It can be an object, like a pitcher of water or a heavy sack of coal, but it can also be a duty or responsibility. In situations characterized by disagreement, the person with the burden of proof is the person who has an obligation, or *onus*, to argue (and in this sense 'prove') that their views are correct.

Burden of proof is a notion that applies to questions of premise acceptability. For when we are attempting to decide whether an argument has acceptable premises we must ask whether the burden of proof lies with the arguer who has provided the premises, or with those who might challenge the premises. Put another way, should the arguer assume the burden of proving that the premise is acceptable, or should a challenger assume the burden of proving that it is *not* acceptable? You may already realize that a parallel question arises in systems of criminal justice, and is resolved in different ways in different countries. In England, for example, a defendant and their lawyer are not required to prove that the accused is innocent. That is assumed unless the prosecution is able to prove their guilt. In France, by way of contrast, the accused is assumed guilty unless they can demonstrate their innocence.

We will explore burden of proof in greater detail in Chapter 11. For the moment, we propose a simple test that will help you decide where the burden of proof lies on issues of premise acceptability. For each premise an arguer puts forward, you should ask, 'Will the audience to whom this argument is directed (assuming it is reasonable) accept the premise without further support?' Most arguers design their arguments so that they will convince any reasonable person of their conclusion, so this question usually reduces to the question of whether the premise in question is acceptable to reasonable people. If the answer to the proposed question is 'no', then the burden of proving it lies with the arguer. If the answer is 'yes', then the burden of proof lies with any challenger, who must show that it is not acceptable.

4. Valid and Invalid Arguments

The second criterion for strong arguments is 'a conclusion that follows from the premises'. A strong argument must have premises that *lead to* its conclusion. Researchers who study theories of argument often debate the nature of the link between premises and conclusion. Some claim that there is only one kind of link that characterizes all arguments, others that there are two kinds of links, and still others that there are more than two. It is impossible to consider these matters here, so in place of such a discussion we will focus on two commonly distinguished ways in which a conclusion may follow from a set of premises.

Some arguments are structured so that a conclusion *necessarily* follows from some set of premises. In cases of this sort the link between premises and conclusion is so strong that it is impossible for us to accept that the premises are true and still reject the conclusion. We call arguments of this sort *deductively valid* arguments.

Consider the following argument:

(P1) The fetus, even in the case of a pregnancy resulting from rape or incest, is an innocent human being. (P2) The killing of innocent human beings is never permissible. (C) Abortion is never permissible.

In a case like this, someone who accepts P1 and P2 must accept conclusion C. For as soon as you accept that the fetus is, in all cases of abortion, an innocent human being, and that the killing of innocent human beings is never permissible, you must accept the conclusion that abortion is never permissible.

In deductively valid arguments, the link between the premises and the conclusion is as strong as it can be. Anyone who accepts the premises of a deductively valid argument must, unless they are irrational, accept the conclusion. This means that deductively valid arguments always satisfy one of the criteria for strong arguments. This does not, however, mean that all deductively valid arguments are strong arguments. For such an argument may not satisfy the first criterion for strong arguments. In the example we have given, P1 assumes that the fetus is a 'human being', and this has been widely debated. P2 is also controversial, for it may be permissible to kill innocent people in certain circumstances (in times of war, for instance). At the very least, this means that the burden of proof in this case requires the arguer who forwards the argument to justify its premises. Because they are (at least provisionally) not acceptable, the argument is weak even though it is deductively valid.

Deductively *invalid* arguments contain a conclusion that does not necessarily follow from the premises. In these cases, we can reject an argument's conclusion even if we accept that its premises are true. In a deductively invalid argument, the link between an argument's premises and conclusion is not as strong as the link in deductively valid reasoning.

This does not mean that all deductively invalid arguments are to be rejected. An *inductively valid* argument is an argument in which the premises make the conclusion likely. An example is the argument that we should believe a witness because he has usually been reliable in the past. In this case, our past experience makes the conclusion likely, but it is always possible that the witness cannot, in this instance, be trusted (because he has been 'bought', because this is a case where he has something to hide, etc.). Inductively valid arguments are characterized by a more tentative link between their premises and their conclusions. These arguments cannot on this account be dismissed, for they are an essential part of ordinary reasoning and can be strong arguments—i.e. arguments that provide convincing reasons why we should accept some conclusion. In contrast, inductively *invalid* arguments are always weak, for they never satisfy the second criterion for strong arguments.

Relevance and Sufficiency

When we are judging validity of the inductive or deductive variety, we can determine whether a conclusion follows from its premises by using two criteria. First, we can ask whether the premises in an argument are *relevant* to the conclusion. We count a premise or group of premises as relevant when it provides some—that is, any—evidence that makes the conclusion more or less likely. Premises are *positively* relevant when they make a conclusion more likely and *negatively* relevant when they make it less likely. The following statements are all positively relevant to the claim that 'University education is a way to build a better economic future.'

- University graduates have, on average, much higher salaries than people who don't go to university.
- University graduates are more likely to be promoted.
- University graduates are more likely to end up in professional and managerial positions.

A strong argument always proposes premises that are *positively* relevant to the conclusion it proposes. If it did not, it would provide no support for its conclusion. While positively relevant premises provide support for a conclusion, they do not guarantee a strong argument. In strong arguments, premises must also be *sufficient* to establish that a conclusion is more likely than not. This implies something more than positively relevant premises, for they may provide some support for a conclusion without providing *enough* support to convince a reasonable audience. We will, therefore, elaborate the second criterion for strong arguments by saying that a conclusion follows from a set of premises if the premises are (1) relevant to the conclusion and (2) *sufficient* to establish it as probable.

In a deductively valid argument, the premises are always relevant and sufficient to the conclusion, for the conclusion cannot be rejected if the premises are accepted. One cannot have premises that are more relevant and sufficient than this. An inductively valid argument does not have as strong a link between the premises and conclusion, but it may still be a strong argument. In such a case, the premises must be relevant and sufficient to establish the conclusion. In an inductively invalid argument they are not.

The difference between relevant and sufficient premises will be clear in many cases. Consider the following *Vanity Fair* letter, which responds to an article that profiled Kathleen Brown, the 1992 Democratic candidate for California governor. In answer to the article's speculation that she would be able to 'deliver' California's electoral votes to Bill Clinton during the 1996 presidential election campaign, Lawrence H. Wallach wrote:

> No governors will be able to 'deliver' their states' electoral votes to President Clinton or anyone else. Clinton will win or lose California based on the voters' perception of . . . his record. Note that in 1992 Clinton easily carried California even though the state had a Republican governor who fully supported George Bush.

Wallach here claims that governors cannot 'deliver' electoral votes. Because he provides evidence to back his claim, we can extract the following argument from his letter.

P1 = In 1992, the California governor could not deliver his state's electoral votes to President George Bush.

C = No governors are able to deliver their states electoral votes to a particular presidential candidate.

This is a case in which P1 is relevant to the argument's conclusion. It successfully shows that governors sometimes fail to 'deliver' electoral votes to their preferred presidential candidates. The problem is that Wallach makes the much stronger claim that *no* governor can succeed in doing so. Instances like the one he cites are relevant to this claim, but one example is not enough to show that his conclusion is even likely. For all we know, a more comprehensive look at examples might show that this instance is unusual.

Deciding when we have sufficient evidence for a conclusion can be an especially difficult task. In 1992, for example, the Canadian National Breast Screening Study published the results of a major study of screening mammography, which concluded that it is not reliable for women in their forties. Given the careful way in which the study was conducted and the remarkably large number of women surveyed, we might expect that the study provided sufficient evidence for this conclusion. Later research showed that this conclusion was mistaken, however. The major problem was the seven-year follow-up period it examined—a period that was too short to register the positive effects of detecting small tumors that may not become life-threatening for eight or more years.

This example illustrates how difficult it can be to judge when the evidence offered by an argument is sufficient for a conclusion. It underscores the point that we need, here and in other argument contexts, to remain open to the possibility that we should be prepared to revise our judgments in light of any further evidence.

Much more could be said about relevance and sufficiency, but we will leave a detailed discussion for Chapter 11. In the meantime, we will focus on models of inference and argumentation that are deductively valid and do not, therefore, require a weighing of the extent to which a conclusion follows from a set of premises.

EXERCISE 6A

1. For each of the following arguments, discuss whether the burden of proof would lie with the arguer who puts forward the premises, or a challenger who might dispute them.

   a)* [The Omega watch company withdrew its ads from *Vogue* magazine in protest over what it called distasteful pictures of an emaciated model in its June 1996 issue. The brand director of Omega argued as follows (source: *The Times* 31 May 1996):] Since *Vogue* presumably targets an audience that includes young and impressionable females, its creators must surely be aware that they will inevitably be influenced by what laughably passes for fashion in these pages. It was irresponsible for a leading magazine that should be setting an example to select models of anorexic proportions.

b) [from the same news story. The publisher of *Vogue* responded:] [The brand director's] comments appear to be motivated by sour grapes, because he had objected to the way Omega watches had been photographed for a feature on watches.

c) [from 'Deadly Dissidence', an editorial responding to President Thato Mbeki's refusal to address the HIV/AIDS crisis in South Africa on the grounds that the link between the two had not been established, *National Post* (3 Nov. 2000)] Let us be clear: The debate over the link between HIV and AIDS is similar to the debate over the truth of the Holocaust: there is no debate. According to the Durban Declaration, a document signed earlier this year by 5,000 doctors and Ph.D.-level researchers, 'The evidence that AIDS is caused by HIV-1 or HIV-2 is clear-cut, exhaustive and unambiguous, meeting the highest standards of science.'

d)* [David Tracy, in 'Human Cloning and the Public Realm: A Defense of Intu-itions of the Good', *Clones and Clones: Facts and Fantasies about Human Cloning* (W.W. Norton & Company, 1998), p. 194] At least this much seems clear on what seems to constitute a public realm. To produce public discourse is to provide reasons for one's assertions. To provide reasons is to render one's claims shareable and public. To provide reasons is to be willing to engage in argument. Argument is the most obvious form of public discourse. To engage in argument is minimally to make claims and to give the warrants and backings for those claims. To move to explicit argument is the most obvious way to ensure publicness.

2. Using the two basic criteria for strong arguments, judge whether the following argu-ments are instances of good reasoning. Are they valid? Why or why not? When eval-uating premises, indicate where the burden of proof lies. Be sure to explain your judgments in each case.

a)* Since large carnivores like grizzly bears and wolves are majestic creatures in their own right and are also critical to maintaining the health of the ecosystem, it is wrong to indiscriminately destroy them, and there should be stricter guide-lines for their conservation.

b) Medieval portrayals of Plato and Aristotle with haloes cannot be taken to mean that these two were seen as 'Saints'. 'Sainthood', and the attainment of it, is directly related to the following of Christ himself, and thus those who predated him cannot be saints.

c)* We should not extend the status of the family to same-sex couples. There are two reasons for this. First, not all discrimination is bad. It is not wrong to discriminate in favour of what is good and against what is bad for our society, for our country, or for our community. Secondly, on the basis of family status, it is not unfair to treat same-sex couples differently than a mixed-sex couple because they are objectively different.

d)   [from a letter to the *Globe and Mail* (8 Feb. 1997)] An independent Associated Press poll (Dec. 1995) showed that 59 per cent of the American public thought that it was 'always wrong to kill an animal for its fur'. A 1997 fur industry poll, specifically targeting fur coat wearers, found that a mere 17 per cent said that a fur coat represented fashion and 14 per cent said social status. From this information it follows that the public views those who wear coats as callous, showing arrogant disregard for the suffering of fur-bearing animals; and also that fur is no longer a status symbol or fashionable.

e)   [from *The Wall Street Journal* (4 June 2003), p. A3]

> **TAKE A CHANCE ON LOVE.**
> **NOT ON YOUR PRIVATE JET.**
> You have to throw caution to the wind when it comes to affairs of the heart. Purchasing a private jet, however, demands a rational approach. When you choose fractional jet ownership with NetJets, you'll have access to the world's largest fleet of business jets, which means you're guaranteed a plane in as little as four hours. The best-trained pilots in the industry assure your safety and it's all backed by the financial strength of Berkshire Hathaway. Maybe that's why people who can fly any way they want choose NetJets.
> **NETJETS. LEAVE NOTHING TO CHANCE.**

f)   [from *The Wall Street Journal* (4 June 2003), p. A8]

> Considering NetJets? If You Think Performance Matters, Call Flexjet.
> **BOMBARDIER FLEXJET'S HIGH PERFORMANCE FLEET STRETCHES YOUR HOURS.**
> Bombardier is a world-leading expert in the design and manufacturing of sleek, aerodynamically efficient aircraft. The superior speed advantage of Flexjet aircraft significantly shortens your trip time and delivers a lower cost per mile than NetJets. With Flexjet you'll fly faster, higher and more efficiently. So, you can use the hours you save towards more trips.
> Flexjet Gives You the Equivalent of 12% More Hours Per Year.
> Flexjet: Equivalent of 112 Hours
> Netjets: 100 Hours
> **Bombardier Flexjet**

5. Argument Schemes

In judging arguments, we have already seen that we can distinguish questions of acceptability from questions of validity, and that the latter incorporate notions of relevance and sufficiency. In the remaining sections of this chapter, we continue to focus on questions of validity and the ways in which it can be judged.

In many cases, we judge the validity of an argument by relying on our intuition — on our intuitive appreciation of what does and does not follow from a set of premises. This is what Sherlock Holmes tends to do when he reflects on his investigations and announces the unexpected verdict that 'So-and-so committed the crime.' In response to Watson's quizzical response, he claims that his reasoning is 'Elementary, my dear Watson.' By this, Holmes means that the conclusion is easy to see once his argument is properly understood. Typically, Holmes goes on to explain his argument in a way that demonstrates that its conclusion follows from the evidence at hand.

Because we have all listened to and proposed many arguments in our lifetime, and because we have an intuitive appreciation of what makes sense and what does not, we can often tell whether a straightforward and uncomplicated argument is valid or invalid. This is often an easier task than judging whether the premises are acceptable, for we can judge the relationship between premises and conclusion even if we do not know whether the premises are acceptable. We rely on this skill when we follow Holmes' step-by-step explanation of his reasoning. And like Holmes, we use this ability when we try to demonstrate that our own inferences are valid.

Consider the following example: In working through the exercises in this text, you wonder whether the answer to a particular question is included in the answers collected at the back of the book. In the process, suppose you employ the following reasoning:

P1 = All the exercise questions answered at the back of this book are starred.
P2 = Exercise question number 5 is starred.
 C = Exercise question number 5 is answered at the back of the book.

This argument is deductively valid. This is probably obvious. If you are unsure, try to imagine that you accept the premises but reject the conclusion. This would mean that exercise question number 5 is, contrary to what the conclusion states, not answered at the back of the book. But it would also mean that P1 is true, i.e. that all answered questions are starred. It would necessarily follow that question 5 is not starred, but this contradicts P2. This 'mental experiment' shows that it is impossible for C to be false when P1 and P2 are true, i.e. that the argument's conclusion deductively follows from the premises.

Consider another example of a valid argument. Suppose that you have an interest in nuclear science. You have heard that the person who discovered radioactivity won two Nobel prizes. You discover that this person is Marie Sklodowska Currie. You argue with a friend over the date when she discovered radioactivity. To settle the matter, you ask a professor who studies the history of science, who tells you, 'I studied her in grad school, it was 1898.' You go back to your friend and say, 'Marie Currie discovered radioactivity in 1898. Professor Szabo, who studied this in graduate school, told me yesterday.' You have constructed an argument. It is inductively rather than deductively valid, but it is a strong argument. Professor Szabo could have slipped up and confused this date with another of importance, but he is an expert in the matter, has studied the specific issue you have asked about, and betrayed no doubts when you asked him. In all likelihood, you and your friend will not need to be told that this is a strong argument. This is something you intuitively appreciate.

Relying on intuition is one way to judge whether an argument is valid or not. It will work in many cases, but it has limits. It is difficult to intuit whether a long extended argument is valid, especially as intuitions often prove mistaken. One might ask how the principle 'Trust your intuitions' can tell us how to judge weak arguments, for even in these cases, the argument seems intuitively valid to at least one arguer, i.e. the arguer who proposed the argument. In such a context, we need a way to choose *between* the competing intuitions this implies.

Ideally, we want an approach to argument validity that allows us to develop a systematic approach to argument. Among other things, it should tell us whether two arguments are valid or invalid for the same kinds of reasons, or for different reasons. The best approach is one that can tell us how to construct arguments that will be valid, in a deductive or inductive way.

We can achieve these goals by adopting an approach to argument validity that recognizes that arguments come in a variety of patterns. When a particular pattern can be isolated and then treated as a standard for judging and constructing arguments, we call the pattern an *argument scheme*. The argument scheme that characterizes a particular argument is identified by the kinds of premises and conclusions involved. The last two examples are illustrations of this. The valid argument that established the conclusion that Marie Currie discovered radioactivity in 1898 is an instance of a scheme called 'Argument from Authority'. Arguments employing this scheme have premises that provide the word of an authority or expert as evidence for a conclusion (we discuss this scheme in detail in Chapter 13). The previous example, about exercise question 5, was an instance of a scheme that deduces a 'particular affirmative' as a conclusion from a 'universal affirmative' in the premise. We discuss this and similar schemes in Chapter 7.

In the present context, it is worth noting that the latter scheme can be defined in a way that lets us separate the scheme and the particular instance of it conveyed in this argument. We can do so by letting X stand for 'exercise questions answered at the back of this book', letting Y stand for 'starred exercises', and letting Z stand for 'question number 5'. Once we define these letters in this way, we can represent the scheme of our example as follows:

Scheme 1
    PREMISE 1: All X are Y.
    PREMISE 2: Z is X.
    CONCLUSION: Z is Y.

This scheme is sometimes called 'universal instantiation'.

The value in identifying this scheme is that it allows us to see that the example we have given shares its structure with many other arguments that can be represented in the same way. An example is the following argument about BMW automobiles:

> All luxury cars are expensive vehicles. The BMW is a luxury car, so the BMW is an expensive vehicle.

If we let X = luxury cars, Y = expensive vehicles, and Z = the BMW, you will see that this new argument is an instance of 'scheme 1'. Our ability to represent both arguments in the same way shows that they share a common structure even though their contents are different.

Though the comparison might initially seem far-fetched, the distinction between an argument's scheme and its content might be compared to the distinction between a tube and the liquid it is built to carry. The tube is a rigid structure that functions in the same way in different circumstances: it delivers the liquid it contains from one place to another. This being said, there is a way in which the tube may perform drastically different tasks. After all, a tube may carry oil, grease, caulking, model glue, toothpaste, hand cream, or any other liquid. In a similar way, a scheme of argument is an argument pattern or structure that can hold different contents and in this way deliver a variety of conclusions.

Whenever it is possible, it is important to recognize an argument's scheme, for each scheme has a set of standards or criteria that can be used to assess the strength or weakness of particular instances of the scheme. These standards and criteria tell us what kinds of questions we should ask when evaluating an argument that is an instance of that scheme. In judging an argument from authority, for example, we ask questions about the authority's credentials, their trustworthiness, and any illegitimate bias they might possess. By asking these kinds of questions, we can distinguish valid and invalid instances of the scheme.

We can productively employ argument schemes as a guide to help us construct arguments that follow an acceptable pattern of reasoning. Some of the arguments we will discuss in later chapters do not correspond to any argument scheme. Other cases are so complex that identifying an argument scheme requires a substantial amount of interpretation. But as you learn to identify more of the patterns involved in these schemes, you will increase the range and types of arguments that you can construct.

6. Invalid Arguments

In some ways, determining the invalidity of a particular argument is more difficult than determining its validity. We will explain one method of establishing invalidity (the method of 'parallel cases') simply to acquaint you with the issues that it raises. But in the process of argument analysis we will emphasize valid arguments and the construction of strong arguments. In view of this, we will normally determine that an argument is invalid by showing that it fails to meet the basic requirements of validity.

Parallel Cases

Consider the scheme we have identified as 'scheme 1'. Suppose we teach someone—let's call him 'Dave'—this scheme, and he attempts to use it, as intended, as a guide to the construction of one kind of deductively valid argument. So far so good. The plan is a good one, for the scheme we have identified will, if it is followed accurately, always produce valid arguments. Consider it again:

>   PREMISE 1: All X are Y.
>   PREMISE 2: Z is X.
>   CONCLUSION: Z is Y.

Upon reflection, you should see that it will, in any case like this, be impossible for the conclusion to be false (i.e. for Z *not* to be Y) if its premises are true. This is true however X, Y, and Z are defined, for in each and every case, Premise 1 would imply that 'Z is X' and thus clearly confirm Premise 2.

Suppose that Dave decides to use scheme 1 to construct an argument about his friend George and George's attitude to logic. He constructs the following argument:

> All mathematicians love logic. George is not a mathematician. George does not love logic.

Like our examples of scheme 1, this is a simple argument about groups (or 'sets' or 'classes') of things. In this case, we let X = mathematicians, let Y = people who love logic, and let Z = George. We represent the argument as follows:

>   PREMISE 1: All X are Y.
>   PREMISE 2: Z is not X.
>   CONCLUSION: Z is not Y.

This summary should make it clear that Dave has not followed scheme 1 properly, but has constructed an argument that corresponds to a different scheme. The fact that all arguments that correspond to scheme 1 are deductively valid cannot, therefore, show that Dave's argument is deductively valid.

As in the case of scheme 1, many other arguments share the scheme that Dave has used, which we can call 'scheme 2'. Consider the following example:

>   P1 = All people who suffer from AIDS are infected with HIV.
>   P2 = George does not have AIDS.
>   C = George is not infected with HIV.

Such reasoning was common when it was first discovered that AIDS victims were HIV carriers. At first glance, it might seem to be a valid argument. But this impression will not last if you think about it carefully. The problem is that P1 — the claim that all people who suffer from AIDS are infected with HIV — is compatible with the claim that other people, who don't have AIDS, also carry the virus. George can, therefore, be infected with HIV even though he does not have AIDS. It follows that the conclusion of the argument can be false when the premises are true, and that the argument is invalid.

Perhaps you will intuitively see that Dave's argument, as well as our second instance of scheme 2, is deductively invalid. If someone refuses to accept that this is so, it may be useful to back this claim by constructing a similar argument that shows that arguments of this sort may have premises that are obviously acceptable and a conclusion that is not. 'You're arguing like this,' you may say, and then provide a counterexample. We call this the *method of parallel cases*. In the present instance, you may apply it by saying

> You can't argue about George that way. That's like saying, 'All Canadians speak English, the president of the United States is not Canadian, so the President of the United States does not speak English.' Don't you see? Your argument involves the same kind of reasoning!

If the point of this counter-example is not clear, we can show that it is parallel to our initial argument by comparing their components one by one as follows:

PREMISE 1
[original] All people who love logic are mathematicians.
  [new] All Canadians speak English.

PREMISE 2
[original] George is not a mathematician.
  [new] The president of the United States is not Canadian.

CONCLUSION
[original] George does not love logic.
  [new] The president of the United States does not speak English.

Because the structure of these two arguments is the same, we can judge the validity of one by considering the validity of the other.

The same method can be used in other kinds of cases. If someone concludes that a particular kind of automobile is a good car because someone said it was 'the best' on a television advertisement, we may say: 'You can't reason that way. That's like saying that we should accept the claims that someone has been paid to say.'

Parallel cases can be used to demonstrate validity as well as invalidity. In both circumstances, the aim of a parallel argument is the same: to portray the logical structure of the argument one is judging. A good appeal to parallel cases must ensure that the parallel arguments being compared are similar in all the relevant respects. Constructing parallel arguments is one good way to develop logical skills, but we will not dwell on this technique here. We want you to know about parallel cases, but our emphasis in this book is on good reasoning, so we will focus on the basic criteria for valid arguments, and the valid schemes that tend to characterize strong arguments.

MAJOR EXERCISE 6M

1. [adapted from 'Workplace Ethics 101', *Globe and Mail* (4 June 2003), p. C2] Suppose you have a co-worker and friend, Anita, who moonlights for extra money. After Anita began her other job, she began staying at the office after hours to use the computer. Now she's doing some of her 'other' work during office hours. Anita argues that she gets her work done as well as she always has, that she isn't hurting anyone, and that what the boss doesn't know won't hurt her. You feel like an accomplice and wonder if you should tell the boss.

    Another co-worker, Bob, says that you should bite your tongue. Anita's behaviour isn't hurting anyone, he says, and it is not affecting your workload or anybody else's workload, so you have no reason to complain.

    A friend, Ira, tells you that Anita is behaving in an unethical way. She is, in effect, stealing from the company, stealing time that belongs to it as well as its computer and other resources. She is demoralizing another employee (you) and probably others as well. You should take action to stop this or it is going to get worse.
    a)   Diagram and assess Anita's argument in defence of her behaviour.
    b)   Diagram Bob's argument for the conclusion that you should bite your tongue.
    c)   Diagram Ira's argument for the claim that you should take action.
    d)   Construct a short argument of your own, arguing for some course of action in this circumstance.

2. For each of the following topics, construct short arguments that adequately satisfy the two basic criteria for strong arguments. Be sure to consider and meet your obligations with respect to the burden of proof. Once you have done this, exchange your arguments with another member of your class and constructively evaluate each other's efforts. Discuss the results.
    a)* appropriate e-mail etiquette
    b)   the right to smoke in enclosed public spaces
    c)   publicly funded healthcare
    d)   the best student restaurant in town
    e)   the ethics of transplanting organs from one species to another
    f)   our obligations to ensure developing nations have minimal standards of healthcare

3. Each of the following is from the 'Letters' section of *Time* (13 Jan. 2003), and is a response to an article entitled 'Look Who's Cashing in on Indian Casinos'. For each example, discuss whether it contains an argument. Provide a fully supplemented diagram for any argument you find and assess it according to the two criteria for strong arguments.

a)* [from Donna D.] The investigative article by Donald L. Barlett and James B. Steele . . . portrayed 'evil' white men getting rich from Indian casinos while the poor Native Americans still live in poverty. As Indians, we already know this. We put up with it, but why? Because $3 million for a tribe after the backer and the state get their cuts is better than begging from Uncle Sam. Sometimes you have to make a deal with the devil to improve the situation.

b) [from S. Medwid] Some problems of Indian gaming could be solved by tying the size of a tribe's casino to the number of registered members. For example, you could allow one slot machine or gaming table per tribe member. This would remove the financial incentive for a tribe's denying membership to legitimate tribal relatives. And it would prevent such absurdities as a one-woman tribe profiting from a 349–slot-machine casino.

c) [from Tammy M.] While most of the reporting on tribal gaming was accurate, it still gave Indian casinos a bad rap. I'd like to point out the good that the casinos of Minnesota's Mille Lacs Band of Ojibwa have done. Prior to our casinos, we had nothing. There was no source of clean water, we had tar-paper shacks for housing, and there were only dirt roads. Today, 14 years after passage of the Indian Gaming Regulatory Act and the building of the Mille Lacs' casinos, we have all the amenities of a good community. We employ more than 3,500 people, most of whom had few options before our casinos existed. Despite the bad news in your report, in the Mille Lacs Band case, there is another side to the story.

d) [from Andrew C.] How about the US government's legal and moral responsibilities to Native Americans? If the US met those we Indians wouldn't have to depend on tribal casinos to meet our basic needs. Don't hate us for trying to survive.

4. For each of the following arguments from *The Sporting News* (24 July 1995), diagram the argument and assess it as a strong or weak argument. Explain your decisions.

a)* [Dave Kindred, arguing against Major League Baseball's decision to institute new rules designed to speed up the game] There is pleasure knowing that events and not an expiring clock will decide when the evening's entertainment is done.

b) [Mike Schmidt, talking about the content of his speech on his induction into baseball's hall of fame] Children and their dreams must have positive reinforcement from parents, coaches and friends. I truly believe that this reinforcement is not only important, but imperative . . . Without parental encouragement to reach their goals, it is more difficult for children to develop self-esteem and become successful.

c) [letter to 'Voice of the Fan'] So Rockets' general manager John Thomas . . . doesn't think changing the logo after back-to-back titles won't hurt their luck? Well, I subscribe to Crash Davis's theory, as stated in the movie *Bull Durham* — 'Never (mess) with a winning streak.' . . . Ask the Penguins if they're sorry they changed logos. They did after their second consecutive Stanley Cup title but haven't made it past the second round since.

d) [Steve Marantz, defending the view that major-league pitching is better than in the past] Strikeouts are a trademark of power pitching. Games are averaging 12.7 strikeouts this season. . . . Never has the game seen more strikeouts than today.

5. Diagram each of the following arguments and say whether they are valid or invalid. Explain your decision.

a)* The conclusion of the argument can be false when the premises are true, so the argument is invalid.

b) Most people find that their logical abilities improve with practice. So you should do fine if you work regularly on the exercises in this book.

c)* In order to avoid the intricacies of theories of truth, we will rely on our earlier remark that the objective of an argument is to convince an audience. If this is so, then it is sufficient for our purposes that the premises of a good argument be accepted as true by both us and our audience. So this is what we will aim for.

d)* [Greg Gutfeld, in 'Be a Jerk', *Men's Health* (1995)] A long time ago, I had this health problem . . . Almost immediately, my doctor laid my worries to rest. He told me to relax. He sat with me and we talked for a long while. . . . We bonded. We became pals. . . . Over the course of a few months, I began to look forward to my visits . . . But there was a small problem. I was still sick.

Finally, I gave up and went to see another doctor. He was not a pleasant guy, more like a scowl in a white jacket. He took one look at me and spat out a diagnosis . . .

A week later I was cured.

I learned something valuable here: When it comes to your health and other important matters, you can usually count on a jerk . . .

e) [from the same article] Jerks make great bosses. . . . Nice bosses can ruin your career by not challenging you to do better. They won't tell you when your ideas stink, your work has been slacking or your fly is down. . . . A nice-guy boss will happily nod as you explain how elevator shoes for dachshunds is the wave of the future.

6. Construct three examples of arguments that fit each of the following argument schemes. (Replace capital letters with names of groups, replace-lower case letters with sentences.) Say whether each of your examples is valid or not. Explain why.

a)* All X are Y. All Y are Z. Therefore, All X are Z.

b) If x, then y. If y, then z. So if x, then z.

c) Some X are Y. Some X are Z. So some X are Y and Z.

7. For each of the following passages, conduct a complete argument analysis. Begin by deciding whether the passage contains an argument. If it contains an argument, diagram the argument (indicating the audience and opponents) and discuss any issues that arise in view of the topics we have discussed in this and the previous chapters of this book (burden of proof, illegitimate bias, etc.). For any arguments that you find, assess whether they are strong arguments by applying the two basic criteria for strong arguments. Explain any doubts that you may have.

a) [from a letter to *Wired* (Jan. 2003), in response to an article on anti-nuclear measures that could guard against nuclear terrorism] The system you describe seems effective at stopping car-delivered nukes. But what happens when a terrorist gets access to a small plane or a helicopter? Even if the system detects gamma rays, law enforcement will have less than 10 minutes to react. While multiple systems need to be developed, the best place to stop loose nukes is 14 miles offshore.

b) [from a letter to *Wired* (Jan. 2003)] Current chipmaking processes may require dangerous substances, but those cited in 'Cleaning Up Clean Rooms' are hardly carcinogenic franken-chemicals. Hydrogen peroxide is what our mommies had us rinse our mouths with (albeit in diluted form) and pour into our ears (full strength) to help remove wax. Isoproply alcohol we swab on cuts and abrasions.

Sometimes just the word chemical frightens people, so we need to be cautious. After all, dihydrogen oxide keeps us alive, but a few years ago a survey revealed that people were terrified of it and would want the FDA to ban it from foods.

c)* Certain non-human primates have been known to exhibit grief at the loss of a family member. But if they do that, then they are capable of abstract thought and must have a sense of self. And if they have those kinds of capabilities, then they are demonstrating some of the key indicators of personhood. Therefore, certain non-human primates are moral agents, since if they exhibit indicators of personhood then they are moral agents.

d) [from an ad for the book *Judaism Beyond God*, by Rabbi Sherwin Wine, in *Humanist* (1987)] Judaism is more than a religion. It's a four thousand year old culture. It has a secular history, secular roots. Einstein and Freud are as much a part of it as Abraham and Moses. Throughout Jewish history there has been a non-establishment pragmatic Jewish humanist tradition. . . . Most Jews, without knowing it, embrace it. You too may be part of the secular Jewish tradition.

e) [Robert F. Hartley, in *Business Ethics: Violations of the Public Trust* (1993)] Lest we conclude that all takeovers involving heavy borrowing are ill-advised, reckless, and imprudent, let us look at a positive example. A&W root beer is part of America's motorized culture . . . In 1986, Lowenkron engineered a leveraged buyout for $74 million, with $35 million in junk bonds . . . By 1989, the company's sales surpassed $110 million, more than triple what they were before the buyout; profits reached $10 million, compared to a small loss in 1986.

f) [Al Bugner, on his heavyweight fight with Frank Bruno, in *Facing Ali*, by Stephen Brunt, p. 160] The fight was the most disgraceful affair ever in a boxing ring. . . . I was rabbit-punched eight or ten times in the back of the head. Even in the eighth round when I was on the ropes he was doing it. There's no doubt in my mind that the whole affair was rigged. It was a set-up.

g)* [from *Life Extension* (Dec. 2002), p. 75] Carnosine may play a role in improving and increasing exercise performance. A study examined 11 healthy men during high-intensity exercise for concentration of carnosine in their skeletal muscle.

. . . Carnosine was able to significantly buffer the acid-base balance in the skeletal muscles, which becomes unbalanced by the overproduction of hydrogen ions occurring in association with the build-up of lactic acid during high-intensity exercise.

h) [from 'No chicken in this game', *Star Weekly* (3 Oct. 1959)] Cock-fighting is one of the oldest and bloodiest sports in the world. The natural spur of the cock is replaced by one of steel, two inches long, which is tied on with leather throngs. The spurs are needle sharp and can do terrible damage. Matches are sometimes over in a few seconds or they may last for over an hour. The fight is always to the finish.

i) [adapted from a letter to the *Brantford Expositor* (9 June 2003), p. 8] I travel Highways 403 and 407 daily from Brantford to Mississauga. I am constantly bombarded by the media virtually every half hour about the SARS problem in Toronto.

Quite frankly, I find the media hype is fuel to the fire with regard to the devastating effect of SARS on the economy.

Not to minimize the tragedy, but as one analyst put it, influenza claims more casualties than SARS.

I am not impressed by the logic.

j) [from an article in the *Wall Street Journal*, 'Poultry in Motion', on automated chicken catching machines (4 June 2003)] Some of the biggest fans are animal rights groups, including People for the Ethical Treatment of Animals. The machines are far more gentle on the birds than human handlers are . . . Chickens hate being caught by human beings because catchers grab them by the feet and carry several birds upside down in each hand. 'Being held upside down freaks out the birds,' says Michael P. Lacy of the University of Georgia's poultry-science department. . . .

Human catchers are expected to snag as many as 1,000 birds an hour. As the men tire during eight-hour shifts, they accidentally slam birds against the cages, breaking wings and legs. Up to 25 per cent of broilers on some farms are hurt in the process. By contrast, a recent study in the British scientific journal Animal Welfare found that a mechanical catcher in use in Germany reduces some injuries by as much as 50 per cent.

That's good news for the birds, and also for the industry. Bruising disqualifies a chicken from the supermarket meat counter, relegating it to less profitable uses such as livestock feed.

k)* [from a personal e-mail on 'why to stop drinking Coke'] In many states the highway patrol carries two gallons of Coke in the trunk to remove blood from the highway after a car accident. You can put a T-bone steak in a bowl of coke and it will be gone in two days. The active ingredient in Coke is phosphoric acid. It's pH is 2.8. It will dissolve a nail in about 4 days.

l)* [from the *Kitchener-Waterloo Record* (4 June 2003), p. A12] Jonathan Gowing's assertion in his June 1 Insight page article that marijuana today is 'up to 700 times more potent' than the stuff my parents smoked is absolutely ridiculous. THC (the chemical responsible for marijuana's psychoactivity) levels in marijuana today are generally higher due to better growing methods. In 1997, the average concentration of THC ... examined by the University of Mississippi's Marijuana Potency Monitoring Project was just under 5 per cent, as opposed to the average concentration of 2–3 per cent found during the 1970s.

Being generous, you could say that marijuana is on average twice as potent as it was during the 1970s. But 700 times more potent? That would mean marijuana today is on average 1,400 per cent THC. That's absolutely absurd.

Gowing also overlooks the fact that higher potency is better for my health: a more potent product means I have to smoke less to get high. . . .

m) [adapted from an article on the legal case against Martha Stewart, in *The Financial Post* (4 June 2003), p. 15] The Martha Stewart case is a crock. She is the wrong target of an unnecessary investigation. The case against Ms Stewart for insider trading being weak, prosecutors are apparently saving face by trying to nab her for not helping them indict her. Sure, she handled this badly. She could, by all accounts, have been much more direct and forthcoming. And it is clear that her story changed—and grew—in the telling. But that doesn't mean she has to help crusading investigators trying to earn departmental points for taking down a domestic biggie.

n) [from an editorial on how to deal with the proliferation of nuclear weapons, in the *Wall Street Journal* (4 June 2003), p. A16] For our part, we don't have much faith in UN inspections, which tend to see only those things the host nation wants to be seen. North Korea hid its clandestine uranium program for years, even as IAEA inspectors 'safeguarded' its plutonium program. Then Pyongyang simply shut off even those TV cameras and booted the inspectors out of the country.

8. Go to your local newspaper or your favourite magazines and find five examples of simple arguments (if you find extended arguments, use the sub-arguments they contain as your examples). Diagram the arguments and assess them as strong or weak.

SYLLOGISMS I:

CLASSIFYING

ARGUMENTS

Chapter 6 distinguished between the acceptability of an argument's premises and its validity. This chapter continues our discussion of deductive validity. Some deductive arguments make claims about different categories, others about the relationships that exist between propositions. The present and next chapters discuss the first kind of deductive validity and the corresponding kind of argument: the categorical syllogism. The focus is on the reasoning involved in such schemes, not the acceptability of the premises. Here, we present

- ♦ categorical statements;
- ♦ immediate inferences;
- ♦ categorical arguments; and
- ♦ tests for validity using Venn diagrams.

This chapter discusses categorical reasoning, which encompasses deductive arguments about classes. We will make no attempt to address such reasoning in the complex ways that characterize contemporary formal logic. That is a topic for a different kind of logic text. Our goal is more modest but also more pertinent to an understanding of ordinary-language reasoning.

To help you understand and evaluate the arguments about classes that occur within such reasoning, we will introduce you to categorical syllogisms, to the argument schemes that characterize them, and to some useful ways in which you can diagram and judge (deductive) validity in such arguments.

Consider the following statements:

All astronomers are highly educated. All highly educated people are assets to society.

If someone sees these two statements, they are likely to bring them together and draw the conclusion that 'All astronomers are assets to society.' Many advertisers depend on this kind of reasoning when planning their campaigns. An advertisement is more effective if potential customers can be expected to see the hidden conclusion and draw it out for themselves.

Consider the following slogan:

Domino's Pizza gets there sooner, and anything that gets there sooner has to be better.

This can be recast as:

All Domino's Pizzas are things that get there sooner.
All things that get there sooner have to be better.

From these two statements the advertiser expects us to draw the hidden conclusion 'All Domino's Pizzas are things that have to be better.' The amounts of money invested in such advertising demonstrates the extent to which advertisers trust us to draw such conclusions. In the process, they demonstrate their trust in the deductive process.

You may have noticed that each of our examples includes, when the hidden components are recognized, three statements, and each statement expresses a relationship between two categories or classes of things. 'Domino's Pizzas' constitute a class of things, as do 'things that get there sooner'. All *categorical syllogisms* express relationships between three classes of things. The statements in such arguments are called *categorical statements*. In the next section we will examine the various types of categorical statements that can make up syllogisms. Later, we will explore the syllogism itself and ways it can be tested for validity. In this chapter we will introduce a simple method for testing deductive validity by means of Venn diagrams. In the next chapter we provide a more technical, but more reliable, method, which employs schematization and rules.

1. Categorical Statements

Categorical statements are subject–predicate statements expressing relationships between classes of things. In the statement 'All crows are black,' 'crows' is the subject and blackness is the predicate that is applied to the subject. Categorical statements always include a *subject class* (crows) and a *predicate class* (black things). The subjects and predicates are always expressed as classes of things. This is particularly important to remember about the predicate class, because it may not be expressed in a way that makes this obvious. In the statement 'Domino's Pizza gets there sooner,' 'Domino's Pizzas' is the subject class. Since 'gets there sooner' cannot be described as a class, we express the predicate class as '*things* that get there sooner'.

Pure Forms

There are four distinct types of categorical statement. We will consider the 'pure form' of each and then consider some of their common variations in ordinary language. In presenting the pure forms, we will use the letter 'S' to represent the subject class of any categorical statement and the letter 'P' to represent the predicate class. We can then formulate the four types of categorical statement as follows:

1. **All S are P.** We call this a *universal affirmative* statement, or **UA**, since it affirms something about all members of S. In a **UA** statement, the *entire* membership of the subject class is *included within* the predicate class. 'All police officers are public servants' is a **UA** statement.
2. **No S are P.** We call this a *universal negative* statement, or **UN**, since it denies something about all members of S. In a **UN** statement, the *entire* membership of the subject class is *excluded from* the predicate class. 'No children are senators' is a **UN** statement.
3. **Some S are P.** We call this a *particular affirmative* statement, or **PA**, since it affirms something about only a portion of the membership of S. In a **PA** statement, at least one member of the subject class is *included within* the predicate class. 'Some animals are carnivores' is a **PA** statement.
4. **Some S are not P.** We call this a *particular negative* statement, or **PN**, since it denies something about only a portion of the membership of S. In a **PN** statement, at least one member of the subject class is *excluded from* the predicate class. 'Some people are not actors' is a **PN** statement.

These are the four 'pure forms' of categorical statements. All statements expressing class relationships are logically equivalent to one or another of these forms. Hereafter we shall refer to the four forms by the letters **UA**, **UN**, **PA** and **PN**. When interpreting these forms there are three points that you should keep in mind. First, we must be careful to distinguish between the statement that *excludes* some S from the class of P and the statement that *includes* some S within the class of 'non-P'. Thus, 'Some S are not P' is read as a **PN** statement, while 'Some S are non-P' is read as a **PA** statement. 'Some penguins are not monogamous' is read as a **PN** statement, while 'Some penguins are non-monogamous' is read as a **PA** statement.

Second, persons, things, and places designated by proper names, such as the President, Apollo 11, and Belgium, as well as defined groups such as 'these cows' or 'the players on the field at the moment' or 'that bus' (said while pointing to a bus), should all be interpreted as referring to an entire class. Statements in which they are subjects will, therefore, be expressed as universal statements. If you think about it, this makes sense, for proper names are names of classes with only one member, and statements with limited phrases denoting the subject term are intended to be universal. Thus 'Belgium is a member of the European Economic Union' is a **UA** statement, and 'No players on the field at the moment are Native Americans' is a **UN** statement.

Finally, note that a **UN** statement is *not* properly expressed as 'All S are not P', because such a statement is ambiguous. It could mean that '*all* S are *excluded* from the class of P,' in which case no S are P. On the other hand, it could mean that it is *not* the case that *all* S are *included* in the class of P, in which case some S are not P. Consider the statement 'All TV evangelists are not frauds.' Does the speaker mean that *all* TV evangelists are excluded from the class of frauds? Or does the speaker exclude only some TV evangelists from the class of frauds? The first alternative would be expressed as the **UN** statement 'No TV evangelists are frauds.' The second interpretation is the **PN** statement 'Some TV evangelists are not frauds'.

Since you should be charitable and not attribute to a writer a stronger claim than may have been intended, you should interpret statements of the 'All S are not P' variety as **PN** statements unless you know that the classes of things denoted by S and P are logically exclusive. 'All triangles are not four-sided figures' is an instance of this exception. It must be interpreted as a **UN** statement because we know that no triangle can, by definition, be a four-sided figure.

Common Variations

We have already seen some of the variations that express categorical relationships. Here are some (but only some) further variations of the pure forms:

UA (Universal Affirmative)

All astronauts are intelligent people.

- Astronauts are intelligent.
- Every astronaut is an intelligent person.
- Anyone who is an astronaut must be intelligent.
- None but intelligent people are astronauts.
- Only intelligent people are astronauts.
- No astronauts are unintelligent people.

UN (Universal Negative)

No astronauts are cowards.

- No one who is an astronaut can be a coward.
- No cowards are astronauts.
- No one who is a coward can be an astronaut.
- All astronauts are non-cowards.
- All cowards are non-astronauts.
- If X is an astronaut, X is not a coward.

PA (Particular Affirmative)

Some women are priests.

- At least one woman is a priest.
- Most women are priests.
- A few women are priests.
- There are some women who are priests.
- Several women are priests.
- Some women are not non-priests.

PN (Particular Negative)

Some women are not priests.

- Many women are not priests.
- Most women are not priests.
- Few women are priests.
- All women are not priests.
- Not all women are priests.
- Some women are non-priests.

These variations do not exhaust all the possibilities. In dealing with particular propositions, it is also important to recognize that though we read 'many', 'few', and 'most' as meaning 'some', the reverse is not the case. If you have a proposition referring to 'some X', you cannot assume that it means 'many' or 'most' unless the context indicates as much. In syllogistic reasoning, 'one', 'few', 'many', and 'most' are treated as equivalent to 'some'. A more powerful logic might distinguish between these 'quantifiers', but that would require a more sophisticated treatment of categories than the one that we are introducing here.

As you read through the next sections of this chapter, you will see how some of the more peculiar variations are equivalent to the pure forms. Where you must decide which pure form you have, ask yourself what relationship between classes is intended. Is the intent of the statement to include or exclude? Is it referring to the entire subject class or only a portion of it? Rather than trying to decide what form a statement is, it is often helpful to eliminate the forms that it is not until you arrive at the form that it must be.

One error that is so common that it should be noted here involves statements that begin with 'Only'. There is a temptation to render 'Only intelligent people are astronauts' as 'All intelligent people are astronauts.' This is wrong. 'Only' indicates the predicate class. While the statement involved is a **UA** statement, the effect of the 'only' is to reverse the classes, giving us 'All astronauts are intelligent people.' To see that this must be so, consider that *only* students at your institution go to the lectures you go to (there are *similar* lectures elsewhere, but not the *same* lectures with the same professor, etc.); however, it would be quite wrong to say that *all* students at your institution are going to the lectures you go to. What can be said is that all students attending these lectures are students at your institution.

Until you become practised at recognizing pure forms, you might want to employ the following three-step process for arriving at them. Take the statement 'Busy people are never at home when you want them.'

Step 1: Determine the classes involved.

[Busy people] are never [at home when you want them = people who are at home when you want them].

Step 2: Determine whether the statement is affirming (including) or negating (excluding).

Busy people are *never* = excluded from people who are at home when you want them.

Step 3: Determine whether the statement is universal or particular.

No Busy people are People who are at home when you want them. **UN**

Exercise 7A

Classify the following statements as **UA**, **UN**, **PA**, or **PN**, and express each in its 'pure form'. Be sure to express both the subject and predicate terms as classes with members.

> **Example**: A few students own Volvos.
> Step 1: A few [students] [own Volvos = Volvo owners].
> Step 2: A few students *are* Volvo owners.
> Step 3: **Some** students are Volvo owners. **PA**

a)* Most dentists have a six-digit income.

b)* Dinosaurs are extinct.

c)* Most people are not prepared to pay higher taxes.

d) No one who has paid attention should be confused.

e) None of my sons is greedy.

f) Laws are made to be broken.

g)* Only the lonely know the way I feel tonight.

h) A few students in this class wish they weren't.

i) There are some extremely wealthy people who pay no income tax.

j) Many wealthy people do not pay income tax.

k) People who live in glass houses shouldn't throw stones.

l) Stephen is far from being fastidious.

m)* New York is in New York.

n)* None but the courageous will survive.

o) Beauty is in the eye of the beholder.

p) Many children of planned pregnancies turn out to be battered children.

q) The vast majority of murders are crimes of passion.

r) All that glitters is not gold.

s) Most labour leaders are not supporters of the North American Free Trade Agreement (NAFTA).

t) Those who support NAFTA see it as a recipe for economic prosperity.

u)* Under no circumstances should the courts deal leniently with people who drive vehicles while inebriated.

v) Several renowned physicists are religious mystics.

w)* Those cars parked on the street whose permits have expired will be towed away.

x)   Lotteries breed avarice.

y)   Whatever will be will be.

z)   Some logicians are not mathematicians.

2. IMMEDIATE INFERENCES

In learning to understand the pure forms, it helps to appreciate the basic relationships between them. You will have to rely on such an understanding when preparing some syllogisms for testing. The relationships between the four forms are usually called immediate inferences. This does not mean that they are immediately obvious to every-one, but that no 'mediate' (i.e. middle, or in-between) term is involved.

In syllogistic logic, the following is the traditional square of opposition:

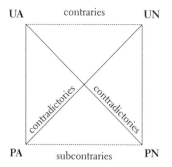

This square allows us to ascertain quickly what must be true when various kinds of categorical statements are accepted as true or false.

From the square, we can see that the **UA** and **UN** statements are 'contraries'. This means that they cannot both be true, but can both be false, and would both be false whenever **PA** and **PN** are both true. The **PA** and **PN** statements are, on the other hand, 'subcontraries', and *cannot* both be false, though they are both true whenever the corresponding **UA** and **UN** statements are both false. In addition, the **UA** statement implies the corresponding **PA** statement, and a **UN** statement implies the corresponding **PN** statement. In contrast, one cannot infer either the **UA** from the **PA** nor the **UN** from the **PN**.

In identifying these and other relationships between different kinds of categorical statements, the square of opposition helps define a variety of deductively valid argument schemes. In saying that a **UA** statement implies a **PA** statement we are, for example, saying that the following argument scheme is deductively valid (i.e. that the conclusion must be true if the premise is true):

UA, therefore **PA**

More generally, we might define this scheme as:

All S are P. Therefore, some S are P.

This scheme indicates that anyone who accepts the premise 'All S are P' must accept the conclusion 'Some S are P'. An instance of this scheme is the following argument:

> All the readers of this page are learning syllogistic logic.
> Therefore, some readers of this page are learning syllogistic logic.

If you substitute other classes for 'S' and 'P' in our definition of the argument scheme, you will see that this scheme defines an indefinite number of deductively valid categorical arguments. We will not formally define all the argument schemes implied by the traditional square of opposition, but you should be able to recognize a variety of schemes that it legitimates.

Contradiction

Another immediate inference you can expect to apply to categorical syllogisms is that of *contradiction*.

Contradiction tells you what statement must be true if a given statement is false, and what statement must be false if a given statement is true. Two statements are 'contradictories' if they cannot both be true and cannot both be false, but one of them must be true and the other false.

You might initially suppose that the contradictory of a **UA** statement is a **UN** statement, but we have already seen that they are contraries rather than contradictories because it is possible for them both to be false. If you examine the square of opposition, you will see that a relationship of contradiction exists not between **UA** and **UN** but between **UA** and **PN**, and **UN** and **PA**.

When it is true that 'All astronauts are intelligent,' it must be false that 'Some astronauts are not intelligent.' The corresponding argument scheme could be defined as:

> **UA**, therefore Not **PN**

Or, more generally, as:

> All S are P. Therefore it is not true that some S are not P.

Likewise, contradiction tells us that if we accept that 'Some astronauts are not intelligent', then we must accept that 'All astronauts are intelligent' is false. The same relationship holds between **UN** and **PA** statements. When we accept it as true that 'No astronauts are cowards,' then we must accept that it is false that 'Some astronauts are cowards.' And if we accept that 'Some astronauts are cowards,' then we must accept that 'No astronauts are cowards' is false.

Obversion

A further immediate inference is called *obversion*. Since a syllogism has three statements expressing relationships between only three classes of things or terms, then the existence of more than three terms means that we do not have a syllogism that can be tested. But sometimes what looks like more than three terms may be reducible to three because the additional terms are alternatives for one or more of the other terms. Obversion is the tool we use to make such reductions. This works when the additional terms are complementaries of one or more of the other terms. The class of 'dogs' has as its complementary class 'non-dogs'. If 'dogs' is the subject class 'S', then the complementary class is written as 'non-S'. Everything in the world can be divided into its class and complementary class: 'presidents' and 'non-presidents', 'things that are amusing' and 'things that are non-amusing', etc. Because we often speak loosely in ordinary language, we may be prepared to take liberties and translate, for example, 'dull people' and 'interesting people' as complementary classes (though, strictly speaking, the complementary class of 'dull people' is 'non-dull people').

We have already seen that 'No astronauts are non-intelligent' is a common variation of 'All astronauts are intelligent.' This is because each is the obverse of the other. They mean the same thing; when we obvert a statement we do not change its meaning. To obvert, you need to

(1) Change the statement from negative to affirmative or from affirmative to negative. That is, if it is a **UA**, make it a **UN**, and vice versa; and if it is a **PA** make it a **PN**, and vice versa.
(2) Negate the predicate term.

For each of the pure forms, obversion works as follows:

	Given		*Obverse*
UA	All S are P	UN	No S are non-P
UN	No S are P	UA	All S are non-P
PA	Some S are P	PN	Some S are not non-P
PN	Some S are not P	PA	Some S are non-P

Conversion

Conversion allows you to switch the position of the S and P terms. In fact, that is how you convert: exchange the position of the S and P.

But conversion is possible only with **UN** and **PA** statements. The converses of **UA** and **PN** statements are not logically equivalent. The **UN** statement converts easily because both classes are being excluded from *each other*. Conversion in this case can be expressed as the argument scheme:

No S are P. Therefore no P are S.

If we accept 'No astronauts are cowards,' it follows that we must also accept that 'No cowards are astronauts.' Likewise, if we accept that 'Some women are priests,' then the converse, 'Some priests are women,' is something we must also accept. To fully appreciate why **UN** and **PA** statements covert so easily, you should read the section on distribution in the next chapter.

The **UA** statement does not convert in this way. While 'All astronauts are intelligent' may be the case, we would not want to say 'All intelligent people are astronauts.' However, the reversal of the terms is possible in a *limited* sense. That is, if we accept that 'All astronauts are intelligent,' we must accept that 'Some intelligent people are astronauts.' So the converse of a **UA** statement is a **PA** statement.

No such qualification is possible with **PN** statements. While 'Some animals are not dogs' is true, we cannot accept the converse, 'Some dogs are not animals.' The converse of the **PN** statement is not its logical equivalent. In other words, it does not convert.

Conversion works as follows:

	Given		Converse
UA	All S are P	**PA**	Some P are S (by limitation)
UN	No S are P	**UN**	No P are S
PA	Some S are P	**PA**	Some P are S
PN	Some S are not P	X	(i.e. no conversion is possible)

Contraposition

A final immediate inference is contraposition. With conversion, the original and the modified statements are logically equivalent in the cases of **UN** and **PA** statements. With contraposition, it is with the **UA** and **PN** statements that this is the case. This is so because contraposition is the result of obverting, then converting, and then obverting once again.

The result of these operations for each of the four forms can be shown as follows:

Given	Obverse	Converse of Obverse	Obverse of Converted Obverse (Contrapositive)
UA All S are P	**UN** No S are non-P	**UN** No non-P are S	**UA** All non-P are non-S
UN No S are P	**UA** All S are non-P	**PA** Some non-P are S	**PN** Some non-P are not non-S
PA Some S are P	**PN** Some S are not non-P	—	—
PN Some S are not P	**PA** Some S are non-P	**PA** Some non-P are S	**PN** Some non-P are not non-S

The **PA** cannot be contraposed because its obverse, a **PN** statement, cannot be converted. The **UN** statement is subject to contraposition with limitation, since its obverse is a **UA** statement that, upon conversion, becomes a **PA**. While contrapositives strike many people as cumbersome, reflection will show you that 'All non-intelligent people are non-astronauts' is simply an alternative, if unusual, way of saying that 'All astronauts are intelligent.'

EXERCISE 7B

1. Define all the argument schemes that are justified by conversion. For each of the schemes defined give three sample arguments that are instances of each scheme. (Show how the sample arguments are instances of the scheme by indicating the substitutions for S and P required in each case.) For three of the sample arguments you give, show how they could be expressed in a manner that is not a direct use of the pure forms of categorical statements.

2. Provide at least two immediate inferences for each of the following:

> EXAMPLE: Some farmers are subsidized.
> (1) Some subsidized people are farmers.
> (2) It is false that No farmers are subsidized people.

a)* Only ticket holders will be admitted.
b)* Many New Yorkers vacation in Florida.
c) No non-famous people are listed in *Who's Who*.
d) Some areas of North America are not populated.
e) It is not true that all hard workers are successful people.
f) Not all play areas are supervised.
g)* Many donors to the club are non-users.
h) No non-citizens are refused legal assistance.
i) The Meadowlake circus is unpopular with animal lovers.
j) It is false to say that some illegal acts are moral.
k) If you haven't paid your fees, you cannot attend class.

3. CATEGORICAL SYLLOGISMS

A categorical syllogism consists of three and only three categorical statements that relate three (and only three) classes of things. More precisely, a categorical syllogism is an argument consisting of three categorical statements related in such a way that two of them, having one class-term in common, entail a third categorical statement relating the other two class-terms.

This may seem a convoluted definition, but it is not difficult to understand what it means in practice. Consider one of our earlier syllogisms:

> All astronomers are highly educated. Highly educated people are assets to society. Therefore: All astronomers are assets to society

Each statement is a **UA** statement. The first two are the premises of the argument, the last one is the conclusion. These three statements relate three classes of things, namely: 'astronomers', 'highly educated people', and 'assets to society'. Each of these classes appears twice in the syllogism. Each of the classes in the conclusion ('astronomers', 'assets to society') appears in a different premise. The remaining class ('highly educated people') appears once in each premise. Depending upon the particular positions the classes occupy in a syllogism, the syllogism will be deductively valid or invalid.

Up to this point we have used S and P to represent the subject and predicate terms for categorical statements. Now we will restrict the use of S and P to the terms that function as the subject and predicate of the conclusion of the syllogism, and we will introduce a third symbol, M, to represent the third class:

> S = subject of the conclusion
> P = predicate of the conclusion
> M = class common to both premises, or 'middle' term

Consistent with this convention, we would identify S, P, and M in the above syllogism as follows:

> S = astronomers
> P = assets to society
> M = highly educated people

This identification of the meanings of S, P, and M we call the *legend*. Note again that each symbol represents a *class* of things and is always expressed in those terms.

The syllogism with which we are working can now be shown to have the following 'symbolic scheme', where the line beneath the second premise separates the premises from the conclusion:

> All S are M   S UA M
> <u>All M are P</u>   or   <u>M UA P</u>
> All S are P   S UA P

Preparing Syllogisms for Testing

The question whether a syllogism is *deductively valid* is a question about its *structure*. We are interested in whether the conclusion follows necessarily from the premises. At this stage we will not worry whether the premises are acceptable (and will, in this way, ignore the first criterion for strong arguments). This in part explains why you may see quite bizarre examples offered as instances of deductively valid syllogisms. The following is a case in point:

> All dogs are highly educated creatures. All highly educated creatures enjoy synchronized swimming. Therefore all dogs enjoy synchronized swimming.

These statements are ridiculous, but as they are represented here, they constitute a deductively valid syllogism. Indeed, this argument has exactly the same *scheme* as the previous argument about 'astronomers', 'assets to society', and 'highly educated people'. That is, it is also of the form

> All S are M
> <u>All M are P</u>
> All S are P

We have already seen that the conclusion of a deductively valid argument follows necessarily from the premises. We would be committed to a contradictory position if we accepted the premises but rejected the conclusion. But deductive validity must not be confused with premise acceptability. They are quite separate concepts. In this and the next chapter, our concern is the difference between syllogistic arguments that are deductively valid and those that are invalid. In such a context, you must try not to be distracted by questions about the acceptability of an argument's premises. Translating the syllogisms into their 'symbolic schema' will help us to concentrate solely on validity.

In preparing to test syllogisms for deductive validity, we need to (1) identify the types of categorical statements included in the syllogism; (2) define S, P, and M in a legend; and then (3) diagram the argument in the manner we have already noted. It is important to begin with the conclusion of the argument, because S and P can be identified by assigning them to the terms of the conclusion. The middle term, M, can *never* appear in the conclusion.

Consider an example:

> The use of physical discipline towards children is known to encourage aggressive tendencies. Aggressive behaviour results in difficulty for the child later in life. Therefore, physical discipline is not good for children. (*Child Development*, 2nd edition, 1991)

As you gain more experience working with syllogisms, you will be increasingly able to recognize examples like this as arguments that relate classes of things. Since we are dealing with ordinary language, we need to make decisions about different phrases and terms that can be interpreted as equivalent. One might compare these decisions to the kinds of decisions we make in diagramming many ordinary arguments that are expressed unclearly. In this particular argument, the conclusion is easily identified by the indicator 'therefore'. It is followed by the statement 'physical discipline is not good for children.'

This tells us that the conclusion relates two classes of things: 'acts of physical discipline' and 'things that are good for children'. We can see that it does so by *excluding* the classes from each other. So the conclusion is either a **UN** or a **PN** statement. Since there is no qualifier to suggest that only some acts of physical discipline are intended, we interpret it as a **UN**. In its categorical form the conclusion reads: 'No acts of physical discipline are things that are good for children.' Once we recognize this, we can assign S and P to the subject and predicate of this conclusion:

    S = acts of physical discipline
    P = things that are good for children

The middle term, M, is the term that both premises have in common. To recognize it we need to determine the premises and cast them in their categorical form. The first of the two remaining statements clearly includes the S term. It tells us that acts of physical discipline (towards children) are things that encourage aggressive tendencies. 'Things that encourage aggressive tendencies' is, then, a candidate for our M class. To decide on this, we would have to interpret the remaining sentence ('Aggressive behaviour results in difficulty for the child later in life') as one that relates the potential M class with P. Assuming that experiencing difficulty in later life is not good for children, we can interpret the ordinary-language statement in the argument as 'No things that encourage aggressive tendencies are things that are good for children.'

This confirms our hypothesis that:

> M = things that encourage aggressive behaviour

Now that we have a full legend and understand the terms of the argument, we can rewrite it in categorical form as:

> All acts of physical discipline are things that encourage aggressive behaviour. No things that encourage aggressive behaviour are things that are good for children. Therefore, no acts of physical discipline are things that are good for children.
>
> All S are M
> No M are P
> No S are P

If we had been unsure how to phrase the second premise, we could have derived it as the hidden premise required to get from the first premise to the conclusion. Having cast the argument in its categorical form, you can use the legend to check that it now has the same meaning as the original formulation.

Any syllogism can be translated into categorical form following this procedure. The critical step is the initial one of identifying the conclusion and thereby defining S and P.

Exercise 7C

Prepare the following syllogisms for testing, identifying **S**, **P**, and **M**.

> **Example:** All members of the United Nations are expected to meet their obligations with respect to peacekeeping. Since the United States is a member of the United Nations, it must therefore meet its peacekeeping obligation.
>
> All members of the United Nations are nations expected to meet their peacekeeping obligations. The United States is a member of the United Nations. Therefore: The United States is a nation expected to meet its peace keeping obligations.
>
> S = the United States
> P = nations expected to meet their peace keeping obligations
> M = members of the United Nations
> All M are P
> All S are M
> All S are P

a) Nobody with a history of heart disease should take up jogging, because jogging is a strenuous form of exercise, and no one with a history of heart disease should engage in strenuous forms of exercise.

b)   Some professional clowns have personality disorders and some people with personality disorders are deeply depressed. So some professional clowns are deeply depressed.

c)* For a vegetable to be considered fresh, it must have been harvested within the last 48 hours. These beans were picked just last night. So they should certainly be considered fresh.

d)   Only healthy people can join the army, and so people suffering from debilitating illnesses cannot join the army, since they are not healthy.

e)   Some polls have been skewed by unrepresentative samples. But any poll like that cannot be trusted. So some polls are untrustworthy.

f)   Get-rich-quick schemes that exploit the gullible are unpopular. But some of them actually work. So, some things that actually work are not popular.

4. VENN DIAGRAMS

We now turn our attention to tests for determining deductive validity or invalidity. Remember that if the syllogism is a deductively valid one, the truth of the premises will guarantee the truth of the conclusion. Consider again our earlier syllogism:

All astronomers are highly educated people. All highly educated people are assets to society. Therefore all astronomers are assets to society.

We can see that if every member of the class of astronomers belongs to the class of highly educated people (Premise 1), and every member of the class of highly educated people belongs to the class of assets to society (Premise 2), then it *must* be the case that every member of the class of astronomers belongs to the class of assets to society, which is what the conclusion tells us. In short, we can see that this is a deductively valid syllogism. Accepting the premises and denying the conclusion will put us in a contradictory position.

To recognize validity is easy with simple arguments, but there are some arguments that seem deductively valid when they are invalid. Consider the next example:

All people who oppose the trade bill are people with conservative values. Smith has conservative values. Therefore Smith opposes the trade bill.

This argument has a superficial appeal to it; it seems right (even more so if we substitute for Smith the name of a well-known conservative). But, as we will see when we test the argument, the conclusion is not guaranteed by the premises and could be rejected by someone who accepted the premises. When it comes to validity and invalidity, we want more than just ways to recognize it: we want to have ways to explain it, ways to make it clear to an audience (which might simply be ourselves).

A more exacting method of testing syllogisms visually portrays the structure of categorical statements. This method is called Venn diagramming, named after the British logician John Venn. Most of the syllogisms you encounter can be tested using this method.

Venn diagrams use circles to depict the relationships between the classes of things represented by S, P, and M. Each circle represents one of these classes. The intersecting, or overlapping, parts of the circles represent the individuals the classes have in common. We shade those portions of circles that our statements tell us are 'empty'. If our statement tells us that 'no sheep are investment bankers', then the overlapping part of two circles, representing 'sheep' and 'investment bankers', is considered empty and is therefore shaded. When we are told that some members of a class either are or are not members of another class, we use **X** to represent this on the diagram. If our statement is 'some sheep are investment bankers', we place an **X** in the overlapping part of our two circles. These points can be illustrated by using two circles to depict each of the four pure forms of categorical statement.

UA

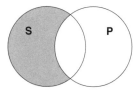

All S are P, so we shade all the circle representing S that is not included in P. This indicates that any portion of S outside of P is 'empty', i.e. that there is nothing in the class of S that is not also a part of the class of P. This is what the **UA** statement tells us.

UN

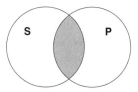

No S are P, so we shade the intersection between the circles representing S and P to show that this area is empty because there is nothing that is both an S and a P.

PA

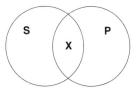

Some S are P, so we put an **X** in the intersection between the circles representing S and P to show that at least one member of the class of S is also P.

PN

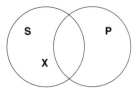

Some S are not P, so we put an **X** in the area of the circle representing S that does not intersect the circle representing P to show that at least one member of S is not P.

A Venn diagram has three circles representing the three classes involved in the syllogism.

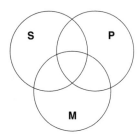

The statements of the syllogism tell us how the classes stand in relation to each other, and as we represent these statements on the three-circle diagram we can look to see whether the premises guarantee the conclusion. In the case of a deductively valid syllogism, once the premises have been represented on the diagram, the conclusion should be *already there*. This is because the conclusion of a deductively valid argument is so strongly implied by the premises that it must, in effect, be accepted as soon as one accepts these premises. This is what a Venn diagram illustrating a deductively valid argument shows. The test for deductive validity using Venn diagrams is expressed as follows: if, after representing the premises, the conclusion is already represented on the diagram, then the argument is *deductively valid*; if the conclusion is not already represented, the argument is *deductively invalid*.

We will begin illustrating this by confirming our judgment of an earlier argument:

> All astronomers are highly educated people. All highly educated people are assets to society. Therefore all astronomers are assets to society.

This argument has the *legend*:   and the *scheme*:

S = astronomers	All S are M
P = assets to society	All M are P
M = highly educated people	All S are P

Each is a **UA** statement, so this is a relatively straightforward example.

P1 is represented
All S are M

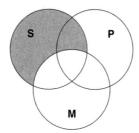

P2 is represented
All M are P

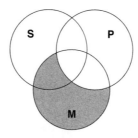

C is represented
All S are P

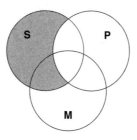

Next, we put P1 and P2 together on a Venn diagram:

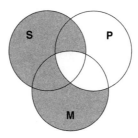

Now, as our test, we look to see whether the conclusion, All S are P, is also represented on this diagram. And it is. The area of S that is outside of P is completely shaded, indicating that it is empty and that, indeed, All S are P. It does not matter that other parts of the diagram are shaded; this shows that there was more information in the premises than in the conclusion. What is important is that the conclusion is contained within the premises, and so, if the premises are correct, the conclusion must also be true. So this syllogism is a *deductively valid* argument. It has a deductively valid scheme or structure, and *any* syllogism of the same scheme will also be deductively valid.

Now we will consider the second example, which is another relatively simple syllogism:

> All people who oppose the trade bill are people with conservative values. Smith has conservative values. Smith opposes the trade bill.

This is another argument with all **UA** statements, but its scheme is different from the previous syllogism.

Legend	*Scheme*
S = Smith	All P are M
P = people who oppose trade bill	<u>All S are M</u>
M = people with conservative values	All S are P

P1
All P are M

P2
All S are M

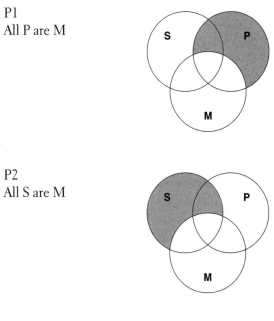

C
All S are P

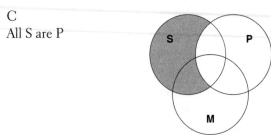

We put P1 and P2 together on a Venn diagram:

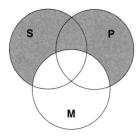

This time we find the conclusion, All S are P, is not already represented on the diagram. The area where S and M intersect, which is outside of P, should be shaded, but it is not. This means that one can accept the premises and not accept the conclusion and, therefore, the conclusion does not follow necessarily from the premises. It follows that the syllogism is *deductively invalid.*

Having shown simple examples of a deductively valid and a deductively invalid syllogism, we can turn to more complex examples. The following is an advertisement from *Vogue* (Oct. 1992):

> No ordinary beauty fluid can deliver the continuous moisture every skin needs to counteract the drying effects of the environment. New Hydra-Renewal Continuous Moisturizing Cream can.

The advertisement makes two claims. The first claim excludes the class of ordinary beauty fluids from the class of beauty fluids that can deliver the continuous moisture every skin needs to counteract the drying effects of the environment. It is a **UN** statement. The second claim includes New Hydra-Renewal Continuous Moisturizing Cream within that second class. It is a **UA** statement. As noted earlier, advertisers expect audiences to draw conclusions from statements that are given. In this case, the obvious hidden conclusion is a **UN** statement that excludes New Hydra-Renewal Continuous Moisturizing Cream from the class of ordinary beauty fluids.

Our procedure requires us to begin with the conclusion, and in this case the conclusion is hidden. But there can be no doubt that the conclusion uncovered here is intended (it is a belief held by the writers). Testing this syllogism will tell us whether the writers have produced their copy wisely.

Legend	*Scheme*
S = new Hydra-Renewal Continuous Moisturizing Cream	No P are M
P = ordinary beauty fluids	All S are M
M = beauty fluids that can deliver the continuous moisture every skin needs to counteract the drying effects of the environment	No S are P

P1
No P are M

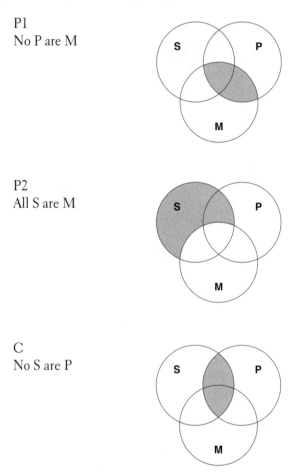

P2
All S are M

C
No S are P

We put P1 and P2 together in a Venn diagram.

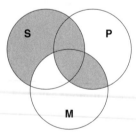

If the syllogism is deductively valid, the conclusion ('No S are P') will already be on the diagram. And it is: the advertisers have correctly identified the conclusion an audience will deduce. The entire area in which S and P intersect is shaded, showing it to be an empty class. As a deductively valid argument, it satisfies one of our two criteria for strong arguments. Of course, a final decision on whether this is a good product will depend on the acceptability of the premises.

The next example is taken from an article in the *Globe and Mail* (17 Mar. 1987, p. A1). The article reported on the rejection of public-service AIDS announcements by a committee that screens commercials for private broadcasters in Canada. The committee's reasoning included the following:

> Most (3 out of 4) public-service AIDS announcements urging the use of condoms condone casual sex. Therefore: Most (3 out of 4) public-service AIDS announcements urging the use of condoms are not acceptable for broadcast.

Since these statements refer to 'most' and not to 'all', we can identify them as particular statements. The first statement (a premise) includes some public-service AIDS announcements within the class of announcements that condone casual sex. It is a **PA** statement. The conclusion, identified by the indicator 'therefore' excludes those announcements from the class of announcements suitable for broadcasting. It is a **PN** statement. With this example we will proceed first to assign S, P, and M (we have enough information to do so), and then decide on how to express the hidden premise.

> Some public-service AIDS announcements urging the use of condoms are announcements condoning casual sex. Therefore: Some public-service announcements urging the use of condoms are not announcements acceptable for broadcast.

Legend	Scheme
S = public-service AIDS announcements urging the use of condoms	
P = announcements acceptable for broadcast	<u>Some S are M</u>
M = announcements condoning casual sex	Some S are not P

The hidden premise must involve a relationship between M and P. What does someone using the expressed reasoning in this argument believe about M and P? It seems likely that they believe the two classes to be mutually exclusive of each other. No announcements acceptable for broadcast are announcements condoning casual sex, and vice versa. Either way, it is a **UN** statement:

No M are P *or* No P are M
(Does it make a difference which way we write this?)

P1
No M are P

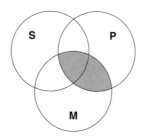

P2
Some S are M

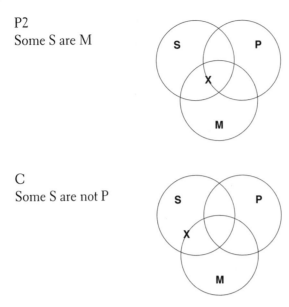

C
Some S are not P

We put P1 and P2 together in a Venn diagram. Notice that when we have a statement that is universal and one that is particular, we always put the universal statement on the diagram first. This is because we often have a choice as to where to place the **X** of a particular statement. If we show the universal statement first, then its shaded area tells us where any **X** cannot go, and thus where it must go.

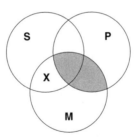

Is there an **X** anywhere in S outside of P, as the conclusion requires? Yes, there is. The argument is valid (as would be the case if we had rendered P1, 'No M are P', as its converse, 'No P are M').

One further example should suffice in illustrating the complexities of the Venn diagram method of testing:

> Some medical professionals are not supporters of euthanasia and some support-
> ers of euthanasia are liberals. From this it follows that it is false to say that all
> medical professionals are liberals.

'It follows that . . .' introduces the conclusion from which we may identify S and P, and M is the class common to the two premises. The conclusion tells us that a **UA** statement ('All medical professionals are liberals') is false. If this is the case, its contradictory statement must be true, and the contradictory of a **UA** statement is a **PN** statement. Now our syllogism is revealed as comprising three particular statements, and we can proceed to the legend and to setting out its form.

Some medical professionals are not supporters of euthanasia. Some supporters of euthanasia are liberals. Therefore: Some medical professionals are not liberals.

Legend
S = medical professionals
P = liberals
M = supporters of euthanasia

Scheme
Some S are not M
<u>Some M are P</u>
Some S are not P

P1
Some S are not M

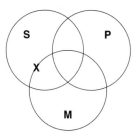

P2
Some M are P

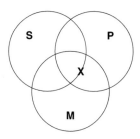

C
Some S are not P

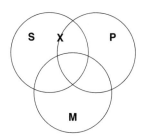

We put P1 and P2 together in a Venn diagram:

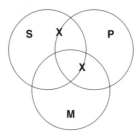

Since there are no universal premises, there are no empty (shaded) areas. So we do not know whether the **X** of P1 should go in the areas of S outside or inside of P. Consequently, we put it on the line. Likewise with P2, we do not know whether the M that is a P is also S, so we put it on the line. Now, for the argument to be valid there should be an **X** in the area of S that is outside of P. But we cannot be sure of this: the **X** is on the line. Thus, this syllogism is invalid because the premises do not guarantee the conclusion. One can accept the premises without accepting the conclusion.

This example shows one of the drawbacks of the Venn diagram method. It has worked well with our other examples, but the possibility of error arises when we are unsure where to place the **X** for particular statements. What we have provided in this chapter is sufficient to introduce the syllogism and equip you for most everyday arguments that involve relationships between classes of things.

MAJOR EXERCISE 7M

1. For each of the following syllogisms:
    (i)   identify S, P, and M in a legend;
    (ii) provide its scheme; and
    (iii) determine its validity using the Venn diagram method.

    EXAMPLE: You will agree that all husbands are married and that no wives are husbands. Surely it follows that no wives are married.

Legend	*Scheme*
S = wives	All M are P
P = married people	No S are M
M = husbands	No S are M

P1
All husbands are
married people

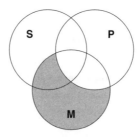

P2
No wives are husbands

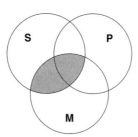

C
No wives are married
people

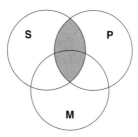

We put P1 and P2 together in a Venn diagram:

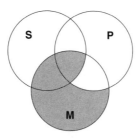

The intersection between S and P is not completely shaded. Therefore, the conclusion is not contained in the premises and this argument is *invalid*.

a)* Some cats aren't pests but all cats are pets, so no pets are pests.

b)* All buildings over 50 feet tall are in violation of the new city bylaw, and the bank building is over 50 feet tall. Therefore, it is in violation of the bylaw.

c) No one who fails this course can major in Psychology, and all Psychology majors are assured a good career, so no one who fails this course is assured a good career.

d) Only courses that involve disciplined thought provide good training for law. And since most philosophy courses involve disciplined thought, so they must provide a good training for law.

e) Some habits are not harmful, and some vices are not habits, so some vices are not harmful.

f) From measuring the footprints we are convinced that the murderer is a man who wears size 9 shoes. That description fits Jim, so he must be the murderer.

g) It is simply not true, as many people suppose, that all professors of political science are socialists. I am convinced of this because, first, it is false to say that no political science professors are money-grubbers, and, second, it is certainly true that no socialists are money-grubbers.

h) No courteous people are rumour mongers, and all discourteous people lack friends. Clearly it must be the case that no rumour mongers have friends.

i) Not all people who are irrational are illogical, since nobody who is illogical is confused, but many irrational people are confused.

j) To make love is to engage in battle! This must be true because it takes two to stage a fight, and it also takes two to make love.

k) Your ideas are immaterial. But whatever is immaterial does not matter. Therefore, your ideas do not matter.

2. Wherever possible, supply the hidden component that would make the following syllogisms complete or valid if possible, and exhibit validity (or invalidity) by the Venn diagram method.

EXAMPLE: Capital punishment is wrong because it is itself a crime.

All acts of Capital Punishment are crimes
All acts of Capital Punishment are wrongful acts

Legend	*Scheme*
S = acts of capital punishment	[ ]
P = wrongful acts	All S are M
M = crimes	All S are P

P
All S are M

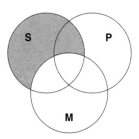

C
All S are P

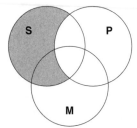

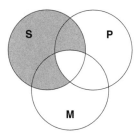

For the conclusion to be contained in the diagram (indicating validity), all of S outside of P must be shaded. The hidden premise must express a relationship between M and P, and the only possible statement that would fit these two requirements is: All M are P.

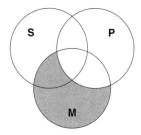

a)* No person who values integrity will go into politics because the realities of political life force people to compromise their principles.

b) [from the *Globe and Mail* (12 May 1988)] Most students can afford to pay more for tuition because most students make between $4,000 and $6,000 each summer.

c) It's not the case that all media stories are reliable because many media reports from foreign news agencies are unreliable.

d) Some of the things parapsychologists tell us about are outlandish because they utterly contradict the laws of nature.

e) [from Canadian Press (8 May 2002): backbench MP Paul Szabo called on Prime Minister Jean Chrétien to declare a free vote on controversial legislation governing new reproductive and genetic technologies.] 'This bill touches on a moral issue, and that is, when does human life begin?' he said. 'All moral votes are free votes.'

f) [adapted from *Time* (13 Jan. 2003), p. 32] You can't conduct a reasoned debate about complex moral issues in a context that is controlled by quacks, clowns, and money. But in the case of cloning, that's what you have—quacks, clowns, and money.

g) [adapted from *Time* (13 Jan. 2003), p. 7] In one forest, orangutans gave a nightly Bronx cheer that does not characterize orangutans elsewhere. Orangutans exhibit different behaviour in different groups, what anthropologists call 'culture'.

3. In each case, construct a valid syllogism by supplying premises for the following conclusions. Prove the validity of your syllogism with a Venn diagram.

    EXAMPLE: All Picasso paintings are costly.

Legend	Scheme
S = Picasso paintings	All M are P
P = Costly things	All S are M
M = Items prized by the world's leading art collectors	All S are P

    a)* This syllogism is valid.
    b) Most trade books are not worth the paper they are printed on.
    c)* No one does wrong voluntarily.
    d) Only cool-headed people will prosper.
    e) Some heavy smokers die of causes other than lung cancer.
    f) Human colonization of the outer planets is currently beyond our capabilities.
    g) All non-union members are non-employees.
    h) You will not get a better deal on a new car than at Dave's Motors.

SYLLOGISMS II:

TESTING

CLASSES

Chapter 7 introduced the categorical syllogism and explained how to construct such arguments and test their validity by means of Venn diagrams. This chapter takes that discussion one step further by introducing a method for testing syllogisms using rules. It discusses

- ♦ schematization;
- ♦ distribution;
- ♦ rules of validity and their application; and
- ♦ some additional procedural points.

1. FULL SCHEMATIZATION

When we introduced the four basic forms of categorical statements, we labelled them **UA**, **UN**, **PA**, and **PN**. Now we will apply their traditional labels as, respectively, **A**, **E**, **I**, and **O** statements (from the Latin for the verbs to 'affirm' and to 'negate': **Aff**I**rmo** and n**E**g**O**). This change will help you learn the features of the remaining parts of this chapter.

A represents the universal affirmative statement 'All S are P'.
E represents the universal negative statement 'No S are P'.
I represents the particular affirmative statement 'Some S are P'.
O represents the particular negative statement 'Some S are not P'.

From this point on we will schematize these statements as:

S **A** P   All S are P.
S **E** P   No S are P.
S **I** P   Some S are P.
S **O** P   Some S are not P.

Distribution

To make the full testing of categorical syllogisms possible, we must add a further component to this schematization. We need some way of indicating whether, in each case, the subject and predicate *terms* (rather than the *statements*) give us information about the entire class of things to which they refer or about only a portion of the class they name. This information is indispensable to applying the rules of validity.

If information is given about an entire membership of a class named by a term, the term is said to be *distributed*. If information is given about only a portion of the membership, the term is said to be *undistributed*. It follows that the subject term of the **A** and **E** statements is 'distributed', for these statements tell us something about *all* S and *no* S. In contrast, the subject term of the **I** and **O** statements is 'undistributed', since these statements only tell us something about *some* of the membership in the subject class.

The predicate term of **E** and **O** statements is distributed because these statements exclude some or all of the membership of the subject class from the *entire* membership of the predicate class. In the **A** and **I** statements, the predicate term is undistributed because such statements do not give us any information about the entire predicate class but only about a portion of the predicate class with which the subject terms of those statements are coincident. All this is conveyed in the following chart:

Statement	Subject term	Predicate term
A	distributed	undistributed
E	distributed	distributed
I	undistributed	undistributed
O	undistributed	distributed

This chart explains why we were only able to apply straightforward conversion to the **E** (**UN**) and **I** (**PA**) statements in Chapter 7. Only with these two statements is the distribution or non-distribution of the subject and predicate classes the same, allowing us to switch them.

In this schematization, we will use a lowercase 'd' following the class symbol to indicate distribution, and a lowercase 'u' to indicate non-distribution. This enables us to complete the schematization of the four types of categorical statement as follows:

A	Sd **A** Pu	All S are P
E	Sd **E** Pd	No S are P
I	Su **I** Pu	Some S are P
O	Su **O** Pd	Some S are not P

Note that whatever S and P (or M) represent, the **A**, **E**, **I**, and **O** statements will *always* be schematized with the distribution/non-distribution indicators shown here. You do not have to decide the distribution of terms in each syllogism you work with, but you need to remember the pattern of distribution/non-distribution associated with each type of statement.

2. Rules of Validity

Particularly when dealing with complex syllogisms, you will find that the rules that determine deductive validity are likely to be more reliable than analyzing language or using Venn diagrams. There are three rules that we will use in this regard.

Rule 1: **The Middle term, M, must be distributed at least once.**
M is the class that is related to each of S and P in the premises of a categorical syllogism. It is on the basis of these relationships that a relationship between S and P is deduced in the conclusion. If the class represented by M in the premises is undistributed in both instances, then each premise could be giving information about a different portion of the M class, and there would be no basis for expressing a relationship between S and P. It is not a violation of Rule 1 if M is distributed in both premises, but it is a minimum requirement that it be distributed at least once. If the M term is undistributed in both of its occurrences, the syllogism is invalid. This type of invalidity is called 'the fallacy of the undistributed middle'.

Consider the following syllogism:

All people who study argument enjoy political debate. Cassie is a person who enjoys political debate. Therefore Cassie studies argument.

In this syllogism, M is the class 'people who enjoy political debate'. If you think about it, you should also see that this is a term that is undistributed in both premises. This tells you that the two premises each refer to only a portion of the people who enjoy political debate. For all we know, they may refer to different portions of this group, which would mean that what is said about the portion in the first premise may not be something that can be said of the portion mentioned in the second premise. For this reason, they cannot be combined, and the conclusion is, by Rule 1, invalid.

Rule 2: **Any term distributed in the conclusion must be distributed in the premise in which it occurs.**
This rule ensures that the conclusion does not contain any information that does not have to be accepted if one accepts the premises. A term that is undistributed in a premise gives information about only a portion of the membership of the class named by that term. If that term is distributed in the conclusion, the conclusion is saying something about the entire membership of that class. Clearly the conclusion cannot legitimately make a claim about *all* members of a class if the premises refer only to *some* of them. Since only S and P appear in the conclusion, it is to these two terms that this rule applies. If a term is distributed in the conclusion but is undistributed in the premise in which it appears, the syllogism is invalid. In this case, the argument is invalidated by what is called 'the fallacy of illicit process'.

Consider the following syllogism:

Bill is guilty of drunk driving. Bill is a man. That just goes to show you that people guilty of drunk driving are men.

In this case, the term 'people guilty of drunk driving' is distributed in the conclusion. The conclusion is a statement about *all* the members of this class. This term arises in the first premise ('Bill is guilty of drunk driving'), but that is a UA statement in which the second term is undistributed, referring to only a portion of this class. It follows, by Rule 2, that this syllogism is invalid.

> *Rule 3:* **There can be only as many negative premises as there are negative conclusions, and if there is a negative conclusion, there must be one negative premise.**

This rule governs the presence of negative statements (**E** or **O**) and needs to be invoked only in the case of syllogisms containing them. There cannot be two negative premises, nor can there be a negative conclusion drawn from two affirmative premises. There can be only one negative premise, in which case there must be a negative conclusion, and vice versa.

Since negative statements *exclude* classes from others, if the S and P classes are both excluded from M, then there would be no basis on which to conclude anything about the relationship between S and P. Likewise, if both premises are affirmative and include S and P in a portion of the M class, then that is no basis for excluding S and P from each other in the conclusion. If, however, one premise expresses a relationship of inclusion and the other a relationship of exclusion, then, given that the other rules are satisfied, the conclusion can legitimately express a relationship of exclusion.

The fallacy involved depends on the specific manner in which the syllogism violates Rule 3. There are, therefore, three fallacy labels associated with violations of Rule 3: 'two negative premises'; 'a negative premise with an affirmative conclusion'; and 'affirmative premises with a negative conclusion'.

Consider the following syllogism:

> No large cats are vegetarians. No vegetarians are ferocious. Therefore: No large cats are ferocious.

This is an example of the fallacy 'two negative premises'. The first premise excludes large cats from the class of 'vegetarians'. The second excludes vegetarians from the class of 'things that are ferocious'. This implies nothing about the relationship between large cats and ferocious things, for the premises only tell us that they are excluded from things vegetarian, and this leaves open the possibility of any independent relationship between them. It follows that the syllogism is invalid, by Rule 3.

3. APPLYING THE RULES

A valid syllogism must satisfy all three of our rules. If any one rule is violated, the syllogism is invalid. We can illustrate the application of the rules by testing two syllogisms we have already shown to be invalid.

EXAMPLE 1

All people who oppose the trade bill are people with conservative values. Smith is a person with conservative values. Therefore: Smith opposes the trade bill.

Legend	*Scheme*
S = Smith	Pd **A** Mu
P = people who oppose the trade bill	Sd **A** Mu
M = people with conservative values	Sd **A** Pu

Note that because they are all **A** statements, the distribution is 'd–u' in each case.

Test

Rule 1: *Violated.* The middle term is undistributed in both premises.

Rule 2: *Okay.* Only S is distributed in the conclusion, and it is also distributed in the premise. [It is not a problem for P to be distributed in the premise but undistributed in the conclusion.]

Rule 3: *Not applicable.* There are no negative statements.

We conclude that this syllogism is *invalid* because it violates Rule 1, thereby committing the fallacy of the undistributed middle.

EXAMPLE 2

Some medical professionals are not supporters of euthanasia. Some supporters of euthanasia are liberals. So: Some medical professionals are not liberals.

Legend	*Scheme:*
S = professionals	Su **O** Md
P = liberals	Mu **I** Pu
M = supporters of euthanasia	Su **O** Pd

Test

Rule 1: *Okay.* The middle term is distributed once in the premises.

Rule 2: *Violated.* P is distributed in the conclusion, but it is undistributed in the premise.

Rule 3: *Okay.* There is only one negative premise, and there is a negative conclusion.

This syllogism is *invalid* because it violates Rule 2, thereby committing the fallacy of illicit process.

A Further Consideration

For many logicians, a syllogism cannot be valid if it has two universal premises (**A** or **E**) and a particular conclusion (**I** or **O**). Such a concern follows from what is called a *hypothetical* interpretation of universal statements. It may have occurred to you that a statement like 'All shoplifters will be prosecuted' does not assume that the class of 'Shoplifters' or the class of 'those who will be prosecuted' has any members. In fact, the statement's intent is to keep both classes empty of members. So we make sense of the statement with a hypothetical reading, i.e. '*If* there is a shoplifter, that person will be prosecuted' (we allowed for such statements in our list of 'Common Variations' in Chapter 7). The hypothetical reading of universal statements does not assume that either class has members. But particular statements, since they refer to *some*, are assumed to have members. Thus a syllogism like the following is invalid—according to a hypothetical reading of universal statements—because the premises *could* refer to classes without members, but the particular conclusion asserts that there *are* members of the classes:

> Not all major diseases are curable because AIDS is a major disease and it is incurable.

After providing the contradictory of the conclusion ('Not all major diseases are curable') and obverting the premise with the complement of the 'P' term ('AIDS is incurable') we derive the following:

> All cases of AIDS (M) are cases of major diseases (S).
> No cases of AIDS (M) are curable diseases (P).
> Therefore: Some major diseases (S) are not curable diseases (P).

Throughout our discussion of categorical syllogisms we have been assuming not a hypothetical reading of universal statements but an *existential* interpretation. That is, we have been assuming that the statements have been expressing assertions about classes with members, about things that are real and exist. This is because most instances of syllogisms drawn from ordinary circumstances (like the AIDS example above) favour the existential interpretation. Unless you know that the universal premises of a syllogism refer, or are intended to refer, to classes that have no members, we suggest you adopt the existential interpretation of those statements. But in cases in which the hypothetical interpretation is clearly warranted, you should invoke a fourth rule:

> *Rule 4:* **A syllogism with two universal premises that do not assume the classes have members cannot have a particular conclusion.**

4. Procedural Points

We will close this chapter with some procedural points that will assist you as you test syllogisms using the rule method.

First, watch for classes and their complementaries in arguments, for example 'suitable things' and 'non-suitable (or unsuitable) things'. Where these appear together in an argument, try using immediate inferences to reduce the number of terms to three, and explain the process you are employing (e.g. contradiction, obversion, conversion, or contraposition).

Second, when assigning symbols in the legend, always identify S, P, and M as positive classes and then, if the complements are present, assign them as non-S, non-P, and non-M. This will avoid the confusion of having, for example, S represent 'immortal beings' and non-S represent 'mortal beings'.

Finally, if a syllogism involves a hidden component, then, wherever possible, use the rules to supply whatever unstated component yields a valid argument. This is a way to give the benefit of doubt to the arguer. But you will find that some syllogisms cannot be made valid, no matter what hidden component is suggested. If providing validity in this way seems overly generous, remember that validity alone is not enough for an argument to be judged a strong one—it must also have acceptable premises.

One last example will illustrate these three procedural points. Consider the following argument:

No problems are welcome because all undesirable things are unwelcome.

In this example, the premise indicator 'because' tells us we have the following premise and conclusion:

PREMISE: All undesirable things are unwelcome
CONCLUSION: No problems are welcome

We have a hidden premise to supply. We also have at least four classes of things: 'problems', 'welcome things', 'undesirable things', and 'unwelcome things'. But 'welcome things' and 'unwelcome things' we can take as complementary classes and look to reduce one to the other by means of immediate inferences.

We have the conclusion, so S and P are identified for us. The remaining class is 'undesirable things', but since this is a negative class, we will assign M to 'desirable things'.

Legend	Scheme
S = problems	All non-M are non-P
P = welcome things	[_____]
non-P = unwelcome things	No S are P
M = desirable things	
non-M = undesirable things	

Our task now is to eliminate non-M and non-P. We can do this by using contraposition (or obversion, conversion, and obversion):

non-Md **A** non-Pu
CONTRAPOSITIVE: Pd **A** Mu

If all undesirable things are unwelcome, then all welcome things are desirable. This gives us the following scheme:

Pd **A** Mu
[_____]
Sd **E** Pd

Now we must ask what hidden premise would be required for this argument to be valid. To decide this, we proceed through each rule, ensuring that it is not violated. The hidden premise must involve S and M. In order for Rule 1 to be satisfied, M must be distributed in the hidden premise, since it is not distributed in the expressed premise. (This means the hidden premise cannot be an **I** statement.) For Rule 2 to be satisfied, S must be distributed because S is distributed in the conclusion. The only statement that would allow both M and S to be distributed is an **E** statement. And we further see that in order for Rule 3 to be satisfied, the hidden premise would have to be either an **E** or an **O** statement. Hence, the hidden premise must be an **E** statement: either 'No problems are desirable things' (Sd **E** Md) or 'No desirable things are problems' (Md **E** Sd). And with this supplied the argument is valid.

MAJOR EXERCISE 8M

Extract at least one syllogism from each of the following passages and test it for validity. Wherever necessary, supply a hidden component.

> EXAMPLE: Since then to fight against neighbours is an evil, and to fight against the Thebans is to fight against neighbours, it is clear that to fight against the Thebans is an evil. (Aristotle, *Prior Analytics*)

> > All acts of fighting against neighbours are evil acts. All acts of fighting against the Thebans are acts of fighting against neighbours. Therefore: All acts of fighting against the Thebans are evil acts.

> > | *Legend* | *Scheme* |
> > |---|---|
> > | S = acts of fighting against the Thebans | Md **A** Pu |
> > | P = evil acts | Sd **A** Mu |
> > | M = acts of fighting against neighbours | Sd **A** Pu |

> *Test*
> Rule 1: *Okay.* The middle term is distributed in the first premise.
> Rule 2: *Okay.* Only S is distributed in the conclusion and it is also distributed in the premise.
> Rule 3: *Not applicable.* There are no negative statements.

> *This syllogism satisfies all the rules and so is valid.*

a)* It's not the case that all valid syllogisms have acceptable premises, nor is it the case that any valid syllogism has a false conclusion. So, no syllogisms with acceptable premises have false conclusions.

b)* Conservatives favour cuts to the education system. Peter does not favour cuts to the education system. Hence, Peter is not a conservative.

c) Nations that violate international law will experience sanctions from the UN, and nations that experience sanctions from the UN will see their populations suffer. So some nations that see their populations suffer are violators of international law.

d) People who smoke are people who deliberately put their health at risk, and anyone who does that is someone who should pay higher insurance premiums. So some of the people who should be paying higher insurance premiums are smokers.

e) Only foreign-owned magazines that have a substantially different Canadian edition are acceptable in Canada under current federal guidelines. Thus, *Sports Illustrated* is unacceptable.

f) Most banks are in a position to reward their customers because any institutions that report high profits are in a position to reward their customers and most banks have reported high profits.

g) [Michael P.T. Leahy, in *Against Liberation: Putting Animals in Perspective* (Routledge, rev. 1994)] Regan sets out Frey's argument schematically as follows: 1. Only those individuals who can have beliefs can have desires. 2. Animals cannot have beliefs. 3. Therefore, animals cannot have desires.

h) [Voltaire, in *Dictionnaire Philosophique*] That man must be extremely ignorant: he answers every question that is put to him.

i) [from an ad for Puerto Rico rums, *Atlantic Monthly* (Nov. 1993)] Only the finest rums come from Puerto Rico. Aging has given our rums a smoothness, whether straight or mixed, that has made them preferred over all others. And only in Puerto Rico, with its heritage of fine rums, is aging guaranteed by law.

j) [The following is adapted from an article by Arthur Schafer, 'There May Be Another Me, But Should There Be Another Ewe?', *Globe and Mail* (28 Feb. 1998). It contains two arguments: that of the 'critics' in the first sentences, and that of the author in the closing sentences. Set out the two arguments, supplying any necessary hidden components, and test both.] Critics warn that no matter what good might come from human cloning, it is wrong in itself. Cloning is said to violate the genetic uniqueness of each human. But what does this mean, exactly? Does anyone seriously believe that the birth of natural-born genetically identical twins is wrong in itself? Yet such identical twins, remember, violate the genetic uniqueness of each human. So it's not the case that all things that violate the genetic uniqueness of each human are wrong in themselves.

k) [from a letter to the *Peterborough Examiner* (22 Mar. 1993)] I am writing with regards to the imposition of a law to make the wearing of a helmet obligatory while riding a bicycle. . . . The concept of 'freedom of choice' must be retained to the greatest degree possible in our society. We cannot and should not remove this right to decide for ourselves except in extreme cases where society at large will suffer drastically from the individuals' bad judgment, which is not the case here.

l)* [Shakespeare, *Richard III*] No beast so foul but knows some pity; / But I know none, and Therefore am no beast.

m) [from a radio ad] Black's paints have been around since 1880, and with that kind of experience you know you're getting the best that money can buy.

n) [On 23 September 1991, then US president George Bush addressed the United Nations on the question of a UN resolution equating Zionism with racism. In concluding that Zionism was not racism, he argued for the historical difference between them.] Zionism . . . is the idea that led to the creation of a home for the Jewish people. . . . And to equate Zionism with the intolerable sin of racism is to twist history and forget the terrible plight of Jews in World War II and indeed throughout history.

o) [Robert Fulford, in *Saturday Night* (Dec. 1986)] A major constitutional challenge, running right up to the Supreme Court, can consume hundreds of thousands of dollars. Only those who can pay exorbitant lawyers' fees will pursue such a challenge; the logical inference is that the Charter will, in the long term, favour the rich.

p)* [from a letter to the *Peterborough Examiner* (24 Nov. 1994)] It is quite incorrect to say 'Violence cannot ever be condoned.' Violence in defence of self or family is usually acceptable. If a sniper is shooting a gun in a crowd of people then it is the duty of the police to shoot back with deadly accuracy to stop the shooting. Going to war to protect your country has an honorable tradition. In retrospect, it is obvious that the killing of Adolf Hitler and his cronies would have prevented World War II and the Holocaust, and would therefore have been quite acceptable.

q) [Judge Bewdley, in the *Globe and Mail* (19 Mar. 1987)] Murder is the unlawful killing of a human being. The murderer has preferred no lawful charge against his victim; given him no right to counsel, no right to cross-examine or make full answer and defence; denied him the right to be tried before an independent, impartial public tribunal; denied him any appeal. The murderer is prosecutor, judge and jury, all without lawful authority. Only such killing can be called murder.

In absolute contrast, society provides an accused murderer with all the rights and safeguards he has denied his victim. If then, after proof of guilt beyond a reasonable doubt, society sentences him to death, that is not murder; it is as far from unlawful killing as it is possible to get. To call this murder is to speak nonsense.

r)* [from the same article] Capital punishment is uncivilized, barbaric, and merely revenge. This is the capital-punishment-is-murder argument all over again. What the abolitionists assert here is: 'Uncivilized barbarians kill; all killing is uncivilized and barbaric; therefore, judicially ordered executions are uncivilized and barbaric.'

s) [adapted from Keith Ward, 'An Irresolvable Dispute?', in *Experiments on Embryos*, ed. A. Dyson and J. Harris (Routledge, 1990)] If there is some entity which has no rational consciousness—which has no consciousness at all—then it is not a person. One might say that it appears to be a necessary condition of having consciousness that you have a brain, so 'no brain, no person'. One can say that a person is dead when the brain stem ceases to function or that if something hasn't got a brain, it is not a person. That seems quite a compelling argument. But the vital point is not the possession of a brain; it is the possession of rational agency. If a person is a rational, sentient agent then nothing which is not a rational sentient agent—and little embryos certainly aren't that—is a person.

PROPOSITIONAL

LOGIC I:

SOME IFS, ANDS, AND BUTS

Strong arguments are valid arguments with acceptable premises. This chapter continues our discussion of validity by looking at a second type of deductive validity, which depends on the relationships between propositions that are expressed by words like 'if', 'then', 'and', 'or', and 'not'. In introducing 'propositional logic', we

♦ define propositional logic arguments;
♦ provide many examples of simple propositional arguments;
♦ distinguish the different kinds of propositions these arguments contain;
♦ show you how to represent the logical structure of these propositions;
♦ present ways of determining whether a particular propositional argument is deductively valid.

This textbook is designed to introduce some key concepts in logic, 'informal logic', critical thinking, rhetoric, and argumentation theory. In this and the following chapter we introduce 'propositional logic', though we make no attempt to provide a detailed account of it. If the material in these chapters piques your curiosity, we recommend a course in formal logic.

In presenting some selected aspects of propositional logic we will ignore many features of it that are of secondary interest when one is attempting to teach the skills that play a central role in good ordinary-language reasoning. (We will not, for example, discuss truth tables, truth trees, and theoretical notions like soundness and completeness.) Our goal is a modest account of some aspects of propositional logic that can help you understand ordinary reasoning in two ways: first, by teaching you some important argument schemes that play a fundamental role in ordinary reasoning; second, by providing an example of the rigorous step-by-step arguments associated with proofs of one kind or another.

1. SIMPLE AND COMPLEX PROPOSITIONS

We have already seen that we can use the methods of syllogistic logic to assess whether arguments that deal with relations between different classes are deductively valid or invalid. In this chapter, we introduce other methods that can be used to determine whether arguments that can be understood in terms of the relations between different propositions are deductively valid.

The basic building blocks of propositional logic arguments are *propositions*. Though philosophers debate the nature of propositions, it will suffice for us to say that a proposition *affirms that something is the case*. Each of the following sentences can be treated as a proposition:

- Nuclear war is the most disastrous calamity imaginable.
- It will continue to snow for the next 24 hours.
- The mail has been delivered.
- I will report your actions to the dean.
- Zeus and Hera head the Olympian family of gods.
- Kellogg's is committed to providing foods of outstanding quality.
- You were reading her e-mail last night.

The propositions expressed by these sentences can be expressed in other ways. In a precise and detailed formal logic, one might make fine distinctions between sentences that have slightly different meanings, but we shall tend to treat them as expressions of the same proposition. We have already dealt with different sentences in this way in earlier examples of argument, when, for example, we recognized different expressions of the same proposition as repetitive, or as alternative ways of stating a premise in the course of diagramming an argument.

Propositional logic arguments depend on a distinction between *complex* and *simple* (sometimes called 'atomic') propositions. Complex propositions are formed by combining simple propositions and 'connectors'. Using two of the propositions we have already listed, and the connector 'If . . . then . . .', we can construct the complex proposition, '*If* you were reading her e-mail last night, *then* I will report your actions to the dean.' This type of proposition is called a 'conditional'. Using the same two propositions and the connector 'and', we can construct the complex proposition, 'You were reading her e-mail last night *and* I will report your actions to the dean.' This kind of proposition is called a 'conjunction'.

In analyzing syllogisms, we introduced ways of representing arguments that allowed us to set out some of the essential features of their premises and conclusions.

In dealing with propositional arguments, we will illustrate the logical structure of complex propositions by letting lowercase letters stand for the simple propositions of which the complex propositions consist. As an aid to your memory, you may pick a letter that you can associate with a key word or particular proposition, as in the following examples:

m = The <u>m</u>ail has been delivered.
c = You will enjoy your course in <u>c</u>ritical thinking.
n = <u>N</u>uclear war is a terrifying possibility.
h = You were reading <u>h</u>er e-mail.
d = I'm going to report you to the <u>d</u>ean.

Definitions of this sort will form our legend when we represent propositional arguments in symbolic form. In order to complete our representation, we will combine our symbols for our simple propositions with symbols for our logical connectors. Using the legend above and the symbol & to represent conjunctions, we can, for example, represent the sentence 'You were reading her e-mail and I'm going to report you to the Dean' as h & d.

In describing propositional logic arguments (and propositional schemes of argument) we will sometimes use the capital letters X, Y, Z, W. They should not be confused with the lowercase letters we use to represent specific simple propositions. The capital letters can stand for any proposition, simple or complex. X could, for example, stand for the proposition h, or (h & d), or any of the complex propositions we will introduce. These 'variables' (so called because they have a variable rather than a set meaning), as you will subsequently see, allow us to more easily define the schemes of argument that characterize propositional arguments.

Negations

In symbolizing the complex propositions that occur in propositional arguments, we will recognize four kinds of complex propositions and the four connectors that make them possible. A *negation* is a proposition that denies another proposition. Let's consider an example. The GNU Project is an attempt to develop copyright-free software for general use. Because the software it has developed (Linux systems) is Unix-like but not Unix, those working on the project coined the name 'GNU', which stands for 'GNU's Not Unix'. The acronym GNU thus represents a negation (the proposition, 'GNU is not Unix'). Like other negations, it denies another proposition, in this case the proposition, 'GNU is Unix'.

In propositional logic, we use the 'tilde', the symbol ~, to represent negations. If we let g = GNU is Unix, we can represent the negation 'GNU is not Unix' as ~g. For any proposition X, ~(X) is its negation, which can be read as 'X is not the case', or, more simply, 'Not X'. If we can drop the brackets without confusion, then we will write the negation ~(X) as ~X.

It is important to recognize that propositions may be expressed in many different ways in ordinary language. Former US president Richard Nixon was famous for declaring, in the midst of the Watergate affair, 'I am not a crook.' If we let c = Richard Nixon is a crook, then we can represent his declaration as $\sim c$. Strictly speaking, this is the proposition 'Richard Nixon is not a crook.' He is able to express it in a different way because he can use the personal pronoun 'I' to refer to himself. One might express the same negation in a variety of other ways that include the sentences 'It's not true that I'm a crook' (spoken by Richard Nixon), and 'Those who say that Richard Nixon is a crook are mistaken.' (In dealing with this last example, there could be contexts in which it would be important to note that the proposition contains a reference to 'those who say', but this need not concern us here).

Within ordinary language, negations may be expressed with a variety of words that include 'no', 'never', 'nothing', 'can't', 'nowhere', and sometimes with the prefix 'un-' (as in 'She is unmotivated,' which is equivalent to 'She is not motivated'). Though each instance of these words must be assessed in its own context, we can generally represent them as instances of the propositional logic $\sim$.

Double Negations

You have probably heard someone complaining about the use of double negatives in ordinary language. Often, in an effort to try and emphasize the negative tone of an assertion, speakers will put an extra negative into their statements. An example of this is the statement 'I *don't* need help from *nobody*.' Using double negatives was considered correct in Shakespeare's time, but it is frowned upon today, especially in essay writing.

Double negatives can be confusing because the negation of a negation is an affirmation. $\sim X$ is the statement 'Not X,' and $\sim \sim X$ is the statement 'Not Not X.' If we spell it out completely, the latter proposition is the claim that 'It is not the case that it is not the case that X,' which is equivalent to the claim, 'It is the case that X.' If we negate the claim $\sim c$, where c = Richard Nixon is a crook, then the result is $\sim \sim c$. It could be expressed as the proposition 'It is not true that Richard Nixon is not a crook,' but we shall instead represent it as the (equivalent) proposition 'Richard Nixon is a crook.'

In a fully developed system of propositional logic, one often has a rule of 'Double Negation' that allows one to move between the propositions X and $\sim \sim X$, but we will instead treat X as the negation of $\sim X$. This is what we do in ordinary language, where we negate an affirmation by adding a negative, and a negative by stating a positive. If I wish to negate your claim that 'Green Day is not a talented band,' for example, I do so by asserting that 'Green Day *is* a talented band,' not by asserting that 'It is not the case that Green Day is not a talented band.'

Conjunctions

Conjunctions have the form X & Y, where X and Y can be any propositions, and the symbol & represents the word 'and'. Each of the two components of a conjunction is called a 'conjunct'. The conjunction X & Y states that both X and Y are true. In accepting a conjunction we accept that this is so.

When we deal with claims in ordinary language, we will treat any proposition that claims that two or more propositions are true as a conjunction. The following conjunctions are taken from the website for MapQuest, a map finder on the web:

- MapQuest is easy to use and offers the most comprehensive coverage of the globe.
- MapQuest.com generates the majority of all Internet mapping page views, licenses its technologies to thousands of business partners and is linked to by hundreds of thousands of other Web sites.
- Through the MapQuest.com site and our business partners, we serve up more than 400 million maps and more than 60 million sets of driving directions every month.

The first two of these conjunctions are easy to represent. If we adopt the legend

e = MapQuest is easy to use.
c = MapQuest offers the most comprehensive coverage of the globe.
m = MapQuest.com generates the majority of all Internet mapping page views.
l = MapQuest licenses its technologies to thousands of business partners.
w = MapQuest is linked to by hundreds of thousands of other Web sites.

then we can represent the first two of our conjunctions as e & c and m & l & w.

Our remaining example is more complex, for it contains two 'and's that must be treated differently. The first 'and' is not a conjunction in the sense in which we use the term in propositional logic, for it is not an 'and' that is used to conjoin two propositions (rather, it is used to link the two subjects of the proposition—MapQuest and its business partners). In contrast the second 'and' does conjoin two propositions. So we can represent the sentence as s & d, where

s = Through the MapQuest.com site and our business partners, we serve up more than 400 million maps every month.
d = Through the MapQuest.com site and our business partners, we serve up more than 60 million sets of driving directions every month.

In ordinary language, propositions may be conjoined in a variety of ways: by the use of semicolons, by the use of connector words like 'but', 'too', 'although', and 'also', or by combining their subjects or predicates. The following sentences are, for example, all instances of the conjunction a & s, where: a = Lewis Carroll wrote *Alice in Wonderland*, and s = Lewis Carroll wrote *Symbolic Logic*:

- Carroll wrote *Alice in Wonderland*; Carroll wrote *Symbolic Logic*.
- Lewis Carroll wrote *Alice in Wonderland* and *Symbolic Logic*.
- Lewis Carroll wrote *Alice in Wonderland* but also *Symbolic Logic*.
- Though Carroll wrote *Alice in Wonderland*, he wrote *Symbolic Logic* too.

All of the conjuncts in the examples of conjunction we have considered thus far are simple propositions. In other cases, conjuncts may be complex propositions. The conjuncts in the conjunction a & $\sim s$ are, for example, a simple proposition (a) and a complex proposition that is a negation ($\sim s$). Using the definitions of a and s above, a & $\sim s$ can be understood as the sentence 'Lewis Carroll wrote *Alice in Wonderland*, but he did not write *Symbolic Logic*.'

Disjunctions

A *disjunction* is a complex proposition that has the form 'X *or* Y'. We call the component propositions, X and Y, the 'disjuncts' of the disjunction. We will use the symbol V (called 'vel') to represent disjunctions in propositional logic. For any X and any Y, the disjunction X *or* Y can be represented as X V Y. We understand a disjunction as the claim that at least one, and perhaps both, of its disjuncts are true. For that reason, the most precise way to understand X V Y in ordinary language is as the proposition that 'X *and/or* Y'.

Consider a remark from a web page containing the records of two regiments during the American Civil War (<http://www.iath.virginia.edu/vshadow2/OR/or.html>). After reading an explanation of 'The Valley Project' that has brought these records together, one reads that: 'You may browse these records at your own pace, or you may search the records for specific keywords from the Official Records Search.' Using the legend

b = You may browse those records at your own pace.

s = You may search the records for specific keywords from the Official Records Search.

we can represent the disjunction on the webpage as b V s.

In ordinary language we often indicate a disjunction by inserting 'or' or a series of 'or's in the subject or predicate portion of a sentence. In such cases a disjunction may have more than two disjuncts. Consider the following two statements:

Jan or Fred or Kaitlin or Monica or Samari will play the piano tonight.
Fred will play piano or drums or guitar or clarinet or xylophone.

Each of these statements is a disjunction with five disjuncts. We can represent the second as p V d V g V c V x if we let

p = Fred will play piano.

d = Fred will play drums.

g = Fred will play guitar.

c = Fred will play clarinet.

x = Fred will play xylophone.

Exclusive Disjunctions

We call the disjunctions we have noted 'inclusive disjunctions' because they incorporate the possibility that their disjuncts are all true. That is why $X \lor Y$ can be understood as the claim that 'X and/or Y'.

When an ordinary-language statement of the form 'X or Y' excludes the possibility that both X and Y are true, we call it an 'exclusive' disjunction. Consider a menu that tells you that you may have 'Soup or Salad' with your meal. Here the 'or' functions as an exclusive disjunction. The restaurant is not telling you that you can have soup and/or salad, but that you can have one or the other.

In such circumstances, the context makes it clear that a disjunction expresses the proposition that one *but not both* of its disjuncts is true. In order to represent this kind of disjunction in propositional logic symbols, we make this exclusion explicit, and render an exclusive disjunction as a proposition of the form $(X \lor Y)\ \&\ \sim(X\ \&\ Y)$. If we let s = You can have soup, and a = You can have salad, then we can represent the disjunction on the menu as $(s \lor a)\ \&\ \sim(s\ \&\ a)$.

Another example of an exclusive disjunction is the following statement, made in conjunction with a television advertisement for Ultramatic beds:

You will be completely satisfied or we will happily refund your money.

If s = You will be completely satisfied, and r = We will happily refund your money, then the statement can be represented as the exclusive disjunction $(s \lor r)\ \&\ \sim(s\ \&\ r)$. In this case we need to represent the disjunction in this way because it is clear that the company is guaranteeing that one, and only one, of s and r is true. If you are completely satisfied, it follows that you cannot expect that your money will be refunded.

Conditionals

A conditional is a complex proposition that has the form 'If X, then Y'. We call X the 'antecedent' of the conditional and Y its 'consequent'. In symbolizing propositions, we will represent conditionals as statements that have the form $X \rightarrow Y$ (you may read this statement as 'If X, then Y' or as 'X arrow Y'). As this kind of symbolism visually suggests, a conditional states what is true if a certain condition (the antecedent) is or was the case.

We included a good example of a conditional in our earlier exercises on bias (Chapter 5). It was the following statement printed on a 'prize envelope' received in the mail:

If you reply in time and win, we'll say . . .

LEO GROARKE, YOU'VE MADE THE FINAL CUT—YOU'RE ONE OF TEN LUCKY PRIZE WINNERS GUARANTEED UP TO $11,000,000!

This is a good example of slanting by distortion. Quite literally, the arguer has distorted the size of the two parts of the proposition. They have done so because they want the reader (in this case, Leo Groarke) to think that he has made the final cut and is one of ten lucky prize winners guaranteed. The qualification in the fine print means, however, that the statement is a conditional rather than a simple affirmation. In this case, the antecedent of the conditional is the conjunction 'you reply in time and win'. We can represent this conditional as $(r \ \& \ w) \rightarrow s$, where r = You reply in time, w = You win, and s = We'll say Leo Groarke, you've made the final cut—you're one of ten lucky prize winners guaranteed up to $11,000,000. In view of this the authors of the sentence can claim, if they are questioned, that the sentence is not just the statement s, but the conditional $(r \ \& \ w) \rightarrow s$, which says only that s is true if r and w are.

Though 'If . . . , then . . .' is a common way of expressing conditionals in ordinary language, many statements express conditionals in other ways. Former Atlanta Brave shortstop Jeff Blauser's remark (reported in *The Sporting News*) that 'If somebody wants to hit me [with a pitch], he's doing me a favour' is naturally represented as $h \rightarrow f$, where h = Somebody wants to hit me with a pitch, and f = He's doing me a favour. The same conditional could, however, be expressed in many different ways, which include the following:

- Someone is doing me a favour if he wants to hit me with a pitch.
- Someone is doing me a favour when he tries to hit me with a pitch.
- Someone who tries to hit me with a pitch is doing me a favour.
- By trying to hit me with a pitch, someone is doing me a favour.

All of these sentences can be represented as the proposition $h \rightarrow f$. You need to recognize ordinary-language conditionals by asking whether they can reasonably be represented by an 'If . . . , then . . .' statement.

Like conjunctions and disjunctions, conditionals may have components that are complex statements, and may be included in other complex propositions. The first example we provided, the proposition $(r \ \& \ w) \rightarrow s$, is a conditional that has a conjunction as its antecedent. Another example that illustrates these complexities is the statement 'Contemporary thinkers are interesting, but Socrates is the greatest philosopher of all time, and you will find ancient accounts of him a good read if you like to see an active mind at work.' If we let

c = Contemporary thinkers are interesting.
s = Socrates is the greatest philosopher of all time.
y = You will find ancient accounts of him a good read.
l = You like to see an active mind at work.

then we can represent this proposition as

$c \ \& \ s \ \& \ (l \rightarrow y)$

You should note that the brackets we use in symbolizing this proposition are needed to ensure that its meaning is clear. If we wrote $c \ \& \ s \ \& \ l \rightarrow y$, then the statement could be read as $c \ \& \ ((s \ \& \ l) \rightarrow y)$, which means something different. We shall have more to say about the use of brackets in propositional logic statements shortly, but first we will ask you to do some exercises, which should make you more comfortable with propositional logic symbols and the basic forms of propositional logic statements.

SIMPLE AND COMPLEX PROPOSITIONS

➤ *Simple statements* are statements that express a proposition that is not a negation, conjunction, disjunction, or conditional. Simple propositions are represented as lowercase letters of the alphabet.

➤ *Negations* deny some other proposition. They are represented as ~X, where X is the proposition that is negated.

➤ *Conjunctions* assert that two or more propositions (its 'conjuncts') are true. They are represented as X & Y.

➤ *Disjunctions* assert that one or more of a number of propositions (its 'disjuncts') are true. They are represented as X V Y.

➤ *Conditionals* are propositions that assert that some proposition (its 'consequent') is true if some other proposition (its 'antecedent') is true. They are represented as X → Y.

EXERCISE 9A

1. Using the legend provided, translate the following propositional logic sentences into English:

    m = Mars is a planet we should explore.
    w = There is water on Mars.
    e = Every living thing needs water.
    s = Space is the final frontier.
    v = Venus is a planet worth exploring.

    a)* m
    b) $\sim w$
    c) $s \& v$
    d)* $m \lor v$
    e) $e \to m$
    f) $(s \& \sim e) \to v$
    g)* $(s \& e \& w) \to \sim v$
    h) $s \& \sim m$
    i) $(s \to v) \& (v \to s)$
    j) $(v \lor m) \to s$
    k) $m \to \sim v$
    l) $v \to \sim m$
    m)* $s; s \to v; therefore\ v$
    n) $\sim(m \lor v)$
    o) $w \& \sim s \& \sim m \& \sim v$
    p) $(m \lor v) \lor \sim s$
    q) $e \to (\sim w \to \sim m)$
    s) $\sim m \& \sim v$
    t) $\sim(m \lor v) \to \sim s$

2. Using the letters indicated to represent simple propositions, represent the following as propositional logic statements. (When you come across exclusive disjunctions, make sure you represent disjunctions as statements in the form X V Y & ~(X & Y).)

a)   You will become a famous writer, or at least a published author. (*f*, *p*)

b)* She's mistaken when she says that Lee Mun Wah didn't produce the film *The Color of Fear*. (*c*)

c)   [from a box of Kellogg's Frosted Flakes] If it doesn't say KELLOGG'S on the box, it's not KELLOGG'S in the box. (*o*, *i*)

d)   [from the same box] If this product in any way falls below the high standards you've come to expect from Kellogg's, please send your comments and both top flaps to: Consumer Affairs, KELLOGG INC. (*f*, *s*)

e)   [a comment on the Welsh Llanelli rugby team] 'Now's the time if we are to ever achieve our ultimate ambition—the European rugby championship.' (*n*, *u*)

f)* If we let *c* = Richard Nixon is a crook, then ~*c* represents Richard Nixon's famous statement 'I am not a crook.' (*l*, *r*)

g)   He is not an untalented guitarist. (*t*)

h)* We define a 'valid argument' as an argument in which the conclusion follows necessarily from the premises. (*v*, *n*)

i)   An argument is *in*valid if it is possible for the premises to be true and the conclusion false. (*i*, *p*)

j)   'The referee didn't allow no cheating.' (*r*)

k)* [from a box of Shredded Wheat] You should try Shredded Wheat with cold milk or with hot milk. (*c*, *h*)

l)   [from *The Economist* (Aug. 1995)] If they do not set these [sugar and peanut] programmes on a path to oblivion, any idea that these Republicans deserve the adjective 'free market' can be dispensed with, once and for all. (*s*, *p*, *f*)

m)   [from an ad in *Mother Jones* (July/Aug. 1995)] If you want to burn up to 79 per cent more calories, WalkFit is your answer. (*b*, *w*)

n)* [Tucker Carlson, of the Heritage Foundation, in a letter to *Mother Jones* (July/Aug. 1995)] 'Safe neighborhoods are organized.' (*s*, *o*)

o)   [Judith Wallerstein, in *Mother Jones* (July/Aug. 1995)] 'It isn't true that divorce is different for a poor child than it is for a rich child in its emotional content . . .' (*d*)

2. TRANSLATION

The process of depicting ordinary propositions in the symbols of propositional logic can be seen as a kind of 'translation'. Especially as propositional logic is a very simple formal logic, and our concern is a very general account of it that can be applied to ordinary statements, the translations that we will use are often approximations, though they capture the sense of the original statements well enough to allow us to investigate their role in propositional arguments.

We have already introduced the basic principles of translation, but some aspects of the process merit further comment, especially as a failure to appreciate them often leads to problems in translation. To underscore the key aspects of translation, we suggest you heed the following 'ten rules' of good translation. If you let them guide your translations, you should have no difficulty translating ordinary sentences and arguments into the appropriate propositional logic symbols.

1. Use lowercase letters to represent simple propositions. This rule of translation may seem obvious, but students often represent complex propositions, most commonly negations, as simple propositions. Remember that it is a mistake to let m = Marcus Aurelius was *not* a good emperor, for this is a negation. The proper way to translate it is by letting m = Marcus Aurelius was a good emperor, and by representing it as $\sim m$.

2. Use brackets to avoid ambiguity. In earlier chapters, we emphasized that it is important to avoid ambiguity in our own arguments, and to recognize ambiguity when it occurs in the reasoning of other arguers. In translating sentences into propositional logic symbols, it is important to use brackets to avoid possible ambiguities when symbolizing particular propositions. The statement $a \rightarrow b \lor c$ is ambiguous because it can be interpreted as the proposition $(a \rightarrow b) \lor c$ or as the proposition $a \rightarrow (b \lor c)$. Because these two propositions mean different things, you must make it clear which you intend when you are translating.

3. Do not confuse indicator words with connector words. Remember that words like 'because' and 'therefore' are logical indicators that arguers use to identify their premises and conclusions. In such cases, they are logical terms, but they are not propositional logic connectors and cannot, therefore, be represented as propositional logic symbols. In propositional arguments they tell us what propositions are premises and conclusions. Propositional logic symbols can then be used to translate these premises and conclusions.

4. Distinguish 'if' and 'only if'. In most ordinary conditionals, the statement that follows the connector word 'if' is the antecedent. An important exception to this rule occurs when conditionals use the connector words 'only if'. In this case, the statement that follows 'only if' is the consequent. The statement 'X only if Y' is, therefore, properly represented as the proposition $X \rightarrow Y$.

You can see why this is the case by considering the conditional 'You can join the Air Force only if you are eighteen.' It would be a mistake to interpret this proposition as the claim that you can join the Air Force if you are eighteen, for this is only one of the requirements (other requirements include good physical health, the passing of entrance exams, and so on). As it is sometimes put, 'X only if Y' states that Y is a necessary—but not sufficient—condition for X. Because X could not, in such circumstances, occur if Y is not true, this is a circumstance in which $X \rightarrow Y$, but need not be a circumstance in which $Y \rightarrow X$.

5. Treat biconditionals as conjunctions with conditional conjuncts. In an ordinary conditional, the implication goes one way: the antecedent implies the consequent. In a 'biconditional' the implication goes both ways: the antecedent implies the consequent and the consequent implies the antecedent. 'If you win the $6 million lotto, you'll be rich,' is a conditional because the consequent ('you'll be rich') does not imply the antecedent ('you win the $6 million lotto'): it does not rule out the possibility that you might become rich in other ways (by receiving $14 million in inheritance, for example). In contrast, one presents a biconditional if one explains the word 'bachelor' by saying, 'You are a bachelor if you are an unmarried man.' For this is a case in which the consequent ('You are a bachelor') does imply the antecedent ('You are an unmarried man').

Biconditionals are a way to express definitions or other equivalences. Logicians often represent biconditionals as statements with the connecting words 'if and only if', but in ordinary language they are more likely to be expressed as conditionals, though the context makes it clear that this is a situation in which the antecedent and the consequent of a conditional are being forwarded as equivalent.

In propositional logic, biconditionals have the form $(X \rightarrow Y) \, \& \, (Y \rightarrow X)$. The informal definition 'An alchemist is the medieval version of the modern chemist' may be rendered as the biconditional $(a \rightarrow m) \, \& \, (m \rightarrow a)$, where

a = A person is an alchemist.
m = A person is the medieval version of the modern chemist.

6. Treat 'unless' statements as conditionals. In ordinary language, the connector word 'unless' precedes an antecedent that is (implicitly) negated. The sentence 'I'll go unless she does' is the conditional 'If she doesn't go, I'll go.' The sentence 'Your kite won't fly unless there's a breeze' is the conditional 'If there is no breeze, then your kite won't fly.' This means that sentences of the form 'Y unless X' are recognized as conditionals of the form $\sim X \rightarrow Y$.

7. Translate sentences that express the same proposition in the same way. In diagramming arguments, we have already seen that the same premise or conclusion is often stated in different ways. In diagramming, we replace these variations with one definition of a premise or conclusion so we can work with a clear statement of the argument. In translating sentences into propositional logic we must similarly recognize that a particular proposition may be expressed in different ways. If s = She got the highest mark in the math exam, then s will also serve as the translation of the sentence 'No one did as well as she did.' If d = She's on the Dean's list, then $s \rightarrow d$ represents both the statement 'If she got the highest mark on the math exam, she's on the Dean's list' and the statement 'She's on the dean's list if it is true that she got the highest mark on the math exam.'

8. Translate logical connectors literally if you can. When ordinary sentences use propositional logic connector words, translate them literally whenever it is clear that the words are used in the same way that connectors are used in propositional logic. If Sherlock Holmes says that 'Either Cecil Jones or Margaret Midgley is the guilty party,' this should be translated as $c \, V \, m$, where

c = Cecil Jones is the guilty party.
m = Margaret Midgley is the guilty party.

The statement $c \lor m$ implies that 'If Cecil Jones isn't the guilty party, then Margaret Midgley is.' This is an inference that we can prove valid in propositional logic, but it would be incorrect to represent Holmes' statement it as $\sim c \rightarrow m$. That is something that is implied by what he said, but it is not what he said.

9. Ignore variations that do not affect the validity of an argument. When you are translating propositional logic arguments, many minor variations will not matter. If there is no obvious way to determine what will and will not matter beforehand, you must simply look at a particular argument and ask yourself what matters to a conclusion and an inference.

Consider the argument 'As the American Anti-Vivisection Society maintains, experiments on animals are justified only if animals feel no pain. As this is certainly mistaken, animal experiments are unjustified.' The general thrust of this argument can be captured by adopting the following legend:

j = Experiments on animals are justified.
p = Animals feel pain.
$\quad\quad j \rightarrow p, \sim p,$ *therefore* $\sim j$

This representation of the argument leaves out some aspects of the argument. Notably, it leaves out the reference to the American Anti-Vivisection Society in the first sentence of the argument and does not capture the full strength of the second premise, which claims that the proposition that animals feel pain is not only true, but 'certain'. In a more sophisticated treatment of this argument, and in a more sophisticated formal logic, these further aspects could be recognized. In working with the limited resources available in propositional logic, however, a rough analogue of the argument must suffice. While this is not the best of all possible situations, it is useful nonetheless, for it can still be used to show that the reasoning in the argument is valid.

10. Check your translation by translating back to ordinary English. If you are unsure of your translation of an ordinary-language sentence or argument, you can check it by translating it back into ordinary English. The result should be a clear instance of the proposition or argument you began with.

Translating Arguments

If you follow our ten translation rules, you should have no difficulty translating ordinary sentences into propositional logic symbols. Once you know how to translate sentences, you will also know how to translate whole arguments, for this requires only that we use the rules to translate the argument's premises and conclusion.

Consider the following argument:

If Samantha moves her rook, James will place her in check with his pawn. If she moves her knight, he'll place her in check with his queen. Those are the only moves open to her, so James's pawn or knight will have her in check in one move.

We can translate this argument into propositional logic symbols as follows:

r = Samantha moves her rook.
k = Samantha moves her knight.
p = James will place her in check by moving his pawn.
q = James will place her in check with his queen.

$r \rightarrow p, k \rightarrow q, r \lor k$, *therefore $p \lor q$*

In creating this translation, you will see that we applied the ten rules for translation to each of the argument's premises and conclusion. In translating the premise 'Those are the only moves open to her' as $r \lor k$, we have, for example, implicitly relied on Rule 7, which tells us to treat different ways of expressing a proposition in the same way. We have recognized that this premise is, even though it does not employ the word 'or', a way of expressing a disjunction, and needs to be represented in this way.

TEN RULES FOR GOOD TRANSLATION

1. Use lowercase letters to represent simple propositions.
2. Use brackets to avoid ambiguity.
3. Do not confuse indicator words with connector words.
4. Distinguish 'if' and 'only if'.
5. Treat biconditionals as conjunctions with conditional conjuncts.
6. Treat 'unless' statements as conditionals.
7. Translate sentences that express the same proposition in the same way.
8. Translate logical connectors literally if you can.
9. Ignore variations that do not affect the validity of an argument.
10. Check your translation by translating back to ordinary English.

EXERCISE 9B

1. Translate the following sentences into propositional logic form using the letters indicated.
   a) If that's Louis, we're in for trouble. If not, we're home free. (l, t)
   b) If Angela and Karl frequent the place, then it's no place I want to go. (a, k, g)
   c) Either you straighten up and get your act together or you're out of here. (s, a, o)
   d) If you want a good time, go to British Columbia or to California. (g, b, c)
   e)* If you have multimedia skills or have worked on video you can apply for the job. (m, v, j)
   f) It's a good wine, but not a great wine. (a, g)
   g) If the greenhouse effect continues to evolve as predicted, the crocuses will bloom in March. (g, c)
   h) If there are any boycotts of the Olympics, the games will lose their credibility. (b, c)

i)* Either I'm paranoid, or you are out to get me. (*p, o*)

j)* They're lying when they say they weren't there. (*t*)

k) North Korea will disarm if and only if South Korea disarms. (*n, s*)

l)* Only those who can stand a lot of pain can get a Ph.D. (*s, p*)

m) The murder can't have been committed by both the chauffeur and the butler. (*c, b*)

n) Whenever it rains there are dark clouds in the sky. (*r, d*)

o) If you go to town, then you'll see the remains of the car on your right side if you turn right on Dundas Street. (*g, r, d*)

p) If he'll buy the chair if I up the price to four hundred dollars, then we'll know that he's guilty and we'll arrest him. (*b, u, g, a*)

q)* I'm not interested in that car unless it is in mint condition. (*i, m*)

r) When it rains there are clouds in the sky, and when it doesn't the sky is clear unless the pollution gets too bad. (*r, c, p*)

s) I'll go only if Joan goes, too. (*g, j*)

t) If you have a headache, it's because you drank too much last night and I can't feel sorry for you when you drink too much. (*h, d, s*)

2. Decide whether the following statements express simple conditionals or biconditionals, and put each into symbols using the letters given.

a)* [Boyle's law] The pressure of a gas varies with its volume at a constant temperature. (*p, v, t*)

b)* An individual is still alive as long as an EEG records brain signals. (*a, s*)

c) You may become a Catholic priest only if you are male. (*p, m*)

d) A figure is a triangle whenever it has only three sides. (*t, i*)

e)* Metal does not expand unless it is heated. (*e, h*)

f)* Abortion is murder if and only if the fertilized ovum is a person. (*m, p*)

g) Whenever it rains, he's in a bad mood. (*r, b*)

h) If there are any more boycotts of the Olympics, the games will have to be cancelled. (*b, c*)

3. Translate the following sentences into propositional logic symbols. Create your own legend.

a) [from the *Literary Review of Canada* (Nov. 2002)] Both the US and Great Britain, but not Canada, had anti-terrorist statutes in place before 11 September.

b) [from a report on the future of footballer Ozalan Alpay, who played for Aston Villa <http://www.ananova.com> (13 Jan. 2003)] 'If I'm still here in the next two or three weeks, I will play for the reserve team.'

c) [from the same report] Villa needs to give him a more realistic value—or he will be stuck at Villa Park until the summer.

d) [from the QuickTime Pro website (14 Jan. 2003)] Whether you use a Macintosh or Windows-based PC, you can harness the power of QuickTime Pro for media authoring and playback of high-quality audio and video.

e) [from the MapQuest website] Consumers . . . can easily access millions of locations around the world, obtain detailed maps and accurate driving directions,
locate places of interest, customize road trip plans, and create, save, download or
email personalized maps.

f)* [Paul Friedman, the public-address announcer at Wrigley Field, in *The Sporting
News*] One thing I've learned is that if you make a mistake, if you say it with a
deep enough voice, you can get away with it.

4. Translate the following propositional logic arguments into propositional logic forms
using the letters indicated.

a) According to the law, she's guilty only if she committed the crime and committed it intentionally. She did commit the crime, but unintentionally, so she's not
guilty. (*g, c, i*)

b) Either you've offended him or he dislikes you. It has to be the latter, for I can't
imagine you offending him. (*o, l*)

c) The Americans or the Germans or the Russians will win the most medals at next
year's Olympics. But I've heard that the Russian team is in disarray, and if that's
true, they won't do well enough to win. Neither will the Americans. I've concluded that the Germans will win the most medals. (*a, g, r, d*)

d) If he moves his rook, she'll move her bishop. And if she moves her bishop, he'll
be forced to move his king. And if he does that, it's checkmate in ten moves. So
its checkmate in ten moves if he moves his rook. (*r, b, k, c*)

e)* In order to avoid the intricacies of such theories we will rely on our earlier
remark that the objective of an argument is to convince an audience. If this is so,
then it is sufficient for our purposes that the premises of a good argument be
accepted as true by both us and our audience. (*o, s*)

f) It should be clear that this new argument is valid, for it is obviously possible for
its two premises to be true when its conclusion is false, and if this is true then the
argument is invalid. (*v, t*)

g)* The Conservatives will win the election if Liberal support declines in urban
ridings. But there's no chance that Liberal support is going to decline in urban
ridings. (*w, d*)

h) You have a problem with your hardware or your software. If it's your software,
only Scott can fix it. If there's a problem with your hardware, only Deb can help.
Either way, it will cost you a bundle. So it's going to cost you a bundle. (*h, y, s,
d, b*)

3. Propositional Schemes and Proofs

In learning how to represent arguments in propositional logic symbols, you have
learned how to represent propositional schemes of argument. For implicit in the translation of any argument is some propositional logic scheme, which defines a class of
arguments that follow a similar pattern of reasoning. Consider, to take an example, the
following argument:

If Jim left, he's gone to Ira's, and if he's gone to Ira's, they are watching *Survivor* again, so they're watching *Survivor* again if Jim has left.

If we let l = Jim has left, i = He's gone to Ira's, and s = They are watching *Survivor* again, then this argument can be properly represented as an argument of the form $l \rightarrow i$, $i \rightarrow s$, so $l \rightarrow s$. But this is not the only argument of this form. There is a large (indeed, infinite) class of arguments that conforms to this scheme. By defining l, i, and s in different ways, we could easily concoct further examples of arguments that are included in this class. (As an exercise, you may want to define l, i, and s in three different ways, noting the three different arguments that result.)

Once we recognize that we identify some general scheme of argument whenever we translate an argument into propositional logic symbols, we can further our analysis of propositional arguments by identifying valid propositional logic schemes. Arguments that conform to these schemes can then be recognized as deductively valid arguments. We can prove that a particular argument is valid by translating it into propositional logic symbols and by showing that it is a variant of a valid scheme, or that one can use valid schemes to deduce its conclusion from its premises. To this end, we will proceed by identifying valid schemes of argument that are associated with each of the propositional logic connectives.

Conjunctions

The two valid schemes of conjunctive argument we will recognize are the most obviously valid propositional arguments, so it is useful to begin with them. The first scheme is 'Conjunction Elimination', or '&E' for short; the second, 'Conjunction Introduction', or '&I' for short.

These two rules can be defined as follows:

&E: X & Y, *therefore X (or Y)*
&I: X, Y, *therefore X & Y*

Both of these schemes are commonly assumed in ordinary reasoning. Both are deductively valid. In the first case, the truth of a conjunction implies that each of its conjuncts must be true, for this is precisely what it asserts. In the second case, the truth of two propositions implies the truth of a conjunction that conjoins them, for it must be true if they are true.

Consider the novel *Arcadia*. Its cover records that the author is Jim Crace. The blurb on the back cover notes that 'He is the author of *Continent* . . . and *The Gift of Stones*.' If we let a = Jim Crace is the author of the novel *Arcadia*, c = Jim Crace is the author of *Continent*, and g = He is the author of *The Gift of Stones*, then this implies that a, and that c & g. Having noted that this is so, we may employ the schemes &I and &E if someone asks us about Jim Crace's works. If someone asks us what Jim Crace has written we may deduce an answer in the following step-by-step way:

1. a P (for 'premise', known from the front cover of *Arcadia*)
2. c & g P (premise, known from the blurb on the back cover)
3. a & c & g 1, 2, &I

This is a very simple propositional logic *proof*. It begins with premises and uses valid propositional schemes of argument (often called 'rules of inference') to arrive, in a step-by-step fashion, at a conclusion. Each of the numbered steps includes a proposition, the insertion of which is assumed or derived in a way that is precisely specified on the right. In this case, the first two propositions, 1 and 2, are assumed on the grounds that they are provided as premises. The insertion of the third is justified by applying the argument scheme &I to propositions 1 and 2.

We implicitly follow the chain of reasoning outlined in our proof when someone asks us what books Jim Crace wrote, and we reason from what we find on the covers of *Arcadia* to the conclusion that 'He wrote *Arcadia, Continent,* and *The Gift of Stones.*' Reasoning about such questions may also employ the scheme &E. Having read that *c* & *g* is true, we may, for example, answer the question whether Jim Crace wrote *The Gift of Stones* by reasoning as follows:

1. *c* & *g*   P
2. *g*   1, &E

This is another simple propositional logic proof. In this case, the proof has one premise, *c* & *g*, and one other proposition that is inferred from it by applying the rule &E.

The argument schemes &I and &E can be used to justify inferences that involve conjunctions of any size. The following is, for example, a propositional logic proof that uses repeated instances of the scheme &I to establish a conjunction with four conjuncts:

1. *j*   P
2. *m*   P
3. *p*   P
4. *a*   P
5. *j* & *m*   1, 2, &I
6. *j* & *m* & *p*   5, 3, &I
7. *j* & *m* & *p* & *a*   6, 4, &I

We have not defined the meaning of the premises in this proof. Instead, we have left this meaning open and used our proof to demonstrate that one can validly move from these premises to the conclusion that *j* & *m* & *p* & *a*, no matter how these simple propositions are defined. We know that this is so because our conclusion (and each of our intermediate conclusions) has been derived by applying a valid scheme of argument (in this case, &I).

Disjunctions

In developing our propositional logic, we will add to &I and &E one scheme of argument that can be used to construct valid disjunctive arguments. It is called 'disjunction elimination' and will be symbolized as 'VE'. We define VE as follows:

VE: X V Y (or Y V X), ~X, *therefore* Y

This is a valid inference because the claim that a disjunction is true and one of its disjuncts false leads inevitably to the conclusion that the remaining disjunct must be true (for the disjunction asserts that at least one of them is true).

Consider the reasoning of an overconfident professor, Dave, who scans his class and sees several students yawning. We might easily imagine him reasoning as follows: 'Either my students are bored or they are tired because they partied late last night. But this is one of the most interesting lectures I've ever given. It must have been some party!'

If we let b = The class is bored with my lecture, and t = The students are tired because they partied late last night, then we can prove that this is a valid chain of reasoning as follows:

1.	$b \lor t$	P
2.	$\sim b$	P
3.	t	1,2, VE

It is important to remember that this proof—and any propositional logic proof—only shows that a particular chain of reasoning is (deductively) valid. It does not prove that an argument must be a strong argument, because that requires both validity and acceptable premises. In this case, students in the class may want to argue that the argument is weak because the premises (that there are only two possible explanations of the students' yawning, and that they cannot be bored) are not acceptable.

The scheme VE can be applied to exclusive as well as inclusive disjunctions. Suppose you are unhappy with the Ultramatic bed you bought under the condition that 'You will be completely satisfied or we will happily refund your money.' We have already seen that the statement can be represented as the exclusive disjunction $(s \lor r)$ & $\sim(s \& r)$, where s = You will be completely satisfied, and r = We will happily refund your money. When you go to return the bed and collect a refund, you will have used this claim as a basis for the conclusion that your money should be happily returned. We can prove the validity of this reasoning as follows:

1.	$(s \lor r)$ & $\sim(s \& r)$	P (the initial guarantee)
2.	$\sim s$	P (your response to your experience with the bed)
3.	$s \lor r$	1, &E
4.	r	3, 2, VE

It is worth noting that the propositional scheme of argument VE does not allow you to move directly from propositions 1 and 2 to r. This is because proposition 1 is, strictly speaking, a conjunction (a conjunction that *contains* a disjunction but is not itself a disjunction), and the scheme VE is applicable only to disjunctions. In using schemes, always remember that you must use them in the precise way they have been defined. In this case, this limitation does not present a significant problem, because we can isolate the disjunction in proposition 1 by using the rule &E, and can then apply the scheme VE. It is by moves of this sort that we can simplify propositions and isolate their elements, and in this way work toward a conclusion in a propositional logic proof.

Conditionals

Our propositional logic will include two basic schemes of argument that employ conditionals. They are called 'Affirming the Antecedent', or 'AA', and 'Denying the Consequent', or 'DC'. (Traditionally, these rules are known as *modus ponens* and *modus tollens*.) These two schemes can be defined as follows:

AA: $X \rightarrow Y$, X, *therefore Y*
DC: $X \rightarrow Y$, $\sim Y$, *therefore* $\sim X$

You should see that both these schemes are deductively valid. A conditional and its antecedent must imply its consequent, for the conditional states that its consequent is true in these specific circumstances. Arguments that match the scheme DC are also valid, for the antecedent of a true conditional cannot be true if the consequent is false, since its truth would (by the scheme AA) imply that the consequent was true.

Consider the following remark by a Chinese commentator on China's move to become a leader in the development of cloning technology (reported in *Wired*, Jan. 2003, p. 121):

> We have a huge population and a one-child policy. Why would you think about making people in a laboratory?

To unravel the argument in these remarks we need to recognize that the question in this quotation is a rhetorical question. The author of the remark is not genuinely asking the question but is suggesting that it *doesn't* make sense to think about making people in a laboratory given the first claim, that China has a huge population and a one-child policy. We can represent the implicit argument as follows:

h = China has a huge population and a one-child policy.
s = It makes sense for China to think about making people in a laboratory.
$$h \rightarrow \sim s, h, \text{ therefore } \sim s$$

As this is a simple instance of the argument scheme AA, we can prove the validity of this reasoning as follows:

1. $h \rightarrow \sim s$ P
2. h P
3. $\sim s$ 1, 2, AA

Every time we use the scheme AA in a propositional logic proof, we state the line numbers for the lines where the relevant conditional and its antecedent appear.

We can illustrate the scheme DC with the following example, from a letter to the *Globe and Mail* (29 Jan. 1987):

> The prize for the most erroneous statement of the week should be shared by economist John Crispo and journalist Jennifer Lewington. Both of them claim that the present value of the Canadian dollar [$0.68 US] gives our exporters an advantage of 30 per cent or more in the US market.
>
> Nothing could be further from the truth. That would be true only if prices and costs had risen by the same amount in both countries. In fact, between

1970 and 1986, the price index of GNP rose 28 per cent more in Canada than it did in the United States.

If we let

e = Economist John Crispo is correct.

j = Journalist Jennifer Lewington is correct.

a = The value of the Canadian dollar gives Canadian exporters an advantage of 30 per cent or more in the US.

s = Prices and costs rise by the same amount in both countries.

then the letter's argument can be translated as $e \rightarrow a; j \rightarrow a; a \rightarrow s; \sim s;$ *therefore* $\sim e$ & $\sim j$. Having determined that the argument has this structure, we can prove its validity as follows:

1. $e \rightarrow a$ P
2. $j \rightarrow a$ P
3. $a \rightarrow s$ P
4. $\sim s$ P
5. $\sim a$ 3, 4, DC
6. $\sim j$ 2, 5, DC
7. $\sim e$ 1, 5, DC
8. $\sim e$ & $\sim j$ 7, 6, &I

In using the schemes AA and DC, keep in mind that the antecedent of a conditional may be a complex rather than a simple proposition. Affirming an antecedent may, in such a case, mean affirming a conjunction, a negation, a disjunction, or a conditional. Denying a consequent may mean denying a proposition of this form. If the conditional one is working with is $(t$ & $h) \rightarrow \sim(q$ V $r)$, then one must affirm the antecedent by affirming $(t$ & $h)$, or deny the consequent by denying $\sim(q$ V $r)$. In the latter case, this requires that we assert $(q$ V $r)$.

The argument scheme DC is prominent in scientific reasoning, where it is used when a theory is rejected by showing that it implies experimental results that are not corroborated. A good historical example is the refutation of 'phlogiston theory' by Lavoisier in 1775. According to phlogiston theory, combustion is a process in which a substance called 'phlogiston' departs from a burning substance. This implies that a substance will lose weight if it combusts (since it has lost phlogiston), but Lavoisier demonstrated that this consequence does not hold in the case of mercury. If we let

p = Phlogiston theory is correct.

w = Mercury will weigh less after combustion.

then we can construct a proof of Lavoisier's reasoning as follows.

1. $p \rightarrow w$ P (on the basis of the theory)
2. $\sim w$ P (established by experiment)
3. $\sim p$ 1, 2, DC

In this case we have a strong argument, for this proves that the argument is valid and it is also the case that both premises are acceptable—the first because it is a clear consequence of Phlogiston theory, the second because it is proved by Lavoisier's experiments.

Conditional Fallacies

In contrast to AA and DC, the alternatives 'affirming the consequent' and 'denying the antecedent' ('AC' and ' DA') are not necessarily valid. You need, therefore, to ensure that you do not confuse them with AA and DC.

The problems with AC and DA can be illustrated with the following conditional:

If you are the host of a popular TV show, then you impressed someone.

This conditional is one that we can reasonably accept as true. For the producers of a popular TV show are not likely to hire you as host unless you've impressed them or someone who works with them. Once we accept the conditional, we can reasonably conclude that you impressed someone if we can establish that you're the host of a popular TV show. This is an instance of AA that illustrates the kind of inference it allows.

Suppose, however, that we accept the conditional and its consequent: i.e. that you impressed someone. In such a context it should be obvious that one cannot validly conclude that you must be the host of a popular television show (!). For similar reasons, one cannot use the negation of the antecedent—i.e. the claim that you are not a popular television show host—to validly conclude that you have not impressed someone. In both cases, you may have impressed someone in ways that have nothing to do with hosting a popular television show (by doing something that is rewarded with a medal of bravery, for example). It follows that the consequent of our conditional does not imply the antecedent, and that the negation of the antecedent does not imply the negation of the consequent.

Biconditionals

The arguments AC and DA are not valid, but similar-looking inferences are valid in the case of biconditionals.

Consider the argument:

This figure is a trapezoid only if it is a quadrilateral with two parallel sides. And it has two parallel sides, a and b, and is a quadrilateral, so it's a trapezoid.

If we let t = This figure is a trapezoid, and q = It is a quadrilateral with two parallel sides, then this might seem to be the following case of AC:

$t \rightarrow q$, q, therefore t

Instead of concluding that this is an invalid argument that is an instance of AC, we can more plausibly conclude that this is an incorrect way of representing the argument, for there is another way to interpret it. For though the conditional with which we began may at first glance seem to be a simple conditional that uses the connector 'only if', it is actually a biconditional. We can see this by recognizing that the conditional in the argument is a definition of 'trapezoid' that can best be represented as the proposition *(t → q) & (q → t)*, for it is true that a figure is a quadrilateral with 2 parallel sides if it is a trapezoid, and that it is a trapezoid if it is a quadrilateral with 2 parallel sides.

Once we recognize our conditional as a biconditional, we need to represent our argument as: *(t → q) & (q → t), q, therefore t*. And this argument can be proved valid as follows, by invoking propositional logic argument schemes we have already introduced:

1. $(t \rightarrow q) \& (q \rightarrow t)$ P
2. q P
3. $q \rightarrow t$ 1, &E
4. t 3, 2, AA

Once we recognize biconditionals and translate them properly into propositional logic symbols, they are relatively easy to work with, for we can use the argument scheme &E to isolate the different conditionals they contain. Once we have done this, we can usually employ conditional argument schemes like AA and DC.

Conditional Series
The last propositional scheme of argument we will introduce in this chapter is called 'conditional series', or 'CS'. It can be defined as follows:

CS: X → Y, Y → Z, *therefore* X → Z

CS is a rule that allows us to reduce two conditionals to one conditional that consists of the antecedent of the first conditional and the consequent of the second. This is a valid inference because the antecedent of a conditional implies not only its consequent but also any further consequent that is entailed by this first consequent. If it is true both that 'If Hitler had attacked Britain two months earlier, he would have won the Battle of Britain,' and that 'If he had won the Battle of Britain he would have won World War II,' then CS allows us to conclude that 'If Hitler had attacked Britain two months earlier he would have won World War II.'

More formally, we can demonstrate the validity of this inference by letting:

t = Hitler attacked Britain two months earlier.
s = Hitler would have won the Battle of Britain.
w = Hitler would have won World War II.

and by constructing the following proof:

1. $t \rightarrow s$ P
2. $s \rightarrow w$ P
3. $t \rightarrow w$ 1, 2, CS

As you will observe in the exercises ahead, it is often useful to employ CS in conjunction with conditional rules of inference like AA and DC.

The scheme CS completes our discussion of the most basic schemes of argument we will include within our introduction to propositional logic. You will find a summary of these rules in a box at the end of this chapter. You may use it as a convenient guide as you begin to construct propositional proofs, but you should learn the schemes well enough to make this unnecessary. The better you know the schemes, the easier it will be to construct the chains of inference that proofs depend on.

Constructing Simple Proofs

Equipped with the argument schemes we have outlined and the ability to translate ordinary sentences into standard propositional logic forms, you should be ready to construct simple proofs that demonstrate the validity of propositional arguments. For those who initially find proofs difficult, we offer the following tips for good proof construction.

1. Remember that good proofs depend on good translations. If you do not translate an argument into propositional symbols properly, your proof cannot (however ingenious it is) prove that an argument is valid. For in that case your proof is dealing with a different argument than the one that you began with. To avoid this, be sure that you translate an argument carefully. In translating argument components, follow the guidelines we introduced in the earlier sections of this chapter. If you know that an argument is valid but cannot construct a proof, check your translation. The problem may be in the translation rather than in your proof.

2. Base your strategy on an argument's premises or conclusion. The validity of an extended argument may be difficult to see. If you are unsure how to proceed, limit your attention to one step at a time. A propositional logic proof proceeds by dividing a larger argument into a series of smaller steps defined by propositional logic argument schemes.

You may find it useful to begin by asking what follows from the stated premises. To determine this, you can derive what you can from an argument's premises and see where this takes you. If a premise is a conjunction, you can isolate each conjunct. If one premise is a conditional and another its antecedent, then AA can be used to derive the consequent. Ask yourself what argument schemes are invited by the premises. After you have established this, you can ask what follows from the propositions you are able to deduce.

Keep track of the premises you have used. In most of the propositional arguments in this book, the conclusion depends on all of the premises. It is probably the premises you have not yet employed that will be the key to progressing with your proof.

Alternatively you may plan your strategy by considering the conclusion. What kind of proposition is it? What argument scheme is likely to justify it? If it is a conjunction, you may need to use the argument scheme &I. That will require you to isolate each conjunction. How can this be done? In this way you can think back from your conclusion until you see a way to arrive at your premises, and can then construct your proof accordingly.

PROPOSITIONAL SCHEMES OF ARGUMENT

&E   X & Y (or Y & X), *therefore* X

&I   X, Y, *therefore* X & Y

VE   X V Y (or Y V X), ~X, *therefore* Y

AA   X → Y, X, *therefore* Y

DC   X → Y, ~Y, *therefore* ~X

CS   X → Y, Y → Z, *therefore* X → Z

EXERCISE 9C

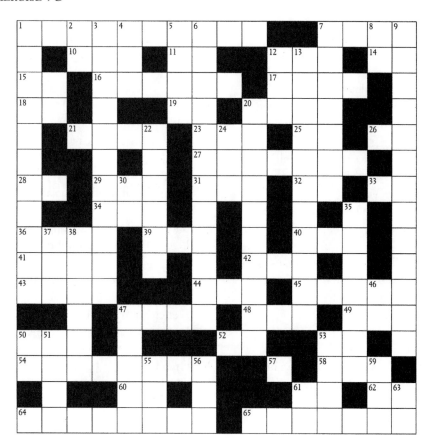

CLUES ACROSS

  1. What follows from premises.

  7. Booby _____ .

10. If g = It's a girl, then ~g = It's a

    _____ .

CLUES DOWN

  1. 'If . . . then' statement.

  2. Latin for 'note well'.

  3. *a & b.*

CLUES ACROSS (*cont.*)

11. If *p* = Paul goes out, *c* = Chris goes out, *m* = Mary goes out, then *m* → (*p* & *c*) and ~*c* imply that Mary is _____ .
12. 'Lion' is equivalent to '_____'.
14. If you have a Ph.D. you are a _____ .
15. If *x* = yes, then ~*x* = _____ .
16. ~(*a* & *b*) _____ s *a* & *b*.
17. _____ Fitzgerald, singer.
18. If *x*, then *y*, ~*y*, so ~*x*.
19. Man's title.
20. _____ of rope.
21. Sounds like our disjunctive connector.
25. Same as 61 down.
26. First word of a proverb equivalent to *h* → *e*, where *h* = You're human.
27. _____ the antecedent.
28. The principles of identity tell us to treat 'that is' as interchangeable with this abbreviation.
29. If *m* = Catch me, then *c* → *m* is a common saying if *c* = you _____ .
31. If *d* = The stock market has its downs, then ~*d* is the statement that the stock market has its _____ .
32. Short for Nova Scotia.
33. (*a* → *b*) & (*b* → *a*) is a _____ conditional.
34. In a race between two individuals, it is a false dilemma to say that one or the other will win, for it may be a _____ .
36. Degree _____ .
39. Word used to form negations.
40. We've discussed conditionals and biconditionals, but not _____ conditionals.
41. Food for Lassie.

CLUES DOWN (*cont.*)

4. Sounds, but is not, equivalent to a dishonest practice.
5. If *t* = Go to Thailand, and *e* = You like exotic places, and it is true that *e* and *e* → *t*, then you should go here.
6. Some propositional rules of inference—e.g. &I—are rules of _____ .
7. Denying the consequent is traditionally called *modus* _____ .
8. The next chapter discusses Reductio _____ Absurdum.
9. The topic of this chapter is _____ logic.
12. Let *g* = Leo, *c* = Chris, and *l* = Linda, and apply VE twice to the following: *g* V *c* V *l*, ~*c*, ~*l*.
13. *a* & *b*, *therefore b* is a case of an _____ .
20. *b*, in *a* → *b*.
22. A word traditionally associated with AA.
24. Short for a Democrat's opposite.
30. Logic plays an important role in _____ research.
35. A rule yet to be introduced: X V Y, X → Z, Y → Z, *therefore* Z.
37. French equivalent to 'island'.
38. Famous baby doctor, Star Trek personality.
46. Grand _____ Opry.
47. The law of the excluded middle says statements can be true or false but not _____ or more false.
50. One of the forms of argument discussed in later chapters of this text is called _____ hominem.
51. Trigonometric function.
53. One might awkwardly say that &E _____ s a conjunction.

CLUES ACROSS (*cont.*)

42. The laws of thought apply
    _____ versally.
43. _____ Uris, famous author.
44. The proposition *a* & *b* can be false in
    three ways. How many ways are there
    for it to be true?
45. $t \rightarrow m$, *t* = you go to a theatre,
    m = you may go to a _____ .
47. '*b* when *a*' is equivalent to 'If *a*,
    _____ *b*'.
48. $\sim(x \,\&\, \sim x)$ is an instance of
    the principle of _____
    -contradiction.
49. $s \rightarrow m$, *s* = She's a Member of the
    Legislative Assembly, *m* = She's an
    _____ .
50. First word of a biblical saying
    equivalent to $a \rightarrow b$, where *b* = shall
    be given.
52. Abbreviation for light.
53. *m* V *a*, where *m* = a form of
    meditation, and *a* = advertising
    abbreviation.
54. Half of *x* V *y*.
57. See 57 down.
58. A rule in propositional logic: Assume
    x, derive $y \,\&\, \sim y$, conclude $\sim x$.
60. If we treated AA as a rule of
    elimination, its abbreviation would be
    this.
61. _____5, British agency.
62. *a* V *i*, where *a* = abbreviation for
    'pound', *i* = first initials of an
    American president.
64. Apply the rule &E to *f* & *d*, where *f*
    and *d* are the names of two great
    logicians, Frege and DeMorgan.
65. Argument building block.

CLUES DOWN (*cont.*)

55. A verb that implies repeated use of
    equivalent propositions.
56. The number of rules of inference
    introduced in this chapter, plus four.
57. First letter of the abbreviation of the
    rule used to derive a consequent.
59. *h* & *p* & *j*, where *h* = Hirt,
    p = Pacino, and *j* = Jolson.
61. If *m* = The culprit is me, *y* = The
    culprit is you, and *s* = The culprit is
    someone else, and $y \rightarrow r$, $r \rightarrow m$,
    $s \rightarrow (s \,\&\, m)$, then we can be sure
    that one culprit is _____ .
63. Hamlet asks whether he should
    x V $\sim$*x*, where *x* = _____ .

Major Exercise 9M

1. Fill in the missing steps in the following proofs. Each '?' indicates a missing step. All the premises are identified.

a)* 1. $a \rightarrow b$ P
     2. a P
     3. ?   ?

b) 1. $c \rightarrow d$ P
     2. $c \rightarrow e$ P
     3. c P
     4. ?   ?, AA
     5. e 2, 3, AA
     6. ?   4, 5, &I

c)* 1. $(e$ or $d)$ & f P
     2. $\sim d$ P
     3. ?   ??
     4. e ??
     5. ?   ??
     6. e & f 4, 5, &I

d) 1. $p \rightarrow s$ P
     2. $r \rightarrow p$ P
     3. $f \rightarrow r$??
     4. f P
     5. r ?, 4, AA
     6. p 2, 5, AA
     7. ?   1, 6, AA

e) 1. $m \rightarrow n$ P
     2. $n \rightarrow o$ P
     3. m & r P
     4. m 3, ?
     5. n 1, 4, ?
     6. o ???

f) 1. a & $\sim c$ P
     2. c V e P
     3. $\sim c$???
     4. ?   2, 3, ?

g)* 1. $a \rightarrow d$ P
     2. $d \rightarrow e$ P
     3. a & b P
     4. a ???
     5. ?   1, 4, AA
     6. ?   ???
     7. a & e 4, 6, ?

h) 1. $(t$ & $h) \rightarrow \sim c$?
     2. t P
     3. h & i P
     4. h 3, ?
     5. t & h ??
     6. $\sim c$??, AA

i) 1. e V f P
     2. $a \rightarrow \sim f$ P
     3. a & b ?
     4. a 3, ?
     5. ?   4, 2, AA
     6. e ??

j) 1. c V q ?
     2. e V $\sim q$ P
     3. f V $\sim e$ P
     4. $\sim f$ P
     5. $\sim e$ 3, 4, ?
     6. $\sim q$??
     7. ?   1, ??

2. Let a = Andrea had a high grade-point average last term, b = Brian did, c = Catharine did, d = David did, and e = Evan did. Translate the following propositional logic arguments from propositional logic symbols into ordinary English, adapting the wording as desirable. After you do the translation, construct a proof that proves the argument valid.

a) $b \rightarrow c$, $c \rightarrow d$, $d \rightarrow e$, b, therefore e
b)* $b \rightarrow c$, $a \rightarrow b$, $d \rightarrow a$, $\sim c$, therefore $\sim d$
c) a & b, b & c, therefore a & c
d) $b \rightarrow c$, $c \rightarrow d$, $\sim d$, a, therefore a & $\sim b$

e)* $a \rightarrow (b \ \& \ c), c \rightarrow e, a$, therefore $a \ \& \ e$
f) $b \ \& \sim c, c \ V \ d, d \rightarrow a$, therefore a
g) $a \rightarrow (b \ \& \sim c), c$ or d, a, therefore d

3. Using the letters given, translate the following arguments into propositional logic and prove them valid. In some cases you will need to recognize hidden premises.

a) If you cut off the top of a triangle with a line that is parallel with its base, you get a quadrilateral with 2 parallel sides. If a figure is a quadrilateral with 2 parallel sides, it is a trapezoid. So if you cut off the top of a triangle with a line that is parallel with its base, then you have a trapezoid. (c, q, t)

b) If the planetary system is not heliocentric, Venus will not show phases. But Venus does show phases. So the planetary system is heliocentric. (h, v)

c) Kaitlin can't be guilty, for she didn't act suspiciously and that's how someone acts when she is guilty. (g, s)

d) If each man had a definite set of rules of conduct by which he regulated his life he would be no better than a machine. We're not machines, so there are no such rules. (d, b)

e) [from an ad in *The Economist* (Aug. 1995)] If you are looking for a bank committed to a straight-forward approach to helping you protect your wealth, consider Bank Julius Baer. (l, b)

f)* If the government minister is not honest, she is not to be trusted, and if she's not to be trusted she should not hold a government post and should be sent back to her law firm. But I know that the minister is not honest, so she should return to her law firm. (h, t, g, r)

g)* As a patriot I can tell you what attitude you should have to this great nation: love it or leave it! Clearly you don't love it, so why don't you leave? (l, g)

h) [from a letter to the *Kitchener-Waterloo Record* (25 Feb. 1995)] The only negative aspect of being a No supporter in the Quebec referendum is finding oneself alongside Brian Mulroney. If keeping Canada together means accepting the company of Mulroney, then maybe we had better rethink our positions. (k, a)

i) [part of the ancient philosopher Timon's directions on how one can be happy] If one wants to be happy, one must pay attention to three connected questions: first, what are things like by nature, second, how should we be disposed towards things, and third, what will be the outcome of this disposition? (h, n, d, o)

4. Construct a proof proving that if a biconditional $(a \rightarrow b) \ \& \ (b \rightarrow a)$ is true and b is false, then a is false.

5. Translate the following arguments into propositional logic symbols using the letters indicated. Construct a proof of their validity.

a)* [Zen Master Dogen in *Dogen*, by Yuho Yokoi] You should listen to the Zen master's teaching without trying to make it conform to your own self-centred viewpoint; otherwise you will be unable to understand what he is saying. (l, a)

b) She's going to the Christmas party only if she has the night off work. And she has the night off work only if David can replace her. But David can replace her only if he doesn't have an exam the next day, and he does. So she isn't going to the Christmas party. (*g, n, d, e*)

c) Humans are mammals, and whales, dolphins, and elephants are mammals, so humans and whales are mammals. (*h, w, d, e*)

d)* In order to avoid the intricacies of such theories we will rely on our earlier remark that the objective of an argument is to convince an audience. If this is so, then it is sufficient for our purposes that the premises of a good argument be accepted as true by our audience. (*o, s*)

e) It should be clear that this new argument is invalid, for it is obviously possible for its two premises to be true while its conclusion is false, and if this is true then the argument is invalid. (*t, v*)

f)* The Liberals will win the election if and only if their leader is attractive to voters in rural ridings. But rural voters will never support a Liberal leader. (*l, a*)

g) There's a problem. It's a problem with your hardware or your software. If it's your software, Deborah can fix it. If there's a problem with your hardware, Scott Reaume can help. But I don't think it's a problem with your software, so Scott can help. (*p, h, s, r, d*)

h) Either you've offended Alex or he simply dislikes you. It must be the latter, for I can't imagine you offending Alex. (*o, l*)

i)* Americans or Germans or Russians will win the most medals at next year's Olympics, but the Russians will not do well enough to win and the Germans will not do well enough to win, so the Americans will win the most medals. (*a, g, r*)

6. Translate into propositional logic symbols and prove valid the following arguments. Use the letters in parentheses to represent your simple propositions. Recognize hidden argument components where necessary.

a)* [adapted from a cartoon by Jules Feiffer (16 Apr. 1972)] We do not want anarchy. When criminals are not punished, the result is rising crime—in a word, anarchy. When corporations don't break the law, the result is falling stocks—in a word, anarchy. So we should punish criminals and support corporate crime! (*a, p, b*)

b) If capital punishment does not deter capital crimes, it is not justified, and if it's not justified it should not be a part of criminal law and should be abolished everywhere. Capital punishment does not, however, deter capital crimes, so it should be abolished everywhere. (*c, j, l, e*)

c)* If you're so smart, why aren't you rich? (*s, r*)

d) Rumour had it that Sam Stone or a look-alike was having dinner at The Steak House. When Tom asked whether he had made a reservation and had showed up on time, the hostess replied affirmatively. 'In that case,' said Tom, 'the person having dinner can't possibly be Sam Stone.' (*s, l, r, t*)

e) If the Rev. Jerry Falwell evaluates his ministry by the money it makes, then he is serving mammon, not God. Now the newspapers reported a complaint by him that his ministry has probably lost $1 million, maybe closer to $2 million, in revenues over the past month as a result of infighting at PTL. If he complains in that way, he is evaluating his ministry by the money it makes. (*e, m, g, c*)

f) [REAL Women is a Canadian organization promoting some of the traditional women's roles] If you belong to REAL Women, you believe in its ideals. But if you believe in its ideals, you believe that men should be our leaders. If you believe that men should be our leaders, you must believe that REAL Women should not lead us. But if you believe that REAL Women shouldn't lead us, you don't really believe in REAL Women. So if you believe in REAL Women, you don't! (*r, i, m, l*)

g)* Zsa Zsa Gabor, who recently got married for the eighth time, gave her age as 54. If that's true, she was only five when she entered and won the Miss Hungary beauty title in 1933. (*z, f*)

h) [adapted from an argument in Trudy Govier's *A Practical Study of Argument*, p. 214] Elephants have been known to bury their dead. But they would do so only if they have a concept of their own species and understand what death means. If they understand what death means, they have a capacity for abstraction, and if they have a capacity for abstraction, they can think. Yet you admit that elephants have no moral rights only if they can't think, so elephants have moral rights. (*b, c, u, a, t, m*)

7. Construct two proofs of the following propositional logic argument, one that uses the rule CS and one that does not.

Campbell was Mayor for the shortest time in the city's history, but it wasn't his fault if his party didn't fully support him. The party didn't fully support him if its president did not support him, so it wasn't his fault. (*c, f, s, p*)

8. Translate the following arguments into propositional logic symbols and prove them valid. Define your own simple propositions.
   a) She can't have many friends if she doesn't respect them. If she doesn't allow them to be themselves, she does not respect them. If she objects to the clothes people wear, she doesn't allow them to be themselves. And she does object to people's clothes. So she can't have many friends.
   b) Robbery or vengeance was the motive for the crime. But the victim had money in her pockets and the motive could not have been robbery if this was so. Clearly, it was a crime of vengeance.
   c) Napoleon can be criticized if he usurped power that did not properly belong to him. If there were no laws that justified his rise to power, he usurped power improperly. But there were no laws of this sort. So Napoleon can be criticized.
   d) If we extend further credit on the Jacobs account, he will feel obliged to accept our bid on the next project. We can count on a larger profit if he feels obliged to accept our bid on the next project. But counting on a larger profit will allow us to improve our financial forecast. So we can improve our financial forecast by extending further credit on the Jacobs account.

PROPOSITIONAL

LOGIC II:

CONDITIONALS, DILEMMAS, AND REDUCTIOS

Chapter 9 introduced some basic propositional schemes of argument. In this chapter we develop our version of propositional logic further by introducing more complex propositional schemes. To that end, we introduce

- conditional proofs;
- reductio ad absurdum arguments;
- reasoning by dilemma; and
- 'De Morgan's Laws'.

Chapter 9 introduced propositional logic connectives and some simple argument schemes that you can use in propositional logic proofs. In this chapter we introduce more complex schemes that are an integral part of ordinary reasoning and can help us capture important aspects of day-to-day discussion and debates. By adding them to our propositional logic, we will make it a system of argument that more closely approximates the kinds of reasoning that characterize ordinary thinking.

1. CONDITIONAL PROOFS

The rules AA and DC may be described as instances of conditional 'elimination'. They allow us to use a conditional to establish the truth of its consequent or the falsity of its antecedent. In the process, we 'eliminate' the conditional and replace it with a related proposition. The scheme 'Conditional Proof', or '→P', is a scheme of conditional 'introduction' that we use when we want prove a conditional. Because we frequently argue for conditionals in ordinary reasoning, →P captures an important argumentative strategy that characterizes ordinary reasoning.

To see how →P works, consider how we might attempt to prove a conditional in the context of an ordinary conversation. Imagine that a group of us are arguing about municipal politics, about what should happen to an old industrial site (a 'brownfield') in the core of the city that we live in. Someone says the city should turn the site into park land. Suppose someone answers, 'No, the city will be better off if they rezone the land and divide it into residential lots.' How can one defend and establish this conditional? One can imagine the conversation continuing as follows:

> Just think about it. The city will be better off if they rezone the land and divide it into residential lots. For suppose they do. The property value will increase dramatically if the land is rezoned and divided into residential lots, so the value of the property will increase dramatically. In those circumstances, private developers will be willing to pay for the development of the property and the city won't have to pay the cost. And the city will be better off if it doesn't have to pay the cost.

This extended argument consists primarily of claims about what would be the case if the antecedent of the proposed conditional were true—i.e. if the city did rezone the land and divide it into residential lots. In arguing in this way, the arguer has adopted the argument scheme →P.

The structure of this argument can be illustrated if we adopt the following legend:

r = The city rezones the land.
d = The city divides the land into residential lots.
i = The value of the property will increase dramatically.
p = Private developers will be willing to pay for the development of the property.
c = The city will pay the cost.
b = The city will be better off.

Using this translation scheme, we can sketch our sample argument as follows:

Conclusion: $(r \& d) \to b$
  For suppose $(r \& d)$
  We know $(r \& d) \to i$
    So i
  But $i \to p$
    So p
  But $p \to \sim c$
    So $\sim c$
  And $\sim c \to b$
    So b
  Therefore $(r \& d) \to b$

You may see that this argument contains a sub-argument that is based on the supposition that *(r & d)* is true. This supposition is used as a temporary premise that the arguer assumes in order to deduce what would be true if *(r & d)* were true. On the basis of this assumption, the propositions *i, p, ~c,* and then *b* are deduced. This allows the arguer to conclude that *b* is true if *(r & d)* is true, i.e. that *(r & d)* → *b*.

In arguing in this way, the arguer has constructed a conditional proof. It is a 'conditional' proof for two reasons—because the proof of *b* is conditional on the supposition that *(r & d)*, and because it is ultimately used to prove the conditional *(r & d)* → *b*. Within a propositional logic proof we prove the validity of arguments like this by defining the argument scheme →P as follows:

→P: X (S/→P), . . . Y, *therefore,* X → Y

This definition can be read as follows: Take any X as a supposition for a conditional proof (S/→P), deduce any proposition Y, and conclude that X → Y. Within a proof we justify the line with X by writing 'S/→P' and the line with X → Y by writing 'x–y, →P', where *x* is the number of the line where X is introduced and *y* is the number of the line where Y occurs.

Using the legend we have already identified, our first example of a conditional proof can be proved as follows:

1.	*(r & d) → i*	P
2.	*i → p*	P
3.	*p → ~c*	P
4.	*~c → b*	P
5.	*r & d*	S/→P
6.	*i*	1, 5, AA
7.	*p*	2, 6, AA
8.	*~c*	3, 7, AA
9.	*b*	4, 8, AA
10.	*(r & d) → b*	5–9, →P

You are already familiar with informal instances of such reasoning, for we construct conditional proofs whenever we assume a proposition 'for the sake of argument' in order to show what follows from it.

In order to ensure that the scheme →P is not used to justify any illegitimate inference in a propositional logic proof, we will stipulate that the lines of a conditional 'subproof' (the lines that extend from our conditional supposition to the consequent we deduce) must not be used elsewhere in the proof. This is a restriction that is needed to ensure that the conditional supposition is employed (explicitly or implicitly) only when we are deducing what would be the case if it were true. In our proof above, this means that the lines 3–7 cannot be employed elsewhere in the proof.

Another example can illustrate →P. Suppose that you believe (1) that we can solve the problems of the world's developing countries and still enjoy a reasonable standard of living if we develop alternative forms of energy, and (2) that there will be a greater chance of lasting peace if we solve the problems of the Third World. If we accept these two premises, we can use the following proof to show that there will be a greater chance of lasting peace if we develop alternative forms of energy:

> a = We develop alternative forms of energy.
> s = We can solve the problems of the Third World.
> e = We will enjoy a reasonable standard of living.
> g = There will be a greater chance of lasting peace.
> 1. $a \rightarrow (s \& e)$ P
> 2. $s \rightarrow g$ P
> 3. a P/$\rightarrow$P
> 4. $s \& e$ 1, 3, AA
> 5. s 4, &E
> 6. g 2, 5, AA
> 7. $a \rightarrow g$ 3–6, $\rightarrow$P

Here as elsewhere, the key to a good conditional proof is the proper use of other propositional rules of inference after we have adopted our initial conditional premise S/$\rightarrow$P.

Exercise 10A

Construct proofs of the following arguments using the rule $\rightarrow$P, and whatever other rules are necessary.

> a)* $a \rightarrow b$, $b \rightarrow c$, therefore $a \rightarrow c$
> b) $a \rightarrow b$, therefore $\sim b \rightarrow c$
> c) $a \rightarrow (b \& c)$, $b \rightarrow c$, $c \rightarrow e$, therefore $a \rightarrow e$
> d) $a \rightarrow (b \lor c)$, $a \rightarrow d$, $d \rightarrow \sim c$, therefore $a \rightarrow c$
> e) $a \rightarrow b$, $a \rightarrow c$, therefore $a \rightarrow (b \& c)$

2. Reductio ad Absurdum

The schemes of argument we have discussed so far offer 'direct' evidence that implies their conclusions. One may also argue for a conclusion by offering 'indirect' evidence that demonstrates that the opposing point of view is mistaken. In our propositional logic, we will include an argument scheme that is designed to allow indirect reasoning in propositional logic proofs. We call this scheme 'reductio ad absurdum', or 'RAA' for short.

Literally, *reductio ad absurdum* means 'reduction to absurdity'. In keeping with this, 'RAA' arguments attempt to establish the absurdity of a position they reject. They disprove a proposition X by assuming it ('for the sake of argument') and deriving a contradiction, a proposition of the form Y & ~Y. Because Y & ~Y is absurd, this allows an arguer to conclude ~X. We can define this scheme as follows:

RAA: X (S/RAA), . . . Y & ~Y, *therefore* ~X

This definition can be read as follows: Take any X as a supposition for a reductio ad absurdum (S/RAA), deduce some contradiction of the form Y & ~Y, and conclude that ~X. Within a proof we justify the line with X by writing 'S/RAA' and the line with ~X, by writing '$x–y$, RAA', where x is the number of the line where X is introduced and y is the number of the line where the contradiction Y & ~Y occurs.

An example may make RAA arguments more intuitive. Some of the clearest examples of reductio ad absurdum arguments are found in mathematical and geometric proofs, but we will restrict ourselves to the kind of arguments that characterize ordinary language. Consider, then, the following regulation on grade-point averages for repeated courses, which is taken from the Wilfrid Laurier University undergraduate calendar (1995–6, p. 35):

> Students in degree programs may repeat courses up to a maximum of two credits. Students who repeat courses above the two credit maximum will have both attempts over the 2.00 limit count toward their GPA.

It should be apparent to you that there is something absurd about this rule. One might try to explain it by arguing as follows:

> The calendar makes no sense. For suppose it did. Then students cannot repeat more than two credits' worth of courses. But if they can have courses above this maximum count toward their GPA, then they can repeat more than two credits worth of courses. But then they both can and cannot repeat more than two credits' worth of courses. And how can one make sense of that!

This is an example of an RAA argument. It shows that a certain proposition (that this calendar makes sense) leads to a contradiction and concludes that this proposition must be false.

We can prove the validity of the proposed argument as follows:

c = The calendar makes sense.
r = Students can repeat more than two credits' worth of courses.
a = They can have courses above this maximum count toward their GPA

1.	$c \rightarrow {\sim}r$	P
2.	$c \rightarrow a$	P
3.	$a \rightarrow r$	P
4.	c	S/RAA
5.	${\sim}r$	1, 4, AA
6.	a	2, 4, AA
7.	r	3, 6, AA
8.	r & ${\sim}r$	7, 5, &I
9.	${\sim}c$	4–8, RAA

Like the scheme $\rightarrow$P, the scheme RAA can be described as a proof within a proof. In one case, the subproof deduces a consequent from an antecedent that is supposed. In the other, it deduces a contradiction from a supposition that is the negation of the conclusion. In both cases, the lines within the subproof cannot be used elsewhere in our proof. In the case of RAA, this means that the lines beginning with S/RAA and ending with Y & ~Y (lines 4–8 in our example) cannot be employed elsewhere in our proof. This stipulation ensures that the conclusions we deduce on the basis of our RAA premise are restricted to conclusions about the situation that would hold if it were true.

Our second example of an RAA argument comes from a debate over cormorants, and the claim that they are birds that should be eradicated or controlled because they destroy freshwater fisheries. One contribution to the debate comes from an article entitled 'Why do we hate big, black birds?' published by Nancy Clark in *Seasons* (Winter 2002, p. 5). In the course of her essay, Clark proposes a theory to account for our different attitudes to different kinds of species:

> My theory is that our views are based on how abundant or rare a species is. People prize rare items, including rare animals, and will spend a great deal of time, effort and money saving a single humpback whale, but hardly any to try to prevent thousands of frogs from being run over. . . . [D]o we admire rock doves, raccoons, and Canada geese for their resourcefulness and adaptability? No, we think they're pests. We don't seem to like species that are too successful.

Is Clark's theory correct? We cannot settle the issue in any definitive way here, but consider the following RAA argument, which uses our attitudes to pets in an argument against it:

> Suppose that Clark is right, that we like animals if and only if they are rare. That means that we like dogs if and only if they are rare. Because dogs are the most common animal we know, it follows that we don't like dogs. But we do. So much for Clark's theory.

This argument could best be understood as a syllogism, but we can also construct the following propositional logic account of it:

c = Clark's theory on our attitudes to animals is correct.
l = We like dogs.
r = Dogs are rare.

1.	$c \rightarrow ((l \rightarrow r) \ \& \ (r \rightarrow l))$	P
2.	l	P
3.	$\sim r$	P
4.	c	S/RAA
5.	$(l \rightarrow r) \ \& \ (r \rightarrow l)$	1, 4, AA
6.	$l \rightarrow r$	5, &E
7.	$\sim l$	6, 3, DC
8.	$l \ \& \ \sim l$	2, 7, &I
9.	$\sim c$	4–8, RAA

RAA is an important scheme of argument, not only in propositional logic, but also in ordinary argument, for it allows us to prove that some views are correct by proving that opposing views are mistaken. In debates between argumentative opponents, RAA is often the argument scheme of choice, for it allows one to undermine the views of one's opponent in a very pointed way. For this reason, RAA arguments are common in political debate.

Exercise 10B

1. Go to exercise 9M, question 2. Prove all of these arguments valid using the argument scheme RAA, and whatever other rules are necessary.

2. Using ordinary language, construct a reductio ad absurdum argument for or against the claim that men with beards cannot be trusted. Translate the argument into propositional logic and construct an RAA proof of its validity.

3. Dilemmas

In ordinary language, a 'dilemma' is a situation that forces us to make a choice between alternatives we would rather avoid. In propositional logic, a 'dilemma' is a scheme of argument that is founded on the two alternatives set out in a disjunction. In dilemma arguments one does not choose between the two disjuncts in a disjunction, but instead shows what follows from the proposition that one or the other disjunction is true. We will include two kinds of dilemma arguments in our propositional logic. One is called 'dilemma' (or 'D' for short), the other 'dilemma to disjunction' (or 'DV'). The two schemes are defined as follows:

$$\textbf{D}: X \vee Y, X \rightarrow Z, Y \rightarrow Z, \textit{therefore } Z$$
$$\textbf{DV}: X \vee Y, X \rightarrow Z, Y \rightarrow W, \textit{therefore } Z \vee W$$

As you can see from these definitions, dilemma arguments combine a disjunction and conditionals in a way that allows us to establish some conclusion that follows even though we do not know which of the disjuncts in the disjunction is true. The validity of such arguments can be understood in terms of our earlier discussion of disjunctions and conditionals. Thus, the initial disjunction in a dilemma argument states that one of the disjuncts is true, but this implies that the antecedent of one of the associated conditionals must be true, and that the same can be said of one of the consequents.

Our first example, which illustrates the scheme D, also illustrates the connection between our ordinary use of the word 'dilemma' and the argument scheme that goes by the same name. Consider the following argument about public speakers, which is taken from a book written by the famous sixteenth-century philosopher Thomas Hobbes (*Principles of Rhetorik*, ch. 24): ''Tis not good to be an Orator, because if he speak the truth, he shall displease Men: If he speak falsely, he shall displease God.' This is a sentence that presents the dilemma of the Orator, whose goal is to convince an audience (something that compels him to say what they would like to hear), but who is morally obligated to speak the truth (which is not what people like to hear).

Hobbes's sentence presents a dilemma argument the Orator has to face. It is indicated by the premise indicator 'because' and can be translated into propositional logic and proved as follows:

t = I speak the truth.
m = I please men.
g = I please God.
s = I am in a good situation.

1. $t \lor \sim t$ P (hidden)
2. $t \rightarrow \sim m$ P
3. $\sim t \rightarrow \sim g$ P
4. $\sim m \rightarrow \sim s$ P (hidden)
5. $\sim g \rightarrow \sim s$ P (hidden)
6. $t \rightarrow \sim s$ 2, 4, CS
7. $\sim t \rightarrow \sim s$ 3, 5, CS
8. $\sim s$ 1, 6, 7, D

Our second example of dilemma is a version of DV taken from a discussion of the suggestion that airports should use face-recognition software to guard against terrorist attack (in *Atlantic Monthly*, Dec. 2002, p. 15). Charles C. Mann writes:

At Logan Airport, in Boston, the software would have scanned the faces of 25 million passengers last year, resulting in 170,000 false identifications. . . . The additional cost and disruption, to passengers and airlines alike, of interrogating and screening those people would be enormous. . . . One could set the criteria to reduce that number of false alarms, but then the risk of missing real terrorists would be dramatically increased—the tradeoff is unavoidable. And a security system that either fails in its principal task or causes major disruptions is not desirable.

In this case, the argument can be converted into propositional logic symbols in the following way:

f = Face-recognition software is used to minimize false alarms.
d = The additional costs and disruption of false identifications would be enormous.
i = The risk of missing real terrorists is dramatically increased.
s = Face-recognition software succeeds in its principal task.
d = Face-recognition software is desirable.

1. $f \lor \sim f$ P (hidden)
2. $f \rightarrow d$ P
3. $\sim f \rightarrow i$ P
4. $i \rightarrow \sim s$ P

$$5. \ (d \lor \sim s) \to \sim d \qquad P$$
$$5. \ \sim f \to \sim s \qquad 3, 4, CS$$
$$6. \ d \lor \sim s \qquad 1, 2, 5, DV$$
$$7. \ \sim d \qquad 5, 6, AA$$

In this and our previous example you may note that the disjunction that is the basis of the dilemma is a hidden premise. This is common in ordinary argument, for the dilemma strategy is so common that audiences will, in normal circumstances, immediately understand that an argument of this form is founded on an assumed disjunction.

Unacceptable Disjunctions and Dilemmas

Like the argument scheme VE, our two kinds of dilemmas are founded on disjunctions. In constructing propositional logic proofs of arguments of this sort, we are proving that they are valid. We have already seen that propositional logic does not prove that an argument is a strong argument, for this requires that an argument be valid *and* have acceptable premises. In dealing with dilemmas and VE arguments, in the course of ordinary argument, this means that you must judge whether the disjunction that is the basis of the dilemma or VE is acceptable.

A disjunction is called a *false dilemma* (or, less frequently, a 'false dichotomy') when it fails to exhaust all alternatives and both disjuncts may be false (because some unstated alternative is true). This is not a concern if the disjunction has the form $X \lor \sim X$, as in the two examples of dilemma we just discussed, for in that case X must be true or false, which means that the disjunction must be true. The same cannot be said in other kinds of cases, however, for they are founded on disjunctions that may have two false disjunctions. This is frequently the case in ordinary reasoning, where false dilemmas are featured in weak arguments that reduce complex issues to simplistic alternatives that overlook other possibilities.

Consider, to take one example, an article in *Mother Jones* discussing ways of making American neighbourhoods safe. In the article, Michael Castleman develops a VE argument, beginning with the disjunction 'We can control crime by reducing criminal opportunity or by addressing poverty,' and arguing that we can't control crime by addressing poverty. He concludes that we must try to control crime by reducing criminal opportunity.

In propositional logic, we can represent Castleman's basic argument as follows:

c = We can control crime by reducing criminal opportunity.
p = We can control crime by addressing poverty.

$$1. \ c \lor p \qquad P$$
$$2. \ \sim p \qquad P$$
$$3. \ c \qquad 1, 2, VE$$

This simple proof shows that Castleman's argument is a valid argument. To determine whether it is a strong argument, it follows that we need to decide whether we should accept its premises as true. In response to Castleman's article, Marc Mauer, the assistant director of the Washington Sentencing Project, wrote the following in a letter to *Mother Jones*:

> Castleman provides some good examples about ways in which neighborhoods can come together in crime prevention efforts. But his suggestion that 'reducing criminal opportunity is our best bet for controlling crime' because of the difficulty of addressing poverty . . . raises a false dichotomy.

This is a good example of a charge of false dilemma, for it suggests that Castleman's disjunction, $c \lor p$, overlooks other alternatives that might be true — in particular the possibility that we could control crime by adopting a mix of measures that fight poverty and control criminal opportunity. As in other cases of false dilemma, the claim is that it is a mistake to think that the alternatives presented in a disjunction are the only possibilities.

In ordinary language, we say that someone *escapes through the horns of a dilemma* when they refute a dilemma argument by rejecting the disjunction it is founded on (by claiming that it is a false dilemma). Consider the argument:

> Today's politician is placed in an impossible position. Either they vote according to their own lights or as their constituents desire. If they vote as their constituents want, they compromise their conscience; but if they vote according to their own lights, they alienate their constituents. So either they compromise their conscience or they alienate their constituents.

This is a clear example of the scheme DV. Though we could prove it a valid argument, one might still try to escape through the horns of the disjunction it is founded on. Politicians can, one might argue, reject the either/or assumption that they have two choices: to vote according to their consciences or as their constituents want. For this overlooks the fact that they may vote in different ways at different times. They might, for example, choose to vote according to their own lights on matters of conscience, but vote as the majority of their constituents want on other issues. By 'escaping between the horns' of the proposed dilemma in this way, a politician need not compromise their conscience and will on many, if not most, issues please their constituents rather than alienate them.

A different problem arises when there are grounds for questioning the conditionals on which a dilemma argument relies. One is said to *take a dilemma by the horns* when one refutes it by rejecting these conditionals (or the premises they are founded on). Here again, the problem is not the validity of the argument, which is guaranteed by the scheme D or DV. The problem is premise acceptability, for the premises might be rejected.

Imagine a woman who does not believe in abortion contemplating an unwanted pregnancy. Suppose she reasons as follows:

> If I have an abortion, I'll be haunted by guilt. But if I don't, I'll ruin my career. If I'm haunted by guilt, my life will be unhappy. If I ruin my career, my life will be unhappy. So I'm going to be unhappy.

If we let:

a = I have an abortion.
r = My career will be ruined.
g = I'll be haunted by guilt.
h = My life will be happy.

then we can prove the validity of this argument as follows:

1. $a \lor \sim a$ P
2. $a \rightarrow g$ P
3. $\sim a \rightarrow r$ P
4. $g \rightarrow \sim h$ P
5. $r \rightarrow \sim h$ P
6. $a \rightarrow \sim h$ 2, 4, CS
7. $\sim a \rightarrow \sim h$ 3, 6, CS
8. $\sim h$ 1, 6, 7, D

In this case, the disjunction that the argument relies on ('Either I'll have an abortion or I won't') is clearly true, so one cannot escape through the horns of the dilemma. It follows that the only way to refute the argument is by taking the dilemma by the horns and arguing that one of its conditionals is false, i.e. that either $a \rightarrow \sim h$ is false, or that $\sim a \rightarrow \sim h$ is false. Because the arguments over these conditionals raise very complex and very controversial issues, we won't develop this strategy in detail here. Suffice it to say that opponents on the different sides of the abortion debate are likely to take hold of different conditionals, and in this sense, different horns of the dilemma.

CRITICIZING DISJUNCTIONS AND DILEMMAS

➤ A *false dilemma* is a false disjunction that overlooks some alternative beyond those incorporated in its disjuncts.
➤ One *escapes between the horns of a dilemma* when one shows that the disjunction a dilemma relies on is a false dilemma.
➤ One *takes a dilemma by the horns* when one refutes it by showing that one (or both) of the conditionals it relies on is not acceptable.

EXERCISE 10C

1. Prove the following arguments valid using the scheme D or DV, and whatever other rules are necessary.
   a)* $a \lor b, a \rightarrow c, b \rightarrow d$, *therefore* $c \lor b$
   b) $a \lor b, a \rightarrow c, c \rightarrow e, e \rightarrow f, b \rightarrow c$, *therefore* $c \lor f$
   c) $a \lor b, \sim c \rightarrow \sim b, a \rightarrow c$, *therefore* c
   d) $a \rightarrow (b \, \& \, (b \rightarrow c)), e \rightarrow c, a \lor e$, *therefore* c
   e) $a \lor b, a \rightarrow c$, *therefore* $c \lor b$

2. Construct a proof proving the validity of the following dilemma argument. How might one escape through its horns or take it by the horns?

> If I tell my boss how I bungled the contract, I'll be fired. If he finds out from someone else, he'll fire me. Either I tell him myself or he'll find out from someone else. Woe is me!

4. De Morgan's Laws

The final scheme of propositional argument we discuss also figures prominently in ordinary reasoning. It consists of one of two forms of argument called 'De Morgan's laws' ('DeM' for short), after the nineteenth-century British logician Augustus De Morgan. There are two variants of the scheme DeM, which can be defined as follows:

DeM: $\sim(X \lor Y)$ *is equivalent to* $\sim X$ & $\sim Y$
$\sim(X$ & $Y)$ *is equivalent to* $\sim X \lor \sim Y$

The word 'equivalent' in each line of this definition means that the two propositions listed can be deduced from each other. The first line tells us that $\sim X$ & $\sim Y$ can be deduced from $\sim(X \lor Y)$, and that $\sim(X \lor Y)$ can be deduced from $\sim X$ & $\sim Y$. The second tells us that $\sim(X$ & $Y)$ can be deduced from $\sim X \lor \sim Y$, and vice versa.

The validity of DeM should be evident. The first part of DeM tells us that the proposition 'I'll go to neither Salzburg nor London' is equivalent to the proposition 'I won't go to Salzburg *and* I won't go to London.' More generally, a disjunction claims that one of its disjuncts is true, so the claim that it is false is equivalent to the claim that the first *and* the second is false. The second part of DeM tells us that the falsity of the claim 'I will go to Salzburg and to London' is equivalent to the claim 'I won't go to Salzburg *or* I won't go to London.' More generally, a conjunction is untrue if and only if one of its conjuncts is false, i.e. the first *or* the second is false.

In propositional logic proofs, the rule DeM is an effective way to move from the negation of a conjunction or disjunction to an equivalent disjunction or conjunction (and vice versa). Suppose we know that you will be going to the opening of a new run of *Hair* if you can find $50 spending money and can make it to the box office four hours before the show begins. If we subsequently discover that you didn't make the show, then De Morgan's laws allow us to deduce that either you didn't find the $50 or you didn't make it to the box office. We can prove this as follows:

f = You find $50 spending money.
m = You make it to the box office four hours before the show begins.
c = You go to the opening of *Hair*.
    1. $(f$ & $m) \rightarrow c$ P
    2. $\sim c$ P
    3. $\sim(f$ & $m)$ 1, 2, DC
    4. $\sim f \lor \sim m$ 3, DeM

Exercise 10D

1. Let *a* = Angela goes to *Hair*, *b* = Brian goes to *Hair*, and *c* = Carla goes to *Hair*. Translate the following arguments into English and construct a proof of their validity using DeM, and whatever other rules are necessary.

    a)* ~(a & b), b, therefore ~a
    b) ~(a V b), ~a → c, therefore c
    c) ~a V ~b, c → (a & b), therefore ~c
    d) ~a & ~b, therefore ~(a & c)
    e) a & b, therefore ~(~a V ~b)

5. Summary: Rules of Inference

We have now introduced all the argument schemes we will include in our version of propositional logic. The complex schemes we have introduced in this chapter are listed in the summary box below. You may use this box as a convenient reference, but you should try to learn the schemes well enough so that you do not need to rely on it.

When you construct propositional logic proofs that use complex schemes, keep in mind the guidelines for proof construction we discussed in our last chapter, for they apply to these kinds of proofs. Construct your proofs in a step-by-step manner, proceeding from your premises to your conclusion. If you are unsure of how you should proceed, you may want to develop your strategy by seeing what you can deduce from your premises, or by thinking backward from the conclusion (asking yourself what kinds of schemes will be needed to prove the conclusion true). The rules RAA and →P are often helpful in difficult cases, for they allow you to introduce a supposition you can work with.

We will end by once again noting that propositional logic proofs establish the validity of particular chains of reasoning, but that this is only one of the two ingredients of strong arguments. To put this in a positive way, we know that an argument that can be proved valid in propositional logic satisfies one of the criteria of strong propositional reasoning. That said, a complete assessment of a propositional argument must consider questions of premise acceptability as well as validity. In the case of dilemmas and disjunctions, that is why we have noted some common issues that arise in this regard. In working with propositional proofs and arguments, we ask you to remember that an instance of good propositional reasoning exists only when one has an argument with premises that are acceptable. If you keep this in mind, then your ability to construct such proofs can provide a good basis for the construction of good arguments.

COMPLEX PROPOSITIONAL SCHEMES

→P*	$X (S/→P)$, . . . Y, *therefore* $X → Y$
RAA*	$X (S/RAA)$, . . . Y & $\sim Y$, *therefore* $\sim X$
D	$X \vee Y, X → Z, Y → Z$, *therefore* Z
DV	$X \vee Y, X → Z, Y → W$, *therefore* $Z \vee W$
DeMV	$\sim(X \vee Y)$ *is equivalent to* $\sim X$ & $\sim Y$
DeM&	$\sim(X$ & $Y)$ *is equivalent ot* $\sim X \vee \sim Y$

* When using →P and RAA, the lines of the subproof cannot be used elsewhere as proof.

Major Exercise 10M

1. Translate into propositional symbols and prove the validity of the following arguments. Use the indicated letters to represent simple sentences and use the scheme specified.

    a) [from an article on determinism—the view that we do not really choose to do what we do because our actions are caused by things beyond our control, such as heredity and environment] If a man could not do otherwise than he in fact did, then he is not responsible for his action. But if determinism is true, then the agent could not have done otherwise in any action. Therefore, if determinism is true, no one is responsible for what he does. (d, o, r; →P)

    b) If Nick does not become a poet, he will become a social worker or a doctor. If he is a social worker or a doctor, he will be financially better off but unhappy. So Nick will be unhappy if he doesn't become a poet. (p, s, d, f, h; →P)

    c)* You can join the Air Force only if you're eighteen, so you can't join the Air Force unless you're eighteen. (j, e; →P)

    d) [adapted from election material that criticized the position taken by a candidate for the Conservative party of Canada] The Conservative candidate says that he would introduce a bill adding five years in prison to the sentence of anyone convicted of a crime committed with a gun; and that he is for fiscal restraint. So much for his credibility. A person who wants to undertake huge expenditures is not for fiscal restraint, and his penal reforms would require the expenditure of hundreds of millions of dollars for the construction and maintenance of new prisons. (i, f, e; RAA)

    e) It's not true that there are moral principles that apply in all cases. If that were true, it would be true that we must always return what we have borrowed. This implies that you should give a gun back if you have borrowed it for target shooting, and the friend you borrowed it from has suffered a nervous breakdown and is determined to kill himself and asks for it back. But in these circumstances it is obvious that we should not give it back. Which shows that moral principles do not apply in all cases. (m, r, g, b, n, k, a; RAA)

f)   [adapted from Peter King, 'Against Intolerance', in *Philosophy Today* (Winter 1994–5)] The main point underlying all this, I think, is that it doesn't make sense to say that we tolerate something. If I say 'I tolerate *x*' I mean both that I judge *x* to be wrong and put up with *x*. If we think *x* is wrong, it makes no sense to say that we tolerate *x*. (*s, j, p, w*; D)

g)* The most unfair question one can ask a spouse is: 'If I die, would you marry again?' It's unfair because if one says 'yes', it will be taken to mean that one is waiting for them to die; and if one says 'no', that will be taken to mean that one's marriage is not a happy one! (*f, y, w, n, h*; DV)

h)   If we censor pornographic films, we will be denying people the right to make their own choices, thereby causing people harm. But if we do not censor pornographic films, we run the risk of exposing society to crimes committed by those who have been influenced by such films, thereby causing people harm. It's unavoidable that some people will be harmed. (*p, m, h, c*; D)

i)   Consider the Chrysler worker with a home and family. Either he tries to sell his home and seek employment elsewhere or he doesn't. If he tries to sell his home and seek employment elsewhere, he faces a substantial financial loss. If he doesn't, then he will have to live with frozen wages and guaranteed layoffs, and then he faces financial disaster. Some choice! (*s, e, f, w, g*; D)

j)   [adapted from Plato's *Apology*, 40c–41a] Death is one of two things. Either it is annihilation, and the dead have no consciousness of anything, or, as we are told, it is really a change—a migration of the soul from this place to another. Now if there is no consciousness but only (something like) a dreamless sleep, there is nothing to fear. . . . If on the other hand death is a removal from here to some other place, then all the dead are there and we should look forward to meeting them. So death is nothing to fear. (*a, c, m, f, d, l*; D)

k)   The robbers didn't take the Ming vase or the Buddhist statue, and she'll be satisfied if they're here. So she'll be satisfied. (*m, b, s*; DeM)

l)   I saw Maryanne in Pittsburgh on the 13th at 2 p.m., so she couldn't have been in Toronto at that time. (*p, t*; DeM)

m)   A professor cannot be both a reputable scholar and a popular teacher. She is popular in the classroom, so she must have abandoned a life of reputable scholarship. (*s, t*; DeM)

n)* Jacinth pulled through without complications, but Francis has a black eye the size of a football, Kirstin has a fever of 39 degrees, and I see that Fred or Paul is in the hospital. So it is false that Fred and Paul are well. (*j, f, k, f, p*; DeM)

2.   Provide a reductio ad absurdum argument for each of the following claims. Construct it in an English paragraph and then translate your argument into propositional logic and construct a proof of its validity.

a)   Every occurrence has a cause.

b)* Religion fulfills some deep human need.

c)   People in medieval times were wrong in thinking Earth saucer-shaped.

3. Provide reductio ad absurdum proofs for all the arguments in question 3 in Exercise
    9M.

4. For each of the dilemmas in question 1 (i.e. examples f, g, h, i, j) explain how one
    might escape through the horns of the dilemma or take it by the horns.

5. Prove the validity of the following arguments:
    a) $(b \rightarrow c)$, $(c \rightarrow b)$, $\sim b$, therefore $\sim c$.
    b) $(a \lor b) \rightarrow c$, $\sim(c \lor d)$, therefore $\sim a$.
    c)* $\sim(a \& b)$, a, therefore $\sim b$.
    d)* $a \& b \& c \& d$, therefore $c \lor e$.
    e) $\sim(a$ or $b)$, $a \lor c$, therefore c.
    f) $b \rightarrow \sim(c \& d)$, $\sim c \rightarrow e$, $\sim d \rightarrow f$, therefore $b \rightarrow (e \lor f)$.
    g) $\sim(a \& b)$, therefore $a \rightarrow \sim b$.
    h) $(b \& c) \rightarrow a$, $\sim a$, therefore $\sim b \rightarrow c$.
    i) $\sim(a \& b)$, $\sim a \rightarrow c$, $\sim b \rightarrow c$, therefore c.

6. Prove the validity of the following arguments. Provide your own legend.
    a) You'll get a passing or a failing grade on the exam. If you get a failing grade, then
        my confidence in you has been misplaced. But I'm sure my confidence has not
        been misplaced, so I'm sure you'll get a passing grade.
    b)* If you do your homework assignments, you'll learn informal logic, and if you
        learn informal logic, you'll be a good reasoner. But if you're a good reasoner,
        you'll probably succeed in your chosen field. So you'll probably succeed in your
        chosen field if you do your homework assignments.
    c) I hope the prime minister can use the forthcoming Commonwealth meetings to
        good advantage by persuading New Zealand to alter its sporting relationships
        with France after the latter's nuclear tests in Tahiti. If New Zealand continues to
        associate with France, Pacific Island nations will boycott the Commonwealth
        Games, and if they do that the Games will be cancelled. But if the Games are
        cancelled, millions of dollars spent in preparation and millions of athlete-hours
        spent in training will go down the drain. So if New Zealand continues to associ-
        ate with France, millions of dollars and millions of athlete-hours will go down
        the drain.
    d)* [look for the hidden conclusion] If you're a great singer, then you're Shake-
        speare and the moon is made out of green cheese. So there.
    e) The murder of Sir Robert was motivated by the hatred he inspired or by a cal-
        culated desire to gain his fortune. If it was a calculated crime, it must have been
        perpetrated by both Lord Byron and his mistress, Kate; but if it was done out of
        hatred, then either the butler, Robert, or Lord Byron's brother, Jonathan, did it.
        Now, Kate was too frightened a woman to have done it and Jonathan has the
        unassailable alibi of being in Brighton on the evening of the murder. Therefore,
        it's obvious the butler did it.

f)   If you enjoyed both Hemingway and Faulkner, you'd like Steinbeck, but you despise Steinbeck, so you must dislike either Hemingway or Faulkner.

g)   It will rain if and only if the wind changes, but the wind will change if and only if a high pressure area moves in and a high pressure area will move in if and only if the arctic front moves southward. It follows that it will rain if the arctic front moves southward.

h)* According to a famous story in Greek philosophy, the great sophist Protagoras agreed to give Euthalus instruction in law on the following terms: Euthalus was to pay half of the fee in advance and the remainder if and when he won his first case. After the instruction, Euthalus did not take any cases and Protagoras grew impatient waiting for the remainder of his payment. He finally took Euthalus to court himself, arguing as follows: The court will decide either for me or against me. If it decides for me, then Euthalus must pay. If it decides against me, then Euthalus has won his first case in court. But if he wins his first case in court, then he must pay me (for that is our agreement). So Euthalus must pay me.

i)   [Euthalus learned his logic well, and replied as follows] Protagoras is wrong, for the court will decide either for or against me. If it decides for me, then I do not have to pay. But if it decides against me, then I have lost my first case in court. But if I lose my first case in court, then I do not have to pay (for that is our agreement). So I do not have to pay.

j)   If the patient has a bacterial infection, she will have a fever. If she does not have a bacterial infection, then a virus is the cause of her illness. So, if she has no fever, she must be ill from a virus.

k)   Either I'll go to France or I won't. If I go, I'll have an interesting time and send you a card from Metz. If I don't go to France, I'll go to Spain and send you a card from Barcelona. But if I go to Barcelona, I'll have an interesting time, so I'll have an interesting time no matter what.

l)   [from the *Toronto Sun* (10 Feb. 1983)] It is wrong to think that we can both value life and be opposed to abortion and birth control. If everyone in the world were against abortion and birth control, can you imagine the terrible poverty, the starvation, the suffering? We would literally have wall-to-wall people, the whole world would be one big slum like we see in South American countries. Life wouldn't be worth living.

m)* [adapted from Jack Miller's Science Column, *Toronto Star* (9 June 1987), p. A14] Kepler offered the theory [that the night sky should be an unbroken canopy of starlight] . . . to disprove the then popular idea that the universe stretched forever and was filled with an infinite number of stars. If that was true, he said, then there would be so many stars that no matter which way you looked at night, you would see one. In every direction there would be a star at some distance or other. There would be no dark spaces between the spots of light, so the sky would be all light. And since the sky obviously is dark at night, the universe does not stretch out forever, or does not have an infinite number of stars in it.

n) [from an article on Senator John Glenn in the *Manchester Guardian Weekly* (23 Oct. 1983)] 'We are not flying into that and there's no way around it,' he told the small band of aides and correspondents. . . . There was no argument . . . When one of the world's greatest pilots says it isn't safe, you don't fly.

7. Using the information provided, deduce by means of propositional logic proofs answers to the questions asked.

   a) *Will someone from the humanities be appointed president of the university you plan to attend?*
   The president has just turned 46. She is a responsible person, but her birthday has been spoiled by a financial scandal. Now she is in trouble with the board of governors or senate. If the board of governors are unhappy, they'll fire her and she'll go somewhere else. If she goes somewhere else, one of the vice-presidents will be appointed president. But the vice-presidents are from the humanities. (The president is from physics.) If the senate is unhappy with the president, they'll make it impossible for her to carry out her programs, and no responsible person will stay in those conditions.

   b)* *Are you likely to survive?*
   You are at sea in a terrible storm. You can run for a lifeboat or stay where you are. If you run for it, then you will be lost at sea. If you don't run you will be safe unless the storm continues. If the storm continues you can survive only if you run to one of the lifeboats. If the sky is dark, the storm is likely to continue. You look up and sea a dark and stormy sky.

8. Prove that the following forms of argument are valid and provide a sample argument to illustrate the scheme in question.

   a)* $(p \lor q)$ & $\sim(p$ & $q)$, p, therefore $\sim q$.
   b) $p \lor q$, therefore $q \lor p$.
   c)* $p \rightarrow q$, therefore $\sim q \rightarrow \sim p$.
   d) $\sim r \rightarrow p$, $\sim p$ & q, $s \rightarrow \sim r$, therefore $\sim s$.
   e) $(a \rightarrow b)$ & $(b \rightarrow a)$, therefore $(a$ & $b) \lor (\sim a$ & $\sim b)$.
   f) The law of the excluded middle [i.e. $X \lor \sim X$], from no premises.
   g)* The law of non-contradiction [i.e. $\sim(X$ & $\sim X)$], from no premises.
   h) p & $(q \lor r)$, therefore $(p$ & $q) \lor (p$ & $r)$.

9.*

THE CASE OF THE MISSING BROTHER
A case from the files of
_____ , *Super Sleuth*
(your name)

I still remember it clearly. That day I burst into your office with the news. I was flustered, but you sat there cool and unmoved.

'Calm down', you said, 'and tell me what's the matter.'

'He's gone,' I spluttered, 'he's disappeared!'

'It happens all the time,' you mused philosophically.

'But he was here just yesterday, and now he's gone—poof—like a little puff of smoke.'

'Calm down,' you said again. 'Calm down and tell me all the details.'

So it began, the case of the missing brother. You've probably had more exciting cases, but it required a tidy bit of deduction, as far as I recall . . .

So much for intro. It's up to you to solve the case. The goal is to determine what happened to Louis, the missing brother. Was he kidnapped? Murdered? Something else? Who perpetrated the crime? What, if any, were the weapons used? And where is Louis now? To deduce the right conclusion, work your way through each day of the case file below. From the information gathered on each day, you should be able to construct a propositional proof that provides some relevant information (e.g. that 'if Mary did it, revenge must have been her motive'). By the time you solve the case, you should be more comfortable constructing proofs in propositional logic.

EXAMPLE

Day 1. You discover that one of the suspects, Joe, would have done something to Louis if and only if (1) he needed a lot of money or (2) he and Louis were still rivals. Yet you discover that Joe doesn't need any money (He's rolling in it!) and that Louis and Joe are no longer rivals.

Let: j = Joe is the culprit.
        m = Joe needs a lot of money.
        r = Joe and Louis are rivals.

Then we can deduce the conclusion that Joe is not the culprit:

1. $(j \rightarrow (m \vee r)) \& ((m \vee r) \rightarrow j)$ P
2. $\sim m \& \sim r$ P
3. $\sim (m \vee r)$ 2, DeM
4. $j \rightarrow (m \vee r)$ 1, &E
5. $\sim j$ 4, 3 DC

Now you're on your own.

Day 2. Louis runs a house for homeless men in Montreal. If he was working on Thursday (the day of his disappearance), he would have been serving the men dinner at 5:00 p.m. If he was serving dinner, then Michael and Leo (two of the homeless men) would have seen him. Michael didn't see him. [If you can't sort out what conclusion you should try to prove, then turn to the answers at the end of the book.]

Day 3. If Louis wasn't working, he must have been headed to the grocery store or have gone for a run when he left on Thursday morning. If he goes for groceries, he walks past 121 rue Frontenac, where there is a big dog chained to the post. Whenever he walks past the big dog at 121 rue Frontenac, it barks furiously. The dog did not bark on Thursday morning. [Begin your deduction with what you proved on Day 2, i.e. use it as your first premise.]

Day 4. A psychic (who's always right) says Louis is kidnapped or lost. If he's lost, he can't be in Montreal (he knows the city too well). If he's kidnapped and in Montreal, the police would have found him. They haven't. [Try an RAA.]

Day 5. I receive a note demanding a ransom of a thousand dollars. The note is either from Louis and the real kidnappers or from someone trying to make some easy money. If they wanted to make some easy money, I wouldn't have received a note asking for a thousand dollars (which will be hard to get from a poor man like myself). If it is from the real kidnappers, then they and Louis are in Quebec City. [Deduce a conjunction answering the following two questions: Is the note from the real kidnappers? and Where is Louis?]

Day 6. Checking on the suspects, you find that Mary is awfully squeamish. This tells you that she had a hand in Louis's disappearance if and only if she hired someone else to do her dirty work. If she hired someone, it would be Joe and Betty Anne, or her brother Ted. But we already know that Joe is not the culprit.

Day 7. An anonymous phone caller tells you that Louis is held captive by some strange cult called Cabala (there's more to this case than meets the eye). If she's right, Chloe will know about it, though she won't say anything. Yet if Chloe or Sam knows about it, Bud will tell you if you slip him a twenty. You slip him a twenty and he has nothing to tell.

Day 8. Arriving in Quebec City, looking for some leads, you see Mugsy. There are three reasons why Mugsy might be here. Either he is going to mail another note or he's helping hold Louis in Quebec City, or he's vacationing. If he's mailing another note, he's a culprit, and if he's helping hold Louis he's a culprit. As you go to find out, Mugsy sees you and runs down an alley before you can apprehend him. He wouldn't be running away if he were vacationing.

Day 9. An anonymous phone caller tells you that the whole case is 'A SP—', but he chokes and the phone goes dead after he gets out the first three letters. No one would have killed the caller unless he was right.

Day 10. Mugsy has been reported going into an old warehouse. You sneak in the back door and along a narrow corridor. There are two doors at the end of the hall. The police have said that Louis must be held in one of these two rooms. A thick layer of dust covers the door on the left.

Day 10½. Your heart pounds, you slip your pistol out of your pocket and bust through the door. Much to your chagrin, there's no one there. [This requires a revision of the conclusion reached on Day 10. Using your new information, go back to it and prove that the police were wrong when they said that Louis must be in one of these two rooms. Use a reductio argument.]

Day 11. You turn to the other door at the back of the warehouse. It leads to the only other room in the warehouse. You know that this is the warehouse Mugsy entered and he would have entered it only if Louis was captive here.

Day 12. The minutes seem like hours as you sneak to the door and quietly open it. You see Louis, Mary, and Mugsy sharing a bottle of good French wine, laughing at how upset I must be. If this were a serious kidnapping, they would not be laughing.

Day 13. Having discovered the whole thing is a spoof, you deduce the motive and the reason why Mary and Ted were involved when you note that either Louis or Mary wanted to fool me; that whoever wanted to fool me must have had a lot of money; that Mary and Mugsy are broke; and that if Louis wanted to fool me, Mary and Mugsy must have participated because he paid them.

Day 14. You wonder whether you should charge me the full rate, given that it was all a spoof. You believe you should get paid the full rate if you did the regular amount of work, however, so . . .

Day 15. Not having my brother's sense of humour, and thinking that one should pay for the consequences of one's actions, I decide that I should . . .

11

ORDINARY

REASONING:

ASSESSING THE BASICS

The last four chapters dealt solely with issues of (deductive) validity. But we have seen that a strong argument is one that is valid and has acceptable premises. In this chapter we take up questions of premise acceptability, and the complexities that arise when we deal with arguments that may be inductively rather than deductively valid. In the process we introduce

- ordinary reasoning,
- acceptability,
- relevance, and
- sufficiency,

and apply a basic account of argument assessment to extended arguments.

In chapters 7, 8 9, and 10 we introduced deductively valid schemes of argument. This is one important aspect of good reasoning, but there are many other features of ordinary reasoning that need to be considered.

Remember that a strong argument is a valid argument with acceptable premises. In deciding that deductively valid arguments are strong or weak (or somewhere between the two), this means that we need to move beyond questions of validity and ask whether such arguments contain premises that are acceptable. A deductively valid argument cannot have true premises and a false conclusion. If the premises are true, then the conclusion must be true. As significant as this is, it is still a big 'if'. We must now address that 'if' by focusing on questions of premise acceptability.

In assessing ordinary reasoning, we must also consider arguments that are inductively, rather than deductively, valid. In judging these arguments we employ methods for assessing the existence of both ingredients necessary for strong arguments. We must, in short, have ways to assess the acceptability of an argument's premises, and principles for assessing whether its conclusion follows from its premises. In order to provide a full-fledged account of ordinary reasoning, we must expand our discussion of validity so that it incorporates arguments that may not be deductively valid.

1. Ordinary Reasoning

Ordinary reasoning is characterized by uncertainty, disagreement, and dispute. Multiple perspectives are involved in public discussion and debate, which inevitably includes arguers who have different religious, political, and moral inclinations, and different opinions about the 'facts' that are relevant to almost any subject that might be discussed. The 'public' is not a homogeneous group of citizens but a conglomerate of many different groups who have different perspectives and vested interests, and these groups often oppose each other. The persistence of debates about issues like abortion, euthanasia, human cloning, and same-sex marriage is in part a result of these differences, which create a situation in which different arguers—and different communities of arguers—approach the same issues in radically different ways. Given this, we cannot expect ordinary arguments to establish certain conclusions and answer the questions of the day.

The uncertainty of ordinary reasoning can be illustrated in the realm of factual claims. Most of the arguments that are used in ordinary discussion have some factual basis. Often, arguments address factual matters—what is the population of the world today, is a vaccine possible for AIDS, how much freshwater is left in the world, does the use of cell phones have negative consequences for our health, etc. And even when arguments address a moral or political issue, they often rely on factual claims. For instance, the conclusion that we should not allow abortion in the fourth month of pregnancy may be founded on claims about the nature of the fetus at that point. Or, the claim that we should or should not support Israeli policy in the West Bank is likely to be founded on claims about the consequences of this policy and the likely consequences if some other policy were adopted. In such contexts, purported and potential facts play a central role in argument and debate.

In judging the acceptability of factual claims, either as premises or on their own, it is important to recognize that we must usually operate in a context of uncertainty. This is the second feature of ordinary reasoning that we need to keep in mind. For though we can establish the acceptability of factual claims in a variety of ways, we can rarely establish them as certain. Some of the most certain factual claims that we can work with are confirmed by observation. We 'see' the facts before us. The claims that visible evidence enables us to make are an important source of acceptable premises when we argue, but a careful reasoner recognizes that observations can be misleading and are not as neutral as our naive views assume. The observations of other people are especially problematic, for we know them only through their reports, and these may be fabricated or biased (as they are often found to be in legal investigations).

In some cases, we may accept a factual claim because it is justified by a deductively valid argument. Here, the deductive validity guarantees that the conclusion of the argument is as certain as the premises, but it is rare that premises are fully certain and this must affect the certainty that we can extend to conclusions. The claim that 'There were 497 billionaires in the world in 2002' might be established by an argument that deduces this from the claim that 'There were 242 billionaires in the United States, 165 in Europe, and 90 elsewhere.' The related claim that the number of billionaires dropped by 41 in 2002 might be justified by arguing that: 'There were 497 billionaires in the world in 2002 and 538 in 2001.' In both cases, these conclusions depend on deductively valid arguments. This does not, however, establish the certainty of the conclusions but only that they are as certain as the premises. And though we might be able to make a reasonable case for the premises (by relying on the data collected annually by *Forbes* magazine, for example), the data is so complex and so difficult to come by that we cannot claim that it is certain.

In still other cases, we may need to establish the acceptability of a factual claim by appealing to inductively valid arguments. Consider the claim that '[C]ontrary to the alarmist predictions of three decades ago, global population is expected to start leveling off at about 8.9 billion in 2050 and stabilize at about 10 billion around 2200' (John Ward Anderson, '6 Billion and Counting—But Slower', *Washington Post*, 12 Oct. 1999, p. A1). This is the kind of claim that could play a pivotal role in arguments about population policy, the future of our environment, and so on. It probably seems a reasonable enough assertion, but how can it be established as acceptable?

Clearly, we cannot know the population of the world in 2050 or 2200. At best we can extrapolate from trends we see now. And we must do so in a way that is fully cognizant of the fact that such predictions may turn out to be mistaken. In 1970, economists at the College of Mexico predicted that Mexico's population would nearly triple from 51 million to 148 million by the year 2000. In the wake of an aggressive population control policy this did not happen, and the population reached only 98 million. This and other factors (environmental change, war, etc.) could undermine the predictions that some scientists are making about the world's population in 2200. Certainly it is logically conceivable that such predictions, even if they are made carefully, will not take into account some factors that will have a significant impact on population growth.

At best, the arguments that are the basis for predictions of population growth yield conclusions that are uncertain. Caution is a good attitude when dealing with uncertain claims of this sort, but such claims are still acceptable if they are backed by reasonable arguments. When we are extrapolating for our experience of the world, high degrees of plausibility or probability must satisfy us. Certainty is not possible because our experience of the world is always open-ended. The future is still to come and our future experiences (or those of others) may lead us to question what we have heretofore assumed and concluded.

It is reasonable to expect that future experience will conform to our past experiences. We expect particles in an experiment to behave the way they have in past experiments. We expect the road to be slippery when it is covered with ice. To a lesser degree, we expect to be happy with our new car if we have been happy with five previous models built by the same manufacturer, and we expect we will enjoy the latest Stephen King novel because we have enjoyed his previous novels. These expectations may be reasonable, but this does not mean that they are certain.

Although our experience of the world does not yield certainty, it does establish factual claims about the world that are reasonable and acceptable, and which can be used as premises in arguments that establish reasonable conclusions. In the context of everyday arguments, much the same can be said of the uncertainties and differences of opinion that characterize moral, political, and religious opinions. Here, too, it would be too much to expect the conclusion of an argument to be certain. Instead of undermining reasoning, the lack of certainty that characterizes ordinary arguments serves to emphasize the need to reason carefully, to consider opposing points of view, and to weigh all the relevant evidence in determining what should and should not be believed.

2. ACCEPTABILITY

In order to judge acceptability, whether we are assessing another's claims or supporting our own, we ask whether the specific audience being addressed, along with a universal audience of reasonable people, would accept the statement without further support.

As we saw in Chapter 6, to ask this question is to ask where the burden of proof lies with respect to a claim. It is just as important to consider this for the arguments we construct. Is a claim we are putting forward as a premise one that we would expect a reasonable audience, and certainly our intended audience, to accept without further support? If it is, then in our minds the onus, or burden of proof, shifts to the audience that is reading or hearing the argument. Any challenger amongst them has the obligation to explain why the premise should not be accepted as it stands. If, on reflection, we recognize that the premise is not acceptable without support, then the burden of proof shifts to us, and we must provide warrants, explanations, or further supporting premises for that premise until we are satisfied that we have provided enough to fulfill our obligation and shift the burden of proof to any challenger. Of course, any supporting premises we provide must themselves be subjected to this same test. The process cannot go on indefinitely, and our arguments should not become unwieldy. The challenge is to ground our arguments in premises that are basic enough that their claims should be accepted by reasonable people.

For each premise provided in support of a conclusion, whether by yourself or by an arguer whose work you are assessing, ask yourself whether there is any evidence that conflicts with the statement and undermines its claim to be acceptable, or whether you lack the evidence needed to decide either way. If you must answer 'yes' to the first question, then the premise is unacceptable and there are grounds for rejecting it. It may conflict with empirical evidence, or it may be rejected by definition, or it may be inconsistent with another premise in the same argument. We will consider each of these ways of being unacceptable in due course. If you must answer 'yes' to the second question, then the premise is questionable. It cannot be accepted as given, but we do not have grounds to judge that the statement itself is unacceptable. However, given that the burden of proof is on the arguer to provide acceptable premises, the presence of questionable ones is a weakness in the argument, and hence something we strive to avoid in our own reasoning.

When evaluating, you must support your judgment that a premise is questionable by stating what evidence is required to make it acceptable. That is, what are you looking for that has not been provided? You may find that when you scrutinize a premise in this way, what you had thought to be questionable is in fact unacceptable, since the evidence that would be required to make it acceptable could not, in principle, exist.

Consider the debate around an essay on democracy and citizenship written by the British Home Secretary David Blunkett ('Integration with Diversity: Globalisation and the Renewal of Democracy and Civil Society', in 'Rethinking Britishness', The Foreign Policy Centre, 16 Sept. 2002). While he accepted that the failure of many Asian families to speak English at home had not been responsible for recent race riots, Blunkett argued that it did prevent those families from participating 'in wider modern culture', and that a fluency in English would help them 'overcome the schizophrenia that bedevils generational relationships'. He supported his claims with a recent citizenship survey that showed that English was not spoken at home in as many as 30 per cent of Asian households in Britain. Critics challenged Blunkett for singling out Asian families and for misapplying a term that refers to a mental illness. In the case of the schizophrenia claim, the critics said that Mr Blunkett had a burden of proof to show that this claim was acceptable. One critic went further and argued that Mr Blunkett should be more concerned with encouraging British people to learn to speak more languages. Part of that argument was as follows:

> Instead of pushing British people to learn new languages, he wants to prevent the rest of us from speaking many. This is, at its best, an obscenity due to Mr Blunkett' s denial of enriching his own people with other, probably richer cultures than his very own. . . . When British people go to other countries, such as Spain for their precious holidays . . . they want to be able to communicate in English and also mingle with an English crowd. If this is what Mr Blunkett tries to preserve, then, all he desires is a nation of non-intelligent, intellectually inferior (certainly in comparison with the rest of the European countries) people. (From a letter to The Observer, 22 Sept. 2002)

Much of this argument is what we will identify later in this chapter as a 'straw argument' since it misrepresents Mr Blunkett's position, which did not in any way imply that people should not speak many languages. But here we are interested in the acceptability of some of the claims put forward by the critic. For example, it is asserted that Mr Blunkett is denying enriching his people 'with other, probably richer cultures than his very own'. This premise appears to be questionable: no support is provided for it, but we have no initial reason to reject it out of hand. But when we ask what sort of evidence we *would* need to accept this statement, we begin to recognize the difficulties involved. How do we measure the richness of cultures, particularly with respect to each other? Minimally, what we require here are some qualitative differences between cultures, perhaps related to languages, since that is the topic in question. Given the qualifying 'probably' of the claim, such evidence might satisfy a charitable audience, although it should be clear that any attempt to decide which cultures are richer will be a complex and debatable undertaking.

But a further claim the arguer makes is even more problematic: 'If this is what Mr Blunkett tries to preserve, then, all he desires is a nation of non-intelligent, intellectually inferior (certainly in comparison with the rest of the European countries) people.' There is an assumption being made here that should be drawn out as a hidden premise, that unilingual people are non-intelligent and intellectually inferior. No matter how charitable we wish to be, this assumption seems unsupportable in principle. It is difficult to conceive of any legitimate evidence that would corroborate this statement. That people have only mastered one language does not prove them to be intellectually inferior. Perhaps such people tend to have more proficiency in the language that they use. And even if they don't, it may be that they have other skills they excel in. It is difficult to say. In this particular case the difficulty is so great that we deem a claim that at first seems questionable as, on reflection, unacceptable.

Remember that it is not enough to simply dismiss a premise as unacceptable or questionable. You must support such judgments by stating the grounds for the unacceptability or by stating what missing evidence or information is needed to determine the acceptability or unacceptability of a premise.

DETERMINING ACCEPTABILITY

There are three decisions we can make with respect to a claim's acceptability:

1. **It is *acceptable* without further support.** The statement itself is of such a nature, or is supported by other statements to such a degree, that a reasonable audience will accept it.
2. **It is *unacceptable*.** The statement conflicts with what is known to be the case such that a reasonable audience (and evaluator) has reason to reject it.
3. **It is *questionable*.** The statement is neither clearly acceptable nor clearly unacceptable because insufficient information is presented to decide either way.

Belief Systems and Acceptability

In judging acceptability, we need to consider it in relation to our audiences. In this context it is useful to distinguish between a 'specific audience' that shares particular commitments and a 'universal audience' that consists of reasonable people. If we want our immediate audience to accept our arguments, we must ensure we build them with premises and assumptions the audience will find acceptable. Our audience must be able to understand the meaning of our premises and assent to them without further support. If our audience consists of rational people, their acceptance of our premises will, of course, remain open to revision in the event that new data come to light.

A central consideration in evaluating acceptability fairly is the role of perspective in reasoning. In addressing ourselves briefly to the problems of vagueness and ambiguity in Chapter 4, we saw that communication is rendered difficult by virtue of the fact that communicators are 'persons', individuals distinct from one another in terms of their heredity, background experiences, conditioning influences, loves, loyalties, values, commitments, politics, religion, and other involvements. These factors constitute for each of us a system of beliefs and commitments.

Systems of belief have an enormous impact on the way we argue and the claims for which we argue, as well as the way we assess acceptability. It is important for us to examine the notion of belief systems in order to become more sensitive to the differences in belief that characterize different audiences. An understanding of belief systems will help us better appreciate the context within which arguments take place. This will in turn prove helpful when we construct arguments and when we evaluate the arguments of others.

All our arguments are formed within a belief system and conform, whether or not we realize it, to the world view or perspective that we have adopted. The make-up of the belief system comprises a number of factors, of which some are with us from early in our development and others are more transitory. Birth determines our sex, race, nationality (although this can change), and, often, our religion. Among the more transitory components are the careers we choose, the organizations and clubs we join, and the friendships we form. We can also think of other associations or commitments that do not fit neatly into either of these categories. Many people reject or change an earlier religious perspective, for example, and this has a major and often dramatic effect on their world view. Again, some of our strongest attachments, such as those to parents or siblings, arise at birth, whereas attachments to our children arise later in life.

Our commitments and beliefs are integrated to the point that it is usually difficult to determine which we have inherited from others and which originate with us. They define our self-identity, constitute our personal perspective, and give rise to the opinions we hold. Strong opinions, in turn, are the embryos from which arguments develop.

Even when we engage in legitimate reasoning, deeply held beliefs may still influence our arguments in ways we do not expect. Quite often this is evident not so much in what we say but in the assumptions behind our reasoning and the consequences that follow from it. Consider the following excerpt from an extended argument by George Grant (from 'The Case Against Abortion', *Today Magazine*, 3 Oct. 1981, 12–13). In arguing against abortions for convenience, Grant introduces into the debate an unusual consideration:

Mankind's greatest political achievement has been to limit ruthlessness by a system of legal rights. The individual was guarded against the abuses of arbitrary power, whether by state or by other individuals. Building this system required the courage of many. *It was fundamentally based on the assumption that human beings are more than just accidental blobs of matter. They have an eternal destiny and therefore the right to rights.* But the large-scale destruction of human beings by abortion questions that view.

We have italicized the two sentences relevant to the present discussion. Our system of legal rights, Grant insists, is 'based on the assumption that human beings are more than accidental blobs of matter.' What this 'more' is, he tells us, is that human beings have a 'right to rights' because they 'have an eternal destiny'. An eternal destiny stands in contrast to being an 'accidental blob'. It implies that we are planned, that our existence is intentional, that there is something eternal or immortal about us, presumably as individuals. All this makes us planned rather than 'accidental blobs'. But planned by whom? Though no mention is made of 'God', belief in a deity is implied.

In drawing out Grant's meaning, we have strayed far from what is stated, but reasonably so. There is ample reason to conclude that Grant's reasoning is grounded in a religious commitment, that he believes we are part of a divine plan. Although this is never stated, it is implied by and follows as a consequence from what is stated.

Elements of our belief systems can have a conscious or unconscious influence on our arguments. Given that our beliefs can show up in the implications and consequences of what we say, it is important that we identify them if we are intent on convincing our audience. If we fail to do so our audience can miss our point or deem unacceptable premises we consider acceptable. Grant's argument needs to be reinforced because his premises are unlikely to be accepted by people who do not share his religious beliefs.

We cannot remove our belief system in order to prevent its influence, nor is it necessary or advisable to try to do so. Our belief system is an integral part of us; to deny it is to deny ourselves. But we must guard against its unconscious or illegitimate influence on our reasoning by being aware of it. Awareness of it requires self-evaluation. We should ask ourselves why we are members of certain audiences. What is it that we hold in common? Which beliefs and commitments do we hold most strongly, and how did they arise? As we construct a profile of our belief system, we can begin to assess the impact of our commitments and associations on our thinking and actions.

Beyond sex, race, religion, and nationality, we should reflect on our educational background—commitments to schools and to a segment of society educated at our level, the beliefs that arise from our economic and social environment and how these influence our views on society, social standing, and politics. We should reflect, too, on our value system—where it comes from, and the commitments it entails, personally and nationally and globally.

Such reflections will give us a profile of our belief systems and help us to understand why we reason as we do. It is one thing to discuss how we would construct arguments defending capital punishment or opposing censorship. But it is quite a different matter to ask why we would come to argue such issues in the first place and why we happen to view the issues the way we do. At some deep level both these activities are connected.

If you catch yourself responding emotionally to an issue instead of employing reasoned argument, you will have to judge the acceptability of your emotive claims. For this, familiarity with your belief system is essential. But we encourage you to test the rationality of your beliefs. Emotional responses are not necessarily irrational. But are they reasonable? Are you able to support your passionately held beliefs with good and sufficient reasons? Don't give up a belief because you can't do this. It may be emotionally satisfying to keep it. But if you cannot support it, you should be aware that this is the case, and that you will have little success convincing a reasonable audience.

Belief Systems and Audiences

What we have said about ourselves as arguers also applies to audiences—both the audiences of which we are a part, and the audiences we may have occasion to address. The belief systems of an audience predispose its members toward certain claims and arguments. Being familiar with the belief system(s) of an audience enables us to judge more accurately what is required to ensure that they will accept the premises of our argument.

If you are a person with a college or university education, you are likely to favour the maintenance and support of universities and colleges and to see them as playing a valuable role in society. You are likely to be sympathetic to arguments proposing a reasonable level of government funding for the university system. The extent of your sympathy is also likely to affect the degree of evidence you will require before you are convinced that there is a need for increased government funding. An arguer does not need to provide you with evidence that a university education is valuable; this can be assumed. She need only provide reasonable grounds for believing the universities are underfunded, and you will agree with her conclusion for increased funding. But convincing people without your educational background may require much more evidence. They are not naturally sympathetic to the cause and will not accept without further support the premise that a university or college education is valuable.

As we saw in the discussion of bias in Chapter 5, our sympathies for a cause or position may interfere with our critical assessment of an argument supporting it. We are not predisposed to give such arguments the same scrutiny we reserve for neutral arguments or those supporting causes we do not favour. It is difficult to be objective in such cases, but it is important that we attempt to be. Just because we believe there are good arguments in favour of a position does not mean that the next argument we see supporting that position will be good. In fact, we can strengthen the general support for a position we hold by pointing out the flaws in arguments made for it and by showing how those flaws may be remedied or avoided. On the basis of other reasons we may accept the conclusion of an argument without accepting the premises supporting it, just as we may agree that a conclusion follows necessarily from its premises but reject the premises.

These comments also apply to our audiences. They, too, have belief systems that a responsible reasoner will not exploit. While our arguments may quite legitimately touch the hearts of our audiences, our primary obligation as responsible thinkers is to consider their minds and speak to them with reasoned arguments. Generally, you can anticipate three types of specific audience: one *sympathetic* to what you are arguing; one not predisposed to your position but *open* to considering it (this is also a key characteristic of the universal audience); and one *hostile* to your position. While each of these audiences requires the same standards of argumentation, it should be easier to convince an audience of the acceptability of a claim if they share your perspective than if they do not. The hostile audience will be the hardest to convince, and your skill as a critical thinker is put to the test when you address such an audience. Doing so demands that you be sensitive to the belief system the members of such an audience share. Quite often, the only way they will be convinced of your point is if you can get them to see it *from their perspective*. Think carefully about the shift of focus this entails. It requires that you think in terms that are hostile to your own position. This audience, more than any other, asks for a reason to be convinced. Its members expect you to consider them and what they believe and argue to *this*.

Audience consideration is not a casual feature of arguing well. Awareness of the belief system of an audience is one of the more important prerequisites for effective argumentation. Without it, all your skills in structuring arguments may prove worthless. Your aim in arguing with a hostile audience is to bring about a change in their thinking. You can best do this by meeting people where they are, understanding the thinking on their side, and leading them from there.

One important qualification concerns the acceptance of standards held by the universal audience—that audience comprising reasonable, objective people. This consideration always has greater priority over any specific audience you address, because the universal audience is governed by the principles of good reasoning. With the specific audience, we respect the beliefs they hold, the assumptions behind their perspective, and the particular knowledge to which they have access. If the principles of good reasoning and the entrenched beliefs of an audience conflict, it is reasonable to favour the former. This way we avoid the apparent trap of treating as 'reasonable' the arguments of fanatics, racists, and their ilk. The following captures this division in a general condition of acceptability:

> *Premise Acceptability*
> A premise is judged acceptable if
> > (1) it would be accepted *without further support* by the audience for which it is intended, given the background knowledge of its members and the beliefs and values they hold, *and*
> > (2) it conforms to (does not violate), alone or in combination with other premises, the principles of good reasoning.

What do we mean here by 'the principles of good reasoning'? Generally, we have been discussing such principles throughout this text and will continue to do so. You should already have a fairly developed sense of the kinds of things a reasonable audience will accept. What follows are some key ways in which a premise can be judged acceptable for a universal (and often, a specific) audience.

Universal Conditions of Acceptability
i) Acceptable by definition, or self-evidently acceptable
Some claims can be established as acceptable by appealing to definitions. We know from the meanings of its component terms that the statement 'All squares are four-sided figures' must be acceptable. Other claims are self-evident for different reasons. 'Your phone bill will be more, less, or the same as last month's bill' is obviously the case because it exhausts all the possibilities with respect to this month's bill. Sometimes we appeal to moral principles we take to be self-evident. 'One should not cause unnecessary pain' is an example of a moral principle many people consider to be self-evident.

A claim that is acceptable by virtue of the meaning of its component terms is acceptable in view of the way in which we use language, and so relies to some extent on what is commonly known by a community of language users (as will be discussed below). This is the strongest type of self-evident claim because the attempt to deny it results in an absurdity. One cannot, for example, deny that 'If Sam is 82 years old, he's an octogenarian,' for this follows from the very meaning of the word 'octogenarian'. An arguer putting forward such a claim as a premise has no burden of proof to support it. Any support would be redundant.

ii) Acceptable as a factual statement reporting an observation or as a statement of personal testimony
Observation is another way of establishing the acceptability of some claims. It is on the basis of this that we would determine whether it is or is not the case that 'There has been virtually no snowfall during the last two hours.' If someone presents us with such a statement, we really have no grounds to reject it unless it contradicts other observations available to us.

This leads to the more difficult cases of claims that are based on a person's own testimony and which are not verifiable by shared observations. While carrying less force as evidential statements for conclusions, such appeals to personal testimony often arise in argumentation, and we need to deal with them. In general, we have no reason to dispute what someone claims to have experienced. If people want to convince audiences, it is in their interests to be truthful, and we can grant statements such as 'I have driven my Toyota every day for two years without any mechanical problem' as acceptable based on the personal testimony of the speaker.

There are obvious qualifications to this, and we need to be cautious. If a person has proved repeatedly that they are untrustworthy, then that is a reason not to accept what they say. Likewise, if the statement lacks plausibility, as with a claim that someone was removed from their car in broad daylight and taken up into an alien space-craft, then we are justified in not accepting it. We expect personal testimony claims to conform to the general structure of experience.

iii) Acceptable by common knowledge

Both of the first two conditions bear on common experience in some way, but common knowledge is so often invoked as a reason for the acceptability of a statement that we need to treat it cautiously. There is a tendency to believe that virtually any claim can form part of some community's shared experience and to judge claims accordingly. This is where we need to look at both the specific audience being addressed and the underlying universal audience. Important also is the distinction between factual claims and evaluative claims. 'The government has proposed a separate justice system for minority groups' is a factual claim. 'The government's proposed separate justice system for minority groups is an outrage' is an evaluative claim. Evaluative claims convey the same information as factual claims but add an expression of it as right or wrong. The first statement may be common knowledge within a community; the second is not.

Under 'common knowledge' we are judging factual claims of a descriptive nature that we can *expect* to be *commonly* known. There are two terms emphasized here that we need to consider in more detail. The breadth of the common knowledge depends on the nature of the topic being argued and the goals of the arguer. We could dismiss a lot of the premises aimed at specific audiences because they report or depend on information not generally known by a larger (universal) audience. But that is being uncharitable. Unless the argument is specifically aimed at a universal audience or has overstepped the boundary between descriptive and evaluative claims, we can allow statements based on the common knowledge of the community being addressed.

At the other extreme, people sometimes reject statements because they are not commonly known by *all* members of an audience. This again is uncharitable and points to the need to consider what we might reasonably *expect* an audience to know. For the most part, we do not know what is actually known by all individuals making up audiences and communities. We cannot see into other minds, and certainly not the minds of large groups of people. To this extent 'common knowledge' is a bit of a misnomer. But we do know what we *expect* people to know, and that is what information they have access to in their daily lives. We live in environments where certain ideas and information are readily available, and by appealing to these environments we can make sense of the common knowledge condition. Thus, when we speak of common knowledge we are not speaking about what people actually know in common, but what we can reasonably expect them to know given the environments in which they live and work. This allows us to accommodate those individuals who don't know what everyone else does.

The common knowledge condition is a judgment we make about environments, and we make that judgment considering the universality of the argument and the audience being addressed. Thus we can, generally, allow statements like 'The Roman

Catholic Church does not allow women to be priests,' or 'The Rolling Stones are a popular rock band,' because these are common bits of information that form part of the environments of most people. More difficult is a statement like 'The United Nations' Fourth World Conference on Women was held in Beijing.' People's access to this kind of information depends on how widely it has been reported in their communities, on how much media exposure it has been given. Also, information about a UN conference will be of greater interest to some audiences than to others. We would allow for these things in judging the use of this statement in a premise. But insofar as the audience is appropriate, and the statement is factual rather than evaluative, it is the kind of statement that could pass as common knowledge for a specific audience.

iv) Acceptable due to its being defended in a reasonable sub-argument
When we judge the acceptability of premises, what we expect is that an arguer will support those premises that would not be otherwise acceptable to the audience being addressed. That is, the audience will recognize her or his burden of proof where required to do so. Where an arguer has fulfilled this obligation, and the support provided is reasonable, then we have grounds for finding the supported premise to be acceptable. Of course, once supported in this way, the premise in question becomes a conclusion, and we would then speak of the sub-argument as being strong. But when we evaluate the acceptability of an argument's premises it is important not to overlook sub-conclusions because these also constitute premises for the main claim. Consider the following:

> It seems jurors are more willing to convict for murder since the abolition of the death penalty. The overall conviction rate for capital punishment was about 10 per cent for 1960–74. From 1976, when capital punishment was abolished, until 1982, the conviction rate for first-degree murder was about 20 per cent. There is reason to believe, then, that the consequence of returning capital punishment to Canada will be to see more murderers sent back onto the streets by reluctant juries. (From a report of the research and statistics group of the Department of the Solicitor-General of Canada. Source: *The Globe and Mail*, 9 Jan. 1987)

We can diagram the four statements of this argument as follows:

(1) [Canadian] jurors are more willing to convict for murder since the abolition of the death penalty.
(2) The overall conviction rate for capital punishment was about 10 per cent for 1960–74.
(3) From 1976, when capital punishment was abolished, until 1982, the conviction rate for first-degree murder was about 20 per cent.
(4) There is reason to believe that the consequence of returning capital punishment to Canada will be to see more murderers sent back onto the streets by reluctant juries.

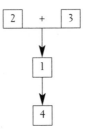

When evaluating the acceptability of the premises in this argument we begin with statement 1, which is a premise in support of the main conclusion, 4. Statement 1, '[Canadian] jurors are more willing to convict for murder since the abolition of the death penalty,' is a controversial, interpretive statement, and even the specific audience of the Canadian public could not accept it as it stands. Recognizing this, the authors have provided the statistical data needed to support 1 in statements 2 and 3. Each describes the conviction rate for murder in Canada, statement 2 prior to the abolition of capital punishment, statement 3 after the abolition. Thus, 2 and 3 represent the kind of premises needed to support the sub-conclusion 1. Of course, attention would then shift to the acceptability of the premises in 2 and 3, and the acceptability of these two factual statements would rely largely on the authority of the source. Such appeals constitute our final condition for acceptability.

v) Acceptable on the authority of an expert

A premise can be accepted because it carries the support of, or appeals to, an expert or authority. The appeal to authority is an argument scheme that will be treated in detail in Chapter 14. Here, we wish only to introduce the notion of expertise and indicate its role in assessing the acceptability of a premise.

Experts are people, institutions, or sources who, by virtue of their authority, knowledge, or experience, can be used to support the claims made in premises. Consider an example:

> As the Surgeon General says, second-hand smoke is bad for your health. So you
> are hurting your children when you smoke at home.

This is actually an extended argument. The main argument is: 'Second-hand smoke is bad for your health, so you are hurting your children when you smoke at home.' Is the premise in this argument acceptable? The arguer attempts to establish its acceptability by appealing to the authority of the Surgeon General. If such an authority is appropriate here—that is, the right kind of authority, speaking on the right issue, with the right motive—then the premise is acceptable. Note that the premise may not be *enough* to carry the conclusion. But in cases—and there are many of them—where we do not have access to the information we would need to judge a premise, or where we simply lack the expertise to make such an assessment ourselves, it is quite legitimate to rely on an authority. Authorities act as proxy support for a premise. The information they have is available somewhere, so their support provides a presumption in favour of the premise. Their information will rarely be enough to carry an argument, but many extended arguments include authoritative sources somewhere.

Experts and authoritative sources come in many forms, like the Department of the Solicitor-General of Canada in the earlier argument, which, as an objective body, gives legitimate support to the premises given there. Other authoritative sources may include religious texts such as the Bible and Koran, professionals who are renowned in their fields, objective consumer advocacy groups, documentaries, dictionaries, and textbooks.

UNIVERSAL CONDITIONS OF ACCEPTABILITY

i)   acceptable by definition, or self-evidently acceptable
ii) acceptable as a factual statement reporting an observation or as a statement of personal testimony
iii) acceptable by common knowledge
iv) acceptable due to its being defended in a reasonable sub-argument
v)   acceptable on the authority of an expert

Universal Conditions of Unacceptability

In some instances, a premise will be judged unacceptable because it fails to satisfy— i.e. it specifically violates—one or more of the conditions of acceptability. In many cases the failure to support a premise with a reasonable sub-argument, or with an appeal to common knowledge, may simply render the premise questionable, but not explicitly unacceptable. The absence of such support prevents us from making a firm judgment. But when a premise contradicts a state of affairs in the world, and the contradiction is apparent from observation or common knowledge, then we have cause to judge the premise unacceptable. Likewise, a premise might be found unacceptable due to the meanings of its component terms, if those meanings were contradictory (for example, if they referred to 'married bachelors', or some such things). Beyond these considerations, there are a few other more specific conditions of unacceptability.

i) Unacceptable due to an inconsistency with another premise

Inconsistency is a weakness in argumentation that is brought to light by carefully reading an argument's components and considering their meaning. It is possible for two (or more) premises in an argument to be perfectly acceptable when considered individually. But when they are appraised together we encounter a situation where they cannot both be acceptable as support for the same conclusion. Consider the inconsistency between the following premises:

P1 = Only claims that can be verified in some way can be trusted.
P2 = Enough people have reported encounters with ghosts to make their existence likely.

These two statements could issue from the belief system of someone who has not carefully evaluated their own beliefs and considered how they sit with each other. At first glance, P2 might seem to be consistent with P1, since a person's experience is a type of verification. But the kind of verification intended by P1 is objective, third-person verification. If claims are to be trusted, there must be some way of subjecting them to testing. As they stand, P1 and P2 appeal to quite different criteria, and if both were to be used in a single piece of argumentation, the inconsistency between them would render them unacceptable.

ii) Unacceptable due to begging the question
Begging the question is a violation of the principle of good reasoning that requires us to avoid circularity, or not to assume in our premises what we are attempting to establish in our conclusions. The following argument illustrates this point:

How do we know that [1](we have here in the Bible a right criterion of truth)?

[2](We know because of the Bible's claims for itself).

[3](All through the Scriptures are found . . . expressions such as 'Thus says the Lord', 'The Lord said', and 'God spoke').[4](Such statements occur no less than 1,904 times in the 39 books of the Old Testament).

[adapted from *Decision Magazine*, Jan. 1971]

(1) The Bible is a right criterion of truth.
(2) The Bible claims truth for itself.
(3) All through the Scriptures are found expressions such as 'Thus says the Lord'.
(4) Such statements occur no less than 1,904 times in the Old Testament.

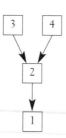

The sub-argument in support of 1 (the main claim) would probably be judged sufficient and accepted by an uncritical audience already sympathetic to it. But the argument would not be—or, at least, should not be—convincing to a universal audience.

By definition, whatever reasons you give to back up a claim must be supporting statements. A statement is not a supporting statement if it merely restates the conclusion or implicitly contains it. What makes statement 2 unacceptable as a premise to a universal audience is that it assumes precisely what it is supposed to prove. It therefore *begs the question.* No reasonable person who has doubts about the truth of the Bible and who is looking for an argument to support the claim that 'the Bible is the right criterion of truth' will be convinced by the argument given. To accept statement 2 as a reason for statement 1, one must already assume that statement 1 has been established.

In order to avoid begging the question, you need to resist the temptation to use premises that merely restate the claim you are trying to establish. The premise: 'People living below the poverty line ought to receive a basic income' is not a separate and distinct reason for the claim: 'The poor should be given financial subsidies up to a pre-established minimum.' It simply recasts the same idea in different language. To use one of these statements as a premise to support the other as a conclusion is to beg the question.

iii) Unacceptable due to problems with language

After reading the discussion of language in Chapter 4 you should be able to recognize a number of semantic problems that would be grounds for finding a premise unacceptable. There may be cases where a specific audience would understand an arguer's meaning while a universal audience would not. But there are also clear-cut examples where no audience could be certain of a premise's meaning, where the statement is essentially vague and the context cannot resolve that vagueness, or where a definition, although not internally contradictory, is too broad or narrow to be persuasive. (A definition that is missing, though, would be a problem of sufficiency. This will be discussed later.)

Even premises that report personal testimony and would otherwise be allowed can be rejected because they fail to communicate clearly. A statement like 'I have driven my 1999 Ford every day for three years without any major problem' founders on the vagueness of 'major problem'. If the person has experienced a constant series of 'minor' problems, that itself might be considered a major problem to someone else.

UNIVERSAL CONDITIONS OF UNACCEPTABILITY

 i)   unacceptable due to an inconsistency with another premise
 ii)   unacceptable due to begging the question
 iii) unacceptable due to problems with language

EXERCISE 11A

1.   Construct audience profiles for each of the following.
        EXAMPLE: professional women
                Professional women are likely to be well educated, to be strongly committed to equal rights for women, to value advancement in their profession, and to be sensitive to the issues that confront women in such careers.

    a)* university students

    b)   Native North Americans

    c)* sports fans

    d)   citizens of industrialized countries

    e)   pet owners

    f)   labour union members

    g)   farmers

    h)   newspaper and media people

2.   Consider your own belief system and construct a detailed profile of its major features.

3.   List the features you would include in the belief system of the universal audience.

4.   Explain the grounds you would use in judging the acceptability, questionability, or unacceptability of each of the following statements:

    a)* The presence of a cause is demonstrated by the existence of its effects.

    b)* The Soviet Union exists today just as it did in 1980.

    c)   [stated by the chief of police] The intersection of these two major roads is the worst location for accidents in the city.

    d)   [from a review of Charlie Russell and Maureen Enns's book *Grizzly Heart*, in the *Literary Review of Canada* (Nov. 2002), p. 20] Russell and Enns have defied the preconceptions of wildlife officials and the general public by living unthreatened—and respected—among the grizzlies of Kamchatka. They demonstrate that it is possible to forge a mutually respectful relationship with these majestic giants, and provide compelling reasons for altering our culture.

    e)   Of all the countries I have visited in South America, I have found the people of Chile to be the most hospitable.

    f)   Human beings cannot always be trusted to tell the truth.

    g)   Several extinct species exist in the rain forest.

    h)* Prisoners in federal penitentiaries should be allowed to vote because they still retain their citizenship and elected officials oversee the regulations that govern the running of penitentiaries.

    i)   Emily Dickinson was an American poet.

    j)   Computer technology will either improve daily life, or it will not.

    k)   Most people prefer the company of those from their own culture.

5.   From the perspective of the universal audience, assess the acceptability of the premises in each of the following arguments. Be sure to explain fully the grounds for your decisions.

    a)   Nobody likes a quitter. So I won't give up smoking.

    b)* To every man unbounded freedom of speech must always be, on the whole, advantageous to the state; for it is highly conducive to the interests of the community that each individual should enjoy a liberty perfectly unlimited of expressing his sentiments.

c)   [Mary Gordon, in *Joan of Arc*, pp. 2–3] Joan's family does not seem to have been of much consequence to her. When she decided to obey her voices and go off to crown the king of France, she left home with a cousin, who was her god-father, employing an ordinary, adolescent lie. She told her parents she was going to help out with the cousin's wife's labor, and then with the new child. She never spoke to her parents again, and when she was asked during her trial if she felt guilty about what could only be construed as a sin of disobedience, she said, 'Since God commanded it, had I had a hundred fathers and a hundred mothers, had I been born a king's daughter, I should have departed.' So we would do well not to linger over Joan's family for explanations of anything.

d)   Since animals can experience pain and are also capable of nurturing relation-ships, it is wrong to use them indiscriminately in experiments, and hence there should be strict guidelines governing such use.

e)   [Marcus Aurelius, in *Meditations*, Book XII] The gods must not be blamed, for they do no wrong, willingly or unwillingly; nor human beings, for they do no wrong except unwillingly. Therefore, no one is to be blamed.

f)   Some diseases have been known to fool even the experienced medical profes-sional. According to the *New England Journal of Medicine*, human error can affect both physicians' diagnoses and laboratory test results. In cases of serious ill-ness, a second opinion is often desirable.

3. Relevance

Beyond having acceptable premises, a strong argument must have a conclusion that follows *from* those premises. In Chapter 6 we saw that a conclusion follows from a set of premises when they are (1) relevant to the conclusion, and (2) sufficient to establish it as plausible. In deductively valid arguments, the premises are both relevant and suf-ficient, for they guarantee the conclusion. Once we accept the premises, this means that we must accept the conclusion. In such cases, it is often said that the premises *entail* the conclusion.

In considering arguments that are, at best, inductively valid, we need to distin-guish between relevance and sufficiency. Like deductive validity, *relevance* is a meas-ure of the relationship between an argument's premises and conclusions. But we can recognize a conclusion's premises to be relevant to it yet still have questions about that conclusion. Consider the following argument:

PREMISE: Six member countries of the UN support the US proposal.
CONCLUSION: Most members of the UN support the US proposal.

For reasons we shall discuss shortly, the premise is relevant to the conclusion: it is the kind of evidence needed to begin establishing the conclusion, and it increases the likelihood of the conclusion. But, it is clear, the premise does not deductively estab-lish the conclusion: that is, we can accept the premise without having to accept the conclusion. We see, then, that relevance is something apart from deductive validity.

Let us add a second premise to our example:

PREMISE 2: The US proposal will soon be debated in the general assembly.

Like the first premise, Premise 2 could be accepted on the basis of common knowledge. But unlike the first premise, the second one makes no obvious contribution to establishing the conclusion—it is not a reason for believing the conclusion. Premise 2, then, is not relevant to the conclusion.

Internal Relevance

Demonstrated above is what we call *internal relevance*: a relation that exists between a premise or set of premises and a conclusion. For premises to be relevant to a conclusion it is not enough for them to be acceptable or to 'talk about the same subject'. The premises must act upon the conclusion so as to increase (or decrease) the probability of the conclusion being accepted.

Usually when we argue, our goal is to increase the degree of likelihood attributed to a claim. But it is possible to introduce evidence that actually undermines the claim, and we have to allow for such instances. Also, when we engage in counter-argumentation we do think of relevance in this negative way as we look to introduce premises that take away from a claim and decrease its likelihood.

Our earlier example illustrates the nature of internal relevance. The first premise, 'Six member countries of the UN support the US proposal,' actively increases the probability that the conclusion will be accepted. If six members support the UN then this goes toward supporting the conclusion that 'Most members of the UN support the US proposal.' It is the kind of positive evidence that we would look for to establish the claim. What we require further is information about the other member nations. As more indicate their support of the proposal, so the likelihood of the conclusion increases further. But if we learn that a number of members oppose the proposal, that counts as negatively relevant evidence that starts to decrease the likelihood of the conclusion.

In contrast to Premise 1, Premise 2, 'The US proposal will soon be debated in the general assembly,' has a neutral relation to the conclusion, neither increasing nor decreasing its likelihood. It simply does not work as a reason for the conclusion, in spite of its being acceptable and related to the conclusion in subject matter. We need to learn from this that premises we have judged acceptable should not be considered relevant because of their acceptability. Relevance is a very different consideration, and acceptable premises can still be found irrelevant to the conclusion they are intended to support. Remember that even if a premise and a conclusion refer to the same subject, this alone does not guarantee that the premise will be relevant to the conclusion in the active way necessary.

In extended arguments you will find that some premises are not relevant to the main claim, because many of them are intended only as support for subsidiary claims. The claim for which a premise is given as evidence is the claim for which the relevance of the premise should be decided. The following example, which is excerpted from an editorial in the *Globe and Mail* (6 Feb. 1987), serves as a fuller application of our rule:

¹ (The right to a lawyer is crucial to our justice system) . . .

² (An accused is vulnerable to intimidation, conscious or not, by the authorities who arrest him).

Since ³ (our society considers him innocent unless proved guilty), and

⁴ (believes he should not be compelled to testify against himself),

⁵ (justice requires that he be counselled by someone who knows the law and can advise him on which questions he must legally answer).

The opening statement appears to be the conclusion for which the reasons that follow are offered as evidence. Diagrammed, the argument looks like this:

1 = (MC) The right to a lawyer is crucial to our justice system.
2 = (P1) An accused person is vulnerable to intimidation, conscious or not, by the authorities who arrest him.
3 = (P2) Our society considers the accused person innocent unless proved guilty.
4 = (P3) Our society believes the accused should not be compelled to testify against himself.
5 = (P4, C1) Justice requires that the accused person be counselled by someone who knows the law and can advise him on which questions he must legally answer.

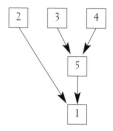

The diagram shows us a subsidiary argument within the main argument. Accordingly, in assessing relevance, we must look at the bearing each of statement 2 and statement 5 has on statement 1, the MC, and the bearing each of statement 3 and statement 4 has on statement 5. Although we may legitimately wonder whether a paralegal could take the place of a lawyer in providing the required service, we have no difficulty seeing that statement 2 and statement 5 are the right kind of evidence needed to increase one's acceptance of statement 1. Likewise, statements 3 and 4 actively increase the likelihood of statement 5 being accepted. Applying our rule of internal relevance, of course, requires judgment on our part. But there seems to be nothing in this argument with which we can legitimately disagree.

RELEVANCE AND HIDDEN PREMISES

If you are still having trouble identifying hidden premises, you may find the rule of internal relevance useful. Before you dismiss a premise as irrelevant to a conclusion consider whether there is a hidden premise that, once drawn out, combines with the explicit premise to support the conclusion. Of course, you won't find this in every case. Consider the following:

¹ It is morally permissible to experiment on human embryos at a developmental stage prior to the formation of the brain, since

² there is no possibility of causing pain or distress to the organism.

(1) It is morally permissible to experiment on human embryos at a developmental stage prior to the formation of the brain.

(2) There is no possibility of causing pain or distress to the organism.

Statement 2 is given as a reason for statement 1, but at first glance we might judge it as irrelevant to that conclusion. How do we get from causing pain to having a brain? What would make the premise relevant to the conclusion (that is, what would provide active support for it) would be an explicit connection between having a brain and feeling pain, which the author has not provided. Drawing out the following hidden premise is, then, a reasonable assumption to attribute to the author. Once drawn out, it combines with the explicit premise to provide relevant support for the conclusion.

HP = A brain is required for any entity to receive messages of [i.e. feel] pain.

Contextual Relevance

Internal relevance is a measure of a premise's relationship to a conclusion. 'Contextual relevance' is a measure of an argument's relationship to the context in which it is situated. An argument can pass the test of internal relevance, with all its premises judged relevant to the conclusion they are intended to support, yet still prove to be contextually irrelevant. The rule here is to ensure that the context of an argument has been correctly recognized and that all components relate to it. If an argument correctly addresses the context in which it arises, including the issue with which it is concerned and any prior argument to which it responds, then it is contextually relevant. If the argument misrepresents the issue or a prior argument and then attacks the misrepresentation, or if it deviates from the issue and doesn't return to address it, then the argument is contextually irrelevant and guilty of being either a 'straw argument' or a 'red herring'.

Straw arguments

We often find ourselves summarizing an opponent's position in order to clarify it or attribute certain consequences to it before arguing against it. When we do this, we must be sure that the opposing position has been fairly and accurately represented. If our version is wrong, whether it is deliberate or through an oversight—if we take our opponent's position to be A when she intended B, and then proceed to attack A—we are guilty of the type of contextual irrelevance known as a 'straw argument'. A straw argument is always a misrepresentation of a position, usually a weakened account of it used to make the response easier and apparently more effective. We saw this earlier in the chapter in the critic's response to David Blunkett's concerns about a lack of English fluency. While Blunkett was concerned that English *as well as* historic mother tongues be spoken in homes, the critic misrepresented him as wanting *only* English to be spoken, a much easier target to attack.

We must address the real argument advanced by a person or held by opponents, not some weakened version of it. The rule of contextual relevance requires that our interpretation of an opposing position be fairly and correctly represented. Consider the following argument, excerpted and adapted from a letter to the *New York Times* (Mar. 1982):

¹ (It should be obvious that the new Medicare Bill will not accomplish the utopia claimed for it),

because ² (it will not make everyone healthy overnight).

Therefore, ³ (the new Medicare Bill should not be passed).

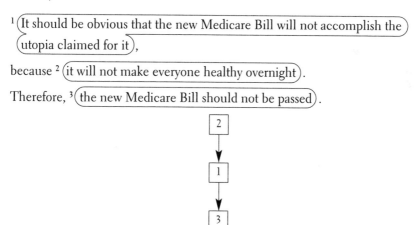

Here we have two arguments: statement 1 in support of statement 3, and statement 2 in support of statement 1. Both arguments satisfy the requirement of internal relevance. Statement 2 is clearly relevant to statement 1, since the failure to make everyone healthy overnight actively increases the likelihood that the bill will not achieve a state of utopia. The internal relevance of statement 1 to statement 3 is less clear, but we may charitably allow that the failure to achieve a promised utopia would be a relevant (though far from sufficient) reason that the bill should not be passed.

But here we pause and wonder about the first argument. Who promised that the Medicare Bill would achieve a utopia? Presumably it was the proponents of the bill, this arguer's opponents. But did they claim this? And if so, did they mean by such a claim that the Medicare Bill would make everyone healthy overnight? It is difficult to imagine anyone making such a strong claim, which suggests a possible exaggeration on the arguer's part. From this point of view, we have a strong reason to think that the arguer has created a caricature of the opposing position in order to attack that mis-representation. In short, we have every reason to suspect that we are dealing with a straw argument that is contextually irrelevant to the real issue.

In the Medicare argument we had to use our judgment to detect an exaggeration. In the next example no such exaggeration is apparent. A sincere attempt to support a position has led to an oversight. The example is a letter to the *Peterborough Examiner* (20 May 1992):

> I am concerned by the recent letters to the editor that portray the Women's Health Care Centre as an abortion clinic.
>
> I would like to point out that the Women's Health Care Centre provides many valuable services . . . pregnancy non-stress testing; colposcopy clinic; lac-tation consultant (breast feeding support); counselling and information on a wide range of health issues of concern to women and their families; workshops covering PMS, menopause, body image, living alone and many others.
>
> I feel that the services provided by the Women's Health Care Centre work in conjunction with physicians and provide comprehensive information and support for the women of Peterborough and the surrounding areas.

The nature of the issue and the context indicate this is an argumentative attempt to defend the Women's Centre against recent attacks. For the most part, that defence is well made. The writer claims that the Centre provides many valuable services, and supports that claim in an internally relevant way with a detailed list of services. But when we consider the context in which the debate arises and the point to be addressed, we are led to ask: '*Is* the Women's Health Care Centre an abortion clinic?' The writer indicates that it is certainly much more than an abortion clinic, and if the charge had been that it was *only* an abortion clinic then her response would have forcefully addressed that charge. But that was not the charge, and it remains that the writer has not addressed the claim that it was an abortion clinic. We do not know whether she agrees with the claim or not. For all its merits, the writer's argument has not addressed the point that the context required to be addressed, and on that ground it is contextually irrelevant.

Red herrings
The second type of contextual irrelevance is what has been traditionally termed the 'red herring'. What distinguishes this from the straw argument is that there is no mis-representation of a prior position or context. Rather, the shift takes place within the

argument as the boundaries of the context are altered through the introduction of a quite irrelevant consideration.

Consider the following example, this time in the form of a dialogue between two speakers, A and B:

> A: Why are you not willing to support the gun-control legislation? Don't you have any feelings at all for the thousands of lives that each year are blotted out by the indiscriminate use of handguns?
>
> B: I just don't understand why you people who get so worked up about lives being blotted out by hand guns don't have the same feelings about the unborn children whose lives are being indiscriminately blotted out? Is not the sanctity of human life involved in both issues? Why have you not supported us in our efforts at abortion legislation?

B does not misrepresent A's position; he simply avoids it by shifting attention to something else altogether. His response is something like:

> P = The lives of unborn children have been indiscriminately blotted out.
> P = You haven't supported our abortion legislation.
> P = The sanctity of human life is involved in both issues.
> HC = I won't support the gun-control legislation.

The conclusion has to be hidden because we can only assume that this is B's reaction. His shifting of topics really allows him to avoid addressing the issue of gun control, so our reconstruction is at best hypothetical.

A red herring arises whenever there is a shift of topic within an argument and the argument is not brought back to the real issue. This is an important point to note. The third premise identified above — 'The sanctity of human life is involved in both issues' — could signal a return to the issue and the start of an argument from analogy. Because such a return is never completed, we bring the charge of red herring. But it will be important later to resist the temptation to judge all arguments from analogy as red herrings. In an argument from analogy the arguer does turn aside to another topic or subject, but does so to suggest a comparison. That comparison then has a bearing on the conclusion where the argument is brought back to its original issue. With red herrings we have no return.

Watch closely for instances of contextual irrelevance. Check that the context is appropriately served by all arguments. Otherwise you may be misled by an argument's internal relevance to accept it as a strong argument when you should not do so.

INTERNAL AND CONTEXTUAL RELEVANCE

Internal Relevance

If a premise increases the likelihood of the conclusion it is intended to support, or if it decreases the likelihood of that conclusion, then the premise is relevant to the conclusion. If neither of these conditions holds, then the premise is not relevant.

> *Contextual Relevance*
>
> If an argument correctly addresses the context in which it arises, including the issue that it concerns and any prior argument to which it responds, then it is contextually relevant. If the argument misrepresents the issue or a prior argument and then attacks the misrepresentation, or if it deviates from the issue and doesn't return to address it, then the argument is contextually irrelevant and is guilty of being either a 'straw argument' or a 'red herring'.

EXERCISE 11B

1. Assess the relevance of the reasons offered for the following claims. For the purposes of this exercise, assume that each reason is acceptable.

   a)* **Claim:** It is wrong to inflict suffering on animals.
   Reasons:
   i)   It is wrong to inflict suffering on any creature that can experience pain.
   ii) All animals can experience pain.
   iii) Circuses exploit animals for human profit.
   iv) Some medical advances for humans can only be achieved at the price of inflicting pain on rats and rabbits.
   v)   Under Christian doctrine, we are to be the stewards of Nature.

   b) **Claim:** There should be stricter gun-control laws.
   Reasons:
   i)   Children already witness too much violence on television.
   ii) Few people would be killed by hand guns if those guns were more rigidly controlled.
   iii) The right to bear arms is written into the Constitution.
   iv) Police associations across North America support stricter gun laws.
   v)   Stricter gun-control laws would assist police in keeping law and order.

   c) **Claim:** Government-sponsored daycare is needed to promote equality of the sexes.
   Reasons:
   i)   Welfare costs will be reduced if single parents are free to take remunerative employment.
   ii) Sexual equality requires that women be free to pursue the same employment opportunities as men.
   iii) The lack of government-sponsored daycare is an impediment to equality of the sexes.
   iv) Daycares provide young children with an environment in which they can learn to interact and acquire essential social skills.
   v)   Economic pressures often force women to choose between Motherhood and a career.

d) **Claim:** Drunk drivers who are convicted of causing accidents in which others are injured should be compelled to compensate the victims or their families.
   Reasons:
   i)   This would force repeat offenders to take responsibility for their actions.
   ii) The costs arise as a result of the drunk driver's actions.
   iii) Courts often treat drunk drivers too leniently.
   iv) Costs incurred in accidents are the responsibility of the insurance companies.
   v)   It's unfair to expect the victims to bear the costs of someone's negligence.

e) **Claim:** Vikings of 1000 BCE visited North America centuries before Columbus did in 1492.
   Reasons:
   i)   The Vikings were exceptional sailors and their ships were built to withstand the travails of long voyages.
   ii) What is believed to be a Norwegian silver penny dating to the reign of Olaf Kyhre, minted between 1065 and 1080 BCE, was found at the Goddard site, a large Indian site in Penobscot Bay, Maine.
   iii) Native North American legends speak of contact with white men long before Columbus.
   iv) Vikings were known to be fearless warriors.
   v)   No replica of a Viking ship has been able to traverse the Atlantic ocean in modern times.

f) **Claim:** Fox hunting is a cruel sport that should be banned in Britain.
   Reasons:
   i)   Fox hunting involves setting a pack of trained dogs against a single small animal that cannot defend itself.
   ii) Fox hunting is destructive to the environment.
   iii) Repeated public opinion polls have shown that 7 out of 10 people in Britain believe that fox hunting is cruel.
   iv) Each year, fox hunting is responsible for the deaths of between 15,000 and 20,000 animals.
   v)   The fox is killed by the lead hound, trained to be first on the scene and snap the neck in less than a second.

g) **Claim:** Fox hunting in Britain provides important services and should be continued.
   Reasons:
   i)   Fox hunting is a sport with 250-year tradition, enjoyed by kings and queens.
   ii) Fox hunting has important economic value to rural Britain.
   iii) In the absence of any other natural predators, environmental checks and balances cannot limit the number of foxes preying on British farm animals.
   iv) Foxes are capable of vicious and wanton destruction of livestock.
   v)   The campaign against fox hunting is merely one of political correctness.

2.   Each of the following examples gives a response to the welfare reform programs proposed in 1999 by Rudolph Giuliani, then mayor of New York (Letters to *The New
York Times Magazine*, 10 Jan. 1999). Set out the argument in each case and then
provide an analysis of internal and contextual relevance. The first letter explains the
background for the other two.

   a)   Workfare participants are working for less than they would receive if they were
being paid the Federal minimum wage. There is something inherently coercive
and unfair in the idea of men and women picking up trash along the West Side
Highway, in their orange vests, 35 hours a week, and being 'paid' what amounts
to slave wages for their efforts. No wonder the unions are concerned; after all,
slaves are far cheaper than union employees.

   b)*   There are two reasons to reform welfare: saving money for Government or
decreasing poverty. New York City keeps very good data on the first and none on
the second. The mayor's goals are clear.

   c)   Bravo to Mayor Giuliani. The poor need work, and we all need a cleaner city.
This Mayor deserves our support when he meets both needs.

4. Sufficiency

In judging whether arguments are inductively—as opposed to deductively—valid, we
need to consider questions of *sufficiency* as well as relevance. Consider our earlier
example:

PREMISE: Six member countries of the UN support the US proposal.
CONCLUSION: Most members of the UN support the US proposal.

Here, we allowed that the premise was acceptable, judged it to be relevant to the
claim, but still felt that the argument fell short of being an instance of strong reasoning. The position of six of almost two hundred members of the United Nations does
not give you enough evidence to establish that most members in the UN are in favour
of the US proposal (even though it provides *some* evidence for the proposed conclusion). By failing to provide *enough* evidence to support the conclusion, the argument
fails to fulfill the criterion of sufficiency.

What a strong argument must do is create a presumption in favour of its conclusion such that its audience is more likely to adopt it than to reject it, and anyone who
does not adopt it has the onus shifted to her or him to provide a counter-argument.
But how much is enough evidence? Experience tells us that this will vary from argument to argument. There are no precise rules for determining when enough evidence
has been put forward. Nor can we think in terms of the number of premises, since a
single premise in one argument can carry as much evidence for its claim as three or
four premises in another argument. But some important considerations can assist you
in making judgments of sufficiency.

1. **Assess the sufficiency of evidence in relation to how strongly the conclusion
has been expressed.** Suppose a resident of an average-size city argues on the basis of

her experience that the postal service is inadequate, by which she means that delivery is slow and unreliable. There is no denying the details of her personal testimony, and we may sympathize with her, given our own frustrations with the postal service. Yet we can see that the evidence of her experience alone is not sufficient to convince a reasonable audience of a general claim about the postal service. In fact, it is difficult to see what non-trivial conclusion can be drawn from her experience.

But suppose the same person undertakes to canvass her neighbourhood and other neighbourhoods throughout the city and finds numerous households with similar complaints. If she can argue on the basis of a broader range of experience, her argument becomes stronger. But it is still not strong enough to support the claim that the postal service in general is inadequate. What she may have is sufficient evidence, if it is representative of all neighbourhoods, to show that the postal service *in her city* is inadequate. Not until she has managed to cull supporting evidence from regions and cities right across the country would she have sufficient evidence to support her claim about the postal service in general. But this, we recognize, would be very difficult for an individual to accomplish.

The point of this example is that what constitutes sufficiency of evidence must be decided relative to the claim the evidence is intended to support. The more general the claim, the more evidence is needed. For this reason you are advised to keep your claims as specific as possible. Without the support of something like a national poll behind you, you are likely to experience difficulty in marshalling sufficient evidence for general claims like this one.

Claims that are expressed with high degrees of certainty are particularly difficult to support without sufficient evidence. Consider the following example:

> Thor Heyerdahl crossed the Atlantic in a raft designed after carvings on an ancient Egyptian tomb. Heyerdahl landed at the island of Barbados. This proves that Barbados was the first landing place for humans in the Western world.

The two premises do not come close to *proving* the conclusion that 'Barbados was the first landing place for humans in the Western world.' But they do provide the right sort of relevant evidence to support a weaker claim such as 'This raises the possibility that . . .'

2. Do not draw a conclusion too hastily. We sometimes find ourselves 'jumping to conclusions' that we afterwards need to modify or withdraw once the excitement abates. Traditionally, arguments of this sort have been termed 'hasty conclusions' or 'hasty generalizations'. They involve conclusions drawn before enough evidence is in. This does not mean that we can't make tentative claims that we test in order to see if we can gather the evidence for them. Scientific progress often proceeds this way, with hypotheses being put forward and then subjected to rigorous testing. But we would be quite alarmed to learn that the latest drug on the market had been tested on only a few subjects before its manufacturers concluded that it 'worked'. In fact, government agencies would not allow this to happen. A similar check needs to be made on our own hypotheses. But still some judgment is required. How many tomatoes in the basket do we have to check before we decide they are a good value? We're generally required to check at least 50 per cent plus one for a reasonable conclusion. But beyond that, circumstances will determine how many we'll have to check before we'll be willing to conclude we have a good buy.

On the other hand, less evidence may be enough to draw negative conclusions. No matter how many times a hypothesis is verified, if there is one instance in which it fails, and the prediction had not allowed for any failures, then that one instance can be enough to reject the hypothesis. In a similar, but not identical, vein, one negative experience of touching a hot stove is enough to convince a child not to do so again. Of course, given the openness of our experience of the world, the next time the hot stove might not burn. But the negativity of the experience is enough to prevent further testing, and we would be reluctant to charge the child with drawing a hasty conclusion, because to do so would be to expect that he should have gathered further evidence.

3. Ensure that the arguer has provided a balanced case and discharged all her or his obligations. Better arguments—that is, arguments that are more likely to receive serious attention from others and to impress them with the arguer's reasonableness—are arguments that try to give a balanced picture of an issue. If you present only the evidence supporting your position and ignore evidence that detracts from it, your audience is likely to be suspicious about what you have left out. It does not help the postal critic's argument if she presents a lot of supporting evidence only to have her opponents present evidence indicating that most people are satisfied with the service.

Selectively presenting only one side of an issue is to engage in what is called 'special pleading'. Consider the following argument:

> The government should not be returned for another term in office. It has hurt the country by paying too much attention to foreign policy and neglecting domestic affairs.

Beyond the vagueness of the charges, the argument makes no attempt to recognize anything positive the government may have done. It is possible that the arguer believes that nothing positive has been done. But a more complete evaluation of the government's performance will have a wider appeal to a broader audience. By explicitly outlining and then addressing the views of those who believe that the government was right to emphasize foreign policy, someone who forwards this particular argument will substantially increase the likelihood that their audiences will find their argument convincing.

We should strive wherever possible to dress our arguments with a sense of objectivity and balance. If there is evidence that goes against your position, honesty demands that you introduce it and respond to it. If you cannot counter it, you probably should not be advancing that argument in the first place. In assessing the arguments of others, however, do not judge them too harshly for not anticipating all the objections to their claim. Rarely are all conditions for sufficiency satisfied, but a well-constructed argument should make a reasonable attempt to respond to key objections.

On the other hand, we do expect arguers to discharge their obligations, particularly those that arise from charges and promises made in the argument. If the arguer claims a position is inconsistent, then the onus is on them to substantiate the charge. The failure to do so is a violation of the sufficiency condition. Likewise, if the arguer promises to show that a position has no reasonable objections to it, then the subsequent argument should be judged on whether that promise is fulfilled.

A final obligation is to define key terms in an argument. If a definition required to establish a claim is omitted, then the evidence for that claim is insufficient.

EXERCISE 11C

1. Assess the sufficiency of different combinations of the premises offered for each of the following claims:

    a)* **Claim:** Boxing should not be outlawed.
        Reasons:
        i)   Boxing gives many young men the opportunity to escape lives of poverty.
        ii)   Boxing is no less dangerous than other contact sports.
        iii) The art of boxing reflects an age-old human love of physical challenge and excellence.
        iv)   While there are some serious injuries, these are relatively rare and proportionately fewer than in other popular sports.
        v)   No one is coerced into boxing or watching the sport.

    b) **Claim:** Critical Thinking courses are certainly the most important courses in the curriculum.
        Reasons:
        i)   Critical Thinking teaches the fundamentals of good reasoning.
        ii)   It helps people learn how to detect bad reasoning in the arguments they hear and read.
        iii) Critical Thinking principles underlie all the academic disciplines.
        iv)   Critical Thinking teaches skills that are useful in the everyday world.
        v)   A Critical Thinking course is part of a well-rounded education.

    c) **Claim:** The service in the local department store is always excellent.
        Reasons:
        i)   I was there yesterday and three assistants asked if they could help me.
        ii)   There's a sign over the main entrance that says 'We Aim to Please'.
        iii) The store is usually busy when I'm there, unlike its competitor.
        iv)   I've always been treated courteously by the sales staff.
        v)   My father has had the same good experience with the store.

    d) **Claim:** Lee Harvey Oswald probably did not act alone in assassinating President John F. Kennedy.

Reasons:

i)   He was alleged to have shot Kennedy from the sixth floor of the Texas School Book Depository where he worked, but shots were also fired from a grassy knoll to the side of the President's car.

ii) Several witnesses report seeing armed men running away from the vicinity of the shooting.

iii) Studies of the direction of the bullets that hit the President indicate they came from more than one direction.

iv) Investigations found that Oswald, who was known to have Cuban sympathies, was involved in the assassination.

v)   The 1976 US senate inquiry concluded that more than one gunman had been involved.

e) **Claim:** A Critical Thinking course is useful for most post-secondary students.

Reasons:

i)   These courses discuss the basic elements used in producing strong, convincing arguments.

ii) Students who have taken a Critical Thinking course generally perform well in other courses.

iii) Such courses force students to defend the decisions they make and the claims they advance.

iv) Such courses aid students in recognizing themselves as thinking creatures with specific beliefs.

v)   Critical Thinking fosters an environment in which students are required to consider the beliefs and perspectives of others.

5. APPLYING THE CRITERIA

In completing this chapter, we want to apply what we have learned about the basic criteria for argument assessment.

The failure of an argument to be relevant to its context is the most detrimental fault of all. Likewise, if there is a major flaw of internal irrelevance, the argument probably cannot be salvaged. But do not assume because one chain of reasoning in an extended argument is internally irrelevant to the main conclusion that the argument has no merits. If there are sufficient other relevant premises, it may be adequately supported, despite the fault in the argument (a fault that you will need to note or, if it is your argument, eliminate).

Likewise, do not take the insufficiency of support for a sub-claim to be reason enough to dismiss an entire argument, nor a few unacceptable premises that play only a minor role in your diagram as rendering the entire argument worthless. Remember that although irrelevance remains a major problem, further premises can often be added to an argument to rectify insufficiency, and premises can be further supported to remedy unacceptability. In the following example we apply the criteria to an extended argument:

¹(Many people dismiss out of hand the suggestion that certain children's stories should be banned because of things like violence and stereotyping).

But ²(there is at least one reason to consider censoring some children's stories).

³(In several common children's stories the stepmother is an evil person who mistreats her stepchildren and wishes them ill).

For example: ⁴(Her stepmother wishes Snow White dead and later tries to poison her).

⁵(Cinderella's stepmother treats her as a servant and mocks her in front of her stepsisters).

And ⁶(the stepmother of Hansel and Gretel has them abandoned in a deep forest).

Since ⁷(children hear these stories at an impressionable age),

⁸(such stories may be instrumental in creating for young children a negative image of stepmothers).

2 = (MC) There is at least one reason to consider censoring some children's stories.
3 = (C1) In several common children's stories the stepmother is an evil person who mistreats her stepchildren and wishes them ill.
4 = (P1) Her stepmother wishes Snow White dead and later tries to poison her.
5 = (P2) Cinderella's stepmother treats her as a servant and mocks her in front of her stepsisters.
6 = (P3) The stepmother of Hansel and Gretel has them abandoned in a deep forest.
7 = (P4) Children hear these stories at an impressionable age.
8 = (C2) Such children's stories may be instrumental in creating for young children a negative image of stepmothers.

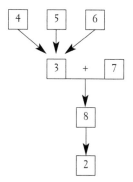

The first statement in this discourse is taken as background. It announces the context in which the argument arises, indicating its controversial nature, and stating the position with which the author disagrees. Statement 1 will be useful in assessing contextual relevance. The context proposed in this statement does not seem exaggerated. We do encounter such charges, particularly during times when children's reading material comes under close scrutiny. The argument as developed responds to this context and without diversion from it. The argument is contextually relevant. We will also assume that the argument arises in the context of a culture in which these stories are popular, judging the audience accordingly.

Given how detrimental to an argument the failure of contextual relevance can be, it is a good idea to start with this as we have done. But for the rest of the analysis, we will proceed in the order that the criteria have been discussed in the chapter, looking first at acceptability, then internal relevance, and then sufficiency.

We have three arguments here: the support proposed for statement 3 by statements 4, 5, and 6; the support proposed for statement 8 by statements 3 and 7; and the support proposed for statement 2, the MC, by statement 8. In judging acceptability, we work backwards through the diagram starting with statement 8.

The claim that certain children's stories may be instrumental in creating a negative image of stepmothers for young children (8) is weakened in a positive sense by the qualifying phrase 'may be'. The writer does not have to establish that the stories *do* have this affect, only that they *may*. While the claim is still not acceptable as it stands (if it were common knowledge, there would be little need to argue for it), it is supported, and we can look to see if that support is reasonable.

The claim that children hear these stories at an impressionable age is unsupported, so it must be evaluated on its own merits. While it may suffer from the vagueness of what constitutes an 'impressionable age', we are prepared to allow the premise on the grounds that people commonly understand young children to be impressionable and these stories are intended for quite young children. A reasonable audience should accept it. To assess statement 3 we need to again consider the evidence offered for it. Each of statements 4, 5, and 6 reports a central and commonly known element in a very popular children's story. Each is acceptable, given the common currency of these stories. And they are enough to establish statement 3 with its reference to 'several common' stories. Together, then, 3 and 7 are acceptable as support for 8 (and, we will soon see, relevant to it). So this argument fares very well on the acceptability condition.

To consider internal relevance we look at the arrows in the diagram. They indicate five decisions to be made about internal relevance. The structure of the diagram is important here. The irrelevance of statement 8 to the MC (2) would be far more detrimental to the argument than the irrelevance of one of the premises given in support of statement 3. As it happens, statement 8 is relevant to the MC. We are told there is at least one reason to consider censoring some children's stories. We expect statement 8 to provide such a reason, and it does. The creation of a negative image for young children is a reason to consider censorship.

Statement 3 and 7 are linked in support of 8. Why should we believe the stories may be instrumental in creating a negative image for young children? The premises give us the kind of information relevant to answering this question: each story portrays the stepmother as an evil character, and children hear this at an impressionable age.

So here, also, the premises are internally relevant to the conclusion they are given to support.

Finally, three arrows lead to statement 3. Statement 3 claims the image of the evil stepmother exists in 'several common' stories. The kind of evidence that would be relevant to establishing this claim would involve examples of such stories. That is exactly what each of statements 4, 5, and 6 provides. So each of them is internally relevant to statement 3. The argument passes the relevance condition for strong arguments.

To complete our assessment, we must decide whether the evidence is sufficient to establish the main claim and its sub-conclusions. It is important to note that both the MC and the sub-conclusion in statement 8 are expressed in a qualified way with no suggestion of certainty. The MC reads that 'there is *at least one* reason to *consider* censoring some children's stories.' It falls short of actually advocating censorship (for which this argument would not be sufficient), nor does it concern all children's stories. Hence, evidence concerning one reason to raise the possibility of censorship would be enough, and this the argument provides. The sub-conclusion in statement 8 states that the stories *may be* instrumental in creating a negative image of stepmothers in young children. Again, it does not suggest a definitive causal relationship between children's stories and negative attitudes toward stepmothers. Such a claim would be harder to defend. Thus, we judge that statements 3 and 7, together, are enough support for 8. To decide otherwise would require us to say what more would be needed, and there is little more that we could expect (beyond, perhaps, the testimony of children or stepmothers who have felt this influence). Whether the three instances cited in statements 4, 5, and 6 are sufficient support for statement 3 is a matter of judgment. But statement 3 refers only to 'several' stories, and the supporting premises provide three.

The argument passes all the conditions for good arguments and is, hence, a strong one. Note that the sufficiency of the evidence in this argument has been judged according to the expectations raised by the argument's own claims. This is a point to take to heart when performing your own assessments. Applying the general criteria to the 'stepmother' argument reveals it to be strong all round. We could charge that it lacks balance because no instances are provided of stories containing good stepmothers, but the many merits uncovered far outweigh this minor defect.

Major Exercise 11M

Assess each of the following passages in terms of the basic criteria of acceptability, relevance, and sufficiency. Be sure to defend your assessments and comment on the overall strength of the argument in each case.

a) [from *Famous* (Jan. 2003), p. 8] As a long-time reader I found the Chantal Kreviazuk article in the October 2002 issue of *Famous* in very bad taste. As a role model for readers of your magazine, her foul language and arrogant diva attitude reveal her to be a person without any class or humility. Pretty much any other . . . singer would exemplify qualities of grace, sensitivity, wit and intelligence and be worthy of an opinion in your magazine. Chantal is simply an embarrassment.

b)* Elementary school teachers should be better paid than university professors. The reasons for this are as follows. The complex material dealt with at university requires that students be well grounded in basic skills of reading and writing. And according to many educators, elementary school teachers teach students in their most formative years when basic skills are best taught. Therefore, the job of elementary school teachers is more important than that of university professors. Furthermore, people should be paid according to the importance of their jobs to society. And lastly, university professors are already over paid.

c)* [Phillip Flower, in *Understanding the Universe* (West Publishing Co., 1990)] Astronomy, however, is accessible to everyone. For only a modest investment, anyone can purchase or build a telescope and begin viewing the sky. . . . Magazines such as *Sky & Telescope* and *Astronomy* are written for amateurs and help them keep up with the latest research results. In addition, many books for the nonscientist have been written on a variety of astronomical subjects, from the origin of the solar system to the future of the universe.

d) [from the *New York Times* (1 Nov. 1992), p. B14] Audiences don't want to see male nudity because it's too private, less attractive than female nudity, and somewhat threatening, so directors avoid it (male nudity) at almost any cost.

e) [from a subscription renewal letter from the *London Review of Books*] The *London Review of Books* is becoming a 'must-read' among scholars, journalists and opinion leaders—not only in Britain but in North America, too. And until recently, you were among this select group, participating in the international exchange of ideas.

You were in an enviable position. Many people who would enjoy the *London Review of Books* do not yet know about it. You did. You took advantage of that.

I can't imagine that you would want to forego the pleasure of subscribing, especially since we have made the renewal rates so attractive. Surely, your not renewing must be an oversight. This is your last chance to correct it.

f) [Daniel D. Polsby, in 'The False Promise of Gun Control', *Atlantic Monthly* (Mar. 1994)] Everyone knows that possessing a handgun makes it easier to intimidate, wound or kill someone. But the implication of this point for social policy has not been so well understood. It is easy to count the bodies of those who have been killed or wounded by guns, but not easy to count the people who have avoided harm because they had access to weapons. Think about uniformed police officers, who carry handguns in plain view not in order to kill people but simply to daunt potential attackers. And it works. Criminals generally do not single out police officers for opportunistic attack. Though officers are expected to draw their guns from time to time, few even in big-city departments will actually fire a shot (except in target practice) in the course of a year. This observation points to an important truth: people who are armed make comparatively unattractive victims. A criminal might not know if one civilian is armed, but if it becomes known that a large number of civilians do carry weapons, criminals will become warier.

g) [In the following piece, from the *Times Literary Supplement* (13 Jan. 1995), the author extracts and assesses the argument attributed to Salman Rushdie. Most of the background is provided, although it may help to know that Imran Khan is a high-profile cricket player.] On July 30 last year, P.D. James . . . wrote a *Spectator* diary meditating upon physical handicaps of one kind and another. 'The depressing fact is that no government can totally compensate for biological disadvantage. And the greatest biological disadvantage is undoubtedly suffered by the ugly and the plain,' she argued, observing that nowadays politicians need perfect teeth. 'We writers are fortunate: beauty is neither required nor expected of us. . . .'

However, she did not leave it there. 'I suspect that few of us are free from the tyranny of the physical self,' she continued. 'I wonder whether Salman Rushdie would have written *The Satanic Verses* if he had been born as handsome as Imran Khan?'

[Rushdie] went ape, sending a letter of complaint to the paper. . . . 'For what I take her remark to mean is that I wrote a novel she considers poor—or, not to mince words, "ugly"—because I was myself lacking in beauty. Ergo, ugly writers write ugly books, and beautiful writers write beautiful ones. Thus, Naomi Campbell is the best novelist in Britain. And we must move swiftly to re-evaluate the novels of, oh let's say P.D. James, in light of her own jacket photographs.'

h) [from an ad in *Good Housekeeping* (Mar. 1992)] Trees aren't the only plants that are good for the atmosphere. Because nuclear plants don't burn anything to make electricity, nuclear plants don't pollute the air.

In fact, America's 111 operating nuclear electric plants displace other power sources and so reduce certain airborne pollutants in the US by more than 19,000 tons every day. Just as important, nuclear plants produce no greenhouse gases.

i)* [from a letter to the *Globe and Mail* (Jan. 1997)] I am interested to see the renewed attempt by the Vatican to defend the bastion of male power that the Roman Catholic Church has always been ('Vatican Says Jesus Didn't Want Women Priests', *Globe and Mail*, 25 Jan. 1997). It's not surprising to see a bishop argue that 'The church does not have the power to modify the practice, uninterrupted for 2,000 years, of calling only men' to the priesthood. The church also seems to lack the power to prevent those men from abusing their positions for their own ends. Stories of the abuse of the young in Maritime orphanages and in Residential schools for natives throughout the land are as sickening as they are numerous. They reveal an institution in which abuse has become endemic. The victims are seen by these men as pure pawns for their own gratification, and their word is rarely believed because of the abuser's 'standing' in the community. This abuse of power has got to stop.

j) [adapted from I.F. Stone, *The Trial of Socrates* (Little, Brown and Company, 1988), p.62] It seems paradoxical for Socrates to say that he was not a teacher. One can imagine three possible reasons for such a claim. They are political, philosophical, and personal. The political reason is tied to Socrates' rejection of democracy. He held that 'one who knows' should rule, but such rule would be undermined if knowledge and virtue were things that one could teach. The philosophical reason is the impossibility of attaining the absolute certainties that Socrates wanted to attain. The personal reason may be Critias and Alcibiades, two of Socrates' students who turned out badly and did Athens a great deal of harm.

k)* [from Norman Kretzmann's introduction to *William of Sherwood's Introduction to Logic* (University of Minnesota Press, 1968), pp. 3–4] Whether or not [William of Sherwood] was a student at the University of Paris, we have several reasons for believing that he was a master there. In the first place, he lived at a time when 'scholars were, indeed, to a degree which is hardly intelligible in modern times, citizens of the world' and when 'almost all the great schoolmen . . . taught at Paris at one period or other of their lives.' Secondly, in each of his two main works Sherwood uses an example with a Parisian setting: in one case the Seine, and in another the university. Finally, all the philosophers who show signs of having been influenced directly by Sherwood or his writings were in Paris at some time during a span of years when he certainly could have been lecturing there.

l) [from a letter to the *Toronto Sun* (17 Nov. 1983)] Canadian military men died in foreign fields because Canada declared war on other countries, not vice versa. The mere fact that we fought does not necessarily make our cause or causes virtuous.

Few Canadians really paused long enough to really investigate the reasons for our foreign adventures.

I had a long talk with a veteran of World War II. He was a hand-to-hand-combat instructor and a guard at Allied headquarters in Italy. I questioned him on the reason for Canada's involvement. He replied unhesitatingly that we fought because Britain told us to. That was the only reason.

It is quite clear that the only reason for world wars is that countries that have no business in the conflict get involved.

m) [Environment Canada, Ottawa, *State of the Environment Reporting Newsletter*, no 7 (Dec. 1991)] Canada is truly a forest nation. The forest sector provides important social, environmental and economic benefits to every Canadian. Forests not only supply wood and fibre, they also provide a habitat for many plants and animals and a retreat from the pressures of daily life. Canada's forests are a backdrop for a multi-million dollar tourism and recreation industry. They also play an important environmental role by recycling carbon, nitrogen and oxygen, influencing temperature and rainfall, protecting soils and supplying energy.

n) [from a generally distributed flyer titled 'Voting Rights or Children'] There is a gaping inconsistency in the logic of our democracy in denying children this fundamental democratic right. Many argue that children haven't the intelligence and experience to vote in a meaningful way. This argument was used years ago as a reason for denying non-male, nonwhite people the right to participate in elections. Nobody's intelligence or experience is of more value that someone else's. We all bring our own attributes to the ballot box when we select a candidate.

Others might say that children don't work and thus don't really contribute to society and therefore shouldn't vote. Well, school is work. And with a double digit unemployment rate and many people on social assistance, this rational is also absurd. Would we deny the unemployed the right to vote?

Some argue that parents or guardians will manipulate or force their children to vote for candidates they themselves endorse. We as adults are constantly bombarded with messages and attempted manipulations by all sorts of media and institutions. Just as we learn to sort out our own beliefs from those of others, so will our children. The issue of pressuring children to vote a particular way would be discussed and become a topic of public discourse. Thus children would come to know their rights and practice these rights in the privacy of the polling booth.

It is time we broaden and enrich our lives by realizing that children's views merit substantial validation.

o) [Samuel V. LaSelva, in 'Pluralism and Hate: Freedom, Censorship, and the Canadian Identity', *Interpreting Censorship in Canada*, ed. K. Petersen and A.C. Hutchinson (University of Toronto Press, 1999), p. 51] [Pluralism] is connected to harm in at least two ways. First, a society that is pluralistic will have a different conception of harm than one that is not. Thus, a society that endorses multiculturalism brings into existence categories of harm and offensiveness that are not universally recognized. Second, a pluralist society not only recognizes distinctive kinds of harm but is itself a source of them. 'One of the difficulties in making multiculturalism politically acceptable', writes Joseph Raz, 'stems from the enmity between members of different cultural groups.' Such enmity is not simply due to ignorance but is endemic to multiculturalism and other forms of value pluralism. By insisting that there is no single scale of value and that different forms of life are worthwhile, multiculturalism requires people to choose between rival values and commitments, and thereby to value what they choose and disapprove of those who choose differently.

12

EMPIRICAL

SCHEMES

OF ARGUMENT:

NOTHING BUT THE FACTS

In this chapter we introduce 'empirical' schemes of argument. They are used when arguers debate factual issues. In each case we outline the basic structure and conditions of the scheme, and sketch the conditions for a good 'counter-argument' that can be used to combat reasoning of this sort. Because the schemes we introduce are allied with scientific reasoning, we include a discussion of its methods of inquiry. The principal topics in this chapter are

- generalizations;
- polling;
- causal reasoning;
- arguments from ignorance; and
- the methods of science.

Chapter 11 discussed the general criteria for strong arguments. Every good argument must have premises that are relevant, acceptable, and sufficient to establish its conclusion. When we deal with a specific argument, we have to apply these criteria to the case at hand.

We can make the task of argument assessment easier by distinguishing different types of argument and specifying conditions of acceptability, relevance, and sufficiency for each type. In doing so, we specify conditions that must be satisfied to construct a strong argument of a particular type. Because these conditions vary from one type of argument to another, the next three chapters introduce three different sets of argument schemes that play a significant role in ordinary reasoning.

In introducing each new scheme, we will describe its structure and the conditions that must be satisfied to construct a strong argument. We will then discuss 'counter-arguments' that may be used to contest conclusions based on each scheme. Because they address the same kinds of issues, counter-arguments can be assessed by asking whether they successfully show that the arguments they respond to fail to meet the conditions necessary for good instances of the scheme in question.

Our first set of schemes applies to 'empirical' or 'factual' issues. This is not the place for a detailed discussion of the nature of such issues (or a lengthy account of the fact–value distinction), so it must suffice to say that empirical issues arise when we debate what happened or will happen in a particular circumstance, what causes certain things to happen, or how individuals or groups think or behave. Because the argument schemes that characterize these contexts are closely related to scientific reasoning, we have ended this chapter with a discussion of the scientific method.

Remember that we are not attempting to provide an exhaustive list of schemes that are used in all factual arguments. Given the complexities of ordinary reasoning, there will be times when you will need to construct or assess empirical arguments that do not match any of the schemes that we will introduce. In such contexts, remember that you already have a way to deal with arguments of this sort, for they can be assessed by using the general criteria for strong arguments introduced in Chapter 11 (i.e. acceptability, relevance, and sufficiency).

1. Generalizations

'Generalization' is the process of moving from specific observations about some individuals within a group to general claims about the members of the group. Occasionally we make generalizations on the basis of a single incident. One painful experience may convince a child not to place their tongue on a frozen lamppost, and one good experience may convince us that The Magic Carpet Cleaning Co. does a good job cleaning carpets. More frequently, generalizations are based on a series of observations or experiences. It is by recording a series of experiences or observations that researchers who conduct polls, surveys, and studies try to determine whether the majority of the population favours capital punishment, whether mandatory seatbelt legislation really reduces injuries in traffic accidents by 40 per cent, and so on.

Generalizations are, by definition, based on an incomplete survey of the evidence. In most cases this is because a complete survey is, for practical reasons, impossible. Consider the following example: Suppose you operate a small business that assembles cell phones, and you have ordered a thousand microchips for them from a firm in Japan. The firm has agreed to produce them to your exact specifications. Upon their arrival, you open one of the 10 boxes at random, pull out five of the 100 chips it contains, and examine each one carefully to ensure that it meets your requirements. You find that all five do. At random you open another box from the 10 and test five more chips, finding once again that they have been properly manufactured. You do the same with a third and a fourth box, with the same results. By this time you have carefully examined 20 of the 1,000 chips and are fully satisfied. Twenty out of 1,000 is a small ratio, but you conclude that 'The computer chips meet our specifications.'

As we shall see shortly, this is a good inference, even though the premises, consisting of limited observations, do not guarantee the truth of your conclusion about the entire order. You could guarantee the truth of the conclusion if you examined all 1,000 of the chips sent and found each and every one to meet your specifications. For practical reasons, we are not usually in a position to undertake such a complete review. Nor is it necessary, given that we have the basis for a reasonable generalization, even though it remains *possible* that a significant portion—indeed, most or even all the remaining chips—are not what you had ordered. You may, by accident, have happened to pick out the only good chips in the entire order. We must accept that this is possible, but the chance of this is very small, so we accept the reasoning and let the generalization stand.

Sometimes, the end result of such a generalization is a *universal* claim. A universal claim has the form 'All Xs are Y'. We discussed syllogistic arguments about such claims in Chapters 7 and 8. In the present example, the universal conclusion would read, 'All the microchips are good.'

Generalizations are also used to support *general* claims. A general claim has the form 'Xs are, in general, Y', or 'Xs are Y', or 'Each X is probably Y'. In the case at hand, you could express a general claim by concluding that 'The microchips meet our specifications.'

In constructing and assessing arguments, it is important to remember that general claims are not as strong as their universal counterparts. The statement 'The microchips meet our specifications' is not as strong a claim as 'All the microchips meet our specifications.' The general claim implies that the microchips are, on the whole, satisfactory. It leaves open the possibility that some chips may be defective. In contrast, the universal claim allows of no exceptions. It is proved mistaken if we can find one microchip that is defective.

General claims do not assert as much as universal claims, so they are easier to defend. When we say that 'Salmon is good to eat,' we mean that it is usually palatable, and our claim is not refuted if we are served a piece of salmon that does not measure up to our general expectations. In making generalizations you should draw general rather than universal conclusions unless you are confident that there are no exceptions to your generalization. In the microchip case, this suggests that you should favour a general conclusion over a universal conclusion, though your sampling of the boxes does provide some support for the universal claim.

In some cases, generalizations lead to neither universal nor general claims but to *proportional* claims. Suppose that you had found a defective microchip among the first five you examined. In that case, you would probably have pulled out a few more—say, four more chips—from the same box and inspected them. Suppose you found them to be satisfactory. From 1 of the 10 boxes you have found 1 out of 9 chips to be defective. Having found one defective chip, you may be more wary than you were. Suppose you open all 10 boxes and at random select a dozen chips from each.

You examine them all, and conclude that the proportion of defective chips is probably 3 out of every 120, or that 2.5 per cent of the chips fail to meet your specifications. More generally, you conclude that the vast majority of the chips meet your specifications, but that some proportion of them is defective. In both cases, you are making a 'proportional' claim.

Representative Samples

We have seen that generalizations can lead to universal, general, or proportional conclusions. In all three cases, the key to a good generalization is a 'representative' sampling of the members of the group in question. We call the sample that is examined in the course of a generalization a *representative sample* if it accurately represents the group as a whole.

Other considerations have to do with what is being sampled. In the case of microchips, which are manufactured using sophisticated technology capable of producing identical items on a production line, we can assume a high level of consistency and predictability. The situation changes if your business is selling fresh fruit rather than computers, and the product you received is not microchips but perishable goods like strawberries or bananas. In this case it is more difficult to assume the consistency of the product, for bananas are not 'produced' identically in the way that microchips are, nor do they retain their quality over an extended period of time. Given that fruit will be affected by many factors that can cause imperfections, there is a greater chance that its quality will vary, and good generalizations will have to depend on a more careful sampling.

In everyday life we are prone to make generalizations without a representative sample. Often this is because our generalizations rely on 'anecdotal evidence', which consists of informal reports of incidents ('anecdotes') that have not been subjected to careful scrutiny. Though anecdotes of this sort are rarely collected in a systematic way, and are sometimes biased and unreliable, they are often used as a basis of generalizations about the unemployed, welfare recipients, professors, women drivers, the very rich, 'deadbeat dads', particular ethnic groups, and so on. You should be very cautious of such generalizations, which are often based on a few specific instances that may have been embellished and slanted according to the prejudices of those who proffer them.

The 'hasty generalizations' that frequently characterize ordinary reasoning have convinced some people that it is wrong to generalize. But bad generalizations do not rule out the possibility of good generalizations, and we can, if we are careful, use our critical faculties and our common sense to decide whether a generalization is based on a representative sample. Two kinds of considerations must play a key role in this assessment.

Sample Size

The first thing you must consider in determining the suitability of a sample is its size. Samples that are too small are unreliable and more likely to be affected by pure chance. In the cell phone example, you examined 20 of 1,000 microchips and concluded that they meet your specifications. Assuming that you have confidence in the firm that manufactured the chips and the process by which they were produced, you have good reason to accept your conclusion, despite the small sample you examined. In contrast, a sample size of one or two or three chips chosen from one box is too susceptible to the luck of the draw. As more and more chips are examined, the chances that your results are mere coincidence diminish.

In the case where you made a proportional generalization, the discovery of a defective chip led you to enlarge your sample. Everyone knows that problems can occur on a production line. So, to get a more accurate picture of the condition of the microchips, you examined more of them. If you had settled for your first five chips, you would have concluded that 20 per cent of the order was defective. As it turns out, a larger sample suggests that there are only problems with 2.5 per cent.

Sample Bias

A sample must be sufficiently large to give us confidence that its characteristics are not due to chance. A representative sample must also avoid bias. Anecdotal evidence is problematic because it tends to be biased. Thus, individuals tend to accept and repeat anecdotes that conform to their own perspective in the process of eliminating counter cases.

In a sample used for generalizations, a bias is some way in which the individuals in the sample differ from other individuals in the larger group specified in the generalization. If the microchips in your order had been made in two distinct ways, 'A' and 'B', and your sample comprised only chips made by process A, then your sample would be biased. This is a serious bias, for each process is likely to have its own potential problems, and you cannot expect to detect problems caused by process B if no process-B chips are included in your sample. In this case, a representative sample must include chips from process A and process B (ideally in equal portions, if the same number of chips were made in each way).

A common source of bias in many generalizations is a natural tendency to generalize from the situations with which we are familiar, without asking whether these situations are representative. When social workers generalize on the basis of their experiences with single-parent families, they must keep in mind that they are working in a specific geographic area with particular social, ethnic, economic, and political characteristics. They must therefore ask themselves whether single mothers and fathers elsewhere share a similar situation. It is only when they have answered in the affirmative that they can use a sample assembled from their own experiences as a basis for a good generalization.

In other cases, bias may enter the process of generalization in subtle ways that are not immediately apparent. An example that illustrates this possibility can be taken from the well-known (ongoing) advertising war between Pepsi and Coke. In Pepsi surveys of customer preference, regular Coke drinkers were asked to choose between a glass of Coke, labelled 'Q', and a glass of Pepsi, labelled 'M'. Over half of those tested picked glass M, and Pepsi made a great deal of this statistic in its advertisements. We can diagram the implicit argument as follows:

where

P1 = Over half of the regular Coke drinkers preferred glass M over glass Q.
P2 = Glass M contained Pepsi, while glass Q contained Coke.
C = Over half of the regular Coke drinkers preferred the taste of Pepsi.

Although this appears, at first glance, to be a reasonable generalization, other researchers detected a bias when they tested the results. These researchers found that people asked to choose between any two glasses of cola marked 'M' and 'Q' generally preferred glass M. It appeared that people—however unconsciously—may have been choosing the letter, not the cola, or somehow making an association between letter and drink. Why people do so is an intriguing question. Is it because 'M' is a common letter associated with pleasant images or positive concepts (such as 'mother', 'magnificent', and 'marvellous'), and that 'Q' is less common and tends to be associated with less positive concepts (such as 'questionable', 'quandary', and 'quack')? For our purposes, it is enough to note that this discovery suggests that the preference is as much for a particular letter as for a particular taste, illustrating just how subtle biases can be.

Bias is particularly problematic when generalizations are made about groups of people. Problems easily arise because humans are not a homogeneous group, and different people are characterized by differences in religious commitment, political affiliation, ethnic background, income, gender, age, and so on. In Chapter 11 we saw that all of these are factors that may contribute to someone's belief system, which affects their opinions and attitudes about virtually anything we may wish to investigate. Consequently, any attempt to generalize about people and their behaviour must carefully avoid a sample that is imbalanced in any way, by taking account of relevant differences and variations in perspective.

Criteria for Good Generalizations

We can summarize our discussion of generalizations by defining good generalizations as strong arguments (i.e. with acceptable, relevant, and sufficient premises) that conform (implicitly or explicitly) to the following scheme:

PREMISE 1: Sample S is a representative sample of Xs.
PREMISE 2: Proportion 1 of Xs in S are Y.
CONCLUSION: Proportion 2 of Xs are Y.

In this scheme,

- *Xs* can be anything whatsoever—dogs, cats, worlds, dreams, cities, etc.
- *Y* is the property that Xs are said to have.
- *Sample S* is the group of Xs that has been considered—the particular microchips selected for examination, the bananas inspected in a shipment, the people questioned in a poll, etc.
- *Proportion 1* and *Proportion 2* refer to some proportion of the Xs—*all* Xs, *some* Xs, *most* Xs, Xs *in general*, etc., or some specified percentage, e.g. 2.5 per cent, 10 per cent, 70 per cent, and so on. Proportion 1 must equal, or be greater than, Proportion 2.

An explicit instance of this scheme would be the following:

P1 = The group of microchips examined (Sample S) is a representative sample of the chips sent (Xs).

P2 = All (Proportion 1) of the microchips examined (i.e. in Sample S) are made to specification (Y).

C = All (Proportion 2) of the microchips sent (Xs) are made to specification (Y).

In this case, Proportion 1 and Proportion 2 are the same proportion, which is normally the case, though it is possible that they will be different. In this example, we could have let Proportion 2 = 'Most', and made our conclusion the general (rather than the universal) claim that 'Most of the microchips sent are made to specifications.'

Our scheme for generalizations raises the question of how we can establish its first premise, i.e. that some sample S is a representative sample of Xs. This question will be explored further in the section on polling, but for now we will simply say that a representative sample is a sample that is (1) large enough not to be overly influenced by chance, and (2) free of bias. In considering whether a generalization is a strong generalization or not we will, therefore, need to spend much of our time considering arguments like the following:

The researchers considered a reasonable number of Xs.
The group of Xs considered is not biased.
Therefore, the sample considered is a representative sample.

In ordinary reasoning, you need to consider the kinds of things that are being sampled in order to decide whether a particular sample of them is reasonable and unbiased.

As you do exercises and consider other examples of ordinary reasoning, you will see that generalizations are often presented in implicit ways in ordinary argument. An arguer may not explicitly address the question whether a sample is biased or reasonably sized. Sometimes they will not even recognize that they have based their general, universal, or proportional claim on a process of generalization that needs to be evaluated. In such contexts, it is up to you to recognize the issues that the implicit generalization raises. In this way you can subject the argument to proper critical assessment.

Counter-Arguments against Generalizations

Given the criteria for good generalizations, we should see that a strong argument against a generalization must show that the conclusion a generalization tries to establish is not supported by strong reasoning. This can be done in one of two ways: (1) by showing that the sample of Xs in question is not characterized by the property alleged (Y); or (2) by showing that the sample of Xs is not representative. In the latter case, we need to argue that the sample is too small, or that it is biased in one way or another. In the process we must, of course, clearly explain why we believe the sample to be inadequate.

GENERALIZATIONS

Generalization is the process of moving from specific observations about some individuals within a group to general claims about members of the group. Generalizations can be the basis for universal, general, or proportional claims. A strong generalization shows

(1) that the individuals in the sample have some property Y, and
(2) that the sample is representative, i.e. that it is (i) of reasonable size, and (ii) free of bias.

A good counter-argument to generalization shows that one or more of these criteria is not met.

EXERCISE 12A

1. For each of the following topics, state whether you are in a position to make a reasonable generalization, and why. In each case, discuss the issues this raises and the problems you may encounter in forming a generalization. Giving examples of possible generalizations, discuss how you could improve the sample in order to yield a more reliable generalization and/or modify your generalization to fit your sample more accurately.
   a) students' work habits
   b) the policies of a particular political party
   c)* bus service where you live
   d) the exams of one of your instructors
   e) psychology courses
   f)* the attitudes of Americans
   g) the spending habits of tourists to California
   h) the colour of squirrels
   i) the price of automobiles
   j) the reliability of your make of car

2. Identify the generalizations contained in the following examples and assess their strength:

a) [from a letter to the *Toronto Star* (17 Nov. 1987)] Vit Wagner's review of the movie *Castaway* (Nov. 10) contains a paragraph that begins: 'From there, things just get worse. While Lucy frollicks (sic) around the island . . .' One thing that keeps getting worse is the standard of spelling in Canadian newspapers.

b)* A month-long poll conducted on people entering the Fitness First health club in Johnsonville found that people worked out on average twice, and sometimes three times a week. The study concluded that people in Johnsonville were very healthy.

c) Tony's first car was a Toyota. It was a very good car. His next car was also a Toyota, and he had very few problems with it. So when his friend Kate needed a car, he recommended a Toyota. Kate took Tony's advice and bought a Toyota, which she is still driving 7 years later. It has had only minor repairs in the course of tune-ups. Tony concludes that the Toyota is an excellent car, and decides never to drive any other car.

d) [from an ad for Madame Zorina Zoltan, 'Tarot-reader for the rich and famous', in *Weekly World News* (24 Mar. 1992)] Her record of accuracy for predicting the future is so incredible: She provided the solutions to unsolved Police Dept. crimes — Predicted to within one block, the whereabouts of kidnap victims.

e) [from the manifesto of the 'Unabomber', taken off the World Wide Web] It is said that we live in a free society because we have a certain number of constitutionally guaranteed rights. But these are not as important as they seem. The degree of personal freedom that exists in a society is determined more by the economic and technological structure of the society than by its laws or its form of government. Most of the Indian nations of New England were monarchies, and many of the cities of the Italian Renaissance were controlled by dictators. But in reading about these societies one gets the impression that they allowed far more personal freedom than our society does.

2. Polling

One context in which generalizations play an important role is polling. Media outlets regularly release the results of professionally conducted polls under headlines that make claims like 'Most Americans Believe the Economy Will Improve in the Next Year', or 'Over 90 per cent of People Support Increased Health Care Spending', or even 'Few People Trust the Results of Polls'. Beneath these headlines we read an array of details that supposedly justify them. They may tell us who was polled (how many), what was asked, how it was asked, who conducted the poll, and how reliable the results are deemed to be (the 'margin of error'). Given the prevalence of conclusions inferred from polls, it is important to learn how to judge them — in order to distinguish strong conclusions from the weak ones, to know what information to expect to be present, and to appreciate when a problem lies in the poll itself or in the way it is being reported.

In deciding whether a poll is a reasonable generalization, we need to begin by identifying three aspects of it:

(1) *the sample*: the group of people polled—who they are, and how many of them there are;

(2) *the population sampled*: the larger group to which the sample belongs and is deemed to be representative of; and

(3) *the property in question*: the opinion or characteristic studied in the poll, about which a conclusion has been drawn.

These three concepts can be illustrated with the following example.

Under the headline '41% of US doctors would aid executions' (*Globe and Mail*, 20 Nov. 2001) we read that 1,000 practising physicians were asked if they would carry out one or more of 10 acts related to lethal injection. In this example, the *sample* is 1,000 practising US physicians, the *population* is all practising US physicians, and the *property* is 'willingness to aid in executions'. As the headline indicates, the researchers conducting the poll concluded that 41 per cent of practising US physicians have the property 'would aid in executions'. They based this conclusion on the fact that 41 per cent of their sample said they would.

Implicitly or explicitly, polling arguments are instances of the general scheme for generalizations. Good arguments from polling are strong arguments that have the form:

PREMISE 1: Sample S is a representative sample of Xs.
PREMISE 2: Proportion 1 of Xs in S are Y.
CONCLUSION: Proportion 2 of Xs are Y.

where:

- **Xs** are the population—the group of people about whom the conclusion is drawn.
- **Y** is the property the people in the population are said to have.
- **Sample S** is the sample of people studied.
- **Proportion 1** and **Proportion 2** are the proportion of people in the sample and the population who are said to have property Y. Proportion 1 must equal, or be greater than, Proportion 2.

In most arguments from polling, Proportion 1 and Proportion 2 are identical. In many arguments, premise 1 (the claim that the sample polled is a representative sample) is a hidden premise.

Because polls may study more than one property in a sample, many arguments from polling will specify not only the proportion of the sample and the population that has the principal property investigated, but also the proportion that has other properties. In trying to determine the percentage of physicians who would act in executions, for example, a poll is likely to reach conclusions about the percentage opposed to such actions, the percentage who have no opinion, and so on. For this reason, the second premise in a polling argument often has the form 'Proportion 1 of Xs in S are Y; Proportion 2 of Xs in S are Z; Proportion 3 of Xs in S are W . . .' In such cases, the conclusion of the polling argument will be 'Proportion 1 of Xs are Y; Proportion 2 of Xs are Z; Proportion 3 of Xs are W . . .'

The structure of arguments from polling can be illustrated with the example we gave above. To find more information on the poll in question, we went to the newspaper's own source, the *Annals of Internal Medicine*. On the basis of the information contained there, we can put the argument of the pollsters into the standard scheme:

P1 = The 1,000 practising US physicians polled constitute a representative sample of practising American physicians.

P2 = Forty-one per cent of the physicians polled indicated that they would perform at least one action related to lethal injection disallowed by the American Medical Association; 25 per cent said they would perform five or more disallowed actions; only 3 per cent knew of any guidelines on the issue.

C = Forty-one per cent of practising US physicians would perform at least one action related to lethal injection disallowed by the American Medical Association; 25 per cent would perform five or more disallowed actions; only 3 per cent know of any guidelines on the issue.

In this case the sample is the physicians polled, the population is practising American physicians, and the properties investigated are the three properties mentioned in premise 2.

Sampling Errors

In determining whether a polling argument is a strong argument, we need to assess the acceptability of the premises. In most cases, there are two kinds of issues that arise in this regard, which correspond to each of our two premises.

The first issue that polls raise is tied to premise 1. It concerns the sample used. In deciding whether it is representative, we need to ask questions like, *Is the sample reliable? Is its size sufficient? How was it selected? Does it include all relevant subgroups? Is the margin of error it allows within reasonable bounds?* If these kinds of questions cannot be answered satisfactorily, we say that the poll contains a *sampling error*. In this case, the polling argument is a weak argument. It can be compared to other kinds of generalizations with samples that are biased or too small.

In many cases, the reports we read of polling results will not give us the answers to all our questions. In considering what has been omitted, remember that sample size is important. As we have seen in our discussion of generalizations, too small a sample will not permit reliable conclusions. How much is enough? For studies like the one on doctors' attitudes to the death penalty, pollsters aim for samples of around 1,000. That may seem small to you, given that the population in question involves a national membership. But as populations grow, the sample sizes required for reliable results increase by only small amounts. A number of 1,000 is adequate for the kinds of national polls you are likely to find reported in the media. Where populations are smaller (such as the number of people in your year at your institution), much smaller samples can be used.

Even when a sample is large enough, there may be problems with the group chosen as a sample. When you judge a sample to determine whether there is a sampling error, consider how it was selected. Did people self-select, say, by voluntarily answering a mail survey or by logging on to a website? If so, you need to judge what kind of people are likely to do so and whether conclusions based on such results actually reflect the populations identified. A certain portion of the public does not use the Internet. Another portion will not answer surveys. These portions of the public will not be represented in a self-selected Internet poll. In such a case, we need to ask whether this creates a bias—whether it means that the sample does not accurately represent the population it is drawn from.

One of the most famous unrepresentative samples in the history of polling is the one the *Literary Digest* used to predict the results of the 1936 US presidential election. It consisted of telephone interviews and written surveys of *Digest* subscribers. Some 10 million individuals registered their opinions, and the pollsters predicted that the election would result in 370 electoral college votes for Landon and 161 for Roosevelt. History showed the pollsters to be drastically mistaken as Roosevelt won hands down. How could this be? How could such a large sample fail to be representative? The answer is that the sample was biased. For in 1936, not everyone could afford a telephone or a magazine subscription; in fact, only individuals of a certain privileged socioeconomic background could. It turned out that the sample represented an economic class that was overwhelmingly predisposed to Landon's Republican party. The error cost the magazine its life.

The preferred means of sample selection is one that is random. A sample is 'random' if every member of the population has an equal chance of being selected. In the survey of American physicians, we are told that the participants were randomly selected. In this and other cases of random sampling, we need to determine whether relevant subgroups of the population have been included. Relevant subgroups can include men, women, and people of a particular age, education, geographical location, etc. As you can imagine, there are many possibilities. In any particular case, the possibilities that matter are those that are likely to affect the property in question. In the poll of US physicians, we would want to know how many of the 1,000 doctors who participated in the survey practise in states that carry out executions, and how many are from states that do not, because it is plausible to suppose that the possibility that one really will be asked to assist with an execution may influence a participant's response.

Because truly random samples are difficult to obtain, polls and surveys conducted by professional pollsters tend to use a method called 'stratified random sampling'. In stratified random sampling, a group of people polled is divided into categories relevant to the property in question, ensuring that a suitable number of individuals from each group is included in the sample. If 25 per cent of Americans have an income under $20,000, then a poll aiming to discover what percentage of Americans support their present government should attempt to have 25 per cent of its surveys answered by Americans with an income under $20,000. The sample should be selected in a way that ensures that all other significant subgroups are considered.

Most reports on polls include a margin of error that gives the confidence level this size of sample allows. While this is a complex matter, it is sufficient for our purposes to understand how to read margins of error. As scientific as polling has become, the results are still approximations that tell us what is *probably* the case. To underscore this point, statisticians report results that fall within a margin of error that is expressed as a percentage ('plus or minus 3 per cent', or '± 3%') that indicates the likelihood that the data they have collected are dependable. The lower the margin of error, the more accurately the views of those surveyed match those of the entire population. Every margin of error has a 'confidence interval', which is usually 95 per cent. This means that if you asked a question from a particular poll 100 times, your results would be the same (within the margin of error) 95 times.

Margin of error is particularly important when it leaves room for very different possibilities, for this raises questions about the significance of the results. For example, if a poll tells us that in the next election 50 per cent of people will vote for party 'A' while 45 per cent will vote for party 'B' (the rest undecided or refusing to tell), and that there is a margin of error of ± 3%, then we need to proceed with caution. For although it looks like party A is ahead, the margin of error tells us that party A's support could be as low as 47 per cent (−3) or as high as 53 per cent (+3); party B's support lies between a low of 42 per cent and a high of 48 per cent. Who is ahead in the polls? In this situation, the overlap makes it too close to call.

Measurement Errors

Assuming that a poll does not contain a sampling error, we still need to ask whether it has attained its results in a manner that is biased or in some other way problematic. Otherwise, the results reported in premise 2 in our polling scheme may be unreliable. Here, we need to ask, *How reliable is the information collected about the measured property? What kinds of questions were asked? How were the results of the immediate questions interpreted? Were the questions or answers affected by biases (of wording, timing, sponsors, etc.)?* If these kinds of questions cannot be answered satisfactorily, we say that the poll contains a *measurement error*. Here the problem may be that the results of the poll are biased because of the way in which the sample was studied.

We know from Chapter 4 that statements can be vague or ambiguous. If survey respondents have been asked questions that lend themselves to different interpretations or are vague ('How do you feel about X?') then we may question the reliability of the results. If a sample of university students is asked whether they 'use condoms regularly', it matters whether the respondents are left to decide what should count as 'regularly' or are given an indication of what the pollster means by the term.

It can also be important to ask how pollsters arrive at percentages from the types of questions asked. To learn that 70 per cent of health club members in a certain city are males seems unproblematic because we can imagine what kind of straightforward question was asked. People tend to know whether they are male or female, and it would be no problem for the pollsters to take the numbers of each and convert them into percentages. But when we are told that 70 per cent of adults are 'largely dissatisfied' with the government's response to crime, then the matter seems not so straight-forward. What questions have the pollsters asked to arrive at this percentage? People may not know their views in quite the same way as they know their sex, and so the clarity of the questions and any directions accompanying them become crucial.

There are other ways in which the questions, or the way they have been posed, may result in a measurement error. Psychologists tell us that people are more likely to answer truthfully when participating in face-to-face interviews. Interviews conducted over the phone are less reliable, as are the results of group interviews, where participants feel pressure to answer certain ways. In judging polls we need, therefore, to ask whether some factors may have influenced people to answer in ways that did not reflect their real behaviour or opinions.

In other cases, a poll may contain a measurement error in view of the time when it was conducted, who conducted it, or who commissioned it. We will usually be told when a poll was conducted. At this point, we should ask ourselves whether there were things occurring at that time that may have influenced the responses. A poll assessing people's views on politicians' trustworthiness conducted in the midst of a political scandal may elicit a different set of responses from those elicited by the same poll conducted at another time. In view of this, the poll may not reflect how people *generally* feel about the issue. Likewise, we may ask whether the group or agency that commissioned the poll released the results in a timely fashion, or held on to them until a time that suited them. If they have waited, the results may no longer be reliable, if intervening events are likely to have altered the views given.

Finally, when dealing with polls that are reported in the media, be charitable. To properly assess a poll you will need a significant amount of information on the way it was conducted. When this information is omitted, ask yourself whether the problem lies with the poll itself or with the media outlet reporting it. Sometimes it is the report that does not give the information we require to properly assess the poll. Our analysis of the reasoning should mention this, and refrain from making conclusions that the information we have will not justify. Also, be alert to how editors and reporters (and those quoted in reports) have themselves interpreted the results of polls in the headlines they choose and the statements they make. Sometimes such headlines and statements are not justified by the information provided, as an analysis of that material, according to the procedures we have explained, will tell you. Our opening headline— '41% of US doctors would aid executions'—is an eye-catching claim. But it also exploits the vagueness of the word 'aid'. The details provided tell us that only 19 per cent of the doctors included in the survey said they would actually give the injection. So the reporter's lead statement that 'More than 40 per cent of US physicians are willing to work as executioners' is misleading.

Counter-Arguments to Polls

Once we understand polls and the ways in which they can support good generalizations, we can also understand how to construct counter-arguments to contest the conclusions based on them. This requires that we show that the features of good arguments from polls are missing in the case at hand. In such cases the poll misreports the results of the polling, or suffers from a sampling or a measurement error. In this way, the criteria for good arguments from polls can help us construct and assess arguments against a poll result.

POLLING

A poll is a kind of generalization that surveys a sample of a larger population in order to establish what proportion of this population has one or more properties. A strong generalization based on a poll shows:

(1) that the individuals polled have the properties in question, to the extent claimed; and

(2) that the sample is representative, i.e. that it is (i) free of sampling errors, and (ii) free of measurement errors.

A good counter-argument to a generalization based on a poll shows that one or more of these criteria is not met.

EXERCISE 12B

1. For each of the polls reported here, identify the sample, population, and property, and set out the argument scheme. Then assess the reliability of the conclusion by means of the questions raised for dealing with polls. Where you identify problems, determine whether they lie with the poll itself or the way it has been reported.

a) [from an article with the headline 'Majority of Muslims view US unfavorably', <http://www.CNN.com> (27 Feb. 2002)] Residents of nine Muslim countries called the United States 'ruthless and arrogant' in a new poll, with most describing themselves as 'resentful' of the superpower. The Gallup poll found that by a 2 to 1 margin, residents in these nations express an unfavorable opinion of the United States, and a majority also indicated their displeasure with President Bush.

Most Muslims surveyed expressed the view that the September 11 terrorist attacks on the United States were not justified morally, but larger majorities labeled US military action in Afghanistan 'morally unjustifiable'. Sixty-one percent said they did not believe Arab groups carried out the September 11 terrorist attacks.

Researchers conducted face-to-face interviews with 9,924 residents of Pakistan, Iran, Indonesia, Turkey, Lebanon, Morocco, Kuwait, Jordan and Saudi Arabia to gauge public opinion in those countries following the September 11 attacks. About half of the world's Muslim population lives in those nine countries. Not every question was asked in every nation.

The overall view was not a positive one for the United States: 53 percent of the people questioned had unfavorable opinions of the United States, while 22 percent had favorable opinions. Most respondents said they thought the United States was aggressive and biased against Islamic values. Specifically, they cited a bias against Palestinians. They also view American values as deeply materialist and secular and American culture as a corrupting influence on their societies, the poll found.

Residents of Lebanon had the highest favorable opinion of the United States, at 41 percent, followed by NATO ally Turkey with 40 percent. The lowest numbers came from Pakistan, at 5 percent. Twenty-eight percent of Kuwaitis, 27 percent of Indonesians, 22 percent of Jordanians, 22 percent of Moroccans, 16 percent of Saudi Arabians and 14 percent of Iranians surveyed had a favorable view of the United States.

On Bush, 58 percent of those surveyed had unfavorable opinions, compared with 11 percent who had favorable views. Of those surveyed, 67 percent saw the September 11 attacks as morally unjustified, while 15 percent of the respondents said they were morally justified. But 77 percent said the US military action in Afghanistan was morally unjustified, compared with 9 percent who said it was morally justified.

The interviews were conducted between December and January. The respondents were randomly selected and did not know a US firm was sponsoring the poll. Gallup said the sampling error was plus or minus 1 percentage point for questions asked in all nine countries and plus or minus 4 percentage points for questions broken down by individual nations.

b)* [from a report in *Nature* (Dec. 1997)] Cheating remains widespread among students at US universities, according to a recent survey of 4,000 students at 31 institutions. The survey found that incidents of serious malpractice have increased significantly over the past three decades and, although highest among students on vocational courses such as business studies and engineering, they are also significant in the natural sciences.

The survey report by Donald McCabe, professor of management at Rutgers University in New Jersey, appears in the current issue of the journal *Science and Engineering Ethics* (4, 433–45; 1997). Based on the experience of the university departments, McCabe concludes that strict penalties are a more effective deterrent than exhortations to behave morally. Cheating is more common at universities without an 'honour code'—a binding code of conduct for students, with penalties for violation. More than half of science students at universities with no honour code admitted falsifying data in laboratory experiments.

More than two-thirds of all students polled said they had cheated in some way. Seventy-three per cent of science students from universities without an honour code admitted 'serious cheating'. The figure for those from universities with a code was 49 per cent. 'Serious cheating' includes copying from someone during an examination, and using crib notes.

c)   [from the article 'Most smokers so addicted they need fast hit', *Globe and Mail* (21 Jan. 1999)] Almost 60 per cent of Canadian smokers are so addicted that they light up within half an hour of wakening, a new study has found. But nearly half of the 5.8 million smokers who indulge their habit every day say they intend to quit smoking within the next six months. If the trends documented in the Statistics Canada survey hold true, however, many of them will be looking for an early morning fix next year.

The National Population Health Survey interviews members of more than 20,000 households every two years. The results from 1996–97, released yesterday, show that 10 per cent of the Canadians who said they were smokers in 1994–95 have quit, and 3 per cent have cut down. But 1.3 million have started or resumed smoking, so in total there has been only a slight decrease in the number of smokers, from 31 per cent to 29 per cent.

Among the other findings:
- Seventy per cent of those who started smoking after the first survey were between 15 and 25.
- Eight per cent of 12- to 14-year-olds say they smoke. Half of these are daily smokers.
- More than 6.7 million Canadians aged 15 and up smoke; 5.8 million of them do so on a daily basis.
- An estimated 29 per cent of teens aged 15 to 19 say they smoke.
- The average number of cigarettes smoked daily is 18.
- Men are more likely than women to smoke.
- Forty-four per cent of Canadians have never smoked.
- Low-income Canadians are more likely to smoke than rich ones.
- Smokers are more likely to be found in jobs such as forestry, fishing, construction and mining than in ones such as teaching, natural sciences and medicine.
- A strong majority of Canadians, including 70 per cent of smokers, believe second-hand smoke is a health concern.
- A third of all children are exposed to second-hand smoke at home.
- Most people think smokers should ask permission before lighting up.
- About 40 per cent of smokers say they sometimes experience unpleasant effects from second-hand smoke.
- The number of cigarettes smoked daily appears to increase with age.
- Smoking is most prevalent in Quebec, where 34 per cent smoke, followed by Nova Scotia and Prince Edward Island at 33 per cent each. British Columbia and Ontario have the lowest rate, at 26 per cent.

3. Causal Reasoning

Often, generalizations are used to establish cause-and-effect relationships. When Pepsi advertises that more than half of the regular Coke drinkers picked Pepsi in their taste test, it suggests that Pepsi's good taste causes them to do so. When a university tells you (or potential students) that graduates earn such-and-such an impressive average income, it is suggesting that a high income is, at least in part, a causal consequence of the stature of their institution and the quality of education it provides.

General Causal Reasoning

General causal arguments attempt to establish general or universal causal claims. We make general causal claims when we say that students from a particular school are better prepared for university, or that wearing seatbelts saves lives. Scientists use general causal reasoning to show that a certain chemical behaves in a specific way under certain conditions, that smoking causes lung cancer, or that car emissions and the burning of other fossil fuels are causing acid rain.

Two kinds of causal conditions play a role in general causal reasoning. A *constant condition* is a causal factor that must be present if an event is to occur. For example, the presence of oxygen is a constant condition for combustion: without oxygen, there cannot be combustion. This gives oxygen an important causal role in combustion, but we would not, under normal circumstances, say that oxygen causes combustion. The event or condition we designate as the cause is the *variable condition*, i.e. the condition that brings about the effect. Since dry foliage is a constant condition for a forest fire and oxygen is a constant condition for combustion, we would normally designate the carelessly tossed match—the variable condition—as the cause of a particular fire.

We call the set of constant and/or variable conditions that produce some event its *composite cause*. A comprehensive account of the composite cause of some event is difficult to produce, for most events are the result of a complex web of causal relationships and a number of constant and/or variable conditions. Often, our interest in a composite cause is determined by our interest in actively affecting the outcomes in some situation. If we can establish that the (variable) condition in the cause of forest fires is the embers from camp fires, we may be able to reduce this risk by educating campers. If we are concerned about spring flooding we must accept that we cannot control the variable conditions that produce such floods (i.e. spring rains and runoff), but we may build dams and reservoirs that allow us to control the constant conditions that make these floods possible (e.g. the height of a river).

In discussing causal arguments, we will begin with arguments for general causal claims, i.e. claims of the form 'X causes Y', where X is either a variable condition or a composite cause. A good general causal argument is a strong argument that establishes (implicitly or explicitly) three points in support of a general causal conclusion. We can summarize these points in the following scheme for general causal reasoning:

PREMISE 1: X is correlated with Y.
PREMISE 2: The correlation between X and Y is not due to chance.
PREMISE 3: The correlation between X and Y is not due to some mutual cause Z.
PREMISE 4: Y is not the cause of X.
CONCLUSION: X causes Y.

In many ways, the key to a good argument for the general claim 'X causes Y' is a demonstration that X and Y are regularly connected. This is captured in the first premise of our scheme, for in such a case we say that there is a *correlation* between X and Y. The claim that gum disease is caused by the build-up of plaque is ultimately based on the work of scientists who have established a correlation between the build-up of plaque and gum disease.

Every causal relationship implies the existence of a correlation between two events, X and Y, but the existence of a correlation does not in itself guarantee a causal relationship. The assumption that this is the case is the most common error made in causal reasoning. The problem is that an observed correlation may be attributable to other factors. Most notably, it may be the result of simple chance or of some third event, Z, which really causes Y or causes both X and Y, and is referred to as a 'second' cause. Our scheme guards against these two possibilities in its second and third premises.

Moreover, given an established correlation between X and Y, we must also have some reason to rule out a causal relationship whereby Y is actually the cause of X. Our fourth premise addresses this. In many instances, the context alone will suffice to support this premise: we can be confident, for example, that house fires do not cause careless smoking. In other cases the relationship may not be so clear and can lead to the problem of confusing cause and effect. Does stress during exams cause errors, or do errors cause stress? The fourth premise requires us to consider carefully whether the causal relationship may be the reverse of what is being concluded.

In many cases, a good argument for the claim that X causes Y will be built on sub-arguments that establish the four premises in our scheme. In arguing that there is a correlation between X and Y, the results of a study or even casual observations may be cited. In arguing that this correlation is not due to chance, a sub-argument may explain why it is plausible to see X and Y as causally connected. In arguing that there is no mutual second cause, a sub-argument may try to eliminate the likely possibilities. And in arguing that Y does not cause X, a sub-argument will aim to show that this is implausible or unlikely.

It is possible to understand the scheme for good general causal reasoning as a variant of the scheme for good generalizations. This is because the correlation that is the heart of an argument for a general causal claim is a sample of the instances of the cause. If we claim that 'Taking a vacation in February is one way to cure the winter blahs,' on the basis of our own experience and the experience of our friends, then we have made a general claim on the basis of a sample of vacations in February (i.e. those taken by ourselves and our friends). In our reasoning, we have used the correlation between these vacations and the curing of the winter blahs as a basis for a causal generalization. In any general causal argument, the correlation between the cause and the observed effect in the sample studied is used to justify the broader claim that the cause always, or in general, leads to the effect. 'X causes Y' is a general claim in which the property 'causes Y' is assigned to X. As in any generalization, we must be sure that the sample offered is representative, that it is not biased in any way and that its connection to the alleged effect is not due to coincidence. The second premise in our scheme discounts the first possibility; the third rules out bias as an explanation for the existence of Y in the correlation.

Given our account of general causal reasoning, good arguments *against* a general causal claim can be constructed by showing that the reasoning the claim depends on violates the conditions for good causal reasoning. In such cases, we will need to show

(1) that the claimed correlation does not exist;
(2) that the correlation is due to chance;
(3) that there is a second cause that accounts for the correlation between the alleged cause and effect; or
(4) that it is more likely that the causal relation is the other way around.

Most problematic causal arguments are undermined by the third possibility.

The problems that frequently arise in general causal reasoning are evident in the following article advocating school uniforms, adapted from an article that the *Globe and Mail* reprinted from the *New York Times* ('Making the case for school uniforms', 13 Sept. 1993). Bear in mind that when the author refers to 'dress codes', he appears to be thinking specifically of school uniforms.

> In many countries where students outperform their American counterparts academically, school dress codes are observed as part of creating the proper learning environment. Their students tend to be neater, less disruptive in class and more disciplined, mainly because their minds are focused more on learning and less on materialism.
>
> Many students [in American schools] seem to pay more attention to what's on their bodies than in their minds . . . The fiercest competition among students is often not over academic achievements, but over who dresses most expensively.
>
> It's time Americans realized that the benefits of safe and effective schools far outweigh any perceived curtailment of freedom of expression brought on by dress codes.

These extended remarks put forward the following causal argument:

P1 = In many countries where students outperform their American counterparts academically, school dress codes are observed as part of creating the proper learning environment.

P2 = Their students tend to be neater, less disruptive in class, and more disciplined, mainly because their minds are focused more on learning and less on materialism.

P3 = Many students [in American schools] seem to pay more attention to what's on their bodies than in their minds.

P4 = The fiercest competition among students [in American schools] is often not over academic achievements, but over who dresses most expensively.

HC1 = There are benefits to school dress codes.

C2 = It's time Americans realized that the benefits of safe and effective schools far outweigh any perceived curtailment of freedom of expression brought on by dress codes.

HMC = American schools should enact dress codes.

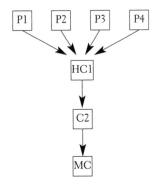

For our purposes, it is the argument for HC1 that matters, for it expresses a causal relationship between the wearing of school uniforms and superior scholarly behaviour and performance. In keeping with the scheme for general causal reasoning, we need to decide if it is a strong argument by asking whether it establishes a correlation between school dress codes and superior behaviour and performance, whether it shows that this correlation is not due to chance, whether it eliminates the possibility that a second cause might account for the correlation it suggests, and whether the proposed causal relationship might work the other way around.

Looked at from this point of view, there are many problems with this argument. It hinges on the acceptance of several related correlations: that students who wear school uniforms are focused more on learning and less on materialism; that students who wear uniforms are also neater and more disciplined; that students who do not wear uniforms are more preoccupied with appearance than with their academic achievements; and finally, that in countries where students outperform American students, their superior performance is related to the fact that those students wear school uniforms. These points imply a causal chain, arguing that wearing uniforms instills in students better discipline, which in turn produces better academic performance. A number of secondary correlations—between uniforms and good behaviour, between uniforms and focus on academic matters—point to the larger correlations between school dress codes and the proper learning environment, and between school dress codes and superior academic performance.

Does this argument establish these correlations? Not in any clear way. The premises that forward these correlations are, at best, questionable. The generalizations having to do with the behaviour and academic performance of some students seem largely anecdotal and would have to be supported by clearer evidence. In general, the arguer seems to take the correlations as obvious, not as things that must be established.

As a result, the argument does not clearly show that students who wear uniforms have superior performance, that students who don't wear uniforms have inferior performance, that students wearing uniforms have better discipline, etc. None of these correlations is sufficiently supported.

Perhaps the argument fares better on the second requirement for good causal reasoning, for it is plausible to suppose that wearing school uniforms might lead to less distraction, to more focus on things other than dress, and to more discipline (because students are more strictly controlled). But even if one ignores the lack of evidence for the correlations and accepts that they are not due to chance, the possibility of a second cause has not been adequately dealt with. The arguer is comparing American students to students in other countries, and this creates the possibility that many other causes might account for the alleged differences between these students.

If it is the case that some American students perform worse academically, we could point to other possible causes, such as poor social or economic conditions, or the possibility that American students are living in a culture that currently tends to undervalue academic achievement. We could argue that cultures where students wear school uniforms also tend to place an extremely high premium on the value and importance of education, with much more public and generalized promotion of educational standards and achievement—more so, perhaps, than in the United States. Conversely, it could be that such encouragement is in fact a form of intense pressure to excel academically, and the same culture that would mandate the wearing of uniforms could be instilling a great deal of pressure in students to succeed. In both cases, the wearing of uniforms would be a secondary, or related, feature of a larger cultural phenomenon. In other words, the wearing of uniforms and academic achievement could both be features or even effects of a larger cause: the cultural context. Finally, this is an example where the context quickly answers the fourth question: it is not plausible to imagine that types of academic performance cause students to dress certain ways. But validating only this fourth condition is not enough to salvage the argument.

In discussing this example, we have tried to construct a strong argument *against* questionable causal reasoning by demonstrating the way or ways in which it fails to meet the requirements for good causal reasoning. We could strengthen our argument further by developing the points we have already made—by citing instances that would tend to undermine the author's overall claim, such as the presence of high academic (and competitive) achievement among American students who were not required to wear uniforms.

A more convincing case of general causal reasoning has been developed by parents and educators who argue that violence on television, in the movies, and in popular video games is fostering violent behaviour in children. For in this case, the evidence cited includes scientific studies based on careful observation, and on documented incidents in which children engaged in violent behaviour that directly imitated violent action or events they had seen on television or in video games. That these children were acquainted with certain video games or watched certain television programs and were directly taking on the names and imitating the behaviour of well-known characters in an effort to reenact the characters' actions can establish the necessary correlation and discount the possibility of coincidence.

In this case, the possibility of a second cause can also be addressed. The most plausible way to argue for one would be to maintain that an aggressive tendency in certain children manifests itself in violent incidents that would occur even if they did not watch television or play video games. But that possibility is discounted by the fact that the parents' observations are, implicitly, a response to a rash of incidents that represent an increase in violent behaviour, a rash that coincides with both an increase in the number and popularity of violent scenes in movies and on television, and in many cases with the direct imitation of the violent actions of well-known television or video characters. In scientific studies, this possibility is discounted by the use of 'control groups'. These studies compare the behaviour of children exposed to violent movies, television, or video games with the behaviour of children who are not exposed to such influences. In view of these kinds of considerations, the parents' causal argument, while not necessarily conclusive, is initially plausible.

GENERAL CAUSAL REASONING

General causal reasoning attempts to establish general causal principles that govern causes and effects. A good general causal argument is an argument that establishes that X causes Y (where X is a variable condition or a composite cause) by showing

(1) that there is a correlation between X and Y;
(2) that this correlation is not the result of mere coincidence;
(3) that there is no second cause, Z, that is the cause of Y or of both X and Y; and
(4) that Y is not the cause of X.

Particular Causal Reasoning

In Chapter 1, we distinguished between arguments and explanations. We saw that many of the indicator words we use in constructing arguments are also used in explanations. One kind of explanation that plays a particularly important role in our day-to-day lives gives the cause of some event or situation. Consider the following statements:

- The fire was the result of smoking in bed.
- He died of a massive coronary.
- You brewed the coffee too long. That's why it's so bitter.
- The reason the car wouldn't start is that the battery was dead.
- Motivated by greed, the banker embezzled the money.

Though none of the above statements uses the word 'cause', they all express causal relationships. Note again that these statements are not arguments. They are explanations; they seek to explain an event by pointing to the cause.

The causal arguments we have discussed so far are arguments for general claims that express general causal principles. When we make particular causal claims, we usually invoke these general principles as a basis for the particular claims. In the most straightforward cases, such reasoning takes the form

X causes Y.
Therefore, this *y* was caused by this *x*.

where '*x*' and '*y*' are instances of the general categories of X and Y. If 'X causes Y' means 'Carelessly tended camp fires (can) cause forest fires,' then 'This *y* was caused by this *x*' means 'This particular forest fire was caused by this (particular) carelessly tended camp fire.' In more complex cases, we may not have obvious general causal principles that we can apply to a particular causal claim. If someone says that 'Sarah was depressed because she did not get an A on her exam,' they are not, thereby, committed to the simple principle that 'Failing to get an A on an exam causes depression.' In cases such as this, we need to investigate the situation further to determine a more complex set of causes and interaction (that may involve Sarah's attitude and upbringing, her rivalries with siblings, and so on) that precipitate the event or circumstance in question. In simple and complex cases, an argument for an explanation of a particular causal claim is dependent on general causal principles.

In view of this, the following scheme captures the essence of a good argument for a particular causal explanation:

PREMISE 1: X causes Y.
PREMISE 2: This is the best explanation of the *y* in question.
CONCLUSION: This *x* caused this *y*.

A strong argument for a particular causal argument establishes (implicitly or explicitly) these two premises and, in view of this, the conclusion.

In keeping with this scheme, a good argument *against* a particular causal explanation must show that it is inconsistent with general causal claims (that the general claim X causes Y is not defensible), or that there is a better causal explanation of the event or circumstance in question. In showing that the general causal claim that a particular causal explanation depends on is problematic we must typically appeal to the conditions for good general causal reasoning and show that there is no strong argument for establishing the general claim in question.

We have found a dubious example of particular causal reasoning in a 1984 newspaper story on speculation that then US President Ronald Reagan, who was first elected in 1980, would not survive his second term in office. The evidence offered for this conclusion was the fact that every US president elected since 1840 in a year ending in zero had died in office. The list began with William Henry Harrison and included Abraham Lincoln, James Garfield, Warren Harding, and Franklin Roosevelt, and ended with John Kennedy. (The proponents of the strange connection noted other striking similarities between Lincoln and Kennedy: Lincoln was elected in 1860, Kennedy in 1960; both Lincoln and Kennedy had vice-presidents named Johnson; Lincoln had a secretary named Kennedy, Kennedy had a secretary named Lincoln; Lincoln's assassin shot him in a theatre and ran to a warehouse, Kennedy's alleged assailant shot from a warehouse and ran to a theatre; and finally, the names of both assailants have the same number of letters.)

The attempt to draw a correlation between the death of a president and the year in which he was elected might be compared to much superstitious reasoning, which confuses coincidence with cause. In the present case, the reasoning is obviously mistaken (for President Reagan did not die in office), but it is still useful to note what is wrong with the reasoning, which might be summarized as follows:

where P1 is the general causal principle 'Presidents elected since 1840 in years ending with a zero die in office,' P2 is the claim that 'President Reagan was elected in a year ending in zero,' and C is the conclusion 'President Reagan will die in office.'

Such reasoning rests, like other arguments for particular causal claims, on general causal principles. In this case, we have represented the causal principle as P1. Given that it differs so radically from normal causes that determine one's time of death, the theory would require very convincing evidence to justify it. But there is little for us to go on. Its proponents list seven presidents who were elected in the years specified and who died in office. That they died while holding office appears to be attributable to little more than coincidence. In view of this, the reasoning for the general causal claim the argument depends on appears to violate the second condition for strong causal arguments (i.e. the condition that a correlation that establishes a causal connection cannot be attributable to coincidence).

The reliability of the proposed causal theory is weakened by several other significant factors: (1) the presidents died in different ways, apparently due to different causal conditions; (2) we know of no more sizable correlation that can add weight to the theory, such as a correlation showing that every head of state elected since 1840 in a year ending in zero died in office; and (3) the 'principle' is concocted specifically to exclude the two earlier presidents elected in years ending in zero (Thomas Jefferson and James Monroe), who did not die in office.

To convincingly show that election in a year ending in zero is a causal factor in a president's demise, one would have to appeal to general causal principles that suggest that there is more than chance at work. It is difficult to imagine what such principles would state and how they could be defended.

> ## PARTICULAR CAUSAL REASONING
>
> Particular causal reasoning attempts to establish the cause of some specific state of affairs. A good instance of particular causal reasoning shows that a certain event or state of affairs, *y*, is caused by *x*, by showing
>
> (1) that this is consistent with good principles; and
> (2) that this provides the most plausible explanation of the state of affairs in question.

EXERCISE 12C

1. For each of the following, identify the causal claim, then evaluate and discuss the reasoning.

   a) After his criminal record was disclosed, the local politician's standing dropped in the polls, and he lost the election to his opponent.

   b) [adapted from Vincent E. Barry, in *The Critical Edge* (Harcourt Brace Jovanovich, 1992)] News item: The jailed owner of a pit bulldog that fatally mauled a 2-1/2-year-old boy has blamed the child's parents for leaving the boy unattended. 'If the parents had kept tabs on this kid, this never would have happened,' said the owner. The child was savagely attacked when he walked past the two pit bulls, tied at the side of the owner's house, and across the front yard.

   c)* Whenever Bob plays poker, he wears his suspenders, because he has never lost at poker while wearing his suspenders.

   d) [Bjørn Lomborg, in *The Skeptical Environmentalist: Measuring the Real State of the World* (Cambridge University Press, 2001), p. 10] Recent research suggests that pesticides cause very little cancer. Moreover, scrapping pesticides would actually result in *more* cases of cancer because fruits and vegetables help to prevent cancer, and without pesticides fruits and vegetables would get more expensive, so that people would eat less of them.

   e) [from the *Globe and Mail* (13 May 1997)] The murder rate in Britain would be at least triple what it is now if it weren't for improvements in medicine and the growing skills of surgeons and paramedics, experts believe. 'The murder rate is artificially low now,' says Professor Bernard Knight, a leading pathologist. 'People say there were far more murders in the old days, but the woundings that happen now would have been murders then,' he told the *Independent* on Sunday. 'If you look at the rise in [the] murder rate, it is very small, but look at the wounding figures and the graph goes up 45 degrees. If that number of woundings had occurred years ago the murder rate would have been massive.'

   f) [from Reuters News Agency (19 Aug. 1996)] LONDON — A British coroner ruled on Monday that a 20-year-old vegetarian who died of the brain-wasting Creutzfeldt-Jakob Disease (CJD) caught it from eating beefburgers as a child.

The verdict, sure to arouse widespread controversy, is the first to legally link a human death to mad cow disease.

Coroner Geoffrey Burt told an inquest in Durham, northeast England, that Peter Hall had died of a new variant of CJD in February. 'I am satisfied that it is more likely than not that Peter contracted this disease prior to 1990 through eating some form of contaminated beef product, such as a beefburger,' Burt told the inquest. He recorded death by misadventure, rather than death by natural causes as would normally be the case with a disease.

In March British government scientists said they had identified a new type of CJD. They said it was likely people caught it from eating beef infected with bovine spongiform encephalopathy (BSE, or mad cow disease). A dozen cases of the new variant affecting people under 40 have been identified. CJD, which can occur naturally, normally affects the elderly because of its long incubation period.

Dr Robert Perry, a neuropathologist at Newcastle General Hospital, examined Hall's brain after his death and confirmed he had died of CJD. He told the inquest it was his personal view that eating infected beef was the 'most credible alternative'. The inquest heard that Hall had been a vegetarian since he was 16. But his father Derek said he had earlier been fond of beef, eating burgers frequently as an after-school snack.

After the new variant of CJD was identified, the government strengthened controls aimed at preventing infected beef from getting into the human food supply. Parts of the cow shown in tests to be infectious have been banned from use since 1990. But some scientists say enough infected beef would have made its way into the food supply before then to potentially infect hundreds of thousands of meat-eaters.

After the hearing, Hall's parents said they would press for a public inquiry, although it was too soon to decide whether to seek compensation. 'This has been a step in the right direction and is more ammunition to get things moving for a public inquiry,' Derek Hall said. 'We want the government to recognise that this has been a problem for a lot of years and should have been dealt with much earlier,' Frances Hall added. 'Our son died because of their mistakes.'

The health ministry and government scientists investigating possible links between BSE and CJD were quick to cast doubt on the verdict. 'No one can just say that,' said one government scientist. 'We won't get answers on the cause of this new strain for 18 months to two years. He's putting two and two together and making 100.'

A Health Department spokesman said a coroner's opinion would not affect government policy. 'The case is scientifically still not proven, but in the interests of public health the government is proceeding as if it were true,' he said. Most scientists say the BSE epidemic, which only affects Britain to a serious degree, was caused by feeding cattle with the remains of sheep infected with scrapie, their own version of the disease. Recent tests have also shown that infected cows can pass the deadly illness to their calves.

4. Appeals to Ignorance

The last empirical argument scheme we will consider in this chapter applies to cases in which we have no specific evidence to use in supporting or rejecting a particular claim. In such contexts, arguments 'from ignorance' (often referred to by their Latin name, as arguments *ad ignorantiam*) take our inability to establish a proposition as evidence for its improbability or, conversely, our inability to disprove it as evidence in favour of it. We construct an argument from ignorance when we argue that ghosts do not exist because no evidence has been given that proves that they do. Traditionally, such arguments have been regarded as fallacious, but there are instances where they constitute good reasoning.

Arguments from ignorance are prominent in legal proceedings, where an accused person is presumed innocent until proven guilty, and in scientific reasoning, where hypotheses may be rejected if no confirming evidence is found. The failure to find evidence of living dodos or of certain kinds of subatomic particles does contribute to the evidence against their (present) existence. More commonplace examples of arguments from ignorance are found in everyday reasoning, in remarks like: 'I've looked for my car keys everywhere and can't find them, so someone must have taken them.' In this case a failure to find evidence confirming that one's keys are where one must or might have put them is used as evidence for the conclusion that they are no longer there.

The criteria for good arguments from ignorance are implicit in these examples. In essence, an argument from ignorance is a good argument when it is the result of a responsible attempt to garner evidence that confirms or disconfirms the claim in question. Accordingly, we define the scheme for good arguments from ignorance as follows:

> PREMISE 1: We have found no evidence to disprove (or prove) proposition P.
> PREMISE 2: There has been a responsible attempt to garner evidence.
> CONCLUSION: Proposition P is improbable (or probable).

It is important to recognize that one can construct a strong argument from ignorance *only* after one has carefully looked for evidence to disprove or prove the proposition that appears in one's conclusion. It would not be convincing to argue that our car keys have been taken on the basis of our failure to see them unless we have made some effort to locate them. It is the responsible attempt to establish a claim that makes an appeal to ignorance plausible.

The first premise in an argument from ignorance is usually indisputable: if someone tells you they have found no evidence for a particular event or circumstance, this must probably be accepted. This means that when we are arguing against an argument from ignorance we will normally need to show that the argument we are criticizing is not founded on a thorough enough investigation of the issue in question. On this basis we can, for example, judge the argument from ignorance in the following letter criticizing comments on 'snuff films' made by the American lawyer Catherine MacKinnon in a speech on pornography (*Globe and Mail*, 24 Mar. 1987):

. . . I wonder if Ms MacKinnon has ever seen a snuff film, especially since no one else seems to have. In the absence of a genuine example, I continue to believe that snuff films are a fabrication of censorship crusaders, the purpose of which is obfuscation. . . .

This is an argument from ignorance because the author uses his *lack* of knowledge of a specific example of a snuff film as a basis for the conclusion that there are no examples. We can dismiss his argument as a weak example because it indicates no serious attempt to investigate the matter. If he had investigated it, he would not have had difficulty finding some examples.

Strong arguments from ignorance can teach us the importance of supporting our rejection of a claim with a responsible attempt to find evidence for it. The extent to which such a search may be carried may be seen in E. Wade Davis's research into the phenomenon of zombies, described and outlined in his book *The Serpent and the Rainbow* (Simon & Schuster, 1985). Before Davis undertook his research, there was little evidence for the existence of zombies other than stories found in Haitian culture. People who became zombies were said to have been killed and buried before reappearing with the characteristic zomboid personality. Because of their inherent strangeness, stories of zombies were given little credence. The implicit reasoning was an appeal to ignorance that can be summarized as the argument 'There is no substantial evidence for the existence of zombies, so they must not exist.'

This is a clear example of an appeal to ignorance. But it is an appeal that was not based on any significant search for evidence. Rather, it was founded on the prejudice that we should reject beliefs that challenge our normal point of view. The shortcomings of this prejudice are highlighted by the research Davis carried out, which included a lengthy investigation that concluded that there are zombies, and that people are transformed into zombies by being poisoned with a potent drug that slows the metabolism of the body to such an extent that the victim appears dead but subsequently exhibits zomboid affectations. Davis's research provides evidence for the existence of zombies that undermines the argument from ignorance that was uncritically assumed to be a good argument.

We cannot be expected to go as far as Davis did in quest of evidence for some claim that is unknown, but our decision not to do so should temper what we profess to know. A good critical thinker is willing to admit that they are not in a position to know much about certain issues. Above all, they will recognize that they should not yield to an all-too-human tendency to hold tenaciously to prejudices and assumptions.

APPEALS TO IGNORANCE

Appeals to ignorance attempt to prove or disprove some claim *x*, by appealing to the *lack* of evidence for or against it. A good appeal to ignorance claims that *x* is probable (or improbable) after the failure of a *responsible* attempt to find evidence for its improbability (or probability).

EXERCISE 12D

Describe specific circumstances in which you would or would not be in a position to construct a good argument from ignorance about each of the following topics.

   a)* ghosts
   b) the alleged racism of a provincial or state ombudsman
   c) the hypothesis that there is a tenth planet
   d) the question of whether someone is guilty of murder
   e) ESP
   f) the irradiation of food

5. THE METHODS OF SCIENCE

The argument schemes in this chapter bear in some way on reasoning about 'the facts'. Arguments of this sort are closely allied to scientific inquiry, which is designed to investigate and establish factual claims and theories. In view of this, some discussion of scientific reasoning is pertinent to a discussion of argument schemes.

There are two general types of scientific reasoning, or reasoning about scientific claims. First, there is the reasoning that scientists engage in as they go about their tasks of discovery and explanation. Second, there is the reasoning that scientists use to communicate their conclusions to others, be they other scientists, the members of the general public, or the members of a research-funding agency. Although we expect scientists to communicate their ideas differently to other scientists than to the general public, a scientist (or someone reporting on scientific findings) must in both cases communicate in a way that reflects the basic principles of scientific research.

The relationship between these two types of reasoning is something that concerns us because the hypotheses scientists formulate and confirm are later communicated to us as claims that we have to assess. In communicating their work, scientists draw from the reasoning they have used to develop their claims. It is important, therefore, to look at the reasoning involved in the discovery and confirmation of scientific hypotheses.

A full range of argument schemes can be combined in the inquiry that is called the 'scientific method', which has become one of the foremost ways to establish facts and theories about them. We should really speak of scientific *methods*. The term 'science' covers such a broad range of disciplines that many different methods are employed for various kinds of problems. Nonetheless, there is a general sequence of steps through which much scientific reasoning proceeds, and which we identify as the scientific method.

The Role of Hypotheses

At the centre of any scientific activity are hypotheses. These are proposed as solutions to a problem or as explanations for some strange or unexpected phenomenon. They are provisional in nature but appear to account for the data available, and they are such that some clear subsequent experience by observation or experiment will either verify or falsify them. Hypothesizing is integral to the scientific theorizing of both social and natural scientists and is evident in the work of researchers as diverse as astronomers, economists, and paleontologists.

Hypotheses are employed in the steps of the scientific method in the following way:

1. Understanding the problem. Scientists begin with a problem or question that presents itself during the examination of some data or phenomena. The problem may be generated by industry or by government, or it may arise in the speculative atmosphere of the laboratory. In all likelihood the scientists have specific data relating to the problem. In this initial phase of the scientific method, scientists rely largely on reasoning about probabilities. They draw on their experience of the world and their own resources to organize the relevant data and understand the problem.

2. Formulating a hypothesis. The next step involves the formulation of a hypothesis. There may be a number of competing hypotheses, each offering a solution to or explanation of the problem. Observation is important here, along with imagination and creativity. Scientists compare what they observe with past phenomena in the hope of detecting common characteristics or behaviour, which will in turn suggest appropriate hypotheses. At the same time, they stretch their imagination in order to conceive possible solutions or explanations that are novel but plausible. Scientists then select the most plausible of these hypotheses for testing.

3. Deducing the implications of the hypothesis. Having selected the most plausible hypothesis, the scientists' next step is to determine what observable consequences would have to follow if it were correct. Such inferences often take the form 'If h is the case, then x would have to occur under such and such conditions.' For example, in 1950 Immanuel Velikovsky, a researcher not recognized by most of the scientific community at the time, published a study in which he argued that Venus had passed close to Earth in human memory. He based this hypothesis on a wealth of data he had culled from the writings of diverse early civilizations and from the geological record. He concluded, among other things, that if his hypothesis was correct, Venus was a very young planet with a high surface temperature. At the time, scientists estimated that Venus had a surface temperature comparable to that of Earth.

4. Testing the hypothesis. Once the scientists have deduced what consequences should follow if the hypothesis is correct, they can devise and conduct tests to ascertain whether these consequences do indeed follow. The tests should be designed to confirm the hypothesis with observable consequences, or to establish that the consequences do not follow. Such observations are not always immediately possible, but if a hypothesis is not testable in practice, it should at least be testable in principle. Scientists have deduced various consequences of the nuclear winter they hypothesize would be the consequence of a large-scale nuclear war. These inferences can be tested in theory by using models and mathematical calculations; however, this is one hypothesis whose consequences, it is to be hoped, will never be observed directly.

The conclusion of Velikovsky's inference was not confirmed until 1961, when radar measurements found the surface temperature of Venus to be at least 600 degrees Fahrenheit, well above that of Earth. In light of subsequent findings, the surface temperature of Venus is now estimated to be nearly 900 degrees Fahrenheit.

Of course, the confirmation of the consequences is no guarantee that the hypothesis is correct. In fact, we know that an argument

If h, then x

x

Therefore, h

is an instance of 'affirming the consequent', which is not, in normal circumstances, a deductively valid argument. As a first step in the testing, however, the confirmation of x does not disconfirm h and is, to that extent, important. This at least tells us that the hypothesis has not yet been disconfirmed or falsified. Ideally, scientists want to present a strong case for a hypothesis by establishing the biconditional '(if h then x) and (if x then h)'.

Velikovsky reasoned conditionally that if Venus had had a close encounter with Earth in recent historical times (e), then its surface temperature would be very high (t), i.e. 'if e, then t'. The consequent, 't', has since been confirmed. If the researchers who have succeeded Velikovsky in his work want to provide a strong case for his hypothesis, they need to establish that the only feasible explanation for the high temperature on Venus is that it had a close encounter with Earth in recent historical times, i.e. '(if e then t) and (if t then e)'. Then the hypothesis would be confirmed. It is difficult, however, to conceive how 'if t then e' could be confirmed this long after the supposed event, and researchers may find it more productive to focus on other consequences of the hypothesis in their efforts to confirm it.

Conversely, the failure of the expected consequence to occur is considered to disconfirm a hypothesis, provided, of course, that the initial conditional is correct. In this case, we would have a deductively valid argument:

If h then x.

$\sim x$.

Therefore, $\sim h$.

Had Venus been discovered to have a surface temperature similar to that of Earth, Velikovsky's hypothesis would have been shown incorrect.

5. Evaluating the hypothesis. Finally, the scientists evaluate their observational and experimental findings and decide to reject the hypothesis, to revise it in some way that the evidence suggests is appropriate, or to consider it confirmed and adopt it as the best current solution to the problem or explanation of the phenomenon.

We can get a better sense of the role of hypotheses in the scientific method if we consider an actual scientific inquiry. In his book *Hunger Fighters* (Harcourt, Brace and Co., 1928), Paul de Kruif recounts the discovery of the cause of pellagra by Dr Joseph

Goldberger. Pellagra, a disease characterized by gastric disturbances, skin eruptions, and nervous derangement, had reached epidemic proportions in the southern United States in the early twentieth century. Its occurrence was endemic, affecting one community while leaving its neighbour untouched. The US Health Service sent Dr Goldberger to Mississippi to discover its cause. We can trace Goldberger's progress through the method of inquiry that has been elaborated:

(1) On his arrival, Dr Goldberger had a problem and specific data with which to work. He had to find the cause of pellagra, the evidence of which was all around him.

(2) From his observations of the disease and the facts at his disposal he devised a hypothesis regarding the cause of the problem. The community orientation of the disease suggested that it may be transmitted by contact, and this led him to hypothesize that the disease was caused by microbes transmitted in this way.

(3) He then deduced the consequences of his hypothesis, reasoning that if pellagra was caused by microbes, persons in close contact with the victims should contract the disease.

(4) Testing this hypothesis, Goldberger noted that in one hospital orderlies, nurses, and doctors who were in close contact with victims did not contract the disease. (Another way of presenting this result is to say that he could not find a correlation between those who had contact and those who contracted the disease.)

(5) Since this test disconfirmed the hypothesis, Goldberger had to discard it. Microbes could not have caused pellagra.

With this discovery, Dr Goldberger had to go back to step 2, make further observations, and formulate another hypothesis. We will denote the second sequences of steps in the inquiry with the prefix 'II':

(II-2) Goldberger noted that the disease was limited to the poor, and that the victims' diet included virtually no milk or fresh meat. At one orphanage he found that only children between the ages of 6 and 12 had the disease. In following up on this, he learned that the children under 6 were given milk and those over 12 were fed meat, but those between the two ages, who were too young to work and too old, supposedly, to require milk, received neither meat nor milk. Thus, Goldberger arrived at the hypothesis that a dietary deficiency in milk and fresh meat was the cause of pellagra.

(II-3) He then deduced that if his hypothesis were correct, remedying these deficiencies would cure the disease.

(II-4) He tested this at the orphanage by providing milk and fresh meat for the children between the ages of 6 and 12.

(II-5) This time his hypothesis was confirmed: all the cases of pellagra at the orphanage disappeared and no further ones developed.

We should note here that, in arriving at his conclusion, Goldberger used good causal reasoning that conforms to the conditions set down in this chapter: he showed a correlation between pellagra and a certain dietary deficiency; he confirmed through testing that this was not coincidence; and he excluded any other second cause.

This outline of the scientific method gives only the bare bones; more varied reasoning is often introduced at different stages. For example, scientists often use models or analogies to draw conclusions about something unknown based on something similar that is better known or understood. Early attempts to describe the structure of atoms included an analogy with the solar system, since it was reasoned that an atom resembled a very small solar system. Like the solar system with its sun, an atom has its positive charge at the centre, and just as the planets move in orbits around the sun, so electrons carry a negative charge around the atom's centre. Such analogies have great illustrative value. Although the context in this example is not clearly argumentative, in other instances it is. Scientists examining the meteorite ALH84001, collected in Antarctica and recognized as originating on Mars, argued for the existence of past life on Mars based on similarities with terrestrial life. Though our emphasis in the next chapter is on moral reasoning, we will spend a portion of it exploring some analogy-based argument schemes that are often used in scientific reasoning.

The scientific method as we have discussed it emphasizes what is observable or can be experienced at least in principle. Some branches of science do not appear to be able to provide immediate observations or experiments that support their conclusions. Historical science is a case in point. Nevertheless, the nineteenth-century philosopher William Whewell argued that historical science can reach conclusions that are just as strong as those that rely on direct observation. His method, termed the 'consilience of inductions', bases conclusions about widely different phenomena on the agreement of general conclusions that can be traced to a common cause. This procedure requires imaginative minds that can sift through diverse data and recognize hints that suggest a common cause. The late Stephen Jay Gould gave an example of this kind of scientific reasoning in *Discover* magazine (Jan. 1987, p.70):

> Since we can't see the past directly or manipulate its events, we must use the different tactic of meeting history's richness head on. . . . Thus plate tectonics can explain magnetic strips on the sea floor, the rise and later erosion of the Appalachians, the earthquakes of Lisbon and San Francisco . . . the presence of large flightless birds only on continents once united as Gondwanaland, and the discovery of fossil coal in Antarctica.

No matter how scientific reasoning varies in its procedures, some hypothesis-forming is always present, whether it be the hypothesis that the solar system is a suitable model for explaining the structure of the atom or that plate tectonics can account for the diverse phenomena identified by Gould. Hypothesizing lies at the heart of scientific reasoning.

Evaluating Scientific Claims

We said earlier that the scientific claims we encounter are reformulations of the reasoning used by researchers who developed those claims. When asked for evidence, they point to tests and studies that demonstrate the plausibility of their claims. If we bear in mind the conditions for good argument schemes like generalizations, causal arguments, and the appeal to ignorance (as well as schemes we will meet in later chapters), we should be able to evaluate the scientific claims that we encounter in the media and elsewhere. We will finish our discussion of the scientific method by noting some general questions you should ask of such claims.

1. Does the scientific claim fit the facts, in the sense that it adequately addresses the problem or data in question? It likely does if the claimants have reached the point of presenting their case to the public, but any claim should still be checked. In doing so, ask whether there is a clear statement of the problem that has allegedly been solved or of the phenomenon that has been explained, and whether the claim made is relevant in this context.

2. Is the claim testable, either directly or in principle? A claim is testable when clear observations or experiments or statistical studies that can confirm or disconfirm the claim in question exist or are conceivable. Assuming that the claim is testable, we will want to be assured that the claim has in fact been confirmed by the tests. Ideally, we will be provided with evidence that this is so. If the claim involves a cancer cure, for example, we want to know how many patients using the drug have gone into remission, for how long, and how these figures compare with the results of patients using other treatments. Of course, some claims given as predictions are not immediately confirmable. Still, insofar as it is possible, the evidence that convinced the researchers to accept the claim should be explained.

3. Is there evidence of agreement among different scientists? If a scientific claim has been received with enthusiasm from a larger scientific community, then this is another reason for accepting it. If it has been received with skepticism by other knowledgeable scientists, then we should be cautious in our evaluation of it. In such contexts, it is important to take note of any counter-claims. If any exist, we must ask whether they have been thrown up as a quick response to the initial claim, or are the result of serious scientific investigation.

Scientific hypotheses express general patterns in the world of nature and in the behaviour of human beings. The descriptive claims we encounter are confirmed hypotheses, nothing more, and we should remember this. If appropriate procedures have been followed, then the hypotheses have been tested and have satisfied the researchers involved. But they are not incontestable and their explanatory power remains subject to revision.

The present overview is intended to give you some sense of what is involved in scientific reasoning. We cannot do full justice to such a complex subject. We hope that our modest discussion will, however, help you understand an important type of reasoning we encounter daily.

THE SCIENTIFIC METHOD

As a general procedure, the scientific method involves five steps for proposing and testing a hypothesis:

(1) *Understanding the problem* that requires a solution or explanation;
(2) *Formulating a hypothesis* to address the problem;
(3) *Deducing consequences* to follow if the hypothesis is correct;
(4) *Testing the hypothesis* for those consequences; and
(5) *Evaluating the hypothesis* with respect to its suitability after testing.

Exercise 12E

1. In Chapter 9 we discussed the phlogiston theory of combustion and the way it was tested and ultimately refuted (see pp. 215–16). Explain how this happened in terms of the steps of scientific reasoning developed in our discussion of the scientific method of testing hypotheses.

2. Find an account of scientific research in a recent magazine (go to a scientific magazine or journal if you need to) or on a science website on the Internet. Explain the research in the terms of the account of the scientific method introduced in this chapter.

3. Analyze the following account of the scientific process of discovery in terms of the five steps of the scientific method:

[Alfred Wallace, in *My Life: A Record of Events and Opinions*, Vol.1 (New York, 1905), pp. 360–2] It was while waiting at Ternate in order to get ready for my next journey, and to decide where I should go, that the idea already referred to occurred to me. It has been shown how, for the preceding eight or nine years, the great problem of the origin of the species had been continually pondered over. . . .

But the exact process of the change [of one species into another] and the cause that led to it were absolutely unknown and appeared almost inconceivable. The great difficulty was to understand how, if one species was gradually changed into another, there continued to be so many quite distinct species, so many that differed from their nearest allies by slight yet perfectly definite and constant characters. . . . The problem then was, not only how and why do species change, but how and why do they change into new and well-defined species, distinguished from each other in so many ways. . . .

One day something brought to my attention Malthus's 'Principles of Population', which I had read twelve years before. I thought of his clear exposition of 'the positive checks to increase'—disease, accidents, war, and famine—which keep down the population of . . . people. It then occurred to me that these causes or their equivalents are continually acting in the case of animals also; and as animals usually breed much more rapidly than does mankind, the destruction every year from these causes must be enormous in order to keep down the number of each species. . . .

Why do some die and some live? And the answer was clearly, that on the whole the best fitted lived. From the effects of disease the most healthy escaped; from enemies, the strongest, the swiftest, or the most cunning; from famine, the best hunters or those with the best digestion; and so on. Then it suddenly flashed upon me that this self-acting process would necessarily *improve the race*, because in every generation the inferior would inevitably be killed off and the superior would remain—that is, *the fittest would survive.*

MAJOR EXERCISE 12M

1. This assignment is intended to test your understanding of argument schemes by using some of them in conjunction with specific normative issues.
   a) Construct short arguments employing the following schemes (one for each argument) in support of the claim 'Public ownership of assault rifles should be prohibited':
      i) generalization
      ii) particular causal argument
      iii) appeal to ignorance.
   b) Employ the same schemes in support of the opposite claim 'Public ownership of assault rifles should be allowed'.
   c) Using any of the argument schemes of this chapter, construct a short argument on one of the following issues:
      i) industrial safety
      ii) nuclear testing
      iii) pollution.

2. Decide whether each of the following passages contains an argument. If it does, assess the reasoning. For any specific argument schemes dealt with in this chapter, explain whether the argument fulfills the conditions for good arguments of that scheme. Note that examples may involve more than one argument scheme, and may also include applications of the scientific method.
   a)* [from 'The corrosion of the death penalty', <http://www.globeandmail.com> (21 May 2002)] This month, the Governor of Maryland temporarily banned the death penalty in his state, over concerns that gross racial disparities exist in the way it is used. Illinois has had a moratorium on the death penalty for two years, after its governor said the risk of executing the innocent was unconscionably high.

These states are opening their eyes to the obvious. Race matters in who is put to death. Between 1977 and 1995, 88 black men were executed for killing whites; just two white men were executed for killing blacks. Two years ago, a federal Justice Department study found that white defendants were almost twice as likely as black ones to be given a plea agreement by federal prosecutors that let them avoid the death penalty. Of the 13 on death row in Maryland, nine are black. Only one of the 13 was convicted of killing a non-white.

b)   [from a letter to the *Globe and Mail* (15 Mar. 1997)] So the Liberals have not come close to making the point that restrictions on tobacco advertising will lead to a reduction in the incidence of smoking among young people (Speaking Freely About Smoking—editorial, March 5). The following Statscan figures are provided with your March 8 front-page article: One in five deaths in Canada are attributed to smoking; in Quebec, the number is one in four. The average age of becoming a 'regular smoker' in Canada is 15; in Quebec, it is 14. Fifty per cent of all sponsorship dollars provided by tobacco companies are spent in Quebec. Coincidence?

c)   [from a letter to *Omni* magazine (Sept. 1983)] I am surprised that a magazine of the scientific stature of *Omni* continues to perpetuate a myth. Bulls do not charge at a red cape because it is red. Bulls, like all bovines, are colour-blind. They see only in shades of black, white, and gray. The reason a bull charges at a red cape is because of the movement of the cape. By the time a matador faces a bull, the animal has been teased into a state of rage by the picadors. They run at it, shout, wave their arms, and prick it with sword points. Any old Kansas farm girl, like me, can attest to the fact that when a bull is enraged it will charge at anything that moves.

d)*   [from the *Windsor Star* (24 Oct. 1995)] Seven out of 10 women wear the wrong size bra, according to surveys by Playtex, a bra manufacturer . . . this statistic was based on women who came to Playtex bra-fitting clinics.

e)   David M. Unwin concludes in *Nature* (May 1987) that the winged reptiles, pterosaurs, spent most of their lives hanging upside down from cliffs and trees because, while they may have been agile in the air, they could do no more than waddle clumsily on the ground.

This conclusion was drawn in part from recent discoveries in Germany and Australia of two relatively uncrushed pterosaur pelvises. In these pelvises, the acetabulum, a socket into which the tip of the femur bone fits, is oriented outward and upward, and this suggests that the pterosaurs' legs were splayed out, giving them a clumsy gait. Had the acetabulum pointed out and down instead, the pelvises would have supported another theory, held since the 1970s, that pterosaurs stood erect with their hind limbs beneath their bodies and were agile on the ground.

f)*   [from the *Globe and Mail* (6 Mar. 1987), from London (Reuters)] Farmer John Coombs claims his cow Primrose is curing his baldness—by licking his head.

Mr Coombs, 56, who farms near Salisbury, in southwestern England, says he made the discovery after Primrose licked some cattle food dust off his pate as he was bending down.

A few weeks later hair was growing in an area that had been bald for years.

The farmer has the whole herd working on the problem now, the *Daily Telegraph* reported yesterday.

Mr Coombs encourages his cows to lick his head every day and believes he will soon have a full head of hair.

g) [from a news report in the *Globe and Mail* (23 Jan. 2003) concerning domestic pressure on President Bush not to go to war against Iraq.] Amid a rising clamour of domestic antiwar protests and increasingly voiced doubts from prominent figures, a poll released yesterday indicates most Americans are unwilling to be rushed into war. The poll found that roughly two out of three Americans do not accept Mr Bush's view that UN inspectors have had enough time or that Baghdad has already failed to comply with a unanimous UN Security Council Resolution requiring it to disarm. 'There is great hesitancy among Americans,' said Andrew Kohut, director of the Pew Research Center for the People and the Press. 'The administration must make the case [for war] and it hasn't done so yet.'

On [Mr Bush's] handling of the Iraq crisis 'support is down by 6 to 8 percentage points in just six weeks,' said Richard Morin, poll analyst for the *Washington Post*, which commissioned the survey by TNS Intersearch along with ABC News. More than 40 per cent of the poll's respondents said that the inspectors should 'have as long as they want'. The poll, conducted January 16–20, is based on telephone interviews with 1,133 randomly selected adults in the United States.

h) [from a cosmetics advertisement] Research among dermatologists reveals a lot of skepticism regarding anti-aging claims. Research also shows that 95% of the doctors surveyed recommended Overnight Success's active ingredient for the relief of dry to clinically dry skin.

The Overnight Success night strength formula dramatically helps diminish fine, dry lines and their aging appearance . . . And after just 3 nights' use, 98% of women tested showed measurable improvements.

Discover Overnight Success tonight. Wake up to softer, smoother, younger looking skin tomorrow.

i) [from a letter to *Saturday Night* (15 July 2000)] According to an article published in the *New England Journal of Medicine*, marking territory with urine may prevent incontinence in old age. The *Journal* looked at two patients' reports of using their urine to keep cats and dogs out of their garden. The male, clad in sandals and kilt, walked around the garden's edge, urinating a small amount every few steps. This constant use of the pubococcygeal muscles keeps the bladder and rectal sphincter strong, and is what scientists believed prevented incontinence among our ancestors.

j) [from a letter to the *Kitchener-Waterloo Record* (1 Dec. 1984)] I would like to respond to the news stories that have warned of possible increases in the taxes of cigarettes and liquor in the next government budget. As a smoker I am very upset. Does the government not realize that if people cannot afford to buy tobacco and stop smoking, many people will be out of work? By raising the price of tobacco, people will have to stop smoking because they cannot afford to buy cigarettes. So the cigarette companies and tobacco farmers will have to lay people off. The government exists to create jobs not to lose them, and if the government raises cigarette prices any more, the unemployment and welfare lines are going to get a lot longer.

k) [from the *Toronto Star* (5 Nov. 1998)] Catholic activists in the United States are furious over this week's *Ally McBeal* episode on Fox-TV that included jokes about nuns having sex and a priest videotaping off-colour confessions. The Catholic League for Religious and Civil Rights in New York complained yesterday about 'a clear and intentional pattern of Catholic bashing' on the hit series.

l) [Tim Radford, 'Genes say boys will be boys and girls will be sensitive', in *The Guardian* (22 June 1997), p. 14] The sensitive sex was born that way. And boys are oafish because they can't help it. Blame nature, not nurture. The gene machine switches on feminine intuition long before birth, British scientists reported last week. The same mechanism switches off in boy babies after conception, leaving them to grow up awkward, gauche and insensitive. The irony is that a girl's talent for tact, social deftness and womanly intuition comes from father, not mother.

'What we might call feminine intuition—the ability to suss out a social situation by observing nuances of expression in voice and so on—is a set of skills of genetic origin that has nothing at all to do with hormones, as far as we know,' said David Skuse of the Institute of Child Health in London. Prof Skuse and colleagues from the Wessex Regional Genetics Laboratory in Salisbury were actually studying Turner's syndrome, a rare condition that affects one female in 2,500.

'A high proportion of girls had serious social adjustment problems, which started around the time they entered school and continued right through to adolescence,' he said. Intelligence was normal, but the girls were often short, and in adult life infertile. As children they were less aware of people's feelings, interrupted conversations, made demands of other people's time, and could not 'read' body language.

Girls have two X chromosomes, boys an X and a Y. But girls with Turner's syndrome have only one. Some inherited their one X from the mother, some from the father. The ones with the mother's X had the more severe problems. So, the researchers reason, there would be a gene or set of genes switched on or off in the egg, according to the parent from whom they are inherited. Girls normally get the switched on version from fathers, and boys inherit a single X chromosome from their mothers, with the genes switched off. 'Others might feel that men are somehow doomed. Well, we can learn social skills,' Prof Skuse said. 'Women will pick them up intuitively.'

This raised an evolutionary puzzle. 'Why would it be advantageous for males to be socially insensitive?' 'If you wanted to recruit boys into an army, a hunting party or a football team, it is an advantage to have those boys socially unskilled so the dominant male in that group can impose a set of social mores,' he said.

m) [Barbara Dority, 'Feminist Moralism, "Pornography", and Censorship', in *The Humanist* (Nov./Dec. 1989) p. 46] In many repressive countries—whether in Central America, Asia, Africa, eastern Europe, or the Middle East—there is practically no 'pornography'. But there is a great deal of sexism and violence against women. In the Netherlands and Scandinavia, where there are almost no restrictions on sexually explicit materials, the rate of sex-related crimes is much lower than in the United States. 'Pornography' is virtually irrelevant to the existence of sexism and violence.

n) [Chandra Wickramasinghe, Milton Wainwright, and Jayant Narlikar, in 'SARS—a clue to its origin?', letter to *The Lancet* vol. 361, no. 9371 (24 May 2003)] Sir—We detected large quantities of viable microorganisms in samples of stratospheric air at an altitude of 41 km.[1,2] We collected the samples in specially designed sterile cryosamplers carried aboard a balloon launched from the Indian Space Research Organisation / Tata Institute Balloon Facility in Hyderabad, India, on Jan. 21, 2001. Although the recovered biomaterial contained many microorganisms, as assessed with standard microbiological tests, we were able to culture only two types; both similar to known terrestrial species.[2] Our findings lend support to the view that microbial material falling from space is, in a Darwinian sense, highly evolved, with an evolutionary history closely related to life that exists on Earth.

We estimate that a tonne of bacterial material falls to Earth from space daily, which translates into some 1019 bacteria, or 20,000 bacteria per square metre of the Earth's surface. Most of this material simply adds to the unculturable or uncultured microbial flora present on Earth.

The injection from space of evolved microorganisms that have well-attested terrestrial affinities raises the possibility that pathogenic bacteria and viruses might also be introduced. The annals of medical history detail many examples of plagues and pestilences that can be attributed to space-incident microbes in this way. New epidemic diseases have a record of abrupt entrances from time to time, and equally abrupt retreats. The patterns of spread of these diseases, as charted by historians, are often difficult to explain simply on the basis of endemic infective agents. Historical epidemics such as the plague of Athens and the plague of Justinian come to mind.

In more recent times the influenza pandemic of 1917–19 bears all the hallmarks of a Space-incident component: 'The influenza pandemic of 1918 occurred in three waves. The first appeared in the winter and spring of

1917–1918 . . . The lethal second wave . . . involved almost the entire world over a very short time . . . Its epidemiologic behaviour was most unusual. Although person-to-person spread occurred in local areas, the disease appeared on the same day in widely separated parts of the world on the one hand, but, on the other, took days to weeks to spread relatively short distances.[3]

Also well documented is that, in the winter of 1918, the disease appeared suddenly in the frozen wastes of Alaska, in villages that had been isolated for several months. Mathematical modelling of epidemics such as the one described invariably involves the ad hoc introduction of many unproven hypotheses—for example, that of the superspreader. In situations where proven infectivity is limited only to close contacts, a superspreader is someone who can, on occasion, simultaneously infect a large number of susceptible individuals, thus causing the sporadic emergence of new clusters of disease. The recognition of a possible vertical input of external origin is conspicuously missing in such explanations.[4,5]

With respect to the SARS outbreak, a prima facie case for a possible space incidence can already be made. First, the virus is unexpectedly novel, and appeared without warning in mainland China. A small amount of the culprit virus introduced into the stratosphere could make a first tentative fall out East of the great mountain range of the Himalayas, where the stratosphere is thinnest, followed by sporadic deposits in neighbouring areas. If the virus is only minimally infective, as it seems to be, the subsequent course of its global progress will depend on stratospheric transport and mixing, leading to a fallout continuing seasonally over a few years. Although all reasonable attempts to contain the infective spread of SARS should be continued, we should remain vigilant for the appearance of new foci (unconnected with infective contacts or with China) almost anywhere on the planet. New cases might continue to appear until the stratospheric supply of the causative agent becomes exhausted.

1   Harris MJ, Wickramasinghe NC, Lloyd D, et al. The detection of living cells in stratospheric samples. Proc. SPIE Conference 2002; 4495: 192–8. [PubMed]

2   Wainwright M, Wickramsinghe NC, Narlikar JV, Rajaratnam P. Microorganisms cultured from stratospheric air samples obtained at 41 km. FEMS Microbiol Lett 2003; 218: 161–5. [PubMed]

3   Weinstein L. Influenza: 1918, a revisit? N Engl J Med 1976; 6: 1058–60. [PubMed]

4   Hoyle F, Wickramasinghe NC. Diseases from Space. London: JM Dent, 1979.

5   Wickramasinghe NC. Cosmic dragons: life and death on our planet. London: Souvenir Press, 2001.

o)   [from C.D.B. Bryan, *Close Encounters of the Fourth Kind: Alien Abduction, UFOs, and the Conference at M.I.T.* (Knopf, 1995) p. 230] During the days immediately following the conference, I am struck by how my perception of the abduction phenomenon has changed: I no longer think it is a joke. This is not to say I now believe UFOs and alien abduction are *real*—'real' in the sense of a reality subject to the physical laws of the universe as we know them—but rather that I feel something very mysterious is going on. And based as much on what has been presented at the conference as on the intelligence, dedication, and sanity of the majority of the presenters, I cannot reject out-of-hand the *possibility* that what is taking place isn't exactly what the abductees are saying is happening to them. And if that is so, the fact that no one has been able to pick up a tailpipe from a UFO does not mean UFOs do not exist. It means only that UFOs might not have tailpipes. As Boston Astronomer Michael Papagiannis insisted, 'The absence of evidence is not evidence of absence'.

p)   [Carl Sagan, in *The Dragons of Eden: Speculations on the Evolution of Human Intelligence* (Random House, 1977) pp. 92–3] So far as I know, childbirth is generally painful in only one of the millions of species on Earth: human beings. This must be a consequence of the recent and continuing increase in cranial volume. Modern men and women have braincases twice the volume of *Homo habilis*'s. Childbirth is painful because the evolution of the human skull has been spectacularly fast and recent. The American anatomist C. Judson Herrick described the development of the neocortex in the following terms: 'Its explosive growth late in phylogeny is one of the most dramatic cases of evolutionary transformation known to comparative anatomy.' The incomplete closure of the skull at birth, the fontanelle, is very likely an imperfect accommodation to this recent brain evolution.

MORAL AND

POLITICAL

REASONING:

SCHEMES OF VALUE

In this chapter we continue our discussion of different schemes of argument by introducing schemes 'of value' that play an important role in ordinary reasoning. Because these schemes play a particularly important role in moral and political reasoning, we focus primarily on examples from these areas. The schemes that we discuss are

- ◆ slippery-slope arguments;
- ◆ arguments from analogy;
- ◆ appeals to precedent;
- ◆ two-wrongs reasoning; and
- ◆ two-wrongs by analogy.

In the last chapter, we discussed schemes of argument that address factual issues. In this chapter, we discuss a set of schemes that are used in reasoning about 'values' or 'morals'. By this we mean that such arguments can be used when we debate what is right and wrong, what *should* be done in particular circumstances, and what policies or laws should be adopted. As it is often said, factual claims and arguments are claims and arguments about what *is* the case; moral (or 'value') claims and arguments are claims and arguments about what *ought* to be the case.

Of course, moral and factual reasoning are not entirely distinct. In ordinary discussion and debate they are usually intertwined. When we debate the political situation in the Middle East, we are likely to debate both factual issues (what are the conditions under which people live, what actually happened in controversial incidents, who controls and acts for whom, etc.) and issues of morality and value (what rights do individuals have, how can one legitimately deal with violent threats, under what circumstances does a group of people have the right to claim a homeland, etc.). In introducing a series of argument schemes that can be applied to moral and political reasoning, we shall see that there are times when these schemes are used to establish factual rather than moral conclusions, and that they often blend empirical and moral reasoning.

As we said at the start of Chapter 12, the schemes that we are introducing are not exhaustive or definitive. They are the basis of a broad range of important moral and political arguments, but in your dealings with ordinary arguments you may find instances of moral and political reasoning that do not fit any of the schemes that we introduce. In such cases, you can assess such arguments by relying on the general criteria for good arguments that we have already identified (i.e. acceptability, relevance, and sufficiency). In fact, each of the schemes in this chapter involves specific applications of the general criteria for a good argument.

1. Slippery-Slope Arguments

The first scheme that we will consider in our account of reasoning about values illustrates the ways in which moral and empirical reasoning are often combined in the discussion of moral and political issues. Because 'slippery-slope arguments' are used in debates about actions and their consequences, they combine causal reasoning about the consequences of particular actions, and moral considerations about the consequences that should or should not be prevented.

Using uppercase letters to refer to actions, we can represent the scheme for slippery-slope arguments as follows:

> PREMISE 1: A causes B, B causes C, and so on to X.
> PREMISE 2: X is undesirable (*or* X is desirable).
> CONCLUSION: A is wrong (*or* right).

Arguments that abide by this scheme are called 'slippery-slope' arguments because the negative version of this argument maintains that a given action, A, initiates our 'sliding down a slippery slope of causal sequences to some inevitable consequence' that we should avoid.

Because a slippery-slope argument can be based on a long chain of cause-and-effect relationships, premise 1 in our scheme will often appear as a series of premises of the form

> A causes B
> B causes C
> C causes D
> D causes X

A strong slippery-slope argument is (explicitly or implicitly) a strong instance of the scheme for such reasoning. Here, we need to consider two questions that correspond to each of our two premises. An answer to the first—*Does the causal chain really hold?*—requires empirical reasoning. The second—*Is the final consequence properly judged to be desirable* (or *undesirable*)?—requires moral reasoning. A good argument *against* slippery-slope reasoning must argue that the claimed causal chain will not develop as proposed, or that the value of its ultimate consequence has been misjudged. The causal chain can be challenged by questioning one of the causal links, either by pointing out that it lacks support or that it is supported by poor causal reasoning.

An example of slippery-slope reasoning in the political arena is found in the following illustration, fashioned after a World War II cartoon by David Low. It is a criticism of the indifference of the English public when Germany moved against Czechoslovakia. Low criticizes this indifference by suggesting that it will precipitate a series of causal effects that will lead to disaster. He does so by drawing (quite literally) a slippery slope that represents the chain of consequences that will transpire if Germany is allowed to take Czechoslovakia.

We can diagram Low's argument as follows:

P1 = If Germany takes Czechoslovakia, then Romania and Poland will fall.
P2 = If Poland and Romania fall, then the French Alliances will fall.
P3 = If the French Alliances fall, then Anglo–French security will be unstable.
P4 = We do not want Anglo–French security to be unstable.
MC = We should not continue to ignore Germany's incursions on Czechoslovakia.

WHAT'S CZECHOSLOVAKIA TO ME, ANYWAY ?

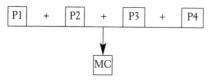

In assessing this argument we need to ask whether the causal chain that it proposes is plausible. In retrospect, history tells us that it was. But at the time, an assessor would have had to judge the likelihood of each step in the causal chain. Given the military might of Germany at that time, combined with the relative weakness of countries like Czechoslovakia, Romania, etc., and given the geographical facts of the situation, a reasoner could indeed have judged each link in the proposed causal chain as plausible. Also the final consequence of this causal chain—the fall of Anglo–French security—is something that is clearly undesirable to Low's audience (the British public) and also to a broader universal audience (which would not, for moral reasons, support the rise of Nazi Germany). We therefore judge Low's argument to be a good instance of slippery-slope reasoning.

Our second example of slippery-slope reasoning is another visual argument, this one taken from a liquor advertisement that we have reproduced below. Like our previous example, this is best understood as a visual metaphor. Understood literally, the image in question makes no sense. Bottles of vodka are not so absurdly large and do not pour their contents down on top of sleepy villages. If they did the result would not be the Manhattan-like streetscape that is the centre-point of this image. In view of this, the image that is the focal point of this advertisement must be understood as a visual metaphor. The message it conveys is one of transformation, the vodka acting as the catalyst that brings about the change. So understood, the message of the advertisement might be summarized as a visual proposition that can be paraphrased as the claim that 'Vodka can transform a sleepy life into one full of cosmopolitan excitement,' or, more personally, as the claim that 'If you add vodka to your life, your sleepy life will be transformed into a life of cosmopolitan excitement.' Clearly, the advertisement is an argument that proposes this claim as a reason for the implicit conclusion that 'You should add vodka to your life.'

To fully appreciate the argument, we need to recognize the hidden premise that 'A life of cosmopolitan excitement is desirable,' for the claim that vodka can give one an exciting night life (the kind associated with the Manhattan-like streetscape the vodka has produced) is a reason for purchasing vodka only if an exciting night life is something that is desirable. Recognizing this hidden assumption, we summarize the argument as follows:

P1 = If you add vodka to your life, your sleepy life will be transformed into a life of cosmopolitan excitement.

HP2 = A life of cosmopolitan excitement is desirable.

C = You should add vodka to your life.

Once we summarize the argument in this way, it can be seen as a clear instance of slippery-slope reasoning, though in ways distinct from our first example. For in this

example the causal chain is associated with one's personal life rather than broader political issues, and this is a case in which the final consequence of the causal chain is claimed to be desirable rather than undesirable.

Our second example is also unlike our first insofar as it is an example of a weak slippery-slope argument. The problem with it is that one might debate the acceptability of its premises. Though the hidden premise may be debated, it might perhaps be acceptable to a particular audience for whom the advertisement is intended. But even in this context, the first premise—the premise that suggests a causal chain—is dubious. Why should we accept that adding vodka to one's life will transform it into a life of cosmopolitan excitement? The consumption of vodka, especially if it is taken too far, is quite likely to have a deleterious effect, in the worst-case scenario resulting in alcohol abuse. Even if it does not have such extreme results, it seems unlikely that vodka will transform one's life in the manner the advertisement has suggested. Certainly it is hard to see how the first premise in the argument is acceptable according to any of the criteria for acceptability we discussed in Chapter 11.

SLIPPERY-SLOPE ARGUMENTS

A slippery-slope argument is one that shows either (1) that an action should not be performed or allowed because it will begin a causal chain leading to an undesirable consequence, or (2) that an action should be performed or allowed because it will begin a chain of causes leading to a desirable end. A good slippery-slope argument must be founded on a plausible causal chain and an acceptable claim about what is or is not desirable.

EXERCISE 13A

1. Assess the slippery-slope arguments in the following passages:
    a)* [adapted from J. Gay-Williams, 'The Wrongfulness of Euthanasia', in *Intervention and Reflection: Basic Issues and Medical Ethics*, ed. Ronald Munson (Wadsworth, 1979)] Euthanasia as a policy is a slippery slope. A person apparently hopelessly ill may be allowed to take his own life. Should he no longer be able to act, he may be permitted to deputize others to do it for him; then the judgment of others becomes the ruling factor. At this point it becomes a matter of others acting 'on behalf of' the patient as they see fit, and this may incline them to act of behalf of other patients who have not authorized them to act on their behalf. It is only a short step, then, from voluntary euthanasia (self-inflicted or authorized), to directed euthanasia administered to a patient who has given no authorization, to involuntary euthanasia conducted as part of a social policy. As social policy, it would give society or its representatives the authority to eliminate all those who might be considered too 'ill' to function normally any longer.
    b) [John Hofsess, in *Maclean's* (Oct. 1973)] If you don't get into the habit of exercising regularly when you're young, you are less likely to keep exercising during your later 20s and 30s when career, home, and family take up more and more time and interest. You'll then tend to become sedentary and physically unfit. That will set you up for various heart and lung diseases during middle age. No one wants to have a heart attack at 45 or 50, so to lessen that danger, you ought to get into the habit of exercising when you're young.
    c) [Arthur Schafer, in 'There can be another me, but should there be another ewe?', the *Globe and Mail* (28 Feb. 1998)] There are some who view the gradual acceptance of such [biomedical] technologies as a slippery slope. We move from rejection to neutrality, and even to approval, it is said. Yes, but is this always a bad thing? The first test-tube baby now leads a normal teenager's life. Does public acceptance of assisted reproduction prove that our moral sensibility has been coarsened? Or have we, rather, discarded an unthinking prejudice?

2. ARGUMENTS FROM ANALOGY

Analogies add richness to our language. An analogy makes a comparison between two different things by identifying similar features they both possess. A neurosurgeon delivering a lecture on the structure of the human brain might introduce her lecture by saying, 'The brain is like a highly efficient and compact computer,' and then organize her lecture around specific similarities.

As long as no conclusion is drawn from the comparison between the brain and a computer we do not have an argument. It is an analogy, but one used simply for elucidation. It is only when the comparison is used as a basis for drawing a conclusion that we have an argument from analogy. Typically, the reasoning is that two things are analogous in a certain respect because they are analogous in one or more other ways. If, based on similarities between the human brain and the computer, the neurosurgeon concluded that 'Humans are (like computers) just complicated machines,' or 'Human beings have the same moral status as a very complex machine,' we would have an argument from analogy.

We call the two things compared in an analogy 'analogues'. In presenting a scheme for analogical arguments, we will label the analogues X and Y. Those respects in which X and Y are said to be alike can be represented as p, q, r, and so on. Each of these letters represents a statement that is true of both X and Y. Since Y is like X in possessing the qualities p, q, r, etc., we conclude that Y possesses some additional property z that we know X possesses. Schematically, the argument can be depicted as follows:

PREMISE 1: X is p, q, r, . . . , z.
PREMISE 2: Y is p, q, r, . . .
CONCLUSION: Y is z.

The analogues do not have to be single entities. One or the other or both may be groups of things, in which case the form of the argument may look like this:

PREMISE 1: X, W, R, S are p, q, r, . . . , z.
PREMISE 2: Y is p, q, r, . . .
CONCLUSION: Y is z.

You must analyze analogical reasoning in terms of the similarities between the analogues. In the extreme case, the analogues, X and Y, will be identical, i.e. the same in all essential characteristics. In that event, the conclusion necessarily follows, for any property of X will be shared by Y. If X and Y are identical ('monozygotic') twins, then finding out something about X's genetic make-up allows us to conclude the same of Y. If X and Y are two actions that are in all morally relevant ways similar, then we can be certain that the conclusion we draw about the rightness or wrongness of one can be applied in the other instance. But the cases we usually consider are cases where X and Y are not identical and where the conclusion that X has property z is only probable, given the premises of the argument.

Arguments by analogy can be used to establish empirical or moral conclusions. In scientific contexts, medical researchers often use discoveries about the effect that particular substances have on rats or other mammals as a basis for conclusions about the effects they will have on humans. In such cases, medical researchers use a species with a physiological system analogous to that of humans, and conclude that humans would probably be similarly affected.

Arguments by analogy also play a central role in moral and legal discourse. The basis of law is the principle that 'justice is blind', which means that the law is obliged to treat similar actions in similar ways. Morality similarly obliges us to judge analogous actions as good or bad or permissible or not permissible. When we are forced to deal with new kinds of moral situation—those that result from new technological innovations, for example—we often proceed by looking for analogous situations with which we are familiar, and by applying relevant moral principles in a similar way to the new circumstance. For instance, if we want to decide whether a new method of dealing with male sterility should be subsidized by the government, we may begin by considering whether this method can be compared to other medical interventions that are (or are not) supported by the government (say, other methods that are supported, or methods used to treat female sterility).

A convincing argument from analogy must enumerate real, and not just apparent, similarities between the analogues. Because different kinds of similarities and differences matter in different contexts, the argument must enumerate the similarities that matter to the case at hand. In sentencing someone convicted of a crime, a judge may decide to look at cases that are similar or different in terms of the seriousness of the offence, premeditation, callousness, the pain caused to innocent victims, etc. Many other similarities and differences will not matter, though the distinction between those that matter and those that don't is not always clear. When Keith Richards of the Rolling Stones was given a suspended sentence for possessing a large quantity of heroin and cocaine, critics argued that the principle that like cases be treated similarly had been violated, because his unexpectedly light sentence was, they claimed, a consequence of the fact that he was a rock star rather than an ordinary addict. Their claim can be expressed as the claim that this kind of difference in personal status is irrelevant when in a court room, where judges are obliged to treat analogous cases in the same way.

In view of these kinds of considerations, a good argument by analogy typically depends on an assumption that we can represent by adding a hidden premise to our standard scheme:

PREMISE 1: X, W, R, S are p, q, r, . . . , z.
PREMISE 2: Y is p, q, r, . . .
HIDDEN PREMISE: p, q, r are the properties relevant to z.
CONCLUSION: Y is z.

This implies that a strong argument of this sort will (implicitly or explicitly) establish z as a property of some Y by pointing out (1) that z applies to X, and (2) that Y is similar to X in sufficient relevant respects, and (3) that X and Y are not relevantly dissimilar. A strong argument from analogy has premises establishing that property z is a property of the first analogue and that the analogues are similar in ways that are relevant to the conclusion, and does not overlook any relevant dissimilarities. Because the premises in an analogical argument must be combined to warrant the conclusion, they will always be linked in a diagram that represents the argument.

One of the most famous historical examples of an argument from analogy is the 'argument from design'. It states that the universe exhibits a particular order, predictability, and design, and maintains that it is reasonable to infer from this the existence of a designer. This designer is, of course, God, and the argument from design is one of the traditional proofs of the existence of God. The eighteenth-century Scottish philosopher David Hume discusses this argument in his *Dialogues Concerning Natural Religion*. His own argument takes place in the context of a dialogue involving several participants, which allows Hume both to present the argument from analogy and then to criticize it. When he presents the argument, he suggests that scientific study shows us that the world is like a machine, with different parts that are made up of other parts that work together in a precise way:

> Look round the world . . . you will find it to be nothing but one great machine, subdivided into an infinite number of lesser machines, which again admit of subdivisions to a degree beyond what human sense and faculties can trace and explain. All these various machines, and even their most minute parts, are adjusted to each other with an accuracy which ravishes into admiration all men who have ever contemplated them. The curious adapting of means to ends, throughout all nature, resembles exactly, though it much exceeds, the productions of human contrivance—of human design, thought, wisdom, and intelligence. Since therefore the effects resemble each other, we are led to infer, by all the rules of analogy, that the causes also resemble, and that the Author of nature is somewhat similar to the mind of man, though possessed of much larger faculties, proportioned to the grandeur of the work which he has executed.

The manner in which everything in nature appears to work together, to happen for a reason, to fulfill a particular purpose, suggests the product of a specific design, akin to human design, but far superior. This resemblance in the origins or causes suggests that the 'Author' of nature is analogous to the human mind, though on a much greater scale, appropriate to the larger scale of creation as a whole. Hume's principal concern is the nature of God: we infer the nature and mind of God by analogy with our nature and mind, extended to divine proportions.

In the next part of Hume's dialogue, another participant, Philo, proclaims that the argument from design is a very weak analogy. Suggesting that analogies weaken the moment we shift our terms of reference, Philo states that we conclude that a house had an architect or builder because this is the kind of effect we have observed to result from that kind of cause. However:

> Surely you will not affirm that the universe bears such a resemblance to a house that we can with the same certainty infer a similar cause, or that the analogy is here entire and perfect. The dissimilitude is so striking that the utmost you can here pretend to is a guess, a conjecture, a presumption concerning a similar cause.

Philo's point is that the dissimilarities between the universe and a house are so great that they threaten to undermine the necessary similarities, and the analogy breaks down; therefore, the attempt to infer, on the basis of one thing, a similar cause in the other—or any cause at all in the case of a proof of God's existence—is fruitless. What we have is a guess, not a fully convincing argument. Hume's discussion goes on to elaborate the ways in which the universe and a house differ, much of it rooted in the basic tenet of his philosophy, that nothing that we cannot know from experience can be proven or accepted. It follows that we can know where houses come from, but cannot say the same about the universe.

One might write a whole book on the argument from design. In the present context, our purpose is to illustrate a basic, and renowned, philosophical example of an argument from analogy. Philo's response to the argument is an example of a counter-argument to analogy, which we will discuss next.

Counter-Arguments to Analogy

Given our understanding of good arguments by analogy, a strong counter-argument *against* an argument from analogy must demonstrate that the criteria for a good argument from analogy are not (or cannot be) met in a specific case. This can be done in two ways.

In some cases, we may criticize an argument by analogy by accepting the proposed analogues but denying that the property emphasized in the conclusion applies to either. Suppose we discipline students for some misbehaviour—say, cheating on an exam—by failing them in our course. Suppose they complain that they have been unfairly treated because other students in the same situation received a zero on the exam but were allowed to complete the course. This is an argument by analogy. It maintains that two groups of students are in analogous situations and should, as a consequence, be treated in an analogous way. As people in these kinds of situation often rely on unreliable anecdotal information, it is easy to imagine that we might respond to the situation by investigating the matter and reporting that 'This is not in fact the case, the students in question were given a failing grade in their course.' In this situation we have constructed a strong counter-argument to an argument by analogy by showing that the analogue that is the basis of the argument does not have the property assigned to it.

More commonly, a counter-argument against analogy will be an *argument by disanalogy*, which attempts to show that two purported analogues are not analogous. This is done by showing that they do not share necessary similarities, or that there are relevant differences that distinguish them. In the case above, we would construct an argument by disanalogy if we told the students who complained that those students they had compared themselves to were not in an analogous situation (say, because their cheating was on a relatively minor test rather than on an exam).

Another example of argument by disanalogy is found in a letter to *Euro Know* (<http://www.euro-know.org/letters017.html>; accessed July 2002). The letter begins with the comment that 'The ideal of the European Union is the integration of, so far, fifteen different political and economic structures not one federal state like the USA controlled by Brussels.' In the rest of his letter the arguer proposes evidence that attempts to show that this analogy does not make sense (that the histories are different, that attitudes are different, and so on). On the basis of this disanalogy, he maintains that it makes no sense for the European Union, as opposed to the United States, to have one currency. The conclusion that it makes no sense to model the European Union on the USA is based upon the argument that the two are not analogous.

We construct an implicit counter-argument to analogy whenever we criticize an argument by analogy. Consider the following letter to the *Toronto Star* (27 Apr. 1983), which focuses on a definition argued from analogy:

> Whether or not a fetus is a human being is a matter of personal opinion but nobody can deny that forcing a woman to carry and give birth to a child against her will is an act of enslavement. Consider: someone approaches you and demands to be hooked up to your life support system for nine months, on the grounds that this is necessary for survival. It would be an unselfish gesture to comply, but you have every right to refuse. After all, it's your body—isn't it?

We can diagram this argument as follows:

P1 = In forcing a woman to carry and give birth to a child and in forcing you to allow someone to be hooked up to your life support system, it is one's own body that is being used.

P2 = In both cases, the use of one's body is necessary to ensure survival, of the person or the fetus.

C1 = Forcing a woman to carry and give birth to a child against the woman's will is like forcing you to allow someone to be hooked up to your life support system for nine months.

P3 = In the second case, you would have the right to refuse to comply (it would be an act of enslavement to force you to comply).

MC = A woman has every right to refuse to carry a child (it would be an act of enslavement to force her to carry it).

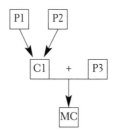

At first glance this argument may seem strong. One of the analogues appears somewhat fanciful, but there are grounds for comparing these two situations because (allowing that the fetus is a person) they both involve the dependence of one person on another. There are, however, two major dissimilarities that have been omitted. Once they are identified, the main conclusion is clearly problematic, and the argument can be recognized as weak.

If someone did approach you and demand to be hooked to your life support system, it would be quite reasonable to first point out that you are in no way responsible for that individual's predicament, and to then require an explanation why that demand should be made specifically of you. A mother carrying a child is in a different situation, for she may bear some responsibility for her situation, in which case the justification for the demand implicitly made by the fetus is quite unlike that in the other analogue. Second, a person approaching you comes from 'the outside' and already has some autonomous existence. But in the case of a pregnancy, the fetus has developed from within and has had no antecedent existence. If the two situations really were analogous, they could not be characterized by such significant dissimilarities. The main conclusion will not, therefore, be acceptable to any reasonable audience. Within the scope of an argument, we could eradicate these differences (imagine, for the moment, that you are responsible for the predicament of the person who needs to be hooked up to your life support system), but in that case it is no longer obvious that it would be wrong to force us to support the sufferer in question.

ARGUMENTS BY ANALOGY

Arguments by analogy are founded on claims that people or situations are analogous. A good argument by analogy supports a conclusion about Y by pointing out (1) that it is true of some X, (2) that Y is similar to X in sufficient relevant respects, and (3) that X and Y are not relevantly dissimilar. A good counter-argument to analogy shows that one or more of the criteria for a strong argument by analogy cannot be satisfied.

EXERCISE 13B

1. Imagine that you are going to buy a new car. You choose to use an argument by analogy to decide what car you should purchase. You decide you want a car that is analogous to one a friend owns. What would be the structure of your argument? What would be the relevant similarities? What differences would not matter?

2. In each case, comment on the appropriateness of arguing the stated claim by means of the analogies suggested.
   a) **Claim:** Marijuana should be legalized.

Analogies:
i)   Legalizing marijuana is like legalizing cocaine.
ii)   Banning marijuana is like banning alcohol.
iii) Making marijuana illegal is like banning novels, in that it entices more users.
iv)   Smoking marijuana is like giving people an easy fix rather than the opportunity to accomplish things by hard work.

b) **Claim:** Rich nations should provide aid to poor ones.
    Analogies:
    i)   Aid is like a handout people don't deserve.
    ii)   Teaching a person to fish is like feeding him for the rest of his life.
    iii) Aiding poor nations is like putting too many people on an already overcrowded lifeboat.
    iv)   Refusing aid is being like a Scrooge, aiding them is being like Jesus Christ.

3. Analyze the analogical reasoning in the following arguments. Are they strong examples of arguments from analogy or disanalogy? Provide your reasons.

a) [from Pliny the Elder's *Natural History*, 7.56] We do not breathe differently from the other animals, and there are some that live longer than us, so why do we not assume they, too are immortal? . . . These [beliefs about the soul] are fictions of childish absurdities.

b) [from a letter to the *Globe and Mail* (11 Mar. 2003)] Crawford Kilian equates the specificity of recruiting a black person as head of the Johnston Chair for Black Canadian Studies at Dalhousie University to establishing segregated public toilets for blacks. The analogy is spurious.

There is nothing black-related about a toilet; there is a great deal black-related about a Department of Black Canadian Studies.

Does Mr Kilian, however painstaking and detailed his study of Canadian blacks, really believe that he, as a non-black, could successfully defend his credibility as head of such a department? Could he accurately communicate the total experience of being black? Indeed, would anyone listen?

In a perfect world, of course, it wouldn't matter that he was white. In a perfect world there would be no such chair for black Canadian studies. It wouldn't be relevant.

Today, alas, it is extremely relevant. And it absolutely requires a black leader.

c) [The cartoonist Gary Larson took legal action to prevent the unauthorized use of his cartoons on the Internet. In appealing to webmasters not to use his cartoons, he sent a letter that has been reproduced on many websites (see, e.g., <http://members.aol.com/HPElzer/letter.html>, <http://www.creators.com/index2_anotefromgarylarson.html>, <http;//fsing.fs.uni-sb.de/~martin/larson/start.html>, <http://farside.lindesign.se/>, <http://www.portmann.com/farside/home.html>, <http://www.fullfont.com/farside.htm>, <http://www.geocities

.com/simmicht/wanted.html>, all accessed 6 July 2002). Assess Larson's reasoning in the following portion of his letter.] These 'cartoons' are my children of sorts, and like a parent I'm concerned about where they go at night without telling me. And seeing them at someone's Web site is like getting the call at 2:00 a.m. that goes 'Uh, Dad, you're not going to like this much, but guess where I am. . . .' Please send my 'kids' home. I'll be eternally grateful.

d) [adapted from a letter to the *Toronto Star* (5 Nov. 1983)] A man who drives his car into the rear of another is not guilty of careless driving if his brakes failed. Similarly, a man should not be found guilty of murder if his mind failed to perceive reality due to mental illness.

e)* [Deane Pollard, in 'Regulating Violent Pornography', *Vanderbilt Law Review*, vol. 43, no. 1 (1990)] Speeding is known to increase the likelihood of car collisions, and drivers are punished for this dangerous behaviour whether or not their particular sprees cause collisions. Violent pornography, like speeding, is intrinsically dangerous, and legislatures may regulate it on the basis of its known propensity for harm without a showing of particular harm.

3. Appeals to Precedent

Morality and law require consistency. In both cases, we are obliged to treat similar cases in a similar way. In view of this, we may appeal to *precedents* (i.e. to previously established decisions) to establish that a particular situation should be treated in a particular way. If an analogous case was treated in a certain way in the past, or if we want to treat future cases as analogous to those that are current, then our reasoning will be based on precedents. If two householders, for example, are granted a permit to add an addition to their house, this sets a precedent for other people in the neighbourhood to do likewise.

When we make an appeal to precedent we are arguing by analogy. In view of this, arguments by precedent are a variant of the scheme we have given for arguments by analogy, i.e.

PREMISE 1: X is p, q, r, . . . , z.
PREMISE 2: Y is p, q, r, . . .
HIDDEN PREMISE: p, q, r are the properties relevant to the moral or legal assessment of X and Y.
CONCLUSION: Y is z.

In the case of appeal to precedent, X is the event or circumstance that is used to establish a precedent. It may be a previous or a future event (if the latter, the argument is used to establish a precedent to ensure that future cases of this sort are treated in a particular way). Y is the analogous event or circumstance that we are faced with. The hidden premise recognizes the assumption that X and Y are relevantly similar.

In dealing with new precedents, one may argue positively for a precedent or negatively against one. In the latter case we argue that some action or decision will set an undesirable precedent, paving the way for actions or situations that are unacceptable. A professor may argue that it would be unfair to accept a late paper from one student because he or she must then accept late papers from other students in similar situations. In other cases, we use appeals to precedent to argue that a given case should be treated in a particular way because it will establish a good precedent for the future. In such a case, we might argue that we should prosecute a particular industrial polluter and not forgive a first offence, since consistency would then demand that we forgive other first offenders.

An example that illustrates how precedents may be used is the 'Powell Doctrine', named after the American secretary of state, Colin Powell. In this case, the precedent appealed to is the Vietnam War and the perceived mistakes committed by the United States both in how the decision to go to war was made and in how the campaign was carried out. These perceived mistakes, which include entering the conflict with little popular support at home and no clearly defined military objective, are said to have had undesirable consequences. According to Powell, the United States was, as a result of these mistakes, trapped in an extended police action, suffering heavy casualties and low morale. On the basis of this understanding of Vietnam, Powell and others have concluded that it sets a negative precedent, i.e. a precedent that establishes how *not* to conduct military action. On the basis of this thinking, the Powell Doctrine holds that the United States should in the future not become involved in military action without a clear and pre-established military objective, a high level of support from the public, and a clearly winnable position. (For more on this see *The New Republic*, 16 Oct. 1995.)

Another example of arguing against a precedent is found in a response to the decision of an Ontario court that ordered that a man's extensive collection of old newspapers, magazines, and papers be seized and destroyed (reported in the *Globe and Mail*, 25 Oct. 1995). The basis of this decision was the argument that the collection, comprising numerous stacks of paper material that he had collected and stored in his basement for years, represented a fire hazard. In response to the decision, other collectors of old books and materials immediately protested, arguing that this decision set an undesirable precedent, one that could be extended potentially to all collectors of any old or antiquarian materials. In this way, the booksellers argued that such a decision could prove a threat for antiquarian collectors, setting a precedent for the suppression of private book collections.

This example highlights the way in which arguments for or against a new precedent share similarities with slippery-slope reasoning insofar as they maintain that some action, used as a precedent, will lead to an undesirable (or desirable) consequence. It is important, though, to distinguish arguments that rely on causal reasoning from those based on analogical reasoning. In most cases, this identification will help us decide whether what we have is principally a slippery-slope argument or an appeal to precedent. While we would not want to rule out the possibility of both types of reasoning arising in a particular argument, we should strive to avoid confusing the two. When constructing your own arguments of these sorts, decide whether the strategy you have in mind is one that uses causal reasoning of a future chain or analogical reasoning of comparing cases, and adopt the appropriate scheme.

As with other cases of analogy, a strong appeal to precedent establishes that the analogues compared—in this case, the precedent and the other situation said to be similar—are in fact analogous, and that a particular moral or legal judgment applies in the situation that is associated with the precedent. Sub-arguments may be used to establish both these claims as acceptable. In constructing a *counter-argument to an appeal to precedent* one must argue against one or both of these claims. In practice, you will find that the strength of most appeals to precedent turns on the question whether the particular case that is said to be a precedent is analogous to the other cases with which we compare it. In particular, you must determine whether there are any relevant dissimilarities that separate the case at hand from the past or future situation(s) to which it is compared.

APPEALS TO PRECEDENT

Appeals to precedent argue for or against a situation or course of action by appealing to previous or future cases that are analogous.

A strong appeal to precedent shows that some action X should be allowed (or disallowed) because some analogous case has been allowed (or disallowed), or because future analogous cases should be allowed (or disallowed).

A strong counter-argument to an appeal to precedent shows that one of these claims is unacceptable because the cases being compared are not relevantly analogous.

EXERCISE 13C

1. Taking the following topics, sketch (i) an appeal to past precedent, (ii) an argument against precedent, and (iii) an argument for a new precedent. In each case, which argument is strongest?
   a) censorship of child pornography on the Internet
   b) medical procedures that transplant tissue from aborted fetuses to patients with Parkinson's disease
   c)* human cloning

2. Evaluate the strengths and weaknesses of the following argument by precedent:

   Several publishers that had been planning books about prominent people or companies have been threatened with lawsuits by their potential subjects. Once threatened, these publishers felt they had no choice but to cancel the plans to publish the controversial books. The situation, known as 'libel chill', will discourage writers, publishers, and commentators in the future from pursuing certain subjects. This situation represents undemocratic media control, censorship, and loss of freedom of expression.

4. TWO-WRONGS REASONING

We use 'two-wrongs reasoning' when we defend or justify a questionable policy or action on the grounds that it is a necessary way of correcting or avoiding some actual or potential injustice. Arguments of this sort are often used by arguers responding to criticism that some action or policy is wrong.

There are two kinds of two-wrongs arguments. In the first kind, the action or policy in question is justified as a response to another wrong it attempts to cancel or alleviate. Such arguments have the following form:

PREMISE: A questionable action or policy X cancels or alleviates some unfairness or injustice.

CONCLUSION: X is justified.

Here, the wrongness of the action or policy defended is explicitly or implicitly acknowledged, but some reasons are given to show that it is permissible or necessary. In the second kind of two-wrongs argument, called 'two-wrongs by analogy', an action is justified by pointing to similar wrong actions that have been allowed. In this case, the argument maintains that consistency justifies the current action. Two-wrongs by analogy is discussed in greater detail below. For the moment, it will help to remember that such arguments are a subset of the more basic two-wrongs argument, and that our comments here apply to both kinds of two-wrongs reasoning.

If correctly argued, two-wrongs reasoning is quite acceptable. Most justifications of self-defence or of civil disobedience take this form. For instance, a government may institute a policy that seriously affects the rights of a group of people. Perhaps their right to vote or assemble in public places is denied. We don't have to look far in the world for examples of people being denied the right to assemble (in India during the time of Gandhi, in the former Soviet Union, in China's Tiananmen Square, in the Philippines). In response to this perceived wrong people defy the government and congregate, and they justify this action by pointing to the wrongness of the policy that restricts them. In another context, a government may justify subsidies that are seen as 'propping up' an industry by arguing that the same practice goes on in other countries and that, regrettably, they must also do so to make the domestic industry competitive on the international market.

These arguments are examples of two-wrongs reasoning. In our first example, the people apparently believed they had no better alternative than to defy what they considered unjust laws. In our second example, a principle of fairness is at stake, and analogical reasoning plays an important role in the argument. In both examples the two-wrongs argument does not deny that the action or policy defended is less than morally ideal. It admits this but still tries to justify the action, maintaining that it is the lesser of two-wrongs and in this way arguing for its acceptability to an impartial universal audience.

In order to be legitimate, two-wrongs arguments must meet three conditions. These conditions are represented by the three premises in the scheme for two-wrongs reasoning, which has the following form:

PREMISE 1: X is a response to another wrong, Y, the unjust consequences of which it is designed to cancel or alleviate.

PREMISE 2: X is less wrong than Y.

PREMISE 3: There is no morally preferable way to respond to Y.

CONCLUSION: X is justified.

A good argument against two-wrongs reasoning must demonstrate that one of the conditions for good two-wrongs reasoning imbedded in the three premises has not been satisfied (i.e. that one of these premises is unacceptable in the case at hand). In this way it is possible to show that the particular wrong being proposed cannot be justified by another wrong.

Clearly, your judgment will play an important role in deciding when the conditions for good two-wrongs reasoning are and are not met. In particular, you will be called on to decide what is 'less' wrong in a specific situation and whether there is (with respect to the third condition) a morally preferable response. These are concerns you will have to heed when constructing your own two-wrongs arguments because, as always, the onus is on you to support adequately your argument on contentious points. The complexities of two-wrongs reasoning illustrate the extent to which the domain of moral argumentation is a domain in which you cannot always expect to easily grasp a right or wrong answer with which everyone will agree. Argument schemes like two-wrongs reasoning shed light on the issue, tell us the kind of questions we should be asking, and facilitate our own reasoning on the issues as we strive to come to reasonable positions on them.

The following two-wrongs argument appeared in an editorial from the *Wall Street Journal* (Jan. 1984) addressing the actions of Bernard Goetz in a famous incident in which he shot four black youths who he believed were going to rob him on a New York subway train:

> If the 'state of nature' has returned to some big cities, can people fairly be blamed for modern vigilantism? Is it more 'civilized' to suffer threats to individual liberty from criminals, or is it an overdose of sophistication to say individuals can never resort to self-protection?

Since this reasoning is phrased in rhetorical questions intended as assertions and the conclusion is hidden, it is important to diagram this argument:

P1 = If the 'state of nature' has returned to some big cities, people cannot be blamed for modern vigilantism.

HP2 = The 'state of nature' has returned to some big cities.

P3 = It is not 'civilized' to have to suffer threats to individual liberty from criminals.

P4 = It is an overdose of sophistication to say individuals can never resort to self-protection.

HC = Self-protection in the form of modern vigilantism is justified.

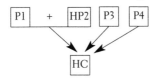

Despite an awkward presentation, the thrust of this reasoning is quite evident. To justify the kind of self-protection in which Goetz engaged, the argument claims that big cities are characterized by a 'state of nature', understood as an everyone-for-his-or-herself struggle to survive. It is important to acknowledge this aspect of the argument because, as a general statement about inner-city life—especially in the big cities of the United States—this claim may appeal to some people.

But Goetz's actions are difficult to justify on the basis of two-wrongs reasoning, for the existence of a first wrong is questionable. When we apply the first condition for a strong two-wrongs argument, we find that it is not clear that Goetz was responding to an actual wrong, since the youths didn't actually rob him but only asked him for five dollars. There are also doubts as to whether the second condition is satisfied. Was Goetz's act less wrong than the one he anticipated? The writer of the editorial clearly believes it was. But the writer also begs the question in an important sense, for P3 already assumes the truth of the conclusion (that the act was justified) when it refers to 'criminals'. There are no clear criminals in this case. To accept Goetz's labelling of people as criminals in a society where the law requires people to be assumed innocent until proven guilty is to grant Goetz status as both judge and executioner. The third condition for strong two-wrongs arguments is also not satisfied. Given that the claim that there is a first wrong is so weak, there are undoubtedly morally preferable ways in which Goetz could have responded (by ignoring the youths, by calling for help, or even by leaving the situation).

We have found a more plausible instance of a two-wrongs argument associated with Maori protests against the British Royal family in Australia and New Zealand. The following is a long excerpt from a discussion of these protests by Augie Fleras in an article entitled '"Crude" Form of Protest a Maori Tradition' (*Kitchener-Waterloo Record*, 1 April 1986):

> The Royal Family has once again experienced several embarrassing incidents while on tour of the South Pacific. Efforts by activists to disrupt the visit of Queen Elizabeth and Prince Philip to New Zealand and Australia have focused worldwide attention on the antipodes.
>
> . . . of the various gestures of defiance exhibited to date, none has attracted the same degree of press coverage as the attempt by a Maori activist to expose his

buttocks to the Queen. . . . Those of us outside of New Zealand might wonder at
the folly of such a seemingly juvenile gesture, more likely to be associated with
drunken 'moons' outside of moving vehicles. Even native New Zealanders
appear perplexed by the audacity of such outrageous behavior.

But as is commonly known among the indigenous population of that country, this behaviour is commensurate with Maori cultural tradition. Exposing
one's buttocks is nothing less than a legitimate and traditional symbol of 'ritual-
ized derision'('whakapohane'). . . .

It is one thing to establish the cultural rationale for 'whakapohane', it is
another to explain why the Royal Family has been singled out for this insulting
treatment.

An understanding of New Zealand history is useful here. In 1840, representatives of the British Crown and a group of Maori leaders signed the Treaty of
Waitangi.

Under the terms of the treaty the Crown acquired the right of sovereignty
over what was known then of New Zealand. The Maori in turn were bestowed
the benefits of imperial protection . . .

They also received the right of access to those resources—land, fish,
forests—necessary to procure their survival. But for the most part successive governments have reneged on their end of the agreement.

Maori land has not been protected from encroachment by land-hungry set-
tlers with the result that only three million acres (of the original 66 million)
remain in Maori possession. . . .

In an effort to vent their frustration and draw royal attention to the plight of
the indigenous people, Maori activists have taken advantage of opportunities to
embarrass the Royal Family and the New Zealand government.

Protest is conducted in a manner consistent with Maori cultural traditions,
and guaranteed to garner maximum exposure.

In this case, the author of the passage is not presenting an argument of his own but
explaining the reasoning behind Maori protests. It should be clear that this reasoning
is an instance of two-wrongs reasoning, for the Maori protesters believe that what
would otherwise be outrageous acts of rudeness are justified because they are a
response to other wrongs—i.e. the wrongs of the Royal Family and the New Zealand
government, who have not kept their side of an agreement they signed with the
Maoris.

To see if this is a good instance of two-wrongs reasoning we need to consider
whether it is a strong instance of the two-wrongs scheme, i.e. an instance that legitimates the conclusion that rude acts of protest against the royal family are justified.
Certainly the first premise required for such an argument is acceptable. The rude
protests are an attempt to respond to a previous wrong, i.e. the Royal Family and the
New Zealand government's failure to respect commitments made to the Maori people. By drawing media attention to their plight they hope to provoke public and inter-

national pressure that will alleviate the unjust circumstances. It is also clear that the second premise necessary for good two-wrongs reasoning is acceptable, for, as rude as it is to expose one's buttocks to the Queen, this is not as wrong as a concerted attempt to deprive a whole people of millions of acres of land and other resources they were promised.

The question whether this argument is a strong two-wrongs argument thus hinges on whether there is a morally preferable way for the Maori protestors to respond to the injustice they are trying to alleviate. We are not in a position to judge this question well (for we do not know what alternative ways of pursuing redress are feasible); however, we can say that it may be plausible to argue that the only way to rectify the injustice is to bring a great deal of political pressure to bear on the situation, and it is conceivable that protests like the one in question are the only feasible way to do so. (The whakapohane protests are, it might be argued, particularly appropriate because they are commensurate with Maori tradition.) In such circumstances, it would be possible to present a strong two-wrongs argument in the following way:

P1 = Rude acts of protest against the British Royal Family are a response to another wrong—the violation of the Treaty of Waitangi and the taking of Maori land and resources—and are an attempt to alleviate this wrong.

P2 = Rude acts of protest are less wrong than the unjust taking of (millions of acres of) Maori land and Maori resources.

P3 = There is no morally preferable way to bring about an attempt to alleviate this injustice.

C = Rude acts of protest against the British Royal Family are justified.

Though our discussion is not in this case definitive, it should help you see what kinds of considerations must play a part in an attempt to construct a good two-wrongs argument.

TWO-WRONGS REASONING

Two-wrongs reasoning attempts to justify an action normally considered wrong by pointing out that it cancels or alleviates some worse wrong. A good two-wrongs argument establishes that (1) the wrong that is said to be permissible is a response to another wrong, the unjust consequences of which it tries to cancel or alleviate; (2) the wrong that is said to be permissible is less wrong than any injustice it attempts to cancel or alleviate; (3) there is no morally preferable way to respond to the injustice in question.

Two-Wrongs by Analogy

'Two-wrongs by analogy' is a more specific kind of this argument that merits separate treatment because it plays an important role in ordinary reasoning. We introduced a two-wrongs-by-analogy argument earlier when we said that one argues by two-wrongs reasoning if one claims that subsidies for one country's industries are legitimate if similar subsidies are offered by other countries to their industries. In this and other circumstances, two-wrongs-by-analogy arguments apply because fairness demands that analogous situations be treated in a similar way. We noted the importance of this principle in our discussion of appeals to precedent. Two-wrongs by analogy differs from an appeal to precedent in its acknowledgement that the action it justifies is less than morally ideal.

Often, two-wrongs by analogy arguments can be diagrammed as follows:

PREMISE 1: An action or policy X is similar to action or policy Y.
PREMISE 2: Y has been accepted/allowed.
CONCLUSION: X should be accepted/allowed.

In many instances of two-wrongs by analogy there are sub-arguments that justify P1 and P2.

We can judge two-wrongs-by-analogy reasoning by appealing directly to the criteria for strong two-wrongs reasoning. In this kind of case, the wrong that is said to be alleviated is the inconsistent treatment of similar situations, and a convincing argument must show that the remedy (allowing some new wrong) is not worse than the inconsistency (the wrong) that is said to have been allowed, and that there is no preferable way to deal with the inconsistency in question. In view of this, a fully explicit two-wrongs-by-analogy argument will conform to the following scheme:

PREMISE 1: A wrong, X, is analogous to other wrongs (Y, Z, W, . . .) that have been permitted.
PREMISE 2: Fairness in the form of consistency is more important than preventing X.
PREMISE 3: There is no morally preferable way to respond to the situation.
CONCLUSION: X should be accepted/allowed.

Both bad and good examples of two-wrongs-by-analogy arguments come readily to mind. If it is common practice not to ticket cars parked illegally on a city lot, it would be unfair to pick one car—a car owned, let us say, by a vocal critic of the municipal administration—and ticket it. In such circumstances, the individual who has been ticketed can reasonably propound the following two-wrongs-by-analogy argument:

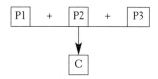

where P1 = Other people who park their cars in the lot are not ticketed, P2 = I am entitled to the same treatment as other people, especially for such a petty wrong, P3 = There is no other way of treating me fairly, and C = I should not have been ticketed.

To refute this argument one would have to show that one or more of the premises is unacceptable. (If they are acceptable, then the argument's adherence to the scheme for good two-wrongs-by-analogy reasoning ensures that they are relevant and sufficient to the conclusion.) One might, for example, argue that the offence is not in fact a petty one (say, because illegal parking is interfering with city workers), and that ticketing a few individuals on a random basis is the morally best way to respond to the situation, given that the city is short of parking officers. It is worth noting that this counter-argument is in fact another instance of two-wrongs reasoning, for it grants that it would be best if all of the individuals who parked in the lot were treated consistently (i.e. if all were given tickets) but justifies a deviation from this policy on the grounds that random ticketing is the morally preferable way to deal with the problem. This counter-argument can, therefore, be assessed by considering the criteria for good two-wrongs arguments.

An example of bad two-wrongs-by-analogy reasoning is the argument that a crackdown on drunk driving is wrong because police and the courts have been lax in prosecuting past offenders. A consistent treatment of future offenders would require that they go free, but such consistency is not as desirable a goal as preventing the potential damage, injury, and loss of life that may be caused by drunk drivers. It follows that the proposed new wrong—turning a blind eye to new offenders—is not preferable to a crackdown. The principle of consistency suggests that it is wrong to treat differently individuals who commit the same offence. If one offender is not charged, then one can argue on these grounds that none of them should be. But in circumstances in which we are dealing with serious offences, a preferable way to deal with the situation would be to charge all offenders. In terms of the criteria for strong, two-wrongs-by-analogy reasoning, the argument that consistency demands that none be prosecuted fails to satisfy the third condition for good reasoning of this kind.

TWO-WRONGS REASONING BY ANALOGY

Two-wrongs reasoning by analogy is a specific form of two-wrongs reasoning that justifies an action normally considered wrong by pointing out that it is analogous to other actions that have been permitted. A good two-wrongs by analogy argument establishes that (1) the wrong that is said to be permissible is analogous to other wrongs that have been permitted; (2) fairness in the form of consistency is more important than preventing the wrong in question; and (3) there is no morally preferable way to respond in the situation.

Counter-Arguments to Two-Wrongs Reasoning

Like arguments that conform to the other argument schemes we have considered, two-wrongs arguments have counterparts that attempt to show that some instance of two-wrongs reasoning is a weak argument. In this case, a good counter-argument will show that some (actual or potential) case of two-wrongs reasoning does not meet the criteria for good two-wrongs arguments embedded in our detailed argument schemes. In practice this means that such an argument will show that some potential wrong is *not* a response to another wrong that attempts to alleviate its unjust consequences, that it is less wrong than the wrong it tries to alleviate, or that there is or was some morally preferable way to handle the wrong in question.

A detailed discussion of counter-arguments to two-wrongs reasoning is beyond the present book, but we will note two ways in which many two-wrongs arguments fail to meet the conditions required for strong instances of this scheme.

1. **Two-wrongs reasoning only justifies 'wrongs' that are an attempt to alleviate other wrongs.** Imagine a student is found guilty of plagiarism on an essay. Suppose they argue, as students often do in such cases, 'I knew seven other people who were guilty of plagiarism.' This is an implicit appeal to the two-wrongs scheme. It maintains that this particular indiscretion is acceptable because others are guilty of the same indiscretion. But there is a fundamental problem with the reasoning, for the wrong that is said to be justified in these circumstances is *not* a response to other wrongs that it tries to minimize or rectify. This is clear, for if the situation really is as the student has suggested, he or she could easily rectify the problem by notifying the course instructor of the indiscretions of the other students. Their failure to do so suggests that their interest is not alleviating other wrongs but excusing a wrong of their own. In such a circumstance, their motivation is fundamentally at odds with the motivation that must lie behind a convincing two-wrongs argument.

One might reply that the student in question can claim that it is wrong that they, but not others, have not been punished for plagiarism, and that this is the wrong that they are trying to eliminate. But how would their marker know this was the case? The marker did not knowingly excuse other students who were clearly guilty of plagiarism, so they cannot, on grounds of consistency, be reasonably asked to do so in this case.

2. **Strong two-wrongs reasoning requires 'proportionality'.** The second and third conditions required for good two-wrongs reasoning imply a 'principle of proportionality' that plays an important role in moral, political, and legal reasoning. If someone commits a crime, society has the right to respond to this, but not in any way whatsoever. It does not, for example, give us the right to torture people or to give them extreme sentences (say, thirty years in jail for smoking in a non-smoking area). We can capture this point by saying that the wrongs that two-wrongs reasoning justifies must always be proportional to the original wrongs. You may legitimately respond to insults by telling someone to leave your office. But not by pulling a revolver from your desk and shooting them. In the latter case, you have violated the principle of proportionality.

COUNTER-ARGUMENTS TO TWO-WRONGS REASONING

A strong counter-argument to two-wrongs reasoning shows that the conditions for good two-wrongs reasoning are not met, or cannot be met, in some instance of (actual or potential) two-wrongs reasoning.

EXERCISE 13D

1. In each of the following scenarios, explain whether the two-wrongs reasoning is legitimate or not. Give reasons for your decisions.

    a)* In response to a law that restricts the immigration of South Americans, forcing many to be sent home to face possible torture and death, citizens hide in their homes people whom they believe to be genuine refugees. They argue that the law is morally wrong.

    b) An elderly man kills his wife of 58 years. She is terminally ill and dying slowly in great pain. He defends himself by arguing that his was an act of euthanasia, and that his wife's suffering was a greater wrong that his action terminated.

    c) *In vitro* fertilization involves the surgical removal of an egg from a woman's ovary, fertilizing it by mixing it with semen in a dish, and then transferring this back to the uterus once it has started to divide. By means of drugs, 'superovulation' can produce several eggs in the same cycle. These can be collected in one surgical operation and then fertilized. Then, one or more of the embryos can be introduced into the uterus while the rest are frozen, either to be introduced into a uterus at a later date or to be used in research. Usually, embryos used in research would then be destroyed. The question arises about the morality of this last activity: producing human embryos for research with no intention of allowing them to develop. But if such research produces a cure for, say, cystic fibrosis—through the discovery of the defective gene, which can then be treated or replaced—then the initial moral wrong of using embryos in research would be justified.

2. Imagine that you wish to be exempted from a final exam in some course you are taking. You know that in the past students have sometimes been exempted due to serious medical conditions. Explain why a two-wrongs-by-analogy argument could or could not be used to defend the claim that you should be exempted for the following reasons:

    a)* Your father is very ill.

    b) You have just gone through an acrimonious divorce.

    c) You panic in test situations.

    d) You have to attend a funeral.

    e) You have been recovering from an accident for the last year.

Major Exercise 13M

1. In support of the claim 'Public ownership of assault rifles should be prohibited' construct a short argument using each of the following schemes:
   a) slippery slope
   b) argument from analogy
   c) appeal to precedent.

2. Use the same argument schemes in support of the opposite claim, 'Public ownership of assault rifles should be allowed'.

3. Construct arguments on the issue of euthanasia using an argument from analogy.

4. A current topic of discussion is the extent to which Western banks and nations should help developing countries by forgiving the huge debt these countries have accumulated. Take each form of reasoning we have discussed and outline how you could use it in your deliberation on the issue. Write a 'Letter to the Editor' using the argument scheme you regard as best suited to justify your position.

5. Construct an argument scrapbook by collecting from magazines and newspapers five examples of the argument schemes we have introduced. In each case, explain whether it is a good or bad argument. If it is a bad argument, explain how it could be strengthened or corrected.

6. Decide whether each of the following passages contains an argument. If it does, assess the reasoning. Using any of the argument forms dealt with in this chapter explain whether the argument fulfills the conditions for good arguments of that form. Note that examples may involve more than one argument form, and that you may need to use the concepts we have introduced in earlier chapters to explain the examples.
   a) [from '10 Songs We Hope We'll Never Hear Again', *Rolling Stone* 912/913 (2003), p. 110] Tom Petty, 'The Last DJ'. Petty's tunes have always been pretty solid, so fans have forgiven his flavorless voice and slightly creepy looks. But he's a hopeless curmudgeon here—that jaded uncle you avoid at family gatherings.
   b) [Arthur Shafer, in 'Top Judges Got it Wrong in this Case' *Toronto Star* (19 Jan 2001). Schafer is commenting on the Robert Latimer case, in which a Saskatchewan man was convicted of murder for killing his 12-year-old daughter to end her suffering from a severe form of cerebral palsy.] Interestingly, however, in the half-dozen or so mercy killing cases in recent Canadian history, some involving doctors who hastened the death of their painfully dying patients with a fatal dose of potassium chloride, not one person served even a single day in prison. Charges have been dropped, or a guilty plea accepted to a lesser charge.
   c) [from *Maclean's* (21 Nov. 1983)] I take exception to Bruce Colebank's letter castigating the United States for dropping two atomic bombs on Japan to shorten the Second World War (Balancing terror, Letters, Oct. 3). As a veteran, let me advise Colebank that both Germany and Japan were endeavouring to build atomic bombs at that time, and only last month a Japanese scientist confessed

that he was working on such a weapon and that Japan would certainly have used it if they had completed theirs first.

d) [Patrick Clawson, in 'Sanctions as Punishment, Enforcement, and Prelude to Further Action', *Ethics & International Affairs* 7 (1993), p. 29. Clawson is asking whether economic sanctions that result in suffering for those affected are justifiable. In the following excerpt he considers sanctions imposed on Iraq after the 1991 Gulf War.] Sanctions by themselves have reduced the living standards of Iraqis by at least one-third. And there is no escaping the fact that despite the humanitarian character of US intentions, those who have suffered most have been ordinary Iraqi civilians, not the Iraqi elite nor the military.

How morally justifiable is this suffering? There is no moral obligation on the part of the world community to permit Iraqis to enjoy a high level of creature comforts so long as the government . . . is ignoring obligations to the community of nations (refusing to destroy weapons of mass destruction and to respect the basic human rights of Kurds and Shiites as required . . . by the Security Council). After all, the Iraqi economy has stabilized at a standard of living not only sufficient to sustain human life but probably as good as the median for all people on the globe.

e) The economist Milton Friedman says the following in his book: 'The individual addict would clearly be far better off if drugs were legal. Today, drugs are both extremely expensive and highly uncertain in quality. Addicts are driven to associate with criminals to get the drugs, and they become criminals themselves to finance the habit. They risk constant danger of death and disease.'

Friedman goes on to say that it is estimated that from one-third to one-half of all violent and property crime in the United States is 'committed either by drug addicts engaged in crime to finance their habit, or by conflicts among competing groups of drug pushers, or in the course of the importation and distribution of illegal drugs. Legalize drugs, and street crime would drop dramatically and immediately.'

In the best of all worlds, we wouldn't legalize drugs, but in this one we should.

f) [This cartoon is a response to the Gary Larson letter quoted in Exercise 13B, 3c (p. 341).]

g) [Kathleen Gow, in *Yes Virginia, There is Right and Wrong* (John Wiley and Sons, 1980), p. 92. In an article discussing various pedagogical techniques, Kathleen Gow questions the use of exercises that put students in imaginary situations where they have to make difficult moral decisions (such as the life raft example).] Children may become so confused by all the qualifications and situational dilemma exercises—many of which are extreme and very far removed from everyday life—that they will decide that the world is totally without moral or social order. As one grade seven student asked, 'Isn't there anything you can count on?'

When we are caring for babies, we do not give them a whole apple to eat. We know that their digestive systems are not sufficiently sophisticated to process the skin, the flesh, and the core. The risk that they will choke is very high. So instead of the whole apple, we give them applesauce—the essence of the apple. This does not mean that we are cheating them of their independence.

h) [Janet George, in 'Saboteurs—the Real Animals', *Manchester Guardian Weekly* (28 Feb.1993), p. 24] People who believe that killing animals for sport is wrong might assume that banning field sports would solve the problem. They are wrong. Hunting is merely the first in a long list of targets . . .

Already, butchers' shop windows are frequent targets for damage, and incendiary devices have been used against department stores selling furs and leather goods. If another private member's bill is introduced successfully, and hunting is banned, animal rights extremists will see it as a vindication of their methods.

i)* [John Searle, in *Minds, Brains and Science* (Harvard University Press, 1984), pp. 37–8] Why would anybody ever have thought that computers could think or have feelings and emotions and all the rest of it? After all, we can do computer simulations of any process whatever that can be given a formal description. So, we can do a computer simulation of . . . the pattern of power distribution in the Labour party. We can do computer simulation of rain storms . . . or warehouse fires . . . Now, in each of these cases, nobody supposes that the computer simulation is actually the real thing; no one supposes that a computer simulation of a storm will leave us all wet . . . Why on earth would anyone in his right mind suppose a computer simulation of mental processes actually had mental processes?

j)* [adapted from a letter to the *Toronto Star*] If pro-choice doctors are allowed to go ahead and open abortion clinics under the banner of women's right to abortion on demand, then members of organized crime should be allowed to open gaming casinos because people have the right to gamble, and producers of pornographic movies to open theatres because people have the right to view what they wish. If pro-abortion groups can do it, so can other groups.

k) [a Low cartoon published in the context of debates over the way Germany should be treated after World War I (reprinted by permission of Atlantic Syndication)]

'PERHAPS IT WOULD GEE-UP BETTER IF WE LET IT TOUCH EARTH.'

l) [St John of Chrysostom, in the *Post-Nicene Fathers* vol. 9, p. 442] To laugh, to speak jocosely, does not seem an acknowledged sin, but it leads to acknowledged sin. Thus laughter often gives birth to foul discourse, and foul discourse to actions still more foul. Often from words and laughter proceed railing and insult; and from railing and insult, blows and wounds; and from blows and wounds, slaughter and murder. If, then, thou wouldst take good counsel for thyself, avoid not merely foul words, and foul deeds, or blows, and wounds, and murders, but unseasonable laughter itself.

m)* [Vincent E. Barry, in *The Critical Edge* (Harcourt Brace Jovanovich, 1992). Barry is making an editorial comment on the colourization of classic black-and-white films, such as *Casablanca* and *Citizen Kane*.] Let this sort of thing go on, and somebody will want to put a mustache on the *Mona Lisa*.

n) Smokers are the most persecuted group on earth. First all the non-smokers decided that we should be segregated to separate parts of restaurants. Then they passed by-laws preventing us from smoking in most public places. Next they'll be storming our houses to arrest us for smoking in the privacy of our home, since even there 'we don't own the air.' This is a bad model for how to set social policy. Once a state begins over-regulating its citizens, the door is opened to any number of infringements on personal liberty and freedom of expression.

o) [Francis Bacon, from *Francis Bacon: A Selection of his Works* (Toronto, 1965), p. 17] There are seven windows given to animals in the domicile of the head, through which the air is admitted to the tabernacle of the body, to enlighten, to warm and to nourish it. What are these parts of the microcosmos: Two nostrils, two eyes, two ears and a mouth. So in the heavens, as in a macrocosmos, there are two favourable stars, two unpropitious, two luminaries, and Mercury unde-cided and indifferent. From this and from many other similarities in nature, such as the seven metals, etc., which it were tedious to enumerate, we gather that the number of planets is necessarily seven.

p) [Gordon Campbell, premier of British Columbia, quoted in the North Bay *Nugget* (13 Jan. 2003), explaining why he wouldn't resign after being charged with drunk driving during a holiday in Maui, even though he had demanded that other politicians who broke conflict of interest laws resign] This took place on my personal vacation. As you know there have been people in the past who have been found to have a conflict of interest that is directly related to their place in office.

q) [from a letter sent out by IIFAR — Incurably Ill For Animal Research (Mar. 1988)] . . . what it all boils down to, after you eliminate all the hype, is that medical research is being conducted to alleviate human suffering, and testing on animals prior to testing on humans is essential. As long as society believes it is okay to kill cows for food, exterminate mice and rats that infect our homes, and kill more than 10 million cats and dogs each year in public pounds because they are nui-sances, it surely must be okay to use animals to find cures for unfortunate human beings who suffer from incurable illnesses.

r) [Gary E. Jones, in 'On the Permissibility of Torture', *Journal of Medical Ethics* 6 (1980), p. 12] Consider, for example, solar energy. It presently suffers from the same poor cost–benefit ratio as the use of torture allegedly does. However, the promise of future benefits from the use of solar energy, along with the assumption that the cost-benefit ratio will improve, are sufficient grounds for many to con-clude that its use should be promoted. Analogously, it could be argued that tech-nical improvements in the methods used to extract information in as humane a way as possible will improve the cost-benefit ratio of the use of torture.

s) [from *World Press Review* (Feb. 2003), p. 18] But there are dangers to China's explosive growth. If the government neglects the growing gap between rich and poor, or the displacement of its massive rural population . . . serious social unrest will ensue. And if China's 1.2 billion people get a taste for SUVs, air condition-ing, and other trappings of its affluent neighbors in the West, the environmental costs alone will be staggering.

Slow steady, patient, controlled: The Chinese government must keep a leash on its economy to avoid self-implosion. If done well, the new century will belong to the dragon. Too much, too fast, too open, and we're all in trouble.

t) [from a letter to the *Globe and Mail* (18 Mar. 2000)] The Ontario government has announced that its funding of universities will be partly tied to graduation rates of their students ('Performance Anxiety Takes On New Meaning', 15 March). This decision will put subtle pressure on university teachers to give stu-dents passing grades to help the university's funding. Over time, it is likely to erode quality. Graduation rates only make sense as an indicator of performance if graduation depends on external examinations completely independent of the institution that prepared the student for graduation.

14

ETHOTIC

SCHEMES:

JUDGING CHARACTER

The last two chapters discussed empirical and moral schemes of arguments. In this chapter we discuss 'ethotic' schemes that, in one way or another, base conclusions on premises about the people who stand behind arguments: those who argue, provide support for premises through their character or expertise, or adjudicate reasoning. The schemes discussed include

- *pro homine*;
- *ad populum* arguments;
- *ad hominem* reasoning;
- appeals to authority; and
- guilt by association.

In Aristotle's *Rhetoric*, one of the most famous books written in the history of argumentation theory, the perceived character of an arguer—his or her *ethos*—is said to play an important role in determining an audience's attitude to an argument. As Aristotle puts it, we are more likely to accept arguments and conclusions offered by people of whom we think highly.

Sometimes the influence of ethos is subtle and implicit. Aristotle's credibility may make us more ready to accept what he says, while disdain for someone we know may make it difficult for us to take their claims and arguments seriously. Sometimes it is important to recognize these implicit aspects of argument and address them. In these circumstances, *ethotic* arguments explicitly address the character of an arguer, using judgments about their *ethos* as a basis for the conclusion that we should treat their claims and arguments in a particular way (that we should accept them, be cautious of them, pay attention to them, reject them outright, and so on). The present chapter provides an introductory account of different kinds of ethotic argument.

Ethotic considerations often play an important role in reasoning. They can arise in circumstances in which we do not have the time, the means, or the ability to investigate a question in sufficient detail to decide the proper answer to it. In circumstances of this sort we may have to accept or reject particular views by considering whether they are offered and defended by individuals or groups we trust or do not trust, or by arguers we do or do not deem competent to address the issue at hand. Such arguments are called '*pro homine*' ('for the person') and '*ad hominem*' ('against the person'), because they defend or attack a claim or point of view by defending or attacking its proponent. As we shall see, there are different kinds of *pro homine* and *ad hominem* reasoning that can usefully be distinguished when we deal with ordinary argument.

1. PRO HOMINE

In 1987, Congressional hearings investigated allegations that the US administration acted improperly and illegally by selling arms to Iran and diverting the money from the sales to rebels trying to overthrow the Sandinista government in Nicaragua. One of the witnesses who testified at the hearings, Lieutenant Colonel Oliver North, became a special focus for media attention. His appearance in Marine uniform, his distinguished military record, and his patriotic fervour captured the imagination of many Americans.

One *New York Times* columnist described North's appeal as the attraction of an 'underdog, true believer, one man against the crowd: there was a lot of Gary Cooper in him, the lonesome cowboy, a lot of Jimmy Stewart, too, the honest man facing down the politicians, and quite a bit of Huck Finn' (6 July 1987). Given that North admitted that he lied to Congress and the public, such a description is ironic and underscores the extent to which a person's 'image' in the media can influence our perceptions of an individual.

Much of the public accepted what North said as true because they were impressed by him as a man. In the process, they relied on *pro homine* reasoning. We engage in such reasoning whenever we defend or accept a conclusion because it is propounded by someone whom we trust to have the correct opinion. Often, *pro homine* arguments have the form 'X believes y, so I accept it too', but a strong *pro homine* must (implicitly or explicitly) be an instance of the following scheme:

> PREMISE 1: X says that y.
> PREMISE 2: X is knowledgeable, trustworthy, and free of bias.
> CONCLUSION: y should be accepted.

In proposing *pro homine* reasoning we take our past experience of certain individuals as intelligent and honest as good grounds for accepting their opinions now and in the future. We rely on *pro homine* reasoning in many informal circumstances, such as trusting an individual's recommendation of restaurants, listening to the commentaries of the sports we watch, or receiving an edifying account of political developments in a particular country.

In deciding whether an argument is a strong or weak *pro homine* we need to consider whether the person whose opinion is appealed to is knowledgeable, trustworthy, and free of bias. This must be judged in different ways in different circumstances, though one consideration that can usually be brought to bear is the quality of a person's reasoning. If the arguer is someone who has in the past demonstrated that they do or do not have a grasp of the difference between weak and strong arguments (say, the difference between reliable and unreliable *pro homine* arguments), then this is evidence to consider when they provide further *pro homine* reasoning. To this extent, the principles this book is trying to teach you are assumed in the judgments that distinguish between good and bad *pro homine* arguments.

What, then, can we make of the *pro homine* appeal to Colonel North that we began with? Although we concede that he was a knowledgeable person, there are some problems with a *pro homine* appeal to his testimony, for one might dispute the claim that he is trustworthy or free of bias. Indeed, it is arguable that patriotism (or any other overriding motive) and obedience to authority—the factors that make North attractive to some—may have blinded him to propriety and made him an untrustworthy judge of what was right and wrong in the circumstances he was involved in. Even more problematic is the question of his bias, for he was himself accused of wrongdoing, a situation that makes it difficult for him to be objective and more difficult for us to know whether his claims are motivated by vested interest or a sincere desire to tell the truth.

Above and beyond the specific problems with a *pro homine* in North's case, there are more general concerns that suggest that we should be cautious in accepting or making any *pro homine* argument. At times, it is reasonable to accept the opinions of individuals we respect in one way or another, but it would be a mistake to slip into an uncritical acceptance of their views. Ultimately, an in-depth investigation of a position cannot be replaced by an appeal to the person who defends it. That said, an appropriate appeal to a person does count as evidence for a position.

PRO HOMINE REASONING

Pro homine reasoning argues for a claim by showing that it is held by some person X. A good *pro homine* argument maintains that it should be accepted because X is

(1) knowledgeable,
(2) trustworthy, and
(3) free of bias.

EXERCISE 14A

Describe a context in which you could make a strong *pro homine* argument for a conclusion about each of the following:
   a)   eating in a particular restaurant
   b)* subscribing to a particular magazine
   c)   believing what an acquaintance says
   d)   reading a particular book
   e)   going on a particular holiday

2. AD POPULUM ARGUMENTS

Ad populum arguments, also called 'appeals to popularity', attempt to establish some conclusion on the basis of its popular appeal. They are an instance of *pro homine* because they justify conclusions by noting that particular people—i.e. most people (or most people in a group)—subscribe to them.

Many appeals to popularity are poor arguments, though even poor instances may be effective, especially when they exploit a strong desire to belong to a group. The following are examples of *ad populum* arguments:

- *25 million people own a Maytag washer. Maybe they know something you don't.*
- **Ruffles**: *America's best-selling chip.*
- *Everyone who's anyone will be there.*
- *Tonight, a special episode of Comedy TV that everyone will be talking about.*

In each of these cases the claim that something is popular among some group is used as a basis for a hidden conclusion (that one should own a Maytag, eat Ruffles, 'be there', or watch the special episode).

Appeals to popularity are problematic because popularity is not a good gauge of what is acceptable or unacceptable, true or false, or right or wrong. Indeed, popular opinion is frequently influenced by prejudice, superstition, outdated theories, and ill-considered judgments. In Columbus's time, the popular view of the world (at least in Europe) was that it was flat. Columbus, like other significant figures in the history of thought, was able to advance our knowledge of the world by refusing to be tied to popular opinions and independently developing his own view.

In a world where we had the time and ability to investigate every issue we had to resolve, such considerations might lead us to reject all *ad populum* arguments. Certainly, appeals to popularity have no significant role to play in scientific investigation or in other attempts to carefully investigate what is true and false. But there are two contexts in which appeal to popular opinion can be reasonable. We have already discussed the first context, for it occurs when we are preparing arguments for a popular audience and need to use its beliefs as premises in our argument. In keeping with our general account of *pro homine*, the second context occurs when we can reasonably proceed on the assumption that popular opinion is knowledgeable, trustworthy, and free of bias.

In such contexts, an *ad populum* argument is an instance of *pro homine* that can be schematized as follows:

PREMISE 1: It is popularly held that y.
PREMISE 2: This is a context in which popular opinion is knowledgeable, trustworthy, and free of bias.
CONCLUSION: y should be accepted.

There are many contexts in which this kind of argument will be weak because premise 2 is not acceptable. But there are also contexts in which this scheme justifies a provisional conclusion. Suppose, for example, that we are in a hardware store buying a handsaw we will use in fixing something for our children. In such a circumstance, we may not have any significant experience with different handsaws and may not have the time to investigate and study the different saws available. In such circumstances, we might reasonably purchase a particular saw because the dealer tells us that 'This is the most popular saw we sell.' In doing so, we accept this as a premise for the conclusion that 'This is the saw I will buy.' In the process we accept an *ad populum* argument.

In reasoning in this way we are accepting, as a hidden premise, the claim that popular opinion about handsaws is knowledgeable, trustworthy, and free of bias. Thus, we assume that the saw in question is the best-selling handsaw because buyers have found it to be a good saw. The group of buyers who have purchased it are in this sense knowledgeable, trustworthy, and free of bias. A critical thinker will recognize that this is not a certain claim. It is always possible that the saw is popular for another reason, say, because the company that produces it has such compelling advertisements, or because it is among the less expensive handsaws. If we were determined to decide which was the best handsaw—because we were comparing handsaws for a consumer magazine, for example—we would eliminate this possibility by testing the saws and not relying on an appeal to popularity. But in a context in which we have limited time at our disposal and want to quickly resolve an issue, it is reasonable to rely on an *ad populum*. In a similar way, the fact that Shakespeare's plays are so popular provides some evidence for their broad appeal, and may be a strong reason for someone to decide to read them.

Because *ad populum* arguments are relatively weak arguments, it is important that you think carefully about particular instances of them. Ask yourself whether this really is a circumstance in which popular opinion is knowledgeable, trustworthy, and free of bias, or at least a circumstance in which there are good practical reasons to rely on this assumption (perhaps because this is the best judge of something that is available in the circumstances).

EXERCISE 14B

For each of the contexts given in Exercise 14A discuss circumstances in which it would and would not be acceptable to use *ad populum* arguments.

3. ARGUMENTS FROM AUTHORITY

Though simple *pro homine* and *ad populum* arguments can be adequate support for a conclusion, they are relatively weak argument schemes. Some of the issues that they raise may be alleviated in 'arguments from authority', a form of *pro homine* argument that recommends a claim on the grounds that it is held by someone who is an authority and is in this more stringent sense knowledgeable about the issues the argument addresses.

As we write this chapter, the United States administration is preparing for war against Iraq. Within the United States and in other nations this has sparked a great deal of debate. Some of this debate concerns the feasibility of such a war from a military point of view. Is the United States likely to prevail in such a war? Might it turn into another Vietnam? Would potential losses to American forces be too great a cost to pay for an uncertain military victory? And even if military victory is achieved, would it ensure the kinds of changes to Iraq that the American government claims to seek (the establishment of an Iraqi democracy, for example)?

In such a context, consider the following remark by retired American general Anthony Zinni on attitudes to the potential conflict (reported in *Rolling Stone* 912/913, 2003, p. 90): 'All the generals see it the same way, and all the others who have never fired a shot and are hot to go to war see it another way.' This remark suggests the generals are not 'hot to go to war', and is a simple argument that can be diagrammed as follows:

P1 = All the generals think we should be cautious about going to war, while all the others who have never fired a shot and are hot to go to war see it another way.

HP2 = We should listen to the generals rather than those who have never fired a shot.

C = We should be cautious about going to war with Iraq.

This is an example of an argument from authority (it also incorporates an *ad hominem* argument, an argument scheme we discuss below). Like other instances of arguments from authority, it is an instance of the basic scheme

PREMISE: X is an authority (expert) who believes and states y.
CONCLUSION: y should be accepted.

In this case, the authorities appealed to are American generals. The claim that is supported by their views is the claim that 'We should be cautious about going to war with Iraq.'

In dealing with arguments from authority, it is important to distinguish 'argument from authority' from arguments *given by* an authority. The latter may not be appeals to authority but other kinds of arguments that back the authority's point of view. In contrast to this, an argument from authority is an appeal to an authority's claim that uses their expertise (rather than their arguments) as a basis for the conclusion that their views should be accepted.

It is arguable that we adopt the majority of our beliefs because we accept the views of authorities who recommend them. We see this in practical affairs, where we depend on doctors, plumbers, electricians, and appliance and automobile mechanics as authorities with special competencies. To a very significant extent, education depends on students accepting the authority and the views of their instructors. Corporations hire consultants. In such cases, we depend on others' views, and it is difficult to see how we could get by without them.

Nonetheless, we must balance our reliance on arguments from authority and general *pro homine* arguments by consistently questioning such appeals. We should keep in mind that the very best appeal to an authority is a secondary way of establishing a conclusion. The suggestion that we accept someone's claim is predicated on the assumption that the person has good reasons for it, and these reasons, rather than the person's authority, ultimately determine the plausibility of their claims. A *pro homine* appeal is simply a promissory note assuring us that the experts—or, in the simple case, 'people with good sense'—have good reasons for their views.

Another problem inherent in some appeals to authorities arises when we are presented with expert opinions that conflict, and we must ask whose judgment we can trust. We all know that there are good and bad doctors, lawyers, plumbers, electricians, and professors, but it can be difficult to sort out the competent from the incompetent. If we know virtually nothing about an issue, we may have little basis for judging who is genuinely knowledgeable and who is not. We can circumvent this problem by appealing to well-established experts and paying particular attention to their views, but even these appeals can be problematic. We tend to think of science as the place where authority is most easily established, but science is characterized by great differences of opinion. Recent philosophers (among them, Thomas Kuhn and Paul Feyerabend) have argued that science suppresses views that go against accepted paradigms, even when they are logically persuasive.

The problem of disagreement among authorities is magnified when we move outside the field of science. The ancient skeptics argued that discrepancies between different people and different authorities show that truth cannot be found. We still face that problem. The views of Kuhn and Feyerabend conflict with those of other scientific authorities who have a more positive view of science and the scientific method. Numerous issues of immense significance to us, such as the best means for preventing nuclear war or motifs for understanding the human psyche, are characterized by disagreement and debate among respected authorities.

We do not raise such problems to dissuade you from using arguments from authority but to alert you to their inherent weaknesses. These problems underscore the importance of constructing and assessing arguments from authority in a way that recognizes their provisional nature and ensures that they are free from common errors. Remember that the basis of any argument from authority is the claim that we should accept someone's views because they have special expertise that makes their claims persuasive. Their expertise is proven by their 'credentials', which are usually educational or professional qualifications.

There are five conditions that must be satisfied, implicitly or explicitly, by a good argument from authority. They can be summarized as follows:

1. A strong argument from authority must identify the authority appealed to and state their credentials.

Anonymous experts lend little weight to a claim, and an audience has no reason to accept the views of the authority if you fail to state the credentials that make them an authority whose opinion should be well regarded.

Often, what is required is relatively straightforward. If you want to establish some basic fact about chemical properties, then it makes sense to use someone with a degree in chemistry as your authority. Perhaps it will be necessary to appeal to someone who specializes in a particular branch of chemistry. On other occasions, specifying credentials may be more complicated. If you are appealing to a panel that has been appointed to investigate a public scandal, you will not be able to say that they have degrees in 'public scandal investigation'. You would have to appeal to the general intelligence, character, and specific knowledge of the members of the panel.

2. A strong argument from authority relies on an authority with credentials that are relevant to the issue discussed.

Many appeals to authority overlook the requirement that strong appeals to authority require relevant specialized knowledge on the part of the authority cited. An advertisement for the diet supplement Xenadrine EFX, which appears in *Alive* (Oct. 2002), features a photo of Hunter Tylo beside the description, 'Actress, Super Model and star of *The Bold and the Beautiful* and *Beverly Hills 90210*.' She is quoted remarking that 'This Stuff Really Works Wonders!' Like most advertisements that display movie stars, athletes, or other celebrities endorsing products, this is a bad argument from authority. For though these experts have established their expertise in some field—acting, sports, etc.—they are usually ill-qualified to judge whether a certain car is more dependable than another, or whether one cereal is more nutritious than the next. If we really want to know whether Xenadrine EFX 'works wonders', we should ask not Hunter Tylo but someone with a doctorate in nutrition who has studied this particular drug.

3. A strong argument from authority appeals to authorities who are not biased.

The most obvious kind of bias arises when individuals have a vested interest, when they stand to gain from expressing some view or making some claim. This is, of course, a further problem with the kinds of endorsements found in advertisements. It is also evident in appeals to the authority of individuals who are in some substantial way committed to one side of a debate, and in this way have a vested interest in it. A good argument could not, for example, cite the authority of scientists employed by the nuclear industry in a debate over the question of whether, say, a nuclear power plant or food irradiation is safe. Such individuals may reasonably argue for a particular view of such an issue, and their arguments may be convincing, but we must use their arguments rather than their authority to defend their conclusions. An appeal to an authority with a vested interest to protect or promote does not carry the same weight as the views of independent authorities and researchers.

4. A strong argument from authority is possible only when there is wide agreement among the relevant experts.

The failure of members of an investigative panel to come to an agreement lessens the extent to which we can appeal to them to decide an issue. A selective appeal to an authority who takes a stand with which other authorities disagree is usually inappropriate. We may say, 'My claim is supported by X, but I must confess that no one else in the field agrees with her on this'; however, such a claim will provide minimal evidence for our view. It would have to be combined with other considerations if it were to be the basis of a convincing argument. This does not mean that lack of agreement is a clear sign that a claim is false. Revolutionary thinkers like Galileo and Darwin, whose claims eventually gained widespread acceptance, stood alone against other contemporary experts. But in such a case it must be an argument scheme other than argument from authority that is used to establish that a claim should be accepted.

5. A strong argument from authority must appeal to an authority who belongs to an area of knowledge where a consensus among authorities is in principle possible because there are universally accepted criteria for making judgments in that field.

In judging and constructing arguments from authority, remember that some topics do not lend themselves to appeals to authority because they refer to fields in which authority is not possible or yet available. Many new areas of inquiry are characterized this way, and some people would hold that this is also the case with disputed fields, like those in parapsychology. Are there, for example, authorities on ghosts? Other people insist that matters of taste are subjective, and that it is not, therefore, possible for authorities to reach a consensus on what constitutes good or bad music, or art, or cuisine. Generally, in appealing to authorities, you must be prepared to argue that the issue at hand is one in which broad agreement is possible because it relates to an appropriate field in which it makes sense to speak of 'authorities'.

Given these conditions, a fully developed strong appeal to authority will be an instance of the following scheme:

> PREMISE 1: X is an authority with credentials c, who believes and states y.
> PREMISE 2: Credentials c are relevant to y.
> PREMISE 3: X is not biased.
> PREMISE 4: There is wide agreement among the relevant experts over y.
> PREMISE 5: y is an appropriate field in which consensus is possible.
> CONCLUSION: y should be accepted.

Many of these premises will be hidden in an ordinary argument. Our earlier example, which argued for the conclusion that we should be cautious about a war with Iraq, is a good illustration of this. Its explicit premise—that 'All the generals see it the same way, and all the others who have never fired a shot and are hot to go to war see it another way'—combines premise 1 and premise 4 in our scheme. The other conditions for good appeals to authority can be assumed. Even though the generals have not been identified, as we would like, their credentials are relevant to y (premise 2), because there is no reason to believe that the generals are biased (premise 3), and because their claimed agreement shows that consensus is possible (premise 5). Assuming that the generals do agree, it follows that this is a good argument from authority.

The kinds of concerns that must be taken into account when we judge authorities have a significant role to play in our interactions with the World Wide Web. It has been a boon to arguers insofar as it has made a remarkable amount of information readily available. At the same time, it is a means of communication that does not clearly separate authoritative and non-authoritative views. Websites may be characterized by a lack of attention to detail, a failure to properly consider opposing points of view, and ill-considered argument. The sources available in a university library have probably been acquired because someone who is an authority (a librarian or a faculty member) has decided that they were significant enough to be included. They have probably been influenced by other experts who write reviews and make recommendations. In contrast, no critical evaluation need inform a site on the Web, which may be constructed in a way that inadvertently or intentionally propagates misinformation.

In dealing with websites it is useful to apply the criteria we have developed in our account of arguments from authority. Remember that any website, whether or not it has been developed by a recognized authority, may have arguments worth considering. But one cannot quote and depend on such sites in the way that we quote and depend on authorities unless these sites satisfy the conditions for good appeals to authority. This means that if you wish to use a website's endorsement of some claim as evidence for a conclusion, the endorsement must be presented in a way that allows you to identify the author and his or her credentials, and to eliminate the possibility of bias and vested interest (which may be evident when you investigate who sponsors a website). The relevance of the author's credentials, the agreement of other experts, and the appropriateness of the field must also be clear if one is to construct a strong argument from authority in such a case. One way to test some of these conditions is by checking other sites on the same topic.

In the final analysis, arguments from authority, like other *pro homine* arguments, are implicit generalizations. An appeal to the claim that certain persons are trustworthy or have certain credentials is a way of saying that they are knowledgeable and have shown good judgment, or that they have acquired the appropriate education or certification and have demonstrated the requisite skills on past occasions. On the basis of this evidence we infer that they deserve our trust and can exercise those skills in the case in question.

ARGUMENTS FROM AUTHORITY

Arguments from authority provide evidence for a claim by establishing that it is endorsed by authorities. A good argument from authority supports a claim on the basis that the person or group that endorses it is deemed to have (1) certain stated credentials, which are (2) relevant to the claim in question, and (3) no biases that are likely to interfere with their assessment of the claim, provided that (4) the claim in question concerns an area in which there is wide agreement among the relevant experts, and that (5) the claim concerns an area of knowledge in which consensus is possible.

EXERCISE 14C

1. Find three instances of argument from authority in a magazine. Diagram them. Are they strong or weak arguments from authority?

2. Find one website that can be used in a strong argument from authority, and one that cannot. Explain why in each case.

4. AD HOMINEM

Ad hominem arguments are counter-arguments to *pro homine* reasoning. An *ad hominem* gives us reasons for not taking someone's position seriously or for dismissing it altogether. A good *ad hominem* bases this claim on premises that show that someone is in some way unreliable. The version of *ad hominem* we call an 'argument *against* authority' argues that a person is not a reliable authority and should not, therefore, be taken seriously.

The general scheme for a good *ad hominem* argument is the reverse of the scheme for a good *pro homine,* and can be represented as follows:

PREMISE 1: X says y.
PREMISE 2: X is unreliable (i.e. not knowledgeable, trustworthy, and/or free of bias).
CONCLUSION: y should not be accepted (on the grounds that X says y).

The essence of an *ad hominem* is an attack against the credibility of a particular individual. We use *ad hominem* for the same reason we employ *pro homine*: it is impossible to investigate every claim we come across. If we hear, for example, that a professor whose work we are familiar with has just published another book on social psychology and decide not to read it because we have read her other six hefty tomes and found reading them a waste of time, we are employing a reasonable *ad hominem*, for we have evidence that she is not knowledgeable.

Good *ad hominem* arguments usually appear in contexts where an appeal to a *pro homine* has occurred or might occur. Consider an advertisement that the Rolling Stones placed in British music publications when the record label Decca released an album called *Stone Age* without the Stones' permission. (The album contained eight songs recorded on other albums and four new releases—see Tony Sanchez, *Up and Down with the Rolling Stones*, p. 214.) The advertisement, paid for by Mick Jagger and signed by all members of the band, read as follows:

> **Beware! Message from the Rolling Stones Re: Stone Age. We didn't know this record was going to be released. It is, in our opinion, below the standard we try to keep up, both in choice of content and cover design.**

This is an interesting argument, for in it the members of the Stones make a *pro homine* appeal to themselves, suggesting that the reader should accept their own judgment that the record in question is of substandard quality.

We can assess this *pro homine* in the way that we assess any other *pro homine*. In this case, it is clear that the Stones made the claim in question, so we must ask whether they are knowledgeable, trustworthy, and free of bias, and in this way individuals whose opinions should be accepted. Though we must accept that they know their own music, and this might seem to make the argument a strong one, this is a case in which one might reasonably question the Stones' status as reliable commentators. Their claim that the music in question is below their normal standard raises, to begin with, the question whether their judgment can be trusted, for the majority of the songs on the record were released on those records that are claimed to be superior. Putting aside the questions that this raises, the most serious problem is one of bias, for the advertisement in question was produced at a time when the Stones had left Decca and established their own competing record company. To that extent they were angered at the release of their songs by a competing record label. But this suggests that they were motivated by their own vested interests, making this a case where a *pro homine* appeal is unreliable.

In producing this criticism of the Stones' advertisement, we have been constructing an *ad hominem* argument that illustrates the logic of such reasoning. That is, we have dismissed the conclusion advanced because we judge the arguer unreliable in the ways we have indicated. There may be other good reasons that could support the Stones' conclusion, but our point is that their say-so is not a good reason to accept it.

In constructing *ad hominem* arguments of this sort, remember that the *ad hominem*, like the *pro homine*, is always a second-best reason for rejecting a particular position. It, too, is only a promissory note we use to conclude that someone's endorsement of a position does not provide evidence for its truth. This is not equivalent to saying that the position is mistaken. Perhaps *Stone Age* was an inferior album. Our *ad hominem* only showed that the remarks of members of the band do not show that this is so. The ultimate determinant of the correctness or incorrectness of a claim must always be found in the reasoning that supports it. This does not mean that we should dispense with all *ad hominem* reasoning, but only that we must keep in mind the provisional nature of *ad hominem* conclusions.

It is important to distinguish *ad hominem* attacks that discredit a person's position because of their character from attacks on the person alone. The latter is often called an *abusive ad hominem* because it does little more than hurl abuse. An example of this occurs in a letter the actor Richard Harris wrote to the British *Sunday Times* (8 June 1995) in response to a feature interview they had conducted with actor Michael Caine. The article discussed Caine's acting career as well as his successes as a businessman and art collector, and it applauded his return to England from a self-imposed exile in Hollywood. In several direct quotations, Caine numbered himself among the premier English actors of his generation (including Harris) and implied that he had out-achieved these men in several respects—as an actor, a television star, and a businessman. In responding, Harris wrote the following:

> Any suggestion that he [Caine] has eclipsed the names of Finney, O'Toole, Burton, Bates, Smith and Courtenay is tantamount to prophesying that Rin-Tin-Tin will be solemnised beyond the memory of Brando . . .
>
>   In truth, he is an over-fat, flatulent 62 year-old windbag, a master of inconsequence now masquerading as a guru, passing off his vast limitations as pious virtues.

These particular remarks are a study in abusive *ad hominem*. They are heavy with insult but don't successfully meet the challenge required by the criteria for a good *ad hominem*—i.e. the challenge to demonstrate that Caine is unknowledgeable, untrustworthy, or biased. Because insult has been substituted for substance, this *ad hominem* is very weak.

Buried in other aspects of Harris's remarks are some indications of more proper *ad hominem* reasoning. In other parts of his letter he argues, for example, that readers should dismiss what Caine is reported to have said about fellow actors because he has tried to achieve greatness by associating with great actors; that Caine is not in a position to criticize the low standard of British television because his own contributions to that medium are part of the problem; and that Caine should not pose as an expert on 'oenology and art' because he admits to buying things for their resale value and so recognizes only their price, not their worth. Each of these cases constitutes a sub-argument that needs to be evaluated. Though the strength of each might be debated, and though Harris's letter is not an example of a better *ad hominem* argument, these aspects of his argument are not abusive in the transparent way that is evident in the remarks provided above.

In your own dealings with *ad hominem* reasoning, be sure to distinguish what is abusive from what is substantial. As always, your goal should be to uncover a clear argument.

AD HOMINEM REASONING

Ad hominem reasoning can be considered the reverse of *pro homine* reasoning. A good *ad hominem* argument establishes that a person's views should not be given credence or should be rejected outright because the person is deemed to be

(1) not knowledgeable,
(2) untrustworthy, or
(3) biased.

EXERCISE 14D

1. For each of the topics listed in Exercise 14A above (p. 362), describe a context in which one could construct a good *ad hominem* argument. Give reasons for your answer.

2. Discuss and evaluate the *ad hominem* in the argument about Iraq above (i.e. 'All the generals see it the same way, and all the others who have never fired a shot and are hot to go to war see it another way').

5. ARGUMENTS AGAINST AUTHORITY

Just as an appeal to authority is a more specific form of the *pro homine*, so an argument against an authority is the more specific form of the *ad hominem*. Its general form is

> PREMISE 1: X is not an authority on y.
> CONCLUSION: X's advocating some claim about y does not provide support for it.

Arguments against authority are counter-arguments that cast doubt on the reliability of a proposed authority's views by showing that an appeal to their opinion fails to meet the criteria we have introduced for good arguments from authority. In view of this, a good argument *against* authority is one that rejects an alleged authority by establishing one of the following:

(1) that the authority's credentials are questionable;
(2) that the credentials cited are irrelevant to the issue in question;
(3) that the alleged authority is biased;
(4) that the topic under scrutiny is one where there is significant disagreement among the relevant experts; or
(5) that the topic is one where expertise cannot be claimed.

These requirements can be understood in light of the considerations we introduced in connection with appeals to authority. Because a failure to satisfy even one of the conditions for a good argument from authority makes such an argument weak, any such failure can be the basis of an argument against authority.

The strength of an argument against authority is a direct function of the extent to which the appeal criticized deviates from the criteria set out in our account of good appeals to authority. Since one of the criteria was widespread agreement among authorities, we can argue that the value of an authority's opinion is lost when the issue is one on which there is virtually no agreement among the experts. If someone does not have the credentials we would associate with authoritative standing in the mathematics field, this is a legitimate reason to take less seriously her views on such topics. And so on.

Our earlier criticism of commercial endorsements by celebrities as representing vested interests was an argument against authority. The following example involves an *ad hominem* and an appeal to authority. It arises in the context of a disagreement among contemporary commentators over the authorship of an ancient text called the *Magna Moralia*. The following, which refers to a passage from the *Magna Moralia*, is from a footnote in a work by one commentator, A.W. Price:

> John Cooper attaches great weight to this passage . . . It is consistent that he ascribes the *Magna Moralia* to Aristotle himself . . . Others will find the author's treatment of 'goodwill' here . . . typical of his [the author of the *Magna Moralia's*] 'constant botching', as Anthony Kenny has termed it. [A.W. Price, *Love and Friendship in Plato and Aristotle* (Oxford: Clarendon Press, 1989), 122–3]

Both Cooper and Kenny can be considered 'experts' in the field by virtue of their published work and its reception. Price thinks that the *Magna Moralia* is not written by Aristotle and backs this claim by invoking Kenny's claim that the author of the *Magna Moralia* is a 'constant botcher' (thereby implying that it is not Aristotle's work). Here then, one has an implicit argument from authority that can be diagrammed as follows:

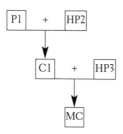

where:

    P1 = Kenny claims that the author of the *Magna Moralia* is a constant botcher.
  HP2 = Kenny is a noted expert.
    C1 = The author of the *Manga Moralia* is a constant botcher.
  HP3 = Aristotle is not a constant botcher.
  MC = Aristotle is not the author of the *Magna Moralia*.

The passage in question contains an implicit argument *against* authority as well as an argument from authority, however, for the appeal to one authority (Kenny) is used to dismiss the views of another (Cooper). The argument against authority can be summarized as the claim that 'The author of the *Magna Moralia* is a constant botcher (C1), so Cooper is not a good judge of the passage in question, and he is not a credible authority.' In essence, this implicit argument calls into question Cooper's credentials by pointing to his alleged poor judgment.

This is, however, a case where appeals to authority are of limited value, for it is a case characterized by disagreements between the authorities. Academia is renowned for its contentious debates, and where disagreements arise it is always important to have both sides of the story. In this case, we have neither the grounds for Cooper's high opinion of the author of the *Magna Moralia* nor the grounds for Kenny's low opinion of the same author. In the face of their disagreement, the fourth condition of good appeals to authority cannot be met. Since the *ad hominem* critique of Cooper's credentials depends on the appeal to authority, it is also problematic. In this instance, Price can better make his point by showing how Cooper's interpretation of the passage could be considered a case of 'botching'. To his credit, it is this that he proceeds to attempt next.

ARGUMENTS AGAINST AUTHORITY

Arguments against authority can be considered the reverse of arguments from authority. A good argument against authority rejects an alleged authority by establishing that

(1) the authority's credentials are questionable; or
(2) the credentials cited are irrelevant to the issue in question; or
(3) the alleged authority is biased; or
(4) the topic under scrutiny is one where there is significant disagreement among the relevant experts; or
(5) the topic is one where expertise cannot be claimed.

EXERCISE 14E

Find three poor examples of arguments from authority in magazines or on websites. Construct a strong argument against authority in response to them. Present your argument in the form of a letter to the editor.

6. GUILT (AND HONOUR) BY ASSOCIATION

An argument scheme closely related to *ad hominem* is what is known as *guilt by association*. As the name implies, this argument attributes 'guilt' to a person or group on the basis of some association that is known or thought to exist between that person or group and some other person or group of dubious beliefs or behaviour. A variant of this scheme of argument that we call 'honour by association' uses a positive association as a basis for the conclusion that they are in some way creditable.

Guilt-by-association arguments are variants of the following scheme:

> PREMISE 1: A person or group X is associated with another person or group Y.
> PREMISE 2: Y has questionable beliefs or behaves in a questionable way.
> CONCLUSION: X's character and/or claims are questionable.

An honour-by-association argument has the form

> PREMISE 1: A person or group X is associated with another person or group Y.
> PREMISE 2: Y has creditable beliefs or behaves in a creditable way.
> CONCLUSION: X's character and/or claims are creditable.

In cases in which the association claimed in premise 1 of either of these arguments exists, guilt or credit can sometimes be legitimately transferred or inferred in the way proposed. But it is important to be wary of such arguments, for they often serve as a vehicle for generalizations based on stereotyping, which should be avoided because they inhibit careful moral assessments.

A guilt-by-association argument is strong when, and only when,

(1) there is good reason to believe that the alleged association between X and Y really does exist;

(2) there is good reason to question the beliefs or the behaviour of Y; and

(3) there is no good reason to differentiate X from Y.

In keeping with these conditions, the conditions for a good honour-by-association argument are the same, except that condition (2) becomes

(2) there is good reason to *credit* the beliefs or the behaviour of Y.

Because many guilt-by-association arguments are problematic, it is a good idea to develop an argument of this sort fully if you decide to use one. In doing so, the main premises in your argument will be variants of the three conditions already noted. These principal premises may have to be backed by sub-arguments that support them.

In dealing with association arguments, remember that they cannot definitively dismiss or establish the views or arguments of a person or group. This can only be accomplished through a critical examination of the views of the person or group in question. But there are still cases in which association arguments are reasonable. For instance, if someone spent twenty years as an active member of the Salvation Army, this does lend credence to their observations about social issues. On the negative side, if someone who offers social criticisms has close connections with extremists, say, because he has acted as a spokesman for an extremist organization, then we have grounds for being skeptical about his analysis of social problems and even his moral character. Especially when we have limited time at our disposal, positive and negative arguments by association can be an important way to determine what arguments we should and should not take the time to consider and discuss.

Difficult cases involve situations in which we might question the relevance of a particular association. Consider the following, taken from Janet George's article on the British anti-hunting campaign, entitled 'Saboteurs—the Real Animals' (*Manchester Guardian Weekly*, 28 Feb. 1993, p. 24):

> . . . one can condemn . . . the dishonesty of the campaign against hunting. If the anti-hunt literature said 'We are against killing animals for any purpose: killing animals for food is morally as unacceptable as killing animals for sport but impossible to ban,' financial and political support for the campaign would be so greatly reduced as to make it unsustainable. Such an extreme view would be held by less than 2 per cent of the population, so a little misrepresentation is necessary to keep funds flowing.
>
> Whatever claims are made by spokesmen of the anti-hunting campaigns, the truth is that more and more hunt saboteurs express their disapproval of legal activities with illegal acts. Anti-hunt organizations pay lip-service to peaceful protest, but by producing emotive and misleading propaganda . . . they must accept some responsibility for the actions of their supporters.

These remarks shift some of the guilt of the 'hunt saboteurs', who have been guilty of increasing violence, onto the anti-hunt organizations who advocate peaceful protest (though there may be some confusion over the identities of the associated parties).

Set out as guilt-by-association reasoning this argument is as follows:

P1 = The anti-hunt organizations are associated with the hunt saboteurs.
P2 = The hunt saboteurs behave in a questionable (violent) way.
 C = The motives of the anti-hunt organizations are questionable.

The first condition for appropriate guilt-by-association arguments requires that the alleged association really does exist. We will grant this for the moment. It seems charitable to allow that the anti-hunt organizations and the anti-hunt 'saboteurs' (accepting that this may be a loaded term and open to challenge) will share ideological views at least to the extent that they are working for the same end.

The second condition asks whether there is good reason to question the behaviour of the one group. There is less doubt here. Although we may shy from the term 'saboteurs', it is established (in the media) that the groups discussed engage in violent acts against property and persons, including law enforcement officers. Such acts are clearly questionable.

The third condition focuses on the relevance of the association in this instance. Is there good reason to disassociate the two groups on this issue? Here we look to the evidence provided by the first paragraph. The link that establishes guilt in George's eyes is the dishonest literature. Although the anti-hunt organizations pay lip-service to peaceful protest, they must accept some responsibility for the violence because they produce misleading and emotive propaganda. Given that she grants that the groups pay lip-service to peaceful protest, we must believe that the propaganda does not explicitly incite violence. So it is difficult to see just how the 'propaganda' establishes a significant enough connection.

The misleading nature of the literature, according to George's first paragraph, lies in its failure to tell the full extent of the group's position. Honesty here would, allegedly, lead to a loss of political and financial support. The people who would disassociate themselves from anti-hunt organizations if the literature was honest are a different group altogether. No connection is established between the failure of the literature to be honest and the violence of the 'saboteurs'. In fact, the literature seems irrelevant to this group, since their actions do not appear to be a result of being misled by any *softer* goal expressed in the literature. At the very least, George has not established the association she requires if she wants to criticize anti-hunt organizations on the basis of their association with violent offenders.

GUILT AND HONOUR BY ASSOCIATION

An argument form that attributes guilt (or credit) to a person or group, X, on the basis of some association that is known or thought to exist between that person or group and some other person or group, Y. In a good guilt-by-association argument,

(1) there is good reason to believe that the alleged association between X and Y really does exist;

(2) there is good reason to question the beliefs or the behaviour of Y; and

(3) there is no good reason to differentiate X from Y.

In a good honour-by-association argument, conditions 1 and 3 remain, and the second condition becomes (2) there is good reason to credit the beliefs or the behaviour of Y.

EXERCISE 14F

1. The well-known German philosopher Martin Heidegger is known to have been a member of the German Nazi party. This has sparked a controversy over whether this association in any way discredits his work as a philosopher. Do you think one could build a strong guilt-by-association argument on this basis? Why or why not?

2.   Assess the different associations and the implicit guilt- and honour-by-association reasoning in the following passage, from <http://www.friesian.com/rockmore. htm> (accessed 4 Feb. 2003):

> The controversy about Martin Heidegger's membership in the German Nazi Party ultimately reveals one very important thing: The very principles that attracted Heidegger to Hitler and the Nazis are also the principles that attract Heidegger's defenders to him. That most of Heidegger's defenders are leftists and 'progressives' (like Richard Rorty) simply reveals a characteristic of the history of the 20th Century: that the Left . . . has far more in common with the far Right . . . than anyone on the Left has ever wanted to admit—except perhaps for Susan Sontag's classic, politically incorrect statement that 'Communism is fascism with a human face'—though one must then explain Alexander Dubcek's claim that the revolution in Czechoslovakia in 1968 was to produce 'Communism with a human face'; presumably he didn't think that it already had one. Since Dubcek had to live under communism and Sontag didn't, we can count on him to have gotten it more right. Sontag, however, who also said that Americans could learn more about the Soviet Union reading *Reader's Digest* than *The Nation*, got it far more right than most of her intellectual peers. (Rockmore: 'Sartre holds that Marxism is unsurpassable as the philosophy of our time', p. 147).

7. OTHER CASES

Our account of guilt-by-association arguments ends our discussion of different argument schemes. In closing, we reiterate the point that some arguments do not fit neatly into the categories we have introduced. Sometimes no specific argument scheme is used, and sometimes the premises contain a mixture of specific schemes. Where there is no specific scheme at all, we must depend on the general criteria of relevance and sufficiency and acceptability in assessing an argument. If an argument is a mixture of a variety of specific schemes, we must appeal to a variety of specific criteria.

To illustrate such complexities, imagine that a homicide investigator argues that White is the murderer the police are looking for on the basis of the following reasoning:

    P1 = Green says White is the murderer.
    P2 = White is a vicious person at the best of times.
    P3 = No one has been able to provide any evidence to the contrary.
    C = White is the murderer.

Note that P1, P2, and P3 appeal to very different sorts of evidence. P1, implicitly appealing to Green as someone who should know who the murderer is, is a *pro homine* argument. P3 is an argument from ignorance. P2 does not conform to any of our specific argument schemes. (Note that it is an attack on White, not an attack on White's views and, hence, not an *ad hominem* argument.)

We diagram the above argument as follows:

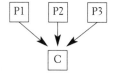

In assessing this argument, we must assess the weight each specific sub-argument lends to the conclusion. Then the overall strength of the argument must be evaluated by asking whether the conclusion is probable, given the cumulative force of the different kinds of evidence introduced to justify it. Individually, each aspect of the total argument may be questionable and, therefore, only marginally convincing. But in conjunction with the others it can contribute to a strong argument, especially if there are no fundamental objections to the reasoning. The strength of the final conclusion is a result of the three separate kinds of considerations providing supporting evidence for it. Thus, although Green may not be the most trustworthy character, his claims must be taken seriously when they are corroborated by other evidence.

Other complications arise when different parts of the conclusion are established by different premises. We can add complexity to the example we have been considering by adding a fourth premise and rewriting the conclusion as a conjunction:

P1 = Green says White is the murderer.
P2 = White is a vicious person at the best of times.
P3 = Nobody has been able to provide any evidence to the contrary.
P4 = All those who have met him agree that Brown could not commit such a heinous crime.
C = White is the murderer and Brown is innocent.

We can now represent the argument as consisting of four premises leading to conclusion C. Premises P1, P2, and P3 clearly go together to establish that White is the murderer, while P4 establishes that Brown is innocent. For purposes of assessing the argument, we can represent Brown's innocence as a hidden conclusion (HC2) following from P4, and the conclusion of our earlier argument, that White is the murderer, as HC1, following from P1, P2, and P3. The final conclusion thus follows from HC1 and HC2, and we can diagram the argument as follows:

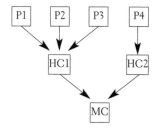

where:

HC1 = White is the murderer.
HC2 = Brown is innocent.
MC = White is the murderer and Brown is innocent.

Using this diagram, we can assess the argument in the normal way.

It is because we need to assess the different premises in such arguments in different ways that we must separate premises that provide different types of support for a conclusion: by appealing to analogies, to causal reasoning, to *pro homine* considerations, and so on. If you keep in mind your goal, which is an honest and logically useful representation, then you should be able to deal effectively with whatever specific argument schemes you come across.

EXERCISE 14G

Construct an argument for the conclusion that 'White is the murderer and Brown is innocent' that has the same form and diagram as the example just given, except that the premises P1–P4 are linked (and not convergent) and in this way establish the plausibility of the conclusion.

MAJOR EXERCISE 14M

1. This assignment is intended to help you test your understanding of the schemes of argument introduced in this chapter by asking you to use some of them in conjunction with specific normative issues.
   a) Construct short arguments employing the following forms (one for each argument) in support of the claim 'Capital punishment should not be reinstated where it is currently disallowed':
      i) *pro homine*
      ii) appeal to authority
      iii) guilt or honour by association.
   b) Employ the same argument forms in support of the opposite claim: 'Capital punishment should be reinstated where it is currently disallowed.'
   c) Using any of the argument forms of this chapter, construct a short argument on one of the following issues:
      i) acid rain
      ii) the rights of indigenous peoples
      iii) insider trading
   d) The Canadian Supreme court decided the 'Ottawa/Quebec Secession-Rights Case' on 28 February 1997. The court was asked to rule on whether the Province of Quebec had the legal right to declare itself separate from Canada. The federal government's argument that it did not have this right was supported

by the opinions of two specialists in international law: James Crawford of the University of Cambridge, and Luzius Wildhaber of the University of Basel in Switzerland (a judge of the European Court of Human Rights). In appealing to these authorities, was the Canadian government making a strong argument from authority?

2. Decide whether each of the following passages contains an argument. If it does, assess the reasoning. Identify any instances of argument schemes dealt with in this chapter, explaining whether they fulfill the conditions for good arguments of that form. Note that examples may involve more than one argument form. Diagram all arguments.

a) [from a letter to the *Toronto Star* (18 Oct. 1990)] The letter by R.T. in the *Star* (Oct. 10) quotes liberal Catholic theologian Dr D. Maguire as stating that a fetus is 'a precious and beautiful form of life but it is not a person'.

    The key word is 'liberal'. Reasoning such as Maguire's is not accepted by the Magisterium of the Roman Catholic Church. When one reads the liberal views of Catholic theologian Maguire, one only needs to consider the source.

b)* [from a flyer advertising 'Astro-Guard Security Systems'] You don't have to be a statistic! The experts admit 'it's not IF you will be the victim of a break-in . . . but WHEN'. Astro-Guard security systems stops burglars BEFORE they get inside. ONE OUT OF FOUR! Those are the statistical chances of you and your family being the victims of a break-in **within the next 12 months** . . . Psychiatrists, Psychologists, Criminologists, Security Experts and Police Officials all agree: 'The Earlier the intruder is discovered, the more effective the security system.'

c) [from a letter to *Toronto Sun* (21 Nov. 1983)] The article 'Hong Kong cash comes oh-so-quietly into Metro' (Nov. 7) is misleading because it does not mention the extensive nature of crime in the Orient. In Hong Kong, for example, organized crime wields tremendous power and influence.

    It has been estimated that one person in six in the colony is a member of the criminal Triad societies. These societies are major heroin traffickers. They have already completely corrupted the Hong Kong police force, and bribing of important officials is routine. Because drugs are so easily obtained, Hong Kong has a serious drug-addiction problem. Many Hong Kong residents, including businessmen, have become extremely wealthy through drug trafficking. If they are permitted to settle here, they would extend Hong Kong's problems to Canada.

    Allowing people into Canada solely on the basis of wealth is very foolish, and could result in the destruction of the moral fibre of our society.

d) [from a letter to the *Peterborough Examiner* (12 Nov. 1994)] What people must understand is that if you support one aspect of the animal rights agenda you are supporting it all. You may not be against fur, but your support is helping animal rights groups in their anti-fur campaigns, and you may be against cosmetic testing, but that support also supports their stand against vital medical research that each and every one of us benefits from every day of our lives.

e) [from an ad in the *Saturday Evening Post* (Feb. 2003)] **Our most popular cookbook FREE when you subscribe.** What could be more appropriate? A better-health cookbook of delicious high-fiber diet recipes to accompany the legendary all-American magazine that has said no to booze and tobacco advertising and replaced those pages with an emphasis on a long, happy, healthy, lifestyle! More than 1,000,000 copies of this 8¼″ × 10¾″ publication attest to the popularity of *The Saturday Evening Post Family Cookbook*, the joint effort of Cory SerVaas, M.D., and Charlotte Turgeon.

f)* [The following, from a letter to the *Toronto Star* (Sept. 1982), concerns a suggestion that noted Canadian doctor Norman Bethune should be honoured for his service to humanity. Bethune died accidentally in 1939 while assisting Communist Chinese forces in their struggle against Japanese invaders.] Is it possible to honour Dr Norman Bethune as a humanitarian, despite the fact that he was a self-confessed Communist? Only a negative rejoinder is possible, for the morality of a person's acts must be judged by their consequences. Thus when Dr Bethune placed his medical skills and humanism at the service of international Communism, he unquestionably contributed to an evil ideology that has produced many mountains of corpses. When Canadians naively eulogize such a person as Dr Bethune, such praise unwittingly constitutes an endorsement of Communist ideology.

g)* [adapted from a report on the effects of smoking on the economy, 'Smoking Benefits Amazing', in the *Peterborough Examiner* (10 Sept. 1994)] According to economist Jean-Pierre Vidal in a study commissioned by Imperial Tobacco, while smoking kills, those deaths have economic benefits for society.

A person who dies of lung cancer at age 70 will not be hospitalized later with another disease and the costs of hospitalization tend to increase substantially for people after the age of 70. Furthermore, wages forfeited by deceased former smokers cost neither the government nor the taxpayer, since they will not be paid for work they will not do.

h) [from a report in the *Kitchener-Waterloo Record* (16 Nov. 1998), D15] . . . meet John Woolsey, . . . an actuary, a profession that looks at life expectancies and mortality rates to help insurance companies set their premiums. He co-wrote a 1996 report on health-care financing for the Canadian Institute of Actuaries. For him, the numbers don't add up. . . . 'Everything I can find that I've looked at indicates that the total cost to society goes down if people smoke.' The reason, Woolsey says with cold logic, is that smokers on average die younger—from five to 15 years depending on whose data you use. 'You eliminate the high costs of medical care for older people because they're already dead.'

i) [Daniel D. Polsby, in 'The False Promise of Gun Control', *The Atlantic Monthly* (Mar. 1994)] If firearms increased violence and crime, then rates of spousal homicide would have skyrocketed, because the stock of privately owned handguns has increased rapidly since the mid-1960s. But according to an authoritative study of spousal homicide in the *American Journal of Public Health*, by

James Mercey and Linda Saltzman, rates of spousal homicide in the years 1976 to 1985 fell. If firearms increase violence and crime, the crime rate should have increased throughout the 1980s, while the national stock of privately owned handguns increased by more than a million units every year of the decade. It did not.

j) [from an ad in the *Saturday Evening Post* (Feb. 2003)] Discover why thousands of people with low vision have purchased the VidoEye power magnification system to continue reading and doing everyday tasks.

k) [from a letter to the *Kitchener-Waterloo Record* (Mar. 1985)] Evolutionists claim that life progressed from one-celled organisms to its highest state, the human being, by means of a series of biological changes taking place over millions of years.

   And they know full well that their claims directly contradict the Bible story of creation. They also state that anyone who puts a literal interpretation on the first two chapters of Genesis is out of touch with reality.

   It's also been proven that most ministers believe the creation story is a fable.

   The Christian belief in creation is not a theory. It is a fact and it doesn't need to be proven, no more than we need to prove that computers have a maker. The computers themselves are the proof.

   There isn't one chance in a billion that a computer could evolve. It demands a maker, and so does our universe.

   In spite of the claims of people such as CBC personality David Suzuki, the so-called missing link between man and beast has never been found. Each species was created with the programmed ability to evolve different types of its own species, but one kind cannot evolve into another. The basic teaching of evolution is based on assumption.

l) [from a letter to the *New York Times* (7 Feb. 1987)] In his Feb. 7 letter, Judge Bruce McM. Wright cites as historical fact the story of Thomas Jefferson's slave mistress, Sally Hemmings. It is simply ridiculous that this patent lie should still be seen in print. Its origin is almost as old as our Republic.

   On July 14, 1798, the Federalist Congress passed the Sedition Act, which made publishing anything false or scandalous against the Government a crime. In May of 1800, James T. Callender, a Scottish immigrant and pamphleteer, went on trial in Richmond for violation of that act.

   Callender was a pathetic creature, an alcoholic and hypochondriac, who never seemed able to extricate himself from debt. Jefferson had befriended him a few years earlier and had advanced him funds to enable him to continue his writing. At his trial . . . Callender was convicted and sentenced to nine months in prison and fined $200.

   When Jefferson became President in 1801, he pardoned Callender. Since Callender had already completed his prison term the effect of this was to refund his fine and clear his name. When Callender received his money three months later, he had grown bitter against Jefferson and his party for the delay and the time he had spent in prison. He decided to chastise the President and succeeded beyond even his expectations.

In September 1802 in the *Richmond Recorder*, he published the story of Sally Hemmings, the slave mistress of the President. Callender cited no support for the story, saying merely that it was 'well known'. He subsequently changed elements of the story repeatedly to bring them into line with the facts of Jefferson's life. Several times he changed the version of how the affair began, and the number of children supposedly produced by it. To those who knew Jefferson's high moral standards and devotion to his dead wife's memory, the story was laughable.

. . . I find it incredible that a story that all reputable historians, led by Jefferson's able biographer Dumas Malone, have discredited for years, should still find its way into print. . . . Without the strictest accuracy, history is worthless.

m) [adapted from a letter to the *New York Times* (Mar. 1982)] As a true American, I wish to speak for what is near and dear to the hearts of Americans. I wish to speak against what is as foreign to these shores as communism, socialism, totalitarianism, and other foreign 'ism's', except of course Americanism. I speak of the Administration's 'medicare bill', better known as 'socialized medicine'.

Socialized medicine would commit us to the complete takeover by government of everything traditionally reserved for the individual. As the late Senator Robert A. Taft—a true American—warned, 'if we are going to give medical care free to all people, why not provide them with free transportation, free housing, free food and clothing, all at the expense of the taxpayer. . . . Socialization is just a question of degree, and we cannot move much further in that direction unless we do wish a completely socialist state.'

If medicare is sound, then a government-sponsored, -financed, and -controlled program is sound for every aspect of our life. But this principle must be rejected. As Americans, freedom must be our watchword. And since freedom means no control, no regulation, no restraint, government programs like medicare are quite contrary to the American concept of freedom.

Unlike pseudo-Americans who want to socialize this country, I believe that socialized medicine would be an insult to true Americans. For true Americans don't want handouts. They want to stand on their own feet. They're willing to meet their obligations. They're willing to work and pay for their medical bills. As convincing proof of this, the AMA has advertised that it will give medical care to anyone who wants it, and practically no one responds to these ads.

We need only look at England to see what effects socialized medicine would have here—to see how it would lower the quality of medical care. For as Dr Lull of the AMA reminds us, the record in Great Britain shows that governmentally dominated medical systems burden doctors with red tape and paper work, thus robbing them of valuable time needed for careful diagnosis and treatment of patients. Not to mention all the freeloaders, hypochondriacs, and malingerers, who daily crowd the hospitals and doctors' offices and thus take away valuable beds and time from those who are really sick. In other words, socialized medicine is not only unnecessary but it would also be undesirable.

It should be obvious that it would not accomplish the utopia claimed for it. Indeed, what proof do we have that it would make everyone healthy overnight? Since there is no conclusive proof, we can only conclude that it would be a dismal failure.

n)* [In May 1987, Klaus Barbie, the so-called 'Butcher of Lyon', was put on trial in France for crimes against humanity during the Second World War. With respect to the defence of Barbie, the following quote from Jacques Verges, Barbie's lawyer, was reported in the *Globe and Mail* (2 May 1987).] We will see during the course of this business that what Mr Barbie did as a loyal officer of his country was no different than what hundreds of loyal officers of this country did during the Algerian war. We will see that Mr Barbie operated under a legally accepted premise at the time and that he was assisted by citizens and officials of France. We will see that even French Jews and members of the Resistance assisted Mr Barbie in his work.

o) [In response to very significant changes to labour laws instituted by Bob Rae's left-leaning Ontario government, groups opposed to the changes printed billboards like the following.]

p) [from a letter to *Globe and Mail* (8 Feb. 1997)] Leaving aside the substance of his testimony, the appearance of Vice-Admiral Larry Murray before the Somalia inquiry provided a rare and revealing glimpse of the kind of man this country promoted to its top military rank.

His responses to questions were uniformly disjointed, qualified, repetitive, digressive, serpentine and interminable. His monotone, rapid-fire delivery, without expression, pace or structure, reflected a personality devoid of presence or style, not to mention charisma.

Over all, after days of hearings, what indelibly comes to mind are not the characteristics of a military leader at all, but those of a bureaucrat. It is a bit of a shock.

q) [Edward Said, in 'Palestinian Elections Now', *Al-Ahram Weekly* (on-line) no. 590 (13–19 June 2002)] . . . it is Yasser Arafat and his circle of associates who have suddenly discovered the virtues (theoretically at least) of democracy and reform. I know that I speak at a great distance from the field of struggle, and I also know all the arguments about the besieged Arafat as a potent symbol of Palestinian resistance against Israeli aggression, but I have come to a point where I think none of that has any meaning anymore. . . . Why anyone for a moment believes that at this stage he is capable of anything different, or that his new streamlined cabinet (dominated by the same old faces of defeat and incompetence) is going to produce actual reform, defies reason. He is the leader of a long suffering people, whom in the past year he has exposed to unacceptable pain and hardship, all of it based on a combination of his absence of a strategic plan and his unforgivable reliance on the tender mercies of Israel and the US via Oslo. . . .

He never really reined in Hamas and Islamic Jihad, and that suited Israel perfectly: it would have a ready-made excuse to use the so-called martyr's (mindless) suicide bombings to further diminish and punish the whole people. If there is one thing along with Arafat's ruinous regime that has done us more harm as a cause it is this calamitous policy of killing Israeli civilians, that further proves to the world that we are indeed terrorists and an immoral movement. . . .

15

ARGUMENTATIVE

WRITING:

ESSAYING AN ARGUMENT

The last important aspect of critical thinking left for us to treat is writing an extended piece of argumentation. Good critical thinkers, after analyzing an argument, are able to write a critical response that incorporates the main features of their evaluation. On other occasions, they will be called upon to write their our own argumentative essays. In this chapter we

- ◆ discuss the evaluative critique;
- ◆ discuss the argumentative essay;
- ◆ apply the techniques discussed to a student essay; and
- ◆ offer our own revision of the essay.

In this text we have focused on the two arms of critical thinking: assessing others' reasoning and presenting reasoning of our own. When we assess another person's argument, we should evaluate the reasoning on its own terms and decide whether we are convinced of the conclusion on the grounds of that reasoning. Although we may consider its context, we should not go beyond the reasoning or add anything to it. When we note hidden premises and assumptions, we should be simply recognizing what is already there (albeit in an implicit way).

After the evaluation, as we organize our critical remarks and *respond*, we will probably go beyond the original argument and bring in other considerations, emphasizing what the arguer has overlooked. We may suggest reasoning that would remedy problems we have found. An *evaluative critique*, then, is an argumentative response that incorporates both the features of our evaluation and our own insights.

The other arm of critical thinking is the construction of our own arguments. The *argumentative essay* captures this activity in its most extensive form. Unlike the evaluative critique, the argumentative essay need not be based on any prior evaluation or response to another's reasoning. It is the form our writing takes when we are setting down the arguments that support a position we hold, engaging in original research on a controversial issue, or conducting an inquiry to arrive at a position we will then hold, perhaps by testing a few hypotheses. In its clearest form the argumentative essay is the first of these, although the other two will often have gone into its earlier drafts.

In this chapter, we will trace the details of both the evaluative critique and the argumentative essay before illustrating these activities by means of a critique of a student essay and then the writing of a revision of that essay.

1. THE GOOD EVALUATIVE CRITIQUE

When preparing for and producing a good evaluative critique there are seven steps to consider. They are

(1) writing an *overview* of the main claim and sub-claims;
(2) diagramming the *macro-structure* and *micro-structure* of the argument;
(3) assessing the *language* of the argument;
(4) assessing the *reasoning* of the argument;
(5) weighing its *strengths and weaknesses*;
(6) deciding on your *response* to the argument; and
(7) preparing the body of your *critique*.

In the following sections we will consider each of these steps in turn.

(1) Overview

In a brief paragraph, set down the main claim that is being put forward and the sub-arguments that are offered in support of it. Also note any specific types of reasoning that have been employed. For example:

> In his article the author is opposing any form of gun-control law because (a) such a law is essentially undemocratic and (b) it will mean innocent members of society receive criminal records. But the bulk of his argument is given to support the contention that (c) gun control is unnecessary because there is no clear connection between guns and crime. The author employs causal reasoning in support of (c). In particular, he attempts to show that any causal claim linking gun ownership to criminal activity is fallacious.

(2) Macro-Structure and Micro-Structure

Depict the structure of the argument in a diagram, showing as much detail as you think is necessary. Minimally, this will involve a diagram of the macro-structure, that is, a diagram showing how the sub-arguments relate to the main claim. It might help you to assign a number or letter to each paragraph of the text with which you are working and to refer to these numbers in your diagram. A micro-structure diagram will be more detailed and will show the supporting premises for each sub-claim.

For example, in the argument referred to in the Overview, each letter represents a sub-argument in support of the main conclusion that 'Gun-control laws are not necessary.' The macro-structure of the reasoning would be depicted in a simple convergent diagram:

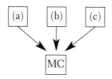

However, each of (a), (b), and (c) could also be depicted in a micro-structure diagram, showing how the respective sub-conclusions are supported by the premises provided for (a), (b), or (c). Since we have not developed the argument in the overview, we have no details to offer here. But you can imagine, for example, a collection of linked or convergent premises supporting (a), which becomes C1 in the micro-structure. We illustrate the value of macro- and micro-structure diagrams later in the chapter.

(3) Language

Some consideration of language may have arisen in the overview if you had trouble with the meaning of the main claim or one or more of the sub-claims. A complete analysis of the extended argument will include a review of its language, even if no problems may be evident.

Watch for vagueness, ambiguity, and heavily loaded language. And be especially alert to poor definitions or the failure to provide the definition of a term that is important to the outcome of the argument. The macro- and micro-structure diagrams will help you assess the importance of terms according to where they occur in the flow of the argument.

(4) Reasoning

Here is the bulk of your analysis: a complete assessment of the reasoning employed that proceeds by considering the various criteria for good reasoning explained in earlier chapters of this text. This will include a general assessment of basic criteria of acceptability, relevance, and sufficiency, as well as the specific criteria associated with deductive and non-deductive argument schemes. If a categorical syllogism has been employed, test it for validity. If the arguer employs an *ad hominem*, ensure that it meets the conditions for good instances of the scheme *ad hominem*. When you assess the reasoning, remember that your goal is to weigh the strengths and weaknesses of the argument, not simply to detect errors. In many cases you will find that it's just as important to note that the arguer has employed arguments appropriately as it is to note that they have employed arguments fallaciously.

(5) Strengths and Weaknesses

Now you have amassed all the information you require to make a decision about the argument and respond to it. Stages 5–7 concern your reaction to the argument. You will want to base your decision about the argument on a balanced appreciation of its strengths and weaknesses. Set out two columns with the headings 'Strengths' and 'Weaknesses', and list under each heading the main discoveries of your analysis. Again, the diagrams will help you determine how detrimental or positive each discovery is. For example, the irrelevance to the main claim of an entire sub-argument is far more detrimental to the overall argument than the irrelevance of just one of many premises to a sub-claim. With some arguments you may find all or most of your entries are in one column. Such cases make for an easy decision. But most ordinary arguments, when fairly assessed, have both strengths and weaknesses that have to be weighed against each other. The weighing should be done objectively. With the most difficult and balanced of arguments, you may want to note that while you may decide one way, a colleague or fellow student evaluating the same argument might decide another way.

(6) Response

Having weighed the strengths and weaknesses, you must next decide both the degree to which you are persuaded by the argument and the manner of your response to it. Stage 5 allowed for a wide range of decisions about the evaluated argument. At the one extreme, the reasoning may be so weak that no reasonable person could be persuaded by it. If the argument happened to have been for a position that you were previously inclined to support, then to continue supporting it you will need to do so on the basis of quite different reasoning. At the other extreme, the reasoning may have such logical strength that if, in your response, you intend to challenge the position it advocates, you will have to counter those strengths with further, even more compelling, argumentation.

As will be clear from the above, this is the stage of evaluation (really post-evaluation) where your prior beliefs and attitudes come into play. You cannot dismiss a strong argument just because you do not like the conclusion (or the arguer!). The process of evaluation has shown you that there can often be quite good arguments advanced in support of positions that you do not support. Coming to such realizations is part of gaining maturity as a critical thinker.

You may agree with the reasoning but not the conclusion. Perhaps the reasoning, while strong, is not strong enough to override other reasons that you have for rejecting the conclusion. Those other reasons will form the core of your response. You may agree with the conclusion but find the argumentation for it weak. Strengthening that argumentation and perhaps adding to it will form the basis of your response. Again, you may allow some of the argumentation but not all of it, and respond accordingly. Or you may allow most of the argumentation but insist that it really supports a reworded claim. As you can see, there are many possible responses between the extremes of complete rejection and agreement. What is important is that your decision is fairly based on both the strengths and the weaknesses, and that you take account of these in your critique.

(7) *Critique*

Criticism is simply the use of critical judgment. It does not have to be negative, although it often carries that connotation. Where a written critique is required, you should write it making use of the six steps we have already discussed. Acknowledge strengths and weaknesses. Use the weaknesses against the arguer in cases where you disagree, and look for ways to remedy or avoid weaknesses where you agree with the arguer's position. Promote the strengths and add to them where you agree, and look to counter them where you disagree. Your critique is where you develop your own extensive argument, and so this is the stage at which the evaluative critique can benefit from many of the considerations that contribute to a good argumentative essay, which we will turn to in the following section.

THE COMPONENTS OF CRITIQUE

1. overview of the main claim and sub-claims
2. macro-structure and micro-structure
3. language
4. reasoning
5. weighing strengths and weaknesses
6. decision
7. the body of the critique

EXERCISE 15A

Following the seven stages outlined in this section, write an evaluative critique for each of the following:

a) Since women and visible minorities have been discriminated against by the system, it is appropriate to institute a policy that involves favouring these groups over others in employment decisions, those others being, for the most part, white males. Some harm is done to those not favoured by this policy, but nothing like the harm the system presently inflicts on the disadvantaged groups. And besides, white males have flourished in the system for so long that even under this policy they will still be fairly well off. The only alternative would be to change the attitudes of society, and thereby the system, at a fundamental level but this would take too long. Therefore, employment equity is currently justified.

b) [A.J. Ayer, in *Language, Truth and Logic* (Dover Publications, 1952)] If the conclusion that a god exists is to be demonstrably certain, then these premises [from which it follows] must be certain. . . . But we know that no empirical proposition can ever be anything more than probable. It is only 'a priori' propositions that are logically certain. But we cannot deduce the existence of god from an 'a priori' proposition. For we know that the reason why 'a priori' propositions are certain is that they are tautologies [statements that are necessarily true]. And from a set of tautologies nothing but a further tautology can be validly deduced. It follows that there is no possibility of demonstrating the existence of god.

c) [During a debate on gun control, one gun owner reacted to a report that 'more guns means more suicide' with the following argument, in a letter to the *Peterborough Examiner* (Mar. 1995).] According to Dr Isaac Safinosky, who presented the Clarke Institute of Psychiatry paper to the American Association of Suicidology, in countries where the suicide rate is rising, control of inflation by the government is the main cause. This creates increased unemployment. As a consequence, he said, 'Society becomes demoralized, so even the employed start to worry, causing people to stop buying. In recent times, inflation has been seen as the major economic threat to society. Monetarist policies have deliberately raised interest rates to cool the economy and reduce inflationary growth; the resulting loss of jobs is seen as a necessary evil in order to bring down wages and prices. Suicide increase in young persons in such countries appears to be the unfortunate concomitant of these policies.'

This study points the finger directly at those people who are blaming us. The economic policies of the government . . . [are] the major cause of the rising rate of suicide.

d) [adapted from a brochure entitled 'Introducing—the Flat Earth Society'] If the Earth were a gigantic globe, then half the world would be living upside-down! Why don't they fall off? Furthermore, one person's 'up' (in the 'southern hemisphere'), would be another person's 'down' (in the 'northern hemisphere'), which is obviously repugnant to Common Sense.

. . . The fantasy of a global Earth that spins (Gyroblobularism) contains even more preposterous absurdities. Thus, with the numbers dreamed up by the Globularists, a person standing at the 'equator' of this 'global' Earth would be whirled around at about 1,000 miles an hour and not know it! At this speed, why does not everything get spun off into space? Or at the very least, why do not all the oceans of the world accumulate at the 'equator' causing a giant tidal wave there?

The Globularists attempt to escape from all these obvious implications by resorting to one sacred word 'gravity' . . . But this feeble attempt at an explanation is nothing more than a circular argument, as an extract from Ambrose Bierce's *The Devil's Dictionary* well explains: 'Gravitation, n. The tendency of all bodies to approach one another with a strength proportioned to the quantity of matter they contain—the quantity of matter they contain being ascertained by the strength of their tendency to approach one another. This is a lovely edifying illustration of how science, having made A the proof of B, makes B the proof of A.'

. . . When one surveys one's own environment with appropriate impartiality, there is an overwhelming *lack of evidence* for the above preposterous fantasies! One can only conclude that they are nothing more than the products of certain people's over-strained feverish imaginations.

e) [from a letter to the University of Waterloo *Imprint* (9 Mar. 1984)] One question that should haunt the atheists as they scan these nicely packaged proofs against God's existence, is the question of whether or not man can trust his own reasoning. For if indeed man has evolved via the process of natural selection, then surely we have a rather shaky foundation to suppose that reasoning is trustworthy. For then our reasoning is no longer based on truth, but rather on its ultimate survival value. Consider the thoughts of Darwin when he wrote: 'The horrid doubt always rises whether the convictions of a man's mind, which has developed from the mind of lower animals, are of any value at all; would anyone trust the convictions of a monkey's mind, if there are any convictions in such a mind?'

Now, the second point that should disturb the atheist is the issues. It is often the case that the atheist likes to have the best of both worlds (Theistic and Atheistic) in this department. Let me illustrate. Man, who can be no more than merely a complex chemical machine, cries out against injustice, hatred, prejudice, etc., now, why is this so? Is there some sort of transcendent worth attached to a heap of chemical reactions contained in what we call the human body? Hitler seemed to believe in building a 'pure' race, one that would be stronger and one that would be white. He, in my mind, was simply following the natural selection rule to the realm of ethics. Yet, many atheists frown upon Hitler's morals and even go as far as to say that he was evil (with a capital 'E'). My point is this: few atheists are willing to accept the notion of relativism in ethics that MUST follow from their presuppositions. Good and evil are relative so how can you criticize Hitler, to whom is he accountable (for he was the law) and besides, he is supposed to be an autonomous free being.

So what if he reduced 6 million Jews to cinders. Tell me that you don't LIKE what he did or that his actions were SOCIALLY unacceptable, but DON'T tell me that he was bad or evil (capital E). These terms do not belong in your world view . . . they went out with God (capital G).

Now, take careful note, this has not been a criticism of atheism as a world view, rather, an attempt to make atheists realize some of the nihilistic implications of that world view.

f) [Robert T. Pennock, in *Tower of Babel: The Evidence Against the New Creationism* (MIT Press, 1999), p.153.] Look around today and you can see for yourself that most of the organisms you come across are not making it into the fossil record. It takes a rather special combination of physical factors—usually those of swamps or estuaries where remains can be buried in sediment, be compacted and, if lucky, remain undisturbed for millions of years—for the bones or imprints of an organism to achieve a measure of immortality in stone. To then become part of the scientific body of evidence, they have to erode in such a way as not to be destroyed, and then found by someone who recognizes their importance. Furthermore, from what we know of evolutionary mechanisms, speciation events are likely to occur in isolated populations, and competition will quickly eliminate the less fit of closely similar forms. Both processes make it even more unlikely that there will be a smooth, continuous fossil record of intermediaries. Thus, it is not at all surprising that there are 'missing links' in the fossil record and this is not good evidence against evolutionary transmutation.

g) [Margaret Sommerville, in *The Ethical Canary: Science, Society and the Human Spirit* (Penguin Books Ltd, 2000), p. 69] . . . creating multiple embryos from the same embryo damages respect for human life itself—even if it does not contravene respect for any one human individual—and for the transmission of human life. It turns a genetically unique living being of human origin into just an object and one that is replicable in multiple copies. It changes the transmission of human life from a mystery to a manufacturing process. It fails to recognize that we are not free to treat life in any way that we see fit, that we do not own life. Rather, we have life and, most importantly, life has us. Recognizing that we owe obligations to life can provide a basis on which to establish respect for life in a secular society. This recognition means that we must ask, 'What must we not do because to do it would contravene respect for human life itself?' I believe that one answer to this question is the use of human embryos for human therapeutic cloning. This cloning can, therefore, be regarded as inherently wrong.

h) [Ian Wilmut, in *The Second Creation: Dolly and the Age of Biological Control*, by Ian Wilmut, Keith Campbell, and Colin Tudge (Farrarr, Straus and Giroux, 2000), pp. 284–5] In the days and weeks that followed Dolly's birth, many a commentator raised this possibility [of cloning crazed dictators] as one of several 'worst-case scenarios', hence the battalion of Hitlers on the cover of *Der Spiegel*. But a cloned dictator would not replicate the original any more than a cloned genius would. It has often been suggested that Hitler might have become a perfectly innocuous landscape painter if only the Vienna Academy of Fine Arts had accepted him as a student before World War I, and we might reasonably hope that the Hitler clone would be luckier in his choice of university.

A genetic nuclear clone of Hitler would not necessarily strive to create a Fourth Reich. This would be most unlikely. If he inherited his clone father's oratorical powers, he might as soon be a school-teacher—or a priest, which was one of Hitler's own boyhood ambitions. If he was fond of dogs, he might become a vet. Of course, the clone's genetic inheritance would set limits on his achievements. Richer postwar nutrition would most likely ensure that a Hitler clone would be taller than the original, but still, he would never shine at basketball, or trouble the Olympic scorers in the high jump. Unless he grew a poky mustache and smeared his hair across his forehead, few would spot the resemblance to his famous father. The Führer's cloned offspring would surely disappoint their clone pater no end.

The cartoonists' vision of an instant battalion of Hitlers is further nonsense. Clones like Dolly may be produced from adult cells, but they begin their lives as one-cell embryos and then develop at the same rate as others of their kind. Adolf Hitler was 44 years old when he became dictator of Germany and 50 at the outbreak of World War II. It would take just as long to produce the doppelgänger as it did to shape the original, and by that time the political moment that brought the first Hitler to power would be well and truly past, as indeed is the case.

2. THE GOOD ARGUMENTATIVE ESSAY

There are five aspects of good argumentative essay writing that you should consider in constructing an extended argument of your own. They are

(1) scope,
(2) clarity,
(3) structure,
(4) argumentation, and
(5) objectivity.

(1) Scope

Before you begin writing, you should have a clear idea of the thesis or claim you are advancing and the way you intend to defend it. Defining the scope of an argument is a matter of establishing manageable boundaries for your reasoning. Given the evidence that you have amassed for your sub-conclusions, what is the main claim you might reasonably be able to defend? And how can you express that claim without promising too much or so little that the argument becomes trivial?

To answer these questions you need to have a clear idea of your intentions and your audience. You will need to have thought through the issue, looked at it from different perspectives (including the opposing viewpoint), and done as much research as your judgment tells you the situation requires.

Be clear about the context of your argument and its most important feature—your *audience*. Are you writing to reinforce the views of a *sympathetic* audience, as when you present an internal paper in a work situation? Are you writing for a *neutral* audience who is predisposed neither to agree nor to disagree but who is open to be persuaded, as when you prepare a paper for an academic jury like a course instructor? Or are you writing for a *hostile* audience of opponents that is predisposed to the opposite position to your own, as in the case of a controversial public debate on a contentious social issue? Think carefully about the audience you will be addressing and decide what information you can assume they have (that is, what will count as shared knowledge for that audience) and how their beliefs and values will lead them to react to what you say.

Given that the hostile audience is the most demanding one to write for, it should be the default audience when you are unsure who you will be addressing, as when your argument is to appear in a public forum or in future contexts that you cannot control.

With your position clear in your own mind and your audience established, you can set down your main claim. State this in an opening paragraph in which you also outline the principal sub-claims that you will advance to support it. Some people like to hold their main point until the end of their argumentative essay, keeping the audience in suspense and building to a climax. This has rhetorical effectiveness and may work for an accomplished and experienced arguer. It would not work for our purposes because it is important for our audience to know our intentions from the outset so that they can appraise the support for our position as it develops. They can only appreciate the relevance of each point as it arises and admire our arguing technique if they are aware from the outset of the claim for which we are arguing.

Given the essay form of the argumentative essay, there is a temptation to *discuss* the topic rather than argue a claim related to it. Avoid this tendency by adopting the language of argumentation in your opening paragraph. For example: 'In the following I will argue . . .'; or 'My conclusion is . . .'; or 'The claim I intend to support is . . .'.

The following are examples of introductory paragraphs that define the scope by presenting a clear conclusion and explaining how it will be supported.

> Advances in medical technology have given rise to new issues that concern society. One of these, perhaps the chief, is human-embryo experimentation. Critics insist this must not be permitted because the consequences may be too horrendous to handle. While I share such concerns, I will argue that, on balance, human-embryo experimentation should be permitted prior to the fourteenth day after fertilization. I will support this with the following sub-claims: (1) prior to the fourteenth day the human embryo is not a person, and (2) only persons are morally significant; (3) the benefits of human-embryo experimentation far outweigh the negative aspects.

*

> In his *Civilization and Its Discontents* Sigmund Freud argues that humans are inherently aggressive. I wish to take issue with this viewpoint and will support the claim that humans are inherently good. To this end I will argue (1) that Freud's conclusion is an overgeneralization based on a selective sample of cases; and (2) that recent studies of children show that aggressive behaviour is learned, not innate.

Reading your introductory paragraph, no one should be in any doubt about what it is you are arguing. You are also giving notice of how your argument is going to be structured, which will aid you in your writing as much as it helps your readers.

(2) Clarity

In order to communicate your intentions clearly you need to think about *how* you are saying things as much as about what it is you are saying. What may be clear to you may not be so clear to your readers, and you should take time to consider this. In earlier chapters we have seen how vague or illegitimately biased language can hurt an otherwise sound argument. When writing an argumentative essay we need to be particularly careful about the way we state claims. One common problem is the tendency to overstate a claim, that is, to claim more than we can support. Often, this can be avoided simply by qualifying our statements. Consider the following pairs of claims:

> A   There are a number of reasons why we should not manipulate the human gene pool.
> B   The human gene pool should never be manipulated.

> A   Freud's examples are rarely convincing.
> B   None of Freud's examples are convincing.

> A   It seems likely that wearing helmets while cycling will save lives.
> B   Clearly, wearing helmets while cycling will save lives.

In each case, statement B is much stronger than statement A. But this is not a positive sense of 'stronger than', because in each case the onus placed on the arguer who would support statement B is much greater. It is more reasonable to expect that we can provide persuasive evidence for the qualified statements in A. When you put down a claim, ask yourself: 'Can I support this, or should I modify it first?'

Another thing to consider is whether you have adequately defined the key terms you are using. Central to the arguments expressed in the introductory paragraphs on medical technology and Freud, above, are the terms 'human embryo' and 'aggressiveness'. You have the obligation to define such terms, because it is likely that the entire extended argument will depend on how your audience understands them. Such definitions should come as early in the argument as possible, perhaps immediately after the introductory paragraph. It is possible for an otherwise clear argumentative essay to leave readers quite unsure about the central terms on which it depends.

(3) Structure

A well-structured argumentative essay is an effective vehicle for the ideas it conveys. Develop your points in a logical order in terms of both strength and dependency. In other words, (1) begin with your strongest point or sub-argument, and (2) where points depend on one another, establish them in an order that shows that dependency and makes sense to the reader.

Beginning with your strongest and most plausible point will capture the reader's attention as well as their conviction. If you succeed in creating a solid foundation for the acceptance of your position, you can build subsequent arguments on it. Starting with your strongest point *for* your claim should not mean that your argument will weaken as it develops. Later arguments that deal with points *against* your claim, or that anticipate and meet objections to what you are saying, may be among the strongest points you will make overall, giving balance and completeness to your reasoning.

For example, in arguing that circuses are undesirable because they mistreat animals, the following claim could be advanced:

C1 = Circuses put animals in unnatural environments and require them to do unnatural things.

Such a claim could be supported by premises that indicate the natural habitats and behaviours of circus animals, and further common-knowledge premises indicating the performance-focused circus environment of such animals. But this argument depends upon a key claim that the argument assumes:

C2 = What is natural is good and what is unnatural is bad/undesirable.

C2 and its supporting evidence should precede C1 or at least be conjoined with it. For C2 to be introduced a page or so later, with other sub-arguments intervening, would be a structural weakness, since the flow of the argumentation would then not be sequential.

While no one would expect you to include a diagram even of the macro-structure, it is a good idea to plot this out for yourself and keep it by your side for reference while you are writing. This will allow you to take advantage of all the benefits of the diagramming technique. You will see how well your argument fits together, how easy (or hard) it is to detect the logical structure, and where support is lacking or overly dependent on one idea. If you have difficulty diagramming your own argument, you can expect someone else to have trouble seeing the connections.

(4) Argumentation

Our purpose in writing an argumentative essay is to convince an audience of our conclusion, or to reinforce the conviction they already hold. If we are to succeed in this, our argument must be strong.

The bulk of this text has dealt with assessing various types of argument. At this point, therefore, we shall simply restate some of the basic principles set forth elsewhere insofar as those principles apply to the writing of the argumentative essay:

- Make sure that your premises are statements that are distinct and separate from your conclusion.
- Ensure that each premise offered in support of a claim must, together with the other reasons, increase the acceptability of that claim.
- Ensure that issues are correctly recognized and directly addressed, and that any version of an opposing argument has been fairly represented.
- Back your claims with as many relevant reasons as necessary to convince your audience.
- Ensure that all your statements, including premises and conclusions, are consistent with each other.
- Do not rely on hidden components: make your assumptions explicit and defend them where necessary.

(5) Objectivity

Besides communicating a sense of fairness and balanced judgment, objectivity in the argumentative essay covers two points.

The first point concerns the views of your opponents. We have all seen overtly one-sided arguments, where all the attention is devoted to *directly* promoting the position held. After all, you might say, the whole point has been to argue for one's position. But in many, if not most, issues there is an opposing point of view with its own considerations. An *indirect* way to further support your case is to consider some of the strongest points of your opponents and show how they can be dealt with or outweighed by your own points. This adds an atmosphere of objectivity to your argument because, if you do it fairly, it shows that you have thought about both sides of the issue and are prepared to recognize the stronger counter-claims.

Naturally, there is a danger of straw-reasoning here. You must only attribute to the opposing viewpoint arguments that you know exist on that side, and you should support that knowledge in some way. It is up to you to judge which of your opponents' arguments are the stronger ones. If you choose those that are obviously weaker and respond to them, or if you attribute to the opposing viewpoint arguments that no one actually holds, then the whole process backfires. Rather than demonstrating objectivity, your argument will appear to the discerning reader to lack objectivity altogether and to be guilty of misrepresentation.

After you have addressed the known arguments of the opposing point of view, A second way to exhibit objectivity is to consider what someone of that persuasion might say in response to what you have specifically said. That is, anticipate objections to your own points. In this way you can demonstrate objectivity by showing that you are prepared to consider criticisms of your own ideas and that you are able to look at your arguments from a different perspective. Quite often such a reading will enable you to detect flaws in your arguments and lead you to make constructive revisions.

Even once you are satisfied with what you have argued, you will still see places where objections might be raised. It is important to note these in your essay: 'Someone might respond to this point by arguing that . . .' You can then counter the objection with a reasonable response. Identifying likely objections—again, without making false attributions—and answering those anticipated objections will add further indirect support to your position.

THE COMPONENTS OF GOOD ARGUMENTATIVE ESSAYS

1. Scope
2. Clarity
3. Structure
4. Argumentation
5. Objectivity

EXERCISE 15B

Think about one of the following topics. Diagram the structure of a macro argument that would express your position on the topic. Next, develop this argument by elaborating micro arguments.

a) objectivity in politics
b) the existence of intelligent life elsewhere in the universe
c) the obligation of wealthier nations to help poorer nations
d) surrogate motherhood
e) prison reform
f) miracles
g) the importance of the United Nations in maintaining peace in the world

3. A Student's Paper

For easy reference in discussing the following paper, each sentence is labelled with a letter, signifying the paragraph, and a digit, signifying the sentence within a given paragraph. Thus 'C' identifies a particular paragraph and 'C3' the third sentence in that paragraph.

Human Cloning

(A1) Human Cloning is an emotional and complex issue. (A2) You can get different views on it depending on who you talk to. (A3) But everyone agrees that there is something very disturbing about it. (A4) Society should think very carefully before it moves in such a direction.

(B1) What is involved here is people making replicas of themselves, or of a child who they have perhaps lost and want to replace. (B2) What they want to do is control what their children will be like.

(C1) The main reason for this is that people do not have the right to decide the identity of another person. (C2) To create identical people in this way is a violation of something very important. (C3) When we have children the proper way there is an element of chance in how something will look and what abilities they will have. (C4) But human cloning takes away that chance and makes a person just like the person they were cloned from.

(D1) People do not have a fundamental right to decide what they want. (D2) There is the freedom to choose. (D3) But this only exists as long as we are not harming anyone else. (D4) When people lose the right to make of themselves what they will and to be surprised by their lives, then they are being harmed.

(E1) Another reason to be concerned is that governments may abuse this technology. (E2) Human cloning will allow the very best qualities of strength and intelligence to be developed in people. (E3) It will be natural for governments to want to build stronger, more talented soldiers. (E4) This is eugenics at its worst.

(F1) Those who support human cloning do so for only one reason. (F2) They wrongly think it will lead to a better society where the tragedies of genetically-transmitted diseases will be gone. (F3) This is a Slippery Slope where the altering of our fundamental nature will become routine. (F4) This will not happen. (F5) Besides, scientists are already finding natural ways to combat diseases and improve the lives of those inflicted by them. (F6) Wouldn't it be better to take this route and avoid the risks of human cloning?

(G1) Health care costs have been steadily rising for decades now and as the Baby Boom generation moves into old age these costs will rise even further. (G2) No decisions should be entirely governed by economic considerations. (G3) But where other problems and risks have been shown to exist, refusing to develop expensive technologies saves society more unnecessary costs.

(H1) In conclusion, there are no good reasons to allow human cloning. (H2) Most people who think seriously about it are repulsed by the idea and their opinion should count.

Critique

There are several positive things that can be said about this paper. The main claim is relatively clear: human cloning should not be permitted. Some attempt is made in paragraph B to define the key idea. Furthermore, the writer has organized the essay neatly around several sub-points, devoting a brief paragraph to each. Also, an attempt is made in paragraph F to deal with the position of those who support human cloning. Nevertheless, there is room for improvement on each feature of a good argumentative essay, as a detailed evaluation will indicate.

Overview

In this essay, the writer argues that there are no good reasons in favour of human cloning and that society should not permit it. To this end, the arguer claims (a) that people have a fundamental right to decide their own identity, and that (b) this overrides any imagined rights that others may have to make such decisions for their offspring. Also, (c) human cloning will lead to abuses on the parts of governments who want to build super armies. Finally, (d) there are economic costs to consider.

The arguer uses analogical reasoning in paragraphs C and F. In comparing reproductive cloning to the 'proper' way to have children and to scientists finding 'natural' ways to combat disease, the writer implies that human cloning is both improper and unnatural.

Structure

We can represent this argument with both the macro- and micro-structure diagrams. Doing so reveals which statements and paragraphs contribute directly to the argument and which do not. We will approach the structure paragraph by paragraph.

Paragraph A *should* have the main conclusion in it. If so, A4 is the only clear candidate. The first two statements report in a general way facts about the issue. A3, if correct, undermines the need for real argumentation since, if everyone did agree, the matter would not be controversial. A4, on the other hand, is a claim that could, and should, be argued. We will come back to it when we look at paragraph H.

Paragraph B is definitional. It attempts to clarify the key term. We will consider this under 'language'.

Paragraph C is the first clear sub-argument. C1 gives the main reason for 'this', which is presumably the main claim. People do not have the right to decide the identity of others because this violates some important element (C2). This, at first vague, element is the chance factor in the lottery of looks and abilities that characterizes 'proper' reproduction. So the micro diagram of paragraph C can be read as follows:

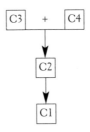

There are two things to note about paragraph D. First, it contains three unsupported independent assertions of 'rights': D1, D3, and D4. (D2 is qualified by D3.) These are crucial claims to the outcome of the argument, especially D4. Second, D1 has been presupposed by C1. D1 asserts the *general* claim that people do not have a fundamental right to make decisions on the basis of their desires. C1 asserts the *specific* claim that people do not have the right to decide the identity of another person. If D1 is accepted, then it serves as support for C1. So, in terms of the argument's structure, D1 is logically prior to C1 and should have been presented (together with an attempt to establish it) before C1. The micro-structure of paragraph D simply consists of three unrelated claims, with D1 leading in the direction of C1, and D2, D3, and D4 giving combined separate support to the main claim.

The four statements of paragraph E deal with the eugenic plans of governments. E1 asserts what may happen, with the other three statements supporting the scenario of abuse.

Paragraph F deals with an opposing argument that human cloning will lead to a healthier society that is free of major diseases. F4 asserts the author's denial of such an outcome. The reason for this denial lies apparently in the author's view that the opposing viewpoint depends on a bad slippery-slope argument (F2 and F3). F5 shifts attention to alternative efforts to bring about the same outcome and supports the claim, hidden in the rhetorical question of F6, that this alternative route will be a better choice. The micro diagram of paragraph F reads as follows:

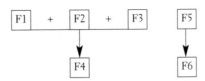

Paragraph G introduces a consideration of the cost to society of the new technology. G3 expresses the author's claim, while G1 and G2 combine as support for it:

In paragraph H we are brought back to the question of the main conclusion. H1 expresses a very strong claim that there are no good reasons to allow human cloning. From reading through the whole argument it seems wise to understand the main conclusion as a hidden one, to the effect that 'Human cloning should not be permitted.' There is no question that the student is arguing for this, although nowhere is it expressly stated. Such a hidden main conclusion captures the sentiment of both A4 and H1. But it also weakens the effect of H1. If we take H1 as the main conclusion, much of the reasoning will not support it. In fact, we will invoke the principle of charity again here and see H1 as the conclusion to only the first argument in paragraph F. This is because H1 asserts there are, in conclusion, no good arguments *for* human cloning, and paragraph F had allowed only one reason for people supporting it.

On the other hand, H2 relates to the earlier statement in A3 in that the writer sees popular opinion opposing human cloning. H2, unlike A3, is expressed like an argument intended as support for the main conclusion: 'their opinion should count.'

If we understand paragraph H this way, we arrive at the macro-structure of the argument:

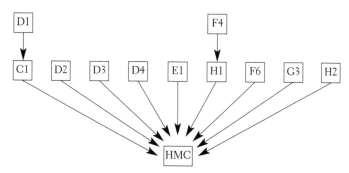

Language

You should have already noted several problems with the language in this argument. We had difficulty identifying the main claim. There are also several statements that are vague, which can be understood only by relying on their context.

While most of the language is neutral in its tone, we have seen two assumptions that indicate an illegitimate bias. These are the references to the 'proper' way to have children (C3) and 'natural' ways to combat diseases (F5). The language of these phrases assumes an unnaturalness about human cloning that cannot just be assumed but needs to be argued for. What actually constitutes 'natural' and why it is to be preferred are important questions in this debate.

The definition in paragraph B, while awkward, is adequate to the student's purpose. It illustrates how 'human cloning' is to be understood with respect to the concerns raised here. It is not a technical definition and would not suffice in other contexts, but it is important that some attempt has been made to explain the key term.

We had to interpret C1 as referring to the main conclusion, as presenting the arguer's main reason for the overall position. Here we used the context to resolve the question of vagueness surrounding 'this' and its referent.

Two other things worth mentioning concern F3 and F6. The charge of slippery slope is unclear. We understand the arguer to be attributing a bad slippery-slope argument to the opposing viewpoint, where human cloning is believed to lead to an unrealistic utopian society. But we had to make this interpretation ourselves using what we know of slippery-slope arguments. The onus was on the arguer to be clearer. F6 is a rhetorical question that masks an assertion. Including F6 as a sub-conclusion involves recognizing that assertion. As a practice, the use of rhetorical questions should be avoided because the audience may miss entirely the statement that is being made.

Reasoning

We will look first at the macro-structure of the argument and consider the sub-arguments as the need arises.

We have taken the hidden main conclusion to be that human cloning should not be permitted. Most of the claims given in support of this are relevant to it. If people do not have the right to decide for others, and if taking away such decisions is a kind of harm, then C1 and the linked premises D2–D4 increase our reasons for holding the HMC. Likewise, if the technology may be abused, then E4 is relevant. H1 certainly increases the case for the HMC, if there are no good reasons for allowing human cloning. Again, F6, G3 and H2 all provide relevant considerations for the HMC. Thus the argument exhibits the general strength of internal relevance of its sub-claims to the HMC.

Where serious concerns arise is when we start to consider whether those claims are acceptable in themselves or adequately supported. Some of these are difficult to decide about. Many audiences would accept C1 as expressing a common value, and added to this, there is the relevant support of D1 that also forms part of the shared values of many audiences. But if we assume a hostile audience for this argument, then both C1 and D1 could be questioned, at least to the extent of requiring further reasons for accepting them. Someone who believes strongly in reproductive freedom may not accept C1, or even D1, and such beliefs can fairly be attributed to the hostile audience for this argument. Given this, it would be wise for the arguer to address the question of whether people have a right to their own reproductive choices, one that overrides any rights that may be conferred on those who do not yet exist.

D3 is another statement with which many would agree: harming others sets a limit to our own freedom. But *is* having one's identity decided for one a harm, as D4 asserts? This claim is very important for the student's position, but it is not supported. Even a sympathetic audience should be bothered by this. Undefended, we have no reason to accept D4. And since it is crucial to the HMC, its questionable status is a serious blow to the sufficiency of the argument.

The sub-argument for E1 introduces the topic of what abuses might result from governments' use of human cloning technology. The reasons provided in the premises are relevant to E1, but at least E3 and E4 are questionable. We are not told why it would be 'natural' for governments to want to use the technology for militaristic ends. This is a scenario that has been popularized in films and fiction, but as a supporting premise it requires its own justification. Nor is it clear why this is eugenics at its worst. The arguer has not specified the meaning of 'eugenics', but this can be readily checked, and in the context of this debate perhaps its meaning can be assumed. As a science of improving the species, eugenics may not be entirely neutral, but 'worst', like 'best', is a comparative value judgment, and all such judgments need support.

The sub-argument leading to H1 is also a concern. H1 claims there are no good reasons to allow human cloning. If correct, it provides very strong evidence for the HMC. But only one reason for human cloning has been considered. While F4 is relevant to H1, it is not sufficient for it, in part because H1 is worded so strongly. The acceptability of F1 becomes important to this sub-argument. We have no reason to accept that there is only one reason for promoting human cloning, and any exposure to the issue will have told us that this is not the case. In fact, in our consideration of C1 and D1 we have already recognized one other. So F1 is contradicted by what we know, and thus it is unacceptable. The one reason given is the slippery-slope argument suggested by F2 and F3. Why the arguer believes the scenario envisioned at the end of this slope will not happen is unclear. The arguer has failed to give any evaluation of the suggested slippery slope. F2 and F3, while relevant to F4, do not provide sufficient support for it, and so F4 cannot be accepted. This renders ineffective an important sub-argument and reveals the arguer's appearance of objectivity to be quite the opposite.

The author expresses in F6 a belief that avoiding the risks of human cloning would be better than any benefits. F5 provides relevant support for this. But again, F5 itself lacks adequate support. The implied analogy with current medical science seems plausible. But we cannot evaluate it unless we have reason to believe that this alternative way of addressing genetic disease itself involves no comparable risks to individuals and society while offering results as good as what might be expected from human cloning technology. Such evidence may exist, but the arguer has not provided any of it, and the acceptability of F5 requires that it be given.

G3, while a very controversial reason, does stand up to scrutiny. G1 reports a common state of affairs, and G2 expresses a value that even a hostile audience is likely to share. Together they provide adequate support for G3. But G3 will be subject to a serious counter-argument just because it is controversial to weigh such costs against human lives.

H2, on the other hand, stands alone. Like A3, it purports to express a general sentiment. But the claim that 'most people' find the idea of human cloning repulsive requires the backing of a recognized poll or survey before we will have reason to accept it.

The final thing to note here, under the condition of sufficiency, is that the arguer fails to anticipate objections to the claims and assumptions being made here. Chief among these is the confusion surrounding questions of nature and nurture. That is, how much of what we are as individuals is due to our genetic make-up, inherited from our parents, and how much is due to the environments in which we develop? The arguer's concerns about loss of identity and choice seem to suggest that nurture has little impact on the developing individual, and that cloned children will replicate their parents in all ways. This would be a likely place for a critic to begin to develop a counter-argument.

Strengths and Weaknesses
We might summarize the strengths and weaknesses of the paper as follows:

Strengths	Weaknesses
• good internal relevance of sub-claims to HMC	• a number of points of vagueness
• attempts to define key term	• key claims D1 and D4 are questionable
• acceptable sub-argument G3	• sub-argument F for H1 is unacceptable
	• sub-argument to F6 is questionable
	• H2 requires statistical support
	• insufficient evidence for HMC

On balance we can see that there are reasons to reject this argument as it stands. This is not due to the longer list of weaknesses but to the more detrimental nature of some of those weaknesses. In spite of being characterized by strong internal relevance, the argument has too many claims that cannot be accepted or whose acceptability cannot be determined. D4 is crucial here, since it deals with the important matter of whether there are harms involved. The appearance of objectivity is lost owing to the inadequacy of the sub-argument to H1. On examination, we see that the arguer has not really considered what is at stake in the opposing viewpoint. The problematic nature of these claims, together with that of F6, means that there is not sufficient evidence for the HMC, and the argument is unpersuasive.

Many of these flaws, however, are of a kind that might be remedied. While the sub-argument H1 rests on the misconception in F1 and would have to be replaced or substantially rewritten, the sub-arguments to C1 (and D1), F6, and H2 could all conceivably be strengthened.

In the light of this critique, the student's draft clearly needs a good deal of polishing. Taking note of our comments, we will rework the argumentative essay we have been analyzing. We are not suggesting that what follows is how the student would rewrite the essay. This is our rewriting of the argument, and in many respects it is more than would be expected in an introductory course on reasoning. But we also have an obligation to discharge: having critiqued the paper, we submit our own version, which we invite you to critique. Usually, a rewrite like this would pass through several drafts. In this case, you will see only the final draft, but in your own revisions you should be aware that rewriting is a progressive job that may require a number of revisions. In proposing the following revision, we must also emphasize that other possible versions could successfully amend the draft with which we began.

Revision

Human Cloning

Since Ian Wilmut and his colleagues announced in the pages of *Nature* that they had successfully cloned Dolly the sheep from a single adult cell[1] public and media attention has been drawn to the prospects of developing this technology for use with humans. Debate has ensued over the social and moral advisability of such development. On the one hand, the technology offers new hope to infertile couples who desire children to whom they are genetically related, and holds the wider promise of removing from the human gene pool hereditary diseases that have afflicted many. On the other hand, people see this as playing God in ways we have never done before—of altering the very nature of human beings and stripping human life of its mystery by reducing it to a commodity.

We hold that human cloning, as it is currently conceived, should not be permitted and that legislation should be introduced to prevent it. We will argue (a) that human cloning has too many possible negative consequences for the cloned individual, including the psychological impact of losing a certain ignorance about one's life and the physical risks of exposure to diseases such as those related to aging; (b) that there will be greater social harms like the diminished value of human life; and (c) that the right to reproductive freedom, while important in its own right, cannot justify the countervailing risks involved.

In this essay, 'human cloning' will be understood to mean 'human reproductive cloning', which is the production of children that are genetically identical to the cell donor. This is in contrast to 'human therapeutic cloning', which involves the production of embryos for research or to manufacture therapeutic products, including tissues and organs. We will not treat therapeutic cloning in this essay.

(a)

Human cloning produces twins—humans who share a genetic identity and then develop distinct personalities and abilities according to the different influences of their environment. But while proponents of human cloning often point to this twinning aspect when arguing that the results of cloning are not unnatural because we already have such people (twins) in society, human cloning produces twins that are relevantly dissimilar from what we have seen before. What we call non-cloned twins share life at the same rate: rarely is there more than a few minutes between their births, and they grow up together, experiencing the surprises of their abilities and of any illnesses as they arise. But, setting aside the cloning of children who are dying or have just died, cloned 'twins' are separated by a generation, and this difference is significant. Their identical other is a parent, an adult, and not a sibling of equal status. The cloned child will already know what it will look like at 10 years of age, as an adolescent, and even as a young adult. It will see its future in the parent in a way that other children simply do not. The mystery of development, of a certain level of wonder, will be taken from the child. We would not say, as some have argued,[2] that we have a 'right' to this ignorance about our future. Rights are too nebulous a concept for this debate. But we would say that in cloning humans, we would be altering the very nature of childhood and changing human development in a way that may have an enormous negative impact on the psyches of those who experience it. Granted we cannot remove all risks from life, but until we have a better sense of how such a fundamental change might affect people, we should not allow human cloning.

There are also physical risks to consider. The technology that produced Dolly and other animals has not been able to prevent the clone from aging at a rate greater than that expected of the donor animal. While such a flaw is likely soon to be corrected, this is simply an example of the kind of unexpected consequence that may arise. We do not know if cloned humans will be more susceptible to certain forms of cancer or other diseases. Again, until we have a much better understanding of the technologies involved, the cloning of humans should not be allowed.

(b)

The arguments above can be seen to be of a 'not yet' variety, warning that it is too soon to countenance the cloning of humans. Consider, also, some 'not ever' arguments, which would not allow human cloning under any circumstances.

One of the great dangers of human cloning is the potential loss of genetic diversity. Ethicist Margaret Somerville writes: 'Many people believe that we must not interfere with the human gene pool . . . because it is the common heritage of humankind and it would be wrong for us to change that heritage. . . . Just from the perspective of practical survival, genetic diversity is important to ensure the integrity and resilience of the human gene pool and, therefore, of human life.'[3] The concern is a real one: we simply do not know what we may be doing by altering the gene pool, even when we remove genes responsible for hereditary diseases. We do not know whether we are dealing with something like an ecological system, where each part has a role to play, and the loss of one element eventually changes the relationships among those that remain.

Beyond this, human cloning threatens a very basic respect that we hold for human life and in turn threatens to alter our basic humanness. Whether or not we allow the buying or selling of cloned embryos, the technology, if developed, allows for the commodification of humans in a way we have never seen before. We may come to think of ourselves in ways we have not done before, and all our attempts to retain and insist on the reverence of human life, through wars and famines, terrorism and disease, may come to nought. When we take control of human life, changing its appearance and nature at will, we commodify it in ways that *in vitro* fertilization and gamete donation never did.

(c)

Critics will point out that such arguments are vague and too generalized, and overlook the human tragedies of couples who are unable to have children of their own. It is argued that reproductive freedom is a basic right that all should enjoy and, therefore, society has an obligation, where possible, to provide the means to overcome infertility. Adoption does not fully address this need—cloning provides a genetic link between family members that adoption cannot. This certainly is a serious consideration and cannot be casually dismissed. But the right to reproductive freedom includes both the choice not to reproduce, through the use of contraception or abortion, for example, as well as to reproduce. As so understood, it is a negative right, meaning that people have a right to act without interference from the government or others. The only reasonable restrictions that might be placed on such liberty are in cases where harm might result to a third party. But this is exactly the concern that we have raised above with respect to the cloned child: there are quite plausible risks that may well result in serious harms. Given the potential seriousness of the consequences of human cloning, we believe that the burden of proof should lie with those who would invoke their right to reproductive freedom to show that real harms will not result.

In conclusion, there are several strong reasons for not allowing human cloning and that justify the introduction of legislation to prevent it. Polls indicate wide public support for such legislation, at least in some countries.[4] We must think very carefully before we take any steps toward altering society in such a radical way.

Notes

1   Wilmut, I. et al. (1997) 'Viable Offspring Derived from Fetal and Adult Mammalian Cells', *Nature* 385: 810–13.

2   Jonas, H. (1974) *Philosophical Essays: From Ancient Creed to Technological Man.* Englewood Cliffs, NJ: Prentice-Hall.

3   Somerville, M. (2000) *The Ethical Canary: Science, Society and the Human Spirit.* Toronto: Penguin Books Canada Ltd.

4   A 1997 Canada-wide telephone poll of 1,516 adults conducted by Ipsos-Reid of Canada found 72 per cent concerned about human cloning. A 1998 poll of Canadians conducted by Pollara found 80 per cent opposed to a person cloning themselves and raising that clone as a child.

4. Conclusion

Human Cloning is a highly controversial and often divisive issue, but it is just the kind of issue that demands clear, critical thinking. We hope you will recognize the benefits of the skills we have discussed throughout this text when you work on issues such as this. Since this is a topic that raises many complex issues, we recognize that good arguments can be constructed for a point of view that opposes the one that has been advocated in our rewrite. It is the interaction between these opposing arguments that, in the long run, is most likely to bring a reasonable resolution to the cloning issue.

Good reasoning is not, however, limited to our thinking about difficult issues. It permeates all corners of our lives, clarifying our ideas and enriching our experiences. We wish you the best in your own encounters with arguments, both those you construct and those you evaluate. We hope you will continue to build on the skills discussed here—something that can be accomplished through practice—and that you will value your development as a critical thinker. Good reasoning is often difficult, but it always matters!

Major Exercise 15M

1. Diagram our revised essay and write an evaluative critique of it.

2. Research and write an evaluative essay that supports the opposite position to that argued in the revision.

3. Select a topic from the list below or propose a controversial topic for approval by your instructor. Research it and reflect on it, and then write an argumentative essay (about four double-spaced pages in length, or 1,000 words). Assume a universal audience.
   a) gun control
   b) human embryo experimentation
   c) homeopathy
   d) the morality of zoos
   e) United Nations peacekeeping
   f) affirmative action
   g) genetically modified food
   h) DNA testing in criminal cases
   i) universal medicare
   j) immigration policies
   k) same-sex marriage

Note: These suggested answers show some measured judgment of the arguments and exercises involved, and illustrate the principles and skills discussed in the text. In many instances, however, alternative possibilities exist. That is to be expected with good critical thinking in societies like our own. Do not hesitate to test your alternatives with instructors and others in your course.

CHAPTER 1

Exercise 1A

2. In the argument suggested, the **premise** is 'killing something is a form of cruelty', and the **conclusion** is 'it is wrong to kill and eat animals'.
   The following argument might be used to address this:

   PREMISE: Killing that is painless and free of suffering is not cruel.
   PREMISE: Animals that are killed for food under government regulations are killed without pain or suffering.
   CONCLUSION: Animals that are killed for food are not treated cruelly.

Exercise 1B

2. The argument here is that 'you' (a reader, assumed to be a parent) should buy new improved Johnson's Baby Shampoo (**conclusion**) because it is hypoallergenic and will protect 'her' scalp from irritation (**premise**), and you have promised to protect her (**premise**).

   Of course, 'you' have not promised to protect the baby in the photo, who is unknown. That is how we can tell the intended audience is new parents who will see the baby as representing their own and so relate to the claim that they have promised to protect their baby. Without that transference the premise would not be at all acceptable.

Exercise 1C

2. a) You'll like the sun. You'll like the beach. You'll like the people. **Therefore,** you'll like Jamaica.

    c) **Because the soldiers taken** have the right to fire and bomb, **they are** soldiers in combat. **Therefore,** they are prisoners of war and not hostages, and **because** proper military procedures make soldiers prisoners of war, not hostages. **Therefore,** the Serbs have responded in accordance with appropriate military procedure.

3. c) This seems to be a report of scientific findings, but there is no obvious premise–conclusion relationship to the statements presented. No reason is given, for example, for why they decided that the mummy received the contaminants from improperly glazed pottery. Therefore, it is not an argument.

    e) This advertisement begins with a significant claim to distinguish Battlefield 1942 from other action games. But, again, no evidence is provided to support the claim. What we have is a description of the game's features.

Exercise 1D

1. b) 'Because' works here as a premise indicator, because the statement that precedes it (drugs should be legal) is a controversial claim that needs to be defended as a conclusion rather than explained. The statement that follows 'because' serves as a reason for the conclusion.

    g) Here, that King does not include a link to the site in question is already known. What stands to be explained is why there is no link. Thus, his reaction to what he takes to be smugness and an offensive tone serves as an explanation for that decision. There are no indicator words.

2. a) *argument*
        (1) Affirmative action programs promote a 'victim mentality' in the minds of those who benefit from them, because they hire individuals on the grounds that they are members of a group that has suffered from injustice.
        (2) Snowy owls are not found this far south. So what you saw must have been some other kind of bird.

    d) *rhetorical question*
        (1) 'She's a democrat, isn't she?' in the remark 'Of course, she's pro-choice. She's a democrat, isn't she?'
        (2) 'Would you trust this man?' in the remark 'He's been convicted of theft ten times, and of assault and battery twice. Would you trust this man?'

    h) *opponents*
        (1) In arguing for a pro-choice position on abortion, one's opponents are those who maintain that abortion should be illegal.

(2) In arguing against new taxes on automobiles that damage the environment, one's opponents are those who advocate those taxes (most probably, environmental groups).

3. a) We have defined an argument as a unit of discourse that contains a conclusion and supporting statements or premises (**premise**). *Since* (**premise indicator**) many groups of sentences do not satisfy this definition and cannot be classified as arguments (**premise**), we must begin learning about arguments in this sense by learning to differentiate between arguments and non-arguments (**conclusion**).

   c) In logic, we have an argument whenever we have reasons suggested as premises for a conclusion (**premise**). Explanations can contain reasoning in this sense (**premise**) and can, *therefore*, (**conclusion indicator**) [Explanations can] be classified as arguments (**conclusion**).

Major Exercise 1M

a) This is an argument. The first statement is a controversial claim that a questioning audience would expect to be supported. The subsequent statements are attempts to provide the required support.

> PREMISE: Historians of religion agree that it had its beginnings in magic and witchcraft.
> PREMISE: Today's religious belief is just an extension of this.
> CONCLUSION: Religion is nothing but superstition.

b) This passage contains no logical indicators. While it does address a controversial issue, it is written as a report of a personal reaction rather than as an argument justifying some conclusion. So we would judge it not to be an argument.

c) This passage is merely a description, not an argument.

f) This is not an argument, but an expression of opinion.

h) This passage contains an argument that can be summarized as follows:

> PREMISE 1: Flattery works like a heat-seeking missile, only what it homes in on is our vanity.
> PREMISE 2: Vanity, as the sages tell us, is the most universal human trait.
> CONCLUSION: Flattery almost always works (i.e. hits its target).

i) This passage contains no premise or conclusion indicators. The only possible evidence offered for a conclusion is the claim that none of the fathers and husbands they know come anywhere close to the definition Pearson proposes. As this would be a weak argument (for how could the reader know that such premises are true?), this is better classified as an expression of opinion.

r) There is an attempt to develop an argument here, supporting the memory of Earhart by challenging the credibility of Elinor Smith. It may have the appearance of a borderline case, but reasons are given here for the view expressed. If we take the regret that Smith was quoted to assert the conclusion that Smith should not have been quoted, then we see several reasons given for this claim:

> PREMISE: Smith has been slinging mud at Earhart and her husband, George Putnam, for years, and I lay it down to jealousy.
>
> PREMISE: Amelia got her pilot's licence in 1923 (not 1929 as Smith once wrote).
>
> CONCLUSION: Elinor Smith should not have been quoted (her views are suspect).

v) Given that this is a remark made in defence of a commitment to the coverage of New Age issues, it is most plausibly interpreted as the following argument:

> PREMISE: When I was going through a recent bout with depression, I sought comfort in Artemis, built an altar to her in my room, burned incense, and meditated, and I found comfort in these ritualistic practices.
>
> CONCLUSION: This type of paganism can be an important tool for women to discover their inner strengths.

CHAPTER 2

Exercise 2A

1. a) *diagram legend*

A 'diagram legend' identifies the premises and conclusions of an argument and assigns them a number: P1, P2, etc.

EXAMPLE 1

Argument

Since we do not know what physical or psychological problems may develop for those treated, and polls tell us that people generally oppose the use of the technology, then society should not permit human or therapeutic cloning in the near future.

Legend
- P1 = We do not know what physical or psychological problems may develop for those treated.
- P2 = Polls tell us that people generally oppose the use of the technology.
- C = Society should not permit human or therapeutic cloning in the near future.

EXAMPLE 2

Argument (and Explanation)

The vineyards of Chile are all planted with French grapes, so you can expect Chilean wine to have the same superior quality as its French counterpart.

Legend
P1 = The vineyards of Chile are all planted with French grapes.
C = You can expect Chilean wine to have the same superior quality as its French counterpart.

2. d) This is not an argument, but a statement about the story of Chicago blues and its relationship to the African-American experience.

e) This is an interesting example. On the one hand, it forwards an argument that can be diagrammed as follows:

P1 = Blues is, at root, a folk idiom that comes from the folk at the grassroots street level (the music got recorded at Chess, VJ, and other labels, but it got created on Maxwell Street).

C1 = If preserving the Chess Studios is essential to the legacy of the Blues, certainly Maxwell Street must be preserved also.

P2 = Hillary Clinton has an appreciation for and understanding of the blues and has played an instrumental role in ensuring that the Chess Studios have been saved and rehabbed.

MC = You should urge Hillary Clinton to Save Maxwell Street, An American Treasure.

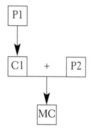

The *audience* for this argument consists of people who will potentially support the saving of Maxwell Street. The *opponents* are those who would oppose such an attempt (perhaps those who would oppose the expenditure of the funds this would require, for example).

The passage is interesting because it suggests another argument (e) that could be used in trying to convince a much more specific audience—i.e. Hillary Clinton— that she should be active in supporting the preservation of Maxwell Street. It is difficult to say who the opponents of such an argument might be, but they could include Hillary Clinton herself (if she is opposed to offering more support). The argument suggested for Hillary Clinton can be diagrammed as follows:

P1 = Blues is, at root, a folk idiom, which comes from the folk at the grassroots street level (the music got recorded at Chess, VJ, and other labels, but it got created on Maxwell Street).

C1 = If preserving the Chess Studios is essential to the legacy of the Blues, certainly Maxwell Street must be preserved also.

P2 = You appreciate and understand the blues and played an instrumental role in ensuring that the Chess Studios have been saved and rehabbed.

MC = You should play an instrumental role in ensuring that Maxwell Street is saved and rehabilitated.

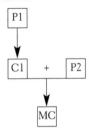

h) This is not an argument, but an explanation. What is in question is not the change in voting pattern, but what produced it.

Exercise 2B

2. a) Admission to a college education depends on demonstrated ability and hence is not simply a right that everyone enjoys. Thus, it should be considered a privilege.

P1 = Admission to a college education depends on demonstrated ability.

C = Admission to a college education is not simply a right that everyone enjoys.

MC = College education should be considered a privilege.

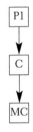

OPPONENTS: those who believe that education generally is a right and there should be no distinction between a college education and the levels of education that precede it

b) Genetic experiments hold great promise for the future of society, and nothing that holds such promise should be banned. Therefore, genetic experiments should not be banned.

P1 = Genetic experiments hold great promise for the future of society.

P2 = Nothing that holds such promise should be banned.

C = Genetic experiments should not be banned.

OPPONENTS: those who challenge the first premise (and conclusion)

c)   In many documented cases, people have been executed for crimes they did not commit. Also, responding to the taking of life by taking still more lives seems just wrong. Therefore, capital punishment is wrong.

> P1 = In many documented cases, people have been executed for crimes they did not commit.
>
> P2 = Also, responding to the taking of life by taking still more lives seems just wrong.
>
> C = Capital punishment is wrong.

OPPONENTS: those who believe that capital punishment is not wrong or avoids greater wrongs by acting as a deterrent

Major Exercise 2M

a)   P1 = The room was sealed from the inside.
P2/C1 = No one could have left it.
MC = The murderer was never in the room.

ARGUER: detective or lawyer
AUDIENCE: colleagues of arguer, or judge or jury
OPPONENTS: skeptic or opposing lawyer

c)   P1 = Literacy skills are essential for the development of productive citizens.

P2 = This program has been teaching people basic literacy skills for over two decades.

C = Providing continued funding for the program is clearly justified.

ARGUER: advocate of literacy skills/program

AUDIENCE: city council or government funding agency

OPPONENTS: those who challenge the claims or have other funding priorities

g)   P1 = In 1994, an international conference of health officials concluded there is no scientific evidence that dental amalgam presents a significant health hazard to the general population, although a small number of patients had mild, temporary allergic reactions.

P2 = The World Health Organization (WHO), in March 1997, reached a similar conclusion. They wrote: 'Dental amalgam restorations are considered safe, but components of amalgam and other dental restorative materials may, in rare instances, cause local side effects or allergic reactions. The small amount of mercury released from amalgam restorations, especially during placement and removal, has not been shown to cause any other adverse health effects.'

P3 = Similar conclusions were reached by the USPHS, the European Commission, the National Board of Health and Welfare in Sweden, the New Zealand Ministry of Health, Health Canada, and the Province of Quebec.

C = The safety of dental amalgams has been reviewed extensively over the past ten years, both nationally and internationally.

MC = No valid scientific evidence has ever shown that amalgams cause harm to patients with dental restorations, except in the rare case of allergy.

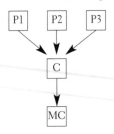

ARGUER: US Food and Drug Administration

AUDIENCE: American public

OPPONENTS: those who believe that dental amalgams pose a health risk

CHAPTER 3

Exercise 3B

1. b)   P1 = Volvos are built to German standards.
       HP = Vehicles built to German standards will last forever (are very durable).
        C = This Volvo will last forever.
       MC = You should buy this Volvo.

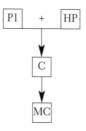

3. a)   P = God is all good.
       HP = Whatever is all good is benevolent.
        C = God is benevolent.

   g)   P = Sports teach discipline.
       HP = Discipline is a good thing for kids to learn.
        C = Sports are good for kids.

   l)   P = It's morally wrong to treat human beings as mere objects.
       HP = Genetic engineering reduces human beings to mere objects.
        C = It is wrong to genetically engineer human beings

Major Exercise 3M

1. b)   This is a borderline case, where we may well take the first statement as a casual observation. But the comparison in the next statement suggests something more serious and recasts the first statement as a criticism of the airlines. Consequently, we can see the following argument:

> P = Airlines make sure you aren't carrying a weapon of destruction and then sell you all the booze you can drink.
>
> HP = Excessive drink can be as dangerous as a weapon.
>
> C = Airlines are inconsistent in their policies.

e)   P1 = Moyers makes virtually no attempt to place the poet in a larger social context—to view poetry as a profession (or, perhaps more to the point, to analyze what it means to say that ours is a culture where it's all but impossible to be a professional poet).

P2 = But as Ezra Pound once pointed out in regard to history, we cannot understand poetry without economics—without some sense of the ebb and flow of the megamercantile society surrounding the poet.

HC = Moyer's program fails to understand poetry.

f)   The second and third statements can be seen as an attempt to provide support for the controversial first statement.

> P1 = The soul does not enter the body until the first breath is taken.
>
> P2 = Up to this point, the fetus is a biological entity only.
>
> HP = An entity without a soul (i.e. one that is only biological) cannot be murdered.
>
> C = Abortion is not murder.

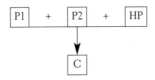

h)   The first statement here makes a strong claim: 'nothing in the world' is as bad as a man's stomach. The second statement does not so much support this as explain the sense of demand in the first. This is Homer's way of saying that no matter what may befall us, we still are slaves to hunger and must eat. This is perhaps an explanation, then. But it's difficult to view the second statement as supporting the first in such a way as to give us an argument.

m)   HP1 = You just noticed this sentence.
     HP2 = This sentence is an example of Bench Advertising.
     HP3 = Advertising that is noticed works.
       C = Bench Advertising works.

CHAPTER 4

Exercise 4B

1. b)   The word 'wealthy' is vague. Its meaning needs to be more precise.
    e)   The sentence is ambiguous. It can mean either that 'Vitamin E is good for elderly people' or that 'Vitamin E is good for making people older'.
    k)   This is another sentence that is ambiguous, in this case because of its structure. In the language characteristic of Shakespeare, it could be the duke who will depose Henry, or Henry who will depose the duke.

2. a)   The sentence is ambiguous, suggesting that the start of treatment in 1983 was the cause of the patient's depression, when the more probable intended meaning is that the patient has been depressed for as long as the treatment has gone on.
    e)   Again, at least two meanings are suggested here: one that is implausible, but which captures the humour, is that the patient, having expired, refused an autopsy. The more likely meaning is that this was a wish expressed prior to death.

3. a)   (1) Convicted criminals must compensate the victims of their crimes.
         (2) Convicted criminals must be dealt with harshly.
    c)   (1) Other people go on living after a person has passed away.
         (2) The soul survives after the body dies.
    e)   (1) Enabling legislation should be introduced to make active euthanasia possible.
         (2) Enabling legislation should be introduced to make passive euthanasia possible.

4. a)   P = As Sigmund Freud pointed out, repression is the price we pay for civilization.
            C = Every society is, of course, repressive to some extent.

    The common word here is 'repression'. The two instances of the term, however, refer to different senses of its meaning. Because of this equivocation, there is no real support between the statements. In the 'premise', 'repression' refers to the necessity of not allowing certain instincts in us to come out, to be 'civil'. This is an activity motivated by the individual. The other statement, however, refers to the ways in which societies repress their members, compelling them to obey the law.

c) Setting aside the opening statement as one that provides the background, we can see the following argument:

> P = When the people of New York pulled together after 11 September, they were displaying not just mutual sympathy, support, and solidarity, but a patriotic commitment to their democracy. By that I mean patriotism in its most decent, and deeply expressed sense, of civil virtue — a commitment to one's community, its values and institutions
>
> C1 = Democracy is not only defended in military terms — it is defended in depth through the commitment of its citizens to its basic values.
>
> MC = The strongest defence of democracy resides in the engagement of every citizen with the community, from activity in the neighbourhood through to participation in formal politics

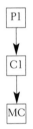

Two terms are important in this argument: 'democracy' and 'patriotism'. While Blunkett does well to clarify how he means 'patriotism' to be understood, the same cannot be said for 'democracy'. This term remains vague throughout.

Exercise 4C

1. b) an intensional definition of 'kitten', by genus (cat) and differentia (immature)
    g) extensional definition

2. a) This definition violates the rule of equivalence, since it is too limiting in restricting child abuse to parental anger and frustration; child abuse can result from other causes and people.
    e) This violates the rules of clarity and neutrality.
    h) This violates the rule of equivalence (other countries — Iceland and Greenland, for example — lie north of the 49th parallel).
    l) This violates the rule of essential characteristics (distance need not be measured by the yard).
    m) This violates the rules of equivalence and of neutrality: 'terrorism' may be a method of war in some circumstances, but it is generally seen to have a wider

application. Also, introducing an 'ought' into the definition opens the door for more subjective judgment.

3. c) This is an argument that strives to define 'person' so as, in its conclusion, to exclude non-human primates from the extension of that term. We are given an intensional definition, one that sets out the characteristics to be shared by all members of the class. It does seem an adequate definition that conforms to the appropriate rules. It meets, for example, the rule of equivalence.

e) The key term here is obviously 'pornography'. The statements begin by excluding certain activities from the extension of 'pornography', which seems reasonable here. But the explicit definition then provided is too narrow (and for some may lack neutrality). By restricting pornography to inappropriate depictions of women, it excludes materials that make similar depictions of men and boys (and children generally).

4. c) Liberalism is a political perspective that emphasizes individual liberty (freedom) over state regulation, and individual choice over social control. Examples of liberalism are found in the writings of John Stuart Mill, Adam Smith, and F.A. Hayek.

f) Objectivity is the presentation of a point of view that is balanced and does not favour any particular perspective on an issue. It particularly avoids the expression of the reporter's own biases or those of the organization he or she represents.

Major Exercise 4M

1 a)   P1 = If people are affected by their environments, by the circumstances of their lives, then they certainly are affected by pornography.

P2 = Even a fool has the sense to see that someone who wallows in filth is going to get dirty.

C1 = Pornography must necessarily effect evil.

MC = People who spend millions of dollars to try to prove otherwise are malicious or misguided, or both.

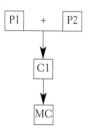

This is clearly a biased argument. The words 'evil', 'necessarily', 'fool', 'wallows', 'filth', and 'malicious' show that the author is not willing to seriously consider the views of many commentators who argue that pornography does not corrupt, either because it is a healthy extension of sexual desires and needs or because individuals can rise above it.

The passage is particularly problematic because some key terms—'common sense', 'intuitive', and 'pornography'—are not defined. If 'common sense' means 'views common to everyone', then it is not the case that common sense dictates that pornography corrupts, for many people think otherwise.

A better argument would also have to make clearer what is meant by pornography, for many would argue that we must distinguish between 'hardcore' and 'softcore' pornography—or 'pornography' and 'erotica'. Hardcore pornography is typically understood as pornography featuring violence as well as sex, and it is frequently argued that it raises concerns not raised by softcore pornography.

b)   P1 = The purpose of critical thinking is to achieve understanding, evaluate viewpoints, and solve problems.

P2 = All three areas involve the asking of questions.

C = Critical thinking is the questioning or inquiry we engage in when we seek to understand, evaluate, or resolve.

Note here that the 'therefore' of the first sentence makes sense only if we understand this as a conclusion from some previous reasoning that has not been provided. The argument we have (clearly indicated by 'since') provides us with a definition of 'critical thinking'—a concept the meaning of which is often debated. The argument assigns 'Critical thinking' to the genus of questioning, while restricting the range of questions involved in the differentia. This way, the definition observes the rule of equivalence. The language here is unproblematic.

g)   P1 = Cybernetics takes as its domain the design or discovery and application of principles of regulation and communication.

P2 = Cybernetics treats not things but ways of behaving. It does not ask 'what is this thing?' but 'what does it do?' and 'what can it do?'

P3 = Numerous systems in the living, social, and technological world may be understood in this way.

C1 = Cybernetics cuts across many traditional disciplinary boundaries.

MC = The concepts that cyberneticians develop form a metadisciplinary language through which we may better understand and modify our world.

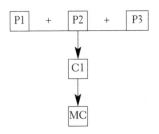

This argument develops an understanding of 'cybernetics' by assigning it to a certain genus (involving the design or discovery and application of principles of regulation and communication) in the first premise. The second premise seems to be an attempt to distinguish it from other things in that genus. It also argues for its value as a 'metadiscipline' for the reasons given. As a stipulative definition, like those developed for many such new concepts, this works well. It clarifies the central term, at least in a way that makes clear how the author is using it.

1)   P1 = The British lion's roar at present is like that of Bottom in Shakespeare's *A Midsummer Night's Dream*—as gentle as any sucking dove.

      P2 = A virile new Britain cannot continue indefinitely to be traduced in the eyes, or rather ears, of the world by the effete languors of Langham Place, brazenly masquerading as 'standard English'.

      P3 = When the Voice of Britain is heard at nine o'clock, better far and infinitely less ludicrous to hear aitches honestly dropped than the present priggish, inflated, inhibited, school-ma'amish arch braying of blameless bashful mewing maidens!

   HC1 = What the world hears of Britain [the English language] is problematic.

    MC = The BBC must be humanized and galvanized.

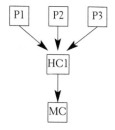

The writer seems to have some concerns about the way the BBC conveys the English language. But our HC here is at best a conjecture, because it is quite difficult to actually determine what the author's concerns are. This, of course, was part of Orwell's point, drawing attention to the irony of someone who commits the same crime of which he or she accuses others. The difficulties lie principally with what we take to be the premises. None of them is clear in its meaning. Each is contaminated by an essential vagueness, to which P3 (and perhaps P1 and P2) adds the feature of emotional language. Since we cannot be sure what the premises mean, it becomes very difficult to determine what really is the conclusion they point to or how well they serve as support for that conclusion.

CHAPTER 5

Major Exercise 5M

1. a)   P1 = Motorists will obey only the speed limits that they perceive as reasonable.

P2 = Such a low speed limit could have the detrimental effect of increasing fuel consumption and exhaust pollution.

C = Reducing the speed to 30 kilometres per hour on city streets would be unreasonable and unenforceable.

ARGUER: Canadian Automobile Association

AUDIENCE: motorists; general public

OPPONENTS: families concerned about speeding on residential streets; city councils; police

There are obvious problems with this argument, not least being that the premises provide no support for part of the conclusion. Our task here, though, is to consider the presence of vested interest and possible bias. This certainly falls within the purview of interest for the CAA, and they have no obvious vested interest in what is being proposed. But we certainly are given only one side of the issue in what is provided here, and this lack of objectivity may have given rise to the tendency to assert rather than provide support. This affects, for example, the circular relationship between P1 and the conclusion, where the premise assumes the very things that it should be supporting.

c)   P1 = Advertising Mail allows you to shop from the comfort of your home.

P2 = Advertising Mail adds $50,000,000 revenue to the Post Office, and that keeps postal rates down.

P3 = Advertising Mail creates employment for tens of thousands of men and women . . . Probably someone you know.

C = The people who send you ads-in-the-mail do a lot of nice things for you, and for us.

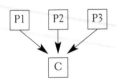

ARGUER: the Post Office

AUDIENCE: homeowners; those who use the postal service

OPPONENTS: disgruntled people fed up with 'junk mail'

This one-sided argument overlooks the obvious objection that a serious consideration of the 'opponents' would bring to light. More particularly, the post office has a clear vested interest here, insofar as the advertisers pay to have their material delivered and this affects the post office's balance sheets.

2. a)   P1 = Our societies ban or restrict any number of activities that are minor irritants: begging, loud music, nudity, skateboarding.

P2 = Although each of these restrictions on individual liberty is the result of intolerance, *The Economist* seldom champions their causes; yet your newspaper seems unable to mention tobacco without commenting on dangers to the rights of smokers.

C = *The Economist*'s assertion that public smoking should not be banned, on the grounds that 'other people's freedoms . . . sometimes get in your eyes,' is biased.

ARGUER: writer to *The Economist*
AUDIENCE: staff and readers of *The Economist*
OPPONENTS: those who advocate smokers' rights

This is an argument about bias. The writer levels a charge of bias against *The Economist* and supports it with premises that seem to show an inconsistency in the magazine's expressed opinions. To avoid the charge, the staff of the magazine would have to show that some of the other 'irritants' mentioned had been defended, or that there was a relevant difference between them and the case of smokers.

e)   P1 = This textbook may discuss evolution, a controversial theory some scientists present as a scientific explanation for the origin of living things, such as plants, animals, and humans.

P2 = No human was present when life first appeared on earth.

C = Any statement about life's origins should be considered a theory, not fact.

ARGUER: Clayton County school authorities
AUDIENCE: users of the textbook
OPPONENTS: those who defend evolution as more than a theory

On the face of it, this looks like an invitation to students to keep an open mind. However, in the struggle for control of the classroom between advocates of evolution and advocates of creation, this takes on a different light—appearing to undermine the authority of evolution. Announcing this as a 'disclaimer' before any evidence is presented creates a problem of bias, since it encourages things to be viewed a certain way in advance. It also presents a controversial notion of 'fact' as something that is observable by humans (rather than what might be inferred from what is observed). Consider what would be excluded as scientific fact on this criterion.

CHAPTER 6

Exercise 6A

1. a) There may be a dispute over what constitutes 'anorexic proportions', but the premise (that follows 'since') asserts what should be generally recognized about the readership of the magazine, and on this point the burden of proof lies with the magazine to challenge this. But insofar as the premise also includes an implicit criticism of *Vogue*'s idea of fashion, then the author needs to defend this charge.

    d) The conclusion of this argument can be gleaned from the first and last statements, relating argument itself and publicness. The intervening statements are premises that would seem to fall within the range of what members of society should allow without question (certainly the readers of this text should allow them!). Hence, the burden of proof lies with anyone who would challenge these premises.

2. a)   P1 = Large carnivores like grizzly bears and wolves are majestic creatures in their own right.

         P2 = Large carnivores like grizzly bears and wolves are critical to maintaining the health of the ecosystem.

          C = It is wrong to indiscriminately destroy them, and there should be stricter guidelines for their conservation.

    This is an inductive argument, and a valid one. While we can accept the premises and still challenge the conclusion, the premises give strong reasons for that conclusion. Both premises are relevant to the conclusion, offering reasons that increase the case against indiscriminate destruction and in favour of guidelines. With respect to acceptability, while the first premise is a judgment on the author's part, it is a judgment that seems consistent with what we know of these creatures, and so the onus should be on someone who would challenge the premise to show otherwise. The second premise, however, might require some clarification regarding the intended meaning of 'critical'; an audience might reasonably expect the author to support this particular claim.

c)   P1 = It is not wrong to discriminate in favour of what is good and against what is bad for our society, for our country, or for our community.
C1 = Not all discrimination is bad.
P2 = Same-sex couples are objectively different.
C2 = On the basis of family status, it is not unfair to treat same-sex couples differently than a heterosexual couple.
MC = We should not extend the status of the family to same-sex couples.

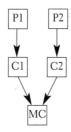

This is an invalid inductive argument that fails on both of the basic criteria. P1 is relevant to C1, since it does increase our reasons for holding it. But this sub-argument is not obviously relevant to the main claim, since it offers no specific reason against extending the status of family to same-sex couples. The same is true of P2, the claim that same-sex couples are 'objectively' different. This would be a relevant reason for treating them differently, but it still does not support the main claim. With respect to acceptability, P1 would seem to pass the test, given its very general pronouncement. But P2 is questionable because of the vagueness of 'objectively' different. Nothing in the argument clarifies the meaning of this term, so the burden of proof lies with the author to explain it.

Major Exercise 6M

2. a) People should always identify themselves in their e-mail address or subject line. This is because so many computer viruses are communicated through e-mail that people are afraid to open messages from names they do not recognize. Moreover, anonymous e-mail might not receive a prompt response from those who are busy.

3. a) As Donna D. indicates, the claim that white men get rich while Native Americans stay in poverty is already known to Indians. Thus, what she does is explain why they accept this situation, using the explanation indicator 'because'. Her explanation is that the money that is received is preferable to begging for handouts from the government.

4. a)   P = There is pleasure in knowing that events and not an expiring clock will decide when the evening's entertainment is done.
C = Major League Baseball shouldn't institute new rules designed to speed up the game.

This is a poor argument, primarily because P is questionable. In basketball, hockey, football, and other sports it is often the race against an expiring clock that adds excitement and pleasure to 'the evening's entertainment'. And if ignoring the clock allows any kind of game to drag on and on, we tend to become bored and exasperated. It follows that the first criterion of good arguments—acceptable premises—is not satisfied in this case.

5. a)   P = The conclusion of the argument can be false when the premises are true.
            C = The argument is invalid.

This argument is valid. By definition, if the premise is correct, then so is the conclusion.

    c)   P1 = The objective of an argument is to convince an audience.
            P2 = If this is so, then it is sufficient for our purposes that the premises of a good argument be accepted as true by both us and our audience.
            C = We will aim for acceptability [it is sufficient for our purposes that the premises of a good argument be accepted as true by both us and our audience].

In fact, this is an explanation of a procedure rather than an argument. But if we take the 'conclusion' to be what is identified in the brackets, then it fits a valid scheme, since the conclusion has to follow if the premises are correct.

    d)   P1 = Doctor A was a nice guy, but he didn't cure me.
            P2 = Doctor B was a jerk, and he cured me.
            C = When it comes to your health and other important matters, you can usually count on a jerk.

This is an invalid argument. The premises may be correct without the conclusion being affected. There is simply too little information in the premises to draw a valid conclusion about what you can 'usually' do.

6. a) All firearms are potentially dangerous things. All potentially dangerous things are to be subject to restrictions. Therefore, all firearms are things to be subject to restrictions.

    This is a valid argument: the conclusion must be accepted if the premises are.

7. c)   P1 = Certain non-human primates have been known to exhibit grief at the loss of a family member.

P2 = If certain non-human primates exhibit grief at the loss of a family member, then they are capable of abstract thought and must have a sense of self.

P3 = If certain non-human primates are capable of abstract thought and have a sense of self, then they are demonstrating some of the key indicators of personhood.

P4 = If certain non-human primates are demonstrating some of the key indicators of personhood, then they are moral agents.

C = Certain non-human primates are moral agents.

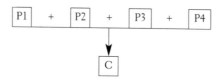

This is a valid deductive argument. If we accept the premises, we must also accept the conclusion. Thus, the argument clearly exhibits one criterion of good arguments quite well. Given the strength of this structure, the premises are relevant to the conclusion. The overall strength of the argument then depends on the acceptability of the premises. Premises 2–4 are what we call hypothetical statements: they indicate what would follow if the prior circumstances were present. The first premise, which starts this chain, appeals to experience. We do not really know the audience for this argument, so we cannot be certain whether the experience referred to is one they would share. But the 'opponents' are those critics of certain animal rights who would challenge the conclusion that certain non-human primates are moral agents. They should recognize the kinds of cases the first premise indicates (even if they would not interpret them the same way). The remaining premises are different in kind. Premise 3 would seem to draw on a common definition of 'personhood' that most would accept. But premises 2 and 4 both make connections that could be viewed as controversial (particularly by the opponents). Why would we assume that if a creature exhibits grief, it must have a sense of self? And why does moral agency follow from personhood? While some audiences would accept these assumptions, they are not straightforward, and the burden of proof lies with the arguer to provide support for them. So, while it has important merits, until this burden of proof is met the argument cannot be considered strong.

g)   P = In a study of 11 healthy men during high-intensity exercise, carnosine was able to significantly buffer the acid-base balance in the skeletal muscles, which becomes unbalanced by the overproduction of hydrogen ions occurring in association with the build-up of lactic acid during high-intensity exercise.

C = Carnosine may play a role in improving and increasing exercise performance.

AUDIENCE: readers of *Life Extension*
OPPONENTS: skeptics of the claims about carnosine

The premise of this inductive argument is relevant to the conclusion: it does increase the likelihood of carnosine playing the role attributed to it. As it stands, though, the premise is not acceptable. The primary problem is that the study is unidentified, thus weakening the appeal to it. Studies of this nature serve as sources of authority, and so it is important that interested people (and opponents) are able to consult the source and verify its claims. This cannot be done here.

k) This is clearly an argument. It is best represented as an argument with an intermediate hidden conclusion, which clarifies the link between the premises (which demonstrate how corrosive Coke is) and the conclusion (that you should stop drinking Coke). So we will diagram the argument as follows:

P1 = In many states, the highway patrol carries two gallons of Coke in the trunk to remove blood from the highway after a car accident.

P2 = You can put a T-bone steak in a bowl of Coke and it will be gone in two days.

P3 = The active ingredient in Coke is phosphoric acid, which has a pH of 2.8 and can dissolve a nail in about 4 days.

HC1 = Coke is very corrosive.

HP4 = Something this corrosive is bad for you.

MC = You should stop drinking Coke.

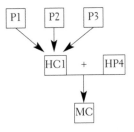

Though this argument may sound impressive, we judge it to be a weak argument that is problematic in terms of both acceptability and validity.

Acceptability. While we are not certain that the initial premises (P1, P2, P3) are true, we will judge them acceptable, as we have no reason to believe they are not true. There is still a problem with the acceptability of the premises, however, for it is not clear that premise HP4 is true. Our own stomach acids are very corrosive, but they aren't bad for us, so it remains to be shown that substances as corrosive as Coke are always bad for one's health.

Validity. One might question whether MC follows from HC1 and HP4, for even if Coke is bad for one's health, one might argue that the harm it causes is relatively minor, and that the pleasure one gets from this outweighs it. One could significantly strengthen the argument, and ensure that MC follows from HC1 and HP4, by adding a convincing argument to this effect.

l) This is an argument against claims made by Jonathan Gowing. The argument can be diagrammed as follows:

P1 = In 1997, the average concentration of THC . . . examined by the University of Mississippi's Marijuana Potency Monitoring Project was just under 5 per cent, as opposed to the average concentration of 2–3 per cent found during the 1970s.

C1 = You could say that marijuana is on average twice as potent as it was during the 1970s, but it is absurd for Gowing to say that it is 700 times more potent (which would mean marijuana today is on average 1,400 per cent THC).

P2 = Gowing also overlooks the fact that higher potency is better for my health: a more potent product means I have to smoke less to get high.

MC = Jonathan Gowing's arguments are not convincing.

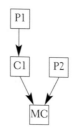

Though the author of the argument makes a mistake (700 per cent more THC would imply 45 per cent THC, not 1400 per cent!), the argument for C1 is relatively strong. P1 is acceptable, as the author cites studies from the University of Mississippi that appear to be authoritative, and C1 clearly follows from P1. The rest of the argument is more problematic, as P2 might be debated (couldn't larger amounts of THC lead to more dependence or other problems?) and in need of support. As one of the premises given for MC (P1) is acceptable and strongly supports MC, the argument is plausible, though P2 would have to be backed in order to make the argument a strong one.

CHAPTER 7

Exercise 7A

a) Some dentists are those who have six-digit incomes. PA
b) All dinosaurs are extinct creatures. UA
c) Some people are not people prepared to pay higher taxes. PN
g) All people who know the way I feel tonight are lonely people. UA
m) All things that are New York (city) are things that are in New York (state). UA
n) All survivors are courageous people. UA

u) No circumstances are circumstances in which the courts should deal leniently with people who drive vehicles while inebriated. UN

w) All cars parked on the street whose permits have expired are cars that will be towed away. UA

Exercise 7B

2. a) **All people who will be admitted are ticket holders.**
    (1) It is false that some ticket holders are not people who will be admitted.
    (2) No people who will be admitted are non–ticket holders.

    b) **Some New Yorkers are people who vacation in Florida.**
    (1) Some people who vacation in Florida are New Yorkers.
    (2) It is false that no New Yorkers are people who vacation in Florida.

    g) **Some donors to the club are non-users.**
    (1) Some donors to the club are not users.
    (2) Some non-users are donors to the club.

Exercise 7C

c)   P1 = All vegetables harvested within the last 48 hours are vegetables that should be considered fresh.

    P2 = All of these beans are vegetables harvested within the last 48 hours.

    C = All of these beans are vegetables that should be considered fresh.

    S = these beans

    P = vegetables that should be considered fresh

    M = vegetables harvested within the last forty-eight hours

    All M are P

    All S are M

    All S are P

Major Exercise 7M

1. a) Some cats aren't pests, but all cats are pets, so no pets are pests.

Legend	Scheme
S = pets	Some cats are not pests
P = pests	All cats are pets
M = cats	No pets are pests

    P1
    Some M are not P

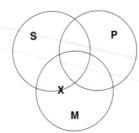

P2
All M are S

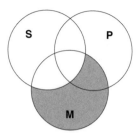

C
No S are P

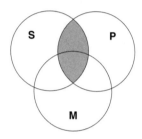

We put P1 and P2 together in a Venn diagram:

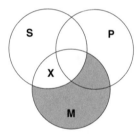

The conclusion is not contained within the premises. Therefore, this argument is *invalid*.

b) All buildings over 50 feet tall are in violation of the new city bylaw, and the bank building is over 50 feet tall. Therefore, it is in violation of the by-law.

Legend	*Scheme*
S = bank building	All buildings over 50ft are buildings in violation of the bylaw.
P = buildings in violation of the bylaw	All of the bank building is a building over 50ft.
M = buildings over 50 ft tall	All of the bank building is a building in violation of the bylaw.

P1
All M are P

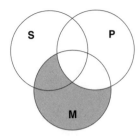

P2
All S are M

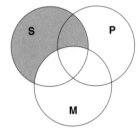

C
All S are P

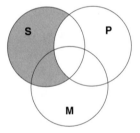

We put P1 and P2 together in a Venn diagram:

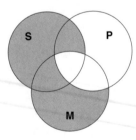

Here we see that the premises shade all of S outside of P, which is what the con-clusion requires. Therefore, this argument is *valid*.

2. a) No person who values integrity will go into politics because the realities of political life force people to compromise their principles.

>   *Legend*
>   S = people who value integrity
>   P = people who will go into politics
>   M = people whose principles are compromised

>   *Scheme*
>   [   ]
>   All P are M
>   No S are P

P
All P are M

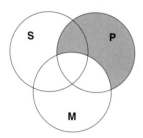

C
No S are P

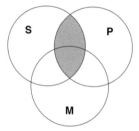

For the conclusion to be contained in the diagram (indicating validity), the hidden premise must relate S and M so as to leave shaded the area shared by S, P, and M. The hidden premise must therefore be: No S are M.

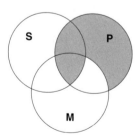

3. a)   This syllogism is valid.

Legend	Scheme
S = this syllogism	All P are M
P = valid syllogisms	All S are M
M = syllogisms with 3 terms	All S are P

c)   No one does wrong voluntarily.

Legend	Scheme
S = people	All P are M
P = those who do wrong voluntarily	No S are M
M = those who are consciously evil	No S are P

CHAPTER 8

Major Exercise 8M

a)   Some valid syllogisms are not syllogisms with a false conclusion. (**A** is false)
Some valid syllogisms are not syllogisms with acceptable premises. (**A** is false)
      C   = No syllogisms with acceptable premises are syllogisms with false
              conclusions.

Legend	Scheme
S = syllogisms with acceptable premises	Md O Pu
P = syllogisms with false conclusions	Md O Su
M = valid syllogisms	Sd E Pd

Test
Rule 1: *Okay.* The middle term is distributed in both premises.
Rule 2: *Violated.* S and P are distributed in the conclusion but not in the premises.
Rule 3: *Violated.* There are two negative premises.

*Argument is **invalid**.*

b)   Conservatives favour cuts to the education system. Peter does not favour cuts to the
education system. Hence, Peter is not a conservative.

Legend	Scheme
S = Peter	Pd A Mu
P = conservatives	Sd E Md
M = those who favour cuts to the education system	Sd E Pd

Test

Rule 1: *Okay.* The middle term is distributed in the second premise.
Rule 2: *Okay.* Both terms are distributed in the conclusion, but also in the premises.
Rule 3: *Okay.* There is a negative premise, but also a negative conclusion.

*Argument is **valid**.*

l) No beast so foul but knows some pity; / But I know none, and therefore am no beast. (Shakespeare, *Richard III*)

Legend   *Scheme*
  S = Richard III   Pd **A** Mu
  P = beasts   Sd **E** Md
  M = creatures that know some pity Sd **E** Pd

Test

Rule 1: *Okay.* The middle term is distributed in the first premise.
Rule 2: *Okay.* Both terms are distributed in the conclusion, but also in the premises.
Rule 3: *Okay.* There is a negative premise, but also a negative conclusion.

*Argument is **valid**.*

p) The writer is arguing that some acts of violence are acceptable because they are a form of self-defence:

  P = Violence in defence of self or family is *usually* acceptable. 'Usually' denotes that this is not a universal statement:
  P = Most acts of violence in defence of self or family are acceptable acts.
  C = [No acts of violence are acts that can ever be condoned] is incorrect.
     = Some acts of violence are acts that can ever be condoned.

[   ]

Most acts of violence in defence of self or family are acceptable acts. Some acts of violence are acceptable acts.

Legend   *Scheme*
  S = acts of violence   [ ]
  P = acts that are acceptable (can ever be condoned) Mu **I** Pu
  M = acts of violence in self-defence Su **I** Pu

Test

Rule 1: To be valid the M term must be distributed in the hidden premise. So it is an **A**, **E**, or **O**.
Rule 2: *Not applicable.*
Rule 3: To be valid the hidden premise cannot be an **E** or an **O**, since there is no other negative statement.

Thus, the hidden premise must be an **A** *statement with the* **M** *term distributed:*
Md **A** Su

r)   The following syllogism can be extracted:
All killings are uncivilized and barbaric acts.
All judicially ordered executions are uncivilized and barbaric acts.

Legend	*Scheme*
S = judicially ordered executions	[ ]
P = uncivilized and barbaric acts	Md **A** Pu
M = killings	Sd **A** Pu

Test
Rule 1: *Okay.* The middle term is already distributed.
Rule 2: S must be distributed in the hidden premise, so it cannot be an **I** statement.
Rule 3: The hidden premise can be neither an **E** nor an **O**, since there is no other negative statement.

Thus, the hidden premise must be an **A** *statement with the* **S** *term distributed:*
Sd **A** Mu

CHAPTER 9

Exercise 9A
1. a)   Mars is a planet we should explore.
    d)   Mars is a planet we should explore or Venus is a planet we should explore.
    g)   If space is the final frontier and every living thing needs water and there is water on Mars, then it is not the case that Venus is a planet we should explore.
    m)   Space is the final frontier. If space is the final frontier, then Venus is a planet we should explore. Therefore, Venus is a planet we should explore.

2. b) c = Lee Mun Wah did produce the film *The Color of Fear*.
            c
            (Note that this is a negation of a negation: the first negation is implied by the phrase 'She's mistaken . . .', the second by the word 'didn't'.)
    f) l = We let c = Richard Nixon is a crook
            $r = \sim c$ represents Richard Nixon's famous statement 'I am not a crook'.
            $l \rightarrow r$
    h) v = An argument is valid.
            n = Its conclusion follows necessarily from the premises.
            $v \rightarrow n$

k) *c* = You should try Shredded Wheat with cold milk.
 h = You should try Shredded Wheat with hot milk.
 c V *h*

n) *s* = A neighbourhood is safe.
 o = A neighbourhood is organized.
 s → *o*

Exercise 9B

1. e) *m* = You have multimedia skills.
 v = You have worked on video.
 a = You can apply for the job.
 (*m* V *v*) → *a*

 i) *p* = I'm paranoid.
 y = You are out to get me.
 (*p* V *y*) & ~(*p* & *y*)

(Note that this is an exclusive disjunction, for if you are out to get me, then I am not paranoid but see things as they are.)

 j) *t* = They were there.
 t

(Note that this is a negation of a negation. The first negation is implied by the word 'lying', the second by the word 'weren't'.)

 l) *s* = You can stand a lot of pain.
 p = You can get a Ph.D.
 p → *s*

(Note that *s* → *p* is incorrect, for this does not imply that you can get a Ph.D. if you can stand a lot of pain: there are many other requirements as well.)

 q) *i* = I'm interested in that car.
 m = It's in mint condition.
 i → *m*

2. a) *t* = The temperature is constant.
 p = The pressure of a gas varies.
 v = The volume of the gas varies.
 t → ((*p* → *v*) & (*v* → *P*))

 b) *a* = An individual is alive.
 s = Their EEG records brain signals.
 (*a* → *s*) & (*s* → *a*)

 e) *e* = Metal expands.
 h = It is heated.
 m → *h*

 f) *m* = Abortion is murder.
 p = The fertilized ovum is a person.
 (*m* → *p*) & (*p* → *m*)

3. f)   *m* = You make a mistake.
         d = You say it with a deep enough voice.
         g = You can get away with it.
              $m \rightarrow (d \rightarrow g)$
4. e)   *o* = The objective of an argument is to convince an audience.
         s = It is sufficient for our purposes that the premises of a good argument be
              accepted as true by our audience.
              $o \rightarrow s$; *o; therefore s*
    g)   *w* = The Conservatives will win the election.
         d = Liberal support will decline in urban ridings.
              $d \rightarrow w, \sim d$

Major Exercise 9M

1.
    a) 1. $a \rightarrow b$ P
        2. *a*   P
        3. *b*   1, 2, AA
    c) 1. $(e \lor d)$ & *f*   P
        2. $\sim d$ P
        3. *e* V *d*   1, &E
        4. *e*   3, 2, VE
        5. *f*   1, &E
        6. *e* & *f*   4, 5, &I
    g) 1. $a \rightarrow d$ P
        2. $d \rightarrow e$ P
        3. *a* & *b*   P
        4. *a*   3, &E
        5. *d*   1, 4, AA
        6. *e*   2, 5, AA
        7. *a* & *e*   4, 6, &E

2. b) $b \rightarrow c, a \rightarrow b, d \rightarrow a, \sim c$, *therefore* $\sim d$
        If Brian had a high grade-point average last term, then Catherine did. If Andrea
        had a high grade-point average last term, then Brian did. If David had a high
        grade-point average last term, then Andrea did. Catherine did not have a high
        grade-point average last term. Therefore, David did not.
             1. $b \rightarrow c$ P
             2. $a \rightarrow b$ P
             3. $e \rightarrow a$ P
             4. $\sim c$ P
             5. $\sim b$ 1, 4, DC
             6. $\sim a$ 2, 5, DC
             7. $\sim e$ 3, 6, DC

e) $a \rightarrow (b \& c), c \rightarrow e, a$, therefore $a \& e$
If Andrea had a high grade-point average last term, then Brian and Catharine did. If Catharine did, then Evan did. Andrea did. Therefore Andrea and Evan did.

1. $a \rightarrow (b \& c)$ P
2. $c \rightarrow e$ P
3. a P
4. $b \& c$ 1, 3, AA
5. c 4, &E
6. e 2, 5, AA
7. $a \& e$ 3, 6, &I

3. f) h = The government minister is not honest.
t = She can be trusted.
g = She holds a government post.
r = She should return to her law firm.

1. $(\sim h \rightarrow \sim t) \& (\sim t \rightarrow (\sim g \& r))$ P
2. $\sim h$ P
3. $\sim h \rightarrow \sim t$ 1, &E
4. $\sim t \rightarrow (\sim g \& r)$ 1, &E
5. $\sim t$ 3, 2, AA
6. $\sim g \& r$ 4, 5, AA
7. r 6, &E

g) l = You love our great nation.
g = You leave it.

1. $l \lor g$ P (what the speaker thinks should be the case)
2. $\sim l$ P
3. g 1, 2, VE (what the speaker thinks should be the case)

As this proof shows, this is a valid argument. But it is also a case of the fallacy of false dilemma, for l and g are not the only two alternatives—if you don't love the nation you might try and change it instead of leaving.

5. a) l = You should listen to the Zen master's teaching without trying to make it conform to your own self-centred viewpoint.
a = You will be able to understand what he is saying.

1. $\sim l \rightarrow \sim a$ P
2. a P (what you want)
3. l 1, 2, DC

d) o = The objective of an argument is to convince an audience.
s = It is sufficient for our purposes that the premises of a good argument be accepted as true by our audience.

1. $o \rightarrow s$ P
2. o P
3. s 1, 2, AA

f) l = The Liberals will win the election.
    a = Their leader is attractive to voters in rural ridings.
    1. $(l \rightarrow a) \,\&\, (a \rightarrow l)$ P
    2. $\sim a$ P
    3. $l \rightarrow a$ 1, &E
    4. $\sim l$ 3, 2, DC

i) a = Americans will win the most medals at next year's Olympics.
    g = Germans will win the most medals at next year's Olympics.
    r = Russians will win the most medals at next year's Olympics.
    1. $a \lor g \lor r$ P
    2. $\sim r \,\&\, \sim g$ P
    3. $\sim r$ 2, &E
    4. $\sim g$ 2, &E
    5. $a \lor g$ 1, 3, VE
    6. a 5, 4, VE

6. a) a = There is anarchy.
        p = Criminals are punished.
        b = Corporations break the law.
        1. $\sim p \rightarrow a$ P
        2. $b \rightarrow a$ P
        3. $\sim a$ P (i.e. we don't want anarchy)
        4. p 1, 3, DC
        5. $\sim b$ 2, 3, DC
        6. $p \,\&\, \sim b$ 4, 5, &I

    c) The implicit argument has the form: If you were so smart, you would be rich. You're not rich. So you're not so smart. It can be proven valid as follows:
        s = You're so smart.
        r = You're rich.
        1. $s \rightarrow r$ P
        2. $\sim r$ P
        3. $\sim s$ 1, 2, DC

    g) z = Zsa Zsa Gabor is 54.
        f = She was only five when she entered and won the Miss Hungary beauty title in 1933.
        1. $z \rightarrow f$ P
        2. $\sim f$ P (a hidden premise)
        3. $\sim z$ 1, 2, DC

Chapter 10

Exercise 10A

a) $a \rightarrow b$, $b \rightarrow c$, therefore $a \rightarrow c$

1.	$a \rightarrow b$	P
2.	$b \rightarrow c$	P
3.	a	P/→P
4.	b	1, 3, AA
5.	c	2, 4, AA
6.	$a \rightarrow c$	3–5, →P

Exercise 10C

1.   a) $a \lor b$, $a \rightarrow c$, $b \rightarrow d$, therefore $c \lor b$

1.	$a \lor b$	P
2.	$a \rightarrow c$	P
3.	$b \rightarrow d$	P
4.	$c \lor b$	1–3, DV

Exercise 10D

1.   a) $\sim(a \ \& \ b)$, b, therefore $\sim a$

It is not the case that both Angela goes to *Hair* and Brian goes to *Hair*. Brian goes to *Hair*. Therefore, Angela does not goes to *Hair*.

1.	$\sim(a \ \& \ b)$	P
2.	b	P
3.	$\sim a \lor \sim b$	1, DeM
4.	$\sim a$	2, 3, VE

Major Exercise 10M

1.   c) j = You can join the Air Force.

e = You're eighteen.

1.	$j \rightarrow e$	P
2.	$\sim e$	P/→P
3.	$\sim j$	1, 2, DC
4.	$\sim e \rightarrow \sim j$	2–3, →P

g) y = You answer 'yes' to the question 'If I die, would you marry again?'

n = You answer 'no' to the question 'If I die, would you marry again?'

w = You will be taken to mean that you are waiting for your spouse to die.

h = You will be taken to mean that your marriage is happy.

1.	$y \lor n$	P
2.	$y \rightarrow w$	P
3.	$n \rightarrow \sim h$	P
4.	$w \lor \sim h$	1, 2, 3, DV

One might try to escape through the horns of the dilemma, though this does not seem promising (the most obvious alternative to y and n is 'I don't know', but it might also be given a negative interpretation, probably by suggesting that it implies that one does not know that one is happily married and may be waiting for one's spouse to die). The best way to answer the dilemma is, therefore, by taking the dilemma by the horns and denying that $y \rightarrow w$ and/or that $n \rightarrow \sim h$. One may, for example, point out that a 'no' answer to the question may mean the opposite of $\sim h$, for one may not want to marry again because one believes that a new marriage could not match the happiness of the present one.

n) j = Jacinth is well.
   f = Francis is well.
   k = Kirstin is well.
   f = Fred is well.
   p = Paul is well.

1.	$j \& \sim f \& \sim k \& (\sim f \vee \sim p)$	P
2.	$\sim f \vee \sim p$	1, &E
3.	$f \& p$	2, DeM

2. b) Religion fulfills some deep human need. For suppose it didn't. Then it wouldn't be found in virtually every human society. But it is found in virtually every human society. So religion must fulfill some deep human need.

   r = Religion fulfills some deep human need.
   f = It is found in virtually every human society.

1.	f	P
2.	$\sim r \rightarrow \sim f$	P
3.	$\sim r$	P/RAA
4.	$\sim f$	2, 3, AA
5.	$f \& \sim f$	1, 4, &I
6.	r	3–5, RAA

5. c) $\sim(a \& b)$, a, therefore $\sim b$

1.	$\sim(a \& b)$	P
2.	a	P
3.	$\sim a \vee \sim b$	1, DeM
4.	$\sim b$	3, 2, VE

d) $a \& b \& c \& d$, therefore $c \vee e$

1.	$a \& b \& c \& d$	P
2.	$\sim(c \vee e)$	P/RAA
3.	$\sim c \& \sim e$	2, DeM
4.	c	1, &E
5.	$\sim c$	3, &E
6.	$c \& \sim c$	4, 5, &I
7.	$c \vee e$	2–6, RAA

6. b) h = You do your homework assignments.
   l = You learn informal logic.

g = You'll be a good reasoner.
s = You succeed in your chosen field.

1. $(h \rightarrow l) \& (l \rightarrow g)$ P
2. $g \rightarrow s$ P
3. $h \rightarrow l$ 1, &E
4. $l \rightarrow g$ 1, &E
5. $h \rightarrow g$ 3, 4, CS
6. $h \rightarrow s$ 5, 2, CS

d) s = You're a great singer.
y = You're Shakespeare.
m = The moon is made out of green cheese.

1. $s \rightarrow (y \& m)$ P
2. $\sim(y \& m)$ P (a hidden premise)
3. $\sim s$ 1, 2, DC

h) d = The court decides for me.
e = Euthalus must pay.
w = Euthalus has won his first case in court.

1. $d \lor \sim d$ P
2. $d \rightarrow e$ P
3. $\sim d \rightarrow w$ P
4. $w \rightarrow e$ P
5. $\sim d \rightarrow e$ 3, 4, CS
6. e 1, 3, 5, D

m) s = The universe stretches forever.
i = The universe contains an infinite number of stars.
w = Whichever way you looked, you would see a star.
l = The sky would be all light.

1. $(s \& i) \rightarrow w$ P
2. $w \rightarrow l$ P
3. $\sim l$ P
4. $(s \& i) \rightarrow l$ 1, 2, CS
5. $\sim(s \& l)$ 4, 3, DC
6. $\sim s \lor \sim l$ 5, DeM

7. b) Like the sky in this example, your predicament is dark. You are unlikely to survive, as the following proof shows.
s = You survive.
r = You run to a lifeboat.
b = You will be blown out to sea.
c = The storm continues.
d = The sky is dark.

1. $r \lor \sim r$ P
2. $r \rightarrow b$ P

3.	$b \rightarrow \sim s$	P (a hidden premise)
4.	$\sim r \rightarrow (\sim s \rightarrow c)$	P
5.	$c \rightarrow (s \rightarrow r)$	P
6.	$d \rightarrow c$	P
7.	d	P
8.	$\sim r$	P/$\rightarrow$P
9.	c	6, 7, AA
10.	$s \rightarrow r$	5, 9, AA
11.	$\sim s$	10, 11, DC
12.	$\sim r \rightarrow \sim s$	8–11, $\rightarrow$P
13.	r	P/$\rightarrow$P
14.	b	2, 13, AA
15.	$\sim s$	3, 15, AA
16.	$r \rightarrow \sim s$	13–15, $\rightarrow$P
17.	$\sim s$	1, 12, 16, D

8. a) *(p V q) & ~(p & q), p, therefore ~q*

1.	$(p \lor q)$ & $\sim(p$ & $q)$	P
2.	p	P
3.	$\sim(p$ & $q)$	1, &E
4.	$\sim p \lor \sim q$	3, DeM
5.	$\sim q$	2, 4, VE

Sample argument

He can spend his money on a present (*p*) or on a video (*q*). He'll spend it on a present, so he won't buy a video.

c) *p → q, therefore ~q → ~p*

1.	$p \rightarrow q$	P
2.	$\sim q$	P/$\rightarrow$P
3.	$\sim p$	1, 2, DC
4.	$\sim q \rightarrow \sim p$	1–3, $\rightarrow$P

Sample argument

If he had climbed out the back window (*p*), there would be footsteps in the flower bed (*q*), so if we don't find any, then he didn't climb out the back window.

g) The law of non-contradiction [i.e. ~(X & ~X)] from no premises.

1.	p & $\sim p$	P/RAA
2.	$\sim(p$ & $\sim p)$	1–1, RAA

Sample argument

She can't be honest and a liar.

9.   THE CASE OF THE MISSING BROTHER

Day 2.   Louis wasn't working the day of his disappearance.

Day 3.   Louis went running when he left the house on Thursday morning.

Day 4.   Louis is not in Montreal.

Day 5.   The note is from the real kidnappers, and they and Louis are in Quebec City.

Day 6.   If Mary had a hand in it she hired her brother Ted.

Day 7.   The anonymous phone call is wrong. (Louis is not held by some strange cult called Cabala.)

Day 8.   Mugsy is a culprit.

Day 9.   The case is a 'SP—'.

Day 10.   You must try the right door.

Day 10½.   The police were wrong. (It's not true that Louis is in one of these two rooms.)

Day 11.   Louis must be in the third room.

Day 12.   This is not a serious kidnapping, but a SPOOF.

Day 13.   Louis paid Mary and Mugsy to fool me.

Day 14.   You charge me the full rate.

Day 15.   . . . send the bill to Louis.

CHAPTER 11

Exercise 11A

1. a) *university students*
    – likely above-average intelligence
    – general basic knowledge
    – interest in issues affecting education
    – likely in late teens to early twenties, but demographic is changing
    – likely to have strong social conscience with an interest in changing things for the better
    – interest in popular culture

    c) *sports fans*
    – a cross-section of all groups and ages in society
    – sense of belonging to a group comprised of strangers
    – sense of competitiveness, perhaps
    – keen on fair play
    – may appreciate the importance of teamwork
    – probably has some sense of how allegiances can be 'irrational' at times

4. a) *Acceptable by definition.* According to the meanings of the terms 'cause' and 'effect', we know this statement to be correct.

    b) *Unacceptable according to common knowledge.* Regardless of how many of the vestiges of the old structure remain, it is generally known that the Soviet Union has changed politically, economically, and even geographically.

    h) The first statement is supported by reasonable premises and is *acceptable* on that basis.

5. b) The premise (second statement) begs the question in relation to the claim (first statement). It expresses the same idea in different language.

Exercise 11B

1. a) Premises *i* and *ii* together connect the ideas of suffering, animals, and experiencing pain. Thus, they increase our reasons for holding the claim and are relevant to it. Premise *iii* is irrelevant to the claim: although it may be acceptable, it does not support the *wrongness* of inflicting suffering. Premise *iv* provides negative relevance for the claim: it weakens the belief that it is wrong to inflict suffering. Being stewards of Nature (premise *v*) in no way entails not inflicting suffering on animals; this statement is irrelevant to the claim and does not increase our support for it.

2. b) The hidden conclusion in this letter is that the mayor's goal in proposing welfare reform is to save the government money. According to the letter-writer, this must be the case because saving money and decreasing poverty are the only reasons for welfare reform (Premise 1), and New York City keeps good data only on the first of these and not on poverty (Premise 2). Contextually, there is no clear problem of irrelevance. Premise 1 is problematic, but it is not attributed to anyone other than the author, so there is no question of a straw argument (and the problem then lies with the acceptability of P1). Internal relevance, however, is a concern. P1 does provide a relevant reason for the conclusion (its problem, as noted, lies elsewhere). But it is not clear how keeping good data on savings, as opposed to no data on poverty, is a reason for believing that the Mayor's motivation is to save money. That is, no connection between keeping records and proposing programs that will save money is evident.

Exercise 11C

1. a) The claim is not qualified in any way. It advocates boxing without conditions. People who support prohibiting the sport argue that it is dangerous (professional boxers die in the ring), aggressive, and demeaning as a 'sport' (watching grown men hurt each other). Arguably, the five reasons offered respond to these concerns.

    The premises provide balance in that they acknowledge the charge of dangerousness (*ii* and *iv*) and respond to it. Premise *iii* can be seen to respond to the charge of aggressiveness, and premise *v* meets the objection that this is not a 'sport'. Both *i* and *iii* offer positive reasons for the claim.

    Still, the support here is contentious, and statements may not be acceptable. We may also doubt that the charges have been adequately met rather than just recognized.

Major Exercise 11M

b) ¹(Elementary school teachers should be better paid than university professors).
The reasons for this are as follows: ²(The complex material dealt with at university requires that students be well grounded in basic skills of reading and writing).
³(And according to many educators), ⁴(elementary school teachers teach students in their most formative years when basic skills are best taught). Therefore,
⁵(the job of elementary school teachers is more important than that of university
professors.)

Furthermore, ⁶(people should be paid according to the importance of their
jobs to society.) And lastly, ⁷(university professors are already over paid).

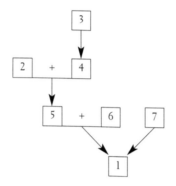

ARGUER: advocate of elementary school teachers
AUDIENCE: general public
OPPONENTS: university professors and other educators

Together, the sub-conclusion 5 and statement 6 are relevant to the MC (1). If one
job is more important than another, and if more important jobs should be better
paid, then elementary school teachers should be better paid.

Again, statements 2 and 4 provide relevant support for 5, increasing its strength.
Although the authority for 4 provided by statement 3 is weak ('many educators' is
vague and unspecified), statement 4 would seem largely a matter of common sense
and to share the common acceptability of 2. However, 2 and 3 are not sufficient support for 5. These premises show that the job done by elementary school teachers is
important, but not that it is *more* important than the job done by university professors; to do this, the premises would need to include an assessment of university professors' contributions that would allow a comparison.

Statement 6 is important to the support 5 provides for the MC. But 6 itself is
unsupported: it is evaluative and certainly does not report a state of affairs. Thus, it
remains questionable until supported. Statement 7 is an interpretation and one that
is irrelevant to the MC.

On balance, the argument has merit but lacks enough support for the sub-conclusion. An assessment of what professors contribute (showing it to be less important) and support of statement 6 would be needed to make the argument a strong one.

c)   1(Astronomy, however, is accessible to everyone). 2(For only a modest investment, anyone can purchase or build a telescope and begin viewing the sky . . .) 3(Magazines such as *Sky & Telescope* and *Astronomy* are written for amateurs and help them keep up with the latest research results). 4(In addition, many books for the nonscientist have been written on a variety of astronomical subjects, from the origin of the solar system to the future of the universe).

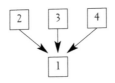

'Accessible' in the conclusion is ambiguous. Does it mean everyone can afford astronomy as a hobby, or that everyone can understand the principles of the science? Statement 2 supports the first of these meanings; statements 3 and 4 the second. So we will charitably understand 'accessible' here in both senses. This understanding allows all three premises to be relevant to the conclusion. Statement 2, though, is questionable, since 'modest investment' is unclear. Given the strong wording of the conclusion—'accessible to *everyone*'—we cannot judge 2 sufficient for the monetary sense of 'accessible' in the conclusion without clarification of what precisely the author means by 'modest'.

Statement 3 appears to report a statement of that which could be checked, so it is acceptable. Common knowledge allows us to accept statement 4. But again, the 'everyone' of the conclusion suggests that the support of 3 and 4 is insufficient. A large segment of the adult population of North America has poor literacy skills, and the premises also exclude most children.

The premises (even statement 2) *would* support a qualified conclusion such as 'Astronomy is accessible to most (many) people.' But the support is insufficient for the conclusion given.

i)   Background (I am interested to see the renewed attempt by the Vatican to defend the bastion of male power that the Roman Catholic Church has always been ('Vatican Says Jesus Didn't Want Women Priests', *Globe and Mail*, 25 Jan. 1997)). ? (It's not surprising to see a bishop argue that 'The church does not have the power to modify the practice, uninterrupted for 2,000 years, of calling only men' to the priesthood).

^{C1}(The church also seems to lack the power to prevent those men from abusing their positions for their own ends). ^{P1}(Stories of the abuse of the young in Maritime orphanages and in Residential schools for natives throughout the land are as sickening as they are numerous). ^{P2}(They reveal an institution in which abuse has become endemic). ^{P3}(The victims are seen by these men as pure pawns for their own gratification, and their word is rarely believed because of the abuser's 'standing' in the community). ^{MC}(This abuse of power has got to stop).

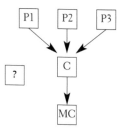

ARGUER: critic of the Roman Catholic Church
AUDIENCE: general public
OPPONENTS: defenders of the Church's doctrinal traditions

This example lets us consider how to capture in our diagram an argument that seems to suffer from contextual irrelevance. We do this with the '?' that hangs off to the side. The issue, as this piece begins, is the Roman Catholic Church's position on the ordination of women. But then we see a switch to another topic, the link being the powerlessness of the Church to change certain behaviours. In fact, though, these are two very different types of 'tradition': the one with respect to women is rooted in doctrine; that which exercises the writer has to do with the actions of some clergy, unrelated in any way to doctrine.

This argument, then, suffers from a fundamental contextual irrelevance: the writer addresses neither the right topic nor one that is relevantly related, but goes off instead on a red herring. The argument that then develops does have some strengths. Setting aside some of the emotive tone (which is a problem to be noted), the principal premises do refer to events that are generally known, and so a reasonable audience will accept them (if not the associated judgments). While these premises do not exactly show that the Church has been powerless, the persistence of the behaviour does indicate a real concern that C1 captures, and the premises are sufficient to support this. The argument would be stronger, however, if it was clearer about the issue to be addressed, either by bringing things back to the original topic, or ignoring the earlier topic altogether.

k)   Whether or not [William of Sherwood] was a student at the University of Paris, we
have several reasons for believing that ᶜ(he was a master there). In the first
place, ᴾ¹(he lived at a time when 'scholars were, indeed, to a degree which is
hardly intelligible in modern times, citizens of the world' and when 'almost all
the great schoolmen ... taught at Paris at one period or other of their lives.'
Secondly, ᴾ²(in each of his two main works Sherwood uses an example with a
Parisian setting: in one case the Seine, and in another the university). Finally,
ᴾ³(all the philosophers who show signs of having been influenced directly by
Sherwood or his writings were in Paris at some time during a span of years when
he certainly could have been lecturing there).

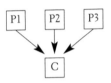

This historical argument requires that we accept the authority of the scholar who
produced it. Since each of the reported facts (and Premises 1, 2, and 3 all report
facts) can be verified, we can accept the premises on the grounds of the reasonableness of the authority.

Each premise provides relevant support for the conclusion. The presence of most
great schoolmen in Paris (P1) increases the probability that Sherwood was there.
Likewise, Parisian settings (P2) suggest an acquaintance with the city. Finally, Paris
seems a common ground for Sherwood and those he influenced (P3).

However, the relevance provided for C is not that strong in the case of P1 and P2,
and they do not directly support the hypothesis that Sherwood was a *master* at the
University of Paris. Only P3 provides direct support for that. So on balance, much
more evidence is required to strengthen the argument.

CHAPTER 12

Exercise 12A

1.   c)   In principle, we should be able to make reasonable generalizations about a topic
like this. We have access to bus schedules and should be able to use our experiences and those of others to track the quality of the service in relation to the
schedule. In acquiring a reasonable sample, it would be important to test the
service across the week and throughout the day and evening. A random test
would be problematic, because different factors can affect service on any day, so
a more systematic approach is required.

f) Constructing generalizations on a topic like this presents serious difficulties, both in terms of the topic and the population involved. To take the latter, 'Americans' is a diverse and complex population, and any good generalization would have to be based on a scientific study of considerable proportions. It would have to canvass opinions from across a broad spectrum of ethnic groups, ages, occupations, etc., and take into account the geographical distribution of such sub-groups. For example, if some states have greater or smaller populations of Hispanic Americans, the sample should account for that. We can begin to imagine the problems involved in arriving at a sample that is reasonably representative.

The second major concern would be the subject matter involved. Generalizing about attitudes is difficult because of the subjective nature of the topic. Serious attention would have to be given to the kinds of questions to be asked, how those questions would be understood by the members of the sample, and how their responses would be interpreted.

2. b) The generalization here is that 'people in Johnsonville were very healthy.' This is based on premises drawn from information about people entering only one health club in the town. This is a very inadequate sample for the conclusion drawn. While the evidence is relevant (of the right kind), it is far from sufficient. Given the premises, a generalization should only be drawn about the members of that club (assuming the month in question was representative of activity there throughout the year). Such a sample is biased towards healthy people, since they would be the kind of people entering such a club. To generalize about the population of the town, we would need a much broader, representative sample that included people who did not enter health clubs.

Exercise 12B

1. b) In this example of polling, the sample is 4,000 students in 31 institutions; the population is US students; and the property cheating, or 'serious cheating', if we restrict ourselves to one of the sub-conclusions. In its broadest claim, the information fits the scheme as follows:

P1 = A sample of 4,000 students at 31 institutions is a representative sample of US students.

P2 = 66 per cent (two-thirds) of the students in the sample admitted to cheating.

C = 66 per cent (two-thirds) of US students have cheated.

We also have information that would allow us to set out the scheme for some sub-groups. For example, we can conclude that 73 per cent of science students from universities without an 'honour code' have been involved in 'serious cheating', based on the information about the sample of science students from universities without an honour code. But this begins to identify some of the problems that prevent us from working with much of the material: we are not told how many of the sample of 4,000 students were science students, nor how many of the 31 institutions were universities with or without honour codes. Hence, the information provided about these sub-groups is of little value. Likewise, claims are made about other sub-groups like business students and engineering students, without our being told what proportion of the sample these involve. It is possible that one or more of these groups is under- (or over-) represented in the sample. More generally, we do not know how the sample was arrived at. Were students contacted directly? Were they sent a survey and asked to return it? Were they guaranteed anonymity? This will lead us to wonder about measurement errors here. There are all kinds of possible ways for such errors to arise, but little information to help us. A subject like cheating is a sensitive one, and this increases the chance that misleading responses have been given. You may also raise concerns about the absence of a margin of error, time of the survey, etc.

Many of these problems may belong to the report more than the poll itself. The report includes claims, for example, that seem to be drawn from more than the poll. How did the survey find that cheating had increased over three decades? Does the sample include responses from over three decades? This seems unlikely. More probable is that this survey is being compared to an earlier one, but we have no information to work on. Likewise, Professor McCabe is reported to have concluded that strict penalties are a more effective deterrent than exhortations to behave morally. But this is based on the experience of the university departments involved, which would not be part of the sample studied.

Exercise 12C

1. c)   There is no evidence that there is any causal connection between Bob wearing his suspenders and winning at poker. It cannot be demonstrated that it is anything more than mere chance or superstition.

Exercise 12D

a)   *Ghosts*
To be in a position to construct a good argument from ignorance about ghosts you would need to have conducted, or have access to the results of, a detailed investigation of the phenomenon. This might involve the study of relevant literature, looking at alleged cases of hauntings and evaluating the results. Or it could involve searching out alleged cases and investigating them firsthand. Then you would be in a position to construct a reasonable argument. If someone had made a concerted effort to demonstrate the existence of ghosts and had failed to come with any evidence, then that would count against the hypothesis.

Simply postulating the non-existence of ghosts on the speculative grounds that no one appears to have proven otherwise would not constitute a good argument from ignorance.

Major Exercise 12M

2. a)   The principal claim for which evidence is provided is that 'Race matters in who is put to death.' From this, we can see being implied the hidden conclusion that the governors of Maryland and Illinois are correct to ban the death penalty over concerns about racial disparities.

The reasoning involved fits the scheme for general causal reasoning. (We take this as general rather than particular because the writer is not concerned with any particular instances.) Basically, the writer shows a correlation between black defendants and the likelihood of facing the death penalty. Of course, it is a big step from this to say that a defendant's being black causes them to be more likely to face execution, but we must also ask how such causal claims could be supported and whether we see that support here. The argument scheme in question can be represented as follows:

> P1 = Being a black defendant is correlated with an increased likelihood of facing the death penalty.
> P2 = The correlation is not due to chance.
> P3 = The correlation is not due to some mutual cause, Z.
> C = Being a black defendant causes someone to be more likely to face the death penalty.

To assess the example, we need to ask whether the premises are corroborated by the information provided. The two claims—that between 1977 and 1995, 88 black men were executed for killing whites while just 2 white men were executed for killing blacks, and that a federal Justice Department study found that white defendants were almost twice as likely as black ones to be given a plea agreement by federal prosecutors—do give credence to both P1 and P2. A correlation is shown to exist, and there is reason to believe it is not a matter of chance. P3 then becomes crucial: is there a hidden factor that could account for the discrepancy? Opponents to the claim may point to poverty as a factor that leads more blacks than whites to commit crimes that warrant the death penalty. But the issue here is more about whether the system treats blacks and whites in the same way once these crimes have been committed. The evidence does not suggest any second cause for this, and the burden of proof would seem to shift to those who would claim blacks are not being disproportionately discriminated against to prove their case. At least that would seem to be part of what is behind the decisions of the governors of Maryland and Illinois.

d)   The survey is undertaken by Playtex, which is one of the leading manufacturers of women's lingerie and is therefore presumably in a position to make judgments about sizing and fitting. Their survey is based on women who came to bra-fitting clinics, which would be an indication that these women were unsure about the size they wore, and indeed may have been wearing the wrong size, thus lending credence to the relatively high finding of 7 out of 10 women. Such high findings have been reported elsewhere also. Whether the sample is too selected is difficult to say—it wouldn't really be possible to poll women outside of such a clinic, or conduct telephone questionnaires on such a topic: most people don't knowingly wear the wrong size of something, so it would seem that polling women at such a sizing clinic is one of the better locations. Where there might be a problem is that we don't really know the size (so to speak) of the sample—how many women were surveyed to arrive at the result? Whether there is bias is less likely, unless we wanted to argue that Playtex was only concluding that women were wearing the wrong size in order to sell them new merchandise. So while this is mostly a plausible generalization, we would need additional information about the size of the sample, the manner in which the survey was conducted, and so forth, before we could reach a final conclusion about the generalization.

f)   It would be quite reasonable to judge this a report and not an argument. But if we look further, we find some interesting causal reasoning on the part of Farmer Coombs. Despite the initial absurdity of the example, it remains the case that, if he is reliable witness, something caused the phenomenon of hair growth. The reasoning structure is quite simple:

P1 = Primrose licked his pate.
P2 = Hair grew in that spot.
C   = Primrose is curing his baldness.

It bears noting that, as a farmer, Mr Coombs would lead a life of fixed routines. Thus, he is likely to notice irregularities in his life. This adds credence to his choice of Primrose licking his head as the key antecedent event prior to the new growth. While there is no correlation to support the causal claim, that is exactly what Mr Coombs is in the process of establishing (or not). So it's too early, perhaps, for a definitive conclusion. Of course, the key factor may be the cattle food dust and not the combination of Primrose's licking and the head. The report does not tell us if Farmer Coombs is including this in his experiment.

Chapter 13

Exercise 13A

1. a) What this argument does is set out the causal steps in the slope that the author believes to characterize euthanasia. While no undesirable consequence is explicitly stated, the author is clearly committed to such a statement, and we have no difficulty supplying the hidden components of the argument scheme:

PREMISES: Voluntary euthanasia will lead to directed euthanasia on behalf of patients who have not authorized it; which will in turn lead to involuntary euthanasia conducted as part of a social policy. Since the elimination of those considered too 'ill' to function is undesirable (hidden), then . . .

HIDDEN CONCLUSION: we should not allow voluntary euthanasia.

We must ask two questions of this: is the consequence foreseen really undesirable, and are the steps in the causal chain plausible so that it is reasonable to believe they will follow once the first step is taken? On the first question, there seems little doubt that the kind of involuntary euthanasia envisaged here is abhorrent to society. But the argument is more problematic when it comes to the other question. Why would we suspect that people who have been deputized by others to assist them in dying might become 'inclined' to assist others who had not made such a request? This is a considerable step, because the second action loses the primary justification of the first, and for responsible individuals this would be crucial. So, the burden of proof lies with the author to support this step in the slope. Likewise, the step to seeing this as part of a social policy involves a far more general acceptance, and the author needs to support his belief that such could follow. Without these modifications, the argument here is weak.

Exercise 13B

3. e)   P1 = Speeding is known to increase the likelihood of car collisions, and drivers are punished for this dangerous behaviour whether or not their particular sprees cause collisions.

   P2 = Violent pornography, like speeding, is intrinsically dangerous.

   C = Legislatures may regulate it on the basis of its known propensity for harm without a showing of particular harm.

When we recast this as the argument from analogy that it is, the scheme is as follows:

   P1 = Violent pornography (**analogue**) is like speeding (**analogue**) in that both are intrinsically dangerous (**similarity**).

   P2 = Speeding drivers are punished whether or not their sprees cause collisions.

   C = Violent pornography should be punished whether or not particular harm can be shown.

Assessment

This argument from analogy is not strong. It is not clear that the claim made in P1 is the case. This may be challenged and needs support. The intrinsic dangerousness of speeding is acknowledged by mention of its known likelihood to increase collisions; no comparable attempt is made to show something like this to be the case with violent pornography. So the similarity is not established. Moreover, speeding is prohibited, not 'regulated': the conclusion suffers from vagueness here. These concerns point to a problem of dissimilarity. Violent pornography is not like speeding exactly because its harmfulness is less direct and not easy to establish. While both analogues are serious societal problems, the difference in types of harm involved are too great for the argument to be strong.

Exercise 13C

1. c) *human cloning*

(i) As a society, we have repeatedly used advances in technology to aid people who are not able to enjoy the rights that the rest of us have. Of particular significance here are technologies like *in vitro* fertilization, which has given the reality of parenthood to many who would not otherwise have enjoyed it. Like *in vitro* fertilization, human cloning technology promises to provide infertile couples (and singles!) with their own genetic offspring. If the argument was compelling with *in vitro* fertilization, it is no different now.

(ii) Human cloning should not be permitted because it would set a dangerous precedent. For all the concerns we may have had about issues like surrogate motherhood, which appear to treat human beings as commercial property, there has never been the real potential for this that would come with human cloning. Suddenly, humans could be mass-produced in ways that pay no recognition to their nature as spiritual beings. Such crass commercialization must be stopped before it can start.

(iii) As much as we have struggled to control disease and disability for thousands of years, we have never really had the opportunity to control and improve our physical well-being that human cloning brings. We stand at the threshold of a new era that promises the elimination of diseases that have haunted us for centuries. We will be able to make medical advances like never before.

Of these three arguments, the one chosen 'strongest' will largely depend on the chooser's position as a person disposed to the technology or opposed to it. The arguments all fit the scheme. But as we know, that scheme is only a frame that allows us to isolate and scrutinize the argument. Ultimately, it depends on how much we are attracted by the alternative visions of the future.

Exercise 13D

1. a) This is the kind of two-wrongs argument that indicates the usefulness of this kind of reasoning when handling difficult moral dilemmas. It gives us a way to think about the issue. This argument satisfies all three conditions. There is a genuine belief on the part of the citizens who hide these people that they are trying to cancel another wrong: the torture and death of those deported. So the first condition is met. Breaking the law by harbouring illegal aliens is a civic wrong, but one that has to be seen as permissible if the alternative involves the deaths of those refugees. This meets the second condition. The third condition is always the hardest. Here, we might imagine morally preferable alternatives like convincing the government to allow these people to stay, or petitioning the United Nations to put pressure on their homeland to change its behaviour. But are these alternatives practical? Many would argue that they are not.

2. a) For a two-wrongs-by-analogy argument to work in this case, you would have to show that the two circumstances are relevantly similar and/or have no relevant dissimilarities. That would be difficult here. The two analogues are 'exemption due to a serious medical condition' and 'exemption due to a sick father'. They are similar in that a sickness is involved, but not to the relevant person. Unless the sickness of the father is expected to be prolonged (which would change the circumstances), the best that might be fairly expected is a postponement of the exam. A serious medical condition in the examinee, however, warrants exemption rather than postponement. Under the circumstances, allowing the one and not the other would not be inconsistent.

Major Exercise 13M

6. i) This is an argument from analogy.

> ANALOGUES: We can do a computer simulation of (C1) the pattern of power distribution in the Labour party, (C2) rain storms (C3), or warehouse fires.
>
> PREMISE: Nobody supposes that the computer simulation is actually the real thing (that a computer simulation of a storm will leave us all wet).
>
> MAIN CONCLUSION: There is no reason to suppose a computer simulation of mental processes actually has mental processes.

The following is a simplified version of this scheme:

P1 = Computer simulations of the pattern of power distribution in the Labour party, rain storms, warehouse fires, and mental processes are all similar in that they can be given a formal description.

P2 = Simulations of power distribution, rain storms, or warehouse fires are not real.

C = Simulations of mental processes are not real.

Assessment
The difficulty lies in organizing the argument more than in analyzing it. The premises do not seem grounded on questionable claims. Searle's claim is that while computers can simulate mental processes, they cannot have them. We could look for dissimilarities in the differences between fires and rain and mental processes. But that would be to miss the point. It is not those things that are involved, but simulations of them. From this point of view, Searle offers a reasonable analogy.

j) This appeal from precedent also bears a resemblance to an argument by analogy and slippery-slope argument. The idea is that opening abortion clinics, as a legal activity, implies social sanction (for the percentage that agreed to legalize abortion clinics). The writer argues that this sets a precedent for opening other venues such as casinos and pornographic theatres. Moreover, it compares the doctors or social workers who open clinics to members of organized crime and porn movie producers—implying, in other words, that the doctors are engaged in immoral and criminal activity, even if it is presently legal. This argument would appear to be problematic, even to one who is pro-life. Even one who is against abortion and feels that the doctors performing it are immoral might concede that it is extreme to liken abortion doctors to organized criminals or porn movie producers. Furthermore, although casinos and porn movie theatres are legal, as are abortion clinics in many places, it is difficult to compare the reasons for frequenting the former with the reasons for going to the latter. And for the same reason, those individuals taking part in the different activities—gamblers, porn movie viewers, and women seeking abortions—would not seem comparable in ways that support the claim that a bad precedent is being set.

m) This could be seen as an appeal to precedent, and even a slippery slope. In the first instance, it's saying that once we allow ourselves to tamper with and change someone else's artistic product, there is a precedent for modifying and changing any work of art, no matter how famous or revered. There is a certain plausibility to this, if we consider that the artist's product is somehow unique and autonomous, and once we have breached that autonomy, there is presumably no difference between changing a movie and changing the Mona Lisa. And to the extent that we could read that last formulation as going from a first-instance case to the extreme, this would be the slippery-slope aspect.

By the same token, it could be argued that there are significant dissimilarities between the case of a movie, which most often is a more collaborative effort, and a painting, which is more the work of an individual artist (although in Leonardo's time, many paintings were the result of collaborative efforts of several studio artists); colorizing a movie could be read as merely the most recent modification or 'improvement' made to the product. Also, movie-making is a more commercial, some might say less high-brow art than the paintings of the Old Masters; and as such, it is arguably less sacred when it comes to outside changes.

In sum, depending on how you argue, and what your presuppositions about art and art forms are, this argument could be construed as an acceptable appeal to precedent, or as one that has some problems.

Chapter 14

Exercise 14A

b) One such context would be a particular company where it was commonly known that the most successful and respected senior members subscribed to a magazine related to the industry or kind of business the company was involved in. You might well conclude that this was a good magazine to read on the basis of its endorsement by such individuals.

Similarly, in an academic context, where certain journals or magazines are favoured by established and respected members of a discipline, that readership may be used as the basis of a *pro homine* argument.

Major Exercise 14M

2. b)   P1 = The experts admit it's not if you will be the victim of a break-in, but when.

HC1 = You will be the victim of a break-in.

P2 = Psychiatrists, Psychologists, Criminologists, Security Experts and Police Officials all agree: 'The Earlier the intruder is discovered, the more effective the security system.'

HC2 = You need a security system that detects the intruder earlier.

HP = The Astro-Guard Security System detects the intruder earlier.

HMC = You should buy an Astro-Guard Security System.

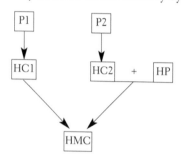

The context indicates that we are dealing with argumentation, but the key claims are hidden, allowing readers to draw the conclusions for themselves. But are these conclusions warranted? Both sub-arguments depend on weak appeals to authorities. P1 is too vague to play any meaningful role as support. Experts must be identified, and here they are not. P2 tells us about the groups being appealed to, but not their specific identities. We do not know whether all members of the groups would agree with the statement, but this seems unlikely. Thus, we cannot even determine whether there is likely to be agreement among the experts.

f)   P1 = Dr Bethune was a self-confessed Communist.

P2 = The morality of a person's acts must be judged by their consequences.

C1 = When Bethune placed his medical skills and humanism at the service of international Communism, he unquestionably contributed to an evil ideology that produced many mountains of corpses.

HC = This involvement in evil shows him to have been immoral.

C2 = It is not possible to honour Dr Bethune as a humanitarian.

MC = When Canadians naively eulogize Dr Bethune they unwittingly endorse Communist ideology.

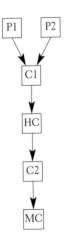

There is a double charge of guilt here, one against Bethune and the other against Canadians who eulogize him. Both are weak. We can accept P1 as common knowledge or at least knowledge that is readily accessible: Bethune was a Communist. The question is whether his association with a rather large and often segmented political ideology implicates him in any of the crimes that are alleged to have been committed by adherents of that ideology.

Following our diagram, we can see that if HC is the case, there is good reason to accept C2. But problems lie with the terms of the association that support HC. In C1 the writer claims that Bethune 'unquestionably' contributed to an ideology that produced many mountains of corpses. As it stands, this is quite unacceptable. The writer neither tells us the extent of that unquestionable contribution nor gives us any evidence for the 'many mountains of corpses'. There is a further problem with P2 in that it is too limiting, because the morality of a person's acts are often judged not by the consequences but in light of the motives behind them. The writer does not even consider this.

The guilt-by-association argument fails here because it is not shown either that the Chinese Communists were immoral or that Dr Bethune was associated with them in an immoral way. In consequence, the further claim that Canadians who praise Bethune become associated with Communism is also unsupported.

g)   [The first statement is background.]

P1 = A person who dies of lung cancer at age 70 will not be hospitalized later with another disease.

P2 = The costs of hospitalization tend to increase substantially for people after the age of 70.

P3 = Wages forfeited by deceased former smokers are a cost for neither the government nor the taxpayer.

MC = While smoking kills, those deaths have economic benefits for society.

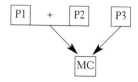

ARGUER: economist Jean-Pierre Vidal, for Imperial Tobacco
AUDIENCE: general public
OPPONENTS: anti-smoking advocates

Assessment

This is principally an appeal to authority. The reasoning rests upon the authority of Vidal. He is the right kind of authority (economist) for the subject matter, but his authority is weakened by potential bias. Since the report was commissioned (and paid for) by Imperial Tobacco, he might have been inclined to produce a report they would find favourable.

Otherwise, the reasoning is strong on the criterion of relevance. Premise 1 is self-evident. But we have only Vidal's authority to accept Premises 2 and 3. Overall, the poor appeal to authority makes this a weak argument.

n) This is a report. But it is a report that contains reasoning: that of Barbie's lawyer. Verges uses two-wrongs reasoning by analogy to justify Barbie's actions during the Second World War. Accordingly, we can set the justification out in the following way:

P1 = Mr Barbie's behaviour was 'no different than' that of loyal French officers during the Algerian war; citizens and officials of France; and even French Jews and members of the Resistance.

P2 = The behaviour of those other three groups has been accepted/allowed.

C = Barbie's behaviour should be accepted/allowed.

Assessment

This appeal for similar treatment falls short of meeting all three of the conditions for assessing such reasoning. It is not clear that Barbie's actions, in sending thousands to death camps and allegedly being involved in executions, was analogous to the comparison cases. The numbers involved, the motive of genocide, and his position in authority over those who may have 'assisted' him all weaken the analogy.

On the question of consistent treatment (condition #2), it is not clear that it is more important to treat this case consistently with the others mentioned, given the widespread view that the events in question are the key act of inhumanity in the twentieth century.

To meet the third condition, Verges would have to argue that there was no morally preferable course of action available to Barbie at the time. In the circumstances, this seems a non-starter. So, on balance, there is nothing to recommend this instance of two-wrongs reasoning by analogy.

INDEX

acceptability, 134–6, 138–9; and belief systems, 252–5; determining, 252; premise, 247, 250–63; universal conditions of, 257–61

ad hominem, 342–4, 345, 349–51, 369–72; abusive, 371

ad populam, 362–3

affirming the antecedent (AA), 214–16, 226

affirming the consequent (AC), 216

ambiguity, 87–93; semantic, 88; syntactic, 87–8

amphibole, 87–8

analogues, 335

analogy: arguments from, 335–40, 342–4, 345, 349–51; counter-arguments to, 338–40

anecdotal evidence, 289, 290

appeals: to popularity, 362–3; to precedent, 93, 342–4

arguer, 5, 43, 44; character of, 359–86

arguments: abbreviated, 56–65; *ad hominem*, 342–4, 345, 349–51, 369–72; *ad ignorantiam*, 313–14; *ad populam*, 362–3; from analogy, 335–40, 342–4, 345, 349–51; assessment of, 133–55, 247–85; against authority, 369–72; from authority, 146, 147, 364–9; borderline, 16–18;

classifying, 156–84; constructing, 77–8, 125–6, 395–9; definition, 2–3, 10; 'from design', 337–8; diagramming, 33–50, 53–65, 68–9, 73–6, 77; dialogues, 55; ethotic, 5, 329–58; and explanations, 20–4; extended, 9–11; implicit components of, 51–82; moral, 329–58; narratives, 24–5; and non-arguments, 13–20; non-verbal elements in, 65–77; *pro homine*, 360–1, 362, 364, 365; schemes of, 144–7, 166–80, 210–19, 226–46, 286–386; 'second-hand', 24–5; simple, 9–11; 'slippery-slope', 330–4; straw(-man), 55, 269–70; strong, 133–6, 138, 140–2, 281, 247–81; translating, 207–8; valid and invalid, 139–44; weak, 133, 137–8

assumptions, 61–2, 63

audiences, 5–7, 9, 10, 43, 44, 252–3, 255–7, 258, 395

authority, 260–1; argument from, 146, 147, 364–9; argument against, 369, 372–4

'begging the question', 262–3

belief systems, 252–7

bias, 109–32; detecting, 116–27; in ethotic arguments, 361, 366, 369, 372; illegitimate, 110–14, 122–6 biconditionals, 205–6, 216–17

categories, 156–7
causes, 20–4; composite, 303
chain, causal, 331–4
character, arguer's, 359–86
charity, principle of, 18
claims, 2–3, 54; controversial, 61; factual, 248–9, 287–93; general, 288; proportional, 288–9; universal, 288; unstated, 60; *see also* conclusions
classes, 156–7; predicate, 157–61; subject, 157–61; testing, 185–94
communication: principles of, 52–6, 66; non-verbal, 65–77
complementaries, 164, 190
components, hidden, 191
conclusions, 3, 10, 34, 134–6, 139–42, 172–80, 187–8; 'hasty', 275–7; hidden, 56–60, 157; main, 36; *see also* claims
conditionals, 196, 201–3, 214–16, 232–6
conditional series (CS), 217–18
conditions, causal, 303
conjunction elimination (&E), 211
conjunction introduction (&I), 211
conjunctions, 196, 198–200, 203, 211–12
connectors, logical, 197, 206
construction, argument, 77–8, 125–6, 395–9
contexts, argumentative, 15, 55
contradiction, 163
contraposition, 165
contraries, 162
conversion, 164–5
critique, evaluative, 387–91

definitions, 83–108, 257; conventional, 96; extensional, 95, 97; formulating, 93–7; by genus and differentia, 95–6; good, 97–9; intensional, 95, 97, 98; rules for, 97–100; stipulative, 96, 97
demonstrations, non-verbal, 67–70, 75, 76
De Morgan's laws (DeM), 237–8
denying the antecedent (DA), 216
denying the consequent (DC), 214–16, 226
diagrams, argument, 33–50, 53–65, 68–9, 73–6, 77, 168; supplemented, 42–4, 47; Venn, 170–84
dialogues, argument, 55
dichotomy, false, 234

dilemmas (D), 232–6; 'to disjunction' (DV), 232; 'false', 234; 'horns' of, 235–6; unacceptable, 234–6
'disanalogy', 94, 338–9
disjunction elimination (VE), 212–13, 234
disjunctions, 200, 203, 232–6; exclusive, 201; unacceptable, 234–6
dispute, verbal, 88–90
distribution, 186–7

elimination, conditional, 226
equivalence, 237–8
equivocation, 88–90
error: margin of, 298; measurement, 298–9; sampling, 296–8
essay, argumentative, 387–8, 395–9
ethos, 5, 359–60
ethotic schemes, 359–86
euphemisms, 85–7
evaluation, argument, 319–21, 387–410
explanations, 20–4

fallacies, 88, 187–8; conditional, 216
flags, argument, 66–7, 75, 76

generalizations, 287–93; counter-arguments against, 292–3; 'hasty', 289; *see also* appeals to ignorance; causal reasoning; polling; scientific reasoning
guilt by association, 374–7

'hasty' conclusions, 275–7
honour by association, 374–7
hypotheses, 315–19
hypothetical interpretation, 189–90

ignorance, appeals to, 313–14
indicators, logical, 13–16
inference, 288; immediate, 162–6; rules of, 238
instantiation, universal, 147
insufficiency, 277
interest: conflict of, 114–16; vested, 112–14
intuition, 145–6
invalidity, 147–50; *see also* validity
irrelevance, 277

language: emotional, 85–7; precision of, 84–104, 389, 396–7

legend, 168, 169, 190, 197
logic: formal, 195; propositional, 195–246
logical indicators, 13–16

meaning, intended, 103–4; *see also* defini-
    tions
metaphors, 71–3, 75, 77
methods, scientific, 315–21
middle term, 167–8; distribution of, 187
morals, 329–30

negations, 197–8, 203; double, 198
'noise', 33–7
non-arguments, 13–20
non-distribution, 186
non-verbal elements, 65–77

objectivity, 276–7
obversion, 163–4
opponent, 9, 10, 43, 44

'parallel cases', 148–50
particular affirmative: (I), 185; (PA),
    158–60, 162–84
particular negative: (O), 185; (PN), 158–60,
    162–84
polling, 294–300
popularity, appeals to, 362–3
population, 295, 296
precedent, appeals to, 93, 342–4
predicate, 157–61, 167, 186
premises, 3, 10, 34, 36; acceptable, 134–6,
    138–9, 247, 250–63; and conclusions,
    139–42; hidden, 56, 60–5, 69, 191–2, 268;
    linked and convergent, 38–42; negative,
    188; universal, 190
principle of charity, 18
pro homine arguments, 360–1, 362; counter-
    arguments to, 369–72
proof, burden of, 138–9, 250–1
proofs: conditional, 226–9; constructing,
    218–19; propositional, 210–19
propaganda, 122
property, 295
proportionality, 352
propositions: atomic, 196; simple and com-
    plex, 196–203; *see also* statements

questions, rhetorical, 17

reasoning: causal, 302–11, 330–4; definition
    of, 2–3; empirical, 286–328; general,
    303–8; ordinary, 247–50; particular,
    308–11
reasons, 20–4
'red herrings', 270–1
reductio ad absurdum (RAA), 229–32
references, symbolic, 70–1, 75, 76
relevance, 140–2, 265–72, 280; contextual,
    268–72; and hidden premises, 268; inter-
    nal, 266–7, 271
rules: for good definitions, 97–100; of infer-
    ence, 238; of good translation, 204–8

samples, 295; and bias, 290–1; errors in,
    296–8; random, 297; representative, 289,
    297; size of, 289–90, 296
schematization, full, 184–5
schemes: argument, 144–7, 166–80; com-
    plex, 239; empirical, 286–328; ethotic,
    359–86; mixed, 378–80; propositional,
    210–19, 226–46; of values, 329–58
science, reasoning methods of, 315–21
slanting: by distortion, 119–22; by omission,
    117–19
'slippery-slope' arguments, 330–4, 343–4
'speech acts', 52–6
square of opposition, 162
statements: categorical, 157–62, 184–5; sim-
    ple, 203; *see also* propositions
straw arguments (*also* straw-man arguments),
    55, 269–70
subcontraries, 162
subject, 157–61, 167, 186
sufficiency, 140–2, 274–7
syllogisms, 185–94; categorical, 156,
    166–84; structure of, 167–70
symbols, 70–1, 75, 76, 197, 204–8

testing validity, 167–84
tilde, 197
translation, 204–8
truth, 138
'two-wrongs' reasoning, 345–53; 'by analogy',
    345, 349–51; counter-arguments to,
    346–7, 351–3

unacceptability, 277; universal conditions of,
    261–3

universal affirmative: (A), 185; (UA), 146,
    158–60, 162–84
universal negative: (E), 185; (UN), 158–61,
    162–84

vagueness, 87–93
validity, 139–47, 156–84, 167–84, 195–225;
    deductive, 156–246; inductive, 247–85;
    rules of, 187–90; testing, 167–84; *see also*
    invalidity

values, schemes of, 329–58
variables, 197
vel, 200
Venn diagrams, 170–84

websites, critical evaluation of, 368
writing, argumentative, 387–410